Photographer's Guide to the Sony DSC-RX100 VI

Photographer's Guide to the Sony DSC-RX100 VI

Getting the Most from Sony's Advanced Compact Camera

Alexander S. White

White Knight Press
Henrico, Virginia

Published by
White Knight Press
9704 Old Club Trace
Henrico, Virginia 23238
www.whiteknightpress.com
contact@whiteknightpress.com

ISBN: 978-1-937986-72-8 (paperback)
978-1-937986-73-5 (ebook)

Printed in the United States of America

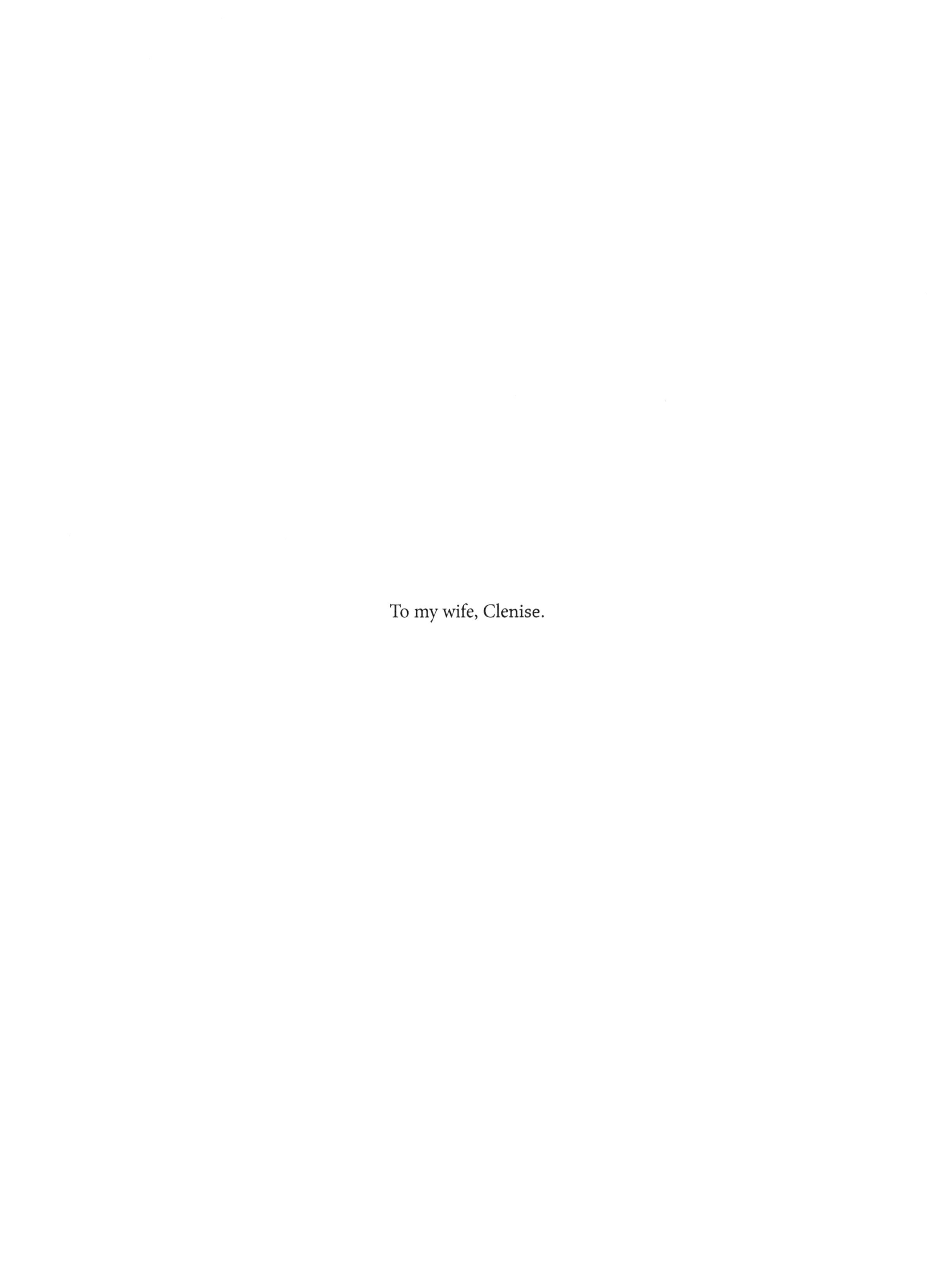

To my wife, Clenise.

Contents

Chapter 4: The Camera Settings1 Menu 43

Chapter 6: Physical Controls 143

Chapter 7: Playback and Printing 160

Chapter 8: The Setup Menu and My Menu 174

Chapter 9: Motion Pictures 196

CHAPTER 10: WI-FI, BLUETOOTH, AND OTHER TOPICS 222

Introduction

This book is a guide to the operation of the Sony Cyber-shot DSC-RX100 VI digital camera. It contains much of the same information as my earlier guide for the RX100 V model, but I have revised it for the RX100 VI with new illustrations and new or revised text where needed to cover this model's new or enhanced features.

The RX100 VI camera continues in the tradition of the RX100 V and earlier models with great portability, excellent image quality, and advanced features for taking stills and videos. It adds several enhancements, including a new lens with an optical zoom range of 24mm – 200mm and an LCD screen with some touch screen features. The RX100 VI can shoot bursts of still images at speeds up to 24 frames per second while adjusting focus and exposure. This model also includes an LSI (large scale integration) chip, which boosts the performance of the sensor and image processor, allowing the camera to shoot a burst of more than 100 shots that can be viewed right after shooting.

The RX100 VI includes a pop-up electronic viewfinder with resolution of 2.3 million dots, and an LCD screen that can tilt up or down and can rotate forward for self-portraits. The lens has a wide-angle setting of 24mm, an f/2.8 aperture at the wide-angle end, and an f/4.5 aperture at the telephoto end. Besides the ability to take short bursts of super-slow-motion video, the RX100 VI comes with several features oriented to advanced video production, including picture profiles with adjustments for gamma curve, knee, black level, and other settings, including the ability to shoot 4K, S-Log, and HLG (hybrid log gamma) video, making this model suitable for use as a second or backup camera for serious videographers.

Despite the addition of several advanced features for still and video photography, the RX100 VI retains the small size of the earlier RX100 models, which leaves the new model as possibly the greatest value available in a camera that can fit into most pockets.

My aim is to provide a complete guide to the camera's features, explaining how they work and when you might want to use them. The book is aimed largely at beginning and intermediate photographers who are not satisfied with the official documentation and prefer a more user-friendly explanation of the camera's controls and menus. For those seeking more advanced information, I discuss some topics that go beyond the basics, and I include in the appendices information about additional resources. I will provide updates and other information at my website, whiteknightpress.com, as warranted.

Chapter 1: Preliminary Setup

When you purchase your Sony DSC-RX100 VI, the box should contain the camera itself, battery, charger, wrist strap, two adapters for attaching a shoulder strap (though no shoulder strap is supplied), micro USB cable, and several brief instruction pamphlets. There is no CD with software or user's guide; the software programs supplied by Sony are accessible through the Internet.

To install Sony's software for viewing and working with images and videos on Windows-based computers, go to the following Internet address: http://www.sony.co.jp/imsoft/Win/. If you have a Macintosh computer, you can get the software at http://www.sony.co.jp/imsoft/Mac/. You can download PlayMemories Home, a program for basic image editing, uploading, and management; Capture One Express, a special Sony-oriented version of Capture One, a sophisticated Raw-processing program from a company known as Phase One; and Imaging Edge, Sony's software package for processing Raw files and for controlling the RX100 VI from your computer when the camera is connected to the computer with its USB cable.

You might want to attach the wrist strap as soon as possible to help you keep a tight grip on the camera. The strap can be attached to the small mounting lug on either the left or right side of the camera. See Appendix A for a discussion of custom grips that can also be of use. If you purchase an optional neck strap, you can attach it to the camera using the strap adapters provided by Sony in the box with the RX100 VI.

Charging and Inserting the Battery

The Sony battery for the DSC-RX100 VI is the NP-BX1. The standard procedure is to charge the battery while it's inside the camera. To do this, you use the supplied micro USB cable, which plugs into the camera and into the Sony charger or a USB port on your computer.

There are pluses and minuses to charging the battery while it is inside the camera. On the positive side, you don't need an external charger, and the camera can charge automatically when it's connected to your computer. Also, many automobiles have USB slots where you can plug in your RX100 VI to keep up its charge. And, you can find portable charging devices with USB ports, as discussed in Appendix A.

On the negative side, with this system you cannot charge a battery outside of the camera, so you cannot be charging a spare battery while using the battery that is inside the camera. One solution to this situation is to purchase at least one extra battery and a device that will charge your batteries externally.

With the RX100 VI, unlike some previous models, you can use the supplied battery charger as an AC adapter that will power the camera. So, if your battery runs completely down, you don't have to wait until you have recharged it to start using the camera again. You can plug the charger into the camera and into an AC outlet or USB power supply, and operate the camera directly from that power source. I'll discuss batteries, chargers, and other accessories in Appendix A.

To charge the battery, insert it into the camera and connect the charger. You first need to open the battery compartment door on the bottom of the camera and put in the battery. You can only insert it fully into the camera one way; what I do is look for the four gold-colored metal contact squares on the end of the battery and insert the battery so those four squares are positioned close to the front of the camera as the battery goes into the compartment, as shown in Figures 1-1 and 1-2. You may have to nudge aside the small blue latch that holds the battery in place, which is seen in Figure 1-3.

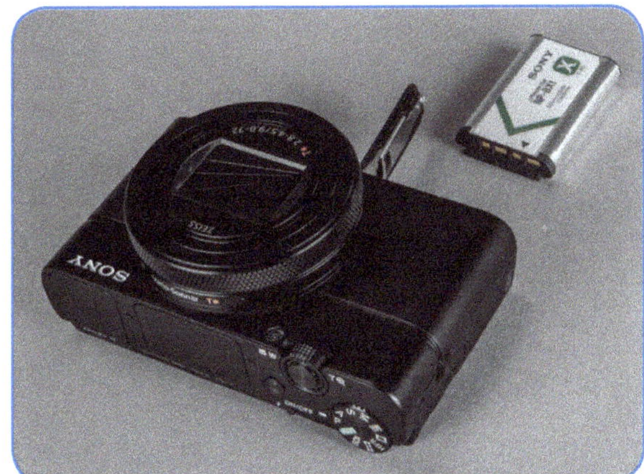

Figure 1-1. Battery Lined Up to Go into Camera

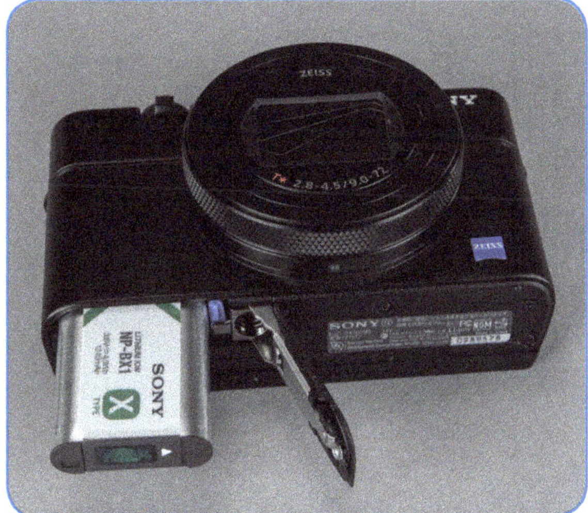

Figure 1-2. Battery Going into Camera

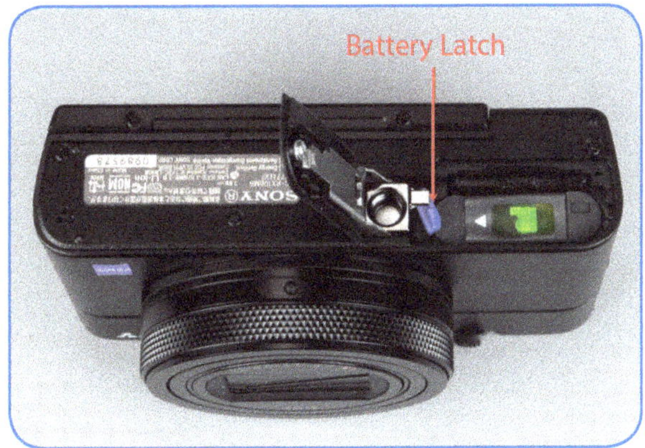

Figure 1-3. Battery Secured by Latch

With the battery inserted and secured by the latch, close the battery compartment door and slide the ridged latch on the door to the closed position. Then plug the larger, rectangular end of the USB cable into the corresponding slot on the provided AC charger, which is model number AC-UUD12 in the United States. Plug the smaller end of the cable into the micro USB port on the upper part of the camera's right side as you hold it in shooting position, as shown in Figure 1-4.

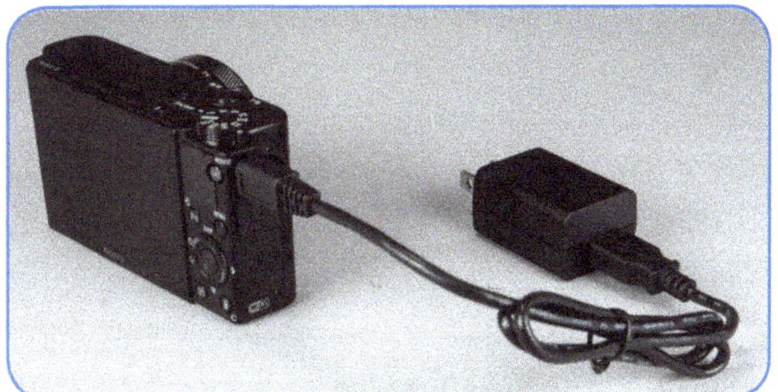

Figure 1-4. Battery Charger Connected to Camera

Plug the charger's prongs into a standard electrical outlet. An orange lamp in the center of the power (On/Off) button on top of the camera will light up steadily while the battery is charging; when it goes out, the battery is fully charged. The full charging cycle should take about 150 minutes. If the charging lamp flashes, that indicates a problem with the charger or a problem with the temperature of the camera's environment.

To charge the battery using a USB power supply such as a USB port on a laptop computer, plug the large end of the camera's USB cable into that power source and the small end into the charging port on the camera, while the camera is turned off.

Choosing and Inserting a Memory Card

The RX100 VI does not ship with a memory card. If you turn the camera on with no card inserted, you will see the message "NO CARD" flashing in the upper left corner of the screen. If you ignore this message and press the shutter button to take a picture, don't be fooled into thinking that the camera is storing it in internal memory. The camera will temporarily store the image and play it back if you press the Playback button, but the image will not be permanently saved. (You cannot even operate the shutter with no card inserted, if the Release w/o Card menu option is set to Disable, as discussed in Chapter 5.)

Some camera models have a small amount of built-in memory so you can take and store a few pictures even without a card, but the RX100 VI does not have that safety net. (In an emergency, if you took one important picture with no card, you might be able to save it. First, don't turn off the camera. Second, play the image, and connect one end of a micro HDMI cable to the camera's HDMI port and the other end to a video capture device.

Then capture the image to that device or to a computer connected to that device. I have done this using a Blackmagic Intensity Pro device, which saved the image to a video capture program. But that process is for emergencies only.)

To avoid the frustration of having a great camera that can't save images, you need to use a memory card. The RX100 VI uses two types of memory storage. First, it can use all varieties of SD cards, which are about the size of a postage stamp. These cards come in several varieties; some examples are shown in Figure 1-5.

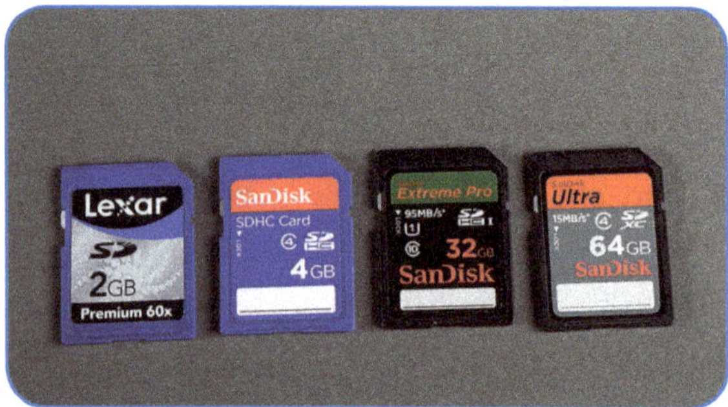

Figure 1-5. Various Types of SD Cards

The standard card, called simply SD, comes in capacities from eight megabytes (MB) to two gigabytes (GB). A higher-capacity card, SDHC, comes in sizes from four GB to 32 GB. The newest, and highest-capacity card, SDXC (for extended capacity) comes in sizes of 48 GB, 64 GB, 128 GB, 256 GB, and 512 GB; this version of the card can have a capacity up to two terabytes (TB), theoretically, and SDXC cards generally have faster transfer speeds than the smaller-capacity cards.

The RX100 VI also can use micro SD cards, which are often used in smartphones and other small devices. These smaller cards operate the same as SD cards, but you need an adapter to use this tiny card in the RX100 VI camera, as shown in Figure 1-6.

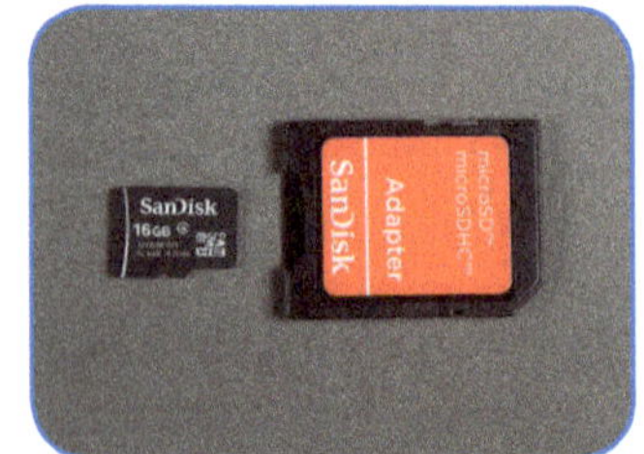

Figure 1-6. Micro SD Card and Adapter

In addition to using SD cards, the RX100 VI, being a Sony camera, also can use Sony's proprietary storage devices, known as Memory Stick cards. These cards are similar in size and capacity to SD cards, but with a slightly different shape, as shown in Figure 1-7.

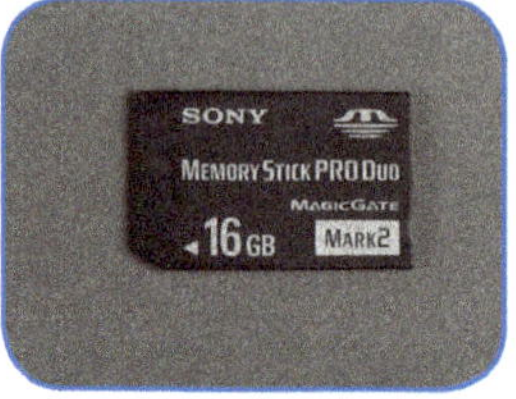

Figure 1-7. Sony Memory Stick Card

Memory Stick cards come in various types, according to their capacities. The ones that can be used in the RX100 VI are the Memory Stick PRO Duo, Memory Stick PRO-HG Duo, and Memory Stick Pro Duo (Mark 2).

There is an important limitation on your choice of a memory card. To record video using the XAVC S format, which provides the highest quality, if you are using an SDHC or SDXC card, you have to use one with a speed of Class 10, UHS Speed Class 1, or faster. If you are using a Memory Stick card, you have to use a Memory Stick PRO-HG Duo.

If you want to record in the XAVC S format using the highest quality of 100 megabits per second (Mbps), you have to use an SDHC or SDXC card rated in UHS Speed Class 3. (There is no Memory Stick card available for use in that situation.) These specifications are not just recommendations; if you try to record in a video format on a card that does not meet the requirements for that format, the camera will display an error message and will not record the video.

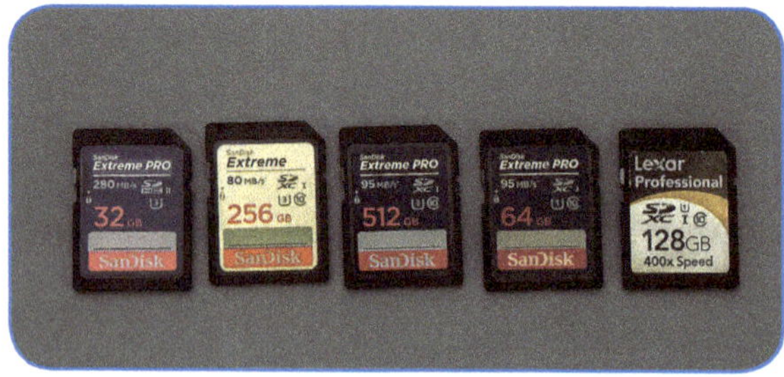

Figure 1-8. High-Speed SDXC Cards

The XAVC S format is worth using if you want high-quality video, and it is a good idea to get one of the high-powered cards that can support its use. Figure 1-8 shows three cards I have tested that can handle all video formats on the RX100 VI—the San Disk Extreme PRO 32 GB SDHC card, the SanDisk Extreme 256 GB SDXC card, and the SanDisk Extreme PRO 512 GB card, all of which are rated in UHS Speed Class 3. This figure also shows two other cards that can handle all video formats except for the 100 Mbps versions of the XAVC S formats—the SanDisk Extreme Pro 64 GB SDXC card, rated in UHS Speed Class 1, and the Lexar Professional 128 GB SDXC card, rated in that same speed class.

If you do not care about using the XAVC S video format, the factors to consider in choosing a card are capacity and speed. If you're planning to record a good deal of HD video or a large number of Raw-format photos, you should get a large-capacity card, but don't get carried away—the largest cards have such huge capacities that you may be wasting money purchasing them.

There are several variables to consider in computing how many images or videos you can store on a particular size of card, such as which aspect ratio you're using (3:2, 4:3, 16:9, or 1:1), image size, and quality. Here are a few examples of what can be stored on a 64 GB SDXC card. If you're using the standard 3:2 aspect ratio, you can store about 2,850 Raw images (the highest quality), 4,150 high-quality JPEG images (Large size and Extra Fine quality), or about 9,600 of the lower-quality Standard images (Large size).

You can fit about 1 hour 15 minutes of the highest-quality XAVC S video on a 64 GB card. That same card will hold about 8 hours 15 minutes of video at the lowest-quality AVCHD setting of 60i 17M (FH), which is still HD (high-definition) quality. Note, though, that the camera is limited to recording no more than about 29 minutes of video in any format in any one sequence. A sequence using one of the highest-quality XAVC S formats can be recorded for no more than about five minutes because of an issue with overheating of the sensor. The video formats and their limitations are discussed in Chapter 9.

The other major consideration is the speed of the card. High speed is important to get good results for recording continuous bursts of images and the highest-quality video with this camera. You should try to find a card that writes data at a rate of six MB/second or faster to record HD video. If you go by the class designation, a Class 4 card should be sufficient for shooting stills, and a Class 6 card should suffice for recording video, except for the requirements discussed above for recording XAVC S video.

If you decide to use a Sony Memory Stick card and want to use it with a card reader, be sure you have a reader that can accept those cards, which, as noted above, are not the same shape as SD cards.

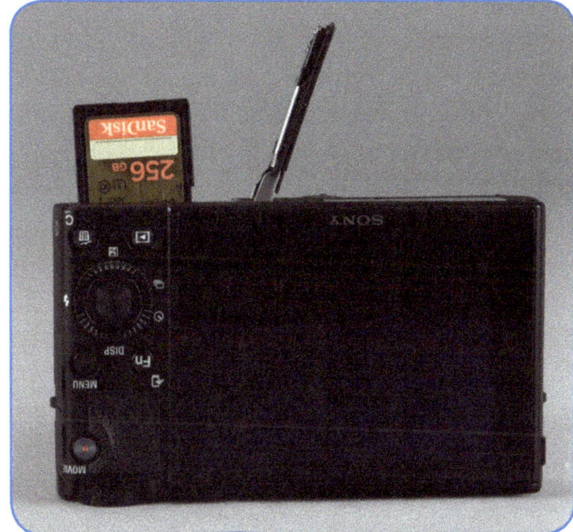

Figure 1-9. SD Card Going into Camera

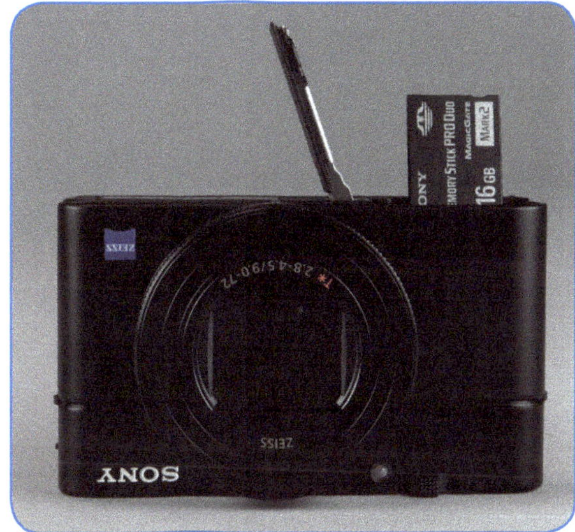

Figure 1-10. Memory Stick Card Going into Camera

Once you have chosen a card, open the same door on the bottom of the camera that covers the battery compartment, and slide the card in until it catches. An SD card is inserted with its label pointing toward the back of the camera, as shown in Figure 1-9; a Memory Stick card is inserted with its label pointing toward the front of the camera, as shown in Figure 1-10.

Once the card has been pushed down until it catches, close the compartment door and slide the latch to the outside position. To remove a card, push down on its edge until it releases and springs up, so you can grab it.

Although the card may work well when newly inserted in the camera, it's a good idea to format a card when first using it in the RX100 VI, so it will have the correct file structure and will have any bad areas blocked off from use. To do this, turn on the camera by pressing the power button, then press the Menu button at the center right of the camera's back. Next, press the Up button (upper edge of the control wheel on the camera's back) multiple times until the highlight has been moved into the line of menu icons at the top of the screen, as shown in Figure 1-11. then press the Right button as many times as necessary to highlight the toolbox icon, as shown in Figure 1-12, which represents the Setup menu.

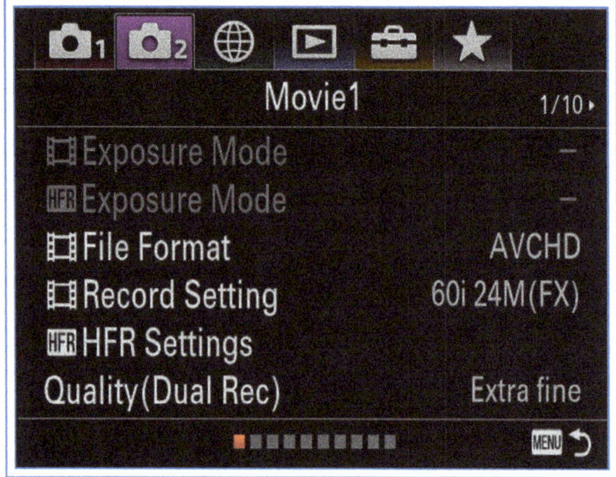

Figure 1-11. Highlight in Line of Menu Icons

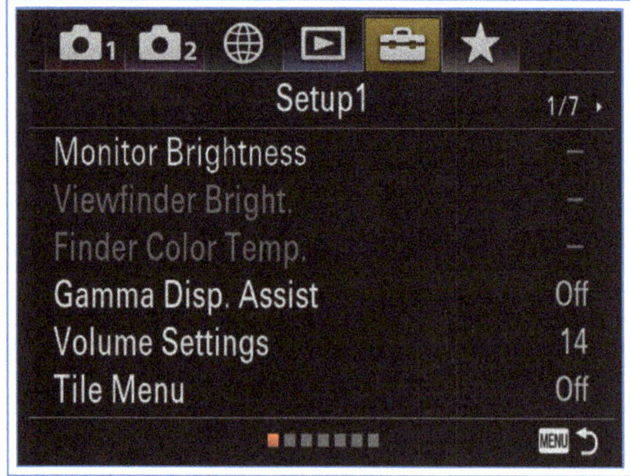

Figure 1-12. Toolbox Icon for Setup Menu Highlighted

When the toolbox icon is highlighted, press the Down button one time to move an orange highlight bar into the main menu screen, as shown in Figure 1-13. Then press the Right button as many times as needed to move the orange highlight bar to screen 5 of the Setup menu, as shown in Figure 1-14. Press the Down button until the Format command is highlighted, then press the button in the center of the control wheel (called the "Center button" in this book). On the next screen, seen in Figure 1-15, highlight Enter and press the Center button again to carry out the command.

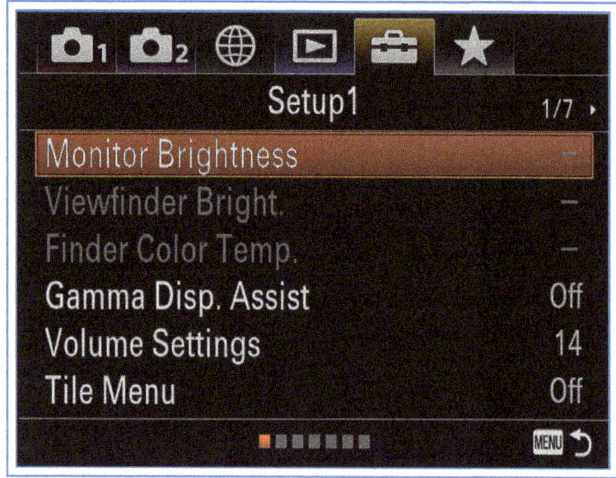

Figure 1-13. Highlight Bar in Setup Menu

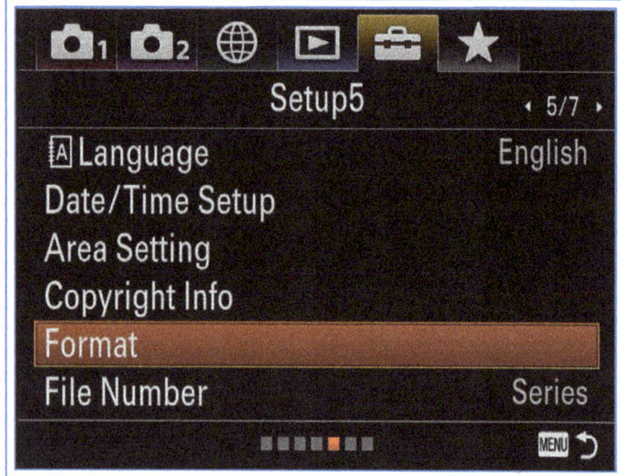

Figure 1-14. Format Option Highlighted on Setup Menu

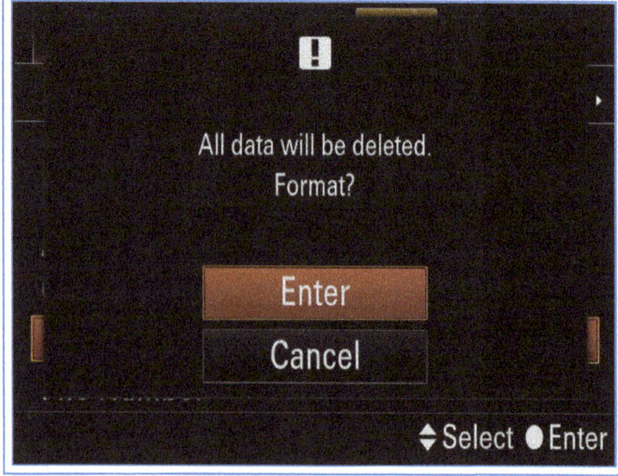

Figure 1-15. Confirmation Screen for Format Option

Setting the Language, Date, and Time

You need to have the date and time set correctly before you take pictures, because the camera records that information invisibly with each image and displays it later if you want. It is, of course, important to have the date (and the time of day) correctly recorded with your digital images. The camera may prompt you to set the date and time the first time you turn it on, but if not, carry out this procedure.

First, follow the same steps with the menu as noted above, but this time highlight the Date/Time Setup item on the second line of screen 5 of the Setup menu. Then press the Center button to move to the next screen. On that screen, select the Date/Time item and press the Center button. You will see a screen like the one in Figure 1-16.

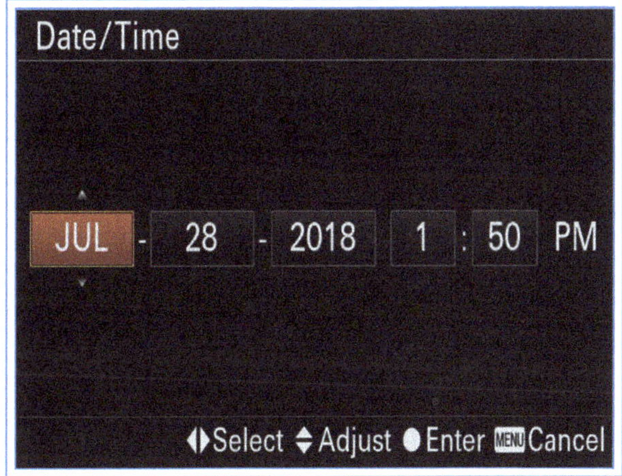

Figure 1-16. Date and Time Settings Screen

On that screen, by pressing the Left and Right buttons or by turning the control wheel, move through the month, day, year, and time settings, and change them by pressing the Up and Down buttons. When those settings have been made, press the Center button to confirm. You can adjust the Daylight Savings Time and Date Format settings on the previous screen if you need to. Then press the Menu button to exit from the menu system.

If you need to change the language the camera uses for menus and other messages, press the Menu button as discussed above to enter the menu system, and navigate to screen 5 of the Setup menu, as shown earlier.

With the direction buttons, move the highlight as needed to the Language item on the first line of the screen and press the Center button to select it. You then can select from the languages on the menu, as shown in Figure 1-17.

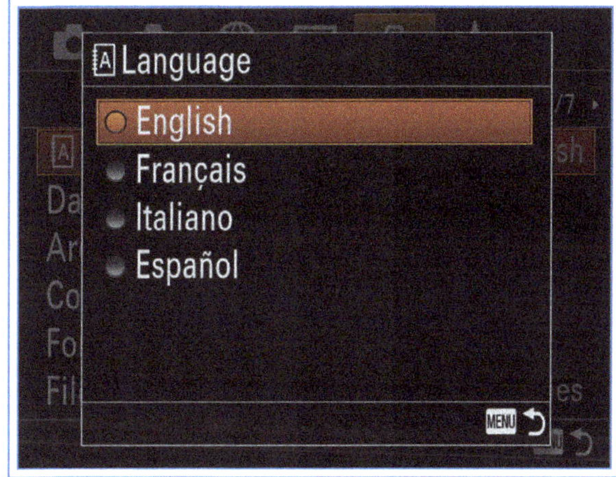

Figure 1-17. Language Selection Screen

Chapter 2: Basic Operations

Now that the Sony RX100 VI has the correct time and date set and a charged battery inserted along with a memory card, I'll discuss the steps to get your camera into action and to capture a usable image to your memory card.

Introduction to Main Controls

Before I discuss settings, I will introduce the camera's main controls to give a better idea of which button or dial is which. I won't discuss the controls in detail here; there is more information in Chapter 6. For now, I will include images showing the buttons, switches, and other controls of the RX100 VI. You may want to refer back to these images for a reminder about each control as you go through this book.

Top of Camera

On top of the camera are some of the most important controls and other features, as shown in Figure 2-1.

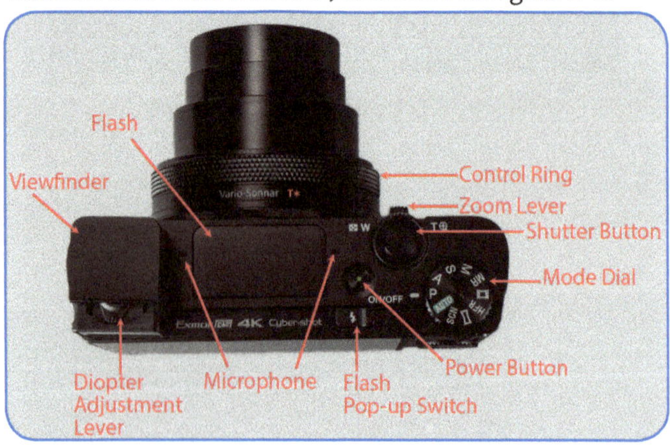

Figure 2-1. Controls on Top of Camera

The mode dial selects a shooting mode for stills or video. For basic shooting without having to make other settings, turn the dial so the AUTO icon is next to the white marker; this sets the camera to its most automatic mode. The large, black shutter release button is used to take pictures. Press it halfway to evaluate focus and exposure; press it all the way to take a picture. The zoom lever, surrounding the shutter button, is used to zoom the lens between its telephoto and wide-angle settings. The lever also is used to change the views of images in playback mode. The control ring, around the lens, can adjust items such as aperture, shutter speed, manual focus, and others, depending on the shooting mode and menu options in effect.

The power button turns the camera on and off. An orange light in the center of the button glows when the battery is being charged in the camera. A green light appears when the camera is powered on. The flash is stored inside the top of the camera; to use it, you have to pop it up using the flash pop-up switch behind the power button. The two small microphone openings are where the camera records sound for movies.

Back of Camera

Figure 2-2 shows the controls on the camera's back.

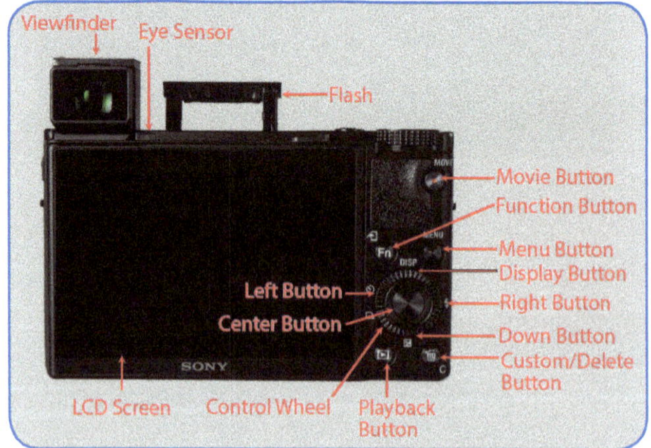

Figure 2-2. Controls on Back of Camera

The built-in electronic viewfinder (EVF) is stored inside the camera's top at the far left side until you pop it up using the Finder switch on the camera's left side. To the right of the viewfinder, in the raised edge just above the LCD screen, is a very small eye sensor, which detects the presence of your head for purposes of switching between the viewfinder and the LCD screen. The Movie button starts or stops a video recording. The

Menu button calls up the menu screens with settings for shooting and other values, such as control button functions, audio features, and others.

In shooting mode, the Function (Fn) button calls up a menu of camera settings for easy access. In playback mode, it activates the Send to Smartphone command, if the command is available, or it can be programmed for another function in playback mode. The Playback button puts the camera into playback mode so you can view recorded images, and it also can turn the camera on, directly into playback mode. The Custom/Delete button, marked with a C and a trash can icon, can be programmed to call up any one of numerous functions in shooting mode. In playback mode, it serves as the Delete button for erasing images.

The control wheel sets values such as aperture and shutter speed and navigates through menus. In addition, its four edges act as buttons when you press them, to control items including flash mode, exposure compensation, continuous shooting, and the display screen. The Center button confirms selections and does other operations. The LCD screen—which displays the live view along with the camera's settings and plays back recorded images—tilts up or down to allow you to hold the camera in a high or low position to view a scene from unusual angles. It also can rotate 180 degrees forward to let you take a self-portrait. It incorporates a touch screen, used for focusing and magnifying images.

Front of Camera

Figure 2-3 shows the items on the camera's front.

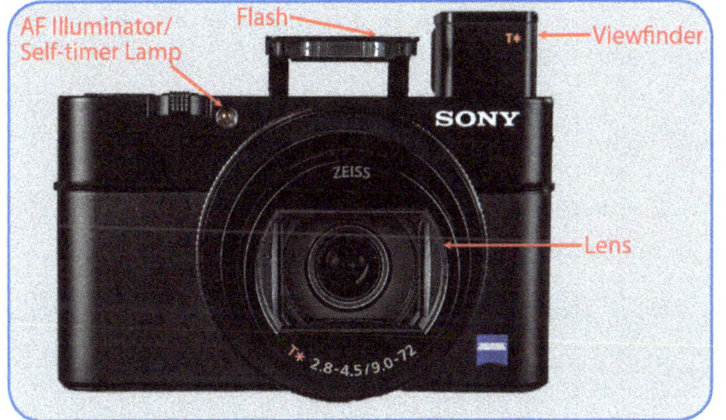

Figure 2-3. Items on Front of Camera

The AF Illuminator/Self-timer Lamp signals operation of the self-timer and provides illumination so the camera can use its autofocus system in dark areas. The lens has a 35mm equivalent focal length range of 24mm to 200mm and an aperture range of f/2.8 to f/11.0. (The actual focal length range of the lens is 9mm to 72mm; the "35mm equivalent" range is commonly used to state the focal length in a way that can easily be compared to lenses of other cameras.)

Right Side of Camera

On the right side of the camera are two small flaps, marked Multi and HDMI, as shown in Figure 2-4. Under those flaps are two ports, as shown in Figure 2-5.

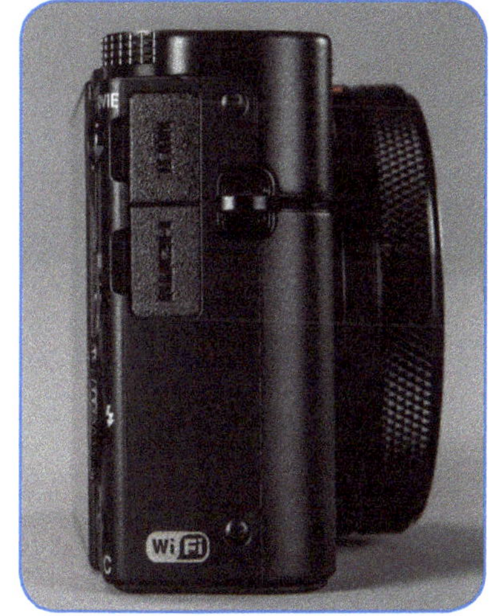

Figure 2-4. Ports on Right Side of Camera - Closed

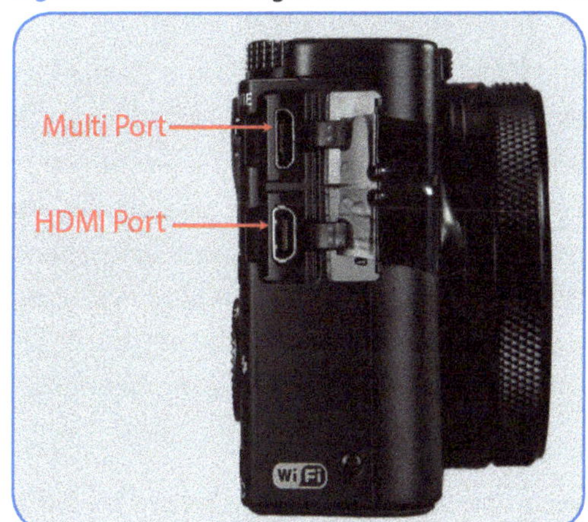

Figure 2-5. Ports on Right Side of Camera - Open

The Multi port or terminal is where you connect the micro USB cable that is supplied with the camera to charge the battery, to power the camera, to connect the camera to a computer to manage images, or to connect to a printer to print images directly from the camera. You also can connect a wired remote control to this port, as discussed in Appendix A. If you download the Imaging Edge software from Sony's website, as mentioned in Chapter 1, you can connect the camera to your computer through this port and control the camera using that Sony software. The HDMI port is for connecting the camera to an HDTV to view images and videos. You can also use this port to output a "clean" video signal to a video recorder as discussed in Chapters 8 and 9, or to a monitor so you can view the shooting information from the camera in shooting mode.

Left Side of Camera

The left side of the camera, shown in Figure 2-6, has two items of interest.

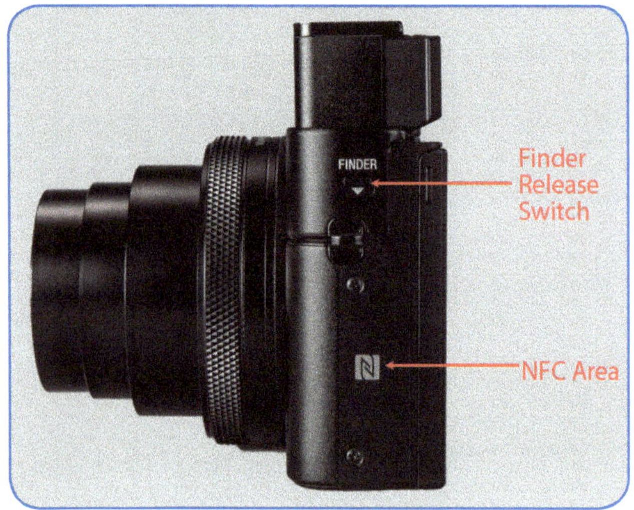

Figure 2-6. Left Side of Camera

The first is the finder release switch, which you press down to release the electronic viewfinder so it will pop up. When the viewfinder pops up, the camera will turn on if it was powered off. When you are finished with the viewfinder, press it back down into the camera's body. When you do this, the camera will turn off or stay powered on, depending on the setting of the menu option called Function for VF Close, the last item on screen 2 of the Setup menu.

The other item of interest on the left side of the RX100 VI is the NFC (near field communication) area, marked by a letter N, where you touch the camera against a smartphone or tablet with NFC capability to establish a Wi-Fi connection automatically. I will discuss this feature in Chapter 10.

Bottom of Camera

Finally, as shown in Figure 2-7, on the bottom of the camera are the tripod socket, the battery/memory card compartment, and the speaker that produces sound for videos. There also is one other item that can't be seen unless the battery compartment is open—the access lamp, located at the outside edge of the compartment, as shown in Figure 2-8.

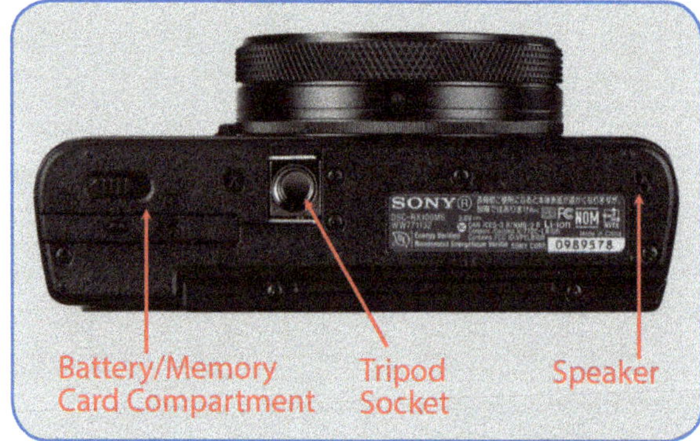

Figure 2-7. Items on Bottom of Camera

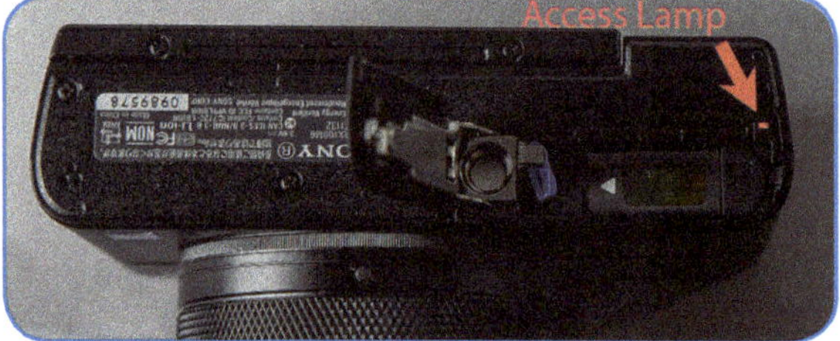

Figure 2-8. Red Access Lamp Inside Battery Compartment

That red lamp lights up when the camera is writing data to the memory card. When the camera has taken a long series of continuous shots, the lamp may stay illuminated for several seconds. During that time, do not remove the battery or the memory card.

Taking Pictures in Intelligent Auto Mode

Now I'll discuss how to use these controls to start taking pictures and videos. First, here is a set of steps for taking still photos if you want to let the camera make most decisions for you. This is a good approach for quick snapshots without fiddling with too many settings.

1. Press the power button on top of the camera. The LCD screen will light up as the camera turns on.
2. Turn the mode dial so the AUTO icon is next to the white indicator line, as shown in Figure 2-9.
3. This sets the camera to the Auto shooting mode. If you see the help screen that describes the mode (called the Mode Dial Guide), as seen in Figure 2-10, press the Center button to dismiss it. (You can dispense with that help screen altogether using

the Mode Dial Guide option on screen 2 of the Setup menu, as discussed in Chapter 8.)

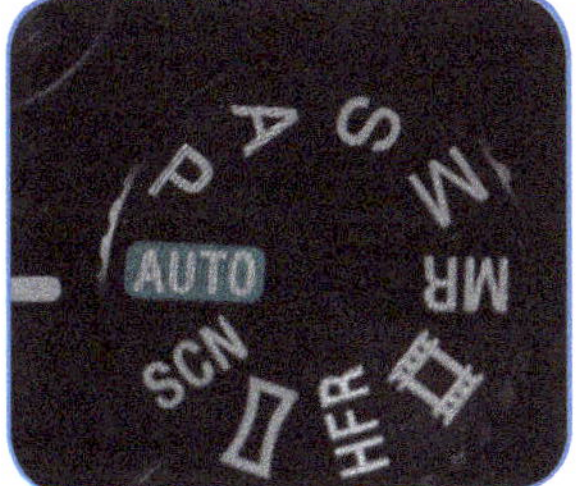

Figure 2-9. Mode Dial at Auto

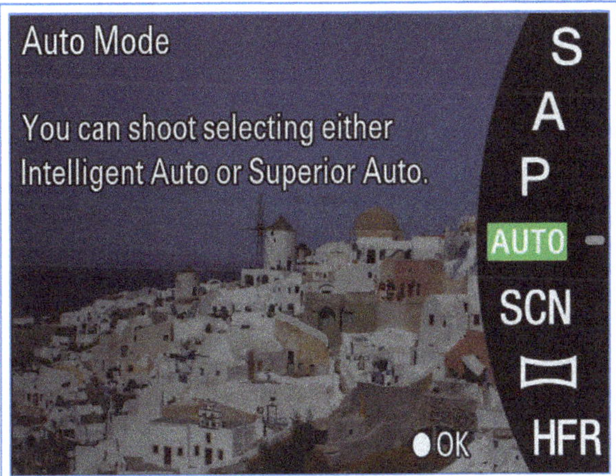

Figure 2-10. Mode Dial Guide for Auto Mode

4. When you first select Auto mode, if the Mode Dial Guide is turned on, after you dismiss the Mode Dial Guide screen, the camera will display the screen shown in Figure 2-11, letting you choose either Intelligent Auto mode (green camera icon) or Superior Auto mode (tan camera icon). For now, leave the green icon highlighted, and press the Center button to dismiss that screen.

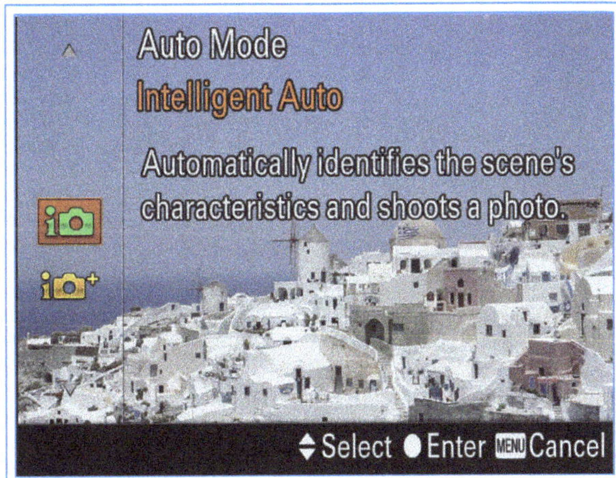

Figure 2-11. Screen to Select Intelligent Auto or Superior Auto

5. Press the Menu button on the camera's back to activate the menu system. As I discussed in Chapter 1, navigate through the menu screens by pressing the Right and Left buttons. The Camera Settings1 and Camera Settings2 menus are headed by a camera icon with a number 1 or 2; the Network menu by the globe icon; the Playback menu by the triangular Playback symbol; the Setup menu by the toolbox icon; and the My Menu option by the star icon.

6. The icon for the currently active menu system is highlighted with a color background and is outlined by a gray line. You can tell which numbered screen of that menu system is active by looking at the numbers separated by a slash mark at the upper right corner of the display, such as the numbers 1/12 shown in Figure 2-12, meaning the camera is displaying the first of 12 menu screens. You also can tell what menu screen is currently displayed by looking at the line of dots at the very bottom of the screen. One of those dots will be orange, to indicate which screen is displayed.

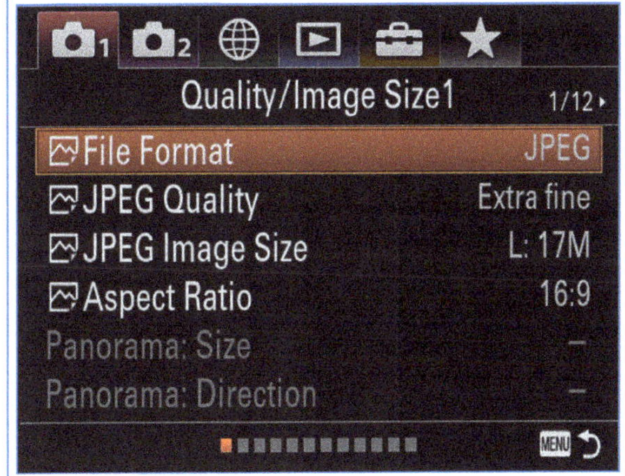

Figure 2-12. Screen 1 of Camera Settings1 Menu

7. When a given menu screen is selected, navigate up and down through the options on that screen by pressing the Up and Down buttons or by turning the control wheel right or left. When the orange selection bar is on the option you want, press the Center button to select that item. Then press the Up and Down buttons or turn the control wheel to highlight the value you want for that option, and press the Center button to confirm it. You can then continue making menu settings; when you are finished with the menu system, press the Menu button to go back to the live view, so you can take pictures.

8. Using the procedure in Step 7, make the settings shown in Table 2-1 for the Camera Settings1 menu. For menu options not listed here, any setting is acceptable for now. I have not listed some settings that are not available for changing in this shooting mode, such as Long Exposure Noise Reduction.

Table 2-1. **Recommended Settings for Taking Pictures in Intelligent Auto Mode: Camera Settings1 Menu**

Menu Option	Setting
File Format (Still Images)	JPEG
JPEG Quality	Extra Fine
JPEG Image Size	L: 20M
Aspect Ratio	3:2
Color Space	sRGB
Auto Mode	Intelligent Auto
Drive Mode	Single Shooting
Bracket Settings	No Setting Needed
Memory	No Setting Needed
Focus Mode	Single-shot AF
AF Illuminator	Auto
Center Lock-on AF	Off
Set Face Priority in AF	No Setting Needed
Pre-AF	Off
AF Area Registration	Off
Del. Reg. AF Area	No Setting Needed
AF Area Auto Clear	Off
Disp. Cont. AF Area	On
Phase Detect. Area	Off
Spot Metering Point	Center
AEL w/Shutter	Auto
Exposure Std. Adjust	No Setting Needed
Flash Mode	Autoflash
Red Eye Reduction	Off
Soft Skin Effect	Off
Focus Magnifier	No Setting Needed
Focus Magnification Time	No Limit
Initial Focus Mag.	x1.0
MF Assist	On
Peaking Setting/Display	On
Peaking Setting/Level	Mid
Peaking Setting/Color	Yellow
Face Registration	No Setting Needed
Registered Faces Priority	Off
Smile Shutter	Off
Auto Obj. Framing	Off
Self-portrait/ -timer	On

9. If you're indoors or in an area with low light, press the flash pop-up switch, located on top of the camera to the right of the built-in flash unit, to release the flash unit and cause it to pop up. If you don't do this, the flash cannot be fired. Then press the Right button on the control wheel, marked with a lightning bolt. A vertical menu will appear at the left side of the screen, as shown in Figure 2-13.

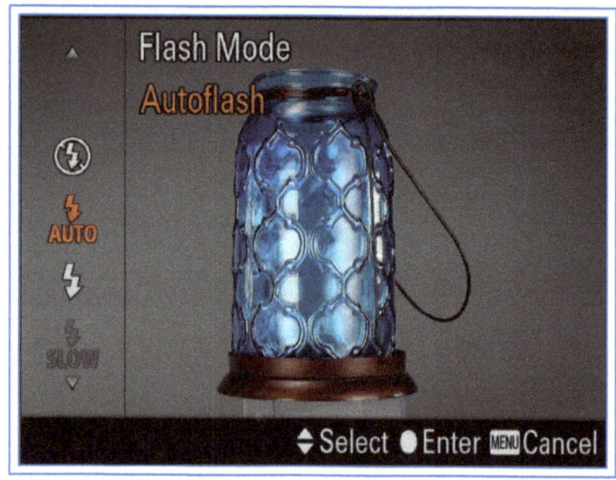

Figure 2-13. Flash Mode Menu

10. Make sure Autoflash is highlighted with the orange selection highlight. If it is not, press the Up or Down button or turn the control wheel to highlight it, so the flash mode is set to Autoflash. Press the Center button to dismiss this menu.

11. Using a procedure like that in Steps 9 and 10, press the Left button, marked with a timer dial and an icon for a stack of images, and make sure the top option, showing a single rectangular frame, is selected, as shown in Figure 2-14. This sets the camera to take single shots, rather than continuous bursts.

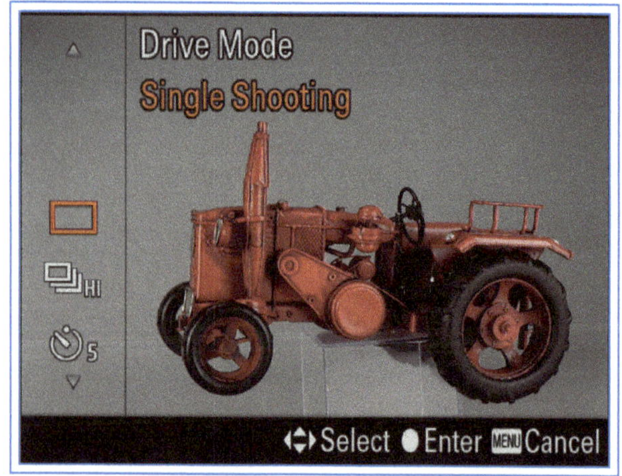

Figure 2-14. Single Shooting Highlighted on Drive Mode Menu

12. If you don't want to make all of these settings, don't worry; you are likely to get usable images even if you don't adjust most of these settings at this point. I have not included any recommendations for the Camera Settings2, Setup, or other menus; the default settings should work well in Intelligent Auto mode. I will discuss all of the menu options later in the book.
13. Press the Menu button again to make the menu disappear, if it hasn't done so already.
14. Aim the camera to compose the picture. Locate the zoom lever on the ring that surrounds the shutter button on the top right of the camera. Push it to the left, toward the letter "W," to get a wider-angle shot (including more of the scene in the picture), or to the right, toward the letter "T," to get a telephoto, zoomed-in shot. Or, if you prefer, turn the control ring (the ridged ring around the lens) to zoom in and out.
15. Once the picture looks good on the display, gently press the shutter button halfway and pause in that position. You should hear a beep and see one or more sets of green focus brackets on the LCD screen indicating that the subject will be in focus, as shown in Figure 2-15.

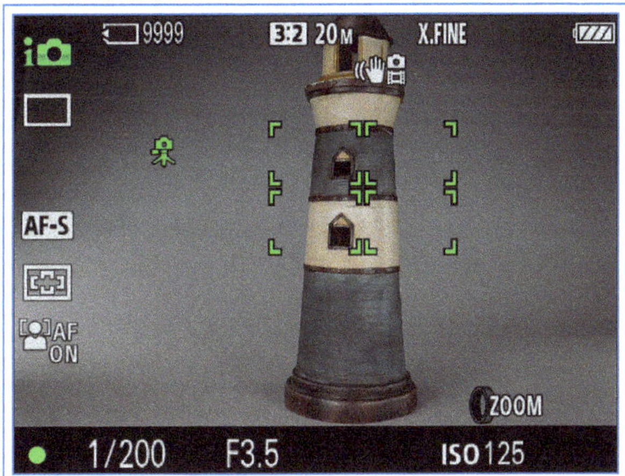

Figure 2-15. Green Brackets Indicating Sharp Focus

16. You also should see a green disc in the extreme lower left corner of the screen. If that green disc lights up steadily, the image is in focus; if it flashes, the camera was unable to focus. In that case, you can re-aim and see if the autofocus system does better from a different distance or angle.
17. After you have made sure the focus is sharp, press the shutter button all the way down to take the picture.

Variations from Fully Automatic

Although the RX100 VI takes care of several settings when it's set to Intelligent Auto mode, this camera, unlike some other compact models, still lets you make a number of adjustments to fine-tune the shooting process.

Focus

With some compact cameras, you have few or no options for focus settings in the most automatic shooting mode. With the RX100 VI, however, you can select any focus mode you want. I will give a brief overview of focus options here, with further discussion in the chapters that discuss menu options and physical controls.

Focus Modes

There are five focus modes available for shooting still images with the RX100 VI, as indicated by the five settings for the focus mode item on screen 4 of the Camera Settings1 menu (AF-S, AF-A, AF-C, DMF, and MF), which are shown in Figure 2-16. Those settings are single-shot autofocus, automatic autofocus, continuous autofocus, direct manual focus, and manual focus. (For movies, the only usable options are the AF-C and MF settings.)

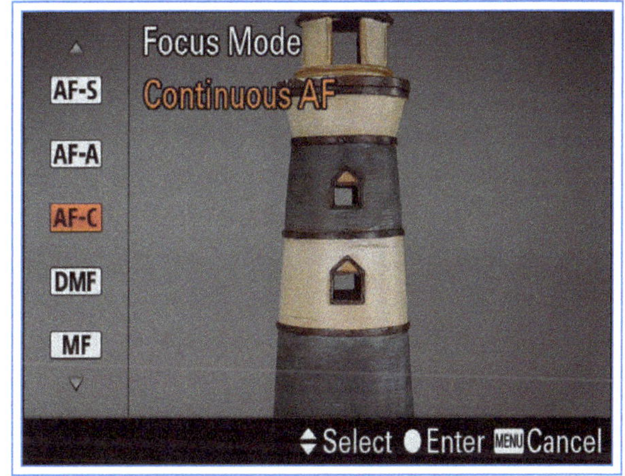

Figure 2-16. Focus Mode Menu

With the AF-S setting, the camera starts to focus when you press the shutter button halfway down. At that point, it tries to achieve sharp focus on an object in the focus area. If it can focus sharply, it beeps and displays one or more green focus frames and a solid green disk. The focus stays locked at that distance as long as you hold the shutter button halfway down; you can then press the button the rest of the way down to take the picture.

With the AF-A setting, the camera combines the AF-S and AF-C settings. That is, it locks focus and keeps it locked if the subject is not moving, as is the case with the AF-S setting. However, if the subject (or the camera) starts to move, the camera operates as if it were using the AF-C setting, discussed below, and continuously adjusts the focus as necessary to keep the subject in focus.

With the AF-C setting, when you press the shutter button halfway, the camera attempts to focus on an object in the focus area, but it then continues to adjust the focus as needed, if the camera or the subject moves. The camera does not lock the focus setting until you press the button all the way down to take the picture. The camera never displays a focus frame on the screen. The green disk appears in the lower left of the display when focus is achieved, but it is surrounded by curving lines to indicate that the camera is continuing to adjust focus.

With the DMF setting, the camera lets you use both the autofocus capability of single autofocus and the manual focusing capability. With this combination of two focus modes, you can press the shutter button halfway to let the camera use autofocus, and then continue to adjust focus by turning the control ring. Or, you can start to adjust focus manually in order to let the camera know approximately where the focus should be centered, and then press the shutter button halfway to let the camera fine-tune the focus on that subject.

Finally, with the MF setting, focusing is entirely up to you. You turn the control ring to bring the image into sharp focus. You might use manual focus in a dark or reflective environment where the camera would have difficulty, or in a situation where the camera might not focus on the subject that is most important to you. Another use of manual focus is for extreme closeup shots, when you need to adjust the focus distance very precisely. As I will discuss in Chapter 4, you can set the camera to assist with manual focusing through several menu options.

My preference is to use the AF-S setting for single autofocus in most situations. In tricky focusing environments, such as taking macro images or pictures of the moon, I often use manual focus with the focus-assisting aids provided by the camera. You may find that continuous autofocus is useful when you are taking pictures of subjects that are moving unpredictably, such as animals or children at play.

Finally, you can touch the screen to tell the camera where to direct its autofocus. For this feature to work, you have to have the touch screen turned on using the Touch Operation option on screen 3 of the Setup menu. Then, below that option, make sure that either the Touch Panel + Pad option or the Touch Panel Only option is turned on. When you touch an area on the screen, the camera will place a focus frame at that point. Then press the shutter button down halfway to focus at that area and all the way down to capture the image. I will discuss the touch focus and other touch operations of the LCD monitor in Chapter 6, where I discuss the camera's physical controls.

Other Settings

There are several other items that can be adjusted in Auto mode, but not many that will have an immediate and noticeable effect on your photography. For example, you can adjust items such as the aspect ratio (shape) of your images as well as the file format, image size, and quality. Those options are important when you want to have more control over your images, but, for general picture-taking in Intelligent Auto mode, they are not critical. I have set forth recommended menu settings in Table 2-1, and I will discuss details of those options in Chapter 4.

However, there are a few menu options you might want to take advantage of when you first use the RX100 VI in Intelligent Auto mode, and I will discuss those briefly now.

You might want to use the Soft Skin Effect option, so the camera will use processing to soften the appearance of skin tones. That option is located on screen 10 of the Camera Settings1 menu. It is effective only when face detection is turned on and a face is detected. (Face detection is automatically turned on in Auto mode.) When the effect is turned on, you can set it to Lo, Mid, or Hi using the Left and Right buttons.

Another setting you might want to try for basic shooting is the Auto Mode option, the first item on screen 3 of the Camera Settings1 menu. Normally, this option is set to Intelligent Auto. If you select the other available setting, Superior Auto, the camera will use the same settings and functions as with Intelligent Auto mode, but it will go one step further. In appropriate conditions, the camera will use its special multiple-shot capability. That is, if the environment is dark or lighted from behind (backlit), the camera may take a rapid burst of shots using a high ISO setting, and combine those shots internally to produce a composite image of higher quality than otherwise would be possible. I will discuss that option in Chapter 3.

Flash

You may want to use the RX100 VI's built-in flash unit if you take pictures in dim lighting or need flash to soften shadows. In Chapter 4 I'll discuss the flash mode settings, Flash Compensation, and the prevention of "red-eye." In Appendix A, I'll discuss how you can use external flash units, even though the camera has no flash shoe.

It's important to remember that the built-in flash unit cannot pop up on its own, even if the flash mode is set to Fill-flash, which requires the flash to fire. You have to use the flash pop-up switch on top of the camera to release the flash before it can fire.

For this discussion, I'm assuming the camera is set to Intelligent Auto mode. In some other situations, such as with some of the Scene mode settings, the Flash menu will not appear; you will see an error message if you press the Right button when the shooting screen is active.

In Intelligent Auto mode, with the flash unit popped up, press the Right button once to call up the flash mode menu, then press the Up and Down buttons or turn the control wheel to select a flash mode from that list. Press the Center button to confirm the selection. (You also can summon the flash mode menu from the Camera Settings1 menu: flash mode is the first item on screen 8 of that menu. See Chapter 4 for a discussion of all items on the screens of that menu.)

The vertical menu at the left of the screen, shown in Figure 2-17, has icons for the five flash modes—a lightning bolt with the "no" sign crossing it out, for Flash Off; a lightning bolt with the word "Auto," for Autoflash; a lightning bolt alone, for Fill-flash (meaning the flash will always fire); a lightning bolt with the word "Slow," for Slow Sync; and a lightning bolt with the word "Rear," for Rear Sync. When the camera is in Intelligent Auto mode, the last two choices will be dimmed; if you highlight one of them and press the Center button, the camera will display a message saying you cannot make that selection in this shooting mode.

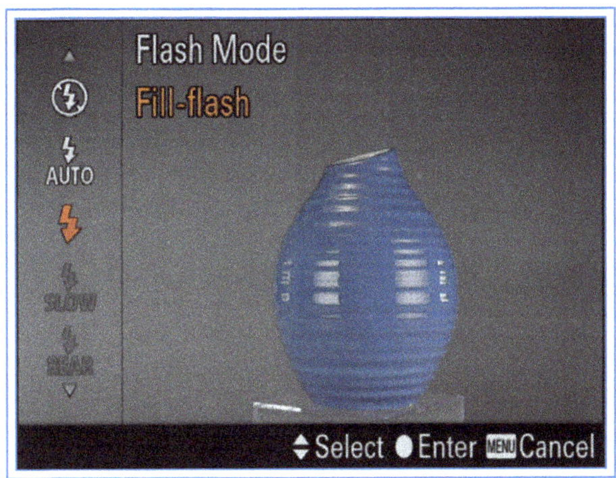

Figure 2-17. Flash Mode Menu

I discussed earlier how to choose Autoflash. If you choose Fill-flash instead, you will see the lightning bolt icon on the screen at all times when the flash is popped up and the detailed display screen is selected. With this setting, the flash will fire regardless of whether the camera's exposure system believes flash is needed. Use this setting when you are certain you want the flash to fire, such as in a dimly lighted room. This setting also can be used in outdoor settings, such as when the sun is shining and you want to reduce the shadows on your subject's face. I will provide an illustration of the use of Fill-flash in Chapter 4.

When the camera is set for using the self-timer with multiple shots, the flash is forced off and cannot be used. If you turn on the flash with burst shooting, the use of flash will drastically limit the shooting speed. Instead of firing a rapid burst, the camera will take multiple images at a slow rate because the flash needs to recycle between shots. In some cases, such as with the Night Scene setting of Scene mode, you cannot even get the flash mode menu to appear; if you press the Flash button, the camera will display a message saying the flash is not available in that shooting mode, as shown in Figure 2-18.

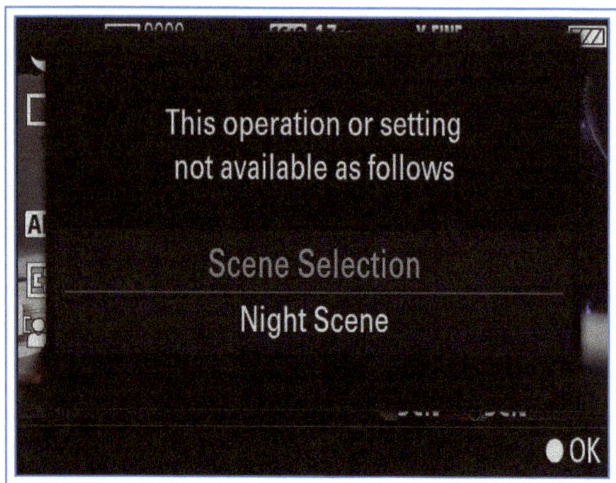

Figure 2-18. Message When Flash Not Available for Use

If you set the mode dial to P, for Program mode, and then press the Right button to select a flash mode, you will see the same five options for flash mode on the menu, but this time the Autoflash option will be dimmed because that selection is not available in that shooting mode.

In summary, when using Intelligent Auto (or Superior Auto) mode, if you don't want the flash to fire because you are in a museum or similar location, you can select the Flash Off mode. You also can just leave the flash stored inside the camera, so it cannot pop up and fire.

If you want to let the camera decide whether to fire the flash, you can select Autoflash mode. To make sure that the flash will fire no matter what, you can select Fill-flash mode. In Chapter 4, I'll explain the other flash options, Slow Sync and Rear Sync, and I'll discuss some other flash-related topics.

Drive Mode: Self-Timer and Continuous Shooting

The drive mode menu option includes more adjustments you can make when using Intelligent Auto mode. If you press the control wheel's Left button, which is marked with a timer dial and an icon that looks like a stack of images, the camera will display a vertical menu for drive mode, as shown in Figure 2-19. Navigate through these options by pressing the Up and Down buttons or by turning the control wheel.

I will discuss the drive mode menu options more fully in Chapter 4. For now, you should be aware of a few of the choices. (I will skip over some others.) If you select the top option, represented by a single rectangular frame, the camera is set for single shooting mode; when you press the shutter button, a single image is captured. With the second option, whose icon looks like a stack of images, the camera is set for continuous shooting and takes a rapid burst of images while you hold down the shutter button. You can use the Left and Right buttons to choose from Hi, Mid, or Lo for the speed of shooting.

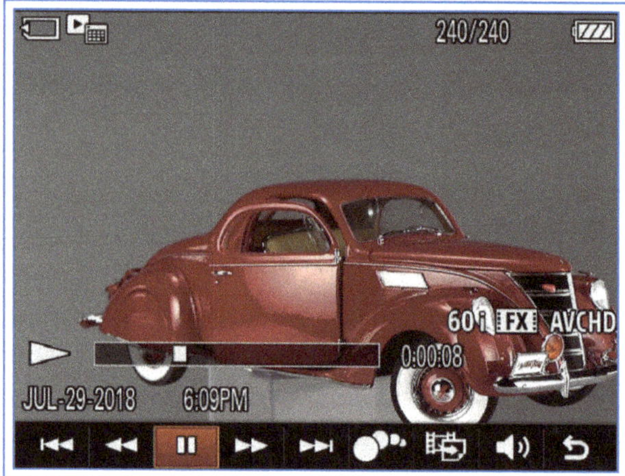

Figure 2-19. Drive Mode Menu

If you choose the third option, whose icon is a timer dial with a number beside it, the camera uses the self-timer. Use the Left and Right buttons to choose two, five, or ten seconds for the timer delay. After the timer has been set, press the shutter button. The shutter will be released after the specified number of seconds. The ten-second or five-second delay is useful when you need to place the camera on a tripod and join a group photo; the two-second delay is useful to make sure the camera is not jiggled by the action of pressing the shutter button. The two-second setting helps greatly when you are taking a picture for which focusing is critical, such as an extreme closeup. I will discuss the use of the self-timer and other drive mode options in more detail in Chapter 4.

The drive mode options also can be reached as the third item on screen 3 of the Camera Settings1 menu.

There are other settings that can be made when the camera is set to Intelligent Auto or Superior Auto mode, including File Format (Still Images), JPEG Quality, JPEG Image Size, Aspect Ratio, and others. I included suggested settings for those items in Table 2-1 earlier in this chapter, and I will discuss the details of those settings in Chapter 4.

Overview of Movie Recording

It is easy to record a movie sequence with the RX100 VI using standard settings. Once the camera is turned on, turn the mode dial to select the green AUTO icon, for Intelligent Auto mode. There is a special Movie mode setting marked by the movie film icon on the mode dial, but you don't have to use that mode for shooting movies; I'll discuss the use of that option and other details about video recording in Chapter 9.

On the first screen of the Camera Settings2 menu, highlight File Format (Movies) and press the Center button to go to the submenu with three choices for the format of movie recording. For now, be sure the third option, AVCHD, is selected, as shown in Figure 2-20; that format provides high quality for your videos without requiring a special memory card. (As discussed in Chapter 1, if you select XAVC S 4K or XAVC S HD for the movie format, you have to use a memory card in Speed Class 10 or greater.)

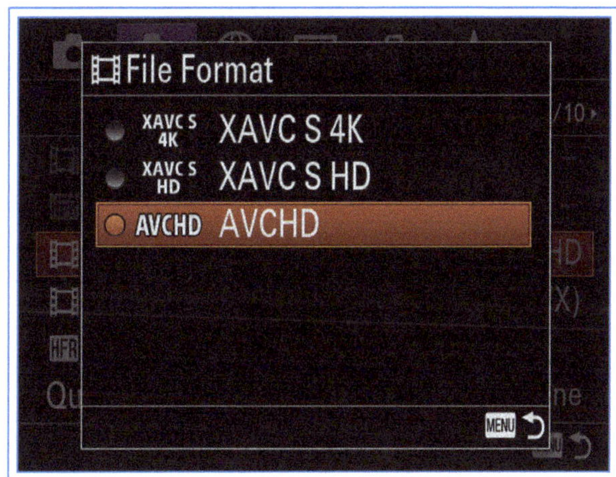

Figure 2-20. AVCHD Highlighted for File Format (Movies)

Using the focus mode option on screen 4 of the Camera Settings1 menu, select AF-S for single autofocus, AF-A for automatic autofocus, AF-C for continuous autofocus, or DMF for direct manual focus. With any of those settings, the camera will use continuous autofocus for recording movies.

For the rest of the settings, I will provide a table like the one included earlier in this chapter for shooting still images. The settings shown in Table 2-2 are standard ones for shooting good-quality movies. All of these settings are found on the Camera Settings2 menu.

Table 2-2. **Suggested Camera Settings2 Menu Settings for Recording Movies in Intelligent Auto Mode**

Menu Option	Setting
File Format	AVCHD
Record Setting	60i 24M (FX)
HFR Settings	No Setting Needed
Quality (Dual Rec)	Extra Fine
Image Size (Dual Rec)	L: 17M
Auto Dual Rec	Off
Proxy Recording	Off
AF Drive Speed	Normal
AF Tracking Sensitivity	Standard
Auto Slow Shutter	On
Audio Recording	On
Micref Level	Normal
Wind Noise Reduction	Off
SteadyShot (Movies)	Standard (Off if on tripod)
Marker Display	Off
Marker Settings	No Setting Needed
Movie w/ Shutter	Off
Shutter Type	Auto
Release w/o Card	Disable
SteadyShot (Still Images)	On
Zoom Setting	Optical Zoom Only
Zoom Speed	Normal
Zoom Func. on Ring	Standard
Display Button	No Setting Needed
Finder/Monitor	Auto
Zebra Setting/Display	Off
Zebra Setting/Level	No Setting Needed
Grid Line	Off
Exposure Settings Guide	Off
Live View Display	Setting Effect On (can't be changed)
Auto Review	2 Sec
Custom Key (Still Images)	No Setting Needed
Custom Key (Movies)	No Setting Needed
Custom Key (Playback)	No Setting Needed
Function Menu Settings	No Setting Needed
Av/Tv Rotate	Normal
Touch Shooting Settings	Touch Focus
Movie Button	Always
Wheel Lock	Unlock
Audio Signals	On: All
Write Date	Off

There are some other settings you can make for still

images on the Camera Settings1 menu that will affect movie recording; I will discuss that topic in Chapter 9. You can leave these items set as they were for shooting still images, as listed in Table 2-1.

After making these settings, aim the camera at your subject, and when you are ready to start recording, press and release the red Movie button at the upper right of the camera's back. (If you see an error message, go to screen 10 of the Camera Settings2 menu, and make sure the Movie Button option is set to Always.)

The screen will display a red REC icon in the lower left corner of the display, above a counter showing the elapsed time in the recording, as shown in Figure 2-21.

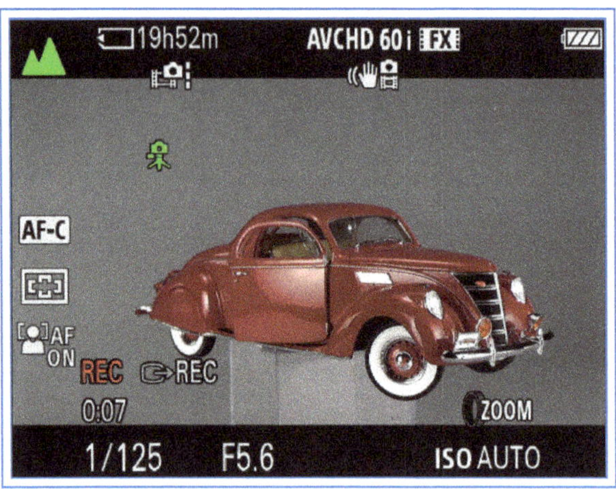

Figure 2-21. Shooting Screen During Video Recording

Hold the camera as steady as possible (or use a tripod) and pan it (move it side to side) smoothly if you need to. The camera will keep shooting until it reaches a recording limit, or until you press the red Movie button again to stop the recording. (The maximum time for continuous recording of any one scene is about 29 minutes.)

The camera will automatically adjust exposure as lighting conditions change. You can zoom the lens in and out as needed, but you should do so sparingly if at all, to avoid distracting the audience and to avoid recording sounds of zooming the lens on the sound track. If the Touch Operation features are turned on through screen 3 of the Setup menu, and the camera is set for autofocus, you can touch the screen where you want the camera to direct its focus. When you are finished recording, press the Movie button again, and the camera will save the footage.

I'll discuss movie options in more detail in Chapter 9.

Viewing Pictures

Before I cover more advanced settings for taking still pictures and movies, as well as other matters of interest, I will discuss the basics of viewing your images in the camera.

Review While in Shooting Mode

Each time you take a still picture, the image will show up on the LCD screen (or in the viewfinder) for a short time, if you have the Auto Review option on screen 8 of the Camera Settings2 menu set to turn on this function. I'll discuss the details of that setting in Chapter 5. By default, the image will stay on the screen for two seconds after you take a new picture. If you prefer, you can set that display to last for five or ten seconds, or to be off altogether.

Reviewing Images in Playback Mode

To review images taken previously, you enter playback mode by pressing the Playback button—the one with the small triangle icon to the lower left of the control wheel. To view all still images and movies for a particular date, go to screen 3 of the Playback menu and set the View Mode option to Date View. If you prefer, you can set View Mode to show only stills, only AVCHD movies, only XAVC S HD movies, or only XAVC S 4K movies.

Once you choose a viewing option, you can scroll through recorded images and movies by pressing the Left and Right buttons or by turning the control wheel. Hold down the Left or Right button to move more quickly through the images. You can enlarge the view of any still image by moving the zoom lever on top of the camera toward the T position, and you can scroll around in the enlarged image using the four direction buttons.

In addition, you can enlarge a still image by tapping quickly twice on the screen, if the touch screen features of the LCD screen are enabled through the Touch Operation item on screen 3 of the Setup menu. After double-tapping the screen, you can scroll the enlarged image around with your fingers, and you can return it to normal size by double-tapping again.

If you press the zoom lever in the other direction, toward the wide-angle setting, an enlarged image will return to normal size. If you press the lever once more in that direction, you will see an index screen with a number of thumbnail images (either 9 or 25, depending on a Playback menu option). A further press brings up a folder view or a calendar screen for selecting images or videos by date, depending on the View Mode setting. You can select images from the index and date screens by pressing the Center button on a highlighted thumbnail image. I'll discuss other playback options in Chapter 7.

Playing Movies

To play movies, move through the files by the methods described above until you find the movie you want to play. You should see a triangular playback icon inside a circle, as shown in Figure 2-22.

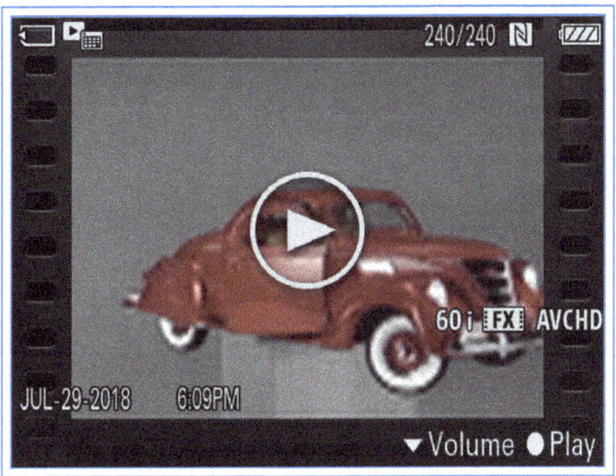

Figure 2-22. Movie Ready to Play in Camera

Press the Center button to start the movie playing. Then, as seen in Figure 2-23, you will see icons at the bottom of the screen for the controls you can use, including the Center button to pause and resume play.

(If you don't see the controls, press the Display button until they appear.) You also can press the Down button to bring up a more detailed set of controls on the screen, as shown in Figure 2-24.

To change the volume, pause the movie and press the Down button to bring up the detailed controls; then navigate to the speaker icon, next to last at the right of those controls, and press the Center button to select it. Then use the control wheel or the Right and Left buttons to adjust the volume. You also can adjust the volume before a movie starts playing, by pressing the Down button to bring up the volume control. To exit from playing the movie, press the Playback button. (I'll discuss other movie playback options in Chapter 9.)

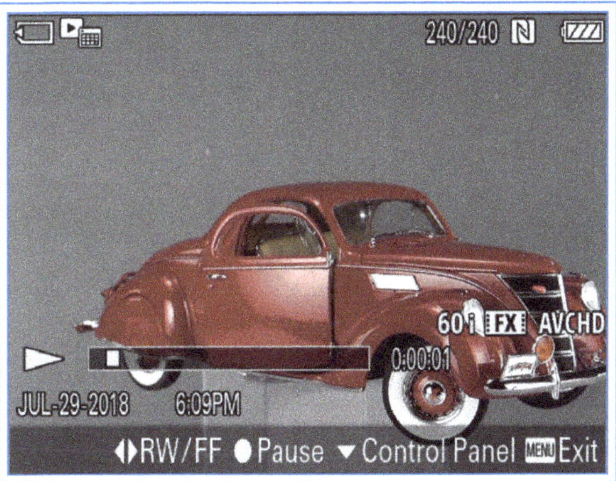

Figure 2-23. Initial Movie Playback Icons

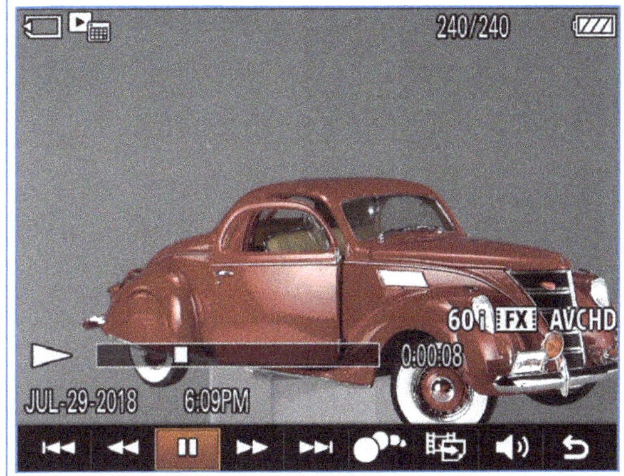

Figure 2-24. Detailed Movie Playback Icons

If you want to play movies on a computer or edit them with video-editing software, you can use the PlayMemories Home software that is provided through the Sony web site. You also can use any program that can deal with AVCHD and XAVC S video files, such as Adobe Premiere Elements, Adobe Premiere Pro, Final Cut Express, Final Cut Pro, iMovie, or Windows Easy Movie Maker, depending on what type of computer you have.

Chapter 3: Shooting Modes for Still Images

Until now, I have discussed the basics of setting up the camera for quick shots, using Intelligent Auto mode to take pictures with settings controlled mostly by the camera's automation. As with other advanced cameras, though, with the Sony RX100 VI there is a large range of other options available. To explain this broad range of features, I need to discuss shooting modes and the Camera Settings1 and Camera Settings2 menu options. In this chapter, I'll discuss the shooting modes; in Chapters 4 and 5, I'll discuss the Camera Settings1 and Camera Settings2 menus.

Whenever you set out to capture still images, you need to select one of the shooting modes available on the mode dial: Intelligent Auto, Program Auto, Aperture Priority, Shutter Priority, Manual exposure, Memory Recall, Sweep Panorama, or Scene Selection. (The other two modes on the dial are for movies, which I will discuss in Chapter 9.) So far, I have discussed primarily the Intelligent Auto mode. Now I will discuss the others, after some review of the first one.

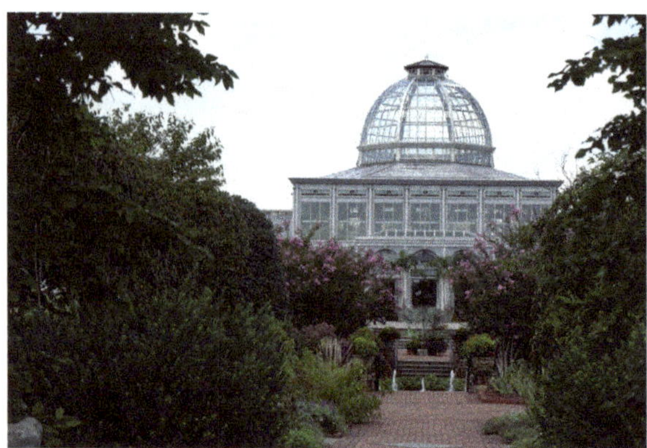

Figure 3-1. Intelligent Auto Example

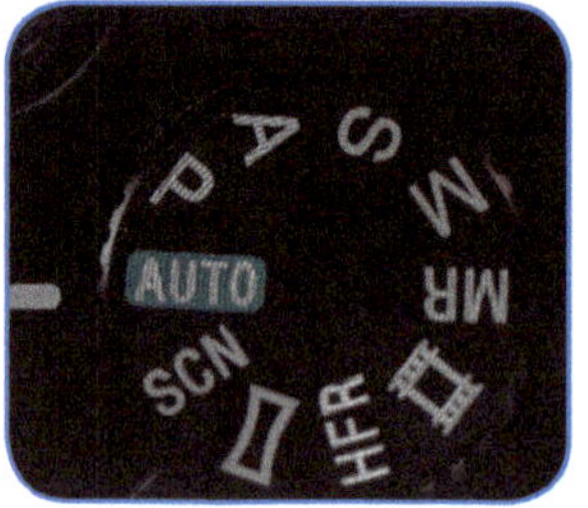

Figure 3-2. Mode Dial at Auto

Intelligent Auto Mode

I've already discussed this shooting mode in some detail. This is a good choice if you need to take a quick shot and don't have much time to fuss with settings such as ISO, white balance, aperture, shutter speed, or focus. It's also a good mode to select when you hand the camera to someone else to take a photo of you and your companions. For example, I used Intelligent Auto mode to get an image of the conservatory building at the local botanical garden, as seen in Figure 3-1.

To make this setting, turn the mode dial to the green AUTO label, as shown in Figure 3-2. When you select this mode, the camera makes several decisions for you and limits your options in some ways. The camera will select the shutter speed, aperture, and ISO setting, along with several other settings over which you will have no control.

For example, you can't set white balance to any value other than Auto, and you can't choose a metering method or use exposure bracketing. You can, however, use quite a few features, as discussed in Chapter 2, including flash mode, some settings of drive mode, focus mode, and others. You also can use sophisticated options such as the Raw file format for images, which I will discuss in Chapter 4 when I discuss the Camera Settings1 menu.

One interesting aspect of this mode is that the camera tries to figure out what sort of subject or scene you are shooting. Some of the subjects the camera will attempt to detect are infant, portrait, night portrait, night scene, landscape, backlight, low light, spotlight, and macro. It also will try to detect certain conditions, such as whether a tripod is in use or whether the subject is walking, and it will display appropriate icons for those situations. So, if you see different icons when you aim at various subjects in this shooting mode, that means the camera is evaluating the scene for factors such as brightness, backlighting, the presence of human subjects, and the like, so it can use the best possible settings for the situation.

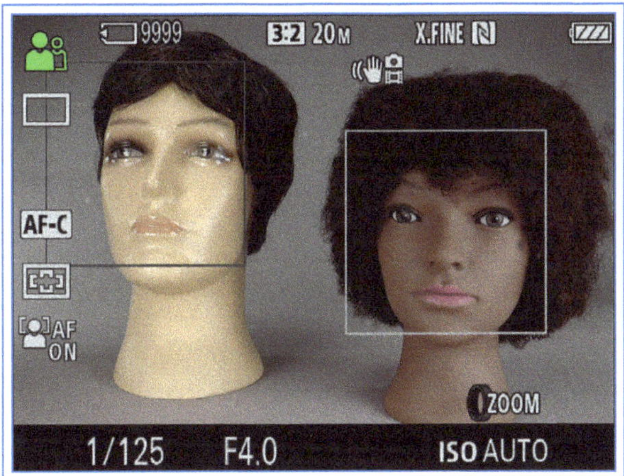

Figure 3-3. Scene Recognition - Portrait

For Figure 3-3, the camera evaluated a scene with two human faces and appropriately used its portrait setting. A portrait icon is in the upper left corner of the screen.

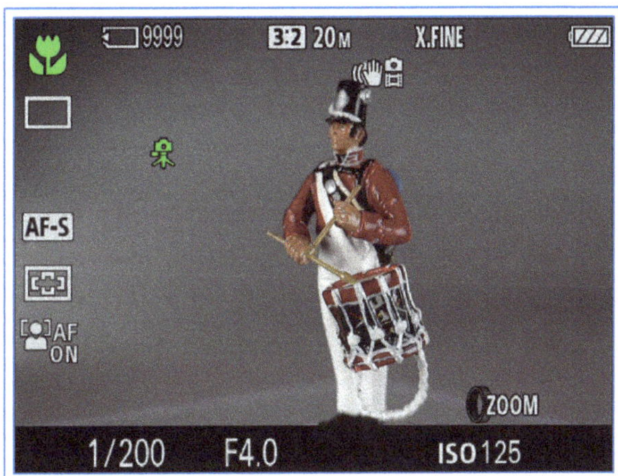

Figure 3-4. Scene Recognition - Macro and Tripod

Figure 3-4 shows the use of automatic scene recognition for a small subject closer to the lens. The camera interpreted the scene as a macro, or closeup shot, and switched automatically into macro mode, indicated by the flower icon. In addition, the camera correctly detected that it was attached to a tripod, as indicated by the tripod icon to the lower right of the macro symbol.

Of course, scene recognition depends on the camera's programming, which may not interpret every scene the same way that you would. If that becomes a problem, you may want to make individual settings using one of the more advanced shooting modes, such as Program, Aperture Priority, Shutter Priority, or Manual. Or, you can use the SCN setting on the mode dial and select a scene setting that better fits the current situation.

Two more points are worth noting for Intelligent Auto mode: First, the camera is programmed to avoid apertures more narrow than f/8.0 in this mode. Therefore, it will vary the shutter speed and ISO settings to avoid having to set the aperture to f/11.0 or other aperture settings above f/8.0. Second, in this shooting mode, the RX100 VI will not use a shutter speed slower than 1/4 second.

Superior Auto Mode

With some Sony cameras, such as the RX100, RX100 II, and RX100 III, there are two Auto settings on the mode dial—one for Intelligent Auto and one for a slightly different mode called Superior Auto. With the RX100 VI, Sony has included this second automatic mode, but has not given it a separate position on the mode dial. Instead, you have to go to screen 3 of the Camera Settings1 menu and select the Auto Mode menu option, as seen in Figure 3-5.

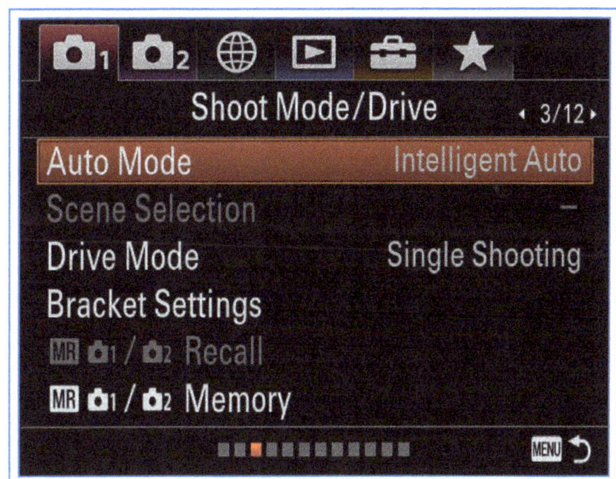

Figure 3-5. Auto Mode Option Highlighted on Menu

When you select that item, you will see a screen for choosing Intelligent Auto or Superior Auto. If you select the lower icon for Superior Auto, as shown in Figure 3-6, the RX100 VI will be set to that mode, and the camera will place a brownish camera icon with a plus sign at its right, in the upper left corner of the display. (That icon may change to an icon showing the current scene recognition, such as a flower for macro, etc.)

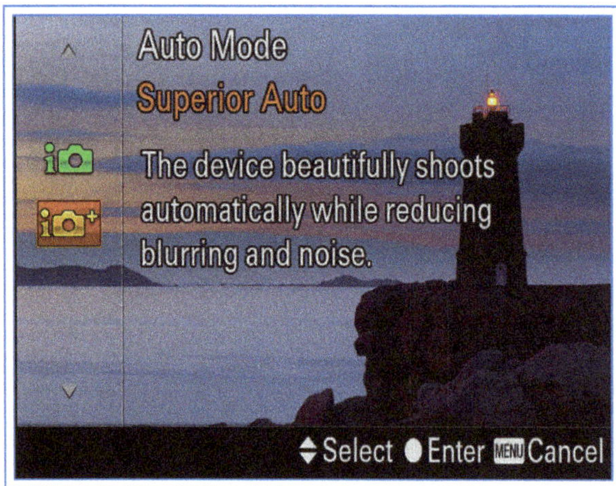

Figure 3-6. Superior Auto Highlighted for Auto Mode

Superior Auto mode includes all features of Intelligent Auto mode, but adds an extra function. In Superior Auto mode, as with Intelligent Auto mode, the camera uses its scene recognition capability to try to determine what subject matter or conditions are present, such as a portrait, a dimly lit scene, and the like.

For many of these scenes, the camera will function just as it does in Intelligent Auto mode. However, in a few specific situations, when lighting is dim, the camera takes a different approach: It captures a rapid burst of shots and combines them internally into a single composite image.

The camera is likely to raise the ISO setting to a fairly high level in order to permit the use of a fast enough shutter speed to capture the scene clearly. The use of this high ISO setting introduces visual "noise" into the image. By taking multiple shots and combining them, the camera averages out and cancels some of the noise, thereby increasing the quality of the final image.

One problem with this system is that you have no control over when the camera decides to use this burst shooting technique. There are three situations in which the camera will do this: when it detects the need for settings called Anti Motion Blur, Hand-held Twilight, or Backlight Correction HDR. When the camera believes this special feature is needed, it fires a burst of shots; you will hear the rapid firing. Then, it will take longer than usual for the camera to process the multiple shots into a single composite image; you may see a message saying "Processing" on a black screen for a second or two. When the camera is using this feature, which Sony calls "Overlay," you will see a small white icon in the upper left corner of the display that looks like a stack of frames with a plus sign at its upper right corner, as shown just below the eagle's head in Figure 3-7.

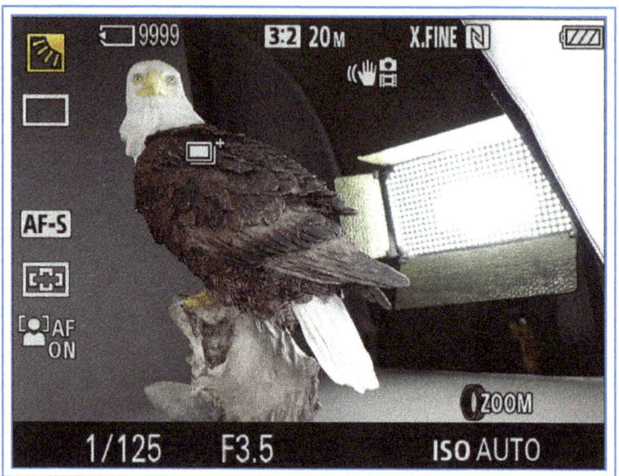

Figure 3-7. Overlay Icon on Shooting Screen

Two of the settings the camera may use in Superior Auto mode—Anti Motion Blur and Hand-held Twilight—are available also as selections in Scene mode, discussed later in this chapter. The third—Backlight Correction HDR—is available only in Superior Auto mode, and only when the camera decides to use it. None of the multiple-shot settings will function when File Format (Still Images) is set to Raw or Raw & JPEG on screen 1 of the Camera Settings1 menu.

I have not found much advantage in using the Superior Auto setting. However, there may be cases when the burst-shooting feature will improve image quality, so it is not a bad idea to use Superior Auto mode when shooting in low light or backlit conditions. As a general rule, though, I prefer to use a mode such as Program, discussed below, and set my own values for items such as DRO, HDR, ISO, and metering mode.

If you want to use Superior Auto mode, there is an easier way to get access to it than selecting Auto Mode from screen 3 of the Camera Settings1 menu. Instead, use the Function Menu Settings option on screen 9 of the Camera Settings2 menu, and set one of the 12 settings for the Function menu to Shoot Mode. Then, when the mode dial is at the AUTO setting, just press the Function button from the shooting screen, and you will see on the Function menu the icon for the current setting for Auto Mode, either Intelligent Auto or Superior Auto. At this point, move the highlight block to that icon using the direction buttons, and, when the icon is highlighted, turn the control wheel or the control ring to cycle through the choices. When your new selection (either Intelligent Auto or Superior Auto) is highlighted, press the Function button to exit to shooting mode.

Program Mode

Choose this mode by turning the mode dial to the P setting, as shown in Figure 3-8.

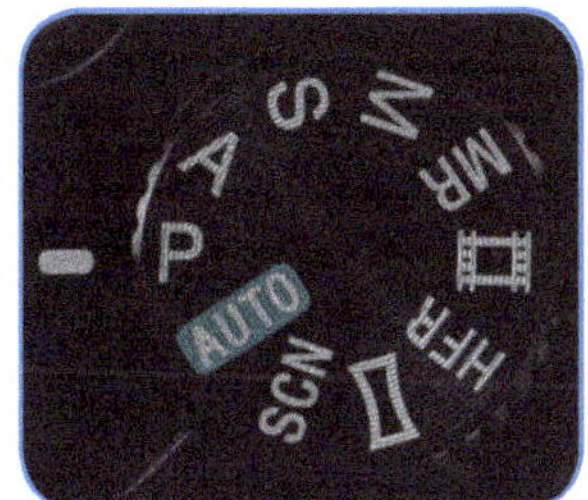

Figure 3-8. Mode Dial at Program

Program mode (sometimes called Program Auto mode) lets you control many of the settings available with the RX100 VI, apart from shutter speed and aperture, which the camera chooses on its own. You still can adjust the camera's automatic exposure to a fair extent by using exposure compensation, as discussed in Chapter 6, as well as exposure bracketing, discussed in Chapter 4, and Program Shift, discussed later in this section. You don't have to make a lot of decisions if you don't want to, because the camera will make reasonable choices for you as defaults.

The camera can choose a shutter speed as long as 30 seconds or as short as 1/32000 second. However, the fastest shutter speed available is 1/2000 second when Shutter Type is set to Mechanical on screen 5 of the Camera Settings2 menu.

In this shooting mode, the camera can choose any aperture in its full range from f/2.8 to f/11.0.

The Program Shift function, which is available only in Program mode, works as follows: When you aim the camera at your subject, the camera will display its chosen settings for shutter speed and aperture in the lower left corner of the display. At that point, turn the control wheel on the back of the camera. The values for shutter speed and aperture will change, if possible under current conditions, to different values for both settings while keeping the same overall exposure of the scene.

You also can use the control ring (the large ring around the lens) to make this setting, if the Control Ring option is set to the Standard setting through the Custom Key (Still Images) item on screen 9 of the Camera Settings2 menu, as discussed in Chapter 5. If you use the control ring for Program Shift, you will see two circular scales on the display, with shutter speed and aperture values that shift as you turn the ring, as shown in Figure 3-9. (A similar display is visible at the bottom of the screen if you use the control wheel, but only if the Exposure Settings Guide menu option is turned on through screen 7 of the Camera Settings2 menu.)

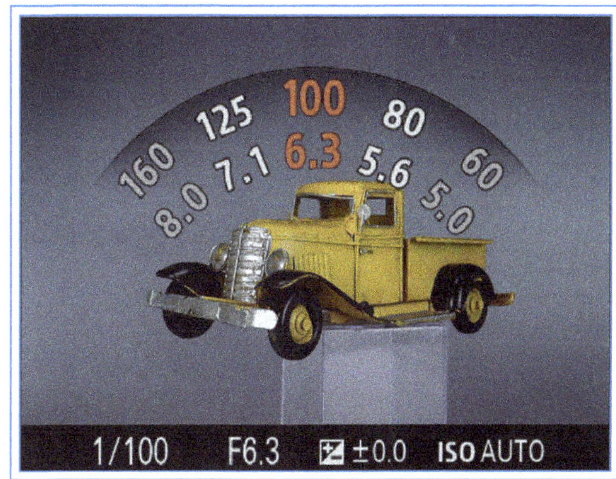

Figure 3-9. Program Shift Display from Using Control Ring

With this option, the camera "shifts" the original exposure to your choice of any of the matched pairs that appear as you turn the control wheel. For example, if the original exposure was f/2.8 at 1/30 second, you may see equivalent pairs of f/3.2 at 1/25, f/3.5 at 1/20, and f/4.0 at 1/15, among others. When Program Shift is in effect, the P icon in the upper left corner of the screen will have an asterisk to its right, as shown in Figure 3-10.

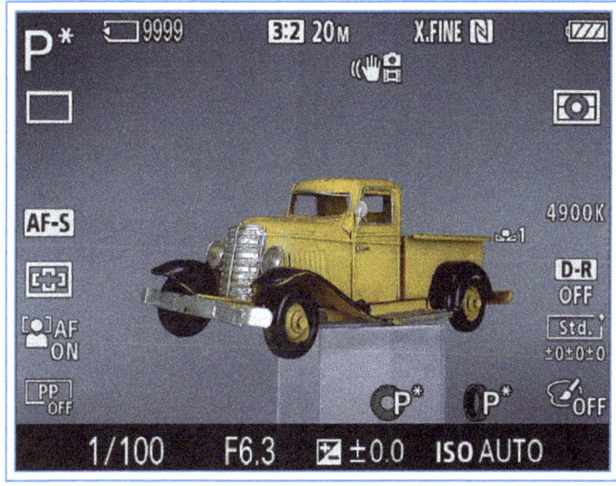

Figure 3-10. Program Shift Icon on Shooting Screen

To cancel Program Shift, turn the control wheel (or control ring) until the original settings are in effect or move the mode dial to another mode, then back to Program. You also can cancel by pressing the flash pop-up button to raise the flash; Program Shift cannot function with flash in use.

Program Shift is useful if you want to use a slightly faster shutter speed to stop action better or a wider aperture to blur the background more, or you might have some other creative reason. This option lets the camera quickly evaluate the exposure, but gives you the option to tweak the shutter speed and aperture to suit your current needs.

Of course, if you need to use a specific shutter speed or aperture, you probably are better off using Aperture Priority, Shutter Priority, or Manual exposure mode. However, having Program Shift available is useful when you're taking pictures quickly using Program mode, and you want a fast way to tweak the settings somewhat.

Another important aspect of Program mode is that it expands the choices available through the Camera Settings1 menu, which controls many of the camera's settings that directly affect your images. You will be able to make choices involving ISO sensitivity, metering mode, DRO/HDR, Creative Style, Picture Effect, and others that are not available in the Auto modes. I won't discuss those settings here; see the discussion of the Camera Settings1 menu in Chapter 4 for information about all of the different selections that are available.

Aperture Priority Mode

You select Aperture Priority shooting mode by turning the mode dial to the A setting, as shown in Figure 3-11.

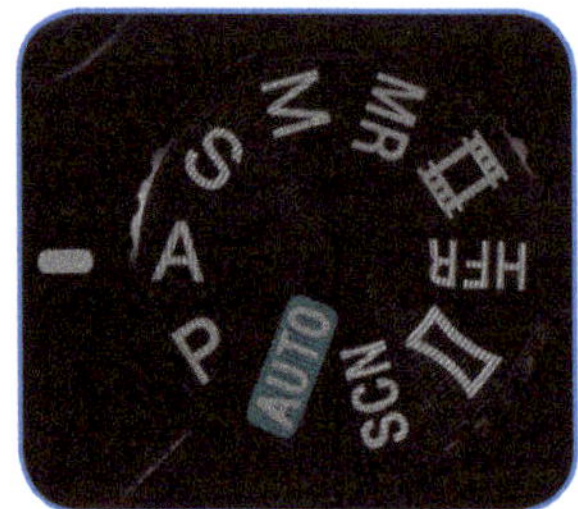

Figure 3-11. Mode Dial at Aperture Priority

In this mode, you select the aperture and the camera chooses a shutter speed for proper exposure. With this mode, you can exercise some control over depth of field of your shots. When you select a narrow aperture, such as f/11.0, the depth of field will be broad, with the result that more items will appear to be in sharp focus at varying distances from the lens. On the other hand, with a wider aperture, such as f/2.8, the depth of field will be relatively shallow, and you may be able to keep only one subject in sharp focus.

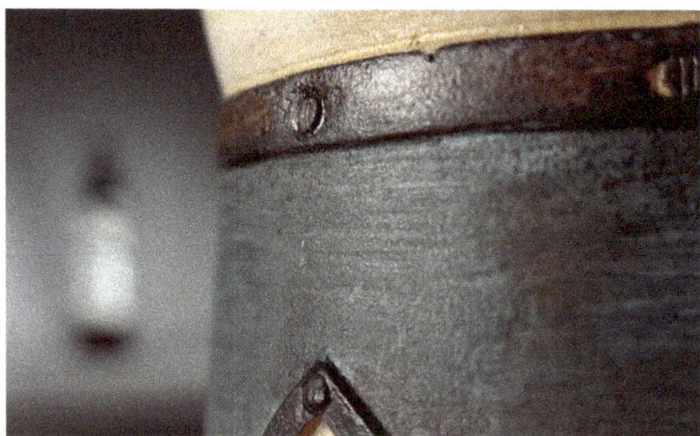

Figure 3-12. Aperture Set to f/2.8

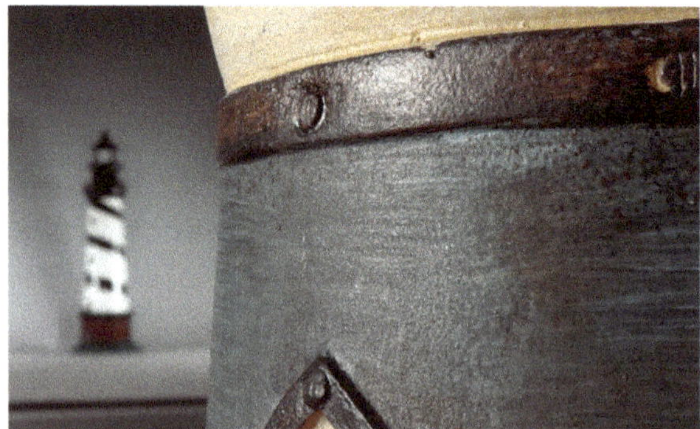

Figure 3-13. Aperture Set to f/11.0

In Figures 3-12 and 3-13, where I photographed two model lighthouses, the settings were the same except for aperture values. I focused on the lighthouse in the foreground in each case. For Figure 3-12, I set the aperture of the RX100 VI to f/2.8, the widest possible. With this setting, because the depth of field at this aperture was quite shallow, the lighthouse in the background is fairly blurry. I took Figure 3-13 with the camera's aperture set to f/11.0, the narrowest possible setting, resulting in a greater depth of field, making the background appear noticeably sharper.

These photos illustrate the effects of varying aperture by setting it wide (low numbers) to blur the background or narrow (high numbers) to enjoy a broad depth of field and keep subjects at varying distances in sharp focus. A need for shallow depth of field arises often in the case of outdoor portraits or photographs of subjects such as flowers. If you can achieve a shallow depth of field by using a wide aperture, you can keep the subject in sharp focus but leave the background blurry, as in Figure 3-12.

This effect is sometimes called "bokeh," a Japanese term for a pleasing blurriness of the background. In this situation, the fuzzy background can be an asset, minimizing distraction from unwanted objects and highlighting the sharply focused portrait of the subject.

You should note that, in order to achieve the long optical zoom range of 200mm, Sony found it necessary to set the widest aperture of the lens for this camera at f/2.8, which is not as wide as with some other models, and it increases as the lens is zoomed in, as discussed below. Therefore, this camera does not readily achieve a heavily blurred background by varying the aperture alone. If you want to blur the background as much as possible, it is advisable to use a long focal length by zooming in the lens to 100mm or more, and move fairly close to the subject, while keeping the subject fairly far in front of the background. An example of this approach is shown in Figure 3-14.

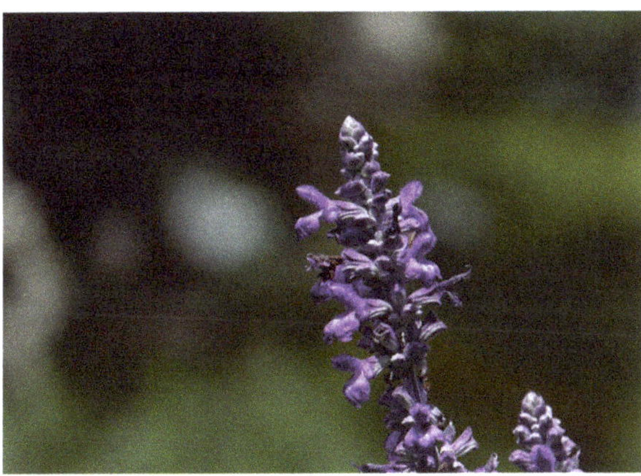

Figure 3-14. Blurred Background from Long Focal Length

Here are the steps to set the aperture. After moving the mode dial to the A setting, use either the control ring or the control wheel to change the aperture. If the control ring does not change the aperture, check the setting for the Control Ring option of the Custom Key (Still Images) item on screen 9 of the Camera Settings2 menu, as discussed in Chapter 5; that menu option has to be set to Standard or Aperture for the ring to carry out this function.

If you use the control ring to set the aperture, the camera will display a circular scale showing the changing aperture values, as seen in Figure 3-15, and the selected value will also appear in the bottom center of the screen.

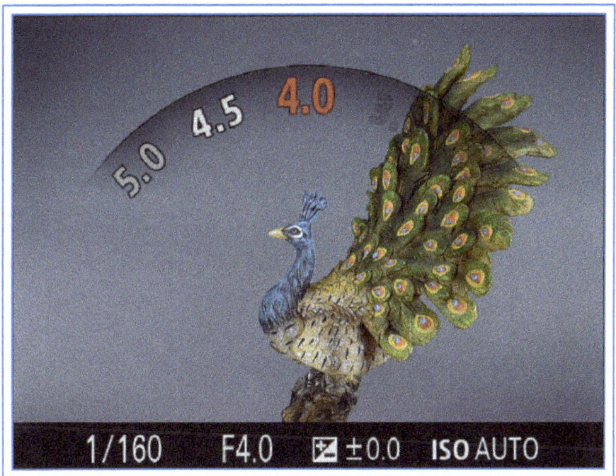

Figure 3-15. Aperture Setting from Using Control Ring

If you use the control wheel instead, the camera will display a sliding scale at the bottom of the screen, if the Exposure Settings Guide option on screen 7 of the Camera Settings2 menu is turned on.

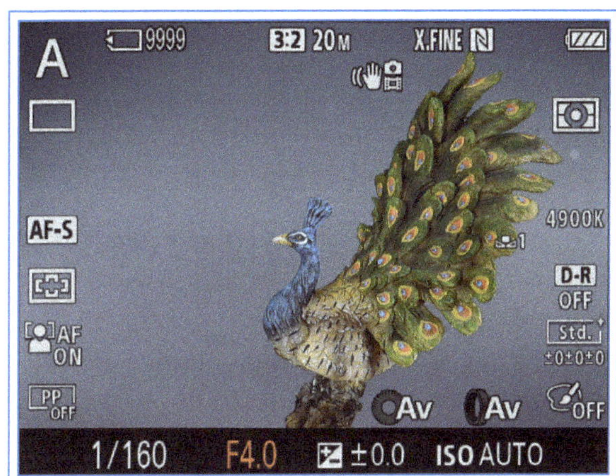

Figure 3-16. Aperture Setting from Using Control Wheel

When you set the aperture, as seen in Figure 3-16, the f-stop (f/4.0 in this case) will appear at the bottom of the screen next to the shutter speed. The camera will select a shutter speed that will result in a normal exposure given the aperture you have set. When the Shutter Type option on screen 5 of the Camera Settings2 menu is set to Auto or Electronic, the camera can choose shutter speeds from 30 seconds to 1/32000 second.

When Shutter Type is set to Mechanical, the range of available shutter speeds is from 30 seconds to 1/2000 second.

Although in most cases the camera will be able to select a corresponding shutter speed that results in a normal exposure, there may be times when this is not possible. For example, if you are taking pictures in a very bright location with the aperture set to f/2.8, the camera may not be able to set a shutter speed fast enough to yield a normal exposure, especially if you are using the mechanical shutter instead of the electronic shutter. In that case, the fastest possible shutter speed (1/2000 second) will flash on the display to show that a normal exposure cannot be made using the chosen aperture. The camera will let you take the picture, but it may be too bright to be usable.

Similarly, if conditions are too dark for a good exposure at the aperture you have selected, the slowest possible shutter speed (30", meaning 30 seconds) will flash.

In situations where conditions are too bright or dark for a good exposure, the camera's display may become bright or dark, giving you notice of the problem. This will happen if the Live View Display item on screen 7 of the Camera Settings2 menu is set to Setting Effect On. If that option is set to Setting Effect Off, the display will remain at normal brightness, even if the exposure settings would result in an excessively bright or dark image. I will discuss that menu option in Chapter 5.

One more note on Aperture Priority mode: Not all apertures are available at all times. In particular, the widest aperture, f/2.8, is available only when the lens is zoomed out to its wide-angle setting (zoom lever moved toward the W). At the highest zoom levels, the widest aperture available is f/4.5.

To see an illustration of this point, here is a quick test. Zoom the lens out by moving the zoom lever all the way to the left, toward the W label. Then select Aperture Priority mode and set the aperture to f/2.8. Now zoom the lens in by moving the zoom lever to the right. After the zoom is finished, the aperture will have changed to f/4.5 because that is the limit for the aperture at the full-telephoto zoom level. (The aperture will change back to f/2.8 if you zoom back to the wide-angle setting.)

Also, when you set an aperture as narrow as f/11 with this camera, lens diffraction comes into play and limits the sharpness of your images. So, unless you have a fairly strong reason to use f/11, such as a need to maximize depth of field in a brightly lighted area, you should try to use apertures no narrower than f/8.0 if possible.

Shutter Priority Mode

In Shutter Priority mode, you choose the shutter speed and the camera will set the corresponding aperture to achieve a proper exposure of the image.

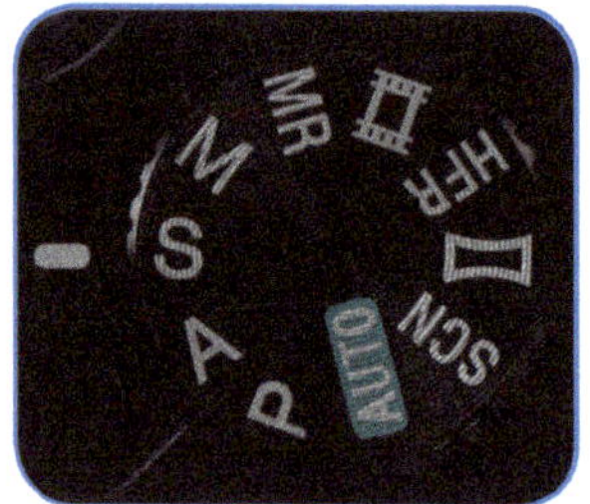

Figure 3-17. Mode Dial at Shutter Priority

In this mode, designated by the S position on the mode dial, as shown in Figure 3-17, you can set the shutter to be open for a time ranging from 30 seconds to 1/32000 of a second, if the Shutter Type menu option is set to Auto or Electronic. If that option is set to Mechanical, the fastest setting available is 1/2000 second.

If the built-in flash is in use, the fastest setting available is 1/100 second with the electronic shutter and 1/2000 second with the mechanical shutter.

If you are photographing fast action, such as a bird in flight, a baseball swing, or a hurdles event at a track meet, and you want to stop the motion with a minimum of blur, you should select a fast shutter speed, such as 1/2000 of a second. For Figure 3-18 and Figure 3-19, I used different shutter speeds in photographing a group of colored beads as I poured them into a large bowl.

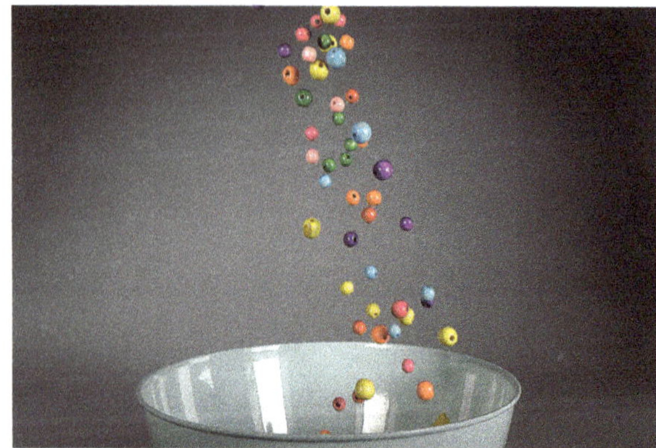

Figure 3-18. Shutter Speed Set to 1/2000 Second

In Figure 3-18, I used a shutter speed setting of 1/2000 second. In this image, you can see the individual beads clearly. In Figure 3-19, with the shutter speed set to 1/60 second, the beads blur together into what looks almost like a continuous stream.

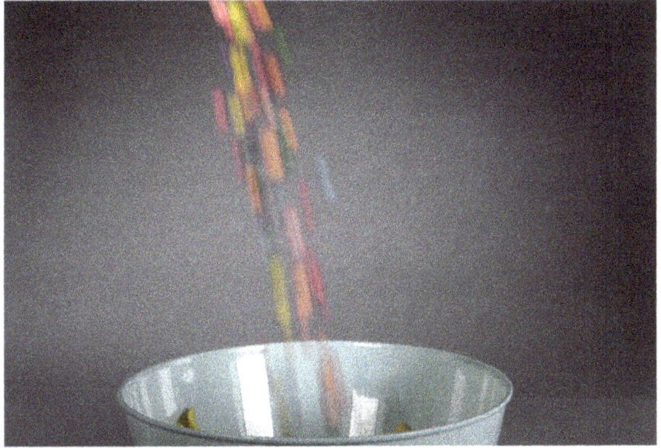

Figure 3-19. Shutter Speed Set to 1/60 Second

Choose this mode by turning the mode dial to the S position, as seen in Figure 3-17. Select the shutter speed by turning the control wheel or the control ring. The Control Ring function must be set to Standard or Shutter Speed using the Custom Key (Still Images) option on screen 9 of the Camera Settings2 menu for the ring to control shutter speed.

As with Aperture Priority mode, the camera will display a sliding scale of shutter speeds as you turn the control wheel if you have the Exposure Settings Guide option turned on in the Camera Settings2 menu. It will always display a circular scale of shutter speeds when you use the control ring to make the setting.

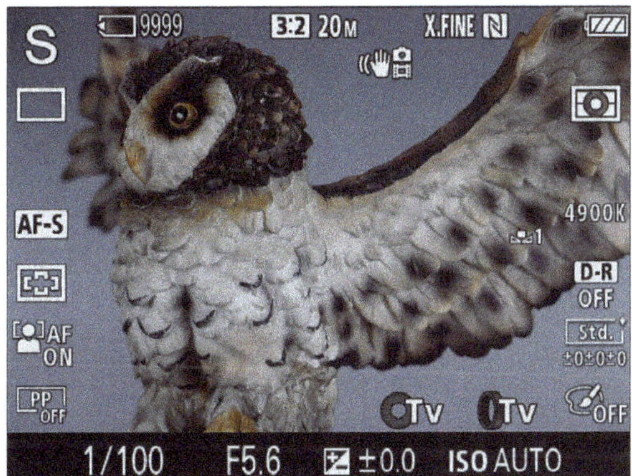

Figure 3-20. Shooting Screen in Shutter Priority Mode

Although the mode dial uses the letter "S" to stand for Shutter Priority, on the detailed display screen, as shown in Figure 3-20, the camera uses the notation Tv (for time value) in the lower right corner, next to the icons showing that the control ring or control wheel can be used to make this setting.

As you cycle through various shutter speeds, the camera will select the appropriate aperture to achieve a normal exposure, if possible. As I discussed in connection with Aperture Priority mode, if you set a shutter speed for which the camera cannot select an aperture that will yield a good exposure, the aperture reading at the bottom of the display will flash. The flashing aperture means that proper exposure at the selected shutter speed is not possible at any available aperture, according to the camera's calculations.

For example, if you set the shutter speed to 1/320 second in a fairly dark indoor environment, the aperture number (which will be f/2.8, the widest setting, if the lens is at its wide-angle setting) may flash, indicating that proper exposure is not possible. As I discussed for Aperture Priority mode, you can still take the picture if you want to, though it may not be usable. A similar situation may take place if you select a slow shutter speed (such as four seconds) in a relatively bright location. (This situation is less likely to happen in Aperture Priority mode, because of the wide range of shutter speeds the camera can use to achieve a good exposure.)

If the current settings in this mode would result in an image that is excessively dark or bright, the LCD display will grow dark or bright to show that effect, but only if the Live View Display option on screen 7 of the Camera Settings2 menu is set to Setting Effect On. If that option is set to Setting Effect Off, the display will show a normal image even in unusually bright or dark conditions.

Manual Exposure Mode

One of the many features of the RX100 VI that distinguish it from more ordinary compact cameras is that it has a fully manual exposure mode, a useful tool for photographers who want to have full creative control over exposure decisions.

To control exposure manually, set the mode dial to the M indicator, as shown in Figure 3-21. You now have to control both shutter speed and aperture by setting them yourself. To set the aperture, turn the control ring around the lens (assuming the control ring is set for this function through the Camera Settings2 menu, as discussed in Chapter 5); to set the shutter speed, turn the control wheel on the back of the camera.

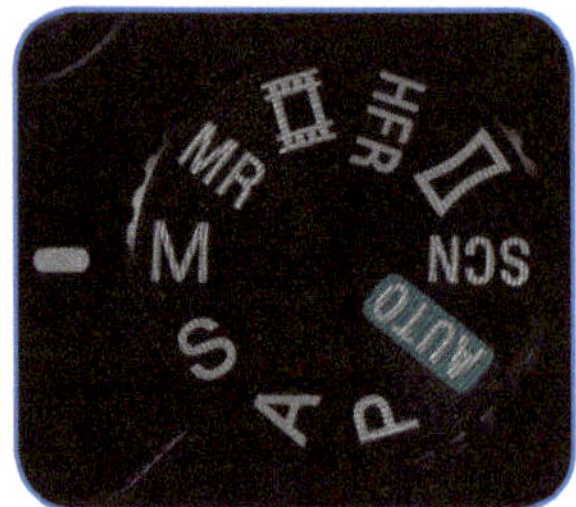

Figure 3-21. Mode Dial at Manual Exposure

If the control ring is not set to control aperture, or if you prefer not to use the ring for that purpose, you can use the control wheel to adjust both aperture and shutter speed. To do that, press the Down button to switch between the two selections.

When you press that button, either the shutter speed number or the aperture number on the display will turn orange for about 10 seconds to show that that value is currently being controlled by the control wheel. Also, the label beside the gray icon for the control wheel in the lower right corner of the display will change between Av (for aperture value) and Tv (for time value) when you press the Down button to switch the wheel's function. Figure 3-22 shows the display when the control wheel is controlling shutter speed.

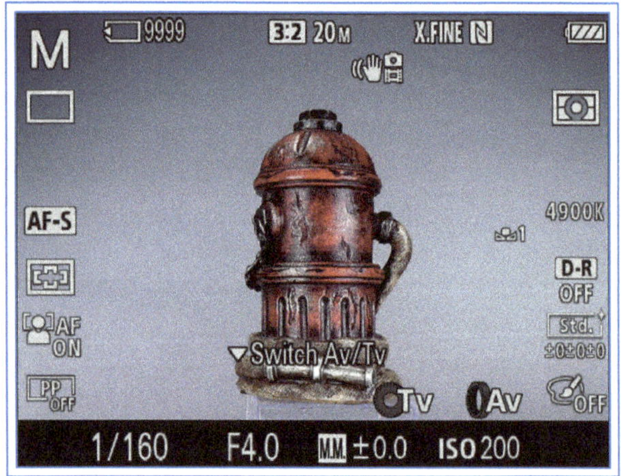

Figure 3-22. Display When Control Wheel Adjusts Shutter Speed

As you adjust shutter speed and aperture, a third value, to the right of the aperture, also may change. That value is a positive, negative, or zero number. The meaning of the number is different depending on the current ISO setting.

In Chapter 4, I'll provide more details about the ISO setting, which controls how sensitive the camera's sensor is to light. With a higher ISO value, the sensor is more sensitive and the image is exposed more quickly, so the shutter speed can be faster or the aperture more narrow, or both.

To set the ISO value, press the Menu button to access the menu system, go to screen 6 of the Camera Settings1 menu, and highlight the ISO item. Press the Center button to bring up the ISO menu, as shown in Figure 3-23, and scroll through the selections using the Up and Down buttons or by turning the control wheel.

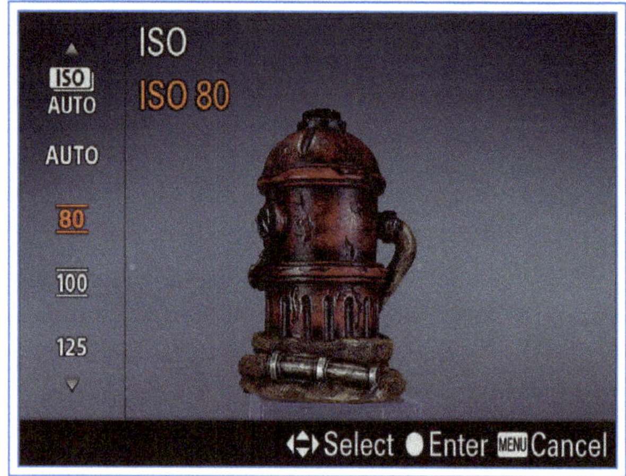

Figure 3-23. ISO Menu

Choose a low number like 125 to maximize image quality when there is plenty of light; use a higher number in dim light. Higher ISO settings are likely to cause visual "noise," or graininess, in your images. Generally speaking, you should try to set ISO no higher than 800 to ensure the highest image quality.

If the ISO value is set to a specific number, such as 125, 200, or 1000, then, in Manual exposure mode, the icon at the bottom center of the display is a box containing the letters "M.M.," which stand for "metered manual," as shown in Figure 3-22.

In this situation, the number next to the M.M. icon represents any deviation from what the camera's metering system considers to be a normal exposure. So, even though you are setting the exposure manually, the camera will still let you know whether the selected aperture and shutter speed will produce a standard exposure.

If the aperture, shutter speed, and ISO values you have selected will result in a darker exposure than normal, the M.M. value will be negative, and vice-versa. This value can vary only by +2.0 or -2.0 EV (exposure value)

units; after that, the value will flash, meaning the camera considers the exposure excessively abnormal.

Of course, you can ignore the M.M. indicator; it is there only to give you an idea of how the camera would meter the scene. You very well may want part or all of the scene to be darker or lighter than the metering would indicate to be "correct."

As with the Aperture Priority and Shutter Priority modes, the camera's display will become unusually bright or dim to indicate that current settings would result in an abnormal exposure, but only when the Live View Display option on screen 7 of the Camera Settings2 menu is set to Setting Effect On. For example, Figure 3-24 shows the camera's display when Manual exposure settings would result in a dark image, with Setting Effect On.

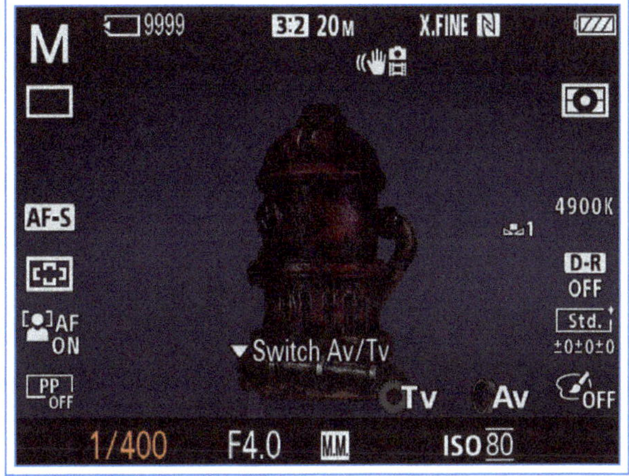

Figure 3-24. Manual Exposure Screen with Setting Effect On

If, instead of a specific value, you have set ISO to Auto ISO, the icon at the bottom center of the screen changes. In this situation, the camera displays the exposure compensation icon, which contains a plus and minus sign, as shown in Figure 3-25. The reason for this change is that, when you use Auto ISO in Manual exposure mode, the camera can likely produce a normal exposure by adjusting the ISO. There is no need to display the M.M. value, which shows deviation from a normal exposure.

Instead, the camera lets you adjust exposure compensation, so you can set the exposure to be darker or brighter than the camera's autoexposure system would produce.

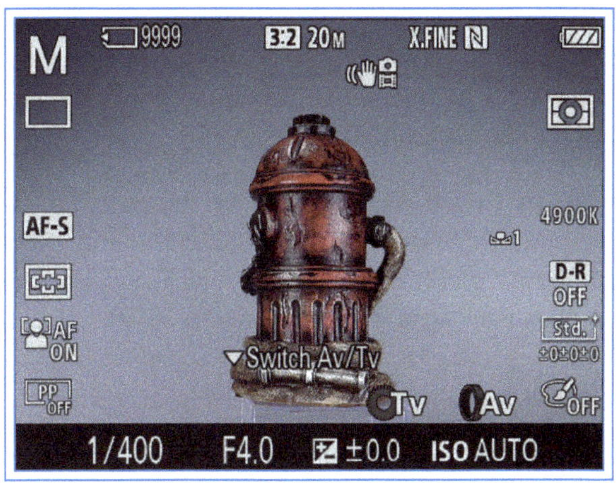

Figure 3-25. Manual Exposure Screen with Auto ISO in Effect

To set exposure compensation in Manual mode, you cannot use the ordinary control for that purpose—the Down button—because that button toggles the function of the control wheel for controlling aperture or shutter speed, as discussed above. To control exposure compensation in Manual mode, you can use the Exposure Compensation item on screen 6 of the Camera Settings1 menu, or you can assign exposure compensation to the control ring or to the Custom, Center, Left, or Right button. You make that assignment using the Custom Key (Still Images) option on screen 9 of the Camera Settings2 menu, as discussed in Chapter 5. You also can use the Function menu to adjust exposure compensation, if that adjustment has been included in that menu, as discussed in Chapter 5.

With Manual exposure mode, the settings for aperture and shutter speed are independent of each other. When you change one, the other one stays unchanged until you adjust it manually. But the effect of this system is different depending on whether you have selected a specific value for ISO as opposed to Auto ISO.

If you select a numerical value for ISO, which can range from 80 to 12800 (or even higher when Multi Frame Noise Reduction is selected for the ISO setting), the camera leaves the creative decision about exposure entirely up to you, even if the resulting photograph would be washed out by excessive exposure or underexposed to the point of near-blackness.

However, if you select Auto ISO for the ISO setting, then, as discussed above, the camera will adjust the ISO to achieve a normal exposure if possible. In this case, Manual exposure mode becomes like a different shooting mode altogether. You might call this the "aperture and shutter speed priority mode," because you are able to set both aperture and shutter speed but still have the camera adjust exposure automatically by changing the ISO value.

The ability to use Auto ISO in Manual exposure mode is very useful. For example, suppose you are taking photographs of a craftsman using tools in a dimly lighted area. You may want to use a narrow aperture such as f/7.1 to achieve a broad depth of field and keep the tools and other items in focus, but you also may want to use a fast shutter speed, such as 1/250 second, to freeze action. If you use Aperture Priority mode, the camera will choose the shutter speed; with Shutter Priority mode, the camera will choose the aperture, and with Program mode, the camera will choose both values. Only by using Manual exposure mode with Auto ISO can you choose both aperture and shutter speed and still have the camera find a good exposure setting automatically.

Even with the ability to use Auto ISO, though, there may be situations in which the camera cannot produce a normal exposure. This could happen if you have limited the scope of the Auto ISO setting by establishing a narrow range between the Minimum and Maximum settings for Auto ISO. It also could happen if you have chosen extreme settings for aperture and shutter speed, such as 1/500 second at f/11.0 in dark conditions. In such situations, the ISO Auto label and the exposure compensation value at the bottom of the display will flash, indicating that a normal exposure cannot be achieved with these settings.

The range of apertures you can set in Manual mode is the same as for Aperture Priority mode: f/2.8 to f/11.0. (As with other shooting modes, the widest apertures are not available when the lens is zoomed in.)

The range of shutter speeds in Manual mode is the same as for Shutter Priority mode: 1/32000 second to 30 seconds if Shutter Type is set to Auto or Electronic and 1/2000 second to 30 seconds if Shutter Type is Mechanical.

If the flash is in use, the fastest setting available is 1/100 second with the electronic shutter and 1/2000 with the mechanical shutter. However, there is one important addition to the range of shutter speeds in this shooting mode. In Manual exposure mode, if Shutter Type is set to Mechanical or Auto, you can set the shutter speed to the BULB setting, just beyond the 30-second mark, as shown in Figure 3-26.

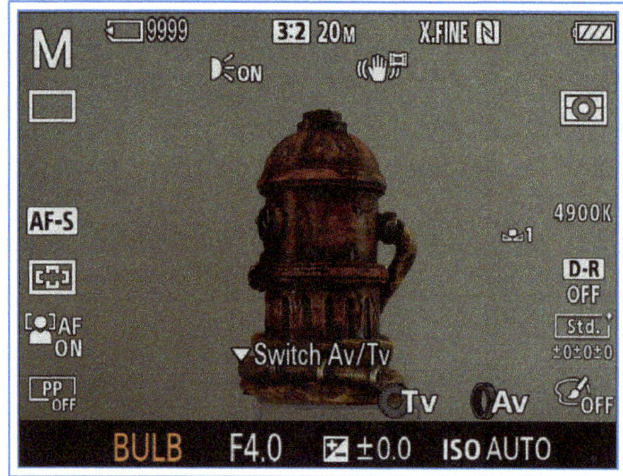

Figure 3-26. Shutter Speed Set to BULB

With the BULB setting, you have to press and hold the shutter button to keep the shutter open. You can use this setting to take photos in dark conditions by holding the shutter open for a minute or more.

One problem is that it is hard to avoid jiggling the camera, causing image blur, even if the camera is on a tripod. In Appendix A, I discuss using a remote control to trigger the camera. After the exposure ends, the camera will process the image for the same length of time as the exposure, to reduce the noise caused by long exposures. You will not be able to take another shot while this processing continues. (You can disable this setting with the Long Exposure Noise Reduction option on screen 2 of the Camera Settings1 menu.)

Another feature available in this mode is Manual Shift, which is similar to Program Shift, discussed earlier. To use Manual Shift, you first have to assign one of the control buttons (Custom or Center) to the AEL (autoexposure lock) Hold or AEL Toggle function using the Custom Key (Still Images) or Custom Key (Movies) option on screen 9 of the Camera Settings2 menu, as discussed in Chapter 5. (The Left or Right button can be assigned to AEL Toggle, but not to AEL Hold.)

Then, after making your aperture and shutter speed settings, change the aperture setting while pressing the button assigned to the AEL function. (If you selected AEL Toggle, you don't have to hold down the button; just press it and release it.)

When you do this, the camera will make new settings with equivalent exposure, if possible. For example, if the original settings were f/3.5 at 1/160 second, when you select Manual Shift and change the aperture to f/3.2, the camera will reset the shutter speed to 1/200 second, maintaining the original exposure. In this way, you can tweak your settings to favor a particular shutter speed or aperture without affecting the overall exposure. An asterisk will appear in the lower right corner of the display while you activate the button that controls AEL.

I use Manual exposure mode often, for various purposes. One use is to take images at different exposures to combine into a composite HDR (high dynamic range) image. I will discuss that technique in Chapter 4.

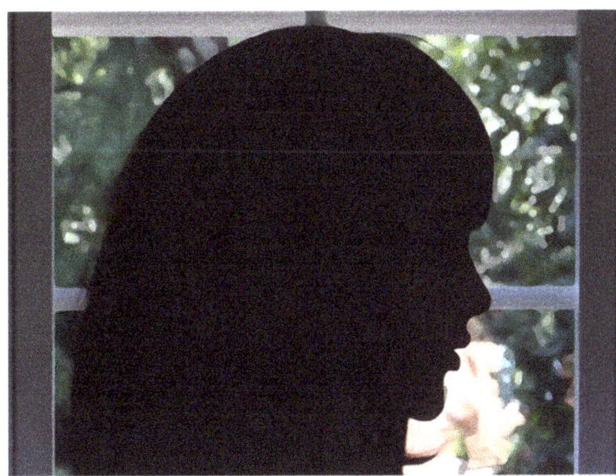

Figure 3-27. Manual Exposure Example

I also use Manual mode when using an external flash, as discussed in Appendix A. In that case, the flash does not interact with the camera's autoexposure system, so I need to set the exposure manually. Manual mode also is useful for some special types of photography, such as making silhouettes, as in Figure 3-27.

Scene Mode

Scene mode, represented by the SCN setting on the mode dial, as shown in Figure 3-28, is different from the other shooting modes I have discussed. This mode does not have a single defining feature, such as permitting control over one or more aspects of exposure. Instead, when you select Scene mode and then choose a particular scene type within that mode, you are telling the camera what sort of environment the picture is being taken in and what type of image you are looking for, and you are letting the camera make the decisions as to what settings to use to produce that result.

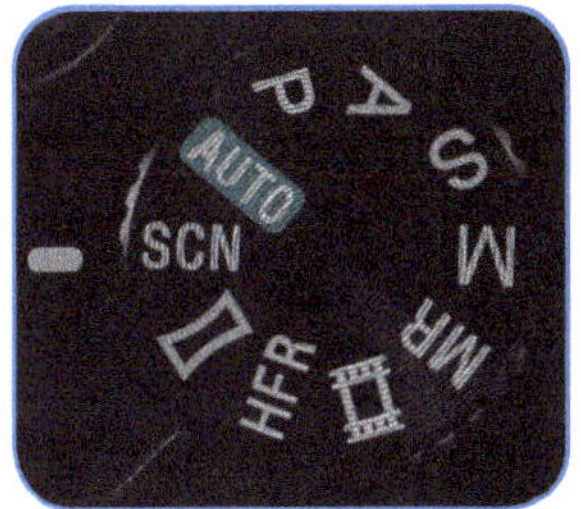

Figure 3-28. Mode Dial at Scene

With most of the Scene mode settings, you cannot select many options that are available in Program, Aperture Priority, Shutter Priority, and Manual exposure mode, such as ISO, DRO, Creative Style, Picture Effect, metering mode, and white balance. There also are some menu settings and control options that are available with certain scene settings but not others, as discussed later in this chapter.

Although some photographers may not like Scene mode because it takes creative decisions away from them, I find it useful in various situations. You don't have to use these scene types only for their labeled purposes; you may find that some of them offer a group of settings that is well suited for shooting scenarios that you regularly encounter. I'll discuss how Scene mode works, and you can decide for yourself whether you might take advantage of it on occasion.

Select Scene mode by turning the mode dial to the SCN indicator, as in Figure 3-28. Now, unless you want to use the setting that is already in place, you need to select from the list of 13 scene options. There are several ways to do this, depending on current settings. If the Mode Dial Guide is turned on through screen 2 of the Setup menu, then, whenever you turn the mode dial to the SCN setting and press the Center button, the Scene Selection menu, shown in Figure 3-29, will appear.

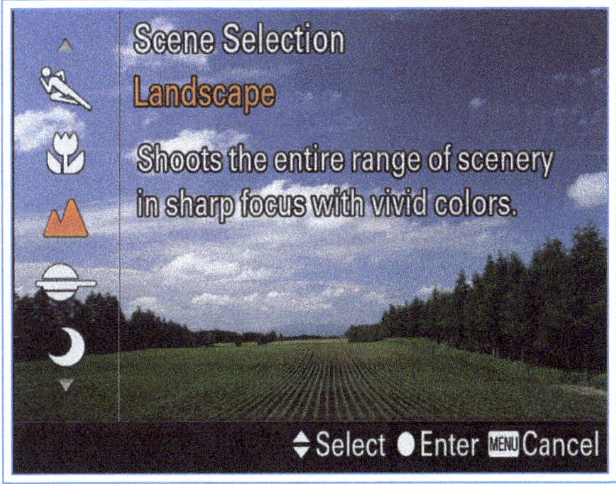

Figure 3-29. Scene Selection Menu

If the Mode Dial Guide is not in use, or if the camera is already set to Scene mode, you can go to screen 3 of the Camera Settings1 menu and call up the Scene Selection item, which produces the same menu as shown in Figure 3-29.

Once the Scene Selection menu is displayed, scroll through the 13 selections using the Up and Down buttons or the control wheel. Press the Center button to select a setting and return to the shooting screen. You will see an icon representing that setting in the upper left corner of the display. (You may need to press the Display button to see the screen that shows the scene setting icon; the icon will disappear after a few seconds on some display screens.) For example, Figure 3-30 shows the display when the Gourmet setting is selected.

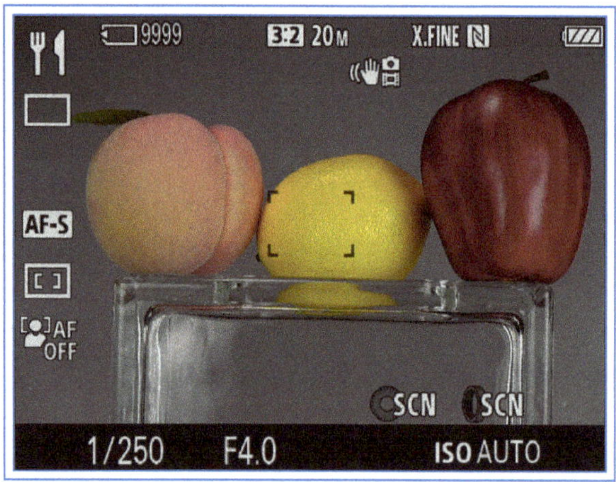

Figure 3-30. Gourmet Scene Type Icon on Shooting Screen

For each scene type the camera displays a screen with a description of the setting's uses as you move the selector over it, as shown in Figure 3-29, so you are not left to puzzle out what each icon represents. As you press the Up or Down button or turn the control wheel to move the selector over the other scene types, when you reach the bottom or top edge of the screen, the selector wraps around to the first or last setting and continues going.

There also are two more ways to select a scene type. If the control ring is set to its Standard setting, then, when the shooting screen is displayed in Scene mode, you can just turn the control ring to cycle through the various scene types. You will see a circular display as the ring turns, as shown in Figure 3-31.

After you stop turning the ring, the icon for the selected scene type will appear in the upper left corner. (If you are using manual focus or DMF this will not work, because the control ring will adjust focus and will not be available to display scene types.) Also, you can turn the control wheel in Scene mode to change scene types, regardless of the function assigned to the control ring. With that option, the camera cycles through the scene types, displaying the menu screen description for each one as the control wheel is turned in shooting mode.

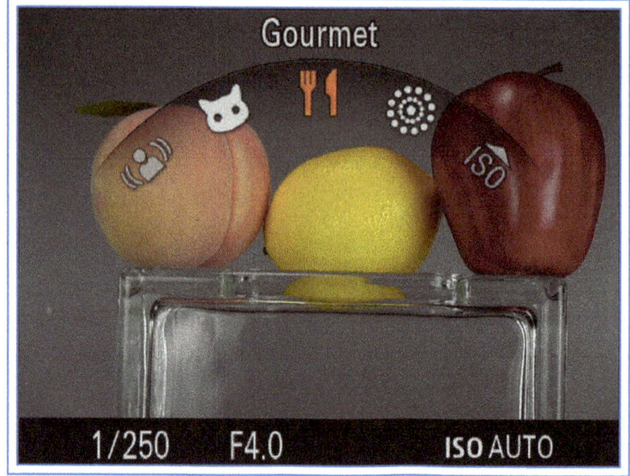

Figure 3-31. Circular Display of Scene Types from Using Control Ring

That's all you have to do to select a scene type. But you need to know something about each option to decide whether it's one you would want to use. In general, each scene type carries with it a variety of values, including things like focus mode, flash status, range of shutter speeds, sensitivity to various colors, and others.

Note that some settings are designed for certain types of shooting, rather than particular subjects such as sunsets or fireworks. For example, the Anti Motion Blur and High Sensitivity settings are designed for difficult shooting environments, such as dimly lighted areas.

Portrait

The Portrait setting is designed to produce flesh tones with a softening effect, as shown in Figure 3-32. You should stand fairly close to the subject and set the zoom to fill the frame with the subject. If you have the Auto Object Framing option turned on through screen 12 of the Camera Settings1 menu, the camera may re-frame the portrait for you and create a second image with what may be a tighter cropping.

The camera will try to use a wide aperture to blur the background. You can use Autoflash or Fill-flash if you want to even out the lighting or reduce shadows on your subject's face. If you are shooting a portrait in front of a busy background, such as a house, try to position the subject's head in front of a plain area, such as a light-colored wall, so the head will be seen clearly.

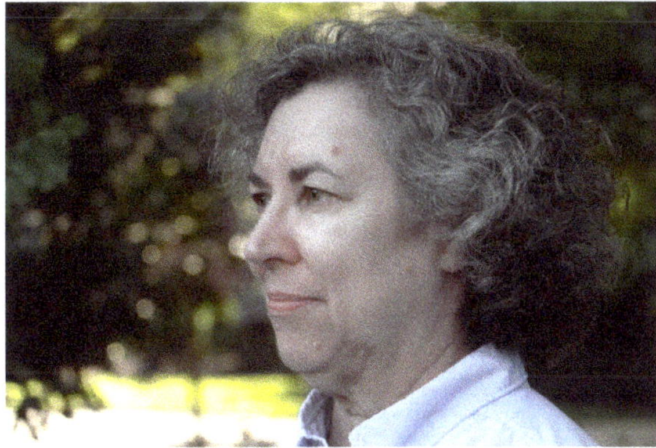

Figure 3-32. Portrait Example

You can use the self-timer, but you cannot use bracketing or continuous shooting. You can use the self-portrait timer feature if it is turned on through screen 12 of the Camera Settings1 menu. To use that feature, flip the LCD screen up so it is facing in the same direction as the lens, and turn the camera so the lens is facing you. Press the shutter button as you see your face, and the shutter will fire after a three-second on-screen countdown.

Sports Action

The Sports Action setting is for use when lighting is bright and you need to freeze the action of athletes, children at play, pets, or other subjects. The camera may set a high ISO value so it can use a fast shutter speed to stop action. You can turn on Fill-flash if you want. The camera sets itself for continuous shooting so you can hold down the shutter button and capture a burst of images. In that way, you increase your chances of capturing the action at a perfect moment. You can switch to any of the three speeds of continuous shooting if you want, but you cannot set drive mode to single shooting or turn on the self-timer. (I'll discuss the drive mode options in Chapter 4.) The camera turns on continuous autofocus, so it adjusts focus automatically as the subject moves. You can switch to manual focus or direct manual focus (DMF), which are discussed in Chapter 4. You cannot turn on single autofocus or automatic autofocus.

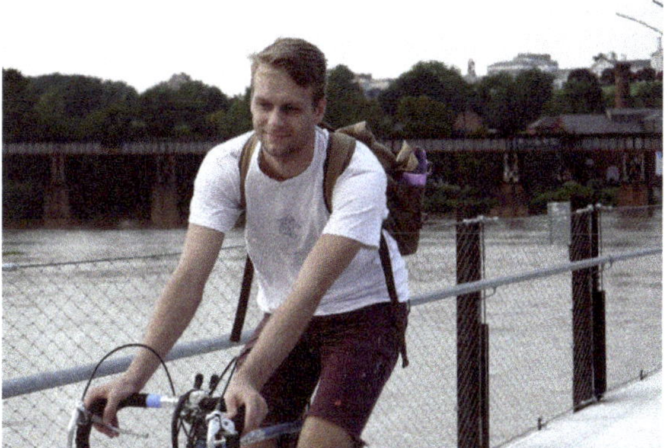

Figure 3-33. Sports Action Example

In Figure 3-33, I used this setting to photograph a man riding his bicycle on a pedestrian bridge over the river. I used the camera's burst setting to capture a quick group of shots as he approached me with little notice.

Macro

Although you can focus at close range in other shooting modes, it is convenient to use this setting to call up a group of options that are suited for extreme closeups of flowers, insects, or other small objects.

When you select the Macro option, the camera will let you set the flash to Forced Off, Autoflash, or Fill-flash. You cannot use continuous shooting or bracketing, but you can use the self-timer.

The camera initially uses single autofocus, but you don't have to use autofocus to take macro shots. You can use manual focus to focus on objects very close to the lens. If you do, however, you lose the benefit of autofocus, and it can be tricky finding the correct focus manually. If you use the DMF setting, you can check focus by pressing the shutter button halfway and having the camera use its autofocus system. You also can take advantage of several aids to manual focusing with the RX100 VI: Peaking, MF Assist, and Focus Magnifier, all of which are on screen 11 of the Camera Settings1 menu, discussed in Chapter 4.

You don't have to use the Macro setting to shoot extreme closeups with the RX100 VI. If you set the camera to one of its autofocus modes—single-shot AF, automatic AF, or continuous AF—it will focus on objects as close as 3.15 inches (8 cm) when the lens is zoomed out and as close as 3.28 feet (100 cm) when the lens is zoomed in to its maximum telephoto range.

When shooting closeups, you should use a tripod if possible because the depth of field is shallow and you need to keep the camera steady to take a usable photograph. It's also a good idea to use the two-second or five-second self-timer. If you take the picture using the self-timer, you will not be touching the camera when the shutter is activated, so the chance of camera shake is minimized. You also can use a wired remote control, as discussed in Appendix A, or control the camera from a smartphone, as discussed in Chapter 10.

If you need artificial illumination, consider using some sort of diffuser over the built-in flash, such as a handkerchief or piece of translucent plastic. Using the flash without some diffusion is likely to result in uneven illumination at such a close range. You might consider using a small lamp that can illuminate the subject without overwhelming it. Another approach is to use an off-camera flash triggered by an optical slave system, as discussed in Appendix A. In that case, you can attach a softbox to the flash to diffuse the light.

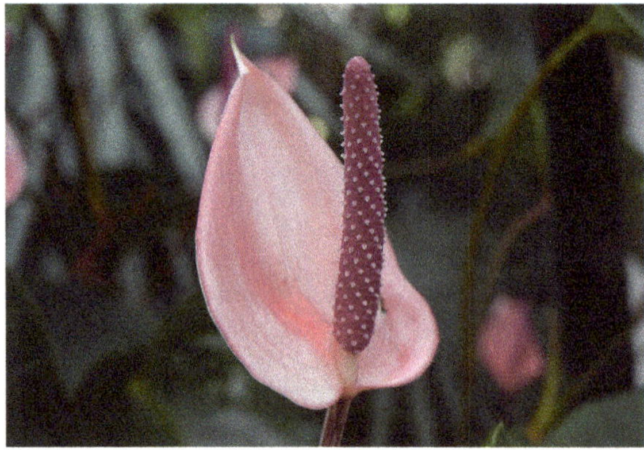

Figure 3-34. Macro Example

In Figure 3-34, I used the Macro setting for a shot of a flower in the botanical garden.

Landscape

Landscape is a Scene mode setting I use often. It is convenient to turn the mode dial to the SCN position and pull up the Landscape setting when I'm at a scenic location. The camera lets you use Fill-flash in case you want to shoot an image of a person as part of your composition, and it boosts the brightness and intensity of the colors somewhat. Otherwise, it limits your choices; you cannot use continuous shooting, but you can use the self-timer. Figure 3-35 is an example taken using the Landscape setting for a shot of a pedestrian bridge across the James River.

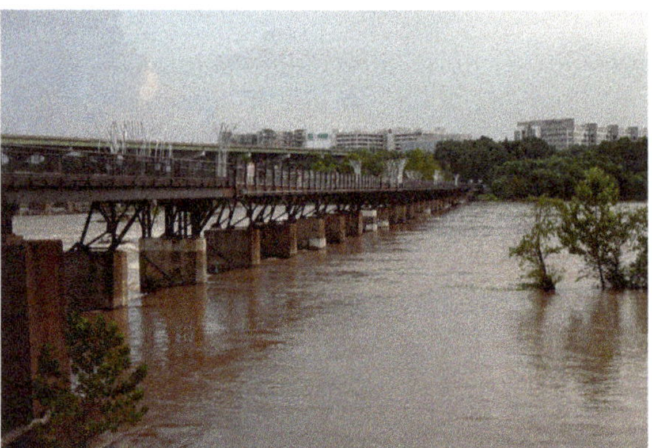

Figure 3-35. Landscape Example

Sunset

This setting enhances reddish hues. You can use Fill-flash to take a portrait with the sunset or sunrise in the background. You cannot use continuous shooting, but you can use the self-timer. As I noted earlier, you don't have to limit this, or any Scene mode setting, to the subject its name implies. If you are photographing reddish leaves in autumn, you might use this option to create an enhanced view of the brightly colored foliage.

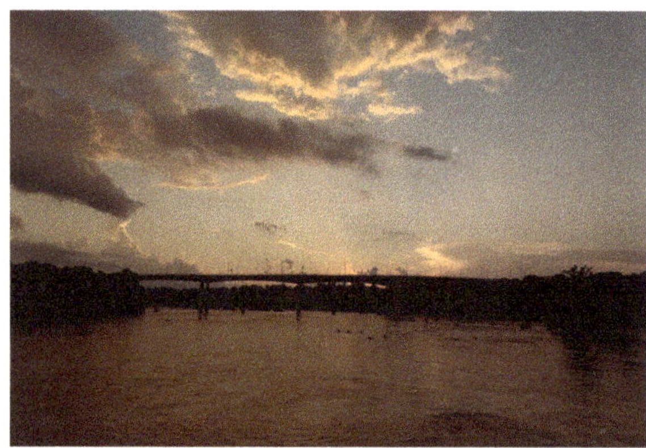

Figure 3-36. Sunset Example

In Figure 3-36, I used the Sunset option for a photograph of a typical evening scene at the river.

Night Scene

The Night Scene option is designed to preserve the natural look of an evening setting. The camera disables the use of the flash completely; if the scene is quite dark, you should use a tripod to avoid camera motion during the long exposure that may be required. You cannot use continuous shooting, but you can use the self-timer. This setting is good for cityscapes and other outdoor scenes after dark when flash would not help. The camera does not raise the ISO or use multiple shots, as it does with other modes used in dim lighting, such as Anti Motion Blur and Hand-held Twilight.

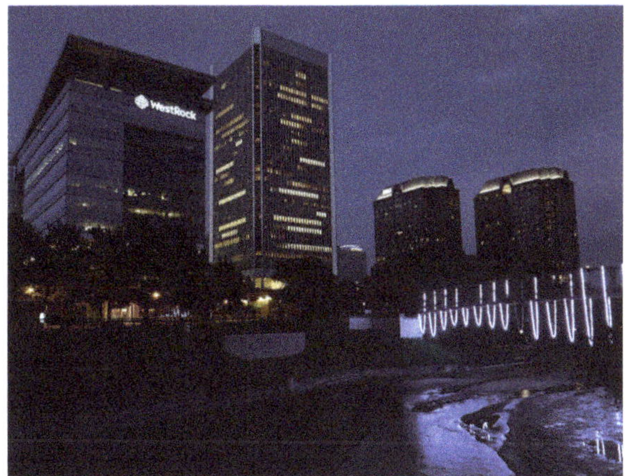

Figure 3-37. Night Scene Example

In Figure 3-37, I used the Night Scene setting to photograph the city skyline after sunset. I had the camera on a tripod, and it exposed the image for one half second at f/3.2, with ISO at 125.

Hand-Held Twilight

This scene type is for taking pictures in low light without flash or tripod. With this special setting, the camera may boost the ISO to a higher level so it can use a fast shutter speed, and it takes a rapid burst of four shots. The camera combines these shots internally into one composite image to counteract the effects of high ISO, which often causes visible "noise," or grain, in an image.

Although the camera tries to select frames with minimal motion blur, the final result with this setting is more likely to show motion blur than a shot made with the Anti Motion Blur setting, discussed later in this section. If the File Format (Still Images) option on the Camera Settings1 menu is set to RAW or Raw & JPEG, the camera resets it to JPEG while using this setting. You can set JPEG Quality to Extra Fine, Fine, or Standard.

Hand-held Twilight is a good option if you are shooting a landscape or other static subject when you cannot use a tripod or flash and the light is dim. If you can use a tripod, you might be better off using the Night Scene setting, discussed above. Or, if you don't mind using flash, you could just use Intelligent Auto, Program, or one of the more ordinary shooting modes. Hand-held Twilight is a useful option when it's needed, but it will not yield the same overall quality as a shot at a lower ISO with the camera on a steady support.

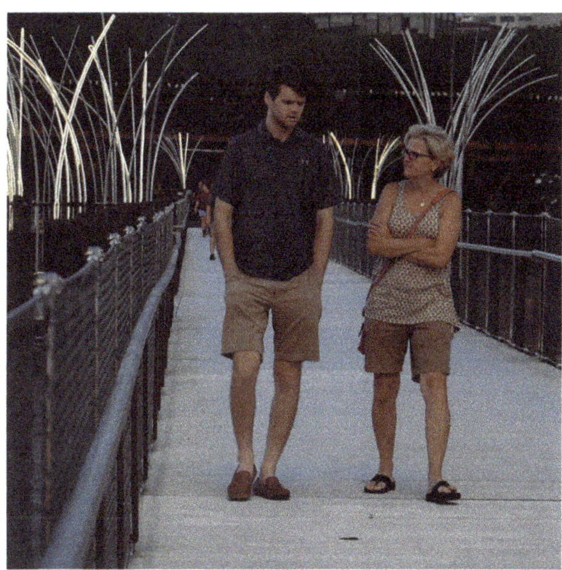

Figure 3-38. Hand-held Twilight Example

In Figure 3-38, I used this setting for a shot of a couple of people on the pedestrian bridge across the river after dark, without using a tripod. The camera set itself to f/4.5 at 1/160 second, with ISO at 400.

Night Portrait

This night-oriented setting is for situations when you are taking a portrait and are willing to use the camera's built-in flash. The main differences from the settings discussed above are that with Night Portrait, the camera takes only one shot and it activates the flash, in Slow Sync mode. You cannot set the flash mode to Flash Off. (However, you can leave the flash unit retracted, and the camera will let you take the shot without flash.)

I will discuss Slow Sync in more detail in Chapter 4. Basically, with this setting, the camera uses a slow shutter speed, so that as the flash illuminates the portrait subject, there is enough time for natural light to illuminate the background also. You can use the self-timer, but not continuous shooting. You also can use Raw for File Format (Still Images) if you wish, so this setting is a good choice for a high-quality portrait outdoors at night. Because of the slow shutter speed, you should use a tripod if possible to avoid motion blur.

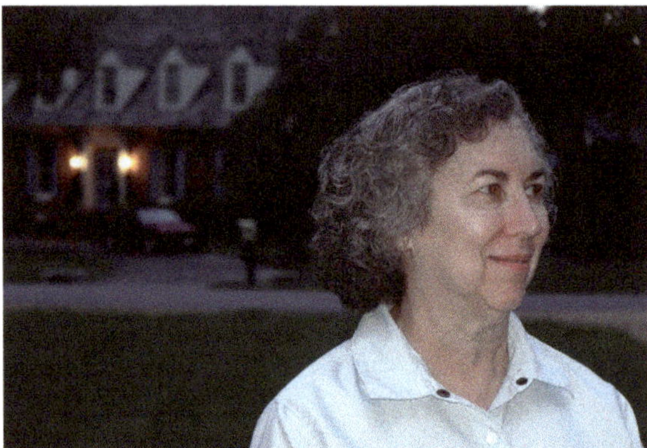

Figure 3-39. Night Portrait Example

In Figure 3-39, I used this setting for a portrait at dusk, with some ambient light in the background. I used the flash, and the camera set the shutter speed to 1/10 second, an exposure long enough to allow some of the background scenery to appear.

Anti Motion Blur

The Anti Motion Blur setting is useful when lighting is dim or the lens is zoomed in to a telephoto setting. In either of those situations, the image is subject to blurring because of camera motion. In dim lighting, blurring can happen when the camera uses a slow shutter speed to expose the image properly, because it is hard to hold the camera steady enough for a sharply focused shot longer than about 1/30 second. In the telephoto case, any camera motion is exaggerated because of the magnification of the image.

To counter the effects of this blurring, with Anti Motion Blur the camera raises the ISO to a higher-than-normal level so the camera can use a fast shutter speed and still let in enough light to expose the image properly. Because higher ISO settings result in increased visual noise, the camera takes a rapid burst of four shots and combines them internally into a single image with reduced noise. The camera also counteracts blur from motion of the subject to a fair extent, by analyzing the shots and rejecting those with motion blur as much as possible.

Anti Motion Blur is useful as the light is fading if you don't want to use flash. It is similar to the Hand-held Twilight setting, discussed above, but the camera is likely to use a higher ISO value with this option, which may result in more noise in the image. For Figure 3-40, I used this setting to capture an image of a kayaker navigating through rapids on the river as darkness fell. The camera used an aperture setting of f/4.5 and a shutter speed of 1/250 second at ISO 800, along with its multiple-shot processing. Because these settings were able to stop the action, the image does not show significant motion blur.

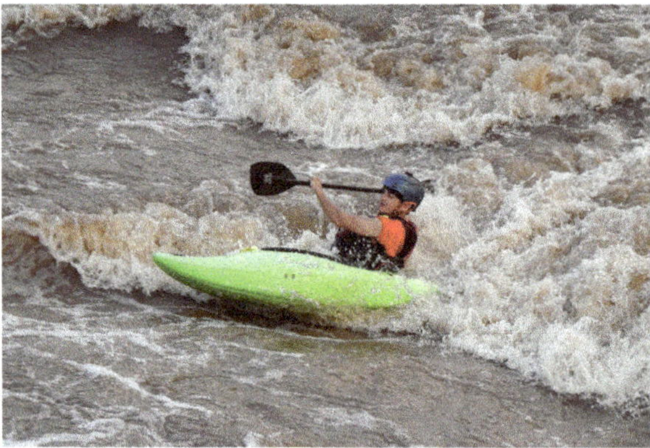

Figure 3-40. Anti Motion Blur Example

You should not expect good results with fast-moving subjects, because the camera will not be able to eliminate motion blur. With slower-moving subjects, though, the RX100 VI can do a good job of reducing blur. With this setting, you cannot set the drive mode options except for the self-timer, and you cannot use the flash. As with the Hand-held Twilight setting, if File Format (Still Images) is set to Raw or Raw & JPEG, the camera resets it to JPEG while this setting is in effect.

Pet

The Pet setting is for taking photos of cats, dogs, and other animals. It is similar to Sports Action in that the flash is off by default, but can be set to Fill-flash. The Pet setting, though, does not let you use continuous shooting. I would recommend this setting for a relatively posed or calm shot of your dog, cat, or other pet; if the animal is running around, you might be better off with the Sports Action selection.

I used this setting for Figure 3-41, a shot of my family's three-year-old spaniel in a fairly quiet pose.

Gourmet

The Gourmet setting, according to Sony, is meant to let you shoot food so that it looks "delicious." In terms of settings, the RX100 VI raises the brightness and vividness of colors to enhance the appearance of food. This setting is useful for people who write food blogs, or who like to record their meals for posterity. The camera lets you have the flash either forced off or set to Fill-flash. Continuous shooting is not available, but you can use the self-timer. In Figure 3-42, the color and brightness enhancements of this setting gave a boost to this image of a plate of artificial fruit.

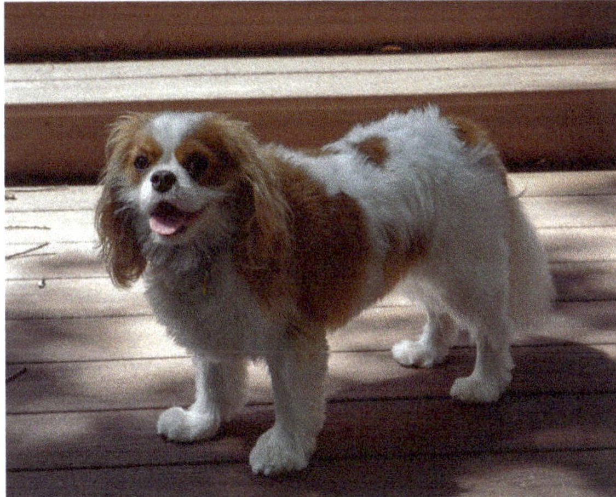

Figure 3-41. Pet Example

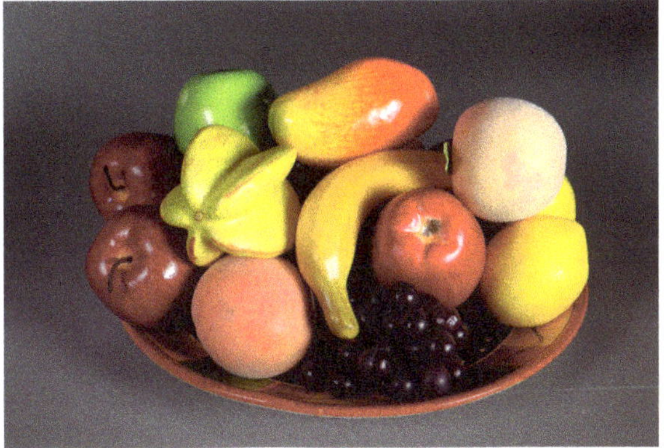

Figure 3-42. Gourmet Example

Fireworks

This scene type is designed to capture vivid images of fireworks bursts. It sets the camera to a two-second shutter speed and intensifies colors. If you can, you should set the camera on a tripod or other sturdy support and turn off the SteadyShot (Still Images) stabilization option on screen 5 of the Camera Settings2 menu. The camera disables the flash and continuous shooting.

This setting is one you can also use as an alternative to the Night Scene setting when you are using a tripod after dark. You might want to try this approach to take advantage of the different color processing that the camera uses with this option. In Figure 3-43, I used this setting for a shot of the pedestrian bridge across the river after dark, with the camera on a tripod, to see how this option would work for a general night scene.

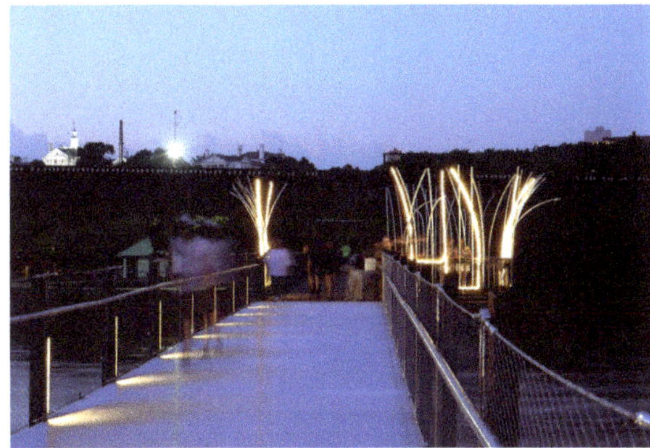

Figure 3-43. Fireworks Example

High Sensitivity

This final Scene mode setting is another option for low-light shooting. The camera disables the flash and continuous shooting, but it allows use of the self-timer. The camera is likely to use an ISO of 3200 or higher, all the way to the maximum of 25600 if the light is dim enough to require it. Unlike the case with Hand-held Twilight and Anti Motion Blur, the camera ordinarily takes only a single shot. However, in very dim lighting, the camera will display the Overlay icon used in Superior Auto mode and take a burst of four shots, which it combines internally to reduce the overall noise. You cannot set File Format (Still Images) to Raw or Raw & JPEG.

If you need to shoot in dim light without a tripod and produce an image that is as smooth and noise-free as possible, you probably should use Hand-held Twilight or Anti Motion Blur instead of High Sensitivity. However, there might be occasions when you don't mind the grainy, noisy appearance that a high ISO can bring. It's good to have various choices available when you are confronted with a dimly lit location.

Note that you cannot set the ISO to 25600 with the ISO setting on the Camera Settings1 menu; as discussed in Chapter 4, the highest setting available on that menu is 12800. To get the camera to use the 25600 value for ISO, you have to use the Multi Frame Noise Reduction setting on the ISO menu or this High Sensitivity setting of Scene mode.

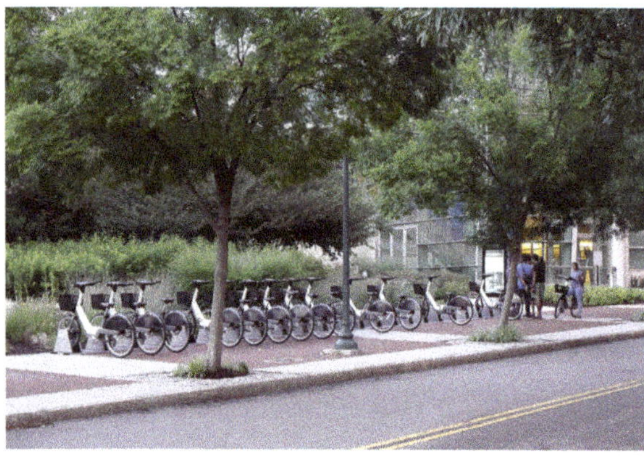

Figure 3-44. High Sensitivity Example

In Figure 3-44, I used the High Sensitivity setting to photograph a small gathering of people near a bicycle stand just after sunset. The camera set the ISO to 3200 with a shutter speed of 1/40 second at f/4.0, so I was able to take the photograph without a tripod.

Sweep Panorama Mode

The next setting on the mode dial is designed for the shooting of panoramic images. If you follow the fairly simple steps involved, the camera will stitch together a series of images internally and produce a high-quality final result with a dramatic, wide (or tall) view of a scenic vista or other subject that lends itself to panoramic depiction.

Because this shooting mode has its own spot on the mode dial, you can quickly set the camera to take panoramas. Just turn the mode dial to select the icon that looks like a long, squeezed rectangle, as shown in Figure 3-45.

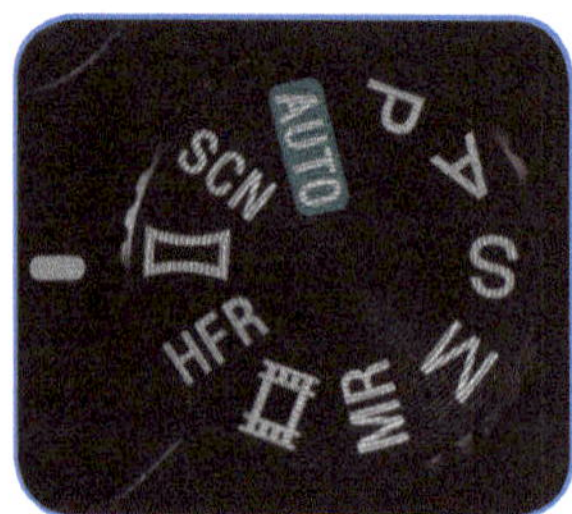

Figure 3-45. Mode Dial at Sweep Panorama

You will see a message telling you to press the shutter button and move the camera in the direction of the arrow that appears on the screen. (If the Mode Dial Guide option is turned on, you will have to press the Center button to dismiss the screen that describes Sweep Panorama mode before this message appears.) At that point, you can follow the directions and likely get excellent results. However, the camera allows you to make a number of choices for your panoramic images using the Camera Settings1 menu. Press the Menu button, and you will go to the menu screen that is currently active.

Navigate to the Camera Settings1 menu, which limits you to fewer choices than in most other shooting modes because several options are not appropriate for panoramas. For example, the File Format (Still Images), JPEG Quality, JPEG Image Size, Aspect Ratio, and ISO settings are dimmed and unavailable. Also, options such as drive mode, focus area, and flash mode are of no use in this situation and cannot be selected. In addition, you will not be able to zoom the lens in; it will be fixed at its wide-angle position. (If the lens was zoomed in previously, it will zoom back out automatically when you switch the mode dial to the Sweep Panorama position.)

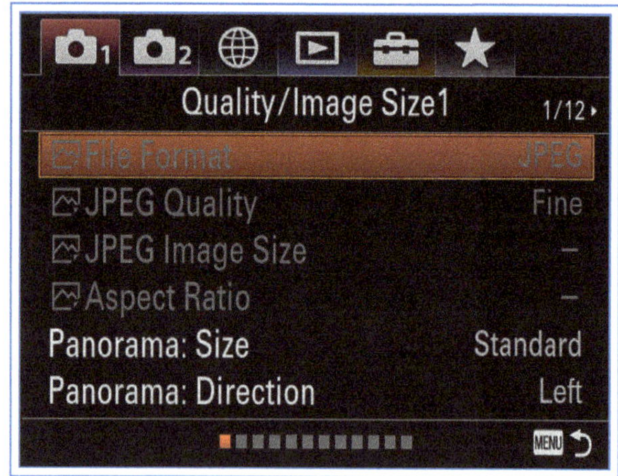

Figure 3-46. Screen 1 of Camera Settings1 Menu in Sweep Panorama Mode

You will, however, see two options on screen 1 of the Camera Settings1 menu that are not available for selection in any other shooting mode: Panorama Size and Panorama Direction, as shown in Figure 3-46.

If you select Panorama Size, you will see two options, Standard and Wide.

With Standard, a horizontal panorama will have a size of 8192 by 1856 pixels, which is a resolution of about 15 megapixels (MP). If you choose Wide, a horizontal panorama will have a size of 12416 by 1856 pixels, resulting in a resolution of about 23 MP. (This figure is larger than the camera's maximum resolution of 20 MP because with the panorama settings, the camera is taking multiple images and stitching them together.)

A vertical panorama at the Standard setting is 3872 by 2160 pixels, or about 8.3 MP; a vertical panorama at the Wide setting is 5536 by 2160 pixels, or about 12 MP.

The Panorama Direction option lets you choose Right, Left, Up, or Down for the direction in which you will sweep the camera to create the panorama.

There is a convenient shortcut for choosing the direction for your panorama. Just turn the control ring or the control wheel while the panorama shooting screen is displayed, and the direction arrow will change to a different position. You can cycle through all four positions with quick turns of this ring. (This function works with the control ring only if it is set to the Standard option through the Control Ring item under Custom Key (Still Images) on screen 9 of the Camera Settings2 menu.)

Also, you can use the Direction setting with various orientations of the camera to get different results than usual. For example, if you set the direction to Up and then hold the camera sideways while you sweep it to the right, you will create a horizontal panorama that has 2160 pixels in its vertical dimension rather than the standard 1856.

Those are the main settings for panoramas. There are other options that are available for selection in this mode on the Camera Settings1 menu, including metering mode, white balance, Creative Style, and others. I will discuss all of these menu options in Chapter 4. You can set the focus mode using the focus mode option on screen 4 of the Camera Settings1 menu, though you cannot select automatic autofocus or continuous autofocus. Table 3-1 provides suggested settings for the Camera Settings1 menu options in Sweep Panorama mode, as a starting point. I am including only the options that are available for setting in this shooting mode.

Table 3-1. **Suggested Camera Settings1 Menu Options for Panoramas**

Menu Option	Setting
Panorama Size	Standard
Panorama Direction	Personal Preference
Color Space	sRGB
Bracket Settings	No Setting Needed
Memory	No Setting Needed
Focus Mode	Single-shot AF
AF Illuminator	Auto
Set Face Priority in AF	No Setting Needed
Pre-AF	Off
AF Area Registration	Off
Delete Reg. AF Area	No Setting Needed
AF Area Auto Clear	Off
Disp. Cont. AF Area	Off
Phase Detect. Area	Off
Exposure Comp.	Adjust if Needed
Metering Mode	Multi
Spot Metering Point	Center
AEL w/Shutter	Auto
Exposure Std. Adjust	No Setting Needed
Red Eye Reduction	Off
White Balance	Auto
Priority Set in AWB	Standard
Creative Style	Standard
Focus Magnifier	No Setting Needed
Focus Magnification Time	No Limit
Initial Focus Mag.	x1.0
MF Assist	On
Peaking Setting	Adjust if Needed
Face Registration	No Setting Needed
Registered Faces Priority	Off

One other setting you can make when shooting panoramas is exposure compensation, using the exposure compensation (Down) button. (I did not specify a setting for the Exposure Compensation menu item in the table above, because I prefer to use the button.) I will discuss that function in Chapter 6. This feature can be useful for panoramas because the camera will not change the exposure if the camera is pointed at areas with varying brightness. So, for example, if you start sweeping from a dark area on the left, the camera will set the exposure for that area. If you then sweep the camera to the right over a bright area, that part of the panorama will be overexposed and possibly washed out in excessive brightness. To correct for this effect, you can reduce the exposure using exposure compensation. In this way, the initial dark area will be underexposed, but the brighter area should be properly exposed. Of course, you have to decide what part of the panorama is the one you most want to have properly exposed.

Another way to deal with this issue is to point the camera at the bright area before starting the shot and press the shutter button halfway to lock the exposure, then go back to the dark area at the left and start sweeping the camera. In that way, the exposure will be locked at the proper level for the bright area.

Once you have made all of the settings you want for your panorama, follow the directions on the screen. Press and release the shutter button and start moving the camera at a steady rate in the direction you have chosen. I tend to shoot my panoramas moving the camera from left to right, but you may have a different preference. You will hear a steady clicking as the camera takes multiple shots during the sweep of the panorama. A white box and arrow will move across the screen; your task is to finish the camera's sweep at the same moment that the box and arrow finish their travel across the scene. If you move the camera too quickly or too slowly, the panorama will not succeed; if that happens, try again.

Generally speaking, panoramas work best when the scene does not contain moving objects such as cars or pedestrians because when items are in motion, the multiple shots are likely to capture images of the same object more than once in different positions.

It is advisable to use a tripod, so you can keep the camera steady in a single plane as it moves. If you don't have a tripod available, you might try using the electronic level that Sony provides with the RX100 VI. You have to activate the level screen using the Display Button option on screen 7 of the Camera Settings2 menu, as discussed in Chapter 5. Then, on the shooting screen, press the Display button until the screen with the electronic level appears. Try to keep the outer tips of the level green as much as possible while shooting the panorama.

In addition to exposure, as discussed above, focus and white balance are fixed as soon as the first image is taken for the panorama. You cannot use the camera's touch focus features in Sweep Panorama mode; touching the screen will have no effect in this mode for purposes of autofocus. (You can use manual focus in this mode, and tapping the screen twice with manual focus in effect will magnify the display, but it's not likely that that action would be useful for panorama shooting.)

When a panoramic shot is played back in the camera, it is initially displayed at a small size so the whole image can fit on the display screen. You can then press the Center button to make the panorama scroll across the display at a larger size, using the full height of the screen.

Figure 3-47 is a sample panorama, shot from left to right using the Standard setting, hand-held.

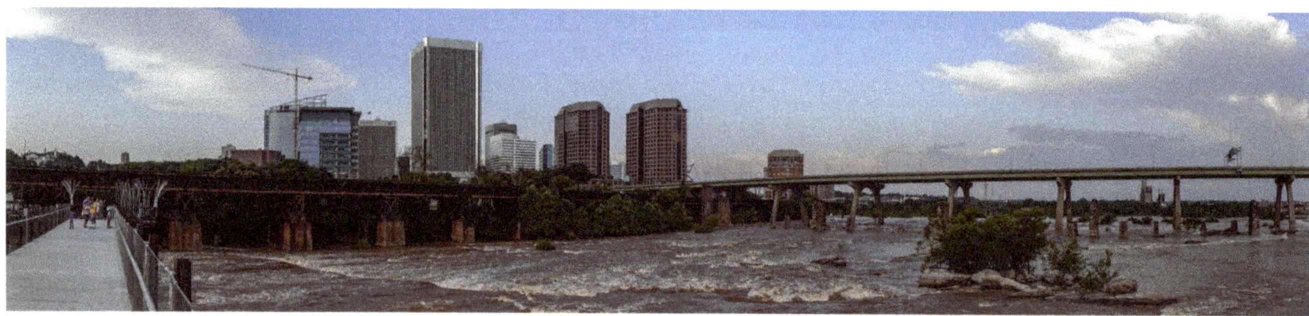

Figure 3-47. Sample Panorama: James River, Richmond, Virginia

Memory Recall Mode

There is one more shooting mode left to discuss, apart from Movie mode and HFR mode, which I will discuss in Chapter 9. This last mode, called Memory Recall, is a powerful tool that gives you expanded options for your photography.

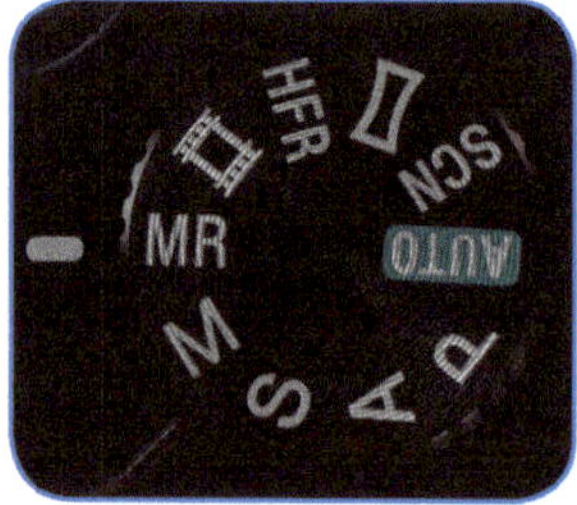

Figure 3-48. Mode Dial at Memory Recall

When you turn the mode dial to the MR position, shown in Figure 3-48, and then select one of the seven groups of settings from the Camera Settings1 and

Camera Settings2 menus that can be stored there, you are, in effect, selecting a custom-made shooting mode that you create with your own favorite settings.

You can set up the camera just as you want it—with stored values for items such as shooting mode, shutter speed, aperture, zoom amount, white balance, ISO, Shutter Type, Zebra, and other settings—and later recall all of those values instantly just by turning the mode dial to the MR position and selecting one of the seven stored memory registers on the Memory Recall screen. With the RX100 VI, unlike some other camera models, you can store settings for any shooting mode, including the Intelligent Auto and Scene modes.

Here is how this works. First, set up the camera with all of the settings you want to recall. For example, suppose you are going to do street photography. You may want to use a fast shutter speed, say 1/250 second, in black and white, at ISO 800, using continuous shooting with autofocus, Large and Extra Fine JPEG images, and shooting in the 4:3 aspect ratio.

The first step is to make all of these settings. Set the mode dial to Shutter Priority and use the control wheel or the control ring to set a shutter speed of 1/250 second. Then press the Menu button to call up the Camera Settings1 menu and, on screen 1, select JPEG for File Format (Still Images), Extra Fine for JPEG Quality, L for JPEG Image Size, and 4:3 for Aspect Ratio.

Then move to screen 3 and choose continuous shooting set to Hi speed for drive mode. On screen 6, set ISO to 800, then on screen 9 set the white balance to Daylight. Next, scroll down three positions below white balance to the Creative Style option and select the B/W setting, for black and white. You also may want to push the zoom lever all the way to the left for wide-angle shooting. You can set any other available Camera Settings1 menu options as you wish, but the ones listed above are the ones I will consider for now.

Once these settings are made, navigate to the Memory item, shown in Figure 3-49, which is the final item on screen 3 of the Camera Settings1 menu. After you press the Center button, you will see a screen like the one in Figure 3-50, showing icons and values for all of the settings currently in effect. The word Memory appears at the upper left of the screen, and the indicators 1, 2, 3, M1, M2, M3, and M4 at the upper right. In the example shown here, the number 1 is highlighted. Now press the Center button, and you will have selected register 1 to store all of the settings you just made. Registers 1, 2, and 3 are stored in the camera's internal memory. Registers M1, M2, M3, and M4 are stored on the memory card that is currently inserted in the camera.

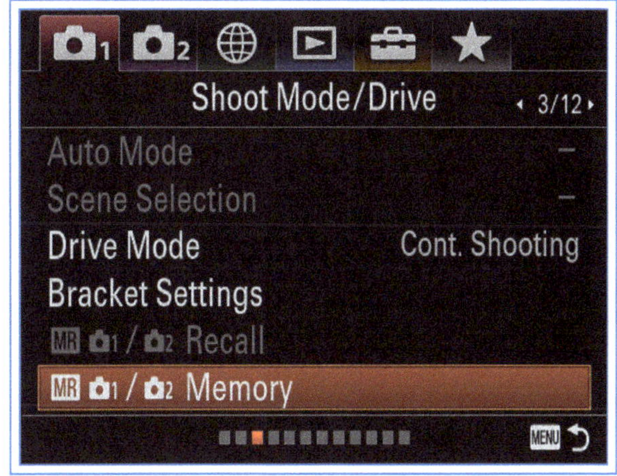

Figure 3-49. Memory Item Highlighted on Menu

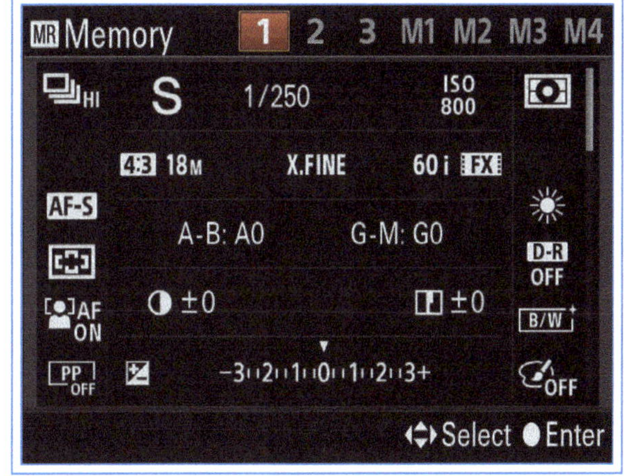

Figure 3-50. Memory Settings Screen

Note the short gray bar at the right side of the Memory screen shown in Figure 3-50. That bar indicates that you can scroll down through other screens to see additional settings that are in effect, such as DRO, Bracket Order, AF Illuminator, Center Lock-on AF, SteadyShot, and many others. Use the Up and Down buttons to scroll through those screens.

Next, to check how this worked, try making some very different settings, such as setting the camera to Manual exposure mode with a shutter speed of one second, Quality set to Raw, continuous shooting turned off, ISO set to Auto ISO, Creative Style set to Vivid, and the zoom lever moved all the way to the right for telephoto. Then turn the mode dial back to the MR position and press the Center button while the number 1 is highlighted for Register 1. You will see that all of the custom settings you made have instantly returned, including the zoom position, shutter speed, and everything else. You can then continue shooting with those settings.

This is a wonderful feature, and it is more powerful than similar options on some other cameras, which can save menu settings but not values such as shutter speed and zoom position, or can save settings only for the less-automatic shooting modes, but not the Scene and Auto modes. What is also quite amazing is that if you now switch back to Manual exposure mode, the camera will restore the settings that you had in that mode before you turned to the MR mode. (The position of the zoom lens will not revert to where it was, though.)

You can store settings from the Camera Settings1 and Camera Settings 2 menu, as well as the aperture, shutter speed and optical zoom settings. So, for example, you could set up one of the seven memory registers to recall Scene mode using the Macro setting, with the lens zoomed back to its wide-angle position. In that way, you could be ready for closeup shooting on a moment's notice.

Note that you can recall the M1, M2, M3, or M4 settings only if the memory card that has those settings saved is inserted in the camera. On the positive side, this means that you can build up an inventory of different groups of settings, and store them in groups of four on different memory cards. If those cards are clearly labeled or indexed, you can select a card with the four groups of settings you may need for a particular shooting session. However, whenever you format a card, the stored settings will be lost.

There are some settings you cannot save to a Memory Recall slot, such as Program Shift and a few menu settings, such as Write Date and a few others that are not that directly involved with shooting. Overall, though, this feature is powerful and useful. With a twist of the mode dial and the press of a button, you can call up a complete group of settings tailored for a particular type of shooting. It is worth your while to experiment with this feature and develop various groups of settings that work well for your shooting needs.

Chapter 4: The Camera Settings1 Menu

With the RX100 VI model, Sony has revised the menu system used on the previous five models in the RX100 series. The new system is similar to the one used on the company's highest-end models, such as the Alpha a9. For those who, like me, were quite familiar with the old system, which had only a single menu of camera settings and a separate Custom menu with more technical options, the new approach takes some getting used to. However, the new system does use somewhat more logical groupings than the older one.

The RX100 VI has six menus: Camera Settings1, Camera Settings2, Network, Playback, Setup, and My Menu. The first two contain settings that affect images and videos, as well as some other options that affect the functioning of various controls, such as the camera's ring, buttons, and wheel. The Network menu has settings that govern the operation of the camera's Wi-Fi and Bluetooth features for remote control and transferring images. The Setup menu has options that affect the camera's operation but that do not affect the image-making and video-recording operations directly, such as settings for camera sounds, monitor brightness, and the formatting of memory cards. Finally, the My Menu system lets you add your most-used menu options to a customized, short menu of your own choices.

I will discuss all of these menus in the various chapters of this book. In this chapter, I will discuss only the Camera Settings1 menu, which mainly offers ways to control the appearance of still images and how you capture them. The available options on this menu will change depending on the setting of the mode dial. For example, if the camera is set to Intelligent Auto mode, the Camera Settings1 menu options are limited because that mode is for a user who wants the camera to make many decisions without input. If the camera is in Sweep Panorama mode, the Camera Settings1 menu options are limited because of the specialized nature of that mode. For this discussion, I'm assuming you have the camera set to Program mode, because with that mode you have access to most of the options on the Camera Settings1 menu.

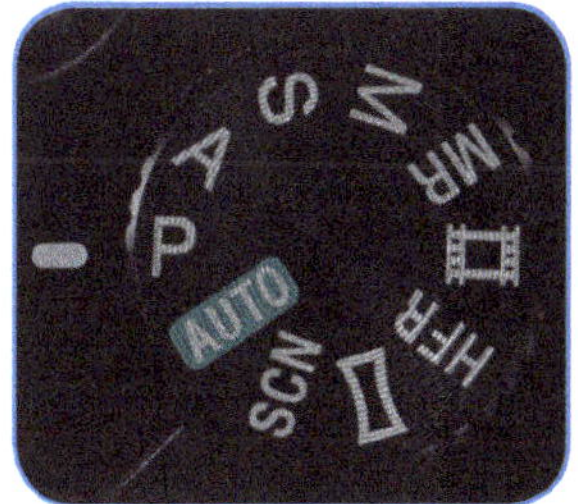

Figure 4-1. Mode Dial at Program

Turn the mode dial on top of the camera to P, which represents Program mode, as shown in Figure 4-1.

Enter the menu system by pressing the Menu button. When the orange highlight bar is visible on a menu screen, you can navigate from one screen to the next by pressing the Right or Left button. As you press either of those buttons, you will see an orange dot at the very bottom of the screen move through a line of gray dots, indicating which screen of the current menu system you are viewing. You also will see a pair of numbers separated by a slash mark at the top right of the menu screen. Those numbers also indicate which screen of the menu is now displayed.

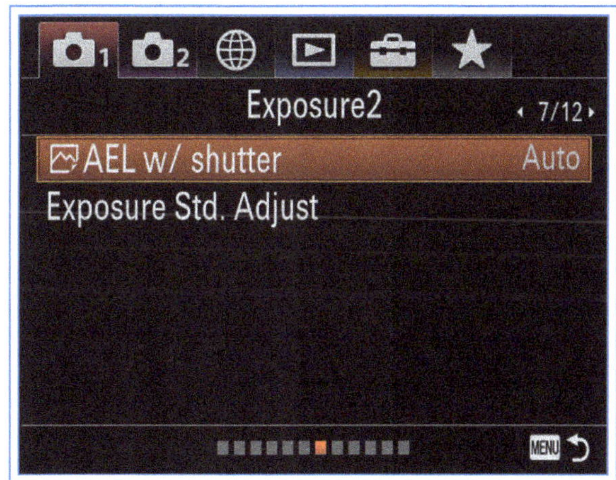

Figure 4-2. Screen 7 of Camera Settings1 Menu

For example, Figure 4-2 shows screen 7 of the Camera Settings1 menu when the camera is in Program mode. The orange dot is in the seventh position from the left at the bottom of the screen, and the numbers at the top right are 7/12, meaning the current screen is the seventh of twelve screens of this menu.

When the menu system first appears, the camera will display the last menu screen that was viewed. If you need to move to a different screen or a different menu, press the Right or Left button to navigate to that screen. As you keep pressing the Right or Left button, the cursor will move through all numbered screens of the various menu systems.

As you move from left to right through the menu screens on the RX100 VI, after the Camera Settings1 menu comes the Camera Settings2 menu, then the Network menu, headed by a globe icon. The last three menus are the Playback menu, marked by a triangle icon; the Setup menu, marked by a toolbox icon, and, finally, the My Menu option, marked by a star icon.

To navigate quickly through these six menu systems, you can press the Up button or turn the control wheel to move the highlight into the line of icons at the top of the screen. When one of those icons is highlighted, and the long, orange highlight bar has disappeared from the screen, you can use the Left and Right buttons to move directly from one menu system to another without going through the various screens of each menu.

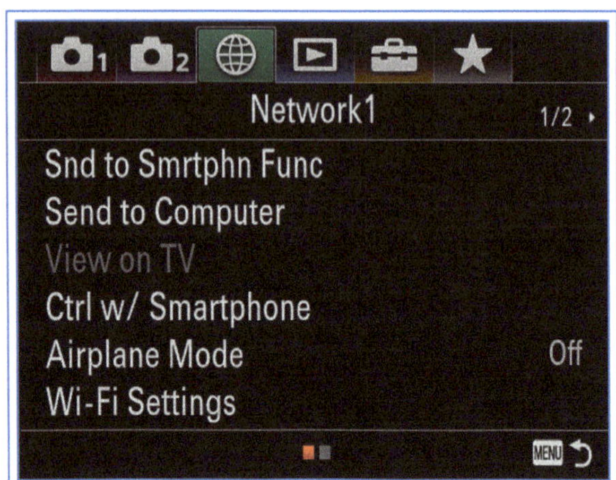

Figure 4-3. Icon for Network Menu Highlighted

For example, in Figure 4-3, the Network menu icon is highlighted. From there, you can press the Left button twice to move the highlight to the camera icon for the Camera Settings1 menu at the far left, as shown in Figure 4-4.

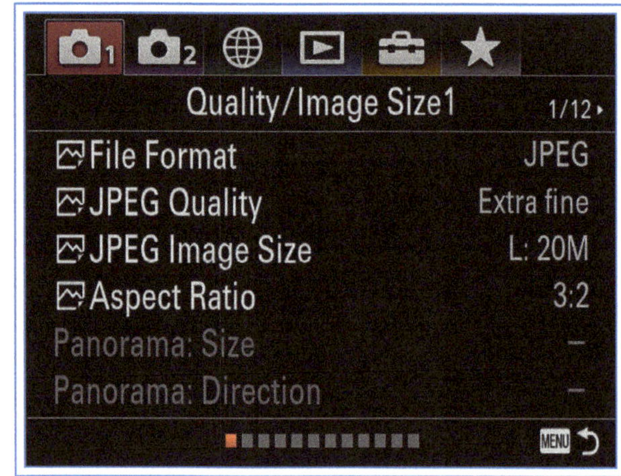

Figure 4-4. Icon for Camera Settings1 Menu Highlighted

Then you can press the Down button or turn the control wheel to move the highlight into the list of items on screen 1 of the Camera Settings1 menu, as shown in Figure 4-5.

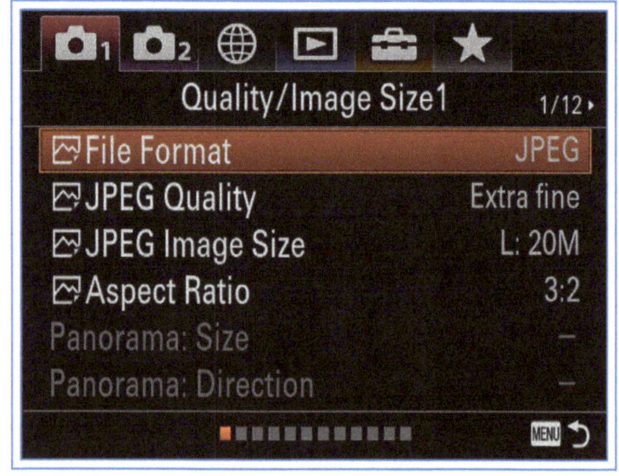

Figure 4-5. Screen 1 of Camera Settings1 Menu

In this chapter, I will discuss only the Camera Settings1 menu; I will discuss the other five menus in Chapter 5 (Camera Settings2), Chapter 7 (Playback), Chapter 8 (Setup and My Menu), and Chapter 10 (Network).

The Camera Settings1 menu has many options on 12 numbered screens. In most cases, each option (such as JPEG Image Size) occupies one line, with its name on the left and current setting (such as L: 20M) on the right. Some items on the menu screens are sometimes dimmed and have only a dash or blank space at the right side, such as the Auto Mode, Scene Selection, and Recall options in Figure 4-6, for example.

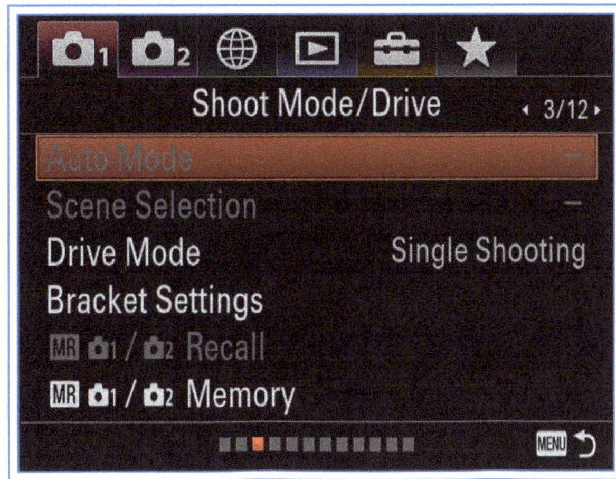

Figure 4-6. Dimmed Items on Menu Screen

This means those options are not available for selection in the current context. In this case, the camera was in Program mode, and those options are available only in Intelligent Auto, Scene, or Memory Recall mode, respectively.

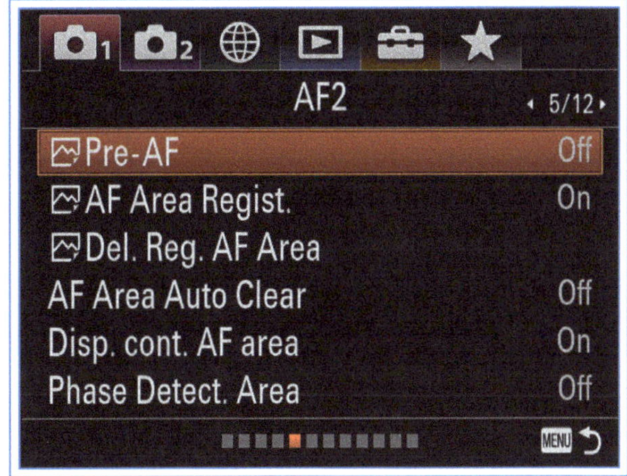

Figure 4-7. Screen 5 of Camera Settings1 Menu

Some items are preceded by an icon that indicates whether they are used for still images, movies, or high frame rate (HFR) movies. For example, Figure 4-7 shows screen 5 of the Camera Settings1 menu, on which the Pre-AF, AF Area Registration, and Delete Registered AF Area items are preceded by an icon showing they are applicable only for still images. When I discuss such options, I will put the category in parentheses when it is not obvious from the context. For example, I will refer to the two File Format items as File Format (Still Images) and File Format (Movies).

Figure 4-8 shows screen 1 of the Camera Settings2 menu, which has three settings (Movie Exposure Mode, File Format, and Record Setting) that apply only for normal movies, and two settings (HFR Exposure Mode and HFR Settings) that apply only for HFR video recording.

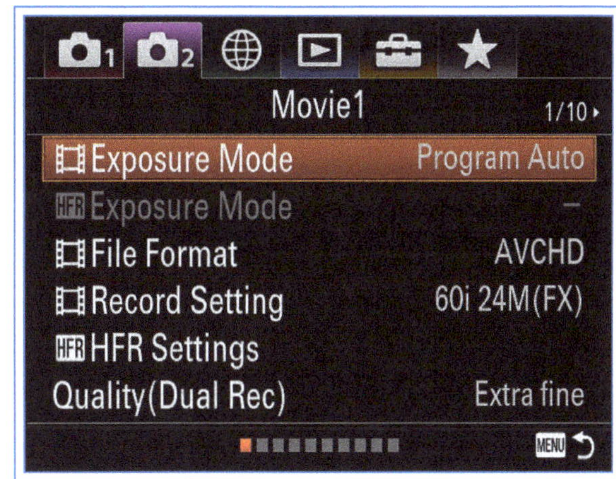

Figure 4-8. Screen 1 of Camera Settings2 Menu

There are a few other icons used for menu options that involve the Memory Recall mode, proxy recording, and the Custom Key assignments. I will discuss those items as they arise in the chapters that follow.

To follow the discussion below of the options on the Camera Settings1 menu, leave the shooting mode set to Program, which gives you access to most of the items on that menu. (I'll also discuss the options that are available only in other modes as I come to them.) I'll start at the top of screen 1 and discuss all of the options on each of the 12 screens of this menu.

File Format (Still Images)

This first option on the Camera Settings1 menu lets you make the important choice of whether to shoot still images using the Raw format, as JPEG files, or in both formats at the same time, as shown in Figure 4-9.

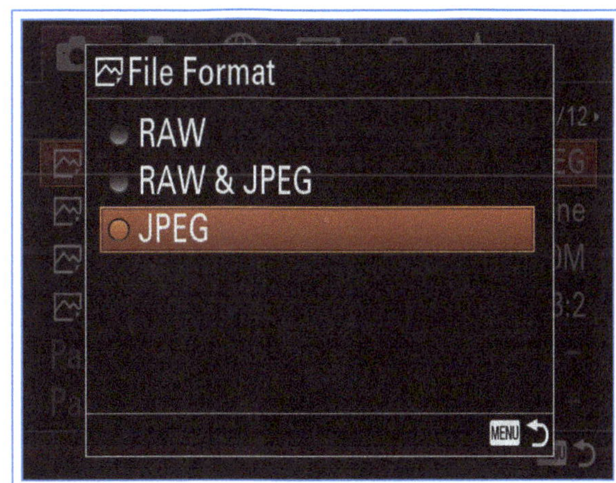

Figure 4-9. File Format (Still Images) Options Screen

As is the case with most camera manufacturers, Sony offers its own special Raw format, which is a file type that preserves as much as possible of the raw data received by the camera through its lens for each still image. If you want to shoot images with the highest possible quality, choose Raw for this menu option. If you want to shoot images that are easier to edit and to share, choose JPEG, which is an industry-standard format that is compatible with a wide range of photo editing programs, email programs, and other software. However, there are some other factors to consider in making this choice.

Raw files are larger than other files, so they take up more space on your memory card, and on your computer, than JPEG files. But Raw files offer advantages over JPEG files. When you shoot in the Raw format, the camera records as much information as it can about the image and preserves that information in the file it saves to the memory card. When you open the Raw file later on your computer, your software can process that information in various ways. For example, you can change the exposure or white balance of the image when you edit it on the computer, just as if you had changed your settings while shooting. In effect, the Raw format gives you what almost amounts to a chance to travel back in time to improve some of the settings that you didn't get quite right when you pressed the shutter button.

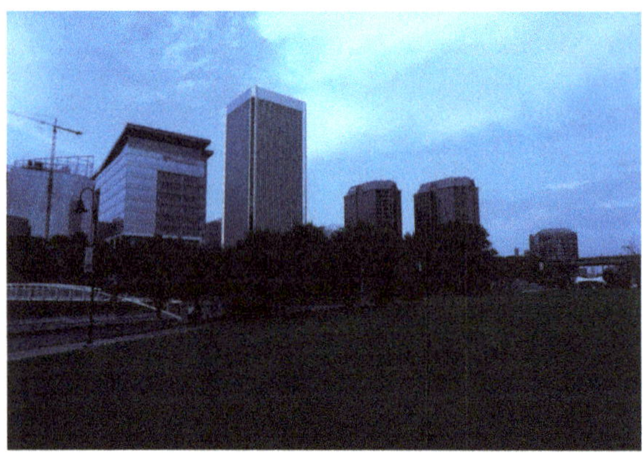

Figure 4-10. Raw Image Taken with Abnormal Settings

For example, Figure 4-10 is an image I took with the RX100 VI using the Raw format, with the exposure purposely set too dark and the white balance set to Incandescent, even though I took the picture outdoors during daylight hours.

Figure 4-11 shows the same image after I opened it in Sony's Imaging Edge software and adjusted the settings to correct the exposure and white balance. The result was an image that looked just as it would have if I had used the correct settings when I shot it.

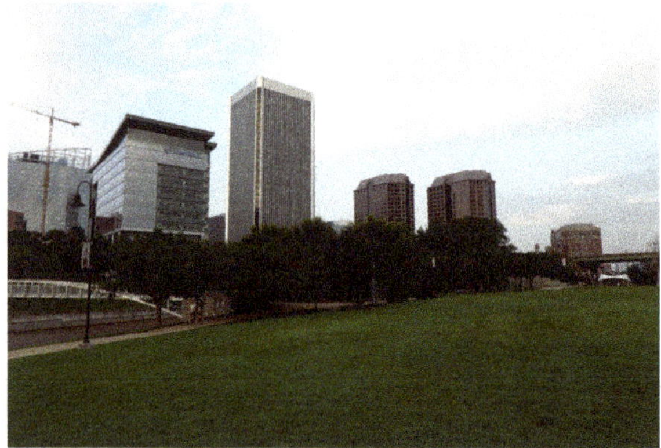

Figure 4-11. Raw Image with Settings Adjusted in Software

Raw is not a cure-all; you cannot fix bad focus or excessive exposure problems. But you can improve some exposure-related issues and white balance with Raw-processing software. You can use Sony's Imaging Edge software to view or edit Raw files, and you also can use other programs, such as Adobe Camera Raw, that have been updated to handle Raw files from this camera.

Using Raw can have disadvantages, also. The files take up a lot of storage space; Raw images taken with the RX100 VI are about 20 MB in size, while Large JPEG images I have taken are between about 4 and 18 MB, depending on the settings used. Also, Raw files have to be processed on a computer; you can't take a Raw image and immediately share it through social media or print it; you first have to use software to convert it to JPEG, TIFF, or some other standard format for manipulating digital photographs. If you are pressed for time, you may not want to take that extra step. Finally, some features of the RX100 VI are not available when you are using the Raw format, such as the Auto HDR, Picture Effect, Soft Skin Effect, and Digital Zoom options.

If you're undecided as to whether to use Raw or JPEG, you have the option of selecting Raw & JPEG, the second choice for the File Format (Still Images) menu item. With that setting, the camera records both a Raw and a JPEG image when you press the shutter button.

The advantage with that approach is that you have a Raw image with maximum quality and the ability to do extensive post-processing, and you also have a JPEG image that you can use for viewing, sharing, printing, and the like. Of course, this setting consumes storage space more quickly than saving your images in just Raw or JPEG format, and it can take the camera longer to store the images, so there may be a slowdown in the rate of continuous shooting, if you are using that option. You also cannot use some menu options that conflict with the Raw setting.

When you choose Raw & JPEG, you can select a JPEG Quality setting and a JPEG Image Size setting (both discussed below) that will apply only to the JPEG image; the Raw image is always at the maximum size and quality.

The best bet for preserving the quality of your images and your options for post-processing and fixing exposure mistakes later is to choose Raw files. However, if you want to use features such as Sweep Panorama mode, some Scene mode types such as Hand-held Twilight, Anti Motion Blur and High Sensitivity, the Picture Effect menu option, and others, which are not available with Raw files, then choose JPEG. If you choose JPEG, I strongly recommend that you choose the Large size and Extra Fine quality, unless you have an urgent need to conserve storage space on your memory card or on your computer. If you want Raw quality and are not concerned about storage space or speed of shooting, choose Raw & JPEG. However, you will still not be able to use Picture Effect and some other options.

JPEG Quality

The second option on this menu, JPEG Quality, is available for selection at any time, though it takes effect only when you are shooting JPEG images. The choices are Extra Fine, Fine, and Standard, as shown in Figure 4-12.

The term "quality" in this context concerns the way in which digital images are processed. In particular, JPEG (non-Raw) images are digitally "compressed" to reduce their size without losing too much information or detail from the picture. However, the more an image is compressed, the greater the loss of detail and clarity in the image. The Extra Fine setting provides the least compression. Images captured with the Fine or Standard setting undergo increasingly more compression, resulting in smaller files with somewhat reduced quality. I recommend always using the Extra Fine setting for JPEG files, unless you have a need to preserve storage space or are taking numerous images that do not need to be of high quality, such as images for photo ID cards or for an inventory of possessions.

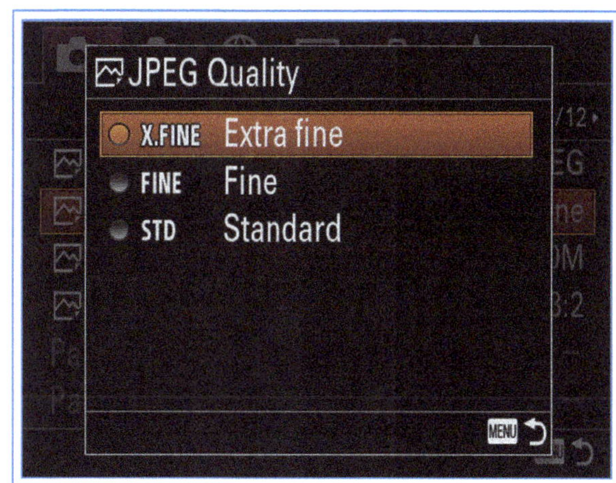

Figure 4-12. JPEG Quality Options Screen

JPEG Image Size

This setting controls the size in pixels of a JPEG still image recorded by the camera. (Raw images are always recorded at the maximum image size.) The Sony RX100 VI has a relatively large digital sensor for a compact camera, and that sensor has a high maximum resolution, or pixel count. The sensor is capable of recording a still image with 5472 pixels, or individual points of light, in the horizontal direction and 3648 pixels vertically. When you multiply those two numbers together, the result is about 20 million pixels, often referred to as megapixels, MP, or M.

The resolution of still images is important mainly when it comes time to enlarge or print your images. If you need to produce large prints (say, 8 by 10 inches or 20 by 25 cm), then you should select a high-resolution setting for JPEG Image Size. You also should choose the largest setting if you may need to crop out a small portion of the image and enlarge it for closer viewing.

For example, if you are shooting photos of wildlife and the animal or bird you are interested in is in the distance, you may need to enlarge the image digitally to see that subject in detail. In that case, you should choose the highest setting (L) for Image Size.

The available settings for Image Size are L, M, S, and VGA, for Large, Medium, Small, and VGA, as shown in Figure 4-13, although, as discussed below, VGA is available only when Aspect Ratio is set to 4:3.

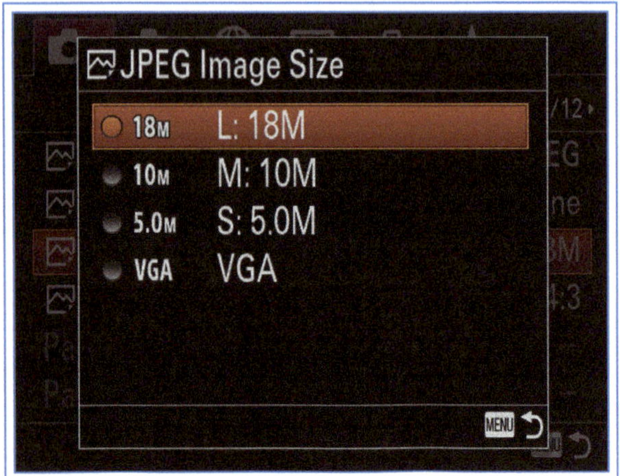

Figure 4-13. JPEG Image Size Options Screen

When you select one of the first three options, the camera displays a setting such as L: 18M, meaning Large: 18 megapixels. The number of megapixels changes depending on the Aspect Ratio setting, discussed below. This is because when the shape of the image changes, the number of horizontal pixels or the number of vertical pixels changes also to form the new shape.

For example, if the Aspect Ratio setting is 3:2, the maximum number of pixels is used because 3:2 is the aspect ratio of the camera's sensor. However, if you set Aspect Ratio to 16:9, the number of horizontal pixels (5472) stays the same, but the number of vertical pixels is reduced from 3648 to 3080 to form the 16:9 ratio of horizontal to vertical pixels. When you multiply those two numbers (5472 and 3080) together, the result is about 17 million pixels, which the camera states as 17M, as seen in Figure 4-14, which shows screen 1 of the Camera Settings1 menu.

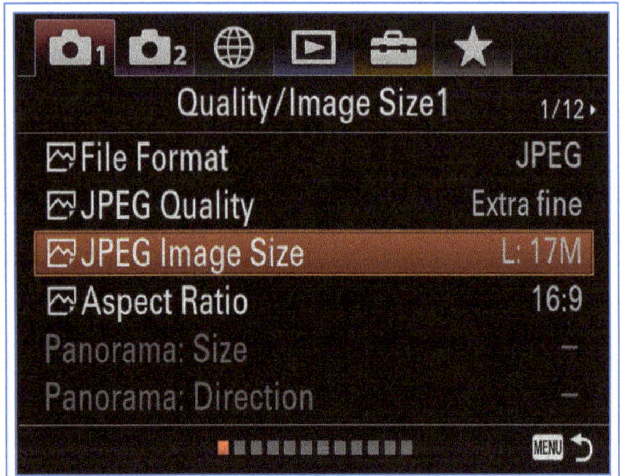

Figure 4-14. JPEG Image Size Value Highlighted on Menu

The VGA option, the smallest size possible, is available only if Aspect Ratio is set to 4:3. Otherwise, this choice does not even appear on the menu option for JPEG Image Size. VGA stands for video graphics array, a designation used for older-style computer screens, which have a 4:3 aspect ratio. The pixel count for this setting is very low—just 640 by 480 pixels, yielding a resolution of 0.3 M, much less than one megapixel. This very small size is suitable if you need to send images by email or need to store a great many images on a memory card.

One of the few reasons to choose a JPEG Image Size setting smaller than L is if you are running out of space on your memory card and need to keep taking pictures in an important situation. Table 4-1 shows approximately how many images can be stored on a 64 GB memory card for various settings.

Table 4-1. **Number of Images that Fit on a 64 GB Card (Image Size vs. Quality at 3:2 Aspect Ratio)**

	Large	Medium	Small
Raw & JPEG (Extra Fine)	1700	2100	2300
Raw	2900	-----	-----
Extra Fine	4300	6700	9999+
Fine	5800	9999+	9999+
Standard	9900	9999+	9999+

As you can see, if you are using a 64 GB memory card, which is a fairly common size nowadays, you can fit about 1700 images on the card even at the maximum settings of 3:2 for Aspect Ratio, Large for Image Size, and Raw & JPEG (Extra Fine) for Quality. If you limit the JPEG image quality to Fine, with no Raw images, you can fit about 5800 images on the card. If you reduce the JPEG Image Size setting to Small, you can store more than 10,000 images. I am unlikely ever to need more than about 300 or 400 images in any one session. And, of course, I can use a larger memory card or multiple memory cards.

If space on your memory card is not a consideration, then I recommend you use the L setting at all times. You never know when you might need the larger-sized image, so you might as well use the L setting and be safe. Your situation might be different, of course. If you were taking photos purely for a business purpose, such as making photo identification cards, you might want to use the Small setting to store the maximum number of images on a memory card and reduce expense. For general photography, I rarely use any setting other than L for Image Size. (One exception could be when I want to increase the range of the optical zoom lens without losing image quality; see the discussion of Smart Zoom and related topics in Chapter 5.)

Aspect Ratio

This third option on the Camera Settings1 menu lets you choose the shape of your still images. The choices are the default of 3:2, as well as 4:3, 16:9, and 1:1, as shown in Figure 4-15. These numbers represent the ratio of the units of width to the units of height. For example, with the 16:9 setting, the image is 16 units wide for every 9 units of height.

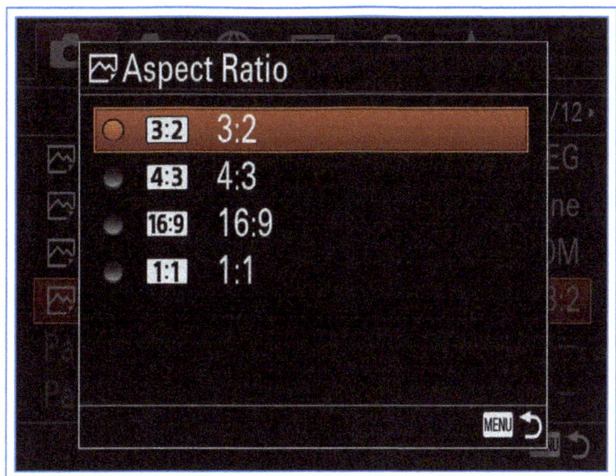

Figure 4-15. Aspect Ratio Options Screen

The aspect ratio that uses all pixels on the image sensor is 3:2; with any other aspect ratio, some pixels are cropped out. So, if you want to record every possible pixel, you should use the 3:2 setting. If you shoot using the 3:2 aspect ratio, you can always alter the shape of the image later in editing software such as Photoshop by cropping away parts of the image. However, if you want to compose your images in a certain shape and don't plan to do post-processing in software, the aspect ratio settings of this menu item can help you frame your images in the camera using the appropriate aspect ratio on the display.

For each of the aspect ratios discussed below, I am including an image I took using that setting in the same location at the same time, to give an idea of what the different aspect ratios look like. The default 3:2 setting, used for Figure 4-16, includes the maximum number of pixels, and is the ratio used by traditional 35mm film. This aspect ratio can be used without cropping to make prints in the common U.S. size of six inches by four inches (15 cm by 10 cm).

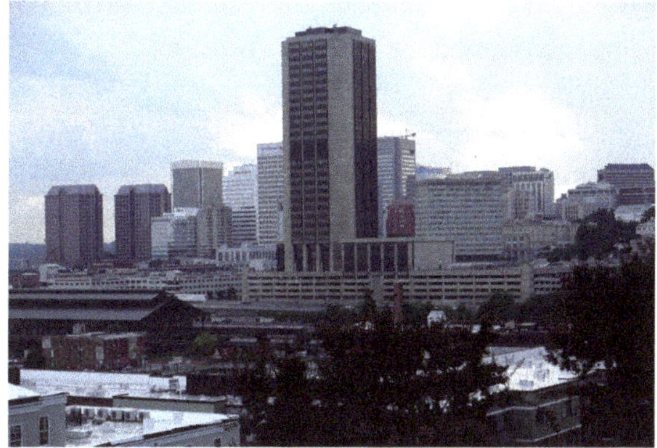

Figure 4-16. Aspect Ratio Set to 3:2

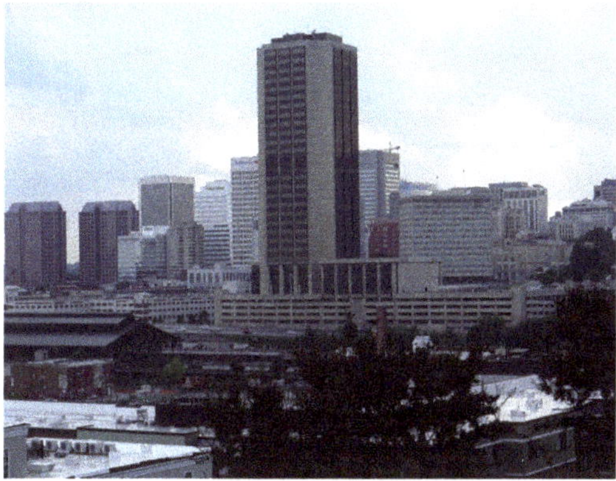

Figure 4-17. Aspect Ratio Set to 4:3

The 4:3 setting, shown in Figure 4-17, is in the shape of a traditional (non-widescreen) computer screen, so if you want to view your images on that sort of display, this may be your preferred setting.

As I noted earlier in discussing JPEG Image Size, if you want to use the VGA setting for Image Size, the camera must be set to the 4:3 aspect ratio. With this setting, some pixels are lost at the left and right sides of the image.

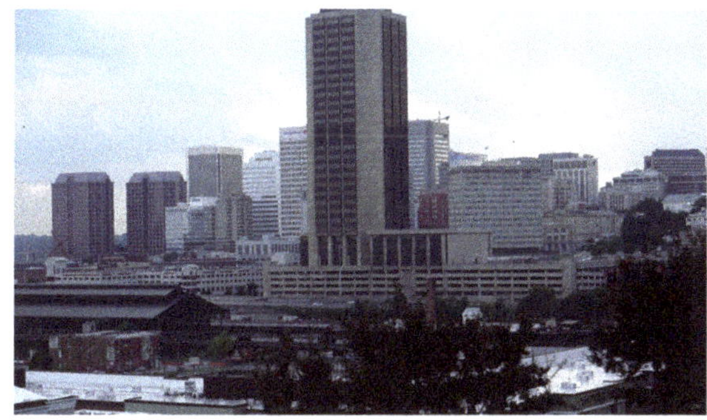

Figure 4-18. Aspect Ratio Set to 16:9

The 16:9 setting, illustrated in Figure 4-18, is the "widescreen" option, like that found on many modern HD television sets. You might use this setting when you plan to show your images on an HDTV set. Or, it might be suitable for a particular composition in which the subject matter is stretched out in a horizontal arrangement. With this setting, some pixels are cropped out at the top and bottom, though none are lost at the left or right.

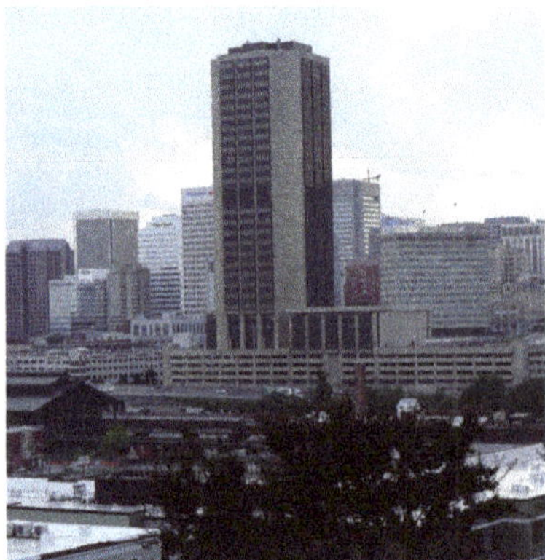

Figure 4-19. Aspect Ratio Set to 1:1

The 1:1 ratio, illustrated in Figure 4-19, produces a square shape, which some photographers prefer because of its symmetry and because the neutrality of the shape leaves open many possibilities for composition. With the 1:1 setting, the camera crops pixels from the left and right sides of the image.

The Aspect Ratio setting is available in all shooting modes except Sweep Panorama. However, although you can set Aspect Ratio when the camera is in Movie mode or HFR mode (mode dial turned to movie-film icon or HFR), that setting will have no effect until you switch to a mode for taking still images, such as Program mode. When the mode dial is set to the Movie position, you cannot take still images other than during movie recording. The aspect ratio of a still image taken while recording a movie is determined by the File Format (Movies) and Record Setting menu options, not by the Aspect Ratio option. With the mode dial at the HFR position, you cannot take still images at all.

Panorama Size and Panorama Direction

The next two commands on this screen of the menu are available only when the mode dial is at Sweep Panorama mode. I discussed these settings in Chapter 3, in connection with that mode. You should not need the Panorama Direction menu option often, because you can always set the panorama direction by turning the control wheel (or the control ring, if it is set to the Standard option) when the camera is in Sweep Panorama mode. You do need the Panorama Size option in order to set the size of the Panorama to Standard or Wide.

Screen 2 of the Camera Settings1 Menu is shown in Figure 4-20.

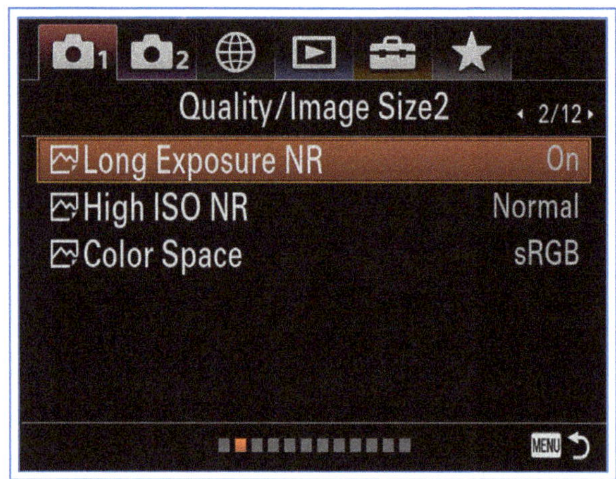

Figure 4-20. Screen 2 of Camera Settings1 Menu

Long Exposure Noise Reduction

This option uses processing to reduce the "noise" that affects images during exposures of 1/3 second or longer. This setting is turned on by default. When it is turned on, the camera processes your shot for a time equal to the time of the exposure. So, if your exposure is for two seconds, the camera will process the shot for an additional two seconds after the image is captured, creating a delay before you can shoot again.

In some cases, this processing may remove details from your image. In addition, in certain situations you may prefer to leave the noise in the image because the graininess can be pleasing in some cases. Or, you may prefer to remove the noise using post-processing software. If you want to turn off this option, use this menu item to do so.

This option is not available for adjustment when the camera is set for continuous shooting, Multi Frame Noise Reduction, exposure bracketing, or in the Auto, Sweep Panorama, or Scene modes. The camera will select a setting for Long Exposure Noise Reduction in those cases. For example, the camera will turn this option off with the Sports Action, Hand-held Twilight, and Anti Motion Blur Scene mode settings, but turn it on with the Portrait and Macro settings.

I recommend you make this setting based on the type of shooting you are doing. If you're taking casual shots or don't want to do post-processing, I suggest you leave this option turned on. But, if you are shooting with Raw quality and want to do processing with software, I recommend turning it off.

High ISO Noise Reduction

This next menu entry has three settings: Normal, Low, or Off; the default is Normal. This option removes noise caused by the use of a high ISO level. One problem with this sort of noise reduction is that it takes time to process your images after they are captured. You may want to set this option to Low or Off to minimize the delay before you can take another picture. If File Format (Still Images) is set to Raw, this option will be unavailable on the menu because this processing is not available for Raw images. It is not available for adjustment on the menu in the Auto, Scene, or Sweep Panorama modes; it is always set to Normal in those modes.

Color Space

With this option, you can choose to record your still images using the sRGB "color space," the more common choice and the default, or the Adobe RGB color space. The sRGB color space has fewer colors than Adobe RGB; therefore, it is more suitable for producing images for the web and other forms of digital display than for printing. If your images are likely to be printed commercially in a book or magazine or it is critical that you be able to match a great many different color variations, you might want to consider using the Adobe RGB color space. I always leave the color space set to sRGB, and I recommend that you do so as well unless you have a specific need to use Adobe RGB, such as a requirement from a printing company that you are using to print your images.

If you are shooting your images with the Raw format, you don't need to worry so much about color space, because you can set it later using your Raw-processing software.

The items on screen 3 of the Camera Settings1 menu are shown in Figure 4-21.

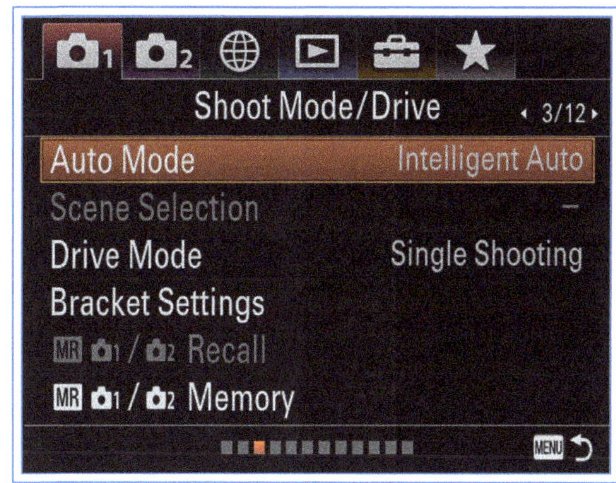

Figure 4-21. Screen 3 of Camera Settings1 Menu

Auto Mode

This option is available for selection only when the mode dial is set to the AUTO position. This menu item lets you choose either Intelligent Auto or Superior Auto for the shooting mode, as discussed in Chapter 3. If the Mode Dial Guide option is turned on through screen 2 of the Setup menu, the screen for choosing between these two modes is automatically displayed whenever you turn the mode dial to the AUTO position and press the Center button when the guide screen appears. If that option is not turned on or the mode dial is already at the AUTO position, you can use the Auto Mode option to choose one or the other of the Auto modes. You also can change between Intelligent Auto and Superior Auto using the Function menu, if the Shoot Mode option appears on that menu, as discussed in Chapter 5.

Scene Selection

As discussed in Chapter 3, this option is used only when the mode dial is at the SCN position. You use this menu item to select one of the settings in that shooting mode, including Portrait, Anti Motion Blur, Sunset, Night Scene, and others. Note that you also can use the control wheel or the control ring (if set to the Standard setting) to change scene types when the shooting screen is displayed. In addition, the Scene Selection menu screen appears automatically when you turn the mode dial to the SCN position and press the Center button, if the Mode Dial Guide option on screen 2 of the Setup menu is turned on. Also, as with Auto

Mode, discussed above, you can choose a scene type using the Shoot Mode option on the Function menu, if that option is included in that menu system.

Drive Mode

This next option on screen 3 of the menu gives access to features of the RX100 VI for shooting bursts of images, bracketing exposures, and using the self-timer.

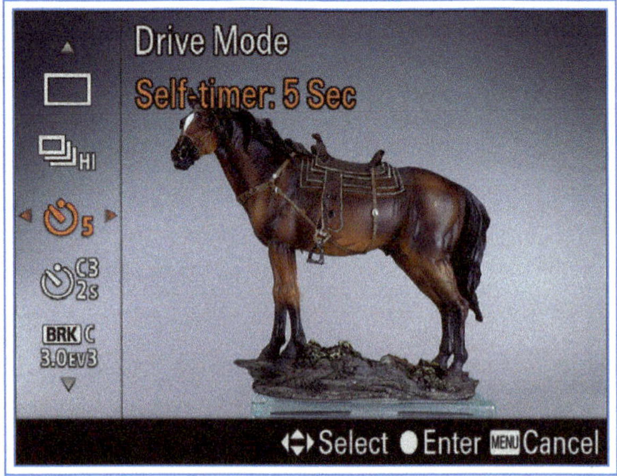

Figure 4-22. Drive Mode Menu

When you highlight this option and press the Center button, a menu appears at the left of the screen as shown in Figure 4-22, with eight choices represented by icons: Single Shooting, Continuous Shooting, Self-timer, Self-timer (Continuous), Continuous Exposure Bracketing, Single Exposure Bracketing, White Balance Bracketing, and DRO Bracketing. Scroll down through this menu using the Up and Down buttons or the control wheel. When the icon for an option is highlighted, you can select sub-options by pressing the Left and Right buttons. (You have to scroll down to see all of the choices on the menu.)

Details for the drive mode settings are discussed below.

Single Shooting

This is the normal mode for shooting still images. Select this top choice on the drive mode menu to turn off all continuous shooting. In some cases, having one of the continuous-shooting options selected will make it impossible to make other settings, such as Soft Skin Effect or Long Exposure Noise Reduction. If you find you cannot make a certain setting, try selecting single shooting to see if that removes the conflict and fixes the problem.

As noted in Chapter 3, this option is not available with the Sports Action setting of Scene mode.

Continuous Shooting

Continuous shooting, sometimes called burst shooting, is one of the most impressive features of the RX100 VI, which provides speeds up to 24 frames per second (fps), with focus and exposure adjusted for each shot. This capability is useful in many contexts, from shooting an action sequence at a sporting event to taking a series of shots of a person in order to capture changing facial expressions. I often use burst shooting for street photography to increase my chances of catching an interesting scene, and when photographing birds, to try to catch them in an interesting position.

To activate burst shooting, scroll down to the second icon on the drive mode menu, which looks like a stack of overlapping frames. When that icon is highlighted, press the Left or Right button to select the speed of shooting—Hi, Mid, or Lo. The Hi setting provides speeds up to 24 fps; Mid has speeds up to 10 fps; and the Lo setting is rated at up to 3 fps. Once a speed is selected, press and hold the shutter button to fire off a burst of shots. The camera will shoot at the selected speed level until its memory buffer fills up, at which point the shooting will change to a considerably slower pace.

If focus mode on screen 4 of the Camera Settings1 menu is set to AF-S for single autofocus, the camera will not adjust its focus during the burst of shots. But, if you set that option to AF-C for continuous autofocus or AF-A for automatic autofocus, the camera will adjust focus for each shot, as long as the aperture value is no higher than f/8.0. The reason for this limitation is that the camera's ability to adjust focus during continuous shooting depends on its use of phase-detection autofocus, which uses 315 special autofocus points covering most of the area of the image sensor. The phase-detection system cannot function at apertures narrower than f/8.0, such as f/9.0 and f/11.0. At those narrower apertures, the camera reverts to using contrast-detection autofocus, which is quite accurate but considerably slower than the phase-detection process. So, if you need to take bursts of continuous shots with autofocus adjustments for all images, you need to ensure that the camera is using an aperture of f/8.0 or lower.

Also note that autofocus will not be accurate in all situations during burst shooting. If the subject is one that is difficult to focus on, the camera may not always focus sharply. But when conditions are reasonably good, the autofocus works very well during burst shooting.

If you want the camera to adjust its exposure during the series of continuous shots, you need to go to screen 7 of the Camera Settings1 menu and check the setting of the AEL w/Shutter menu item. If that item is set to On, the camera will lock exposure when you press the shutter button, and exposure will be locked throughout the burst as it was set for the first image, even if the lighting changes dramatically.

However, if you set AEL w/Shutter to Off, then the camera will adjust its exposure as needed during the burst of shots. If you set AEL w/Shutter to Auto, then the camera will adjust exposure during continuous shooting if the focus mode is set to continuous autofocus or automatic autofocus, and the aperture is f/8.0 or wider. If AEL w/Shutter is set to Auto when you are using single autofocus, then the camera will keep the exposure locked. (Of course, if you want the camera to adjust exposure automatically, you have to use an exposure mode in which the camera normally controls exposure. If you use Manual mode with a fixed ISO value, the exposure will not change.)

Depending on conditions such as image size and quality, lighting, settings for autofocus and autoexposure lock, and the speed of the memory card, the rate of burst shooting can vary considerably. With normal conditions, such as shooting Extra Fine and Large images with a shutter speed of 1/400 second using continuous autofocus, in my testing the camera shot at full speed until the memory buffer filled. Then the rate slowed down drastically to a few frames per second. When shooting with Quality set to Raw & JPEG, I found that the shooting speed slowed down after about 105 shots. The following table shows the results of my testing with various settings. I carried out these tests using a SanDisk ExtremePRO 32 GB SDHC card, rated in UHS Speed Class 3. The aspect ratio was set to 3:2 for all shots.

Table 4-2. **Results of RX100 VI Continuous Shooting Tests**

Continuous Speed	Quality	Shots Before Slowdown	Focus Setting	AEL w/ Shutter
Hi	Raw & JPEG	105	AF-C	Auto
Hi	Raw	108	AF-C	Auto
Hi	Extra Fine	228	AF-C	Auto
Hi	Fine	235	AF-C	Auto
Hi	Raw & JPEG	106	AF-S	On
Hi	Extra Fine	232	AF-S	On
Mid	Raw & JPEG	112	AF-C	Auto
Mid	Extra Fine	263	AF-C	Auto
Lo	Extra Fine	656+	AF-C	Auto

Based on these tests, I found there was not much advantage in choosing a speed slower than Hi, unless that choice is the most appropriate for the shooting session. For example, if you are shooting a relatively slow-moving activity and don't want to load up your memory card with hundreds of images, you may want to choose the Mid or Lo letting. However, if you are shooting sporting events, running children or pets, birds in flight, or other fast-moving subjects, the Hi setting yields excellent results with continuous focus and exposure adjustments.

Although you can turn on the flash when the Continuous Shooting option is selected, and the camera will actually take a series of shots with flash as you hold down the shutter button, the time between shots may be several seconds because the flash cannot recycle quickly enough to take a rapid series of shots.

After taking a burst of shots, it can take the camera a while to save them to the memory card. The access lamp inside the battery/memory card compartment lights up in red while the camera is writing to the card. In addition, the camera will display a series of small vertical lines along with a series of changing numbers in the upper left corner of the display, indicating the number of images remaining to be written from the buffer to the memory card. While the access lamp is illuminated and the buffer-emptying display is active, be sure not to remove the battery or the memory card. While the buffer is being emptied, you can take additional shots, and you can enter playback mode to view images that have already been written to the memory card, but you cannot use the menu system.

When you have captured a series of continuous shots, the way they are displayed in playback mode depends on a menu setting called Display Continuous Shooting Group, on screen 3 of the Playback menu. If that option is turned on, as it is by default, then, once the burst of shots is captured and written to the memory card, the camera will display all of the shots in the group as a single item that appears like a stacked group of images. In the lower right corner of the display, the camera displays the word Expand next to a round icon, as shown in Figure 4-23. These indications mean that you can press the Center button to open up the group so you can see the individual images inside it.

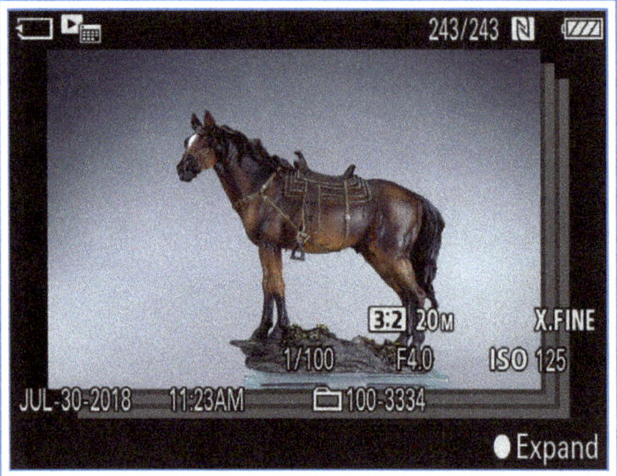

Figure 4-23. Burst of Images Displayed as Single Group

If you don't press the Center button, the group, which may contain hundreds of images, will behave like a single image for purposes of scrolling through images and deleting them. If you press the Center button, the group opens up and you can view each individual image within the group.

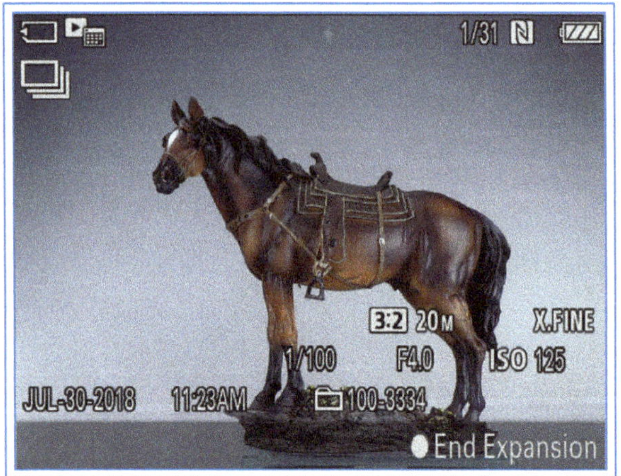

Figure 4-24. Burst of Images Displayed Individually

The camera will display a set of numbers in the upper right corner of the display, such as 1/31, indicating which image is being viewed out of how many total images in the group, as shown in Figure 4-24. To end the expansion and group the images back into a single item, press the Center button again.

For Figure 4-25, I used continuous shooting to take a series of images of two men playing basketball in a park. Using the high-speed burst setting, I was able to get a picture showing them both in mid-air.

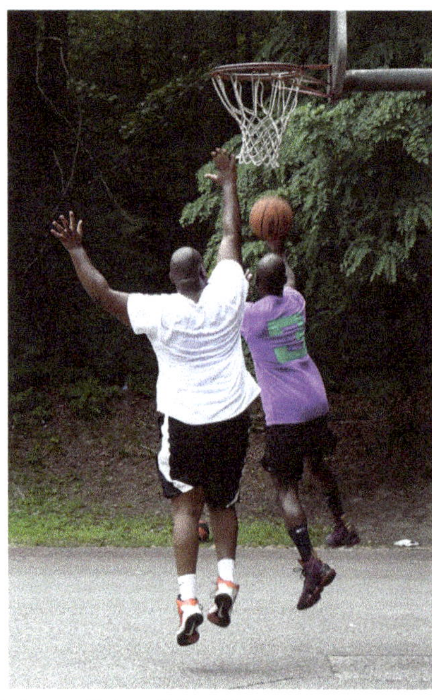

Figure 4-25. Image Taken Using High-speed Continuous Shooting

Continuous shooting is not available in Sweep Panorama mode, in Scene Selection mode (except for the Sports Action setting), with certain Picture Effect settings, with Auto HDR turned on, with ISO set to Multi Frame Noise Reduction, or when the Smile Shutter is turned on. When the Shutter Type option on screen 5 of the Camera Settings2 menu is set to Mechanical, the Hi setting for continuous shooting cannot be used.

Self-Timer

The next icon down on the menu of drive mode options represents the self-timer, as shown in Figure 4-26. The self-timer is useful when you need to be the photographer and also appear in a group photograph. You can place the RX100 VI on a tripod, set the timer for five or ten seconds, and insert yourself into the group before the shutter clicks. The self-timer also is helpful when you don't want to cause image blur by jiggling the camera as you press the shutter button.

For example, when you're taking a macro shot very close to the subject, focusing can be critical, and any bump to the camera could cause motion blur. Using the self-timer gives the camera a chance to settle down after the shutter button is pressed, before the image is recorded.

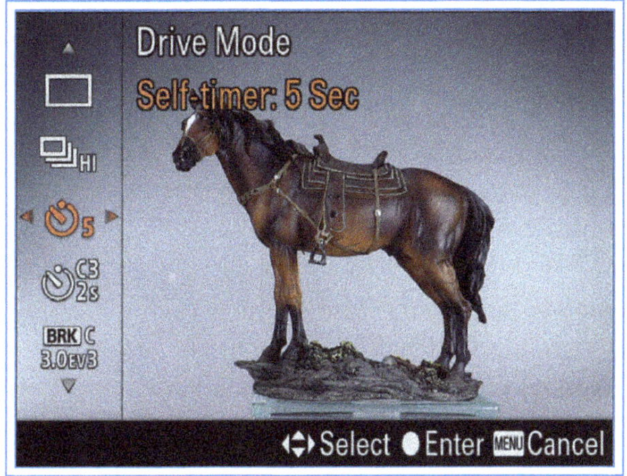

Figure 4-26. Self-timer Icon Highlighted on Drive Mode Menu

The self-timer option presents you with three choices: ten seconds, five seconds, and two seconds. When the self-timer icon is highlighted, press the Left or Right button to highlight one of these options, and press the Center button to select it. After you make this selection, the self-timer icon will appear in the upper left corner of the display with the chosen number of seconds (10, 5, or 2) displayed next to the icon, as shown in Figure 4-27. (If you don't see the icon, press the Display button until the screen with the various shooting icons appears.)

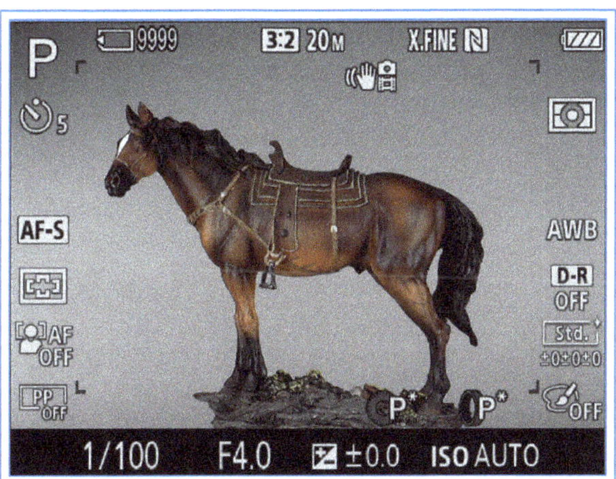

Figure 4-27. Self-timer Icon on Shooting Screen

Once the self-timer is set, when you press the shutter button, the timer will count down for the specified number of seconds and then take the picture. The reddish lamp on the front of the camera will blink, and the camera will beep during the countdown, unless the beeps have been silenced with the Audio Signals option on screen 10 of the Camera Settings2 menu.

The self-timer is not available in Sweep Panorama mode, with the Sports Action setting of Scene mode, when the Smile Shutter is activated or for recording a movie, and you cannot select continuous autofocus when the self-timer is turned on.

Self-Timer (Continuous)

The next item down on the drive mode menu, shown in Figure 4-28, is another variation on the self-timer. With this option, you can set the timer to take multiple shots after the countdown ends. You can choose any of the three time intervals, and you can set the camera to take either three or five shots after the delay. When you highlight this option, you will see a horizontal triangle indicating that, by pressing the Left and Right buttons, you can select one of six combinations of the number of shots and the timer interval. For example, the option designated as C3/2S sets the camera to take three shots after the timer counts down for two seconds; C5/10S sets it for five shots after a ten-second delay.

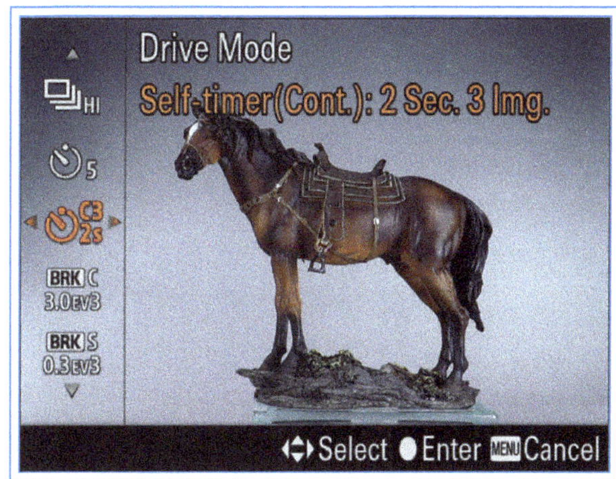

Figure 4-28. Self-timer (Continuous) Icon on Drive Mode Menu

This option is useful for group photos; when a series of shots is taken, you increase your chances of getting at least one shot in which everyone is looking at the camera and smiling. You can choose any settings you want for Image Size and Quality, including Raw & JPEG, and you will still get three or five rapidly fired shots, though the speed of the shooting will decrease slightly at the highest File Format and JPEG Quality settings.

Continuous Exposure Bracketing

This next option on the drive mode menu, shown in Figure 4-29, sets the camera to take three, five, or nine images with one press of the shutter button but with a different exposure level for each image, giving you a greater chance of having one image that is properly exposed.

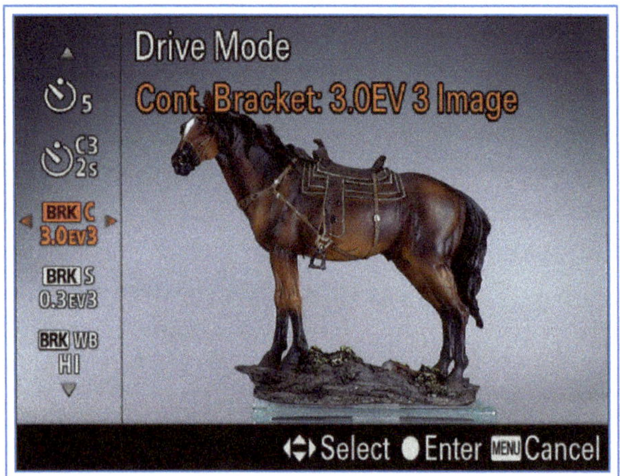

Figure 4-29. Continuous Exposure Bracketing Icon on Drive Mode Menu

When you highlight this option, you will see a horizontal triangle meaning that you can use the Left and Right buttons to select one of 13 combinations of the difference in exposure value and the number of images in the bracket. The first nine choices include exposure value (EV) intervals of 0.3, 0.7, or 1.0, each with a bracket of three, five, or nine exposures. The other four choices are for EV intervals of 2.0 or 3.0 EV, each with a bracket of three or five exposures.

The decimal numbers represent the difference in EV among the multiple exposures (three, five, or nine) that the camera will take. (With the larger EV intervals of 2.0 or 3.0 EV, the available numbers of shots are three or five; there is no option for choosing nine shots, because the overall exposure range would be too great, given the larger EV interval.)

For example, if you select 0.7 EV as the interval for three exposures, the camera will take three shots—one at the metered exposure level; one at a level 0.7 EV (or f-stop) below that, resulting in a darker image; and one at a level 0.7 EV above that, resulting in a brighter image. If you want the maximum exposure difference among the shots, select 3.0 EV as the interval for the three or five shots.

Once you have set this option as you want it and composed your scene, press and hold the shutter button and the camera will take the three, five, or nine shots in rapid succession while you hold down the button.

If you set this option for three exposures, the first one will be at the metered value, the second one underexposed by the selected interval, and the third one overexposed to the same extent. If you set it for five exposures, the first three shots will have the values noted above, the fourth will have the most negative EV, and the fifth will have the most positive EV. With nine exposures, the pattern will be similar, with the final two exposures having the most negative and positive EV settings, respectively. (You can change this order using the Bracket Settings menu option, discussed later in this chapter.)

You can use exposure compensation, in which case the camera will use the image with exposure compensation as the base level, and then take exposures that deviate under and over the exposure of the image with exposure compensation.

If you pop up the flash and set it to fire, using the Fill-flash setting for example, the flash will fire for each of the bracketed shots and the exposure will be varied, but you have to press the shutter button for each shot, after the flash has recycled. (The orange dot to the right of the flash icon on the screen shows when the flash is ready to fire again.) With this approach, the camera will vary the output of the flash unit rather than the exposure value of the images themselves.

When using Manual exposure mode with ISO set to Auto, the camera adjusts the ISO setting to achieve the different exposure levels for the multiple images. If ISO is set to a specific value, the camera varies the shutter speeds for the multiple shots.

Single Exposure Bracketing

The next option is similar to the previous one, except that, with this selection, you have to press the shutter button for each shot; the camera will not take multiple shots while you hold down the shutter button. You have the same 13 choices for combinations of EV intervals and numbers of exposures. You might want to choose this option when you need to pause between shots for some reason, such as if you are using a model who needs to have some costume or makeup adjustments for each exposure. It also could be useful if you want to look at the resulting image after each shot to see if you need to make further adjustments to your settings.

Apart from using individual shutter presses, this option works the same as continuous exposure bracketing. For example, you can use flash and you can change the order of the exposures using the Bracket Settings menu option.

None of the bracketing options—exposure, white balance, or DRO—is available in the Auto, Scene, or Sweep Panorama shooting mode.

White Balance Bracketing

The next option on the drive mode menu, White Balance Bracketing, whose icon is highlighted in Figure 4-30, is similar to Continuous Exposure Bracketing, except that only three images can be taken and the value that is varied for the three shots is white balance rather than exposure.

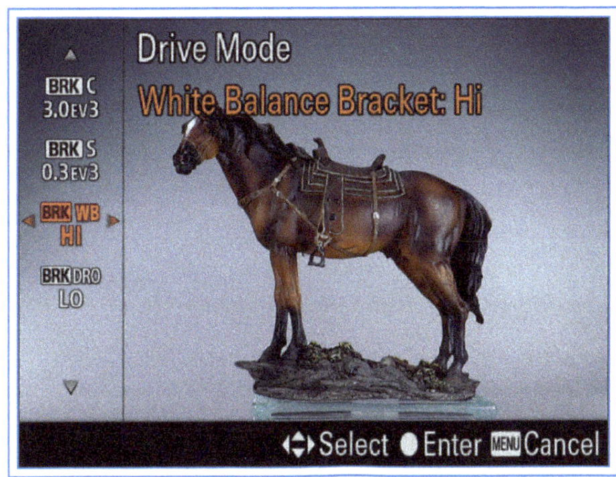

Figure 4-30. White Balance Bracketing Icon on Drive Mode Menu

Using the Left and Right buttons, select either Lo or Hi for the amount of deviation from the normal white balance setting. Then, when you press the shutter button (you don't have to hold it down), the camera will take a series of three shots—one at the normal setting; the next one with a lower color temperature, resulting in a "cooler," more bluish image; and the last one with a higher color temperature, resulting in a "warmer," more reddish image. When you use this form of bracketing, unlike exposure bracketing, you will hear only one shutter sound because the camera takes just one image, with one quick shutter press, and then electronically creates the other two exposures with the different white balance values.

You can change the order of the exposures using the Bracket Settings menu option, discussed later in this chapter.

DRO Bracketing

This final option on the drive mode menu, whose icon is shown in Figure 4-31, sets the RX100 VI to take a series of three shots at different settings of the DRO (dynamic range optimizer) option. I'll discuss DRO later in this chapter. Essentially, DRO alters the RX100 VI's image processing to even out the contrast between shadowed and bright areas. It can be difficult to decide how much DRO processing to use, and this option gives you a way to experiment with several different settings before you decide on the amount of DRO for your final image.

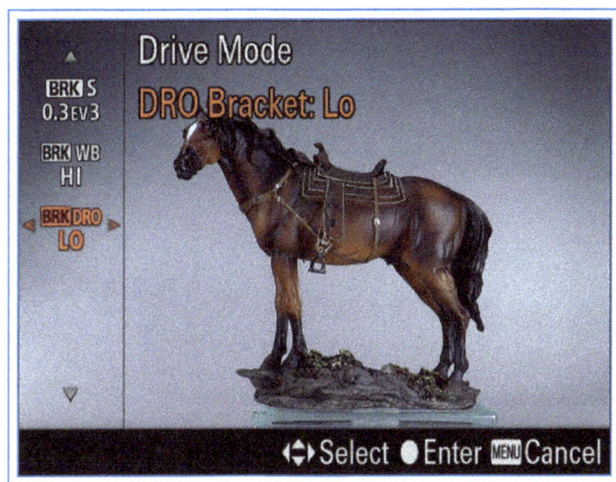

Figure 4-31. DRO Bracketing Icon on Drive Mode Menu

As with White Balance Bracketing, you can select Hi or Lo for the DRO interval. Also, as with White Balance Bracketing, you only need to press the shutter button once, briefly; the camera will record the three different exposures electronically. The order of these exposures is not affected by the Bracket Order menu option.

Bracket Settings

The next option on this menu screen includes two settings for how bracketed exposures are taken. When you select Bracket Settings, you will see two sub-options: Self-timer During Bracket, and Bracket Order, as shown in Figure 4-32.

The Self-timer During Bracket option, whose options screen is shown in Figure 4-33, lets you use the self-timer with bracket shooting. Without this option you could not use bracketing and the self-timer at the same time, because they are selected by different options on the drive mode menu.

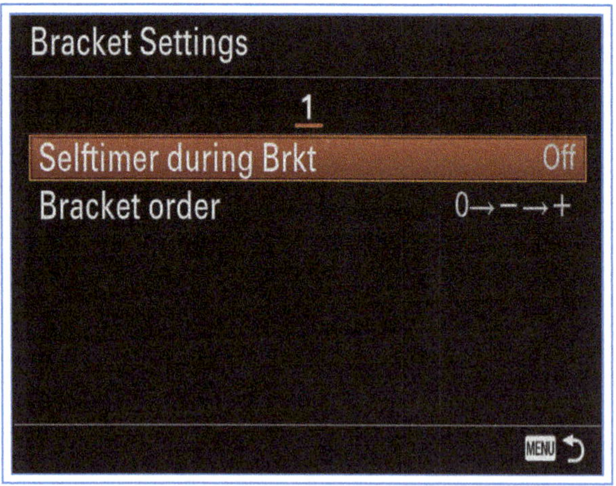

Figure 4-32. Bracket Settings Options Screen

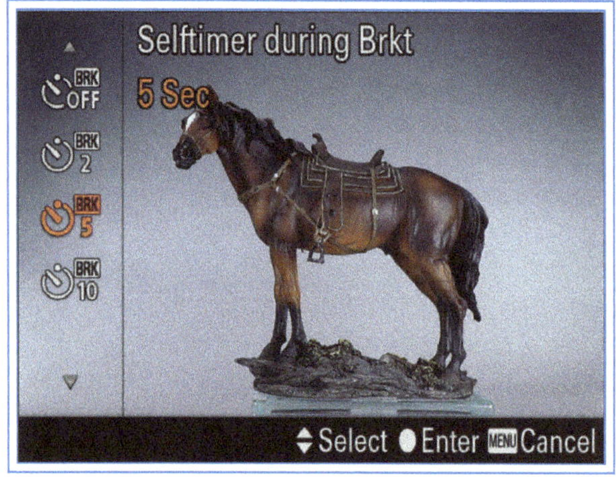

Figure 4-33. Self-timer During Bracket Options Screen

With this menu item you can have the self-timer set for two, five, or ten seconds before the first bracket shot is triggered, or you can leave the self-timer turned off. This setting turns on the self-timer for any type of bracket shooting you choose from the drive mode menu—exposure, white balance, or DRO.

The second sub-option, Bracket Order, lets you alter the sequence of the bracketed shots. As shown in Figure 4-34, there are two choices.

The first one is the default setting, with which the first shot is at the normal setting, the next is more negative (or with lower color temperature), the one after that is more positive (or with higher color temperature), and so on, ending with the most negative setting and, finally, the most positive setting. If you choose the second option, the images are shot in a strictly ascending series, moving from the most negative setting to the most positive setting.

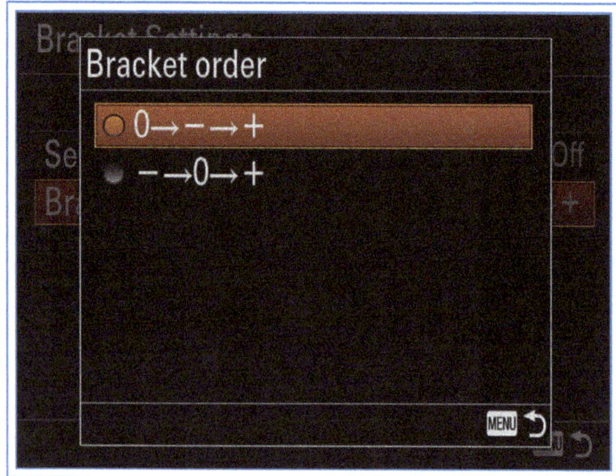

Figure 4-34. Bracket Order Options Screen

The Bracket Order option affects the order for exposure bracketing and white balance bracketing, but not for DRO bracketing.

Recall

The Recall option is used only when the mode dial is set to MR. Using this option, you can recall the camera settings that you stored to one of the seven slots for the Memory Recall mode, as discussed in Chapter 3.

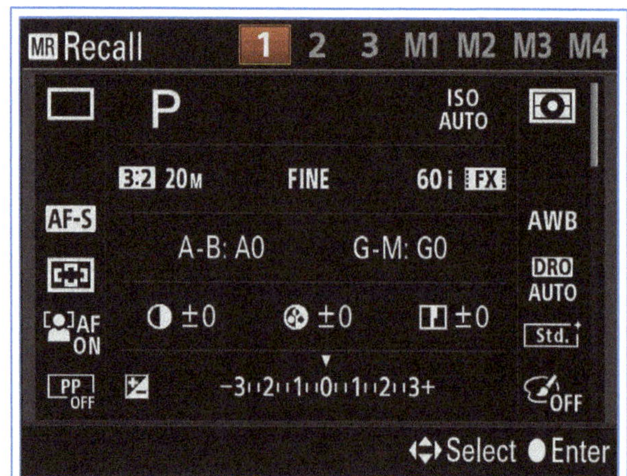

Figure 4-35. Recall Settings Screen

When the mode dial is first turned to MR, this option's main screen appears on the camera's display with one of the seven indicators at the upper right highlighted, as shown in Figure 4-35. (If the Mode Dial Guide option is turned on through screen 2 of the Setup menu, the Mode Dial Guide screen will appear first; you then have to press the Center button to make this screen appear.)

If the mode dial is already at MR and you want to change to another memory register, you can use this menu option. Once the Memory Recall screen is displayed, either by turning the mode dial to MR or by using this menu option, use the direction buttons or the control wheel to select register 1, 2, 3, M1, M2, M3, or M4 at the upper right of the screen. The settings for registers 1, 2, and 3 are stored in the camera's internal memory; the settings for registers M1 through M4 are stored on a memory card. Of course, you have to make sure the appropriate memory card is in the camera if you want to use M1 through M4.

When the register whose saved settings you want to recall for use is highlighted, press the Center button, and the new group of settings that were stored to that register will take effect.

Memory

The final option on screen 3 of the Camera Settings1 menu, Memory, was discussed in Chapter 3 in connection with the Memory Recall shooting mode. Once you have set up the RX100 VI with the settings you want to store to a register of the MR mode, select the Memory option and choose one of the seven numbered registers, as shown in Figure 4-36.

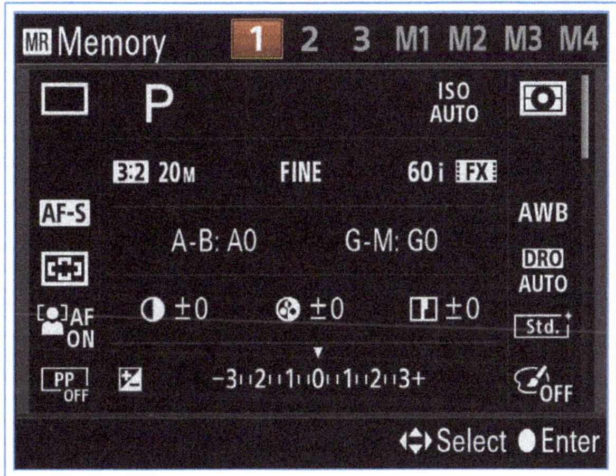

Figure 4-36. Memory Settings Screen

Press the Center button, and all of the current settings will be stored to that register for the Memory Recall mode. You can recall those settings at any time by turning the mode dial to the MR position (or selecting the Memory Recall menu option if the mode dial is already at that position) and selecting register 1, 2, or 3, or M1, M2, M3, or M4. As noted above, the contents of the first three registers are stored to the camera's internal memory, while the contents of M1 through M4 are stored to a memory card in the camera.

With either the Recall or Memory option, you can scroll to additional screens using the Down button to see other settings currently in effect.

The items on screen 4 of the Camera Settings1 menu are shown in Figure 4-37.

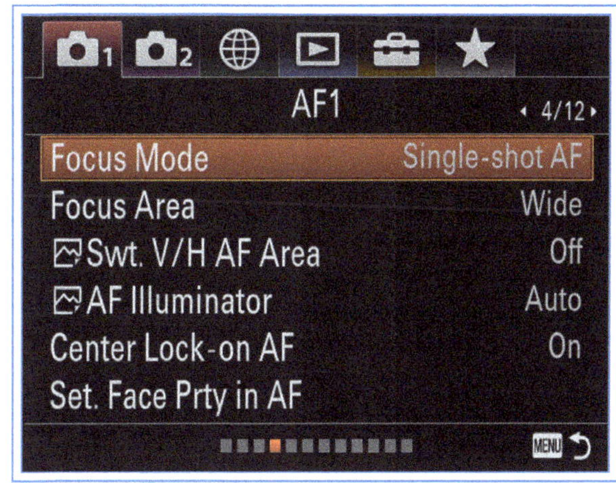

Figure 4-37. Screen 4 of Camera Settings1 Menu

Focus Mode

The focus mode option gives you five choices for the method the camera uses for focusing. This is one of the more important choices you can make for your photography. Following are details about each of the five selections, which are shown in Figure 4-38.

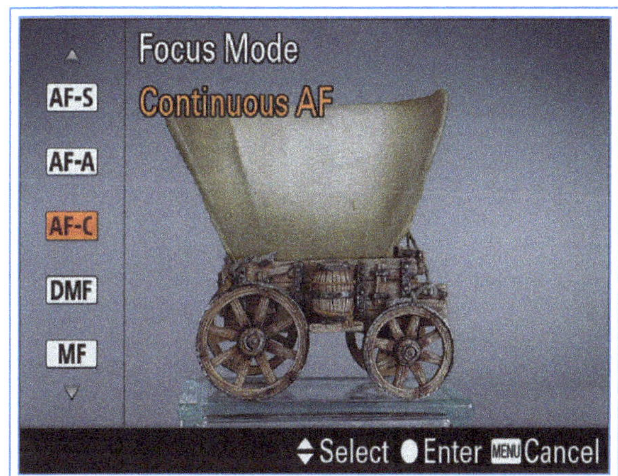

Figure 4-38. Focus Mode Options Screen

Single-Shot AF

The first focus mode option is single-shot AF, indicated by the AF-S icon. With this option, the camera tries to focus on the scene using the focus area that is selected using the focus area menu option, discussed below. If the Pre-AF option on screen 5 of the Camera Settings1 menu is turned on, the camera will continuously adjust focus, even before you press the shutter button halfway down. When you do press the button halfway down, the camera will lock in the focus and keep it locked as long as you keep the button pressed halfway.

If the Pre-AF menu option is not turned on, then the camera will not make any attempt to adjust focus until you press the shutter button halfway down.

Once you press the shutter button halfway down, you will see one or more green focus brackets on the screen indicating the point or points where the camera achieved sharp focus, as shown in Figure 4-39, and you will hear a beep (unless beeps have been turned off through the Setup menu, as discussed in Chapter 8).

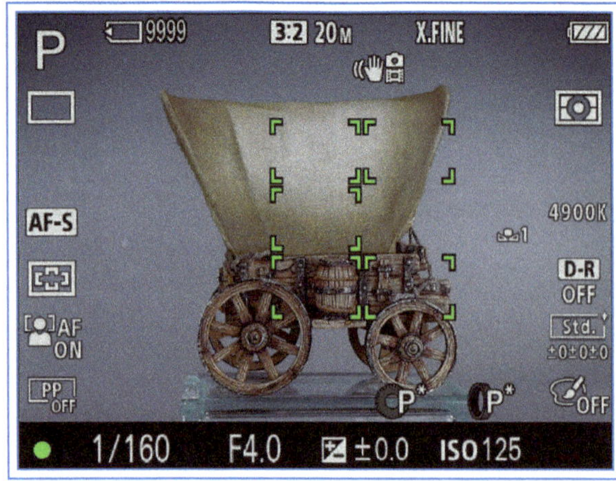

Figure 4-39. Green Frames Showing Sharp Focus

In addition, a green disc in the lower left corner of the display will light up steadily indicating that focus is confirmed. If focus cannot be achieved, the green disc will blink and no focus brackets will appear on the screen.

Once you have pressed the shutter button halfway to lock focus, you can use the locked focus on a different subject that is at the same distance as the one the camera originally locked its focus on. For example, if you have focused on a person at a distance of 15 feet (4.6 m), and then you decide you want to include another person or object in the scene, once you have locked the focus on the first person by pressing the shutter button halfway down, you can move the camera to include the other person or object in the scene as long as you keep the camera at about the same distance from the subject. The focus will remain locked at that distance until you press the shutter button the rest of the way down to take the picture.

Automatic AF

The second option for focus mode, automatic AF, designated by the AF-A icon, is a mixture of the first and third options, single AF and continuous AF. With automatic AF, the camera locks focus on the subject as with single AF, but, if the subject or camera then moves in a way that changes the focus point, the camera will continue to adjust focus, as with continuous AF. I generally prefer to use either single AF or continuous AF, so I will know whether the camera is going to be adjusting focus, rather than relying on its electronic judgment as to whether focus needs to be changed. But, in a case where the subject initially is stationary but may be moving, this mode could be useful.

Continuous AF

The next option for focus mode, continuous AF, is designated by the AF-C icon on the menu. With this option, as with single-shot AF, the RX100 VI focuses continuously before you press the shutter button if the Pre-AF menu option is turned on. If that option is turned off, the camera does not adjust focus until you press the shutter button halfway.

The difference with this mode is that the camera does not lock in the focus when you press the shutter button halfway. Instead, the focus will continue to be adjusted if the subject moves or the distance to the subject changes through camera motion. You will not hear a beep or see any focus brackets to confirm focus. Instead, the green disc in the lower left corner of the display will change its appearance to show the focus status.

If the green disc is surrounded by curved lines, as shown in Figure 4-40, that means focus is currently sharp but is subject to adjustment if needed.

If only the curved lines appear, that means the camera is still trying to achieve focus. If the green disc flashes, that means the camera is having trouble focusing.

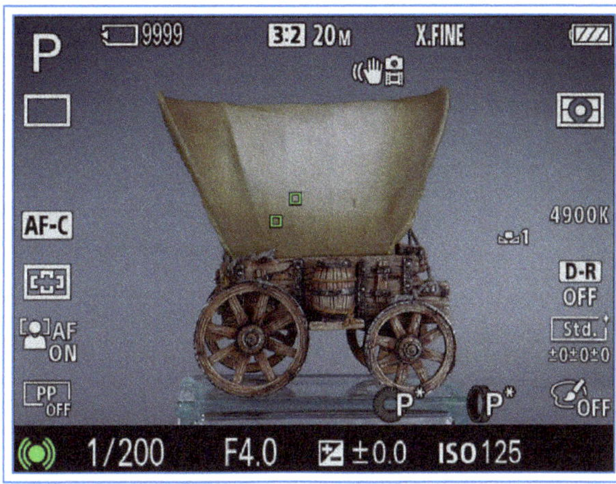

Figure 4-40. Green Disc with Curves for Continuous AF

This focusing mode can be useful when you are shooting a moving subject. With this option, you can get the RX100 VI to fix its focus on the subject, but you don't have to let up the shutter button to refocus; instead, you can hold the button down halfway until the instant when you take the picture. In this way, you may save some time, rather than having to keep starting the focus and exposure process over by pressing the shutter button halfway again. Continuous AF is the only autofocus option available for recording movies.

DMF

The third option for focus mode is DMF, which stands for direct manual focus. This feature lets you use a combination of autofocus and manual focus. DMF can be helpful if you are shooting an extreme closeup of a small object, when focus can be critical and hard to achieve. With the DMF option, you can start the focusing process by pressing the shutter button halfway down. The camera will make its best attempt to focus sharply using the autofocus mechanism. Then you can use the camera's manual focusing mechanism (turning the control ring, as discussed below in this section) to fine-tune the focus, concentrating on the parts of the subject that you want to be most sharply focused.

DMF also is useful when you are shooting a scene with objects at varying distances and you want to focus on one of the more distant ones. In that case, you can start out using manual focus, adjusting it for the most important object, to let the camera know which item to focus on. Then you can press the shutter button halfway to let the camera take over and use autofocus to improve the sharpness of the focus.

When DMF is activated, you can turn on Peaking through screen 11 of the Camera Settings1 menu, as discussed below, and that feature will function for autofocus as well as for manual focus. You also can use the MF Assist feature from that same menu screen with DMF. That feature is discussed below in connection with manual focus. If you use MF Assist with DMF, you have to hold the shutter button halfway down while turning the control ring to focus, in order for the screen to be enlarged. If you turn the control ring without holding the shutter button halfway, the focus will be adjusted, but without the enlargement of the screen.

Manual Focus

The final selection on the focus mode menu is Manual Focus. As I indicated in the discussion of DMF, there are situations in which you may achieve sharper focus by adjusting it on your own rather than by relying on the camera's autofocus system. Those situations include shooting extreme closeups; shooting a group of objects at differing distances; or shooting through a barrier such as glass or a wire fence.

Also, manual focus gives you the freedom to use a soft focus effect purposely. As I will discuss later in this chapter, the RX100 VI includes a setting on the Picture Effect menu called "Soft Focus," which adds a pleasing softness to your image. If you would rather create this effect on your own by controlling the focus directly, you can set the camera for manual focus and defocus the subject in precisely the way you want.

To use manual focus with the RX100 VI, all you have to do is turn the control ring—the large ring around the lens, next to the camera's body. This action is intuitive, and it is similar to the way most lenses were focused in the days before autofocus existed.

In addition, there are several functions available to assist with manual focusing. I will discuss those menu options separately later in this chapter, but I will briefly describe them here so you can get started with manual focus.

The first option, MF Assist, is controlled through the fourth item on screen 11 of the Camera Settings1 menu. With MF Assist turned on, whenever you start turning the control ring to adjust focus in manual focus mode, the image on the display is magnified 5.3 times, as shown in Figure 4-41, so you can more clearly check the focus.

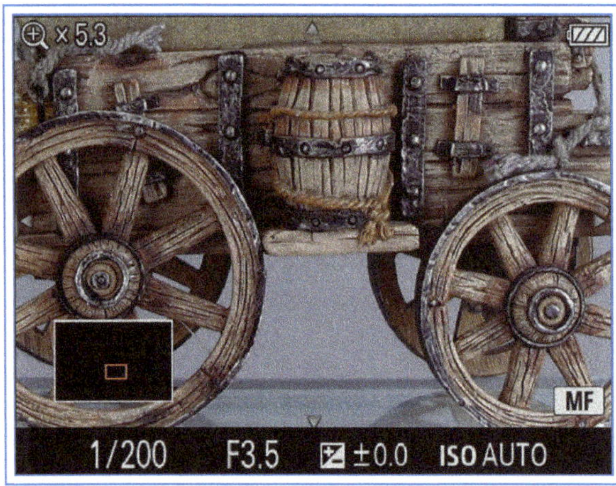

Figure 4-41. MF Assist Screen with 5.3x Magnification

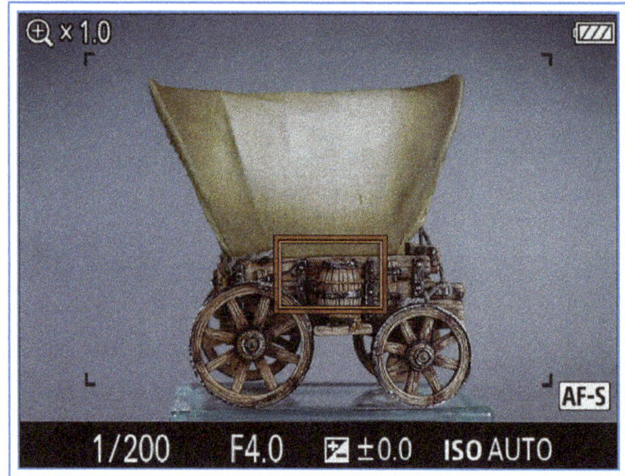

Figure 4-42. Focus Magnifier Frame on Display

Once the magnified image is displayed, if you press the Center button, the image is magnified further to 10.7 times normal. Press the Center button again to return to the 5.3-times view and press the shutter button halfway to return the display to normal size. You can adjust how long the magnified display stays on the screen using the Focus Magnification Time option, also found on screen 11 of the Camera Settings1 menu. I prefer to set the time to No Limit, so the magnification does not disappear just as I am getting the focus adjusted as I want it. With the No Limit setting, the magnification remains on the screen until you dismiss it by pressing the shutter button halfway.

If you don't want the camera to enlarge the image as soon as you start focusing, you can use the Focus Magnifier option instead of MF Assist. You can find Focus Magnifier on screen 11 of the Camera Settings1 menu, or you can assign it to a control button using the Custom Key (Still Images) option on screen 9 of the Camera Settings2 menu. You can set the Custom, Center, Left, or Right button to activate the Focus Magnifier option.

Once Focus Magnifier is activated, a small orange frame appears on the screen, as shown in Figure 4-42. You can move that frame around the screen with the control wheel or the direction buttons, or by dragging it with your finger if touch screen operations are turned on. The frame represents the area that will be magnified when you press the Center button. By pressing the Center button, you can switch magnification to various levels, as discussed later in this chapter.

You can use both MF Assist and Focus Magnifier, though I see no need to do so. My preference is to use only the MF Assist option. I prefer not to go through the steps to turn on the Focus Magnifier option, which does not add that much to the focusing options. However, when I am faced with a challenging task such as shooting in dim lighting, I sometimes use the Focus Magnifier option because it is easier to deal with that situation by being able to see the subject clearly at its normal size and selecting the focus point before using magnification and starting to focus.

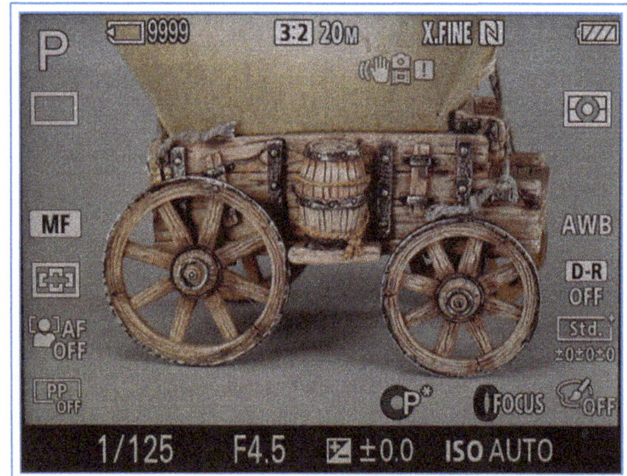

Figure 4-43. Peaking Turned Off

The RX100 VI provides one more aid to manual focusing, called Peaking, which is controlled using the Peaking Setting option on screen 11 of the Camera Settings1 menu. It has three sub-options: Peaking Display, Peaking Level, and Peaking Color. Peaking Display can be on or off, and Peaking Level can be set to Low, Mid, or High. When Peaking Level is turned on at any of those levels, then, when you are using manual focus or DMF, the camera places bright pixels around the areas of the image that it judges to be in focus, as shown in Figure 4-43 (without Peaking) and Figure 4-44 (with Peaking Level set to High).

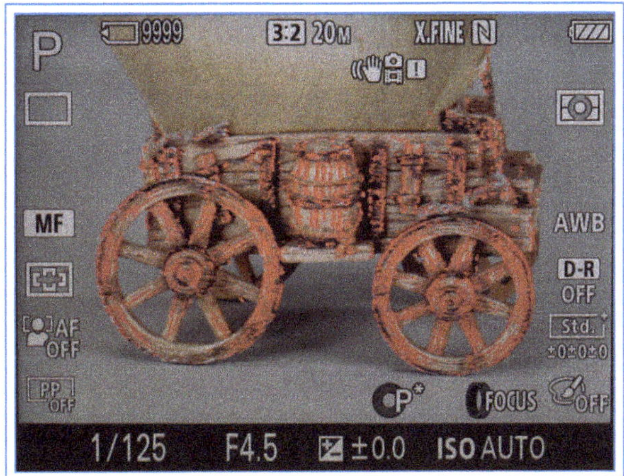

Figure 4-44. Peaking Level Set to High

Besides setting the intensity of this display, you can set its color—white, red, or yellow—using the Peaking Color option. I find Peaking to be especially useful in dark conditions because the Peaking effect contrasts with the dark display. Also, as noted above, Peaking works with both the autofocus and manual focus aspects of the DMF option. I will discuss Peaking further later in this chapter.

Finally, there is another way to customize the use of manual focus with the RX100 VI. On screen 9 of the Camera Settings2 menu, as noted above, you can use the Custom Key (Still Images) menu option to assign the Custom, Center, Left, or Right button to control any one item from a long list of functions. One of those functions, called AF/MF Control Toggle, is useful if you need to switch back and forth between autofocus and manual focus on frequent occasions. When this function is assigned to a button, you can press the button to switch instantly between these two focus modes. This is so much more convenient than going back to the Shooting menu and using the focus mode menu option, that it may be worthwhile dedicating a button to this use.

Focus Area

The second option on this menu screen, focus area, lets you choose the area the camera focuses on when using an autofocus setting or DMF, as selected with the focus mode menu option. The three autofocus modes are single, automatic, and continuous. Direct manual focus, or DMF, is a mode that lets you use both manual focus and autofocus. The focus area option sets the focus area for all four of those focus modes.

Before I discuss the various choices for the focus area menu option, it is important to note that these settings were originally designed for use with a camera that does not have any touch screen features. If you don't want to use the touch screen for focusing, that is fine—you can just use the focus area setting to control where the camera directs its focus. However, you can use the touch screen for focusing to some extent, with any of these settings in place.

I will discuss touch screen options in more detail in Chapter 6, where I discuss the LCD screen and other physical features of the camera. Briefly, when shooting still images with an autofocus mode in effect, if focus area is set to Wide or Center (or the Wide or Center setting for Lock-on AF), you can choose the focus point by touching the screen. Just put your finger on the screen at the chosen point, and the camera will place a focus frame there. You can then drag that frame around the screen if you want. Then press the shutter button to focus and take the picture.

If focus area is set to Flexible Spot or Expand Flexible Spot (or the Flexible Spot or Expand Flexible Spot setting for Lock-on AF), you can drag the focus frame on the screen to move it, or tap the screen to place the frame at a new location. If focus area is set to Zone, you can touch the screen to move the focus zone. The situation is similar for video recording, with a few variations, as discussed in Chapter 6.

In the following discussion of focus area options, I will not often mention the touch focus feature, but remember that it is available as an alternative way to use autofocus.

The choices for focus area are Wide, Zone, Center, Flexible Spot, Expand Flexible Spot, and Lock-on AF. Figure 4-45 shows five of these options; you have to scroll down to see the last one.

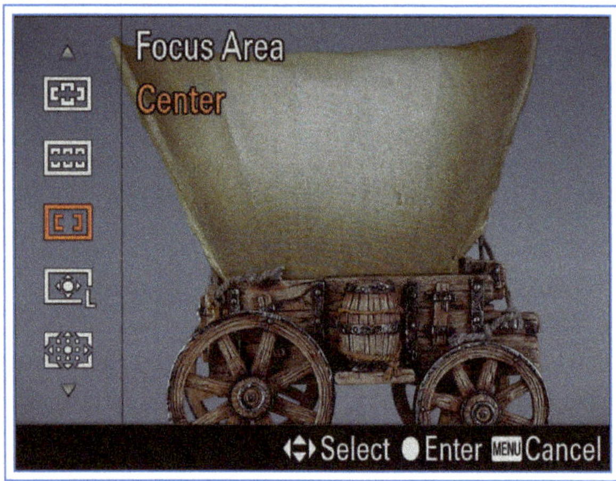

Figure 4-45. Focus Area Options Screen

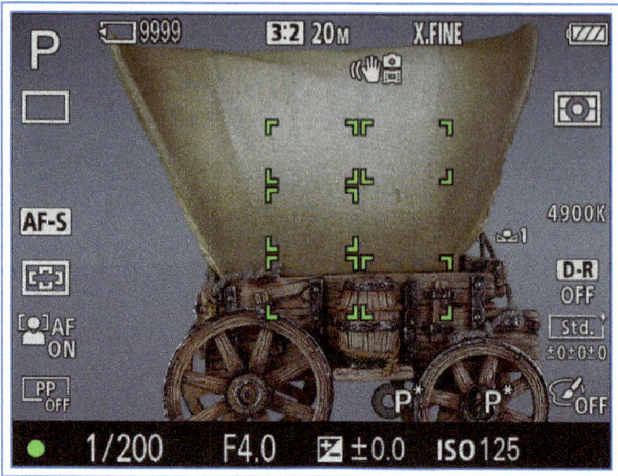

Figure 4-46. Focus Frames with Focus Area Set to Wide

The ways these selections operate vary somewhat depending on whether you select single autofocus, automatic autofocus, continuous autofocus, or DMF for focus mode on the menu. If you select DMF, you can use autofocus in the same way as with single autofocus, so DMF is the same as single autofocus with respect to focus area. I will discuss the following options assuming at first that you are using single autofocus or DMF as your focus mode. I will also assume that face detection and face detection frame display are turned off through the Set Face Priority in AF option on screen 4 of the Camera Settings1 menu; if they are turned on and a face is detected, a face detection frame will be seen instead of the focus area frame.

Wide

With the Wide setting for focus area, the RX100 VI uses multiple focus zones that cover the whole screen, and tries to detect one or more items within the scene to focus on based on their locations. When it has achieved sharp focus on one or more subjects, the camera displays a green frame indicating each focus point. You may see one or several green frames, depending on how many focus points are detected at the same distance. An example with multiple frames is shown in Figure 4-46.

When you are using single autofocus, the Wide option is good for shots of landscapes, buildings, and the like. In continuous autofocus mode, the RX100 VI does not display a focus frame with the Wide setting. (It will display small, moving blocks where focus is located, if Display Continuous AF Area is turned on through screen 5 of the Camera Settings1 menu.) The camera tries to focus on subjects that appear to be the main ones.

Zone

The Zone setting is similar to Wide, but the camera displays an area that uses only part of the screen. With this setting, the camera will be limited to focusing on a subject within the designated zone. When you select this option, the camera displays a set of gray frames that outline the overall focus zone. with arrows pointing to the four edges of the display, as shown in Figure 4-47.

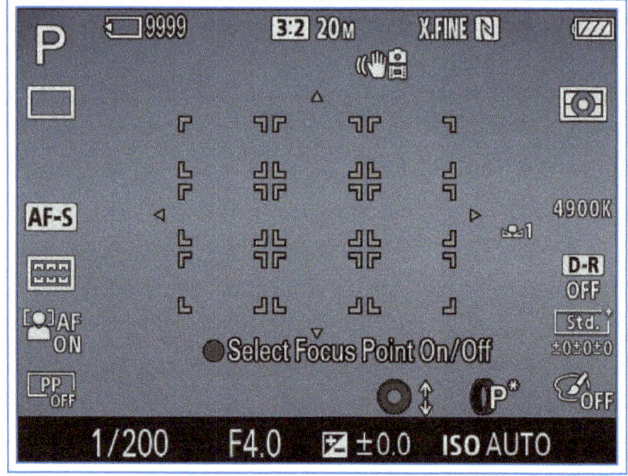

Figure 4-47. Focus Area Set to Zone

Use the four direction buttons to move the focus zone around the display. You also can turn the control wheel to move the frame up and down on the screen. If touch screen operations are turned on, you can drag the zone around the screen. If you press the Custom/Delete button while the zone is activated for moving, it will move back to the center of the display. When the zone is located where you want it, press the Center button to fix it in place. The camera will display a black frame in the chosen location, as shown in Figure 4-48. When you press the shutter button halfway to focus, the camera will display green frames that indicate where focus is sharp within the designated zone.

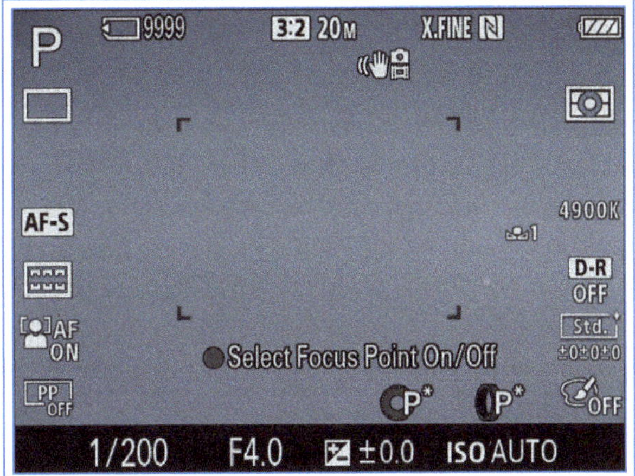

Figure 4-48. Black Focus Frame for Zone Setting

This setting is useful when you want to focus within a certain area, but the location of the actual subject is not certain. For example, if you are photographing a show in which the performers are located on the right side of the stage, you can set the zone to the right side and let the camera direct its focus to the action within that limited area.

Center

If you select Center for the focus area setting, the camera places a black focus frame in the center of the display, as shown in Figure 4-49, and focuses on whatever it finds within that frame.

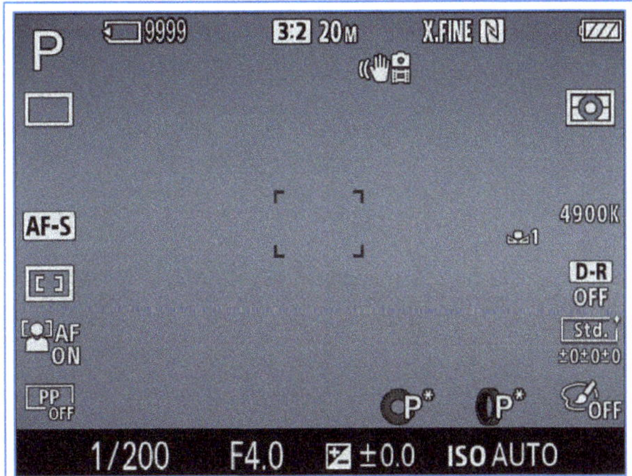

Figure 4-49. Focus Frame for Center Setting

When you press the shutter button halfway, if the camera can focus it will beep and the frame will turn green. This option is useful for an object in the center of the scene.

Even if you need to focus on an off-center object, you can use this setting. To focus on an object at the right, center that object in the focus frame and press the shutter button halfway to lock focus. Keeping the button pressed halfway, move the camera so the object is on the right, and press the button to take the picture.

If you turn on continuous autofocus with the Center setting, the camera still will display a black focus frame. When you press the shutter button halfway, the frame will turn green when focus is sharp, but the camera will not beep. As the camera or subject moves, the camera will continue to re-focus as you hold the shutter button halfway down. You can use this technique to carry out your own focus tracking, by moving the camera to keep the center frame targeted on a moving subject.

Flexible Spot

The Flexible Spot option gives you more control over the focus area, with a frame you can move around the screen and resize. After you highlight this option on the Camera Settings1 menu, press the Right or Left button to select the size of the Flexible Spot focus frame: L, M, or S, for Large, Medium, or Small.

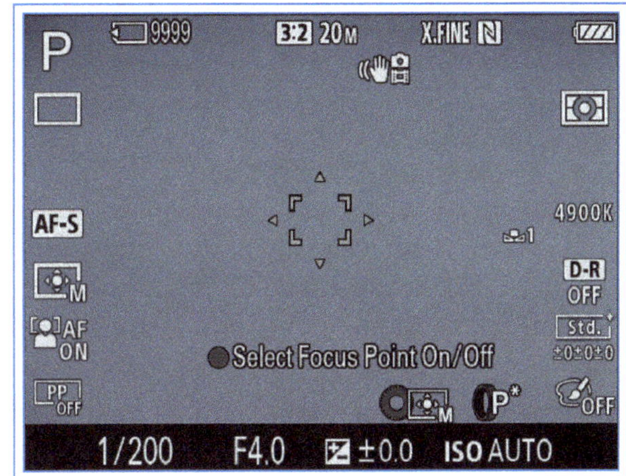

Figure 4-50. Focus Frame for Flexible Spot Setting - Movable

After choosing a size, press the Center button and you will see a screen like that in Figure 4-50, with a gray focus frame of that size with arrows pointing to the four edges of the display.

Use the four direction buttons to move the frame around the display. You also can turn the control wheel to change the size of the frame, no matter what size you initially selected from the menu. When the frame is located and sized as you want it, press the Center button to fix it in place. The camera will display a black frame of the chosen size in the chosen location. When you press the shutter button halfway to focus, the focus frame will turn green when focus is sharp.

This frame operates the same way as the frame for the Center option, except for the ability to change the location and size. To return the frame quickly to the center of the screen, press the Custom/Delete button while the frame is activated for moving, and it will move back to the center of the display.

This option is useful for focusing on a particular point, such as an object at the far right, without having to move the camera to place a focus frame over that object. This might help if you are using a tripod, for example, and need to set up the shot with precision, focusing on an off-center subject. If the subject is small, using the smallest focus frame can make the process even easier.

If you use continuous autofocus, the Flexible Spot option works the same way as the Center option, discussed above, but with the added ability to change the size and location of the frame.

One problem with the Flexible Spot option is that it can be cumbersome to move the frame again once you have fixed it in place. One way to do this is to select the focus area menu option and repeat all of the steps discussed above. There are several quicker ways to move the frame, though.

The easiest way to do this is to have the Touch Operation and Touch Panel items turned on through screen 3 of the Setup menu. With those settings active, you can touch the LCD screen with your finger to choose a new focus point, or drag the focus frame to a new location. (If the Touch Pad is also activated through that menu screen, you can move the focus frame by touching the LCD screen when you are using the viewfinder to view the scene.)

Another easy way to move the focus frame, without using the touch screen, is to go to screen 9 of the Camera Settings2 menu and select the Custom Key (Still Images) option. On the next screen, select the Custom or Center button, and assign the Focus Standard setting to that button. Then, whenever Flexible Spot is in effect, just press the assigned button when the shooting screen is displayed, and the screen for moving the focus frame will appear. You can quickly use the direction buttons to move the frame where you want it, and you can turn the control wheel to resize it. You can press the Custom/ Delete button to center it on the display.

Another option for moving the focus frame is to assign focus area to a control button using the Custom Key (Still Images) menu option. Then, when you press the assigned button, the camera displays the focus area menu, from which you can choose the size and location of the Flexible Spot frame. Or, you can assign focus area to the Function menu, which is called up by pressing the Function button. I will discuss that menu in Chapter 6.

My preference is to use the touch screen, which is simple and does not require using a control button for the Focus Standard option. As an alternative, I recommend assigning the Focus Standard setting to the Center button. Then, to move the focus frame, just press that button and it is an easy matter to adjust the frame's location and size. I will discuss the Custom Key menu options further in Chapters 5 and 6.

Expand Flexible Spot

This next option for focus area is a variation of the previous one, Flexible Spot. It operates in the same way, except that the frame size is small and it cannot be resized. You can move it around the display with the direction buttons and the control wheel.

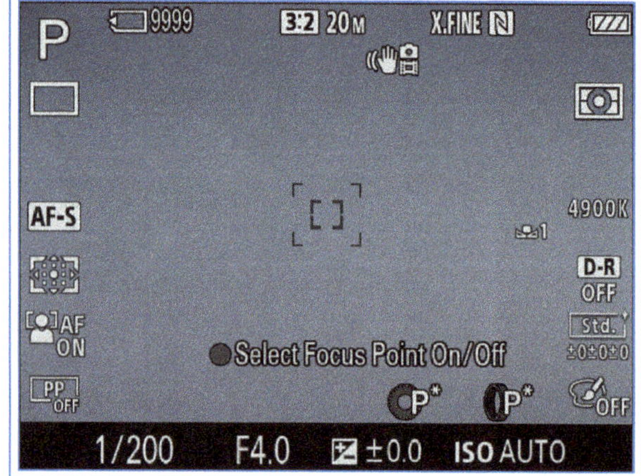

Figure 4-51. Focus Frame for Expand Flexible Spot Setting

When you use this frame to fix the focus for your shot, the camera will first try to focus on a subject within the frame. If it cannot find a focus point in that small area, it will expand its scope and try to focus on a subject within the area immediately surrounding the frame. That area is outlined by four small brackets outside the corners of the focus frame, as shown in Figure 4-51.

This option can be of use when you want to focus on a small area, but you don't want the focusing to fail if focus can't be achieved in that exact spot.

Lock-on AF

The final option for focus area is Lock-on AF, which sets up the camera to track a moving object. This option is available for selection only when the focus mode is set to Continuous AF. When you highlight this option on the menu, as shown in Figure 4-52, the camera gives you seven choices for the Lock-on focus frame: Wide, Zone, Center, Flexible Spot Small, Flexible Spot Medium, Flexible Spot Large, or Expand Flexible Spot. These frames correspond to the other choices for focus area, discussed above, and they also include the Lock-on frame's ability to "lock on" to a subject and track it as it moves.

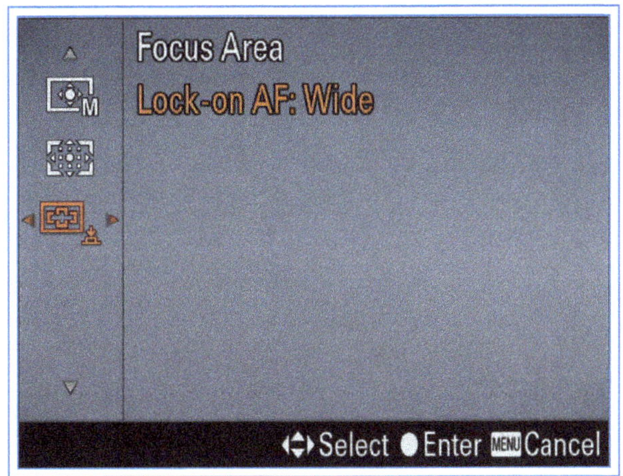

Figure 4-52. Icon for Lock-on AF Highlighted on Focus Area Menu

After choosing one of these seven settings, aim the camera at the subject, place the focus frame (if there is one) over it, and press the shutter button halfway. The camera will try to keep the subject in focus as the subject or camera moves. The camera may occasionally display a double-bordered focus frame that moves with the subject. It also will display small green blocks that track the subject, if you have turned on the Display Continuous AF Area option on screen 5 of the Camera Settings1 menu. When you are ready to take the picture, press the shutter button all the way. If the autofocus system worked as expected, the image should be in focus.

When you are deciding which of the seven sub-options to choose for Lock-on AF, consider the subject that you want the camera to lock on to, and choose accordingly. For example, if the subject is an automobile that is not too far away, you can probably choose Wide. If the subject is a person some distance away, you may want to choose Flexible Spot Small or Medium. Note that this choice affects only how the camera selects the subject to lock on to. Once it has locked onto that subject, the camera will attempt to track whatever subject it has selected, as the subject moves around. So, even if you started with the Flexible Spot Small setting, if the camera locks on to a nearby face, the camera should continue to track the face, even if the face is larger than the initial focus frame.

If you select an option with a movable focus frame or zone, such as Zone, Flexible Spot, or Expand Flexible Spot, you can move that frame around the screen in the same way as described earlier for those focus area options.

The Lock-on AF option will not give good results if the subject moves too rapidly or erratically, or moves completely out of the frame. But, for subjects that are moving moderately in stable patterns, the Lock-on AF system is worth trying. This option is not available when recording movies.

If this feature does not produce the results you want, you can consider using the Center Lock-on AF option, found on screen 4 of the Camera Settings1 menu, discussed later in this chapter.

The only focus area setting available is Wide when the camera is in Auto or Scene mode, when the Smile Shutter is in use, or when the mode dial is at Movie and Auto Dual Recording is turned on through screen 2 of the Camera Settings2 menu.

Switch Vertical/Horizontal AF Area

This next option on screen 4 of the Camera Settings1 menu is designed for photographers who need to change the orientation of the camera between horizontal and vertical fairly often, and would like to have the camera automatically move the focus point and/or the focus area when that happens. For example, this feature could be useful for a person who is shooting sporting events or weddings, and often uses a focus point in the upper middle of the LCD screen when shooting horizontally. If the camera is then rotated to the left, with the side with the shutter button held up in the right hand, that focus point will have moved to the left side of the screen. To compensate for that effect, you can use this menu option, which causes the camera to memorize the focus points and sizes of focus frames that you specify for each orientation.

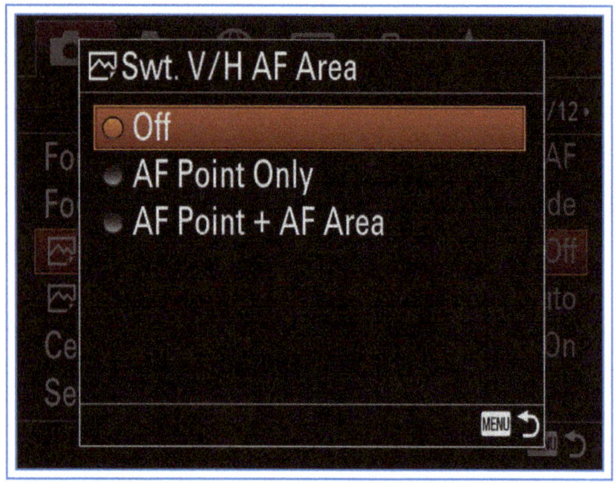

Figure 4-53. Switch Vertical/Horizontal AF Area Options Screen

To do this, select either AF Point Only or AF Point + AF Area, as shown in Figure 4-53, and press the Menu button to return to the shooting screen. Then, assuming you chose AF Point + AF Area, first, with the camera in its normal, horizontal orientation, select a setting for the focus area menu option (Wide, Zone, Center, Flexible Spot, etc.). Also, if you selected a setting with a movable focus zone or frame, such as Zone or Flexible Spot, move the focus area where you want it on the display. (Use any technique available to move the focus frame—the touch screen, the Focus Standard option assigned to a control button, or the focus area menu option, as discussed in connection with the focus area menu option.)

Then, tilt the camera to a different orientation (left or right). Select the focus area setting you want for that orientation, and, if applicable, move the focus frame where you want it. Finally, tilt the camera to the third orientation (right or left), and again select a focus area setting and, if applicable, a location for the focus frame.

Then, as long as this menu option is turned on, the camera will automatically use the focus area menu option you selected for a given orientation when you move the camera between the vertical and horizontal orientations, and it will move the focus point if that was selected as well. If you later change the setting for this menu option, the focus area settings and focus frame positions you selected will not be retained. However, they are retained when the camera is powered off and back on, as long as the menu option setting has not been changed.

This option does not work with the Auto modes, video recording, digital zoom, and in several other situations.

I don't do enough shooting in different orientations that I would find this feature useful, but it is available if you need it.

AF Illuminator

The AF Illuminator item lets you disable the reddish lamp on the front of the camera for autofocusing. By default, this option is set to Auto, which means that when you are shooting a still image in a dim area, the camera will turn on the lamp briefly if needed to light the subject and assist the autofocus mechanism in gauging the distance to the subject. If you want to make sure the light never comes on for that purpose—to avoid causing distractions in a museum or other sensitive area, or to avoid alerting a subject of candid photography—set this option to Off. In that case, the lamp will never light up for focusing assistance, though it will still illuminate if the self-timer is activated.

Center Lock-on AF

This option is similar to the Lock-on AF setting discussed earlier in this chapter, but there are differences. Lock-on AF is a sub-option for the focus area menu item, discussed above. Lock-on AF is available only with continuous autofocus. When it is activated, the camera uses the selected focus area setting to lock on to a subject. When you half-press the shutter button, the camera will try to keep the subject in focus as it moves.

The option being discussed here, Center Lock-on AF, is a separate menu option. It is not available when the Lock-on AF option has been selected for focus area. However, unlike the other option, Center Lock-on AF is available with single autofocus and automatic autofocus, as well as with continuous autofocus.

In order to make use of this feature, apart from turning on the menu option, you should assign one of the control buttons to the Focus Standard option, using the Custom Key (Still Images) option on screen 9 of the Camera Settings2 menu. I usually assign the Center button to that function. (If you don't assign a button to Focus Standard, you have to turn on Center Lock-on AF through the menu system each time you want to lock on to a new subject or resume tracking a subject for which tracking has stopped.) However, the Focus Standard option works for this purpose only when focus area is set to Wide or Center. (With other focus area settings, pressing the Focus Standard button activates the focus frame or zone for moving around the screen.)

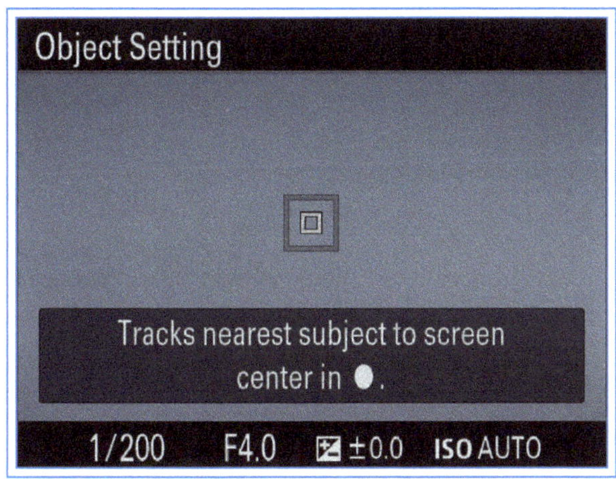

Figure 4-54. Message to Press Button to Lock Focus

To use Center Lock-on AF, select this menu option and turn it on. The camera will display a message that you can press the Center button to lock on to the subject, as shown in Figure 4-54. At that point, place the focus frame over the subject and press the Center button. The camera will display a double-bordered frame that will move around the display and expand as needed to keep the subject inside the frame and in focus. You can half-press the shutter button to lock focus at the current focus distance. When you are ready to take the picture, press the shutter button. To cancel the tracking, press the Center button. To start tracking again, from the shooting screen press the button assigned to Focus Standard to reactivate the feature.

This option can be more convenient to use than the Lock-on AF option, because you can use it with either single or continuous autofocus and you don't have to select a particular type of focus frame. You can just press the button assigned to Focus Standard and the tracking function will start.

If Touch Operation on screen 3 of the Setup menu is set to activate the touch features of the LCD screen and Touch Shooting Settings on screen 9 of the Camera Settings2 menu is set to Touch Focus, once tracking has started, you can touch your finger to the screen to select a new subject to be tracked or to re-start tracking after it has been canceled.

There is one area of potential confusion with this feature: Although you can assign the Center button to the Focus Standard option, you do not have to use that button for that option; the Custom button can be assigned to Focus Standard as well. However, no matter which of those buttons is assigned to Focus Standard, you still have to use the Center button (or the touch screen) to initiate the tracking of the subject. So, you may have to press the Custom button to activate the Center Lock-on AF feature, and then press the Center button to start the tracking. You can then press the Custom button or the Center button to cancel tracking. But, as I noted earlier, I just use the Center button for Focus Standard, to avoid having to use two buttons for this one function.

Center Lock-on AF does not work with Sweep Panorama mode or with the Hand-held Twilight or Anti Motion Blur settings of Scene mode. It also does not operate when Digital Zoom, Clear Image Zoom, or the Smart Teleconverter option is in use with the lens zoomed beyond the optical zoom range; in Movie mode with SteadyShot (Movies) set to Intelligent Active; with high frame rate video recording; or when Record Setting is set to one of the 120p options (100p for PAL systems).

Set Face Priority in AF

This option lets you choose whether or not the camera focuses on detected faces with higher priority than other subjects. This menu item has two sub-options, as shown in Figure 4-55: Face Priority in AF, and Face Detection Frame Display, either of which can be turned on or off. If Face Priority in AF is turned on, the camera will attempt to achieve sharp focus for the face that has the highest priority, either because you have registered it using other menu options, or because of the camera's own system for prioritizing faces, which chooses the face closest to the camera.

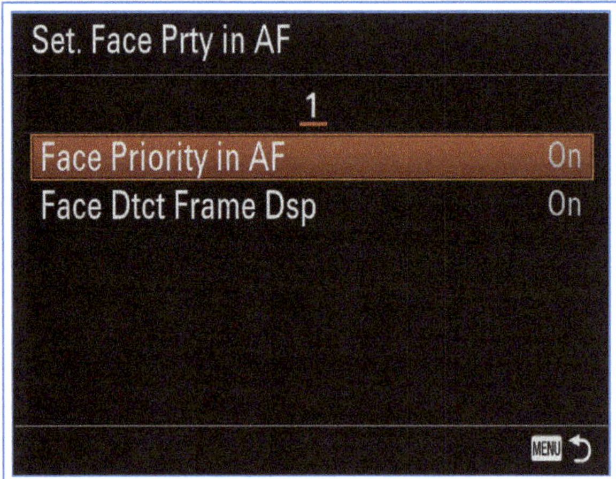

Figure 4-55. Set Face Priority in AF Options Screen

If you want the camera to give focus priority to registered faces, you have to first register them using the Face Registration item on screen 12 of the Camera Settings1 menu, and you also have to turn on the Registered Faces Priority option on that same menu screen.

If Face Priority in AF is turned off, the camera will not direct its focus to a face, unless the face happens to be the subject that would receive focus priority anyway based on its location and the focus area setting.

If Face Detection Frame Display is turned on and Face Priority in AF is also activated, the camera will display a square focus frame for any face it detects. If Face Detection Frame Display is turned off, the camera will not display face detection frames, although it will display green frames for faces in focus. As shown in Figure 4-56, the camera can detect as many as eight human faces and select one as the main face to concentrate its settings on.

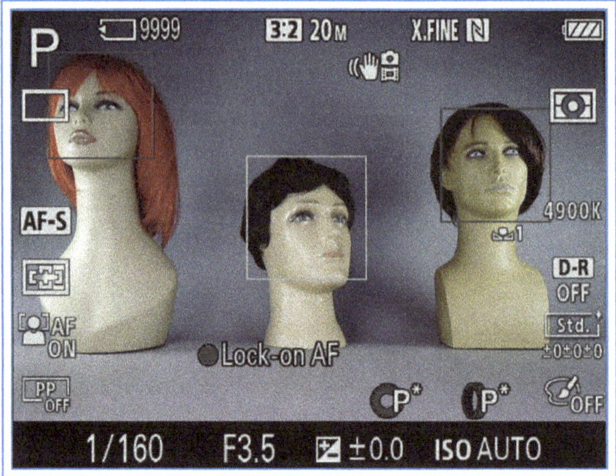

Figure 4-56. Face Detection Frames on Display

Before you press the shutter button, the camera will display white or gray frames around any faces it finds. When you press the shutter button halfway to lock focus and exposure, the frame over the face the camera has selected as the main face will turn green. The camera may place multiple green frames if there are multiple faces at the same distance from the camera. If the touch operations are turned on through screen 3 of the Setup menu, you can touch the face you want the camera to focus on, and the camera will direct its focus to that face.

When using face detection, you need to be aware of the setting for focus area on screen 4 of the Camera Settings1 menu. If it is set to Wide, the camera will find a face and focus on it. However, if focus area is set to an option such as Zone, Center, Flexible Spot, or Expand Flexible Spot, the camera will not focus on a face unless the face is within the area of the focus zone or frame. So, if you want to rely on the camera to find and focus on faces, you should set focus area to Wide. Of course, you can always use touch focus to touch a face you want the camera to focus on, no matter what focus area setting is in use, as long as touch operations are enabled.

Face detection does not work when some other settings are in use. For example, it does not work with the Landscape, Night Scene, or Sunset scene settings, when Picture Effect is set to Posterization, when Digital Zoom or Clear Image Zoom is in use, when the Sweep Panorama mode is in use, or when using the Focus Magnifier option. It also does not function when recording a video with Record Setting set to 120p (100p if the PAL system is in use).

In summary, if you want the camera to focus on human faces, turn on both sub-options of this menu item.

Screen 5 of the Camera Settings1 menu is shown in Figure 4-57.

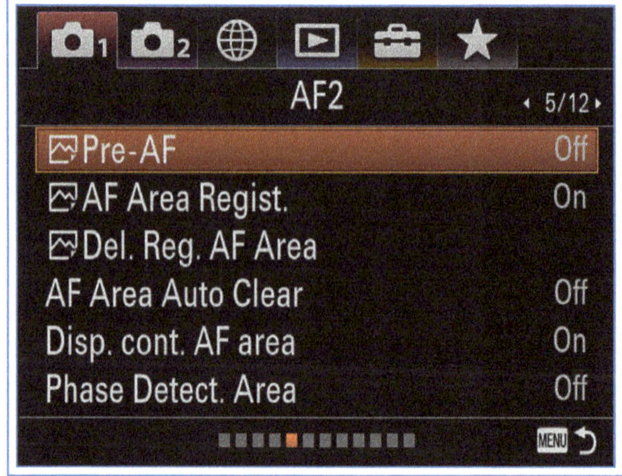

Figure 4-57. Screen 5 of Camera Settings1 Menu

Pre-AF

The Pre-AF setting affects the way the RX100 VI uses autofocus for capturing still images. When this option is turned on and focus mode is set to AF-S, AF-A, or AF-C, for single-shot, automatic, or continuous autofocus, the camera continuously tries to focus on a subject, even before you press the shutter button halfway. With this setting, the camera's battery is depleted more quickly than normal, but the final focusing operation may be speeded up because the camera can reach an approximate focus adjustment before you press the shutter button to evaluate focus and take the picture.

If this setting is turned off, then the camera makes no attempt to use its autofocus mechanism until you press the shutter button halfway to check focus. I usually leave this setting off to avoid running the battery down too soon. But, if I were taking pictures of moving subjects, I might activate this setting to speed up the focusing process.

When the camera is recording movies, it always uses the equivalent of the Pre-AF setting; this menu option has no effect for movie recording.

AF Area Registration

This option lets you register a location for a movable focus frame, so you can assign a button to instantly place the frame on the display at that location. This is a two-step process. First, you have to set this menu option to On. Then, go to the shooting screen and position a movable focus frame, such as Flexible Spot, in the location you want on the display. Then, press and hold the Function (Fn) button for a second or two. The camera will then display a message saying the AF area has been registered.

Next, go to the Custom Key (Still Images) option on screen 9 of the Camera Settings2 menu and assign either the Custom or Center button to the option called Registered AF Area Hold. (The Left and Right buttons cannot be assigned to that function.) Then, when the camera is in shooting mode, you can press the assigned button and the focus frame will instantly appear at the registered location as long as you hold down the button.

If you don't want to have to hold down the assigned button, you can choose the Registered AF Area Toggle option, in which case you only need to press and release the button.

You cannot call up a registered AF area when the mode dial is at the Auto, Movie, or HFR position.

Delete Registered AF Area

This option lets you delete an AF area registration that you set up using the previous menu option. Although you can always register a new location, which will remove the current registration, you might want to just delete the current registration, because, even if the registered AF area is not assigned to a control button, the camera causes the registered area to flash on the shooting screen, as a reminder that there is a registered AF area available for assignment to a button. The flashing can be quite distracting, so I am glad to be able to delete the registration.

AF Area Auto Clear

This option controls whether or not the camera continues to display one or more green focus frames after it has achieved sharp focus when the focus mode is set to AF-S, AF-A, or DMF. By default, this option is turned off, so the autofocus area is not cleared from the display when focus is achieved; the green frame or frames remain on the display until you press the shutter button all the way down to capture an image. If you turn this option on through the menu, then the frame or frames will disappear from the display after about one second, so you can have a clear view of the subject before you press the shutter button all the way down to take the picture.

If the focus mode is set to AF-C, the green focus blocks or focus frame will stay on the screen even if this option is turned on, because the camera continues to evaluate focus in that mode until you press the shutter button all the way.

The setting you use for this option is a matter of personal preference. I usually don't mind seeing the green focus frames on the display, so I leave this option turned off most of the time. There could be situations, though, when you want to confirm focus by viewing the green frame(s) but then want to see the subject clearly without the frames, before you actually capture an image.

Display Continuous AF Area

This option can be turned either on or off. When it is turned on, it controls whether the camera displays small, green focus blocks to show what area of the scene is in focus, when the focus mode is set to continuous autofocus and the focus area option is set to Wide or Zone. If this option is turned off, the camera does not display any focus frames or blocks under those conditions.

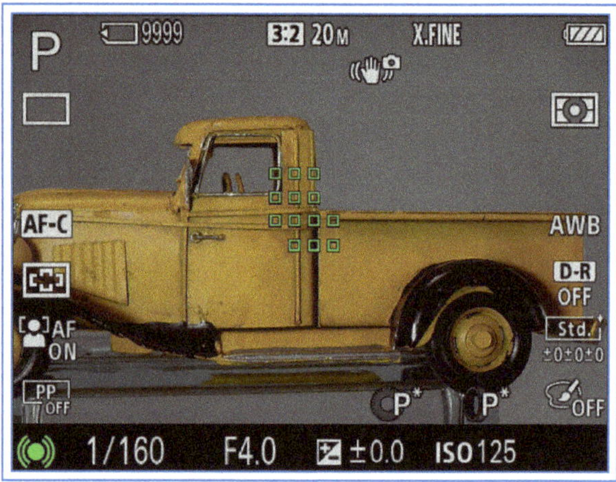

Figure 4-58. Green Blocks for Continuous Autofocus

I find this option useful, because, without it, there is no obvious way to tell what part of the scene or subject is currently in focus. With continuous autofocus in effect and focus area set to Wide or Zone, the camera's autofocus mechanism adjusts constantly as you half-press the shutter button, and there is no frame or other indicator that shows where the focus is being set, other than judging with your eyes what parts of the image look sharper than others. When this menu option is turned on, the camera displays a constantly changing set of focus blocks, as shown in Figure 4-58, as the autofocus mechanism selects a main subject to focus on within the boundaries of the Wide or Zone focus area setting.

Phase Detection Area

One of the prime features of the Sony RX100 VI camera is its fast and efficient autofocus system. The RX100 VI uses both contrast detection and phase detection for autofocus. With contrast detection, which uses 25 focus points, the camera looks for areas of contrast in the subject and focuses the image by checking the contrast level as the focus distance changes. With phase detection, the camera uses 315 individual focus points, at which the camera checks to see if the image is in focus by comparing two signals to see if they are in phase. Phase detection is considerably faster than contrast detection, so it can be useful to know exactly where the phase detection focus points are located. Phase detection functions only when the aperture is set to f/8.0 or wider (lower f-numbers).

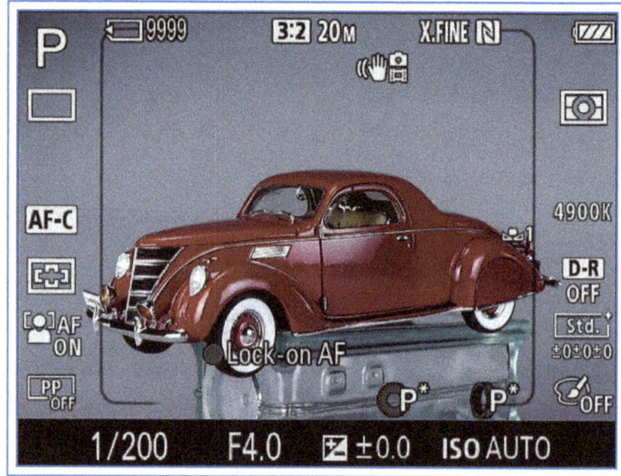

Figure 4-59. Phase Detection Area Frame

With this menu option, you can turn on or off a display that shows the area where the 315 phase detection focus points are located. When it is turned on, the shooting screen looks like Figure 4-59, with a large frame that shows the boundaries of the area containing the 315 focus points. When this option is turned off, that frame is not displayed. The frame is not displayed while recording movies.

Whether or not to display this frame is a personal preference. For general use, you may not need it, and it could prove slightly distracting. If you are photographing a difficult subject and may need to know whether the phase detection focus points will be able to cover the subject, this option could be worth using.

The items on screen 6 of the Camera Settings1 menu are shown in Figure 4-60.

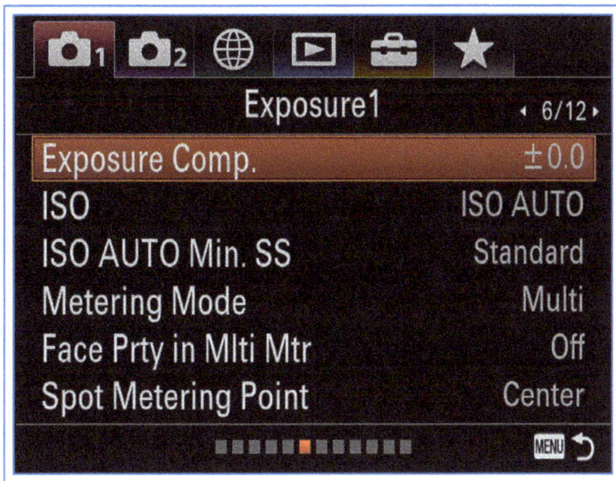

Figure 4-60. Screen 6 of Camera Settings1 Menu

Exposure Compensation

This next option on the Camera Settings1 menu gives you an alternative way to adjust exposure compensation. As I will discuss in Chapter 6, the primary way to adjust this option is by pressing the Down button. You also can use the Custom Key (Still Images) menu option to assign one of the control buttons or the control ring to adjust exposure compensation, or you can use the Function menu for that purpose, as discussed in Chapter 6. This menu option is yet another way to adjust this value.

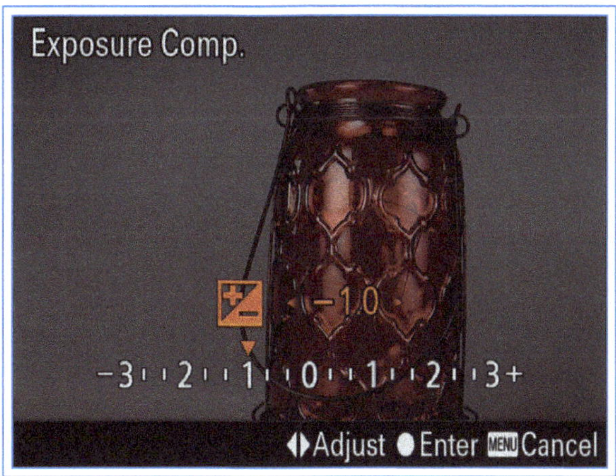

Figure 4-61. Exposure Compensation Scale on Display

When you use the Exposure Compensation menu option, there is no difference from the procedure when you use a physical control to make the adjustment. Once the EV (exposure value) scale appears on the display, as shown in Figure 4-61, use the Left and Right buttons or the control wheel to set the amount of positive or negative compensation, to make the image brighter or darker than it would be otherwise.

Exposure compensation can be adjusted up to 3.0 EV plus or minus for still images, but only up to 2.0 EV in either direction for movies. It cannot be adjusted at all in Auto or Scene mode. In Manual mode, it can be adjusted only when ISO is set to Auto ISO. It cannot be adjusted with the Down button in that mode, because that button is used to switch functions of the control wheel.

When you adjust exposure compensation using this menu option or a physical control, the value you set will be retained in memory after the camera is powered off and back on again, so be sure to set it back to zero when the compensation is no longer needed.

ISO

ISO is a measure of the sensor's sensitivity to light. When ISO is set to higher values, the camera's sensor needs less light to capture an image and the camera can use faster shutter speeds and narrower apertures. The problem with higher values is that their use produces visual "noise" that can reduce the clarity and detail in your images, adding a grainy, textured appearance.

In practical terms, shoot with low ISO settings (around 125) when possible; shoot with high ISO settings (800 or higher) when necessary to allow a fast shutter speed to stop action and avoid motion blur, or when desired to achieve a creative effect with graininess.

As is discussed in Chapters 5 and 6, with the RX100 VI you can get quick access to certain important settings, such as ISO, using the Function menu, the Quick Navi system, or by assigning the setting to a control button or the control ring using the Custom Key (Still Images) option on screen 9 of the Camera Settings2 menu. However, you can also set ISO from the Camera Settings1 menu, and you can get access to some additional ISO settings only from this menu. So, it's important to understand how to use this menu item.

ISO is the second item on screen 6 of the Camera Settings1 menu. After you highlight it, press the Center button to bring up the vertical ISO menu at the left of the screen, as seen in Figure 4-62. Scroll through the options by turning the control wheel or by pressing the Up and Down buttons to select a value ranging from one of the top two options—Multi Frame Noise Reduction and Auto ISO—through 80, 100, 125, 160, 200, and other specific values, to a maximum of 12800 at the bottom of the scale. (If you want to use an ISO value higher than 12800, you need to use the Multi Frame Noise Reduction feature, discussed below, or the High Sensitivity setting of Scene mode.)

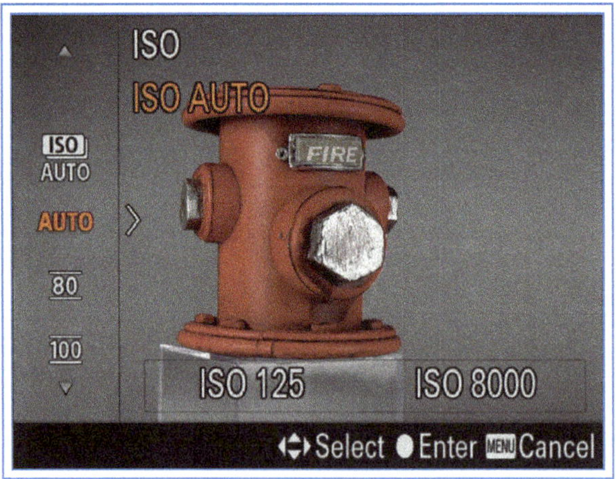

Figure 4-62. ISO Menu

If you choose Auto ISO (the second option on the menu, highlighted in Figure 4-62), the camera will select a numerical value automatically depending on the lighting conditions and other camera settings. You can select both the minimum and maximum levels for Auto ISO. In other words, you can set the camera to choose the ISO value automatically within a defined range such as, say, ISO 200 to ISO 1600. In that way, you can be assured that the camera will not select a value outside that range, but you will still leave some flexibility for the setting.

To set minimum and maximum values, while the orange highlight is on the Auto ISO option, press the Right button to move the highlight to the right side of the screen, where there are two rectangles labeled (when highlighted) ISO Auto Minimum and ISO Auto Maximum, as shown in Figure 4-63.

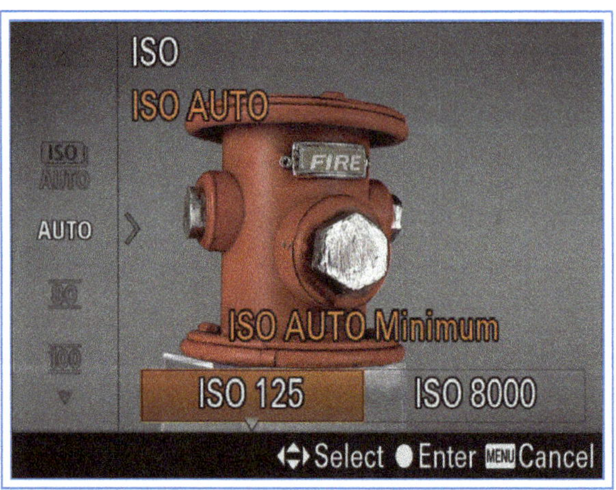

Figure 4-63. Block for ISO Auto Minimum Highlighted

Move the highlight to each of these blocks in turn using the Right button and change the value as you wish, by pressing the Up and Down buttons or turning the control wheel. You can set both the minimum and the maximum to values from 125 to 12800, when using normal settings for still images. The ranges are different when using Picture Profile settings, as discussed later in this chapter. When both values have been set, press the Center button to move to the shooting screen.

Once the minimum and maximum values are set, the camera will keep the ISO level within the range you have specified whenever you select Auto ISO or the Auto setting for Multi Frame Noise Reduction, discussed below. Of course, you can always set a specific ISO value at any other level by selecting it from the ISO menu.

Multi Frame Noise Reduction

The top item on the ISO menu, whose icon includes the ISO label and a stack of frames, as shown in Figure 4-64, is a special setting called Multi Frame Noise Reduction (MFNR). With this option, the camera uses the ISO value you select and also uses a different type of image capture to enhance the quality of the shot.

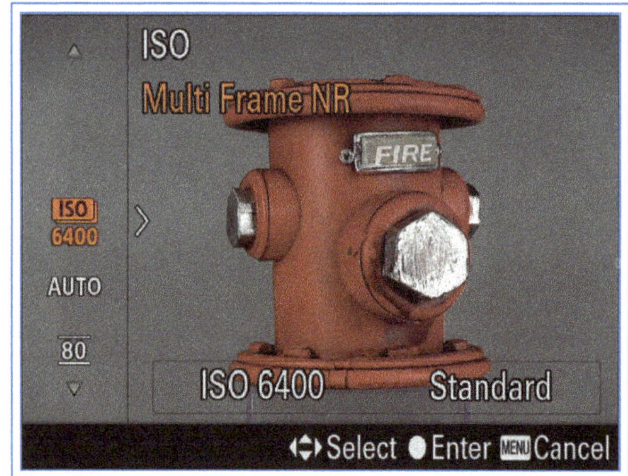

Figure 4-64. Icon for Multi Frame Noise Reduction Highlighted

With this option, you can set an ISO value as high as 25600, twice as high as the maximum value on the standard ISO menu. When you use MFNR, the camera takes multiple shots in a rapid burst and creates a composite image with reduced noise. The camera also attempts to select frames with minimal motion blur.

After you have highlighted MFNR on the menu, use the Right button to move the highlight to the right side of the screen, on the selection block for the ISO value to be used, as shown in Figure 4-65.

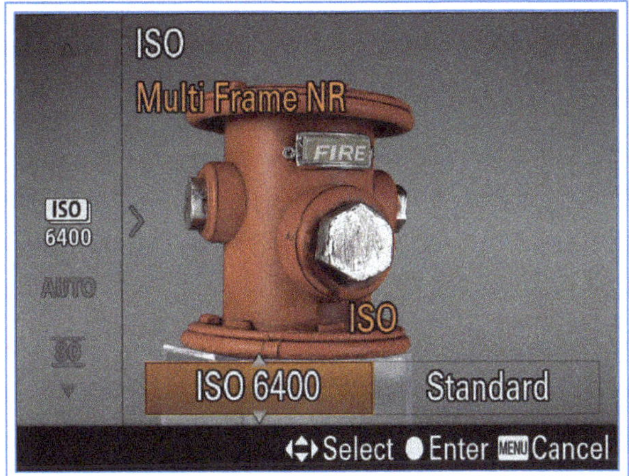

Figure 4-65. Selection Block for MFNR ISO Value Highlighted

Use the Up and Down buttons or turn the control wheel to select a value, which can be Auto or a specific value from 200 all the way up to 25600. If you choose Auto, the camera will select an ISO value within the limits set for ISO Auto Minimum and Maximum, and it will take multiple shots using that value. You cannot use the flash when MFNR is in effect. Also, you cannot use Raw for File Format (Still Images), DRO, HDR, Picture Profile, Picture Effect, or continuous shooting with this setting.

After selecting the ISO value for MFNR, press the Right button one more time to move the highlight to the block for NR Effect, as shown in Figure 4-66. For this value you can select Standard or High, to specify how much noise reduction is applied to the MFNR images you capture.

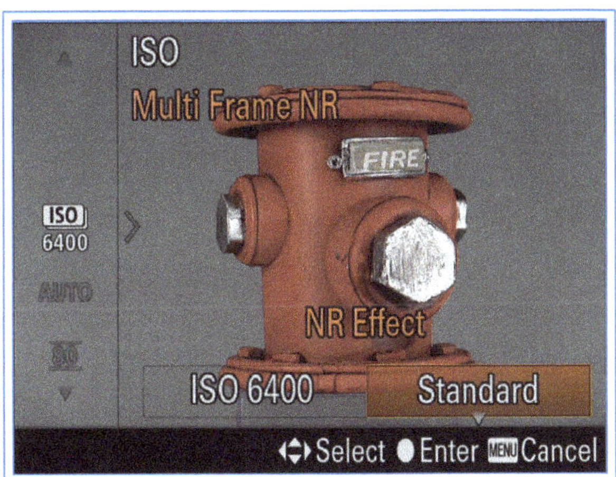

Figure 4-66. Selection Block for NR Effect Value Highlighted

The MFNR setting is the only way to set the RX100 VI to an ISO above 12800. If you are faced with the prospect of taking pictures in a dark environment, consider using this specialized setting, which really is more akin to a shooting mode than to an ISO setting. (You can use the High Sensitivity setting of Scene mode, which may use a setting this high, but you cannot directly set that ISO value.)

For Figure 4-67, I used this setting to capture a view of a couple of people strolling on the pedestrian bridge across the river after dark. The camera exposed the image for 1/50 second at f/4.5, using an ISO setting of 8000.

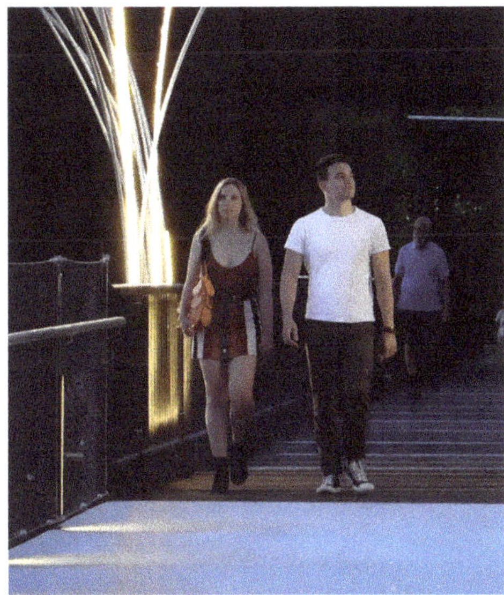

Figure 4-67. Multi Frame Noise Reduction Example

Here are some more notes on ISO. As I discussed in Chapter 3, with the RX100 VI, you can select Auto ISO in Manual exposure mode. In that way, you can set both the shutter speed and aperture, and still have the camera set the exposure automatically by varying the ISO level. In the Auto, Scene, and Sweep Panorama modes, Auto ISO is automatically set, and you cannot adjust the ISO setting. The available ISO settings for movie recording are different from those for stills; I will discuss that point in Chapter 9.

Also, note that the settings for ISO 80 and 100 are surrounded by lines on the menu, as shown in Figure 4-62. The lines indicate that those two settings are not "native" to the RX100 VI's sensor, whose base ISO is 125. So, although using the two lower settings reduces the sensor's sensitivity to light, it does not improve dynamic range or reduce noise in your images significantly.

My recommendation is to use Auto ISO for general photography when the main consideration is to have a properly exposed image. When you know you will need a fast shutter speed, select a high ISO setting as necessary. When you need to use a wide aperture to blur the background or a slow shutter speed to smooth out the appearance of flowing water, use a low ISO setting. When you are shooting in unusually dark conditions, consider using the MFNR setting with a high setting for ISO, even as high as 25600 in extreme cases.

ISO Auto Minimum Shutter Speed

The next option on screen 6 of the Camera Settings1 menu lets you set a minimum shutter speed, or shutter speed range, for the camera to use when ISO is set to ISO Auto or to MFNR with the value set to Auto. This option is available for selection only when the shooting mode is set to Program or Aperture Priority, the only two advanced shooting modes in which the camera chooses the shutter speed. The purpose of this setting is to ensure that the camera uses a shutter speed fast enough to stop the action for the scene you are shooting.

For example, if you are shooting images of children at play with the camera set to Program mode and ISO Auto in effect with a range from 200 minimum to 1600 maximum, the camera ordinarily may choose a relatively low ISO setting in order to maintain high image quality and low noise. However, using that setting may result in the use of a fairly slow shutter speed, such as 1/30 second, in order to provide enough light for the exposure. With the ISO Auto Minimum Shutter Speed setting, you can set the minimum shutter speed you want the camera to use, such as, say, 1/125 second, to avoid motion blur. You also can specify a more general range of shutter speeds, using several categories, as discussed below.

To use this option, make sure the shooting mode is set to Program or Aperture Priority and that ISO is set to Auto ISO, or to Multi Frame Noise Reduction, with Auto ISO in effect for that setting. Then, highlight this option and press the Center button. You will see the menu shown in Figure 4-68, which includes numerous options as you scroll down through several screens.

All but one of the options are specific shutter speeds, ranging from 1/32000 second to 30 seconds. If you select one of those values, the camera will try to use a shutter speed at least that fast for each shot while maintaining the minimum ISO setting. Once the camera has found it necessary to lower the shutter speed to the minimum value, it will start raising the ISO level as needed. If the camera has set the ISO value to the upper range specified for Maximum ISO and still cannot expose the image properly at the ISO Auto Minimum Shutter Speed, the camera will set a shutter speed slower than the minimum value, in order to achieve a proper exposure.

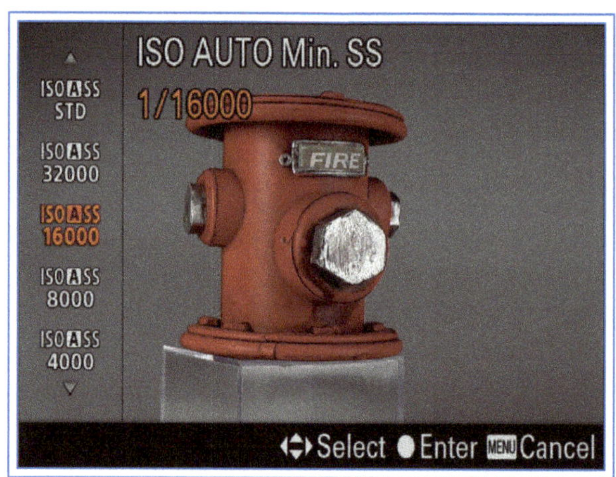

Figure 4-68. ISO Auto Minimum Shutter Speed Options Screen

For example, in the situation discussed above, using ISO Auto with a range from 200 to 1600, if there is plenty of light, the camera may select shutter speeds such as 1/250 second or 1/500 second. It will maintain the ISO at 200 if possible, and it will not select a shutter speed slower than 1/125 second. If the lighting conditions become such that the camera needs to lower the shutter speed all the way to the minimum setting of 1/125 second, the camera will raise the ISO as needed. If the light becomes too dim, the camera may set the ISO to the top of its Auto ISO range at 1600 but still find it impossible to get a good exposure using 1/125 second for the shutter speed. In that case, the camera will use a slower setting, such as 1/60 second or 1/30 second, as needed.

The item at the top of the menu for this option lists settings that are not specific shutter speeds: Standard, Fast, Faster, Slower, and Slow. You can use one of these if you don't need to specify a particular shutter speed but just want to set general guidance for the camera to use. If you choose Standard, the camera tries to maintain a normal shutter speed based on the current focal length of the lens. So, if the lens is at its 24mm wide-angle setting, the camera will try to maintain a shutter speed faster than 1/24 second. If it is zoomed in to 200mm, it will try to use a speed faster than 1/200 second. If you choose Fast or Faster, the camera attempts to maintain a faster shutter speed than with Standard; Slow or Slower has the opposite effect.

I generally leave this setting at Standard, unless I am faced with a situation in which I definitely need a particularly fast shutter speed.

Metering Mode

This option lets you choose among the five patterns of exposure metering offered by the RX100 VI—Multi, Center, Spot, Entire Screen Average, and Highlight—as shown in Figure 4-69.

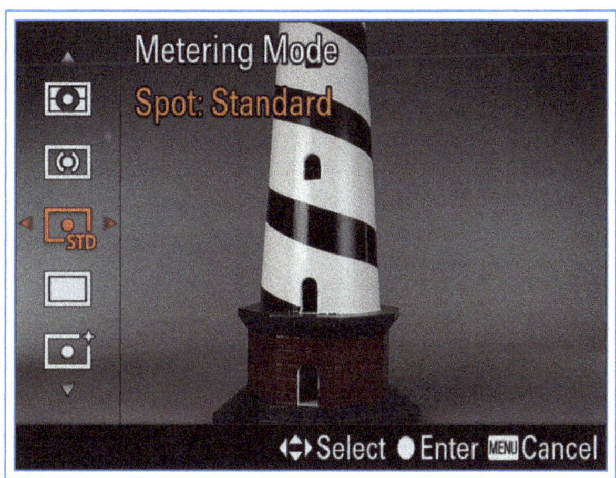

Figure 4-69. Metering Mode Options Screen

This choice tells the camera's automatic exposure system what part of the scene to consider when setting the exposure. With Multi, the camera uses the entire scene that is visible on the display, but it divides that area into segments and analyzes the pattern of the segments in order to determine the optimum exposure. If you turn on the Face Priority in Multi Meter option, discussed below, the camera will optimize exposure for the face or faces it has detected.

With Center, the camera still measures all of the light from the scene, but it gives additional weight to the center portion of the image on the theory that your main subject is in or near the center.

With Spot, the camera evaluates only the light that is found within the spot metering zone. You can change the size of that zone between Standard and Large by pressing the Left and Right buttons when the Spot icon is highlighted. Figure 4-70 shows the Spot setting in use with the Standard setting for the metering zone.

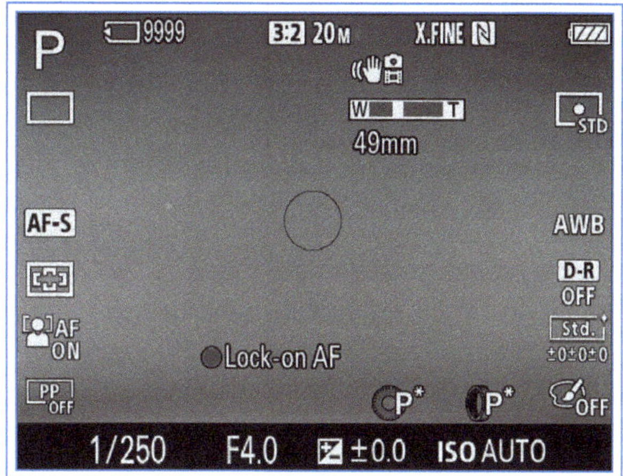

Figure 4-70. Spot Metering Standard Circle on Display

With the Spot option, particularly with the Standard setting, you can see the effects of the exposure system clearly by selecting Program exposure mode and aiming the small circle at various points, some bright and some dark, and seeing how sharply the brightness of the scene on the camera's display changes. If you try the same experiment using Multi, Center, or Entire Screen Average mode, you will see more subtle and gradual changes.

If you choose Spot metering, the circle you will see is different from the rectangular frames the camera uses to indicate the Center, Flexible Spot, or Expand Flexible Spot focus area settings. If you make one of those focus area settings at the same time as the Spot metering setting, you will see both a spot-metering circle and an autofocus frame on the LCD screen, as in Figure 4-71, which shows the screen with the Spot metering and Flexible Spot focus area settings in effect.

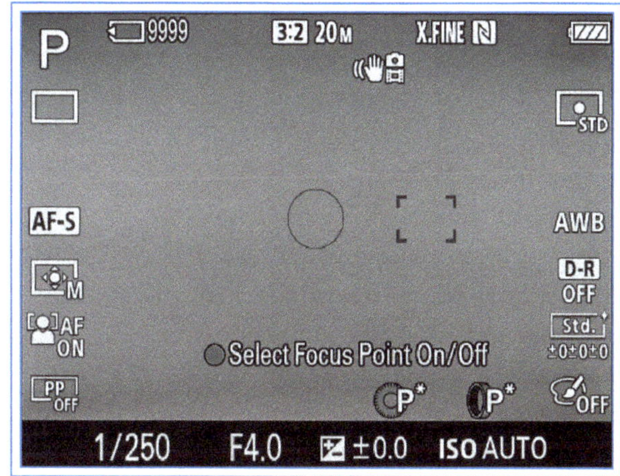

Figure 4-71. Spot Metering Circle and Center Focus Area Frame

Be aware of which one of these settings is in effect, if a circle or a frame is visible on the shooting screen. Remember that the circle is for Spot metering, and the rectangular bracket is for Center, Flexible Spot, or Expand Flexible Spot autofocus (or an equivalent Lock-on AF setting). You can use the Spot Metering Point menu option, discussed later in this chapter, to set the Spot metering point to move along with the Flexible Spot or Expand Flexible Spot focus frame.

The next choice for metering mode, Entire Screen Average, bases the exposure on the overall brightness of the entire screen, without regard to where the subject is located. This option may be useful if the scene is uniform in its brightness or if you know from past experience that basing the exposure on the average brightness will yield a good result.

The last option, Highlight, causes the camera to base the exposure on the brightest point in the scene, regardless of its location. This setting is especially useful for a situation such as a stage performance that is illuminated by one or more spotlights, to avoid overexposure. However, you need to be careful if there is a situation in which the most important subject is not the brightest object in the scene. In that case, you might want to switch to Spot metering and move the Spot metering circle over the subject.

In Auto mode and all varieties of Scene mode, the only metering method available is Multi. That method also is the only one available when Clear Image Zoom or Digital Zoom is in use. (The conflict arises only when the lens is actually zoomed beyond the limit of optical zoom; at that point, the camera will change the metering method to Multi, and will change it back when the lens is zoomed back within the optical zoom limit.)

The Multi setting is best for scenes with relatively even contrast, such as landscapes, and for action shots, when the location of the main subject may move through different parts of the frame. It also works well for shots of people, if you activate the Face Priority in Multi Meter option, discussed below. The Center setting is good for sunrise and sunset scenes, and other situations with a large, central subject that exhibits considerable contrast with the rest of the scene. The Spot setting is good for portraits, macro shots, and other images in which there is a relatively small part of the scene where exposure is critical. Spot metering also is useful when lighting is intense in one portion of a scene, such as when a concert performer is lit by a spotlight. However, the Highlight option may be preferable for scenes with stage lighting.

Face Priority in Multi Meter

This option works in a way similar to the Set Face Priority in AF, discussed earlier in this chapter. This option lets you set whether or not the camera optimizes exposure for a detected face, when metering mode is set to Multi. If it is turned on, the camera ignores the overall exposure reading and concentrates the exposure setting based on the highest-priority face. If it is turned off, the camera ignores the faces, and uses the standard algorithm for metering based on the overall scene. In Intelligent Auto or Superior Auto mode, this option is turned on and cannot be disabled.

Spot Metering Point

When Spot metering is in effect, you can use the Spot Metering Point menu option to set the Spot circle to move along with the Flexible Spot or Expand Flexible Spot focus frame, whenever either of those frames is in use for focus area. This menu option has two choices—Center or Focus Point Link. If you choose Center, then the Spot circle will always stay in the center of the frame. If you choose Focus Point Link, then the Spot Circle will move as you move the Flexible Spot or Expand Flexible Spot focus frame, as shown in Figure 4-72. If touch screen operations are active, you can move the Spot metering circle and focus frame by dragging a finger on the screen.

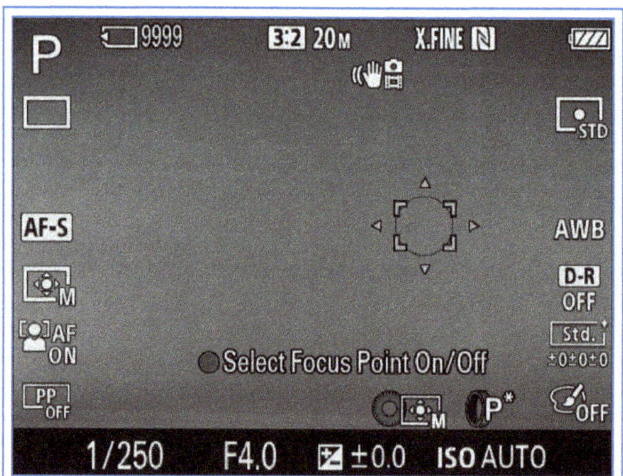

Figure 4-72. Spot Metering Circle Moved with Focus Frame

If focus area is set to Lock-on AF with the Flexible Spot or Expand Flexible Spot sub-option, with the Focus Point Link option the Spot metering circle will be located where the focus frame is before focus tracking begins, but the metering area will not move as focus is tracked.

The items on screen 7 of the Camera Settings1 menu are shown in Figure 4-73.

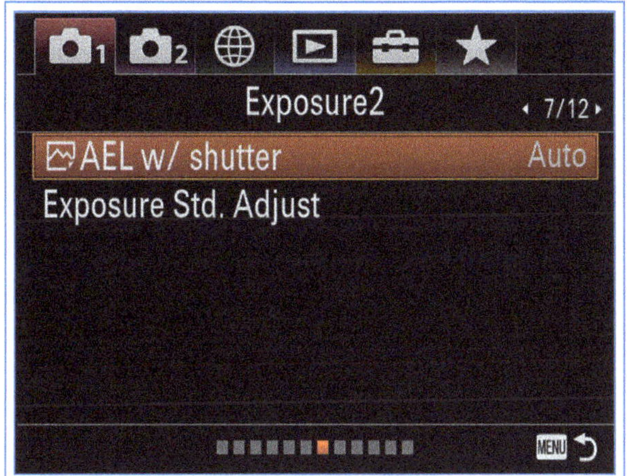

Figure 4-73. Screen 7 of Camera Settings1 Menu

AEL with Shutter

This menu item, whose options screen is shown in Figure 4-74, controls how the shutter button handles autoexposure lock. There are three possible settings for this feature: Auto, On, and Off.

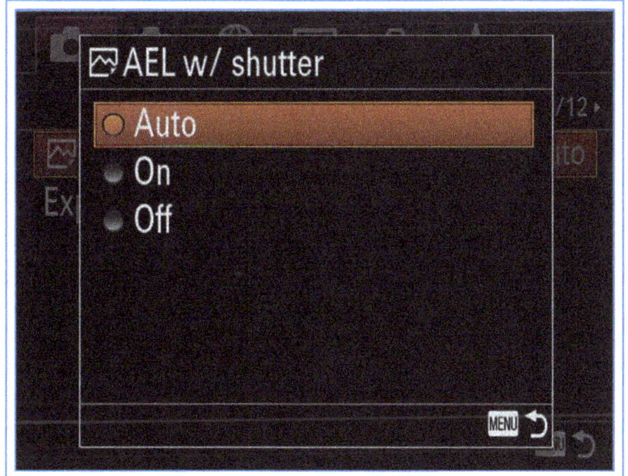

Figure 4-74. AEL with Shutter Options Screen

With the default option, Auto, pressing the shutter button halfway locks exposure when focus mode is set to AF-S for single-shot autofocus or DMF for direct manual focus. When the focus mode is set to AF-C for continuous autofocus or MF for manual focus, pressing the shutter button halfway does not lock exposure. When the focus mode is set to A for automatic autofocus, pressing the shutter button halfway locks exposure as long as the subject does not move. If the subject starts to move, the exposure will no longer be locked.

If AEL with Shutter is set to On, then pressing the shutter button halfway locks exposure in all situations, regardless of what focus mode is in place. So, for example, if focus mode is set to AF-C, pressing the shutter button halfway locks exposure, though the focus mechanism will continue adjusting focus. If focus mode is set to MF, pressing the shutter button halfway locks exposure, even though focus is not adjusted.

If this menu option is set to Off, then pressing the shutter button halfway never locks exposure, in any focus mode. You may want to use this setting when you need to press the shutter button halfway to lock focus and then move the camera to change the composition somewhat. You might want the camera to re-evaluate the exposure, even though you have already locked the focus.

Another important use for the Off setting is when you are using the continuous shooting settings of drive mode. As I discussed earlier in this chapter, if you want the camera to adjust its exposure for each shot in a continuous burst, you need to set AEL with Shutter to Off, or set it to Auto with focus mode set to AF-C or AF-A. Otherwise, the camera will lock exposure with the first shot, and will not adjust it if the lighting changes during the burst.

Of course, you may not want to use the Off or Auto setting in that scenario, because it can slow down the burst of shots, and, depending on the situation, it may not be likely that the lighting will change during a brief burst of shots. But this option is available for those times when you want the camera to keep adjusting exposure while you take a burst of shots.

Exposure Standard Adjustment

This second and final item on screen 7 of the Camera Settings1 menu lets you fine-tune the exposure settings for the various metering modes. You can use this option to program in an adjustment of up to one stop of EV (exposure value) for each of the camera's five metering modes: Multi, Center, Spot, Entire Screen Average, and Highlight.

This adjustment ordinarily should not be necessary, but it is included for photographers who know that, when they use a particular metering mode, their exposure generally needs a particular adjustment. For example, a photojournalist who covers rock concerts may have found that her shots need to be adjusted upward by 0.5 EV so the non-highlighted areas on the stage are not lost in shadows when she is using the Highlight setting for metering mode. She can use this menu option to set a positive adjustment in that amount.

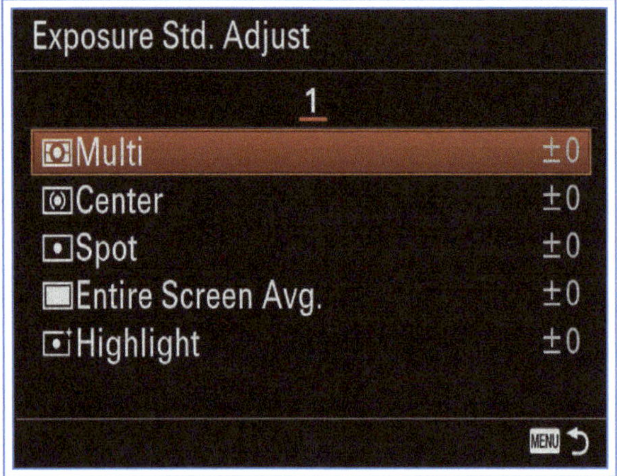

Figure 4-75. Exposure Standard Adjustment - List of Modes

To make this adjustment, select this menu option and press the Right button to move to a screen with a message saying this adjustment is usually not necessary; then select the OK label to move to the screen listing the metering modes, shown in Figure 4-75.

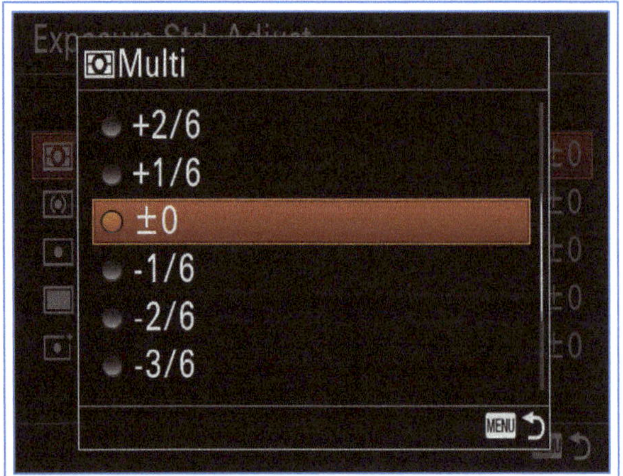

Figure 4-76. Exposure Standard Adjustment - Adjustment Screen

On that screen, select the metering mode you want to adjust, and move to the adjustment screen, shown in Figure 4-76, where you can select the adjustment you want. Then press the Menu button repeatedly, or just press the shutter button halfway, to return to the shooting screen.

I consider this option to be a somewhat esoteric one, which I don't recommend using unless you have a definite need for it.

The items on screen 8 of the Camera Settings1 menu are shown in Figure 4-77.

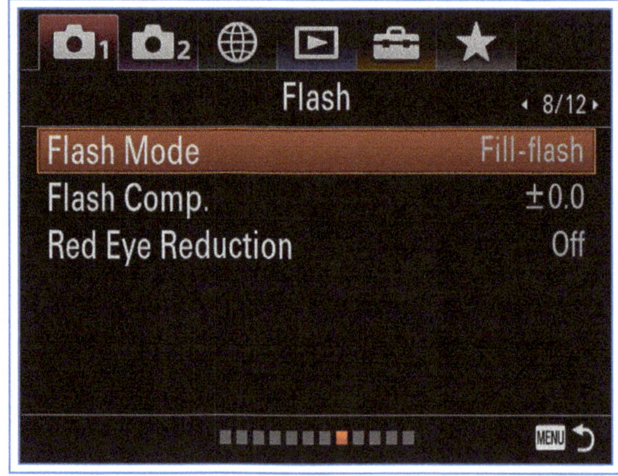

Figure 4-77. Screen 8 of Camera Settings1 Menu

Flash Mode

This option controls the behavior of the camera's flash unit. There are five choices—Flash Off, Autoflash, Fill-flash, Slow Sync, and Rear Sync—as seen in Figure 4-78. Autoflash is dimmed on this screen, because it is not available for selection in Program mode, illustrated here.

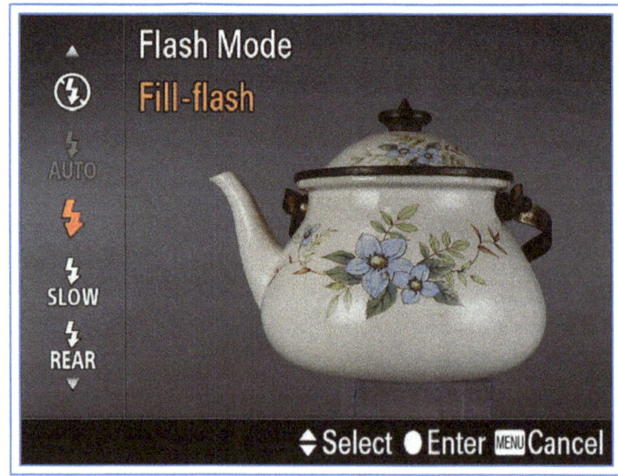

Figure 4-78. Flash Mode Menu

There is no shooting mode in which all five options are available. You can also get access to this menu by pressing the Right button on the back of the camera when the shooting screen is displayed, unless the Right button has been assigned to a different setting from its default setting of flash mode, using the Custom Key (Still Images) option on the Camera Settings2 menu.

Flash Off

To make sure the flash will not fire, choose Flash Off. This is a good choice when you are in a museum or other place where you don't want the flash to fire, or if you know you will not be using flash. It also can be helpful to avoid depleting a battery that is running low. This option is available for selection in Auto, Program, Aperture Priority, and Shutter Priority mode and with the Portrait, Sports Action, Macro, Landscape, and Sunset settings of Scene mode. Of course, with the RX100 VI you also have the option of just not raising the flash with the flash pop-up switch, which will have the same effect as using this flash mode option.

Autoflash

With Autoflash, you leave it up to the camera to decide whether to fire the flash. The camera will analyze the lighting and other aspects of the scene and decide whether to use flash without further input from you. This selection is available only in Auto mode, and with the Portrait and Macro settings of Scene mode.

Fill-Flash

With Fill-flash, you are making a decision to use flash no matter what the lighting conditions are. If you choose this option, the flash will fire every time you press the shutter button, if the flash is popped up. This is the setting to use when the sun is shining and you need to soften shadows on a subject's face, or when you need to correct the lighting when a subject is backlit.

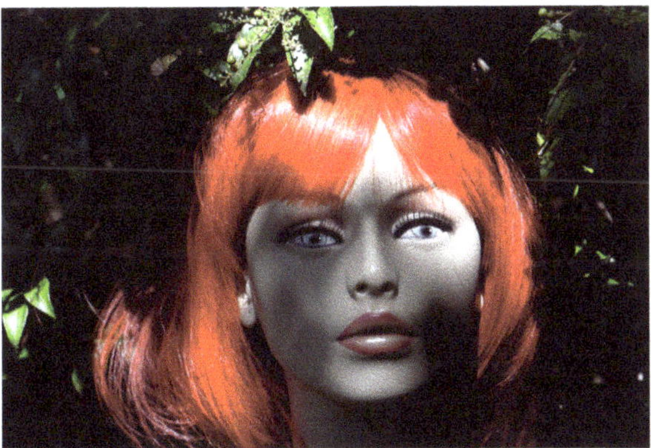

Figure 4-79. Image Taken With Flash Off

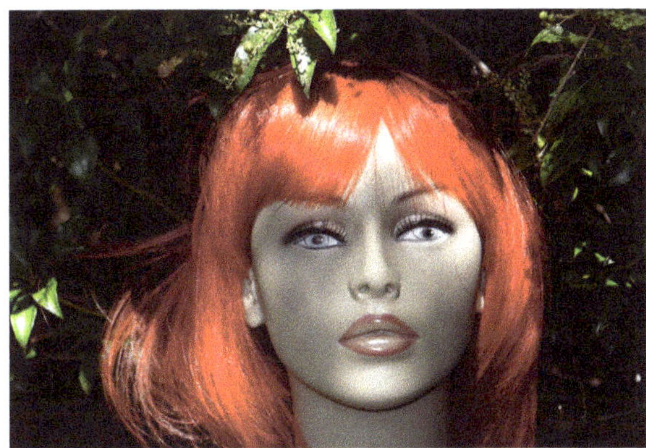

Figure 4-80. Image Take with Fill-flash

For example, for Figures 4-79 and 4-80 I took two shots of a mannequin in mixed sunlight and shade. The second shot, with fill-flash, is more evenly exposed because the shadows were reduced by the light from the flash.

Fill-flash is available with all still-shooting modes except Sweep Panorama and the Scene mode settings of Night Scene, Hand-held Twilight, Night Portrait, Anti Motion Blur, Anti Motion Blur, and High Sensitivity.

Slow Sync

The Slow Sync option is useful when you are taking a flash photograph of a subject at night or in dim lighting, when there is some natural light in the background.

With this setting, the camera uses a relatively slow shutter speed so the ambient (natural) lighting will have time to register on the image. In other words, if you're in a fairly dark environment and fire the flash normally, it will likely light up the subject (such as a person), but because the exposure time is short, the surrounding scene may be black. If you use the Slow Sync setting, the slower shutter speed allows the surrounding scene to be visible also.

I took the two images in Figures 4-81 and 4-82 with identical lighting and camera settings, except that I took the first image with the flash set to Fill-flash and shutter speed at 1/50 second, and I took the second image with the flash set to Slow Sync, resulting in a longer shutter speed of 1/4 second.

In Figure 4-81, the flash illuminated the mannequin in the foreground, but the background is dark. In Figure 4-82, the room behind the mannequin is illuminated by ambient light because of the slower shutter speed.

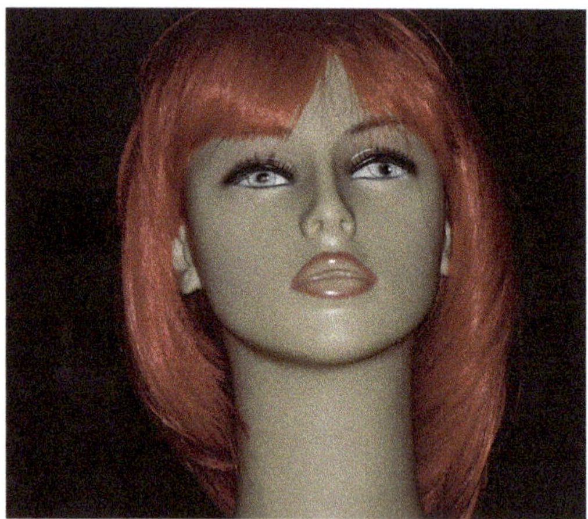
Figure 4-81. Image Taken with Normal Flash

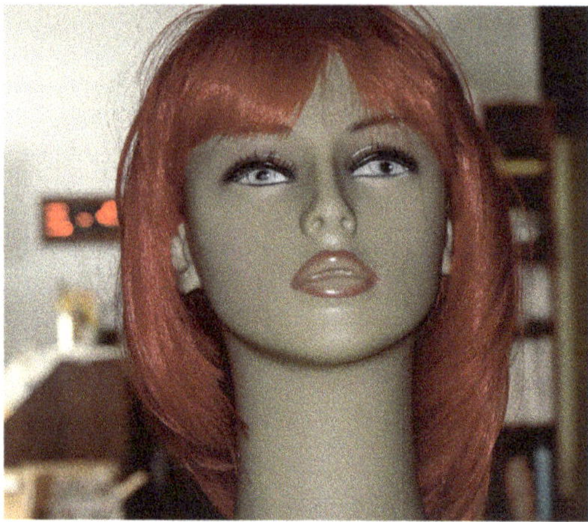
Figure 4-82. Image Taken with Slow-sync Flash

When you use Slow Sync, you should use a tripod because the camera may choose a very slow shutter speed, such as three seconds or longer. Note that you can choose Slow Sync even in Shutter Priority mode. If you do so, you should select a slow shutter speed because the point is to use a long exposure to light the background with ambient light. With Shutter Priority mode you can choose any shutter speed, but it would not make sense to select a relatively fast one, such as, say, 1/30 second. The same considerations apply for Manual exposure mode, in which you also can select Slow Sync.

Slow Sync can be selected only in the Program, Aperture Priority, Shutter Priority, and Manual exposure modes. With the Night Portrait setting of Scene mode, Slow Sync is set by the camera and cannot be changed.

Rear Sync

The next setting for flash mode is Rear Sync. You should not need this option unless you encounter the special situation it is designed for. If you don't activate this setting (that is, if you select any other flash mode in which the flash fires), the camera uses the unnamed default setting, which could be called "Front Sync." In that case, the flash fires very soon after the shutter opens to expose the image. If you choose the Rear Sync setting instead, the flash fires later—just before the shutter closes.

Rear Sync helps avoid a strange-looking result in some situations. This issue arises, for example, with a relatively long exposure, say one-half second, of a subject with lights, such as a car or motorcycle at night, moving across your field of view. With normal (Front) sync, the flash will fire early in the process, freezing the vehicle in a clear image. However, as the shutter remains open while the vehicle keeps going, the camera will capture the moving lights in a stream extending in front of the vehicle.

If, instead, you use Rear Sync, the initial part of the exposure will capture the lights in a trail that appears behind the vehicle, while the vehicle itself is not frozen by the flash until later in the exposure. With Rear Sync in this particular situation, if the lights in question are taillights that look more natural behind the vehicle, the final image is likely to look more natural than with the Front Sync (default) setting.

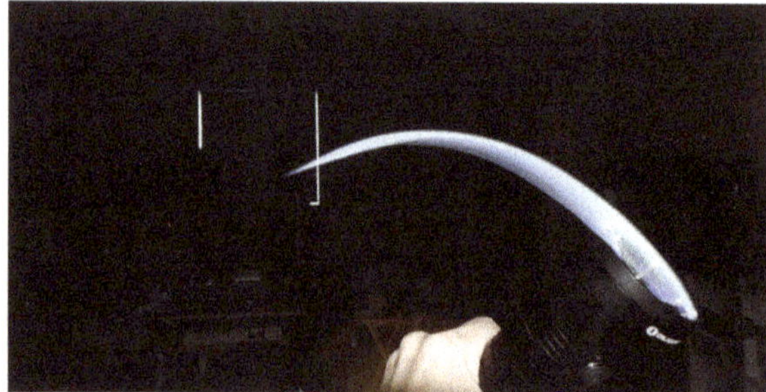
Figure 4-83. Image Taken with Normal Flash

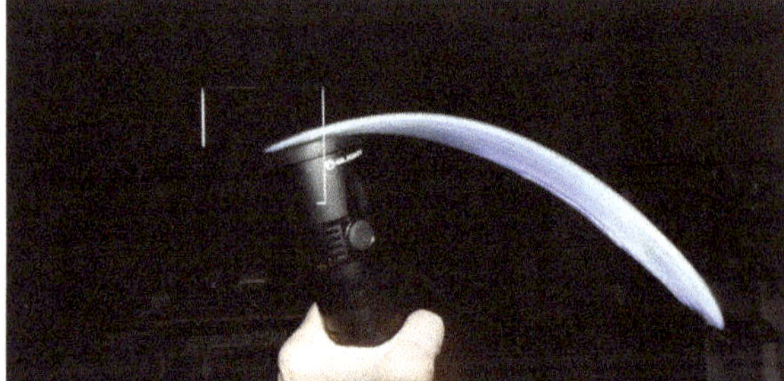
Figure 4-84. Image Taken with Rear-sync Flash

The images in Figures 4-83 and 4-84 illustrate this concept using a flashlight. I took both pictures using the built-in flash, with a shutter speed of 0.8 second. For each shot, I waved the flashlight from right to left. In Figure 4-83, using the normal (Fill-flash) setting, the flash fired quickly, making a clear image of the flashlight at the right of the image, and the light beam continued on to the left during the long exposure to make a light trail in front of the flashlight's path of movement.

In Figure 4-84, using Rear Sync, the flash did not fire until the flashlight had traveled all the way to the left, and the trail of light from its beam appeared behind the flashlight's path of motion. If you are trying to convey a sense of natural movement, the Rear Sync setting, as seen here, is likely to give you better results than the default setting.

A good general rule is to use Rear Sync only when you have a definite need for it. Using this option makes it harder to compose and set up the shot, because you have to anticipate where the main subject will be when the flash finally fires late in the exposure process. But, in the relatively rare situations when it is useful, Rear Sync can make a dramatic difference. Rear Sync is available only in the more advanced shooting modes: Program, Aperture Priority, Shutter Priority, and Manual exposure.

Flash Compensation

This menu item lets you control the output of the camera's built-in flash unit. This function works similarly to exposure compensation, which is available in the more advanced shooting modes. (Exposure compensation is discussed in Chapter 6.) The difference between the two options is that flash compensation varies only the brightness of the light emitted by the flash, while exposure compensation varies the overall exposure of a given shot, whether or not flash is used.

Flash compensation is useful when you don't want the subject overwhelmed with light from the flash. I sometimes use this setting when I am shooting a portrait outdoors with the Fill-flash setting to reduce shadows on the subject. With a bit of negative flash compensation, I can keep the flash from overexposing the image or casting a harsh light on the subject's face.

To use this option, highlight it on the menu screen and press the Center button. On the next screen, shown in Figure 4-85, press the Left and Right buttons or turn the control wheel to set the amount of positive or negative compensation you want.

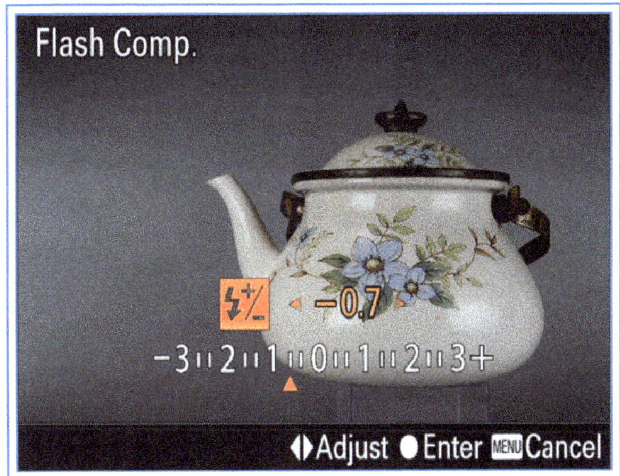

Figure 4-85. Flash Compensation Adjustment Screen

When the flash is popped up, an icon in the upper right corner of the shooting screen shows the amount of compensation in effect, even if it is zero, as shown in Figure 4-86, where it is -0.7. Be careful to set the value back to zero when you are done with the setting, because any setting you make will stay in place even after the camera has been powered off and back on again.

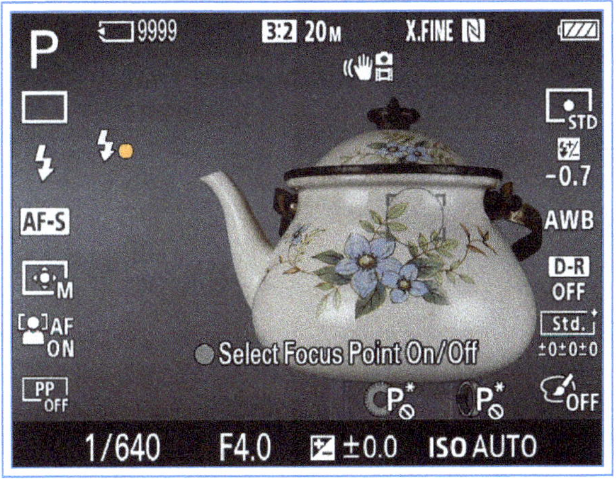

Figure 4-86. Flash Compensation Icon on Shooting Screen

The Flash Compensation option is not available in the Auto, Scene, or Sweep Panorama modes.

Red Eye Reduction

This final option on screen 8 of the Camera Settings1 menu is designed to combat "red-eye"—the eerie red glow in human eyes that appears in images when on-camera flash lights up the blood vessels on the retinas. This menu item can be set to either On or Off. If it is turned on, then, whenever the flash is used, it fires a few times before the actual flash that illuminates the image. The pre-flashes cause the subject's pupils to narrow, reducing the ability of the later, full flash to enter the pupils, bounce off the retinas, and produce the unwanted red glow in the eyes.

I prefer to leave this option turned off and deal with any red-eye effects using editing software. However, if you will be taking flash photos at a party, you may want to use this menu option to minimize the occurrence of red-eye effects in the first place.

Figure 4-87 shows screen 9 of the Camera Settings1 menu.

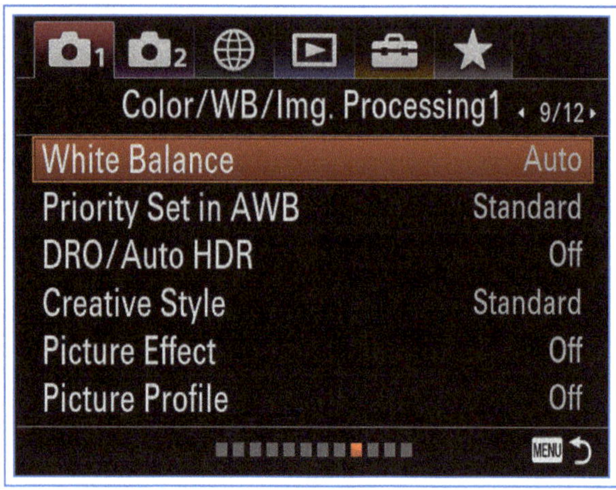

Figure 4-87. Screen 9 of Camera Settings1 Menu

White Balance

The White Balance menu option is needed because cameras record colors of objects differently according to the color temperature of the light illuminating those objects. Color temperature is a value expressed in Kelvin (K) units. A light source with a lower K rating produces a "warmer," or more reddish light. A source with a higher rating produces a "cooler," or more bluish light. Candlelight is rated about 1,800 K, indoor tungsten light (ordinary light bulb) is rated about 3,000 K, outdoor sunlight and electronic flash are rated about 5,500 K, and outdoor shade is rated about 7,000 K. If the camera is using a white balance setting that is not designed for the light source that illuminates the scene, the colors of the recorded image are likely to be inaccurate.

The RX100 VI, like most cameras, has an Auto White Balance setting that chooses the proper color correction for any given light source. The Auto White Balance setting works well, and it will produce good results in many situations, especially if you are taking snapshots whose colors are not critical.

If you need more precision in the white balance of your shots, the RX100 VI has settings for common light sources, as well as options for setting white balance by color temperature and for setting a custom white balance based on the existing light source.

Once you have highlighted this menu option, press the Center button to bring up the vertical menu at the left of the screen, as shown in Figure 4-88.

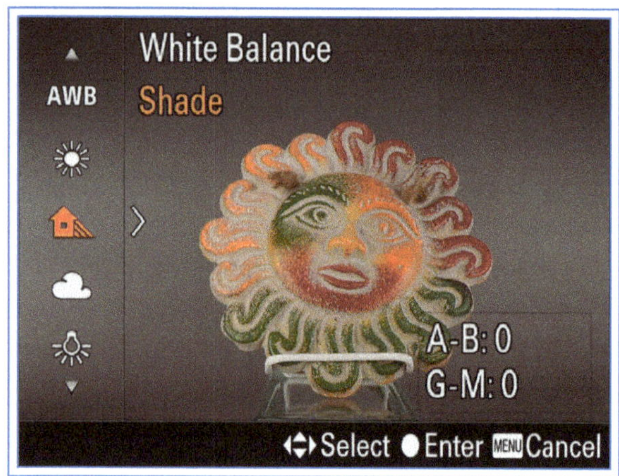

Figure 4-88. First Group of White Balance Menu Options

Press the Up and Down buttons or turn the control wheel to scroll through the choices in the first group: Auto White Balance (AWB), Daylight (sun icon), Shade (house icon), Cloudy (cloud icon), and Incandescent (round light bulb icon).

The second group, seen in Figure 4-89, includes Fluorescent Warm White (bulb icon with -1), Fluorescent Cool White (same, with 0), Fluorescent Day White (same, with +1), Fluorescent Daylight (same, with +2), and Flash (WB with lightning icon).

The choices in the third group, shown in Figure 4-90, are Underwater Auto White Balance (AWB with fish icon), Color Temperature/Filter (K and filter icon) and three numbered custom choices.

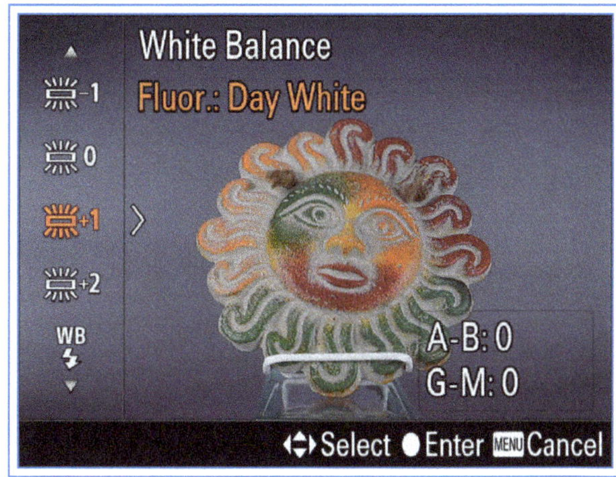

Figure 4-89. Second Group of White Balance Menu Options

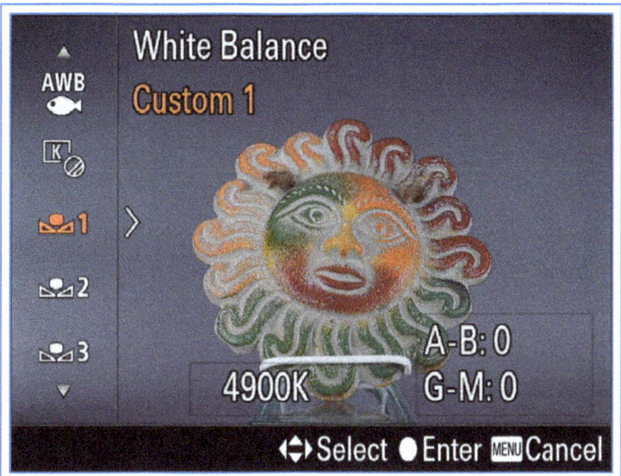

Figure 4-90. Third Group of White Balance Menu Options

Finally, if you scroll past the above choices, there is an icon with the word "SET," which represents the option for setting a custom value.

To select a setting without making any further adjustments, highlight it and press the Center button. Most of the settings describe a light source in common use. There are four settings for fluorescent bulbs, so you should be able to find a good setting for any fluorescent light, though you may need to experiment to find the best setting for a given bulb. For settings such as Daylight, Shade, Cloudy, and Incandescent, select the setting that matches the dominant light in your location. If you are indoors and using only incandescent lights, this decision will be easy. If you have a variety of lights turned on and sunlight coming in the windows, you may want to use either the Color Temperature/ Filter setting or the Custom option.

The Color Temperature/Filter option lets you set the camera's white balance according to the color temperature of the light source. One way to determine that value is with a device like the Sekonic C-700 color meter shown in Figure 4-91.

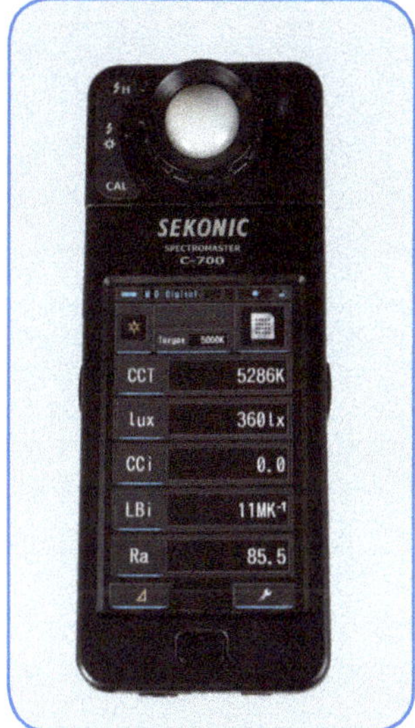

Figure 4-91. Sekonic C-700 Color Meter

That meter works well when you need extra accuracy in your white balance settings. If you don't want to use a meter, you can still use the Color Temperature/ Filter option, but you will have to do some guesswork or use your own sense of color. For example, if you are shooting under lighting that is largely incandescent, you can use the value of 3,000 K as a starting point, because, as noted earlier in this discussion, that is an approximate value for the color temperature of that light source. Then you can try setting the color temperature figure higher or lower, and watch the camera's display to see how natural the colors look.

As you lower the color temperature setting, the image will become more "cool," or bluish; as you raise it, the image will appear more "warm," or reddish. Once you find the best setting, leave it in place and take your shots. (The Live View Display option on screen 7 of the Camera Settings2 menu must be set to Setting Effect On for these changes to appear on the display, as discussed in Chapter 5.)

To make this setting, after you highlight the icon for Color Temperature/Filter, press the Right button to move the orange highlight to the right side of the camera's screen so that it highlights the color temperature value bar, as shown in Figure 4-92.

Raise or lower that number by pressing the Up and Down buttons or by turning the control wheel, and press the Center button to select that value.

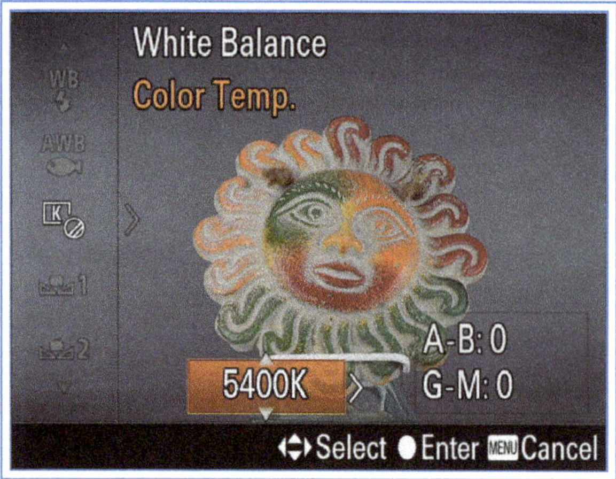

Figure 4-92. Color Temperature Adjustment Scale

If you don't want to use color temperatures, you can set a custom white balance. This process can be confusing, because the custom setting has several icons on the White Balance menu. The first three custom icons, just below the Color Temperature/Filter icon, are used to set the camera to one of three currently stored custom white balance settings. The fourth icon, with the word "SET", is the one to use to measure and store a new reading for one of the custom settings using the camera's special procedure for setting that value. Before you can use any of the three upper custom icons, you need to use the lowest custom icon to set the custom white balance value as you want it.

To set and store a custom white balance, highlight the SET icon at the end of the White Balance menu. Press the Center button to select this option, and the camera will display a message saying "Press the [Center] button to capture data of central area of screen," as shown in Figure 4-93. Aim the camera at a gray or white surface, lit by the light source you are measuring, that fills the circle on the screen. Press the Center button, and the camera will set the white balance.

The lower area of the screen will show the measured color temperature along with letters and numbers indicating variations along two color axes. If there is some variation, you will see an indication such as G-M: G1, meaning one unit of variation toward green along the green-magenta axis. If there is no variation, it will say A-B: 0 and G-M: 0, as shown in Figure 4-94.

Press the Right and Left buttons or turn the control wheel to select register 1, 2, or 3. Press the Center button to store the new setting to that register, replacing the existing setting. To use the custom white balance setting you saved, select the 1, 2, or 3 custom icon on the White Balance menu, depending on the slot you used to save the setting. You can change any of the custom settings whenever you want to, if you are shooting under different lighting conditions.

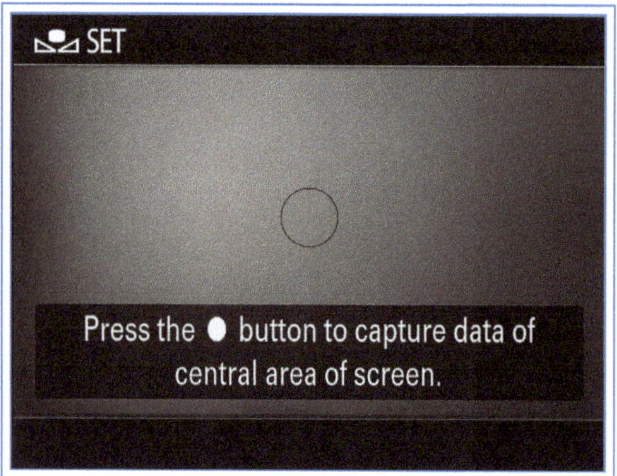

Figure 4-93. Message to Capture Data for Custom White Balance

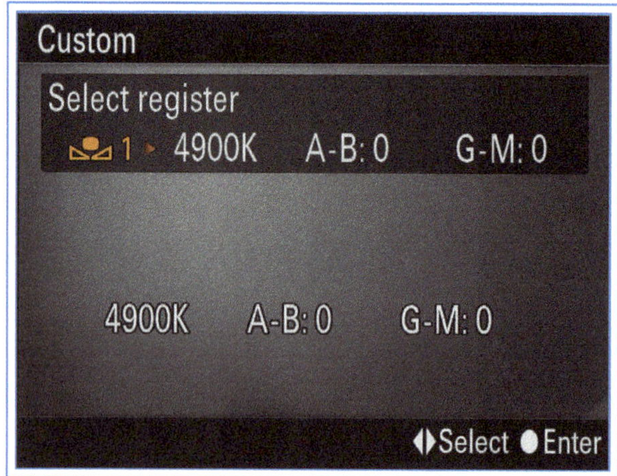

Figure 4-94. Message After Setting Custom White Balance

There is one more way to adjust the white balance setting by taking advantage of the two color axes discussed above. If you want to tweak the white balance setting to the nth degree, when you have highlighted your desired setting on the White Balance menu (whether a preset, color temperature, or custom setting), press the Right button, and you will see a screen for fine adjustments, as shown in Figure 4-95.

This screen has a pair of axes that intersect at a zero point marked by an orange dot. The axes are labeled G, B, M, and A for green, blue, magenta, and amber.

You can now use all four direction buttons to move the orange dot along either of the axes to adjust these four values until you have the color balance exactly how you want it. You also can use the control wheel to adjust the G-M axis. Press the Center button to confirm the setting.

Figure 4-95. Screen to Fine-tune White Balance Setting

Be careful to undo any adjustments using these axes when they are no longer needed; otherwise, the adjustments will alter the colors of all of your images that are shot with this white balance setting in a shooting mode for which white balance can be adjusted, even after the camera has been powered off and then back on.

Some final notes about white balance: First, if you shoot using Raw quality, you can always correct the white balance after the fact in your Raw software. So, if you are using Raw, you don't have to worry so much about what setting you are using for white balance. Still, it's a good idea always to check the setting before shooting to avoid getting caught with incorrect white balance when you are not using the Raw format.

Second, before you decide to use the "correct" white balance in every situation, consider whether that is the best course of action to get the results you want. For example, I know of one photographer who generally keeps his camera set for Daylight white balance even when shooting indoors because he likes the "warmer" appearance that comes from using that setting. I don't necessarily recommend that approach, but it's not a bad idea to give some thought to straying from a strict approach to white balance, at least on occasion.

The white balance setting is fixed to Auto White Balance in the Auto and Scene modes.

Before I leave this topic, I am including a chart in Figure 4-96 that shows how white balance settings affect images taken by the RX100 VI. I took the photos in the chart under daylight-balanced light using each available white balance setting, as indicated on the chart.

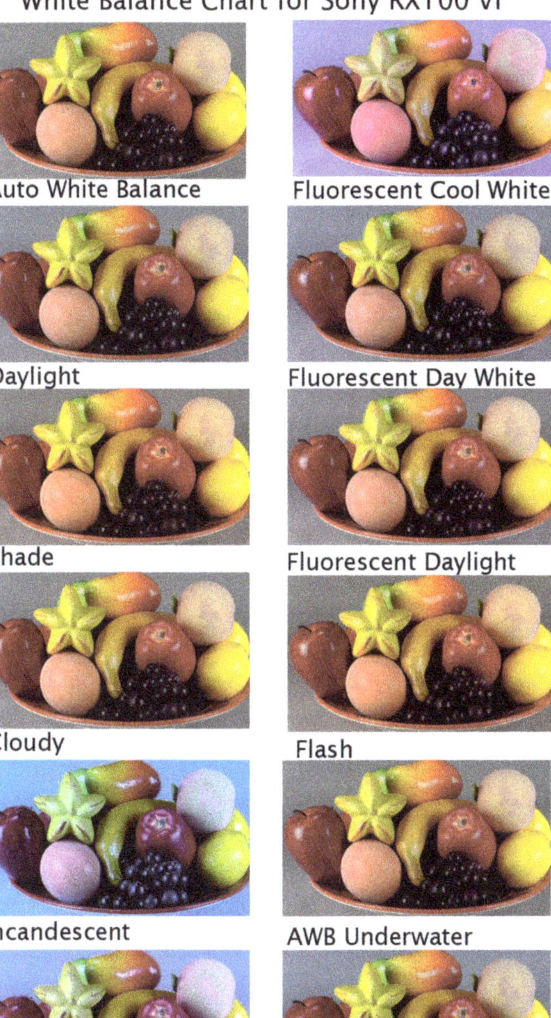

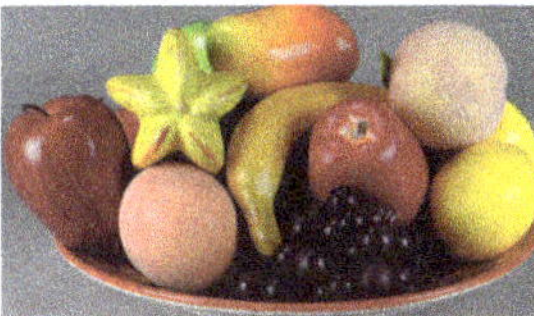

Figure 4-96. White Balance Comparison Chart

Most of the settings yielded acceptable results. The only ones that clearly look incorrect for this light source are the Incandescent, Fluorescent Warm White, and Fluorescent Cool White settings. The other settings produced variations that might be appropriate, depending on how you plan to use the images.

Priority Set in Auto White Balance

This option gives you a way to tweak the white balance of shots taken using the Auto White Balance setting. You can leave it set to its default setting of Standard, or set it to Ambient or White. It is intended for use when you are shooting a scene illuminated by incandescent lighting. If you set this option to Standard, the camera makes no change to its normal Auto White Balance setting. With Ambient, the camera adjusts the white balance to the warmer side, making the shot appear a bit more yellowish than it would otherwise. With the White setting, the camera adjusts to the cooler side, producing a more ice-tinged white.

I generally leave this setting at the Standard option, but if you are doing extensive shooting under incandescent lighting using the Auto White Balance setting, this menu item gives you a way to make a mild adjustment to the color balance of your images. When you set this option to Ambient or White, the camera displays an AWB icon on the detailed shooting screen that reflects that setting.

DRO/Auto HDR

The next option on the Camera Settings1 menu lets you control the dynamic range of your shots using the DRO/HDR processing of the RX100 VI. These settings can help correct problems with excessive contrast in your images. Such issues arise because digital cameras cannot easily process a wide range of dark and light areas in the same image—that is, their "dynamic range" is limited. So, if you are taking a picture in an area that is partly lit by bright sunlight and partly in deep shade, the resulting image is likely to have some dark areas in which details are lost in the shadows, or some areas in which highlights, or bright areas, are excessively bright, or "blown out," so, again, the details of the image are lost.

One way to deal with this situation is to use high dynamic range (HDR) techniques, in which multiple photographs of the same scene with different exposures are combined into a composite image that has clear details throughout the entire scene. The RX100 VI can take HDR shots on its own, or you can take separate exposures yourself and combine them in software on a computer into a composite HDR image. I will discuss those HDR techniques later in this chapter.

The RX100 VI's DRO (dynamic range optimizer) setting gives you another way to deal with the problem of uneven lighting, with special processing in the camera that can boost details in dark areas and reduce overexposure in bright areas at the same time, resulting in a single image with better-balanced exposure than would be possible otherwise. To do this, the DRO setting uses digital processing to reduce highlight blowout and pull details out of the shadows.

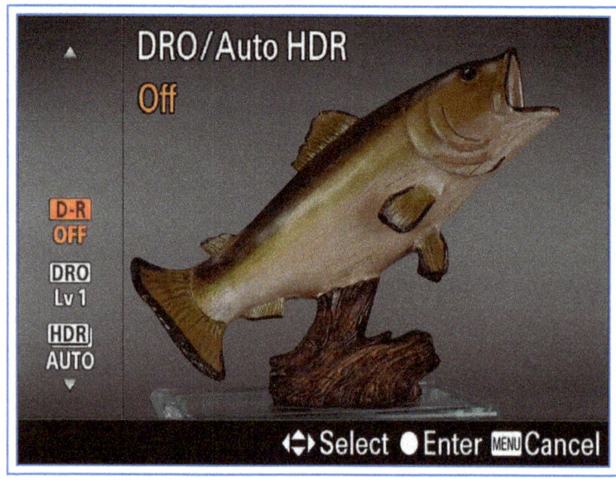

Figure 4-97. DRO/Auto HDR Menu

To use the DRO feature, press the Menu button and highlight this option, then press the Center button to bring the DRO/Auto HDR menu up on the camera's display, as shown in Figure 4-97. Scroll through the options on that menu using the Up and Down buttons or by turning the control wheel.

With DRO Off, no special processing is used. With the second choice, press the Right and Left buttons to move through the DRO choices: Auto, or Level 1 through Level 5. With the Auto setting, the camera analyzes the scene to pick an appropriate amount of DRO processing. Otherwise, you can pick the level; the higher the number, the greater the processing to even out contrast between light and dark areas.

Figures 4-98 through 4-100 are examples of various levels of DRO processing for images taken under conditions of bright sunlight and shadows, ranging from Off to Level 5. As you can see, the greater the level of DRO used, the more evenly the RX100 VI processed lighting in the scene, primarily by enhancing details in the shadowy areas.

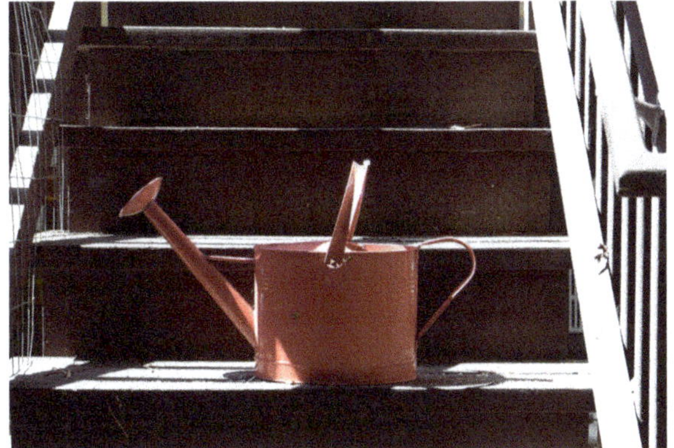

Figure 4-98. DRO Turned Off

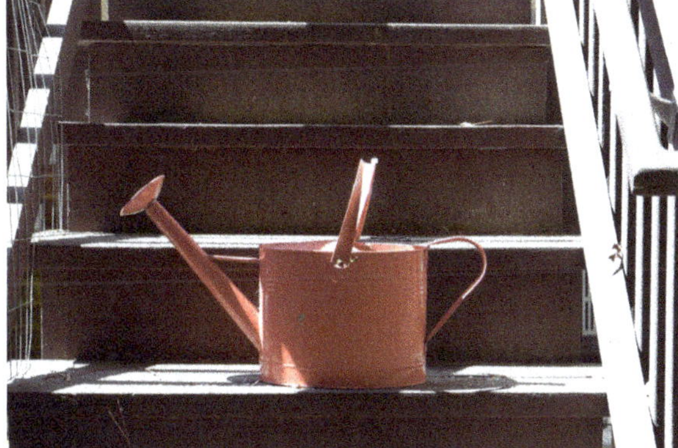

Figure 4-99. DRO Set to LV3

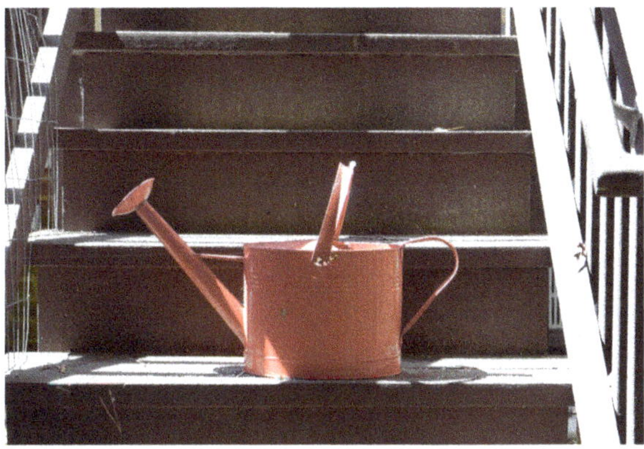

Figure 4-100. DRO Set to LV5

There is some risk of increasing visual noise in the dark areas with this sort of processing, but the RX100 VI does not seem to do badly in this respect; I have not seen increased noise levels in images processed with the DRO feature.

The final option for this item, HDR, involves in-camera HDR processing. With traditional HDR processing, the photographer takes two or more shots of a scene with contrasting lighting, some underexposed and others overexposed, and merges them using Photoshop or HDR software to blend differently exposed portions from all of the images. The end result is a composite HDR image with clear details throughout all parts of the photograph.

Because of the popularity of HDR, many makers have incorporated some degree of HDR processing into their cameras in an attempt to help the cameras even out areas of excessive brightness and darkness to preserve details. With the RX100 VI, Sony has provided an automatic method for taking multiple shots that the camera combines internally to achieve one HDR composite image. To use this feature, highlight the bottom option on the DRO/Auto HDR menu, as shown in Figure 4-101.

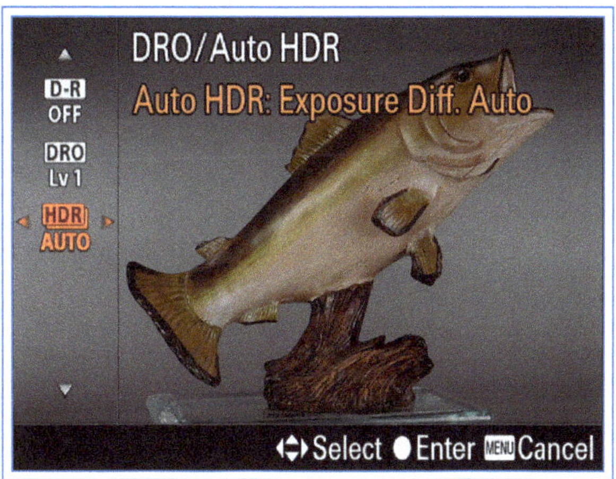

Figure 4-101. HDR Option Highlighted on Menu

Press the Right and Left buttons to scroll through the various options for the HDR setting until you have highlighted the one you want, then press the Center button to select that option and exit to the shooting screen. The available options are Auto HDR and HDR with EV settings from 1.0 through 6.0.

If you select Auto HDR, the camera will analyze the scene and the lighting conditions and select a level of exposure difference on its own. If you select a specific level from 1.0 to 6.0, the camera will use that level as the overall difference among the three shots it takes.

For example, if you select 1.0 EV for the exposure difference, the camera will take three shots, each 0.5 EV level (f-stop) different in exposure from the next—one shot at the metered EV level, one shot at 0.5 EV lower, and one shot at 0.5 EV higher. If you choose the maximum exposure difference of 6.0 EV, then the shots will be 3.0 EV apart in their brightness levels.

When you press the shutter button, the camera will take three shots in a quick burst; you should either use a tripod or hold the camera very steady. When it has finished processing the shots, the camera will save the composite image as well as the single image that was taken at the metered exposure.

For Figure 4-102 through Figure 4-105, I took shots of a birdhouse in an area that was partly in bright light and partly in shade, to illustrate the effectiveness of the HDR settings. For Figure 4-102, HDR was turned off; for Figure 4-103, it was set at 3.0EV; for Figure 4-104, HDR was set to its highest value, 6.0EV. The image using HDR at 6.0EV gave the best results in terms of pulling details out of the shadows.

For comparison, I took several shots of the subject using a range of exposure levels in Manual exposure mode. I merged those images together in Photomatix Pro software and tweaked the result until I got what seemed to be the optimal dynamic range.

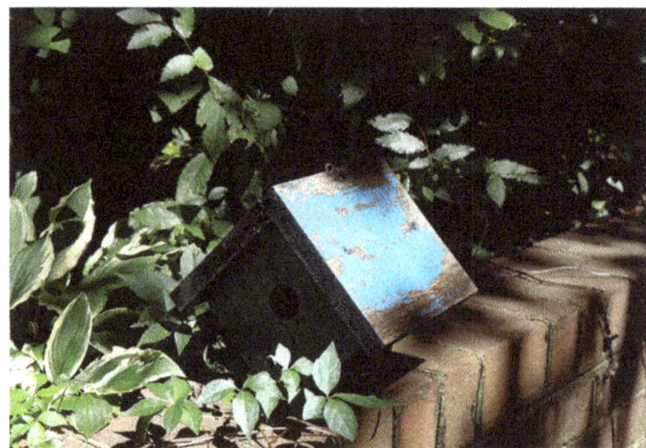

Figure 4-102. HDR Turned Off

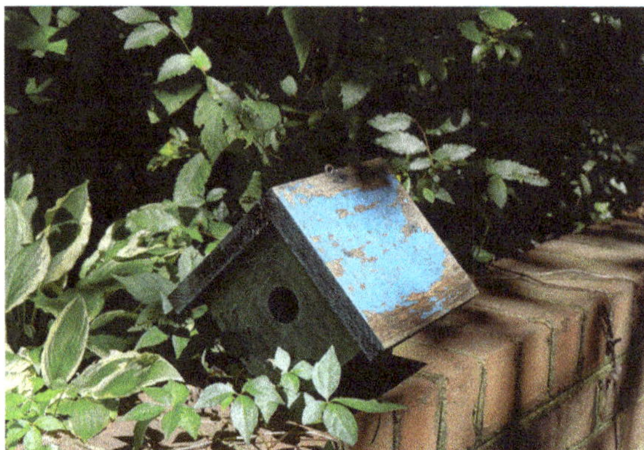

Figure 4-103. HDR Set to 3.0EV

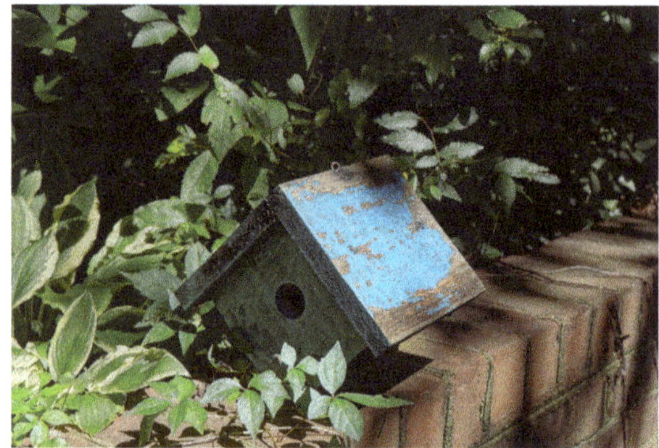

Figure 4-104. HDR Set to 6.0EV

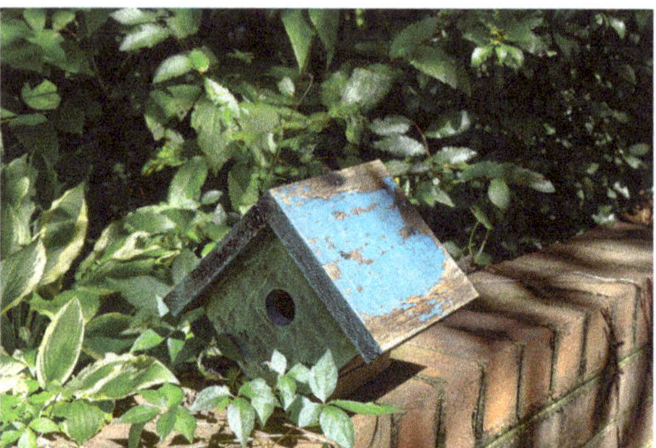

Figure 4-105. Composite Image from Photomatix Pro Software

In my opinion, the HDR image done in software, shown in Figure 4-105, did a better job of evening out the contrast than the Auto HDR images processed in the camera. However, these images were taken under fairly extreme conditions. The in-camera HDR option is an excellent option for subjects that are partly shaded and partly in sunlight, when you don't have the time or inclination to take multiple pictures and combine them later with HDR software into a composite image.

My recommendation is to leave the DRO Auto setting turned on for general shooting, especially if you don't plan to do post-processing. If the contrast in lighting for a given scene is extreme, then try at least some shots using the Auto HDR feature.

If you are planning to do post-processing, you may want to use the Raw setting for File Format (Still Images) so you can work with the shots later using software to achieve evenly exposed final images. You also could use Manual exposure mode or exposure bracketing to take shots at different exposures and merge them with Photoshop, Photomatix, or other HDR software. The RX100 VI provides high levels of dynamic range in its Raw files, particularly if you shoot with low ISO settings. Therefore, you very well may be able to bring details out of the shadows and reduce overexposure in highlighted areas using your Raw processing software.

Note that the Auto HDR setting cannot be used if you are using the Raw format for your images. The other DRO settings do work with Raw images, but they will have no effect on the Raw images unless you process them with Sony's Imaging Edge software or some other software that has been programmed to recognize the DRO settings embedded in the Raw files. When I used Adobe Camera Raw to open a Raw file taken by the RX100 VI with DRO set to LV5, the image did not show any effects of the DRO processing.

You cannot adjust DRO and Auto HDR settings in the Auto, Scene, and Sweep Panorama modes. With the Sunset, Night Scene, Hand-held Twilight, Night Portrait, Anti Motion Blur, and Fireworks settings, and in Sweep Panorama mode, DRO/Auto HDR is turned off. With other scene types and in Auto mode, DRO is turned on. DRO/HDR cannot be used when Multi Frame Noise Reduction, Picture Effect, or Picture Profile is active. You can use flash with the DRO/HDR settings, but it will fire only for the first HDR shot, and it defeats the purpose of the settings to use flash, so you probably should not do so.

Creative Style

The Creative Style setting provides options for altering the appearance of images with in-camera adjustments to their contrast, saturation (color intensity), and sharpness. Using these settings, you can add or subtract intensity of color or make subtle changes to the look of your images, as well as shoot in monochrome. Of course, if you plan to edit your images on a computer using software such as Photoshop, you can duplicate these effects readily at that stage. But, if you don't want to spend time processing your images in that way, having the ability to alter the look of your shots using this menu option can add a good deal to the enjoyment of your photos.

To use this feature, highlight Creative Style on screen 9 of the Camera Settings1 menu and press the Center button to go to the next screen, as shown in Figure 4-106. Using the Up and Down buttons or turning the control wheel, scroll through the 13 main settings: Standard, Vivid, Neutral, Clear, Deep, Light, Portrait, Landscape, Sunset, Night Scene, Autumn Leaves, Black and White, and Sepia. If you want to choose one of these settings with no further adjustment, just press the Center button when your chosen option is highlighted.

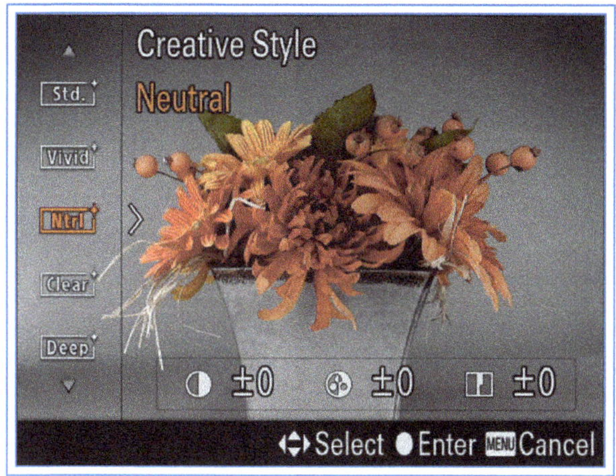

Figure 4-106. Creative Style Menu

If you use an option other than Standard, you may see a change on the display in shooting mode. For example, if you choose Sepia or Black and White, the screen will have that coloration.

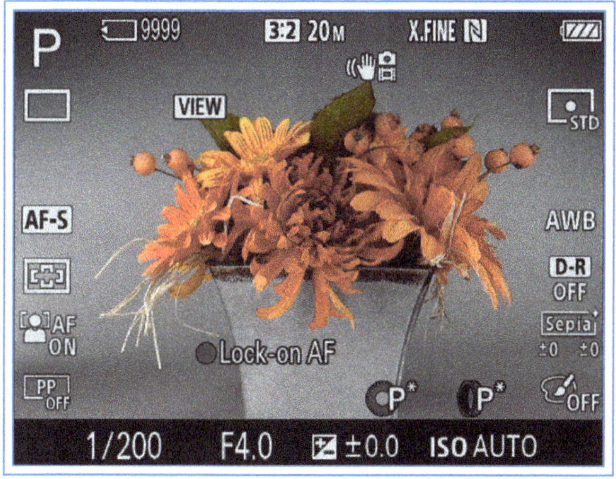

Figure 4-107. Shooting Screen with Setting Effect Off

This effect will be visible, though, only if the Live View Display option on screen 7 of the Camera Settings2 menu is set to Setting Effect On. If that menu option is set to Setting Effect Off, the display will not show any change from the Creative Style setting. You will still see an icon showing which setting is in effect, in the lower right of the screen. For example, Figure 4-107 shows the display when the Sepia setting is active but Setting Effect is off. (The VIEW indicator in the upper middle of the display indicates that Setting Effect is turned off.)

Adjusting Contrast, Saturation, and Sharpness

To fine-tune contrast, saturation, or sharpness for a Creative Style setting, move the highlight bar to the setting, such as Portrait, and press the Right button to put a new bar on the right of the screen. You will see a label above a line of icons at the bottom of the screen, as shown in Figure 4-108.

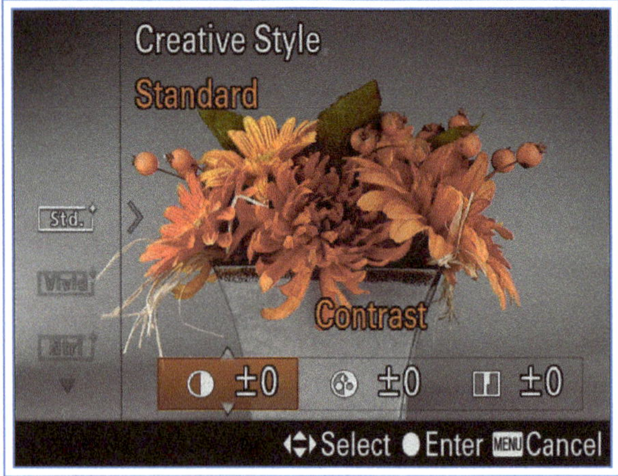

Figure 4-108. Creative Style Adjustments Screen

As you move the highlight over each icon with the Left and Right buttons, the label will change to show which value is active and ready to be adjusted. When the chosen value (contrast, saturation, or sharpness) is highlighted, use the Up and Down buttons or turn the control wheel to adjust the value upward or downward by up to three units. When the Black and White or Sepia setting is active, there are only two adjustments available—contrast and sharpness. Saturation is not available because it adjusts the intensity of colors and there are no colors to adjust for those two settings.

By varying the amounts of these three parameters, you can achieve a range of different appearances for your images. For example, by increasing saturation, you can add punch and make colors stand out. By adding contrast and/or sharpness, you can impose a "harder" appearance on your images, making them look grittier and more realistic. Figure 4-109 was taken with the Standard setting with all three parameters adjusted to their minimums, and Figure 4-110 was taken with the same setting, but with the contrast, sharpness, and saturation all adjusted to their maximum levels of +3 units. As you can see, Figure 4-110 is noticeably brighter, with a crisper look than that in Figure 4-109.

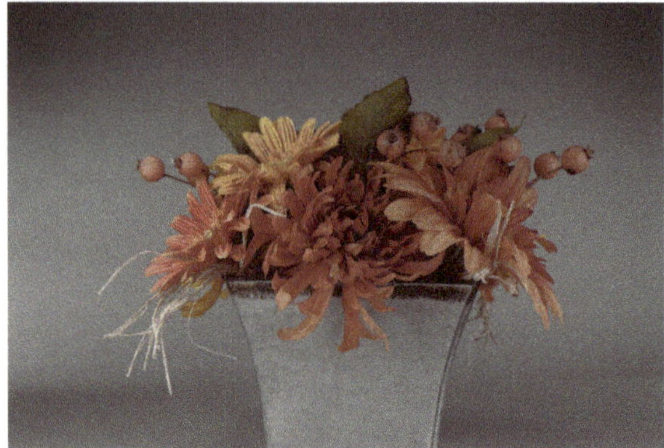

Figure 4-109. Creative Style Adjustments at Minimums

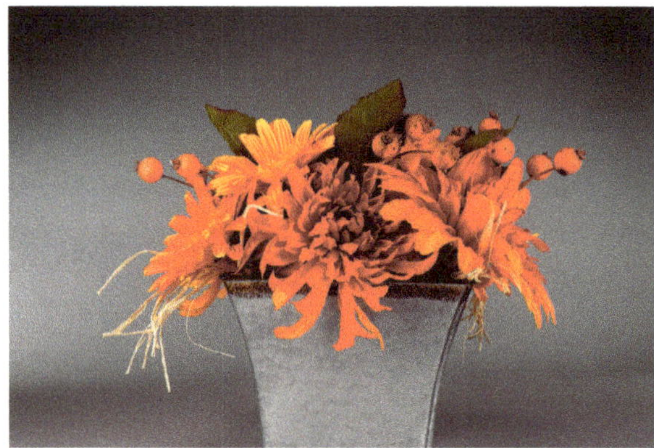

Figure 4-110. Creative Style Adjustments at Maximums

If you want to save the adjusted settings for future use, you can create and save six different custom versions, using any of the 13 basic settings with whatever adjustments you want. To do this, scroll down on the Creative Style menu to the numbered items, starting just below the Sepia item, as shown in Figure 4-111.

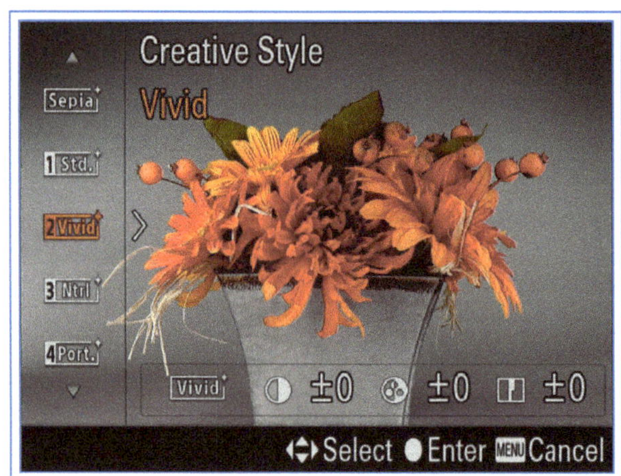

Figure 4-111. Numbered Icons for Storing Custom Creative Style Settings

There are six numbered icons, of which the first four are visible on the screen shown here. They all work in the same way. Highlight a numbered icon, then, using the

Right button, move the highlight to the right side of the screen, on the name of the setting (Vivid, Neutral, Deep, etc.). Use the control wheel or the Up and Down buttons to select any one of the 13 basic Creative Style settings. Then scroll to the right and adjust contrast, saturation, and sharpness as you want them. When all the adjustments are made, press the Center button to accept them. Whenever you want to recall that customized setting for later use, call up the Creative Style menu and scroll to the numbered icon for the style you adjusted.

The Creative Style option works with all shooting modes except Auto mode and Scene mode. You can use it with the Raw format, but the results will vary depending on the Raw-conversion software you use. For example, when I shot a Raw image in Program mode using the Black and White setting, the image showed up in black and white on the camera's screen. However, when I opened the image in Adobe Camera Raw software, the image was in color; that software ignored the information in the image's data about the Creative Style setting.

When I opened the image using Sony's Imaging Edge software, though, the image appeared in black and white, because Sony's software recognized the Creative Style information recorded by the camera. So, if you want to use this menu option with Raw files, be aware that not all software will use that data when processing the images.

The Creative Style menu option cannot be used when the Picture Effect or Picture Profile option is in use.

Figures 4-112 and 4-113 include comparison photos showing each Creative Style setting as applied to the same subject under the same lighting conditions to illustrate the different effects you can achieve with each variation. General descriptions of these effects are provided after the comparison charts.

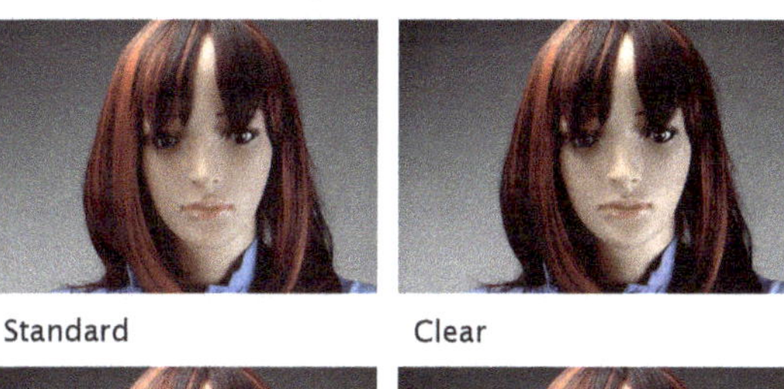

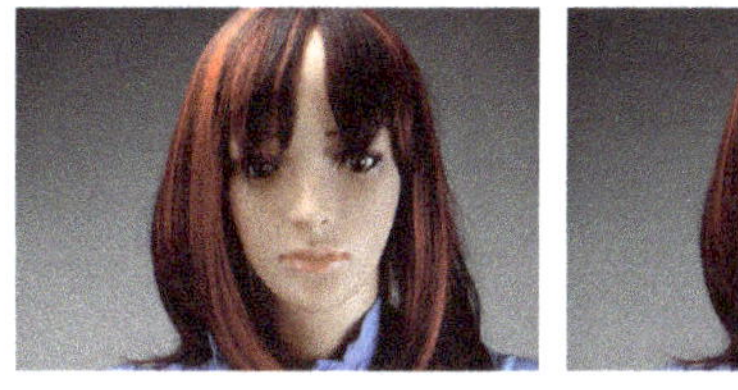

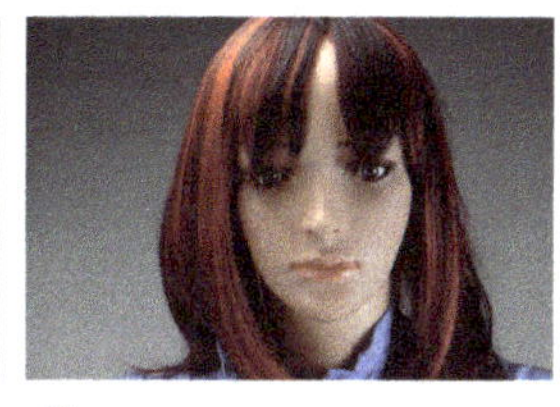

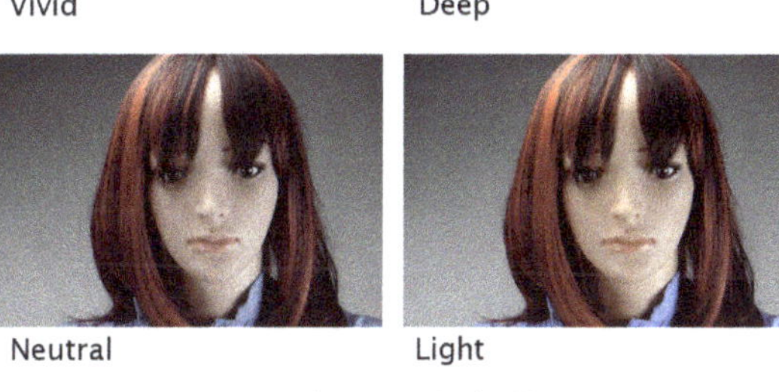

Figure 4-112. Creative Style Chart - Part 1

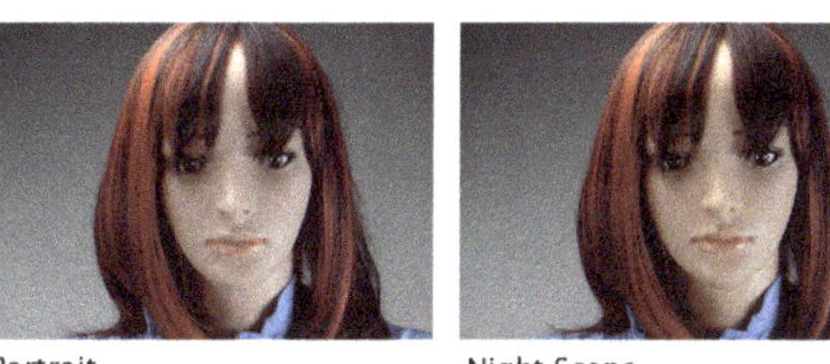

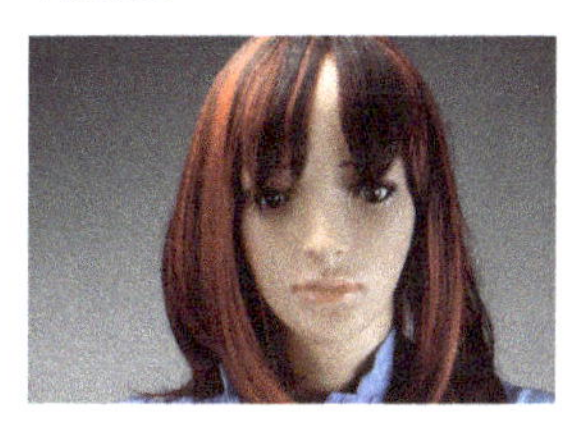

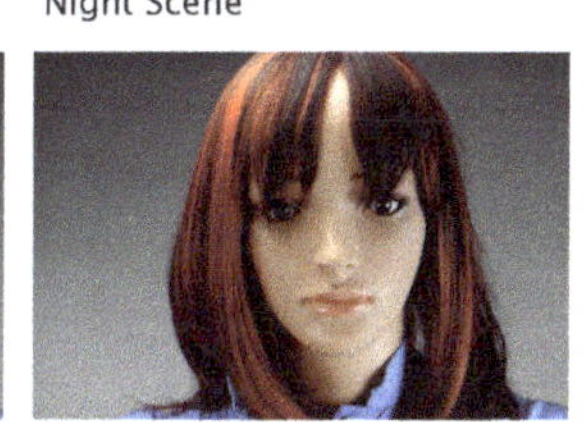

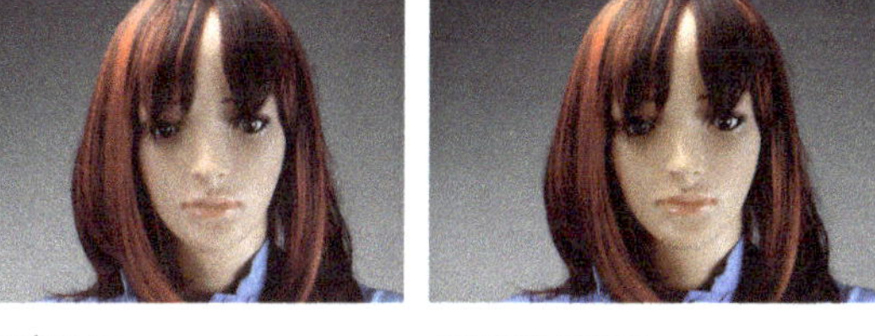

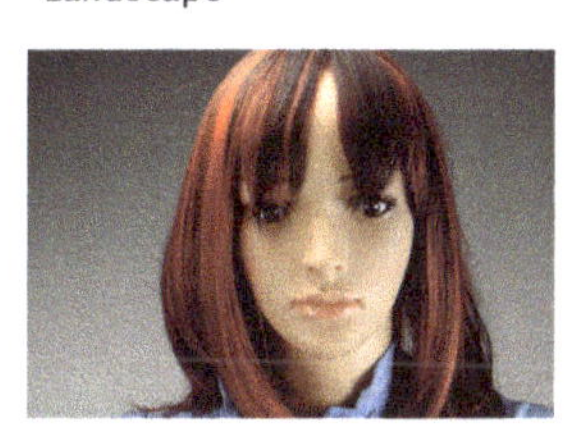

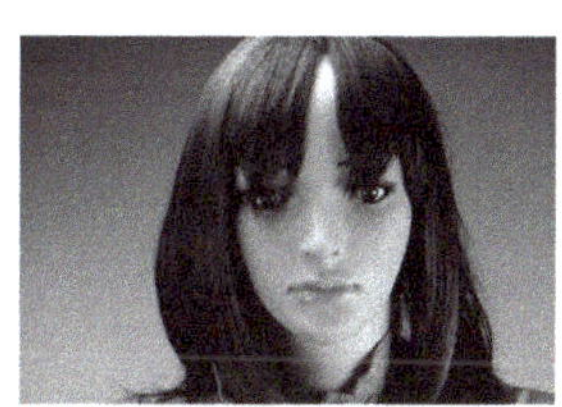

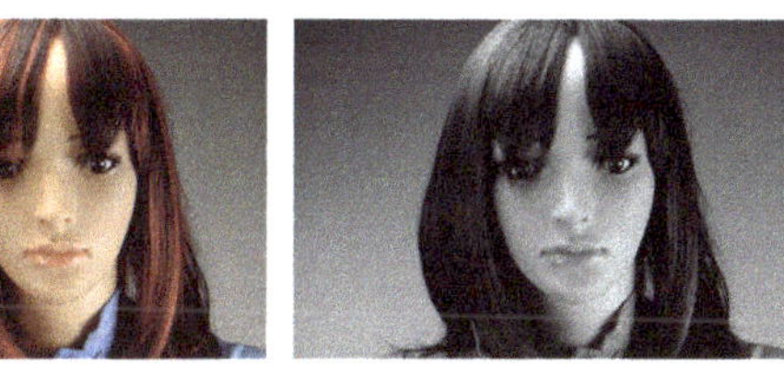

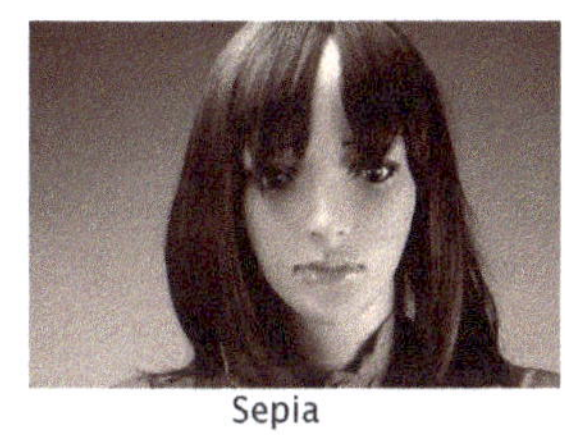

Figure 4-113. Creative Style Chart - Part 2

Standard

The Standard setting uses what Sony considers to be appropriate processing to give a pleasing overall appearance for everyday photographs, with some enhancements to make color photographs appear bright and sharp. This option is intended to be a good default setting for general purposes.

Vivid

The Vivid setting increases the saturation, or intensity, of all colors in the image, as well as the contrast. As you can see from the samples, it calls attention to the scene, though it does not produce dramatic effects. The Vivid setting might work well to emphasize the colors in images taken at a birthday party or at a carnival.

Neutral

With the Neutral setting, the RX100 VI leaves images with reduced saturation and sharpness, so you can process them to your own taste using software.

Clear

The Clear option emphasizes the highlighted areas in an image, giving them added intensity. Some users feel this setting yields images with more intensity than the Vivid setting.

Deep

Sony says that this setting is intended to show the "solid presence" of the subject. In effect, it emphasizes the shadow tones and lowers the overall brightness of the image.

Light

This setting is the opposite of Deep; it emphasizes the highlight tones and results in a brighter, lighter appearance.

Portrait

The main feature of the Portrait setting is a reduction in the saturation and sharpness of colors to soften the appearance of skin tones. You might want to use this setting to take portraits that are flattering rather than harsh and realistic. Because this setting provides midrange values for the colors and contrast, some photographers find this to be their favored Creative Style setting for general photography.

Landscape

With the Landscape setting, the RX100 VI increases all three values—contrast, saturation, and sharpness—to make the features of a landscape, such as trees and mountains, stand out with clear, sharp outlines. It is similar to Portrait in its processing of colors, but the sharper outlines and contrast might be too strong for portraits.

Sunset

With the Sunset option, the camera increases the saturation to emphasize the red hues of the sunset. In my opinion, this setting produces more changes in color images than any of the others.

Night Scene

Night Scene lowers contrast in an attempt to soften the harsh effect that may result from shots taken in dark surroundings, without affecting the saturation or hues of the colors.

Autumn Leaves

This setting, designed for enhancing shots of fall foliage, increases the intensity of existing red and yellow tones in the image, but does not alter the color balance or introduce new reddish shades, as the Sunset setting does.

B/W

This setting removes all color, converting the scene to black and white. Some photographers use this setting to achieve a realistic look for their street photography.

Sepia

This second monochrome setting also removes the color from the image, but adds a sepia tone that gives an old-fashioned appearance to the shot.

The RX100 VI also has settings for Portrait, Landscape, Sunset, and Night Scene in Scene mode, discussed in Chapter 3. However, the similar settings of the Creative Style option are available in the more advanced shooting modes, including Program, Aperture Priority, Shutter Priority, and Manual exposure, so you have access to settings such as ISO, metering mode, and others. And, as noted above, you can tweak Creative Style settings by fine-tuning contrast, saturation, and sharpness.

I don't often use the Creative Style settings, because I prefer to shoot with the Raw format and process my images in software such as Photoshop. I occasionally use the Sunset setting to enhance an evening view. The Creative Style settings are of value to a photographer who needs to take numerous photographs with a certain appearance and process them quickly. For example, a wedding or sports photographer may not have time to process images in software; he or she may need to capture hundreds of images in a particular visual style and have them ready for a client or a publication without delay. For this type of application, the Creative Style settings are invaluable. The settings also are useful for any photographer who wants to maintain a consistent appearance of his or her images and is not satisfied with how the JPEG files look when captured with the factory-standard settings.

Picture Effect

The Picture Effect menu option includes a rich array of settings for shooting images with in-camera special effects. The Sony RX100 VI gives you a variety of ways to add creative touches to your shots, and the Picture Effect settings can produce excellent results.

The Picture Effect settings are not available in the Auto, Scene, or Sweep Panorama modes and do not work with Raw images. If you set a Picture Effect option and then select Raw (or Raw & JPEG) for Quality, the Picture Effect setting will be canceled. However, with a Picture Effect setting turned on, you still have control over many of the most important settings, including JPEG Image Size, white balance, ISO, and even, in most cases, drive mode. So, unlike the situation with the Scene mode settings, when you select a Picture Effect option, you are still free to control the means of taking your images as well as other aspects of their appearance.

To use these effects, select the Picture Effect menu option as seen in Figure 4-114, and scroll through the choices at the left using the control wheel or the Up and Down buttons.

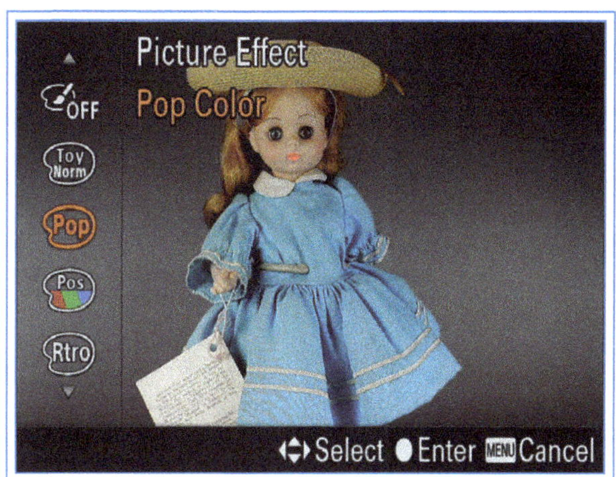

Figure 4-114. Picture Effect Menu

Some selections have no other options, and some have sub-settings that you can choose by pressing the Left and Right buttons.

I will discuss each option in turn and include sample images taken with each of the effects.

Off

The top setting on the Picture Effect menu is used to cancel all Picture Effect settings. When you are engaged in ordinary picture-taking or video shooting, you should make sure the Off setting is selected so that no unwanted special effects interfere with your images.

Toy Camera

The Toy Camera option is an alternative to using one of the "toy" film cameras such as the Holga, Diana, or Lomo, which are popular with hobbyists and artists who use them to take photos with grainy, low-resolution appearances. With all of the Toy Camera settings, the RX100 VI processes the image so it looks as if it were taken by a camera with a cheap lens: The image is dark at the corners and somewhat blurry.

The several sub-settings for Toy Camera, reached by pressing the Right and Left buttons, act as follows:

Normal: No additional processing.

Cool: Adjusts color to the "cool" side, resulting in a bluish tint.

Warm: Uses a "warm" white balance, giving a reddish hue.

Green: Adds a green tint, similar to dialing in an adjustment on the green axis for white balance.

Magenta: Similar to the Green setting, but adjustment is along the magenta axis.

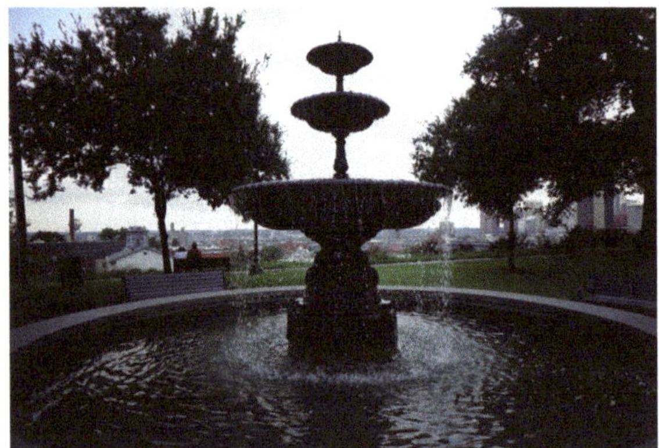

Figure 4-115. Toy Camera Example

I took Figure 4-115 with the Toy Camera option using its Normal setting. This setting seemed appropriate to add a vignetting effect to an image of a fountain in a public park.

Pop Color

This setting, according to Sony, is meant to give a "vivid look" through emphasis on bright colors. As you can see in Figure 4-116, which shows a colorful sculpture in the botanical garden, this setting is another way to add "punch" and intensity, along with added brightness, to color images.

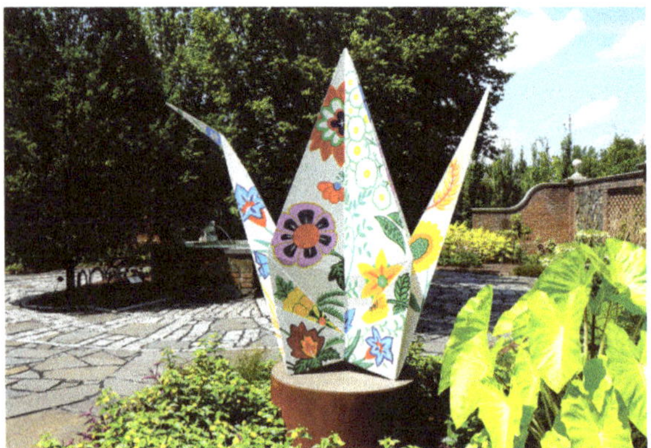

Figure 4-116. Pop Color Example

Posterization

This is a dramatic effect. Using the Right and Left buttons, you can choose to apply this effect in color or in black and white. In either case, the camera places extra emphasis on colors (or dark and light areas if you select black and white) and uses a high-contrast, pastel-like look. It is somewhat like an exotic type of HDR processing. The number of different colors (or shades of gray) used in the image is decreased to make it look as if the image were created from just a few poster paints; the result has an unrealistic but dramatic effect, as you can see in Figure 4-117, with its view of chairs in front of a brick wall, taken with -0.7 EV of exposure compensation.

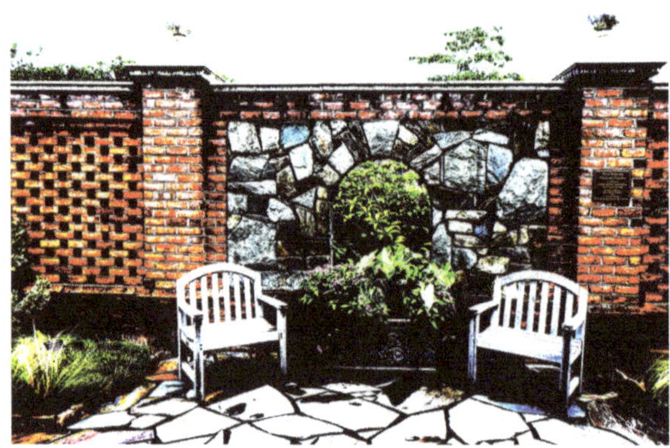

Figure 4-117. Posterization Example

Remember that with all Picture Effect settings, you can adjust other settings, including white balance, exposure compensation, and others. With Posterization, you might use exposure compensation, which can change the appearance of this effect dramatically. I have found the results with this setting often are improved by using negative exposure compensation to avoid excessive brightness, as I did with this image. I recommend using Posterization to achieve a striking effect, perhaps for a distinctive-looking poster or greeting card.

Retro Photo

With this setting, the RX100 VI uses sepia tint and reduced contrast to mimic the appearance of an aging photo. This effect is not as pronounced as the sepia effects I have seen on other cameras; with the RX100 VI, a good deal of the image's original color still shows up, but there is subtle softening of the image with the sepia coloration.

In Figure 4-118 I used this effect for a shot of the city skyline from an elevated viewpoint, trying to convey an aura of an old-time photograph.

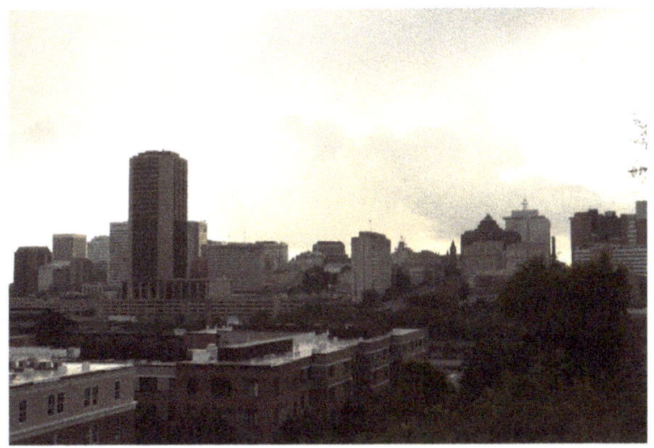
Figure 4-118. Retro Photo Example

Soft High-Key

"High key" is a technique that uses bright lighting throughout a scene for an overall look with light colors and few shadows. With the RX100 VI, Sony has added softness to give the image a light appearance without the harshness that might otherwise result from the unusually bright exposure. In Figure 4-119, I used this setting for a photo of pool surrounded by rocks in an indoor garden setting. This option was useful in adding softness and brightness to a subject that might have looked excessively dark without some such lightening.

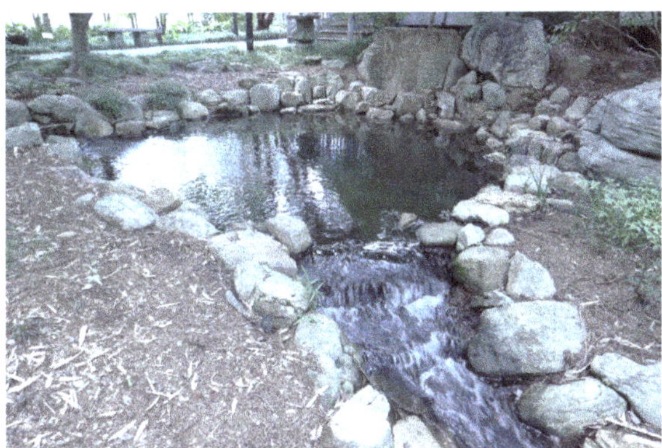
Figure 4-119. Soft High-key Example

Partial Color

The Partial Color effect lets you choose a single color to retain in an image; the camera reduces the saturation of all other colors to monochrome, so that only objects of that single hue remain in color in the image. I really enjoy this setting, which can be used to isolate a particular object with dramatic effect. In Figure 4-120, I used this setting to emphasize the red color of a train-themed playground structure in a city park.

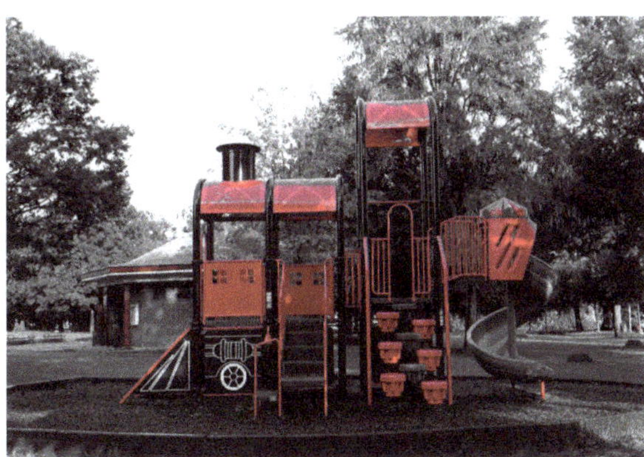
Figure 4-120. Partial Color Example

The choices for the color to be retained are red, green, blue, and yellow; use the Left and Right buttons to select one of those colors. When you aim the camera at your subject, you will see on the display what objects will show up in color, if the Live View Display menu option is set to Setting Effect On.

There is no direct way to adjust the color tolerance of this setting, so you cannot, for example, set the camera to accept a broad range of reds to be retained in the image. However, if you change the white balance setting, the camera will perceive colors differently.

So, if there is a particular object that you want to depict in color, but the camera does not "see" it as red, green, blue, or yellow, you can try selecting a different white balance setting and see if the color will be retained. You also can fine-tune the white balance using the color axes to add or subtract these hues if you want to bring a particular object within the range of the color that will be retained.

By choosing a color that does not appear in the scene at all, you can take a straight monochrome photograph.

High Contrast Monochrome

This setting lets you take black and white photographs with a stark, high-contrast appearance. You might want to consider this setting for street photography or any other situation in which you are not looking for a soft or flattering appearance.

I used this setting for Figure 4-121, an image of a group of industrial machines installed in a line near the riverfront, to emphasize their geometrical arrangement.

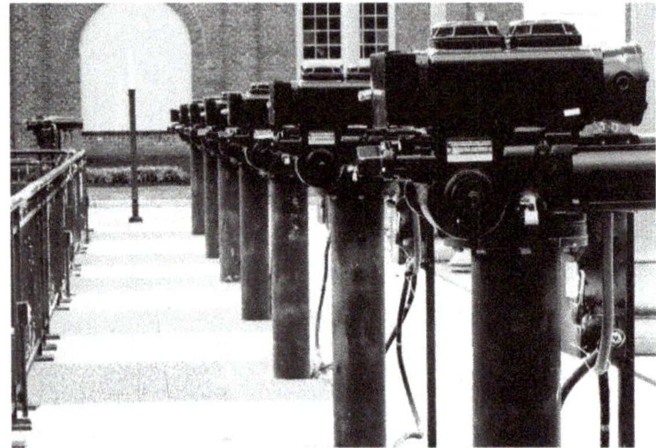

Figure 4-121. High Contrast Monochrome Example

Soft Focus

The Soft Focus effect is another setting that is variable; you can select either Low, Mid, or High by pressing the Right and Left buttons. This effect is straightforward; the camera blurs the focus to achieve a dreamlike aura. This is the first of several Picture Effect settings that cannot be previewed on the screen; you have to take the picture and then play it back to see the results of the Soft Focus setting. (As an alternative to using this setting, you can set focus mode to manual focus and defocus the image to your own taste to achieve a similar effect.)

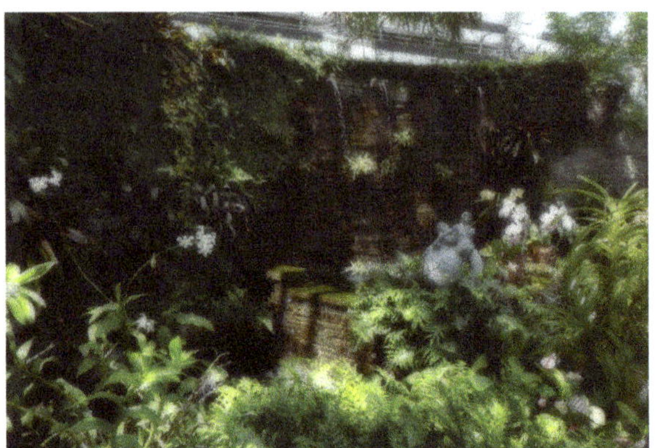

Figure 4-122. Soft Focus Example

For Figure 4-122, I used this option with its Mid setting for an image of an indoor garden and waterfall. I find that this effect is often good for adding a feeling of peacefulness to a scene.

HDR Painting

The HDR Painting setting is similar to the HDR setting of the DRO/Auto HDR menu option. With this option, the camera takes a burst of three shots at different exposure settings and combines them internally into a single image to achieve even exposure over a range of areas with differing brightness. Unlike the more standard HDR setting, this one does not let you select the specific exposure differential for the three shots, but it lets you choose Low, Mid, or High for the intensity of the effect. Also, it adds stylized processing to give the final image a painterly appearance.

I often have good results with this setting when I shoot from an indoor area through a window on a sunny day, especially when there is a variety of colorful items outside. For Figure 4-123, though, I used the Mid setting for a view of the city skyline on a day with some dramatic clouds.

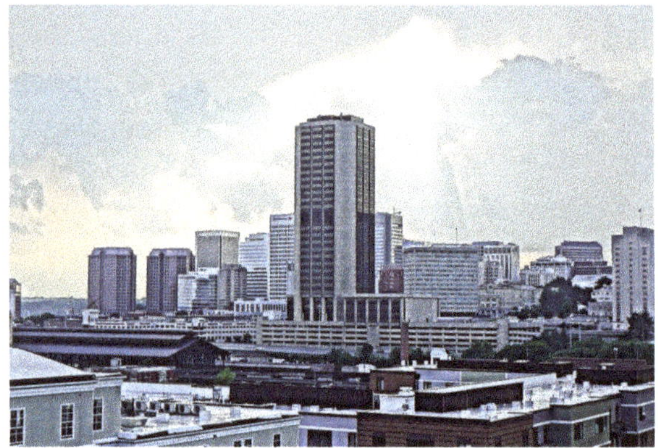

Figure 4-123. HDR Painting Example

Because the camera takes multiple images with this option, you can't preview the results on the screen before taking the picture. Using a tripod is advisable to avoid blur from camera motion while the three shots are being taken.

Rich-Tone Monochrome

The Rich-tone Monochrome setting can be viewed as a black and white version of the HDR Painting setting. With this option, like that one, the RX100 VI takes three shots at different exposures and combines them into a single composite photo with a broader dynamic range than would otherwise be possible. Unlike the color setting, though, this one does not let you select the intensity of the effect. I used it in Figure 4-124 for an image of the same view shown in the previous figure, for comparison. This setting is good for producing traditional, postcard-like views of scenic subjects.

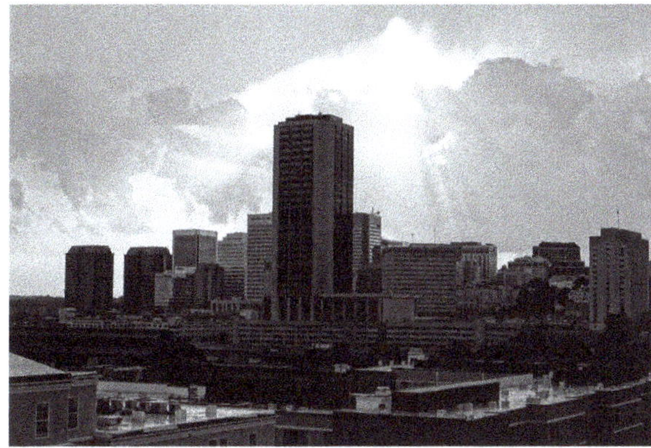

Figure 4-124. Rich-tone Monochrome Example

Miniature Effect

With the Miniature Effect option, the camera adds blurring at one or more sides or the top or bottom of an image to simulate the look of a photograph of a tabletop model or miniature. Such images often appear hazy in one or more areas, either because of the narrow depth of field of these closeup photos, or because of the use of a tilt-and-shift lens, which causes blurring at the edges.

For this feature to work well, you need an appropriate subject. I have found that this effect looks interesting when applied to something like a street scene or a train, which might actually be reproduced in a tabletop model. For example, if you are able to get a high vantage point above a road intersection or a railroad, you may be able to use this processing to make it look as if you had photographed a high-quality tabletop display.

After highlighting this option on the Camera Settings1 menu, press the Right and Left buttons to choose either Top, Middle (Horizontal), Bottom, Right, Middle (Vertical), Left, or Auto for the configuration of the effect. If you choose a specific area, that area will remain sharp.

For example, if you choose Top, then, after you take the picture, the top area (roughly one-third) will remain sharp, and the rest of the image below that area will appear blurred. If you choose Auto, the camera will select the area to remain sharp based on the area that was focused on by the autofocus system and by the camera's sensing how you are holding the camera.

You will not see how the effect will alter the image while viewing the scene, though the camera will place gray areas on the parts of the image that will ultimately be blurred to give an idea of how the final product will look. In Figure 4-125, I used this setting for an image of a city street from a high vantage point. This effect can provide a lot of fun if you experiment with it; it can take some work to find the right subject and the best arrangement of sharp and blurry areas to achieve a satisfying result.

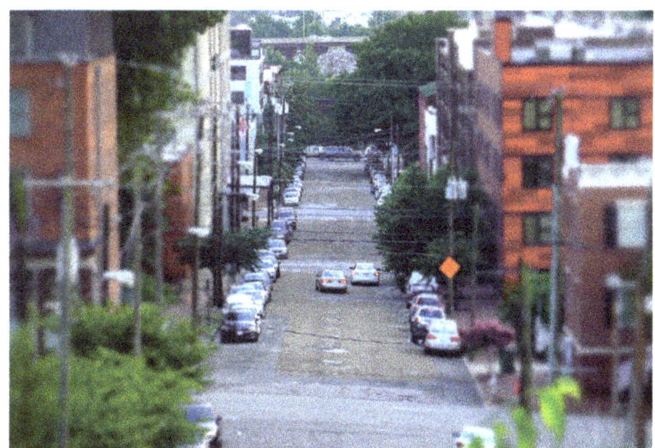

Figure 4-125. Miniature Effect Example

Watercolor

The Watercolor effect blurs the colors of an image to make it look as if it were painted with watercolors that are bleeding together. You need to choose a subject that lends itself to this sort of distortion. For example, I have found that the faces of dolls and other figures can be pleasantly altered to have an impressionistic appearance. I have also had some pleasing results with plants and trees. In Figure 4-126, I used this setting for an image of a picturesque building in the botanical garden.

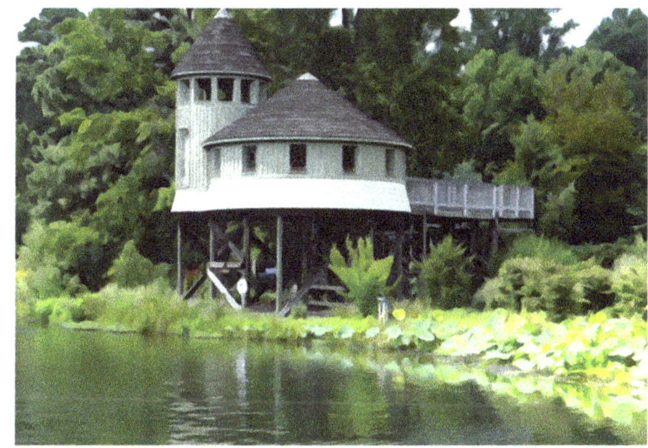

Figure 4-126. Watercolor Example

Illustration

This final option for the Picture Effect setting finds edges of objects in the scene and adds contrast to them, making the image seem like a pen-and-ink illustration that has been colored in. You can set the intensity of the effect to Low, Mid, or High using the Right and Left buttons. If you choose a subject with edges that can be outlined and a repeating pattern, you can achieve a pleasing result. This is another effect whose final result you cannot judge while viewing the live scene; you need to see the recorded image to know what the actual effect will look like.

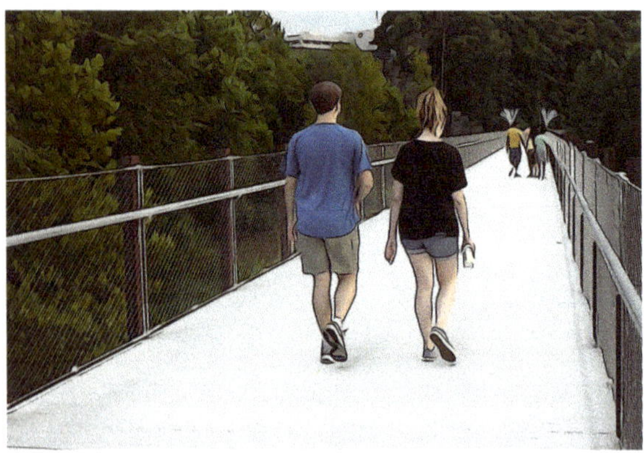

Figure 4-127. Illustration Example

As you can see in Figure 4-127, taken with Illustration set to Mid, this effect can transform an ordinary view into a stylized image while leaving the scene recognizable. The images produced with this effect may be more suited as decorative items than as depictions of actual objects or locations, but their appearance can be very striking and unusual. This setting often produces good results when people are included in the scene, especially if they are wearing clothes with bright colors.

Several of the Picture Effect options are not available for shooting movies: Soft Focus, HDR Painting, Rich-tone Monochrome, Miniature Effect, Watercolor, and Illustration. If one of those effects is turned on when you press the Movie button, the camera will turn off the effect while the movie is being recorded, and turn it back on after the recording has ended. You also cannot use continuous shooting or any type of bracketing with any of those six effects.

Picture Profile

The Picture Profile option, the final item on the ninth screen of the Camera Settings1 menu, provides powerful tools for adjusting the appearance of your files, particularly video footage. This option is similar in some ways to the Creative Style option, which provides a separate set of preset adjustments that affect image processing, as discussed earlier in this chapter. Like Creative Style, the Picture Profile option includes several presets from which you can easily choose one that suits your current needs and instantly apply it to all videos and images you record using that setting. You also can adjust several parameters within any of the Picture Profile settings, just as you can with the Creative Style settings, and you can save the adjusted settings for future use.

However, apart from those similarities, the Picture Profile option is considerably different from the Creative Style feature. Creative Style is straightforward in the adjustments it provides, both in its 13 preset options (Standard, Vivid, Neutral, etc.) and in the adjustments you can make to those settings (contrast, saturation, and sharpness). It is easy to understand what is being adjusted for the presets and to see the resulting differences in the appearance of your images and videos.

The Picture Profile option does not provide such easily categorized adjustments. These adjustments are technical ones intended for use by experienced videographers, to produce footage that is ready for post-processing, or that matches footage from other cameras using the same profile.

In this section, I will explain how to apply a Picture Profile setting and how to adjust one, and I will discuss parameters that can be tweaked for each profile. I will not try to give a detailed explanation of all possible adjustments for the various settings involved, such as gamma, knee, and detail.

To use this setting, highlight Picture Profile on the menu screen and press the Center button to display the vertical menu of settings, as shown in Figure 4-128.

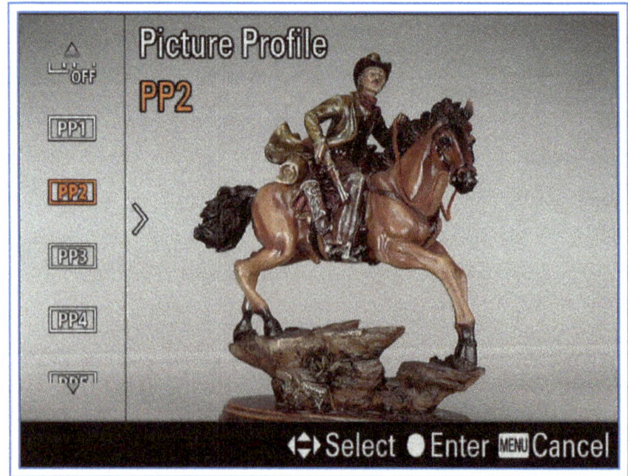

Figure 4-128. Picture Profile Menu

Use the control wheel or the Up and Down buttons to scroll through the eleven settings, including PP Off and PP1 through PP10.

If you don't need or want to bother with setting a profile, just leave this item set to PP Off and you won't have to deal with it further. To use one of the ten preset profiles, scroll to that setting and press the Center button to choose it. That profile will then be displayed in an icon in the lower left corner of the detailed shooting screen, as shown in Figure 4-129.

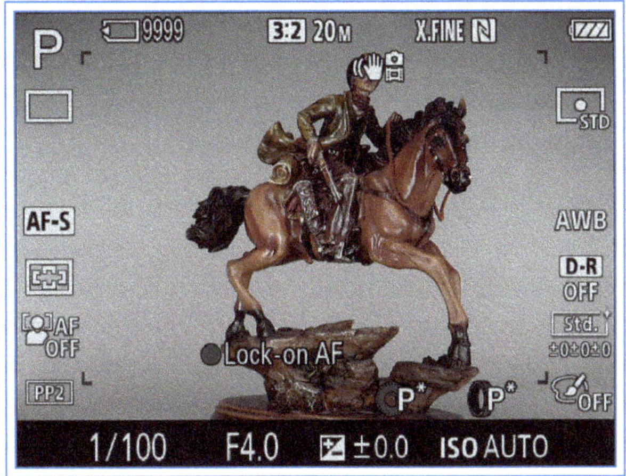

Figure 4-129. Picture Profile Icon on Shooting Screen

The basic characteristics of the ten preset profiles that come with the camera are as follows:

PP1 Uses the standard gamma curve for movies.

PP2 Uses the standard gamma curve for still images.

PP3 Uses ITU709 gamma curve for natural color tone. The ITU709 standard is the normal set of specifications for HD television. This is a good profile to use for shooting that won't need extensive post-processing. This is also good for matching footage with that of other cameras.

PP4 Uses the ITU709 standard for color tone. Should not need much post-processing for color tone.

PP5 Uses Cine1 gamma curve to reduce contrast in dark areas and modify bright areas to produce a "relaxed" color effect. Good for sunny days and conditions with high contrast.

PP6 Uses Cine2 gamma curve, optimized for editing with up to 100% video signal; generally similar to Cine1, for use with less need for post-processing to avoid clipping highlights.

PP7 Uses S-Log2 gamma curve, designed to yield increased dynamic range, for footage that will be adjusted with post-processing software.

PP8 Uses S-Log3 gamma curve, which is similar to S-Log2 but has some technical differences. See the links in Appendix C for a discussion of the differences between those two settings. This profile has Color Mode set to S-Gamut3.Cine, as opposed to PP9, which has a different setting for Color Mode.

PP9 Uses S-Log3 gamma curve with Color Mode set to S-Gamut3.

PP10 Uses HLG2 gamma curve, which can be used as the basis for recording HDR footage or images.

You should be able to get good results for general footage with any of the first four Picture Profile settings. On a particularly bright day or in contrasty conditions, you might try PP5, which uses the Cine1 gamma, designed to compress the dynamic range to avoid clipping highlights, or PP6, which uses the Cine2 gamma, which compresses the range even more.

If you will be doing post-processing to correct the color of your footage, you may want to use PP7, PP8, or PP9, which use the S-Log2 or S-Log3 gamma curve settings. With any of these options, your footage will look dull and somewhat dark as shot, but its dynamic range will be considerably greater than normal, so you will have excellent options for producing good-looking footage with your post-processing software. However, because of the way these settings expand dynamic range, they require the use of an ISO setting of 1000 or greater. So, if you use PP7, PP8, PP9, or any profile that includes S-Log2 or S-Log 3 gamma, the camera will not set the ISO any lower than 1000, and will reset a lower ISO value to 1000. (There also are some limits on ISO settings available with various other gamma settings, but those limits are not as severe as for the S-Log settings.)

If you want to record HDR video footage, you can use PP10, which includes a gamma setting of HLG2. For HDR recording, the Picture Profile setting has to include a gamma setting of HLG, HLG1, HLG2, or HLG3. PP10 is provided as a preset option that is ready to use for HDR recording. Or, you can modify it to use one of the other HLG settings for gamma.

The chart in Figure 4-130 shows the effects of the ten preset Picture Profile settings, as well as the same image with no Picture Profile in place, to give a general idea of how these settings affect an image.

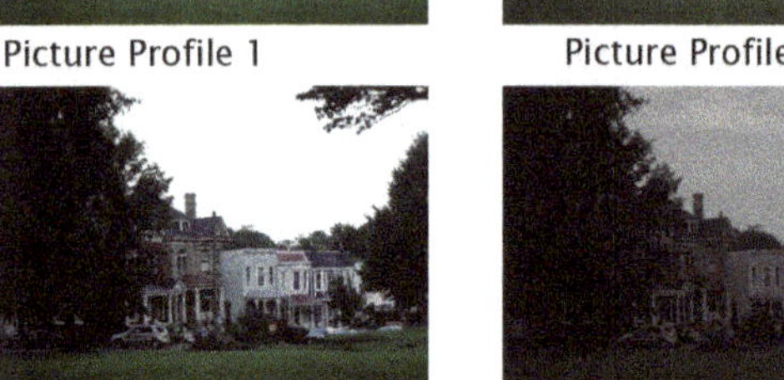
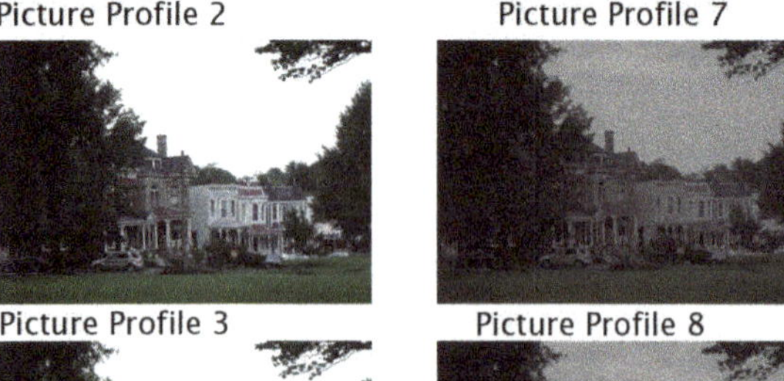
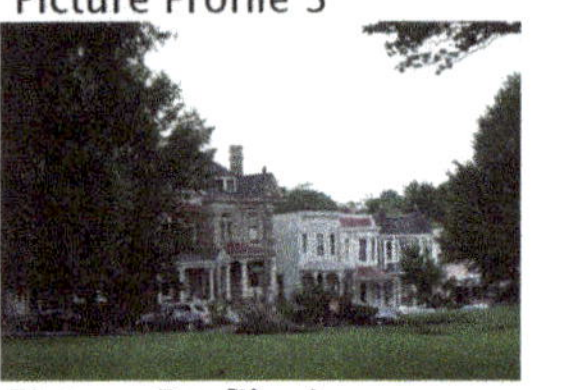
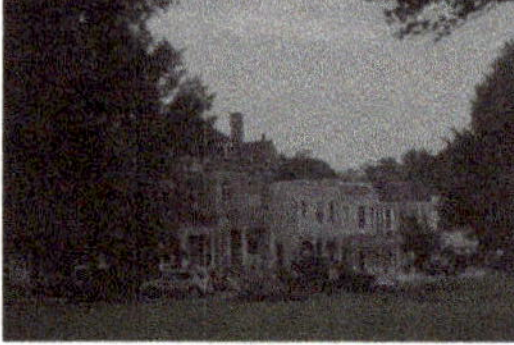
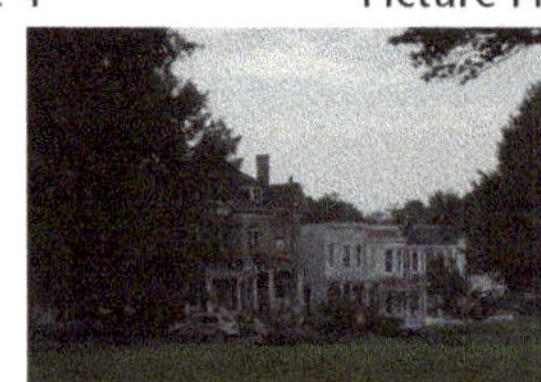

Figure 4-130. Picture Profile Comparison Chart

As you can see, PP7, PP8, and PP9, which use S-Log2 or S-Log 3 gamma, and PP10, which uses HLG2 gamma, produce a dark image on the camera's display. When you are using any of those four settings, you can activate the Gamma Display Assist feature, which sets the display to a higher level of contrast, so you can compose your shot accurately. That feature is found on screen 1 of the Setup menu. You also can assign it to a control button using the Custom Key (Still Images) or Custom Key (Movies) option on screen 9 of the Camera Settings2 menu, as discussed in Chapter 5.

If you are serious about video production, you may not be content with any of the ten preset Picture Profile settings. You can easily modify any of them in the camera. I don't recommend that you do this unless you are knowledgeable about video production, but the option is available. I will discuss the mechanics of how to adjust the various parameters for the Picture Profile settings, but I will not engage in a technical discussion of when and why to adjust them. (Appendix C has links to resources with further information.)

To adjust a Picture Profile setting, first highlight the Picture Profile menu option and press the Center button to display the menu of Picture Profile options, as shown in Figure 4-128. Scroll to the one you want to adjust and press the Right button. You will then see a screen like that in Figure 4-131, listing the first six parameters that can be adjusted: black level, gamma, black gamma, knee, color mode, and saturation.

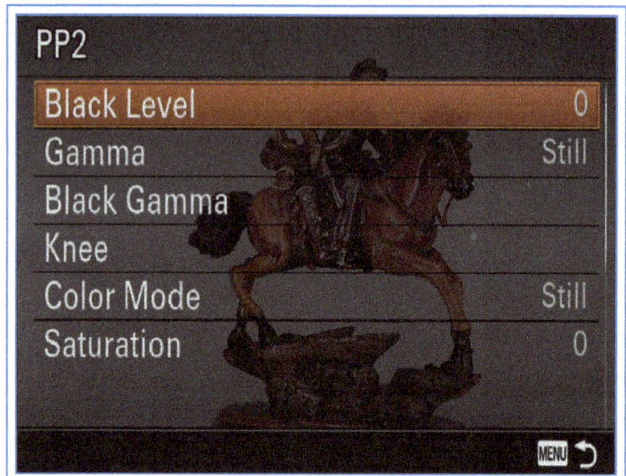

Figure 4-131. Picture Profile Parameters Adjustment Screen

Turn the control wheel or press the Up and Down buttons to scroll through this list and on to the remaining parameters: color phase, color depth, and detail. The last two options, copy and reset, are for copying the settings or restoring the default settings.

When you have highlighted a parameter to adjust, such as gamma, press the Right button or the Center button to bring up the adjustment screen, as shown in Figure 4-132.

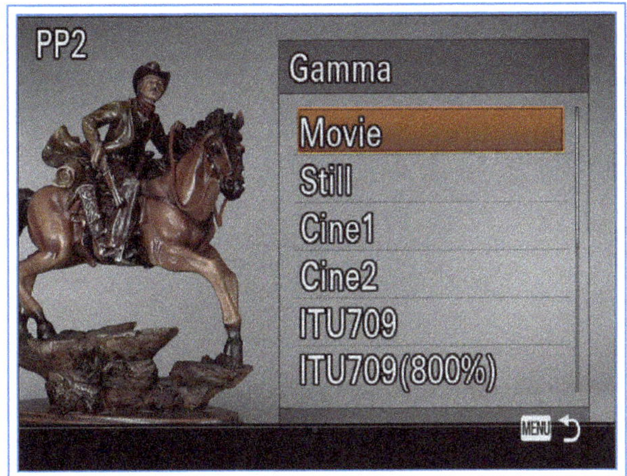

Figure 4-132. Adjustment Screen for Gamma

Use the control wheel or the Up and Down buttons to choose the value to set, and press the Center button to set the value and return to the previous screen. Continue scrolling through the parameters to set each as you want it. Once you have made the adjustments, the Picture Profile number you adjusted will retain those changes, even if the camera is turned off and back on. If you want to copy the settings from one Picture Profile slot to another, use the copy item near the bottom of the list of parameters. Use the reset option to restore the Picture Profile setting to its default values.

Following are general descriptions of the nine parameters that you can adjust for each Picture Profile setting:

Black Level. Default 0; adjustment from -15 to +15. Adjusting in the negative direction strengthens the black color in the image; adjusting in the positive direction fades or weakens it.

Gamma. No default. Choices are Movie, Still, Cine1, Cine2, ITU709, ITU709 (800%), S-Log2, S-Log3, HLG, HLG1, HLG2, or HLG3. The gamma curve is an adjustment to the video signal to account for the difference between recorded video and the output characteristics of various display devices, such as cathode ray tubes, HDTVs, etc. The first two choices are self-explanatory. Cine1 has the signal compressed to avoid clipping of highlights; Cine2 is compressed further for the same purpose. The ITU709 setting is a standard one for HDTV. The ITU709 (800%) option provides greater dynamic range than ITU709. It applies standard contrast and color levels to the video signal and turns off the knee circuit. It can be used as the finished product for video production. You may need to use this standard or S-Log2 when recording to certain external recorders. The S-Log2 standard, which provides greater-than-normal dynamic range, produces a flat, somewhat dark signal. This standard is for use when you will adjust the appearance of the video file with post-processing software. S-Log3 is similar to S-Log2 with some technical differences; see Appendix C for further information. The HLG options are variations of an industry standard setting known as Hybrid Log-Gamma. These settings are designed to provide a wider dynamic range than other settings, in a way similar to the function of the HDR setting for still images. HLG is the basic setting. Each of the other three options provides additional dynamic range, but also introduces more possibility of visual noise in the scene because of the use of lesser amounts of noise reduction. As noted earlier, PP10 includes the HLG2 setting by default.

Black Gamma. Range default is Middle; can be set to Wide or Narrow. Level default is 0; can be set from -7 to +7. Increasing Level brightens the image and decreasing Level darkens it. Adjusting Range determines whether the Level adjustment affects only blacks (Narrow) or a wider range of grays. The black gamma value is fixed at 0 when gamma is set to HLG, HLG1, HLG2, or HLG3.

Knee. The knee adjustment sets a curve for compressing the signal in the brightest parts of the video image to avoid clipping or washing out of highlights. The Mode can be set to Auto or Manual. If you select Auto, then you need to use the Auto Set option to choose the Max Point and Sensitivity. If you choose Manual, you need to use the Manual Set option to set the Point and Slope.

Color Mode. No default. Can be set to Movie, Still, Cinema, Pro, ITU709 Matrix, Black & White, S-Gamut, S-Gamut3.Cine, S-Gamut3, BT.2020, or 709. Movie is designed for use with the Movie setting for Gamma; Still for the Still setting; Cinema for the Cine1 setting; Pro for the gamma curve of Sony professional video cameras; ITU709 Matrix for use with the ITU709 gamma curve; Black & White for shooting in monochrome; S-Gamut for shooting with the S-Log2 gamma curve; S-Gamut3.Cine and S-Gamut3 for use with the S-Log3 gamma curve. BT.2020 and 709 are the only color mode settings available when gamma is set to HLG, HLG1, HLG2, or HLG3. If you select the Black & White setting, the video will be shot in black and white.

Saturation. Default 0. Can be set from -32 to +32. This adjustment is similar to the saturation adjustment available with the Creative Style menu option. A negative setting lowers the intensity of colors, reducing them almost completely to black and white at the -32 level, while a positive value increases their intensity.

Color Phase. Default 0. Can be set from -7 to +7. Adjusting in the negative or positive direction makes the colors shift their hues. You can use this setting to match the color output of the RX100 VI to that of another camera you are using for video production.

Color Depth. Default 0. Can be set from -7 to +7 for each of six colors: red, green, blue, cyan, magenta, and yellow. A higher number makes the color darker and richer; a lower number makes it brighter and paler.

Detail. There are two main settings: Level and Adjust. Level has a default of 0 and can be adjusted from -7 to +7. This setting affects the sharpness of edges in the image. A lower number softens the image and a higher number gives it sharper contrast. The other main setting, Adjust, has several settings, starting with Mode, which can be set to Auto or Manual. If you set Mode to Auto, you can ignore the other settings. If you set it to Manual, you can adjust V/H Balance, B/W Balance, Limit, Crispening (misspelled on the camera's menu), and Hi-Light Detail. Sony's user's guide recommends changing only the Level setting, at least at first, but the guide provides details on the other settings. You can see those details at Sony's website, http://helpguide.sony.net/di/pp/v1/en/index.html. If you are planning to use software to process your video, you may want to reduce Level to -7 so you can determine the proper amount of sharpening on your own.

The good news about the Picture Profile setting is that you do not need to worry about it if you don't want to. If you are shooting primarily still images or videos for your own use, you don't have to select any Picture Profile setting. However, if you are using the RX100 VI for professional video production, perhaps as a second camera, you may need to set the Picture Profile so the camera's output will match that of your other cameras.

Picture Profile cannot be used when DRO/HDR, Creative Style (other than Standard), or Picture Effect is in use. Picture Profile settings affect Raw files, but the black level, black gamma, knee, and color depth settings are not reflected in Raw images.

If you want to explore Picture Profile in greater detail, check out the resources listed in Appendix C.

The single item on screen 10 of the Camera Settings1 menu is shown in Figure 4-133.

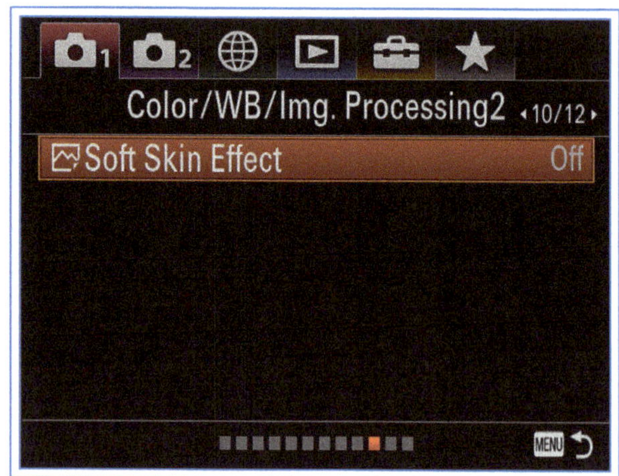

Figure 4-133. Screen 10 of Camera Settings1 Menu

Soft Skin Effect

This menu option softens skin tones in the faces of subjects for still images. The option is dimmed and unavailable in some situations, such as when one of the continuous shooting options or the Raw setting for File Format (Still Images) is selected. After you select it and turn it on, you can use the Right and Left buttons to set the level at Lo, Mid, or Hi, from the screen shown in Figure 4-134.

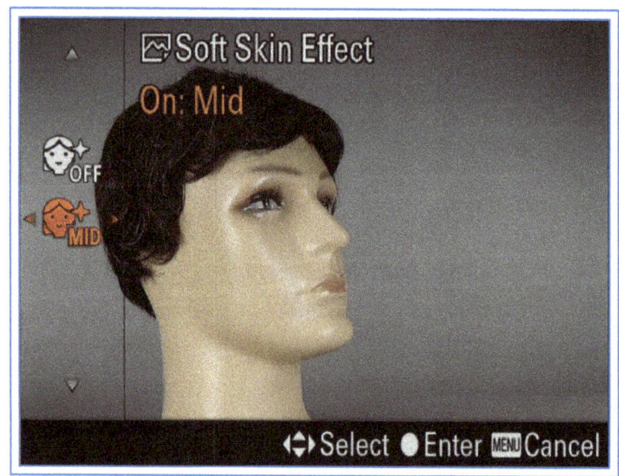

Figure 4-134. Soft Skin Effect Options Screen

However, even if you turn the Soft Skin Effect option on, it will not produce any changes in your images unless you also have Set Face Priority in AF turned on through screen 4 of the Camera Settings1 menu, and the RX100 VI has detected a face.

When it works, this setting reduces sharpness and contrast in areas that the camera perceives as skin tones. It can do a good job of smoothing out wrinkles. Figures 4-135 and 4-136 show the results of a test I made. Figure 4-135 was taken with the effect turned off; Figure 4-136 had the setting at its Hi level.

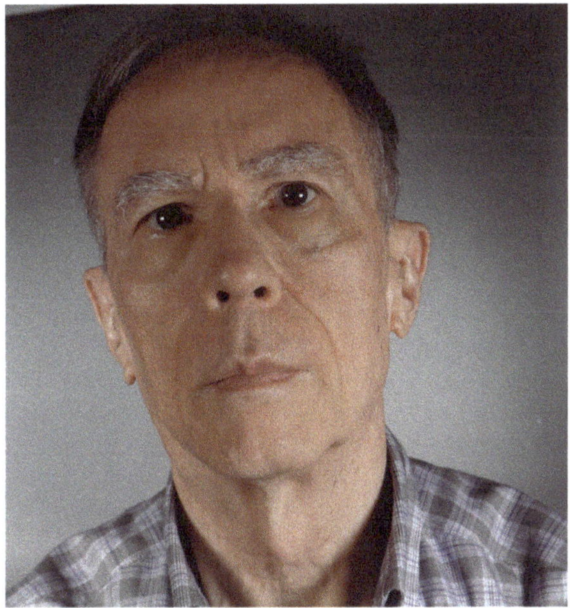

Figure 4-135. Soft Skin Effect Turned Off

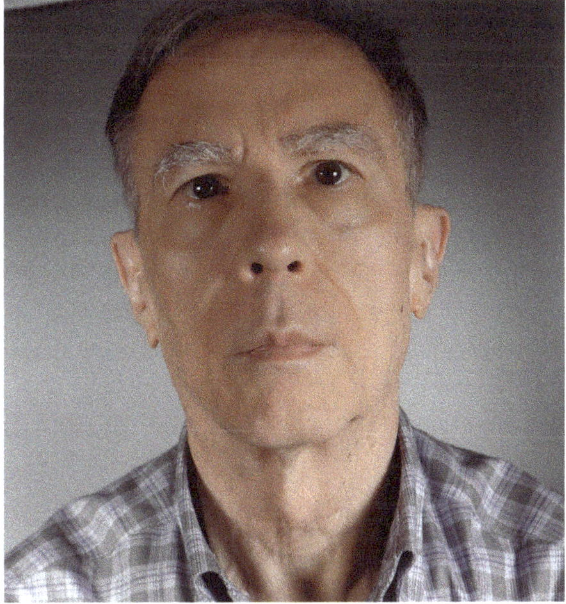

Figure 4-136. Soft Skin Effect Set to Hi

This can be a useful option for doing some basic retouching of your JPEG portraits in the camera.

The items on screen 11 of the Camera Settings1 menu are shown in Figure 4-137.

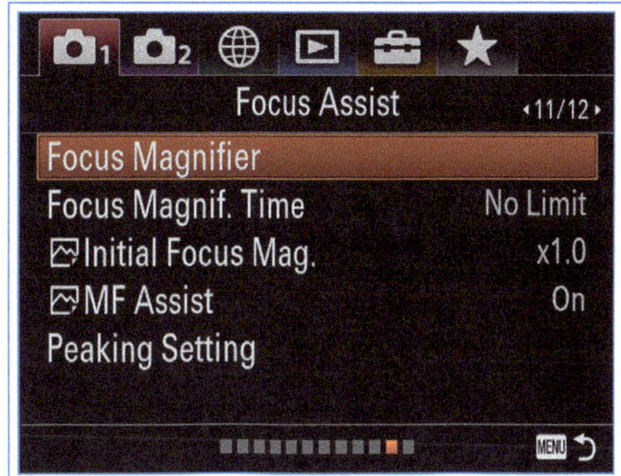

Figure 4-137. Screen 11 of Camera Settings1 Menu

Focus Magnifier

The Focus Magnifier option gives you a way to enlarge a small portion of the shooting screen display so you can check the focus of that area. It is useful primarily when using manual focus or direct manual focus (DMF), but it can also be used when focus mode is set to AF-S or AF-A. It cannot be used with the AF-C setting. This option works somewhat differently when recording movies, as discussed later in this section. For this discussion, I'm assuming the Initial Focus Magnification menu option, discussed later in this section, is set to x1.0.

When you select this menu option, the camera places an orange frame on the display, as seen in Figure 4-138.

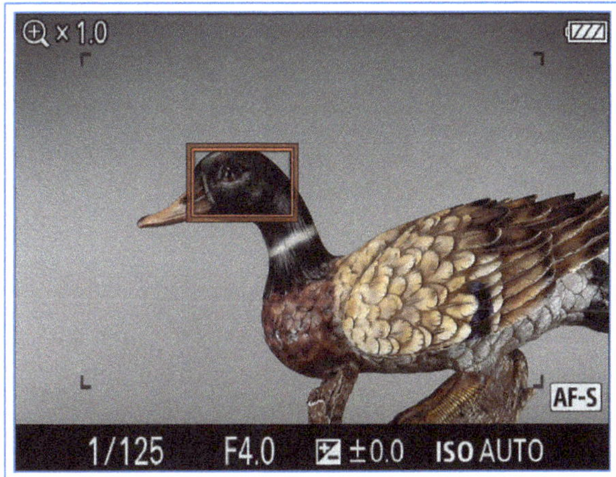

Figure 4-138. Focus Magnifier Frame on Display

You can move the frame to any position on the display using the direction buttons and the control wheel. When the frame is over the area where you want to check focus, press the Center button. The camera will then enlarge the area within the frame to 5.3 times normal, as shown in Figure 4-139. (The enlargement factor is different when shooting movies; see discussion below.)

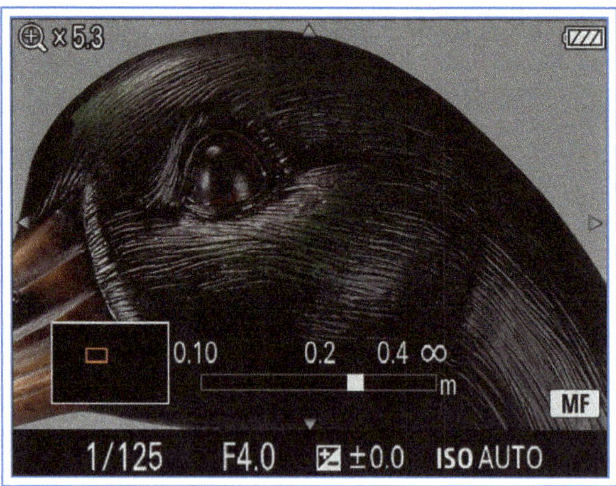

Figure 4-139. Focus Magnifier Screen at 5.3x Magnification

An inset square will show the position of the Focus Magnifier frame. You can scroll the display around while it is enlarged, and you can recall the frame to the center of the display by pressing the Custom/Delete button. Press the Center button again, and the focus area will be magnified to 10.7 times normal. A final press will restore the display to normal size and dismiss the magnifier frame. You also can dismiss the frame by pressing the shutter button halfway. You can then call the magnifier frame up again using this menu option if you want to.

When you have activated the Focus Magnifier frame, you can also move it around the screen by dragging it with your finger, if the touch operation features are turned on through screen 3 of the Setup menu. That function works in any focus mode, including autofocus. When the camera is set to manual focus mode, you can activate Focus Magnifier at the 5.3x magnification factor just by tapping twice quickly on the screen. Then you can drag the magnified area around the screen; tap twice quickly again to dismiss the magnification.

The Focus Magnifier option can be a bit confusing because it acts in a similar way to another option, which is activated from an item further down on the same menu screen, called MF Assist. As I will discuss later in this chapter and in Chapter 6, when you turn on MF Assist with manual focus in effect, the focus area is enlarged to 5.3 times normal as soon as you start turning the control ring to adjust the focus. Then, once the focus area is enlarged with that option, pressing the Center button will magnify the focus area to 10.7 times normal. You can toggle between the 5.3 and 10.7 magnifications using the Center button, and exit to the shooting screen by half-pressing the shutter button.

In other words, if the MF Assist menu option is active, the Center button always acts to magnify the focus area once you have started to adjust focus in manual focus mode. If you select the Focus Magnifier menu option, the difference is that pressing the Center button will magnify the display before you start focusing.

The advantage of using the Focus Magnifier menu option is that you can select the position of the enlarged focus area before you start adjusting focus. If you use the MF Assist option, the camera will enlarge the display as soon as you start turning the lens ring to adjust focus, and you will not be able to choose the location of the enlarged focus area until the display is already enlarged.

The MF Assist option works well for me, because it operates as soon as I start adjusting focus. However, if you prefer to be able to adjust the location of the frame for the enlarged focus area before starting to adjust focus, the Focus Magnifier option is useful. In addition, as noted earlier, you can use Focus Magnifier even with autofocus, although you cannot adjust autofocus with the frame on the display, because the frame disappears when you half-press the shutter button to cause the camera to focus.

The Focus Magnifier feature is easier to use if you assign it to one of the control buttons. For example, you can use the Custom Key (Still Images) option on screen 9 of the Camera Settings2 menu to assign Focus Magnifier to the Left button. Then, you can just press that button to bring the enlargement frame up on the display. You can quickly adjust the position of the frame, press the Center button once or twice to enlarge that area, and then adjust the focus (if using manual focus or DMF) and take the picture.

You can adjust the length of time the screen stays enlarged with this feature by using the Focus Magnification Time option, discussed immediately below. I prefer to set the time to No Limit so the magnification lasts as long as I need it. You also can set the Focus Magnifier option to use an initial magnification factor of 1.0x or 5.3x using the Initial Focus Magnification item, discussed below.

As noted above, Focus Magnifier works slightly differently for movies than for still images. If you assign this option to a control button, you can call it up while recording a movie to check the focus of the area within the frame. The only magnification factor when shooting movies is 4.0x, rather than 5.3x and 10.7x, the factors when shooting still images.

Focus Magnification Time

This option lets you select how long the display stays magnified when you use either the Focus Magnifier option, discussed above, or the MF Assist option, discussed below. The choices are two or five seconds or No Limit, as shown in Figure 4-140. The default option is two seconds.

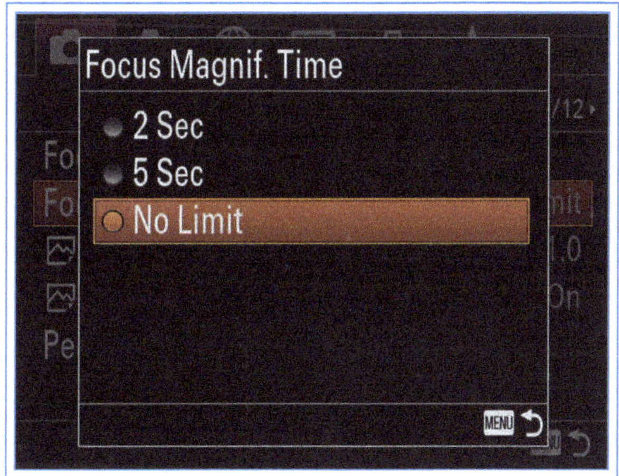

Figure 4-140. Focus Magnification Time Options Screen

With No Limit, the image will stay magnified until you press the shutter button all the way to take the picture, or press it halfway to dismiss the enlarged view. When using manual focus, the time limit of two or five seconds starts once you stop adjusting focus with the control ring. My preference is to use the No Limit option, so I can take my time in adjusting manual focus precisely, even if I stop turning the ring.

Initial Focus Magnification

This menu option lets you select either x1.0 or x5.3 as the initial magnification factor for the Focus Magnifier frame when it first appears on the screen. If you select the default of x1.0 for this menu option, the Focus Magnifier frame will appear on the display with no magnification until you press the Center button. The area within the frame is then magnified to 5.3 times, and a second press magnifies it to 10.7 times; a third press removes the frame from the display. If you select x5.3 for this option, the frame will appear with the 5.3 times magnification already in effect.

Note: If you use the In-Camera Guide help system, which can be assigned to a control button using the Custom Key (Still Images) option, and press that button when this menu item is highlighted, you will see that the help system says that this option controls the initial magnification for the Focus Magnifier option and for the MF Assist option. However, this option controls the initial magnification only for the Focus Magnifier option. The MF Assist screen always displays initially at the 5.3x magnification, regardless of the setting for this option.

MF Assist

The MF Assist option is useful when manual focus or DMF is in use. When MF Assist is turned on in manual focus mode, the RX100 VI enlarges the image on the display screen to 5.3 times normal size as soon as you start turning the control ring, as shown in Figure 4-141.

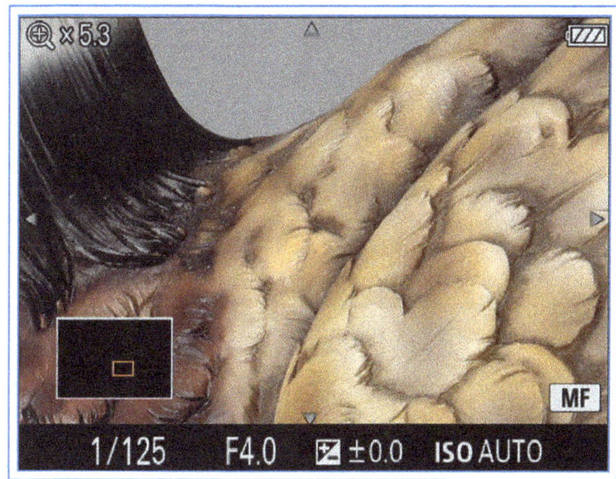

Figure 4-141. MF Assist Screen at 5.3 x Magnification

To increase magnification to 10.7 times, press the Center button; press that button again to return to the 5.3 enlargement factor. Press the shutter button halfway down to return the image to normal size. This feature is helpful in judging whether a particular area is in sharp focus. If you turn this option off, you can use another focusing aid, such as Focus Magnifier, discussed above, or Peaking, discussed immediately below.

Or, you can use this option and Peaking at the same time, to provide even more assistance.

When DMF is in effect, you have to keep the shutter button pressed halfway down while turning the control ring to use the MF Assist enlargement feature.

Note that, as discussed above in connection with the Focus Magnifier option, when the camera is in manual focus mode, you can tap twice on the screen to magnify the image to 5.3 times normal, and drag the magnified area around the screen with your finger; tap twice again to return the size to normal.

I find MF Assist helpful, especially when I set the camera to leave the enlarged screen in place indefinitely using the Focus Magnification Time option, discussed above. However, the Focus Magnifier option also is helpful, and may be preferable in one way because the screen does not become magnified until you select the area to be magnified using the orange frame and press the Center button to magnify the screen. (You can change that behavior with the Initial Focus Magnification menu option, discussed above.)

In some cases, where a subject (like the moon) does not have clear edges or other features to focus on, enlarging the view may not be that much help. In those situations, Peaking may be more useful. Or, you may find that using Peaking in conjunction with MF Assist is the most useful approach of all. You should experiment with the various options to find what works best for you.

MF Assist is not available when recording movies. You can use Focus Magnifier in that situation, if it is assigned to a control button.

Peaking Setting

The Peaking Setting menu option, whose main options screen in shown in Figure 4-142, controls the use of the Peaking display to assist with manual focus. When Peaking is turned on with focus mode set to manual focus or DMF, the camera displays bright pixels at areas where focus is sharp, to help you adjust focus. The Peaking Display option controls whether the Peaking feature is activated or not; the Peaking Level option controls the intensity of the display; and Peaking Color determines the color of the pixels that are displayed.

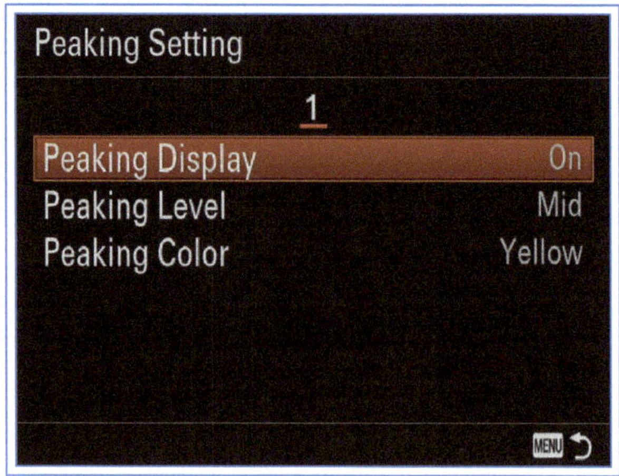

Figure 4-142. Peaking Setting Options Screen

You can set the level to Low, Mid, or High and the color to red, yellow, or white. Figures 4-143 and 4-144 illustrate this feature. Peaking Level is turned off for Figure 4-143 and set to High for Figure 4-144.

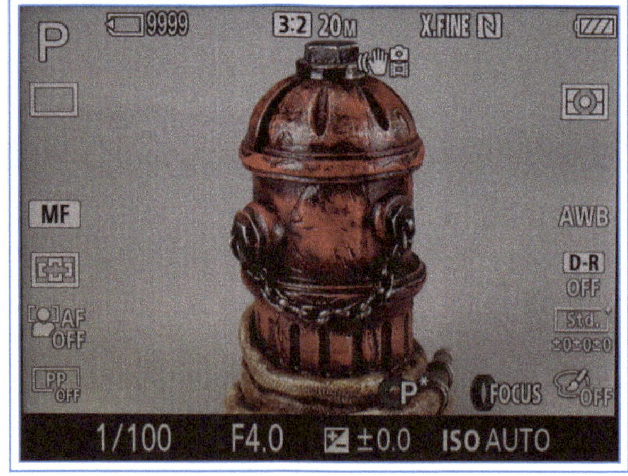

Figure 4-143. Peaking Turned Off

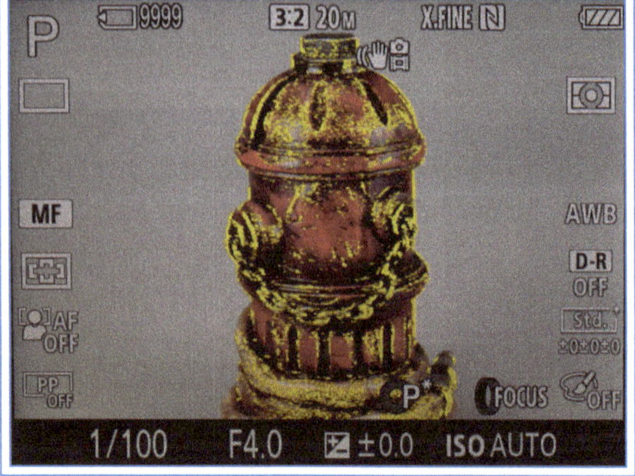

Figure 4-144. Peaking Set to High

The idea is that these lines provide a more definite indication that the focus is sharp than just relying on your judgment of sharpness. Some photographers set Creative Style to black and white while focusing so the Peaking color will stand out, and some set Peaking Level to Low so the color is not overwhelming, letting them see when the color just starts to appear. Some turn on MF Assist to enlarge the screen when using Peaking. You should experiment to find what approach works best for you.

For a good demonstration of how Peaking works, see this YouTube video posted by a participant in the Sony Cyber-shot Talk forum at dpreview.com at http://youtu.be/jMAlMQev7Kw.

Note that Peaking also works with DMF, even if you are using the autofocus function of that setting.

The items on screen 12 of the Camera Settings1 menu are shown in Figure 4-145.

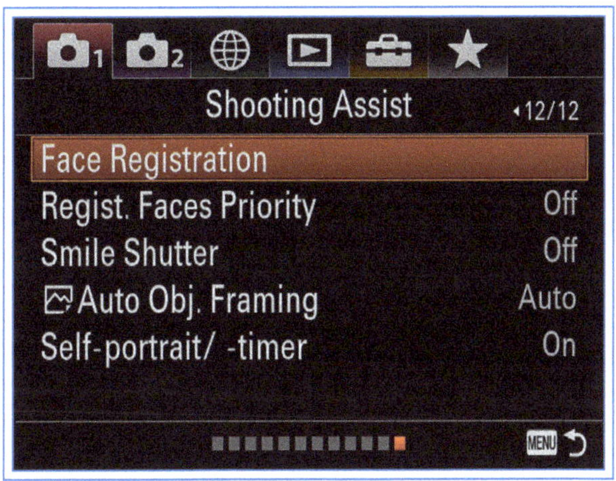

Figure 4-145. Screen 12 of Camera Settings1 Menu

Face Registration

This first option on screen 12 of the Camera Settings1 menu lets you register human faces so the RX100 VI can give those faces priority when it uses face detection. You can register up to eight faces and assign each one a priority from one to eight, with one being the highest. Then, when you turn on the menu option for Set Face Priority in AF, discussed earlier in this chapter, the camera will try to detect the registered faces first, in the order you have assigned them. This feature could be useful if, for example, you take pictures at school functions and you want to make sure the camera focuses on your own children rather than on other kids.

To use this setting, select this menu option, and on the next screen, shown in Figure 4-146, select New Registration.

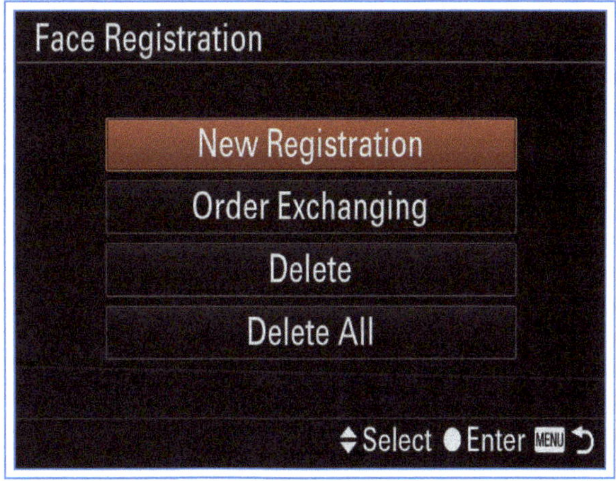

Figure 4-146. Face Registration Options Screen

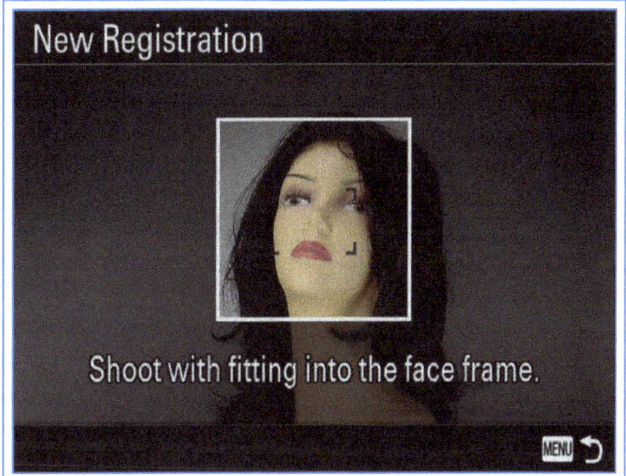

Figure 4-147. Screen to Register a Face

Press the Center button, and the camera will place a square frame on the screen. Compose a shot with the face to be registered in that frame, as shown in Figure 4-147, and press the shutter button to take a picture of the face. If the process succeeds, the camera will display the face with the message "Register face?" Highlight the Enter bar on that screen and press the Center button to complete the registration process.

Later, you can use the Order Exchanging option to change the priorities of the registered faces, and you can delete registered faces using other menu options.

Registered Faces Priority

This next menu option can be turned either on or off. If it is turned on, then faces registered with the Face

Registration option, discussed above, will be given priority when the camera focuses on faces when Face Priority in AF is turned on through screen 4 of the Camera Settings1 menu.

Smile Shutter

The next option on this menu screen is Smile Shutter, which is a sort of self-timer that is activated when the subject smiles. It can be turned either on or off.

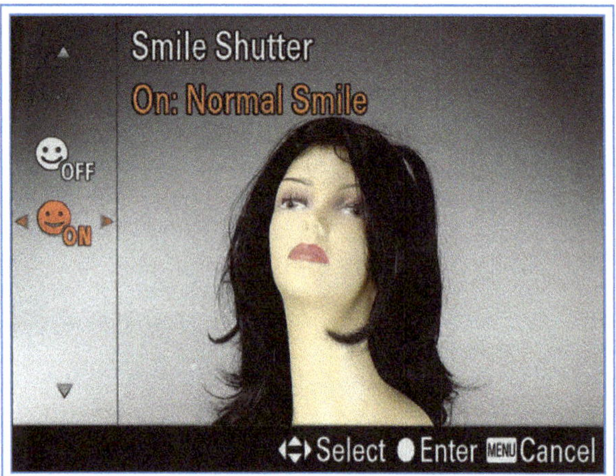

Figure 4-148. Smile Shutter Options Screen

After highlighting the On icon for this option as shown in Figure 4-148, use the Left and Right buttons to choose the level of smile that is needed to trigger the camera—Slight Smile, Normal Smile, or Big Smile. Then press the Center button to exit back to the shooting screen, and aim the camera at the subject or subjects. (You can, of course, put the camera on a tripod and aim it at yourself, if you want.)

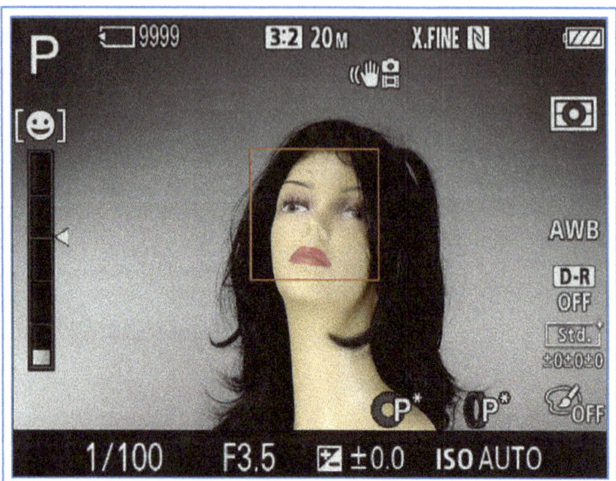

Figure 4-149. Smile Shutter Meter on Shooting Screen

As shown in Figure 4-149, the camera will show a meter at the left of the screen with a pointer to indicate how large a smile is needed to trigger a shot.

As soon as the camera detects a big enough smile from any person, the shutter will fire. If a person smiles again, the camera will be triggered again, with no limit on the number of shots that can be taken. In effect, this feature acts as a limited kind of remote control with one specific function. I consider this option to be something of a novelty, which can be entertaining but is not necessary for everyday photography.

Auto Object Framing

This next menu option provides a somewhat unusual function: It rearranges the composition of your shot based on the camera's electronic judgment. To activate it, set it to Auto on the menu. Then, after you capture your image, the camera will display a white cropping frame around what it believes to be the subject if it finds that the image can benefit by being trimmed to fit the subject better. For this feature to work with faces, you need to have Face Priority in AF turned on through screen 4 of the Camera Settings1 menu. Besides faces, Sony says that the feature will work with macro shots and objects tracked with Lock-on AF.

When you take a picture of the face or other subject, the camera may, if it finds it possible, crop the image and produce a new version of the image with the frame trimmed and resized to emphasize the subject in a more pleasing way.

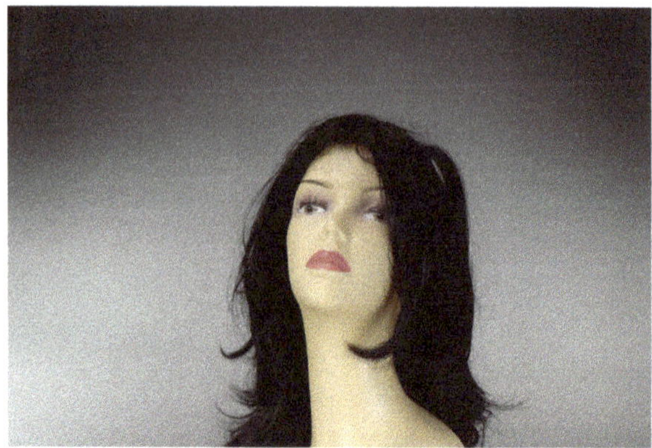

Figure 4-150. Auto Object Framing Example - Before

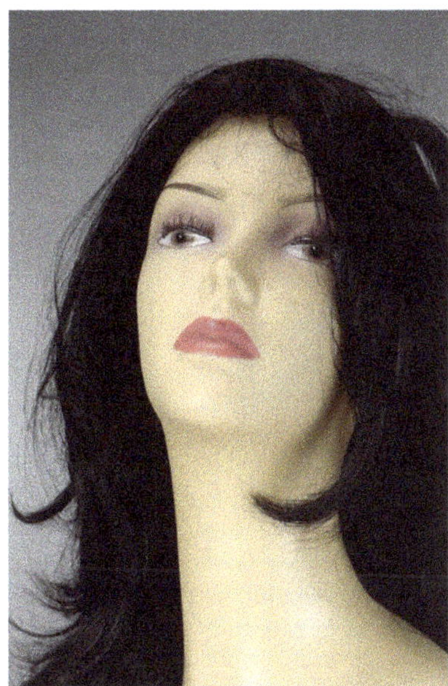

Figure 4-151. Auto Object Framing Example - After

An example is shown in Figure 4-150 and Figure 4-151, which show the uncropped and cropped versions, respectively, of a mannequin head I photographed with Face Priority in AF activated. The camera's cropping looks appropriate, but I would rather do the cropping myself in Photoshop or just compose the image in this way to begin with.

The camera saves both versions, so there is no harm in using this feature. It could be useful if you are pressed for time or are unable to get into position to take the shot you want. If you need a more nicely cropped version of the image quickly for a slide show, perhaps, this could be a good way to fill that need.

This feature is available for selection only if the camera is set for autofocus with JPEG images. It does not work with Raw images or when the lens is zoomed beyond the full optical zoom range. It also does not work when the camera is set for a feature that involves multiple shots, such as continuous shooting, HDR, or Multi Frame Noise Reduction, or certain Picture Effect settings.

Self-portrait Timer

This last option on the Camera Settings1 menu can be turned either on or off. If it is turned on, then, when you rotate the LCD screen so it faces forward, the camera will display a large three-step countdown timer when you press the shutter button, so you can get ready for a self-portrait. The timer screen, shown in Figure 4-152, includes a three-second self-timer icon in the upper left corner. If this menu option is turned off, you can still take a self-portrait, but without the on-screen timer.

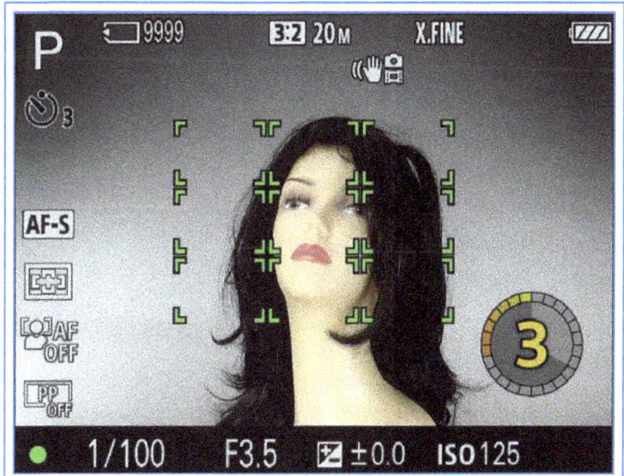

Figure 4-152. Self-portrait Timer in Use

When you use this option, the camera locks focus when you press the shutter button to start the timer, and, if your position changes during the countdown, the focus may be incorrect.

To avoid this problem, you can turn off this option and take the picture with no delay. Another approach is to control the camera from a smartphone via Wi-Fi as discussed in Chapter 10, or to use a wired remote control as discussed in Appendix A. Or, you can just make sure your face does not change its distance from the camera after you press the shutter button to start the self-portrait timer.

Chapter 5: The Camera Settings2 Menu

The second menu that is represented by a camera icon deserves a separate chapter, because its settings are not just a continuation of those on the Camera Settings1 menu. The Camera Settings2 menu contains all of the settings that directly affect video recording, such as file formats, audio recording options, and the like. This menu system also includes a number of settings that affect still photography as well as video recording, such as options for the speed of zooming and switching between the LCD screen and viewfinder. Each of these options is discussed below. However, I do not discuss in this chapter the details of options that are strictly used for video recording. I will mention those items below, but I will discuss them in detail in Chapter 9, where I discuss movie making. Screen 1 of this menu is shown in Figure 5-1.

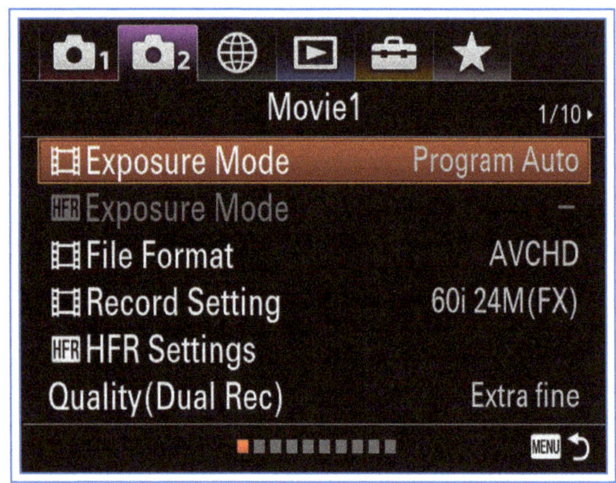

Figure 5-1. Screen 1 of Camera Settings2 Menu

Exposure Mode (Movies)

This first menu item on this screen is available for selection only when the mode dial is set to Movie mode (the position marked by a movie film icon). It lets you select one of the four available exposure settings for recording movies in that mode: Program Auto, Aperture Priority, Shutter Priority, or Manual Exposure. The Movie mode is for recording movies at normal speeds, as opposed to the high frame rates used for slow-motion movies recorded in the HFR mode. I will discuss this option in Chapter 9.

Exposure Mode (HFR)

This second item on the Camera Settings2 menu is another mode-specific one. It is available for selection only when the mode dial is set to HFR, for high frame rate movie recording. This option lets you choose one of the four exposure modes for recording super-slow-motion movies, which are similar to those mentioned above for Movie mode. I will discuss those settings, as well as other aspects of HFR recording, in Chapter 9.

File Format (Movies)

This next option also applies only for movies. I will discuss the details of this setting in Chapter 9. For now, you should know that XAVC S (either 4K or HD) gives the highest quality but is available only if you are using an SDHC or SDXC card rated in Speed Class 10 or UHS Speed Class 1 (UHS Speed Class 3 for some settings). The AVCHD option yields high quality also and does not require a special memory card.

Record Setting

This option is related to the File Format option, discussed above. I will discuss the details of this option in Chapter 9. The available settings will be different depending on whether you choose XAVC S 4K, XAVC S HD, or AVCHD for File Format. They also will be different if you have set the NTSC/PAL Selector option, on screen 3 of the Setup menu, to PAL, the TV system used in much of Europe and some other locations. In this book, I will discuss the video options that are applicable for the NTSC system, as used in the United States, Japan, and elsewhere.

HFR Settings

This menu option controls the settings for HFR, or high frame rate video recording, when the mode dial is set to the HFR position. I will discuss this option and other aspects of HFR recording in Chapter 9.

Quality (Dual Recording)

This next option on the Camera Settings2 menu sets the quality of still images that are captured during video recording. When you have started recording a video, you can press the shutter button at any time to capture a still image. You also can use the Auto Dual Recording option, discussed below, to set the camera to capture still images automatically during video recording. There are some limitations on these capabilities, which are discussed in Chapter 9. The options available for this setting are Extra Fine, Fine, and Standard. The Raw setting is not available.

The items on screen 2 of the Camera Settings2 menu are shown in Figure 5-2.

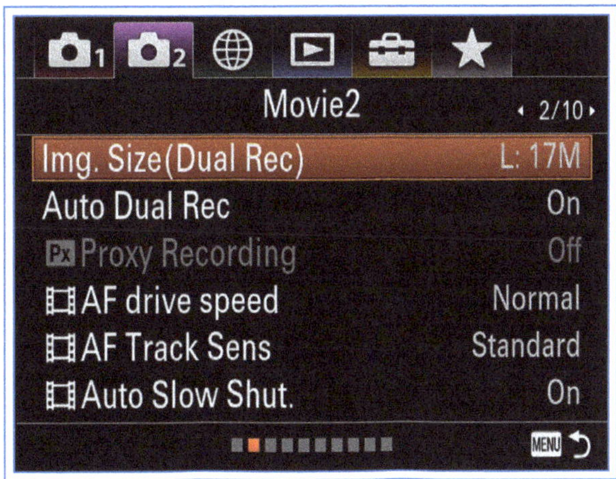

Figure 5-2. Screen 2 of Camera Settings2 Menu

Image Size (Dual Recording)

This next option on the Camera Settings2 menu is related to the previous one. This option sets the size of still images that are captured during video recording. Choices for Image Size, seen in Figure 5-3, are L:17M, M:7.5M, and S:4.2M, for Large, Medium, and Small.

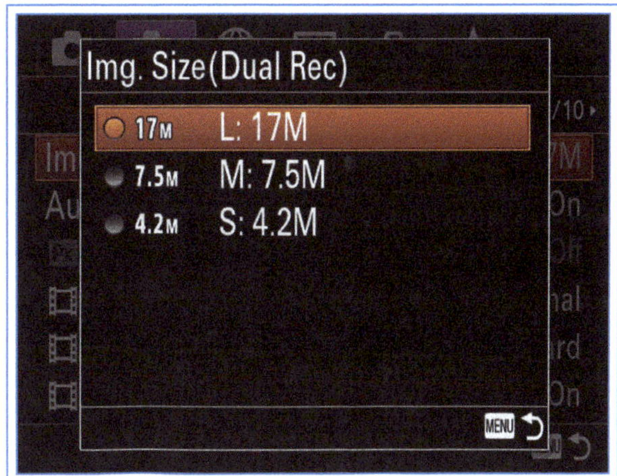

Figure 5-3. Image Size (Dual Recording) Options Screen

Auto Dual Recording

This menu option lets you set the camera to capture still images automatically during a video recording, when the camera detects what it considers to be "impressive compositions, including people." I will discuss this option in Chapter 9, in connection with video recording.

Proxy Recording

This option can be used to set the camera to record a smaller-sized video file at the same time as a high-quality version, so you can share the smaller file quickly or use it for proxy editing. I will discuss this option in Chapter 9.

AF Drive Speed

This option controls the speed at which the camera's autofocus system changes focus when recording video. I will discuss it in Chapter 9.

AF Tracking Sensitivity

This option, located after AF Drive Speed on the menu, controls how quickly the autofocus system tracks a moving subject when recording video. I will discuss it in Chapter 9.

Auto Slow Shutter

This option lets the camera automatically set a slower shutter speed than normal when shooting a movie, in order to compensate for dim lighting. I will discuss this option in Chapter 9.

The items on screen 3 of the Camera Settings2 menu are shown in Figure 5-4.

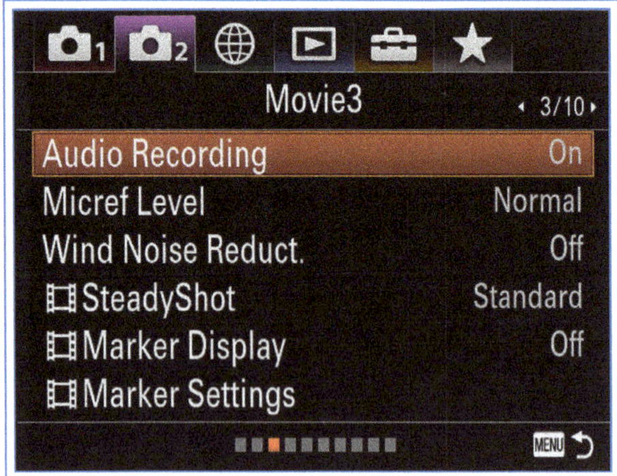

Figure 5-4. Screen 3 of Camera Settings2 Menu

Audio Recording

The Audio Recording item on the Camera Settings2 menu can be set either on or off. If you are certain you won't need the sound recorded by the camera, then you can turn this option off. I never turn it off, because I can always turn down the volume of the recorded sound when playing the video. Or, if I am editing the video on a computer, I can delete the sound and replace it as needed—but there is no way to recapture the original audio after the fact if this option was turned off during the recording.

Micref Level

This option lets you control the sound level for movies that you record with the camera, either in Movie mode or when the mode dial is set to a still-shooting mode. I will discuss its use in Chapter 9.

Wind Noise Reduction

This option also is one that applies only to movies. I will discuss it in Chapter 9.

SteadyShot (Movies)

This next option controls the use of the camera's built-in image stabilization system, for movies only. This menu item has a movie film icon in front of its name, whereas the other SteadyShot menu option, for still images, which is on screen 5 of the Camera Settings2 menu, has a mountain-landscape icon in front of its name. I will discuss this video-oriented SteadyShot option in Chapter 9.

Marker Display

This option, which can be turned either on or off, determines whether or not various informative guidelines, called "markers," are displayed on the camera's screen for movie recording. I will discuss the details of this option in Chapter 9.

Marker Settings

This menu option works together with the Marker Display option, discussed above. This option lets you activate any or all of the four available markers—Center, Aspect, Safety Zone, and Guideframe. I will discuss this setting in Chapter 9.

The single item on screen 4 of the Camera Settings2 menu is shown in Figure 5-5.

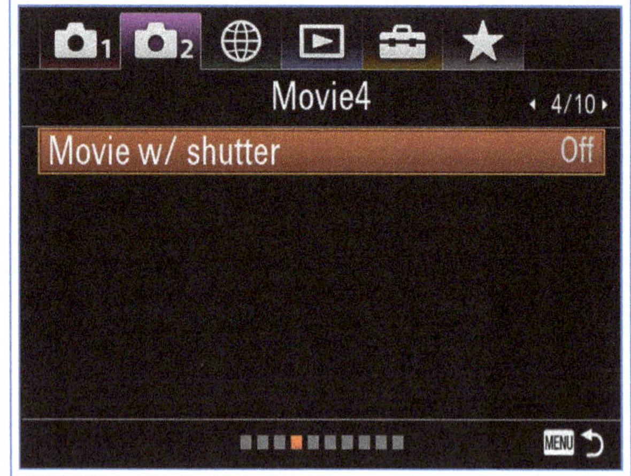

Figure 5-5. Screen 4 of Camera Settings2 Menu

Movie w/Shutter

This only option on screen 4 of the Camera Settings2 menu can be turned either on or off. If it is turned on, you can start and stop movie recording by pressing the shutter button when the camera is set to Movie mode or HFR mode, for high frame rate. I will discuss this option in Chapter 9.

The items on screen 5 of the Camera Settings2 menu are shown in Figure 5-6.

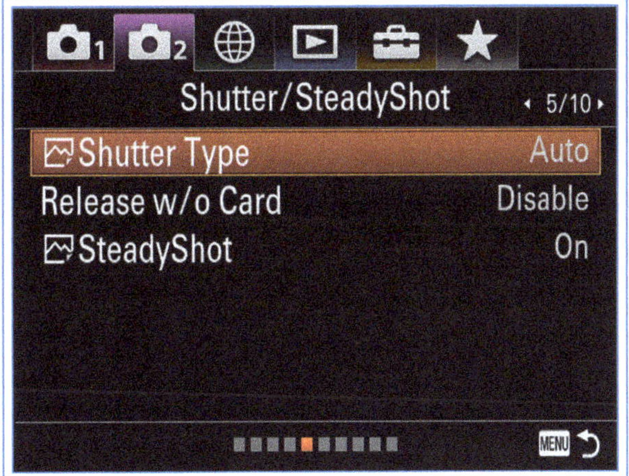

Figure 5-6. Screen 5 of Camera Settings2 Menu

Shutter Type

This next option lets you determine whether the RX100 VI uses its mechanical shutter or its electronic shutter for still images. One of the distinctive features of this camera is that it is equipped with both types of shutter, giving you flexibility for various scenarios.

With the mechanical shutter, the camera can use shutter speeds from 1/2000 second to 30 seconds, plus the BULB setting, with which you can hold the shutter open as long as you need to. In addition, the camera can synchronize its flash with the mechanical shutter at any setting, including 1/2000 second.

With the electronic shutter, the camera can use shutter speeds from 1/32000 second to 30 seconds, but with no BULB setting, and it can synchronize with its flash only at speeds of 1/100 second or slower.

There are several considerations for choosing mechanical or electronic for the shutter type. First, if you need a super-fast shutter speed such as 1/16000 second, you need to use the electronic shutter. You might want a speed in that range if you are taking photos in very bright conditions but still want to use a fairly wide aperture to blur the background. You also might want to use a very fast shutter speed in order to maximize the rate of continuous shooting, or to ensure that you get sharp images of fast action at a sporting event.

Also, you can use the electronic shutter when you want to minimize the sounds made by the camera, such as if you are shooting in a museum or other place where sounds should be kept to a minimum. The mechanical shutter makes a sound that cannot be disabled; you can disable the sound of the electronic shutter using the Audio Signals option on screen 10 of the Camera Settings2 menu. However, the sound of the mechanical shutter is not that loud, and I have not found the shutter sound to be a major factor in choosing a shutter type.

You might use the mechanical shutter if you need the BULB setting for exposures longer than 30 seconds, or if you need to synchronize the flash with a shutter speed faster than 1/100 second. You also might use the mechanical shutter to avoid distortion that can take place in some cases from use of the electronic shutter, such as when shooting under fluorescent lighting.

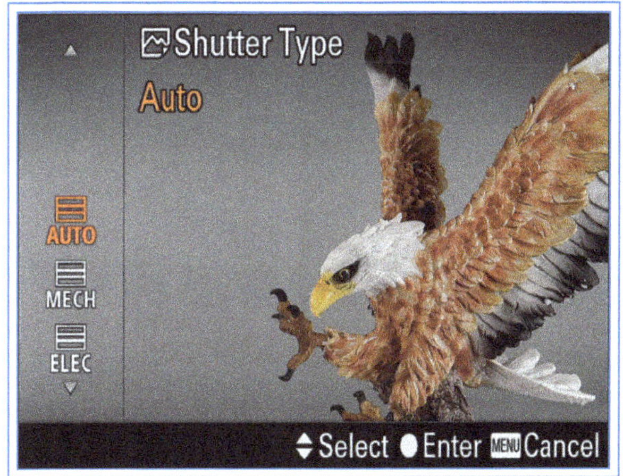

Figure 5-7. Shutter Type Options Screen

This option has three choices, shown in Figure 5-7: Auto, Mechanical Shutter, or Electronic Shutter. With Auto, the camera decides which shutter type to use based on current conditions, including what shutter speed is called for by the exposure reading. With Mechanical Shutter or Electronic Shutter, the specified shutter type is always used, with two exceptions. Even if Shutter Type is set to Electronic Shutter, the mechanical shutter will be used when you press the Center button to save a custom white balance, or you press the shutter button to register a new face with the Face Registration option. When Shutter Type is set to Electronic Shutter, Long Exposure Noise Reduction is not available. I usually leave this setting at Auto, unless there is a particular need for the Mechanical or Electronic setting.

Release without Card

This option can be set to either Enable or Disable. If it is set to Enable, you can operate the camera's shutter release button even if there is no memory card inserted in the camera. In that case, the camera will display a NO CARD warning message, but it will let you operate the shutter and an image will be saved temporarily. This setting is useful if the camera is on display in a retail store, so customers can operate the controls and see how a saved image would look, without having to have an expensive memory card left in the camera. As I noted in Chapter 1, there is no easy way to save an image taken when this setting is active, although in an emergency you may be able to send the image through the HDMI port to a video capture device.

If you select Disable for this item, the NO CARD warning is still displayed. In addition, if you try to press the shutter button, the camera will display a warning message advising that the shutter cannot be operated with no memory card inserted, as shown in figure 5-8. This setting is the safest one to use, because it protects you against operating the camera when there is no card inserted to save images or videos.

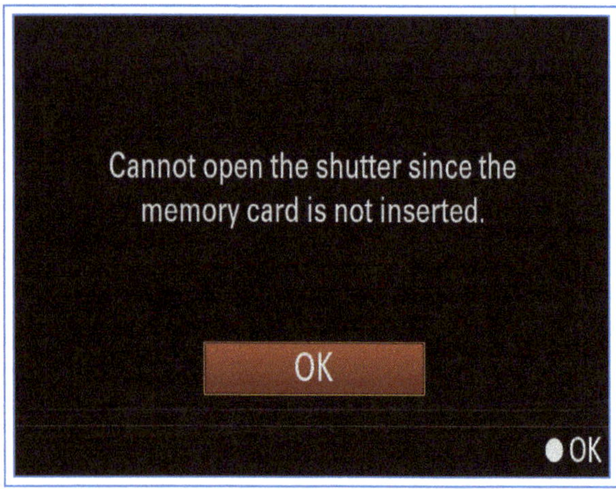

Figure 5-8. Warning Message for Operating with No Card

However, if you have the camera connected to a computer using the PC Remote feature with Sony's Imaging Edge software, you can capture images with the camera through the software controls, even if there is no card in the camera and Release without Card is set to Disable. In that situation, you have to go to the PC Remote Settings option on screen 4 of the Setup menu and set the Still Image Save Destination to PC Only. If that option is set to PC + Camera, you cannot capture images using Sony's Imaging Edge software with no memory card installed in the camera, even with this option set to Enable. The PC Remote feature is discussed in Chapter 8, in connection with the USB Connection item on the Setup menu.

SteadyShot (Still Images)

SteadyShot is Sony's optical image stabilization system, which compensates for small movements of the camera to avoid motion blur, especially during exposures of longer than about 1/30 second. This setting is turned on by default, and I recommend leaving it on at all times, except when the camera is on a tripod. In that case, SteadyShot is not needed, and there is some chance it can "fool" the camera and cause it to try to correct for motion that does not exist, resulting in image blur.

The items on screen 6 of the Camera Settings2 menu are shown in Figure 5-9.

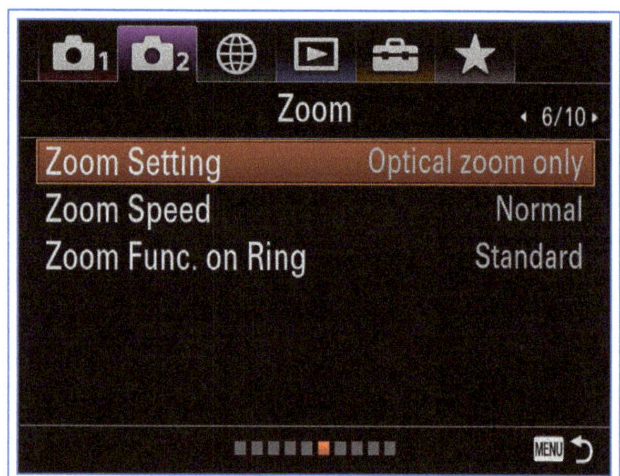

Figure 5-9. Screen 6 of Camera Settings2 Menu

Zoom Setting

The first option on screen 6 of the Camera Settings2 menu, Zoom Setting, provides two ways to give the RX100 VI extra zoom range, using features called Clear Image Zoom and Digital Zoom. To explain these features in context, I will discuss all three zoom methods that the camera offers—optical zoom, Clear Image Zoom, and Digital Zoom. (I will also discuss a fourth feature related to these, called Smart Zoom.)

Optical zoom is the camera's "natural" zoom capability—moving the lens elements so they magnify the image, just as binoculars do. You can call optical zoom a "real" zoom because it increases the amount of information that the lens gathers. The optical zoom of the RX100 VI operates within a range from 24mm at the wide-angle setting to the fully zoomed-in telephoto setting of 200mm.

To complicate matters a bit, I should point out that the actual optical zoom range of the RX100 VI's lens is 9.0mm to 72mm; you can see those numbers on the end of the lens. But the numbers that are almost always used to describe the zoom range of a compact camera's lens are the "35mm-equivalent" figures, which translate the actual zoom range into what the range would be if this were a lens on a camera that uses 35mm film. This translation is done because so many photographers are familiar with the zoom ranges and focal lengths of lenses for traditional 35mm cameras, on which a 50mm lens is considered "normal." I use the 35mm-equivalent figures throughout this book.

The Digital Zoom feature on the RX100 VI magnifies the image electronically without any special processing to improve the quality. This type of zoom does not really increase the information gathered by the lens; rather, it just increases the apparent size of the image by enlarging the pixels within the area captured by the lens. On some cameras, the amount of digital zoom can be very large, such as 50 times normal, but such a large figure should be considered as a marketing ploy to lure customers, rather than as a feature of real value to the photographer.

The other option on the RX100 VI, Clear Image Zoom, is a special type of digital zoom developed by Sony. With this feature, the RX100 VI does not just magnify the area of the image; rather, the camera uses an algorithm based on analysis of the image to add pixels through interpolation, so the pixels are not just multiplied. The enlargement is performed in a way that produces a smoother, more realistic enlargement than the Digital Zoom feature. Therefore, with Clear Image Zoom, the camera achieves greater quality than with Digital Zoom, though not as much as with the "pure" optical zoom.

Finally, there is another way the RX100 VI can have a zoom range greater than the normal range of optical zoom, with no reduction in image quality. The standard range of 24mm to 200mm is available when JPEG Image Size is set to Large. However, if JPEG Image Size is set to Medium, Small, or VGA, the camera needs only a portion of the pixels on the image sensor to create the image at the reduced size. It can use the "extra" pixels to enlarge the view of the scene. This process, which Sony calls Smart Zoom in its documentation, is similar to what you can do using editing software such as Photoshop. If the final image does not need to be at the Large size, you can crop out some pixels from the center (or other area) of the image and enlarge them, thereby retaining the same final image size with a magnified view of the scene.

So, with Smart Zoom, if you set JPEG Image Size to VGA, M, or S, the camera can zoom to a greater range than with JPEG Image Size set to L and still retain the full quality of the optical zoom. You will, of course, end up with lower-resolution images, but that may not be a problem if you are going to post them on a website or share them via e-mail.

In short, optical zoom provides the best quality for magnifying the scene; Clear Image Zoom gives excellent quality; and Digital Zoom produces magnification accompanied by deterioration of the image. Smart Zoom lets you get greater zoom range with no image deterioration, but at the expense of resolution.

Here is how to use these settings. I will assume for now that you are leaving JPEG Image Size set to L, because that is the best setting for excellent results in printing and editing your images.

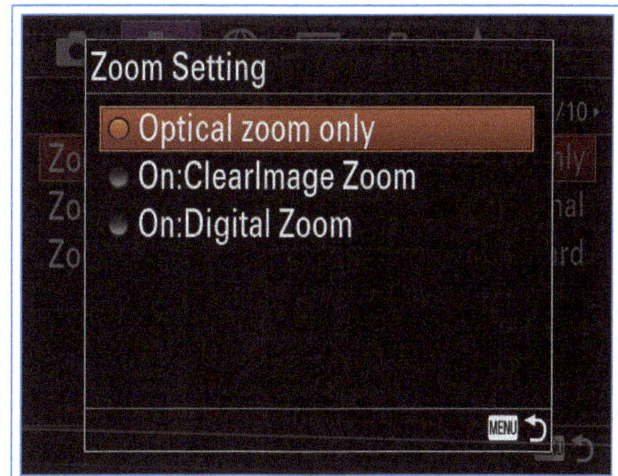

Figure 5-10. Zoom Setting Options Screen

When you select the Zoom Setting menu option and press the Center button, the camera displays the screen shown in Figure 5-10, giving you the choice of Optical Zoom Only; On: Clear Image Zoom; or On: Digital Zoom. If you turn on Digital Zoom, Clear Image Zoom will automatically be activated also. Optical Zoom is always available, no matter what settings are used.

If you turn on only Clear Image Zoom, you will have greater zoom range than normal, as discussed above, with minimal quality loss. If you also turn on Digital Zoom, you will get even greater zoom range, but quality will suffer as the lens is zoomed past the Clear Image Zoom range. When these various settings are in effect, you will see different indications on the camera's display.

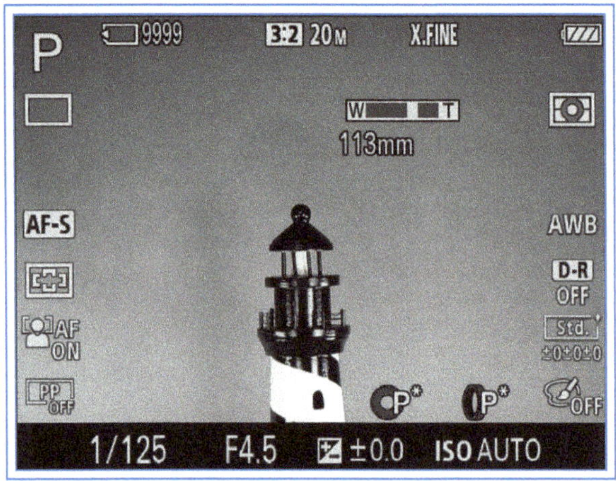

Figure 5-11. Zoom Scale: Optical Zoom Only

In Figure 5-11, JPEG Image Size is set to L with Clear Image Zoom and Digital Zoom turned off. The zoom indicator at the top of the screen goes only as far as 200mm.

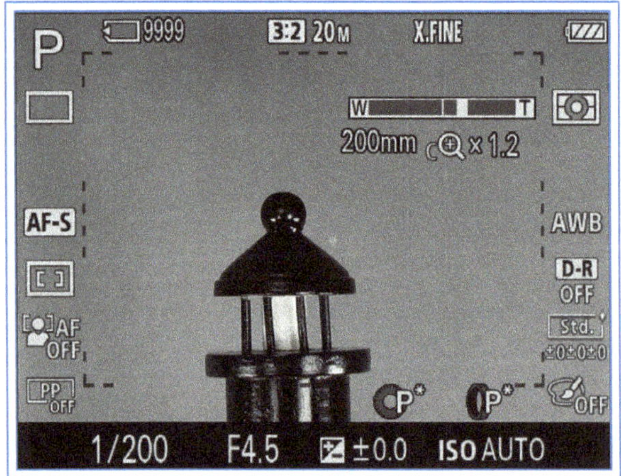

Figure 5-12. Zoom Scale: Clear Image Zoom

In Figure 5-12, Clear Image Zoom is turned on. The lens can be zoomed to two times the normal range. There is a small vertical line in the center of the zoom scale marking the point where the zoom changes from optical-only to expanded (either Clear Image Zoom or Digital Zoom, depending on the settings). The magnifying glass icon with the "C" beneath the scale means Clear Image Zoom is turned on. Also, once the lens zooms past the optical zoom range, the sound of the zoom mechanism stops, so you can tell by listening when the camera has entered the range of Clear Image Zoom and Digital Zoom.

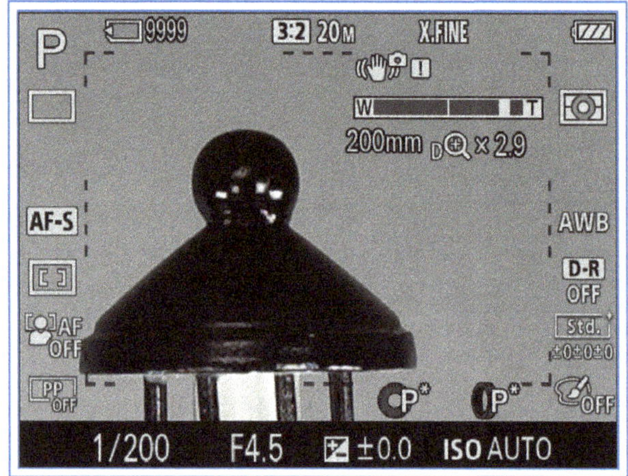

Figure 5-13. Zoom Scale: Digital Zoom

In Figure 5-13, both Clear Image Zoom and Digital Zoom are turned on, and the zoom indicator goes up to four times normal. The magnifying glass icon beneath the scale has a "D" beside it, indicating that Digital Zoom is now in effect.

With a JPEG Image Size setting smaller than Large, the zoom scale will use an S to show that the camera is using Smart Zoom, as the zoom range extends beyond the standard optical zoom limit.

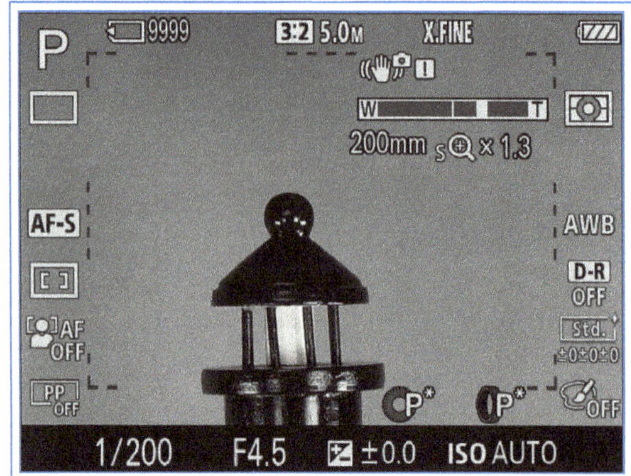

Figure 5-14. Zoom Scale: Smart Zoom

For example, in Figure 5-14, with Image Size set to Small, the lens is zoomed in to 1.3 times the optical range, and the zoom indicator displays an S to indicate that Smart Zoom is in effect. When Smart Zoom is in use, the ranges of Clear Image Zoom and Digital Zoom also are expanded.

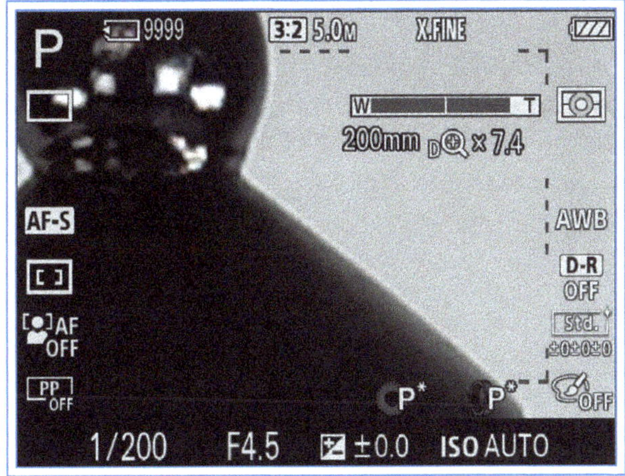

Figure 5-15. Zoom Scale: Smart Zoom and Digital Zoom

For example, as shown in Figure 5-15, with JPEG Image Size set to Small and Digital Zoom turned on, the lens can be zoomed in to 8.0 times the normal optical range.

Table 5-1 shows the zoom ranges with JPEG Image Size at L, M, S, and VGA, for Optical Zoom, Clear Image Zoom, and Digital Zoom. For the L, M, and S figures, Aspect Ratio was 3:2; with other Aspect Ratio settings, results would be different. For the VGA figures, Aspect Ratio was 4:3, the only setting for which VGA is available.

Table 5-1. **Zoom Ranges at Various Settings for JPEG Image Size**

	Large	Medium	Small	VGA
Optical Zoom (with no deterioration)	200mm	275mm	400mm	1520mm
Clear Image Zoom (with minimal deterioration)	400mm	550mm	800mm	3000mm
Digital Zoom (with significant deterioration)	800mm	1120mm	1600mm	3000mm

To summarize the situation with zoom, when JPEG Image Size is set to Large, you can zoom up to 200mm with no deterioration using optical zoom; you can zoom to 400mm with minimal deterioration using Clear Image Zoom; and you can zoom to 800mm using Digital Zoom but with significant deterioration.

My preference is to limit the camera to optical zoom and avoid any deterioration. However, many photographers have found that Clear Image Zoom yields good results, and it is worth using when you cannot get close to your subject. I do not like to use Digital Zoom to take a picture. However, it can be useful to zoom in to meter a specific area of a distant subject, or to check the composition of your shot before zooming back out and taking the shot using Clear Image Zoom or optical zoom.

Clear Image Zoom and Digital Zoom are not available in several situations, including with Raw images, when the Smile Shutter is turned on, and in Sweep Panorama or HFR mode. They also are unavailable when the Smart Teleconverter option has been assigned to a control button. The Smart Teleconverter option, discussed later in this chapter, is itself a form of Digital Zoom.

When the lens is zoomed in to the range of Clear Image Zoom or Digital Zoom and autofocus is in use, the focus area menu option is disabled and the camera uses a broad focus frame, which is represented by a dotted area like that seen in Figure 5-16.

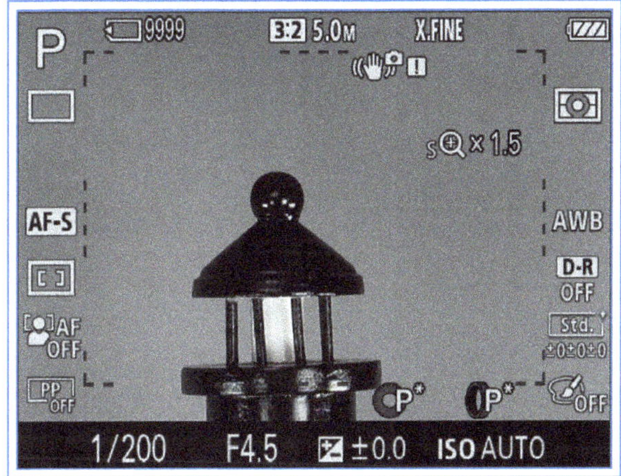

Figure 5-16. Large, Dotted Focus Frame for Non-optical Zoom

Zoom Speed

This option, which can be set to Normal or Fast, controls how quickly the lens zooms in or out when you move the zoom lever. It also controls the speed of the lens when you are using an optional Sony remote control that has a zoom function, as discussed in Appendix A. The setting for this item depends on your preference. You may prefer the slower zooming of the Normal setting, especially if you want to set a specific, intermediate focal length for your shots. But, if you like to change focal lengths quickly to zoom all the way in or out, the Fast setting will save some time.

To increase the speed of zooming using the control ring, use the Zoom Function on Ring option, discussed below, and set the value to Quick instead of Standard.

Zoom Function on Ring

This last item on screen 6 of the Camera Settings2 menu determines the way the control ring operates when you are using it to zoom the lens in and out. As I will discuss later in this chapter, the action assigned to the control ring is determined by the Custom Key (Still Images) and Custom Key (Movies) settings on screen 9 of the Camera Settings2 menu. When the control ring's function is set to Standard, it controls zoom only in Auto mode. In any other shooting mode, you have to set the control ring's function to zoom to enable it to zoom the lens.

When the ring is set to control zoom, you can use the Zoom Function on Ring menu option to choose between Standard, Quick, and Step for the way the zoom operates, as shown in Figure 5-17. With Standard, when the control ring is used to zoom the lens, it does so continuously, just as the zoom lever does. That is, as you turn the ring, the lens zooms through all focal lengths that are available.

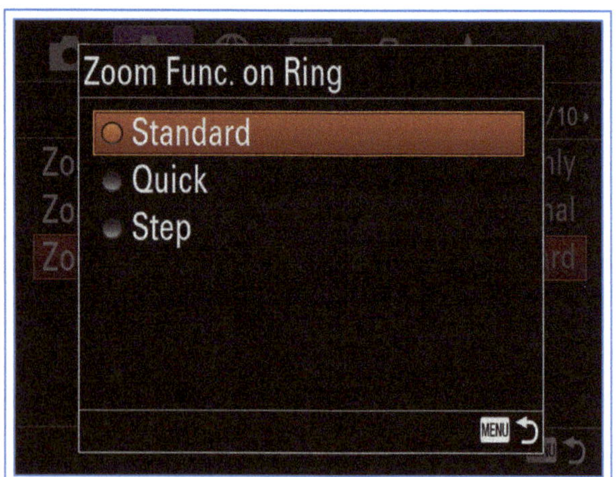

Figure 5-17. Zoom Function on Ring Options Screen

With optical zoom, that means it will zoom from the 24mm wide-angle setting to the 200mm telephoto setting in continuous increments. With Clear Image Zoom and Digital Zoom, the zoom levels increase beyond the 200mm point.

If you choose Quick, the control ring still zooms continuously, but at a faster rate. You might choose this option if you often need to zoom the lens all the way in or all the way out and are not so concerned with setting intermediate focal lengths or making precise adjustments. (This is similar to the setting called Fast for the zoom lever, which is set through the Zoom Speed menu option, discussed above.)

If you set the Zoom Function on Ring menu option to Step, then the control ring zooms the lens only to certain preset values: 24mm, 28mm, 35mm, 50mm, 70mm, 100mm, 135mm, and 200mm. When you nudge the ring toward the wide-angle or telephoto side, the zoom will move to the next preset focal length. You should give the ring a quick nudge and then release it; if you keep turning it, it will move past the next value and go on to the one after that.

There are some limitations with the Step Zoom function on the RX100 VI. First, if you set the camera for manual focus or DMF using the focus mode menu option, the control ring will control manual focus and will not zoom the lens.

Next, the Step Zoom feature works only for the control ring; the zoom lever will always zoom the lens continuously. Also, the Step Zoom feature does not work when shooting movies.

Finally, if you turn on Clear Image Zoom or Digital Zoom using the Zoom Setting option on screen 6 of the Camera Settings2 menu, or use Smart Zoom, the Step Zoom feature will not include specific increments for the zoom range beyond the optical limit of 200mm. Instead, as shown in Figure 5-18, where Digital Zoom is in use, the camera displays the range of preset increments along with an area at the right side of the scale extending from the 200mm mark to a magnifying glass icon at the far right, showing a general area of extended zoom range.

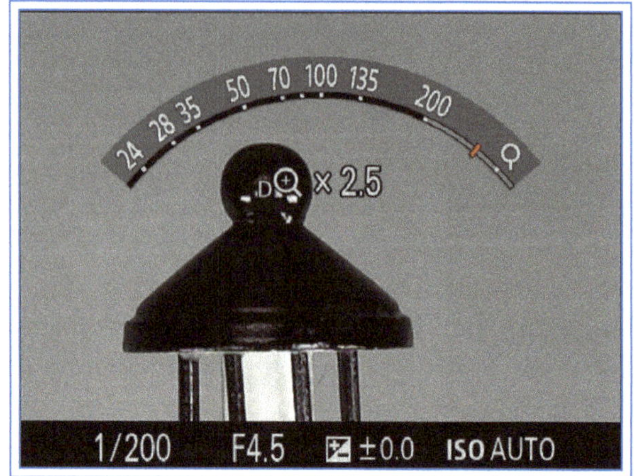

Figure 5-18. Zoom Scale: Step Zoom and Smart Zoom

Step zoom is useful if you want to make sure you have the lens zoomed to the exact focal length you want. Of course, this feature is of use only if your desired focal length is 28mm, 35mm, 50mm, 70mm, 100mm, or 135mm; it is easy to set the focal length to 24mm or 200mm using the normal zoom method because those focal lengths are at the two extremes of the camera's optical zoom range.

You might want to choose a focal length of 50mm, for example, to compare shots from the RX100 VI against shots from another camera using that same setting.

The items on screen 7 of the Camera Settings2 menu are shown in Figure 5-19.

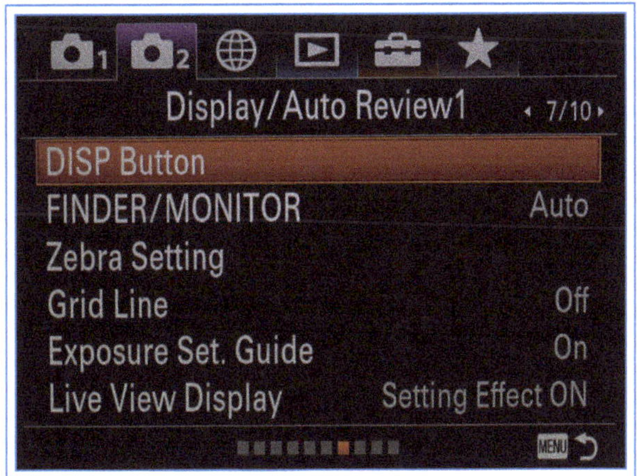

Figure 5-19. Screen 7 of Camera Settings2 Menu

Display Button

This option lets you choose what screens appear in shooting mode as you press the Display button. There are sub-options for the monitor (LCD) and viewfinder, as seen in Figure 5-20.

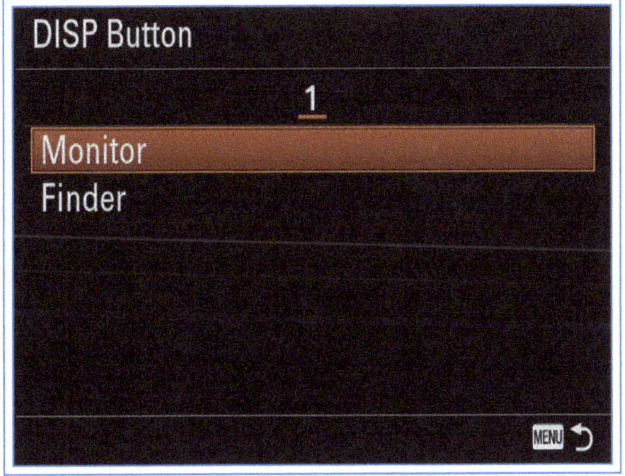

Figure 5-20. Display Button Options Screen

You can make different choices for the LCD and viewfinder, so pressing the Display button when you are using the monitor may bring up different screens than when you are using the viewfinder. After you decide to choose screens for the monitor or the viewfinder, you will see a screen like that shown in Figure 5-21.

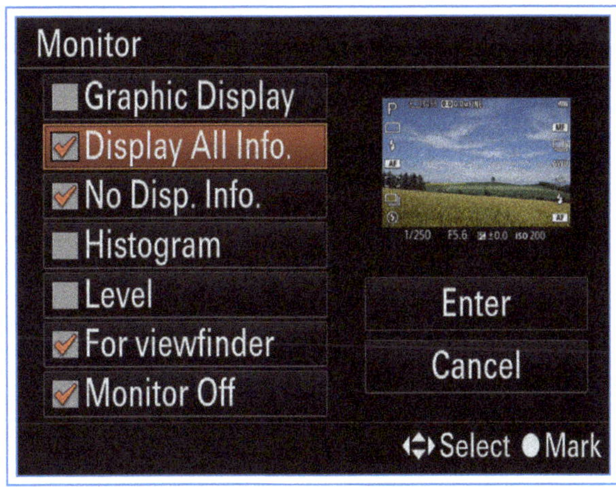

Figure 5-21. Monitor Display Screen Options

This screen shows the seven display screens you can select for the monitor. The selection screen for the viewfinder is identical to this one, except that the sixth and seventh choices, For Viewfinder and Monitor Off, are not available as choices to appear in the viewfinder. The For Viewfinder display screen is designed to appear on the monitor to provide shooting information when you are viewing the live view through the viewfinder, and the Monitor Off screen is designed to black out the monitor to avoid distracting those around you when it is not needed, such as when the camera is on a tripod and you don't need to make any further adjustments.

Five of the seven display screens available for the monitor are shown in Figure 5-22 through Figure 5-26. The screens displaying just the image with no information and showing a black monitor are not shown here. Figure 5-22 shows the version of the screen with the Graphic Display in the lower right corner; that display is supposed to illustrate the use of faster shutter speeds to stop action and the use of wider apertures to blur backgrounds. I find it distracting and not especially helpful, but if it is useful to you, by all means select it.

I find the Display All Information screen, shown in Figure 5-23, to be cluttered, but it has useful information. You can always move away from this screen by pressing the Display button (if there is at least one other display screen available), and I like to have it available for times when I need to see what settings are in effect.

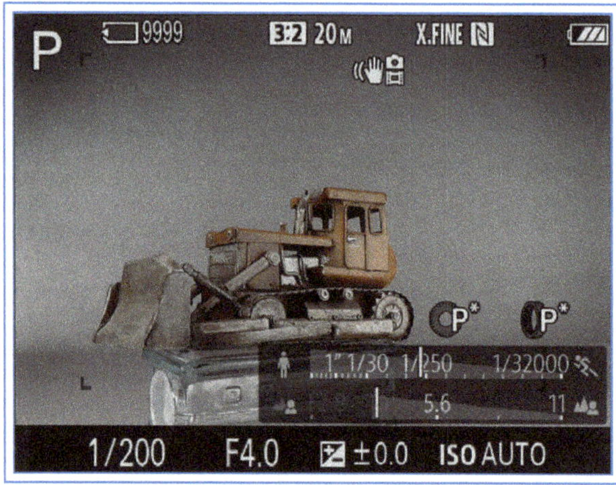

Figure 5-22. Graphic Display Screen

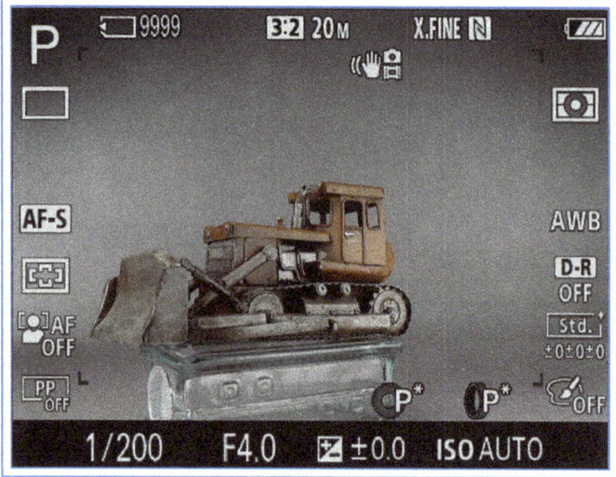

Figure 5-23. Display All Information Screen

The third option, displaying only the image, isn't shown here. This display is good for focusing and composing your shot. I always include it in the cycle of screens.

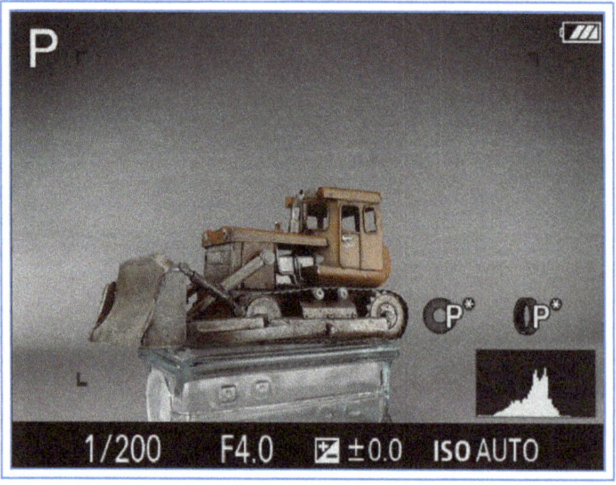

Figure 5-24. Histogram Screen

The fourth screen, shown in Figure 5-24, displays the histogram. This shooting-mode histogram, unlike the one displayed in playback mode, shows only basic exposure information with no color data. However, it gives you an idea of whether your image will be well exposed, letting you adjust exposure compensation and other settings as appropriate while watching the live histogram on the screen. If you can make the histogram display look like a triangular mountain centered in the box, you are likely to have a good result.

You should try to keep the body of the histogram away from the right and left edges of the graph, in most cases. If the histogram runs into the left edge, that means shadow areas are clipping and details in those areas are being lost. If it hits the right edge, you are losing details in highlights. If you have to choose, it is best to keep the graph away from the right edge because it is harder to recover details from clipped highlights than from clipped shadows.

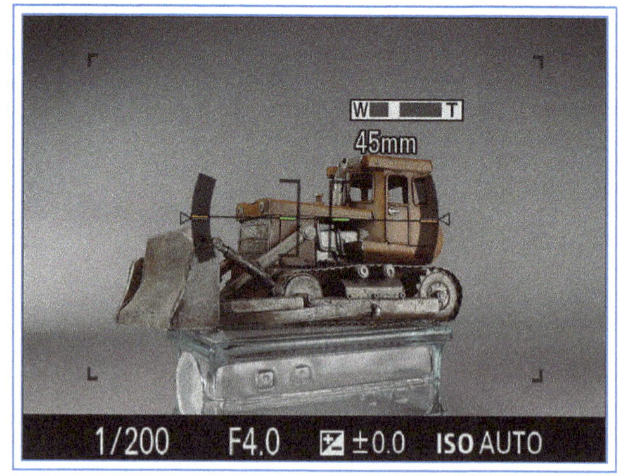

Figure 5-25. Level Screen

The fifth available display screen, shown in Figure 5-25, includes the RX100 VI's level, which is a useful tool for leveling the camera both side-to-side and front-to-back.

Watch the small orange lines on the screen; when the outer two ones have turned green, the camera is level side-to-side; when the inner two lines are green, the camera is level front-to-back.

The sixth choice, shown in Figure 5-26, which is available only for the monitor, is called For Viewfinder.

This option is the only one that provides shooting information but does not include the live view in shooting mode. Instead, it displays a black screen with detailed information about the camera's settings, so you can check your settings after (or before) you look at the live view in the viewfinder. In addition, as I will discuss in Chapter 6, this screen includes the Quick Navi system.

When you press the Function button, the settings on the screen become active. You can navigate through the settings using the direction buttons and adjust them using the control wheel and the control ring.

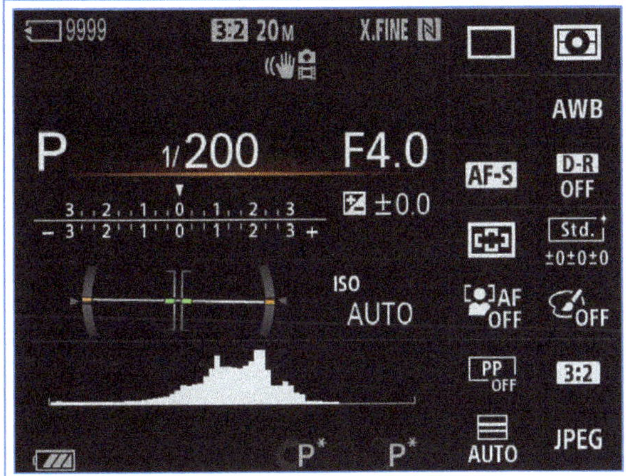

Figure 5-26. For Viewfinder Screen

The seventh and final option, not illustrated here, is the blank screen, which is available only for the monitor. It is provided for when you want to turn the display completely off to avoid distracting or disrupting people around you, or to preserve battery life.

Once you select the Display Button option and choose whether to select screens for the monitor or viewfinder, you can scroll through the seven (monitor) or five (viewfinder) choices using the control wheel or the direction buttons. When a screen you want to have displayed is highlighted, press the Center button to put an orange check mark in the box to the left of the screen's label, as seen earlier in Figure 5-21.

You can also press that button to unmark a box. The camera will let you uncheck all seven of the items for the monitor (or all five for the viewfinder), but if you do that, you will see an error message as you try to exit the menu screen. You have to check at least one box so that some screen will display when the camera is in shooting mode.

After you select from one to seven screens for the monitor and from one to five for the viewfinder, highlight the Enter block and press the Center button. Then, whenever the camera is in shooting mode, the selected screens will be displayed; you cycle through them by pressing the Display button (Up button). If you have selected only one screen, pressing the Display button will have no effect in shooting mode.

If you select for the monitor only the screen that includes the live view but no shooting information, the camera will still always display the shutter speed, aperture, exposure compensation, and ISO; all of those values are displayed in the black strip below the area where the image is displayed. However, if you select the screen that blanks out the monitor completely, not even that basic shooting information will be displayed.

Finder/Monitor

This next option, shown in Figure 5-27, lets you choose whether to view shooting and playback displays on the RX100 VI's LCD screen or in the viewfinder.

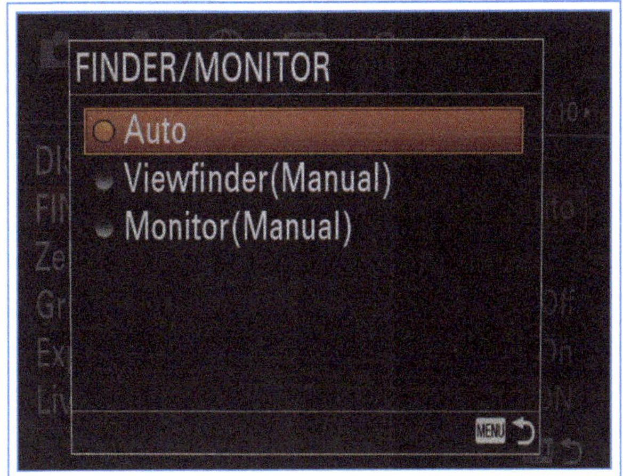

Figure 5-27. Finder/Monitor Options Screen

The viewfinder can provide the same information as the LCD screen, but its display is viewed inside an eye-level window that is shaded from daylight, giving you a clear view of the shooting, playback, and menu screens.

By default, this menu option is set to Auto, which means the camera switches to the viewfinder automatically when you move your head near the eye sensor to the right of the viewfinder. The camera turns on the viewfinder display and blacks out the LCD.

If you prefer to use either the viewfinder or the LCD screen at all times, set this menu option to Viewfinder (Manual) or Monitor (Manual), according to your preference. With either of those settings, the camera will not switch to the other method of viewing unless you go back to this menu option and change the setting, or change it using a control button that is assigned to that function, as discussed later in this chapter.

For me, the Auto option works well, and I rarely change that setting. But if you will be using the LCD while working with your head (or another object) close to the camera's viewfinder, you might prefer the Monitor (Manual) option so the screen does not blank out unexpectedly. Or, if you know you will not be using the monitor, you can choose Viewfinder (Manual).

Zebra Setting

This next Camera Settings2 menu option gives you a tool for measuring the exposure level of an image or video when you are composing your shots. This menu item has two sub-options, Zebra Display and Zebra Level, as shown in Figure 5-28.

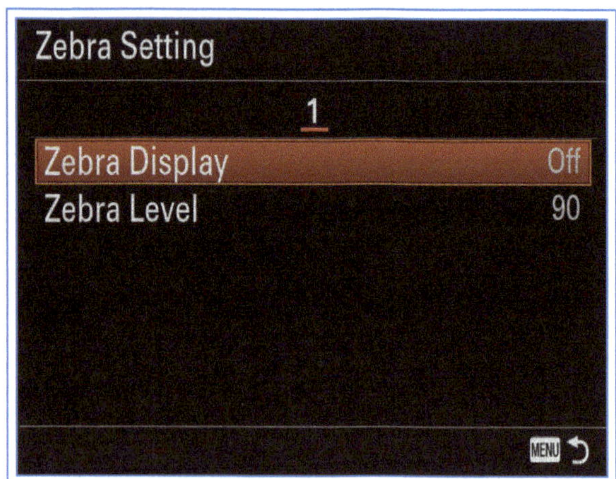

Figure 5-28. Zebra Setting Options Screen

Zebra Display can be turned either on or off, to determine whether the Zebra stripes are displayed on the shooting screen. The Zebra Level option can be set to a value from 70 to 100 IRE in five-unit increments, or 100+ for values greater than 100. The IRE units are a measure of relative brightness or exposure, with 0 representing black and 100 representing white.

You also can save and later use two custom values, C1 and C2, as discussed below. Figure 5-29 shows the screen for selecting values up to 90.

When you turn Zebra Display on at any level, you very likely will see, in some parts of the display, the black-and-white "zebra" stripes that give this feature its name.

Zebra stripes originally were created as a feature for professional video cameras, so the videographer could see whether the scene would be properly exposed. This tool often is used in the context of recording an interview, when proper exposure of a human face is the main concern.

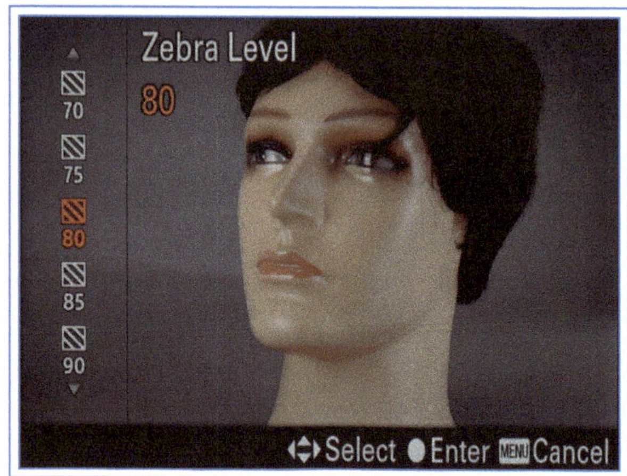

Figure 5-29. Zebra Level Options Screen

There are various approaches to using these stripes. Some videographers like to set the zebra function to 90 IRE and adjust the exposure so the stripes barely appear in the brightest parts of the image. Another recommendation is to set the option to 75 IRE for a scene with Caucasian skin, and expose so that the stripes barely appear in the area of the skin.

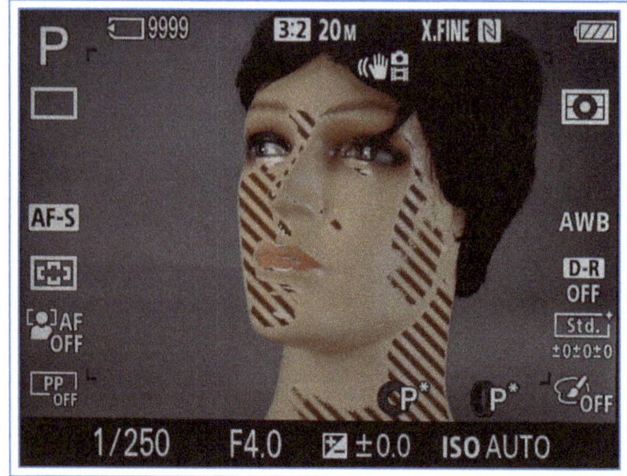

Figure 5-30. Zebra in Use at Level 75

In Figure 5-30, I set IRE to 75 and exposed to have the stripes appear clearly on the mannequin's face and neck.

As the brightness of the lighting increases for a subject, there may be no stripes at first, then they will gradually appear until they cover the subject, then they will seem to disappear, because the exposure is so bright that the subject is surrounded by an outline of "marching ants" rather than having stripes in its interior.

If you want to save customized values for Zebra, you can save settings to the C1 and C2 slots. A standard way to use these two values is to set C1 to a value for exposure confirmation and C2 to a value for flare confirmation.

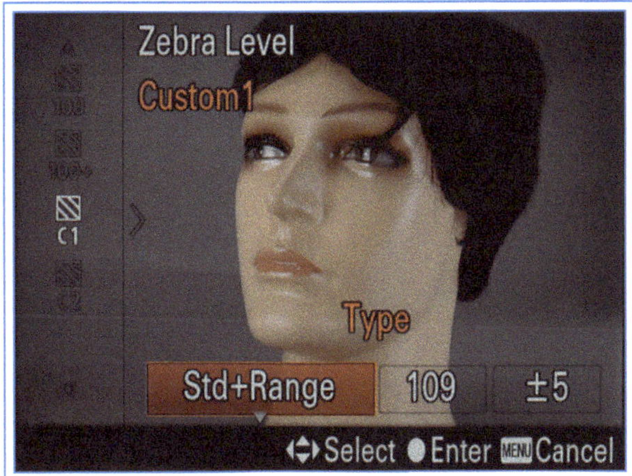

Figure 5-31. Standard + Range Block Highlighted

To set C1 for exposure confirmation, select Zebra Level, scroll down to the C1 block and press the Right button. You will see a screen like that in Figure 5-31, with the Std+Range block highlighted in orange. (Press the Up or Down button or turn the control wheel if necessary to bring that label into the block.)

With the Std+Range block highlighted, press the Right button to move to the next block, and use the Up and Down buttons or the control wheel to set a value, which can be from zero to 109, in one-unit increments. Then press the Right button to move to the next block and select a range, which can be from ±1 to ±10.

For example, you might set the first block to 77 and the second block to ±5, so the Zebra pattern would appear when the brightness of the scene was within five units of 77, plus or minus. You could then set Zebra to C1 to confirm that the scene's exposure is within that range.

To set the C2 value for flare confirmation, scroll down to that block and press the Right button. Make sure the highlighted block contains the Lower Limit label, as shown in Figure 5-32.

Then press the Right button to move to the second block and select a setting from 50+ to 109+ in one-unit increments. That value represents the brightness level that you don't want to exceed. You can then set Zebra to the C2 block and check the scene to make sure the lighting stays within that limit, to avoid flare. The Zebra pattern will appear if that limit is exceeded.

Zebra is a feature to consider, especially for video recording, but the RX100 VI has an excellent metering system, including both live and playback histograms, so you can manage without this option if you don't want to deal with its learning curve.

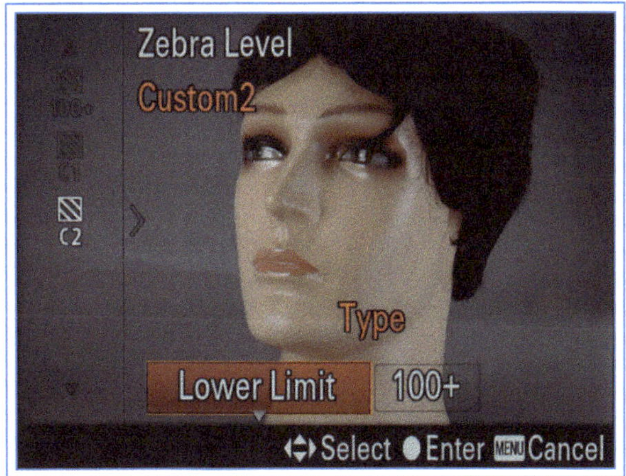

Figure 5-32. Lower Limit Block Highlighted

Grid Line

With this option, you can select one of four settings for a grid to be superimposed on the shooting screen. By default, there is no grid. If you choose one of the grid options, the lines will appear in your chosen configuration whenever the camera is showing the live view in shooting mode, whether the detailed display screen is selected or not. Of course, the grid does not appear when the For Viewfinder display, with its black screen full of shooting information, is displayed, or when the blank screen is selected. The four options are seen in Figure 5-33.

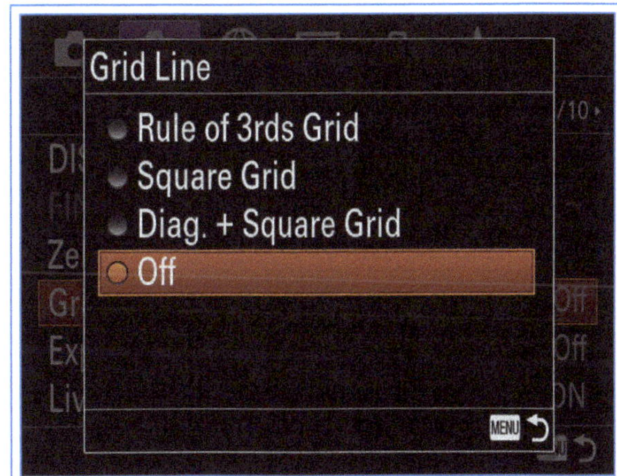

Figure 5-33. Grid Line Options Screen

Following are descriptions of these choices, other than Off, which leaves the screen with no grid.

Rule of Thirds Grid

This arrangement has two vertical lines and two horizontal lines, dividing the screen into nine blocks, as shown in Figure 5-34.

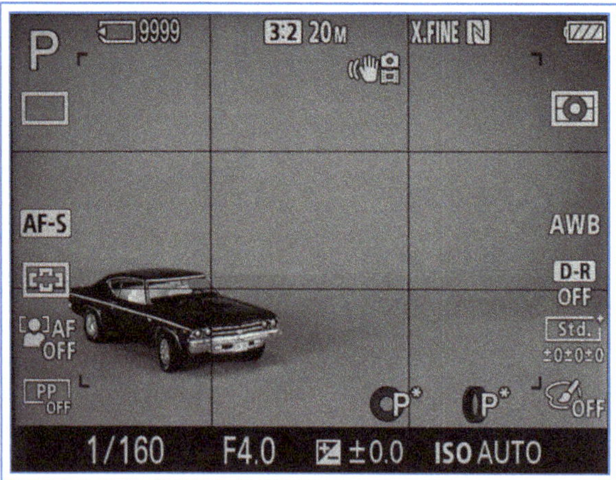

Figure 5-34. Rule of Thirds Grid in Use

This grid follows a rule of composition that calls for locating an important subject at an intersection of these lines, which will place the subject one-third of the way from the edge of the image. This arrangement can add interest and asymmetry to an image.

Square Grid

With this setting, the grid has five vertical lines and three horizontal lines, dividing the display into 24 blocks, as seen in Figure 5-35. In this way, you can still use the Rule of Thirds, but you have additional lines available for lining up items, such as the horizon or the edge of a building, that need to be straight.

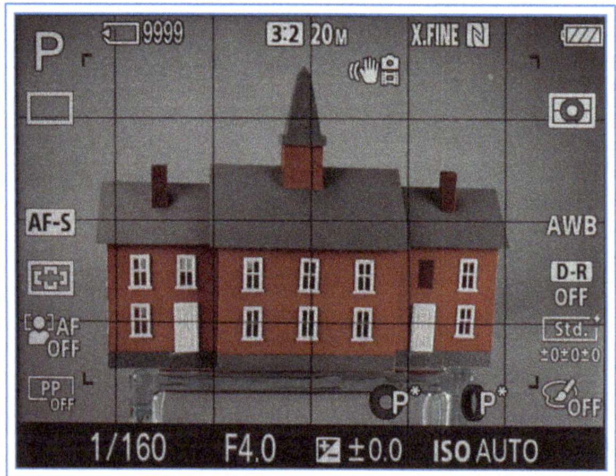

Figure 5-35. Square Grid in Use

Diagonal Plus Square Grid

The last option gives you a square grid of four blocks in each direction and adds two diagonal lines, as shown in Figure 5-36.

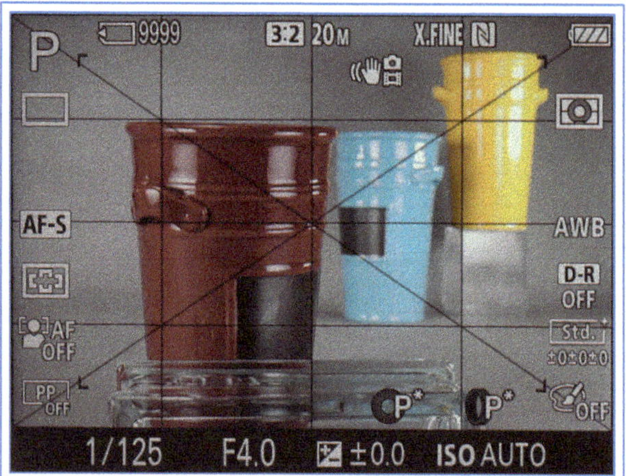

Figure 5-36. Diagonal Plus Square Grid in Use

The idea is that placing a subject or, more likely, a string of subjects along one of the diagonals can add interest to the image by drawing the viewer's eye into the image along the diagonal line.

Exposure Settings Guide

The next option on the Custom menu, when turned on, activates a graphic display to simulate one or two sliding bands near the bottom of the screen, showing the settings for aperture, shutter speed, or both, when you adjust those settings using the control wheel. (When you adjust any of the above values using the control ring, the camera always displays a circular scale in the top half of the screen, regardless of the setting of this menu option.)

The display varies according to the shooting mode. In Program mode, two bands display aperture and shutter speed when you activate Program Shift using the control wheel. In Shutter Priority mode, a single band displays shutter speed as you adjust it. In Aperture Priority mode, a single band shows the aperture as you adjust it. In Manual mode, the display varies according to which value is currently being adjusted by the control wheel.

Figure 5-37 shows the display when shutter speed is being adjusted. I find this display distracting, so I leave it turned off, but it might be useful to see this display to let you know what value is being set, in some circumstances.

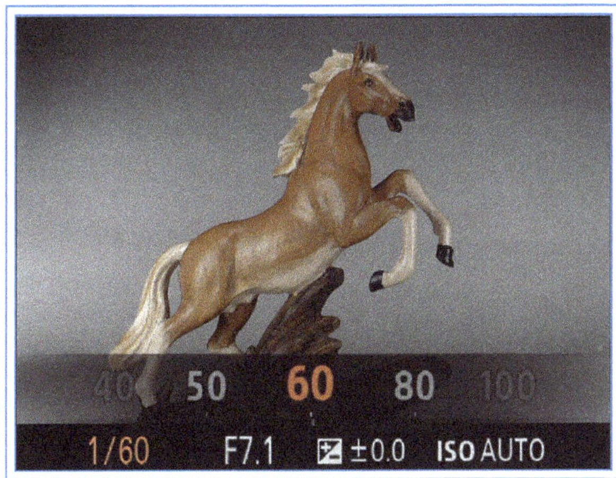

Figure 5-37. Exposure Settings Guide in Use

Live View Display

This menu option can be important for getting results that match your expectations. It lets you choose whether or not the camera displays the effects that certain settings will have on your final image, while you are composing the image.

When you select this option, you will see two sub-options on the next screen: Setting Effect On and Setting Effect Off, as shown in Figure 5-38.

If you select Setting Effect On, then, when you are using Program, Aperture Priority, Shutter Priority, or Manual exposure mode, the camera's display in shooting mode will show the effects of exposure compensation, white balance, Creative Style, and Picture Effect, with some limitations. In addition, it will show the effects of exposure changes in Manual exposure mode and other advanced modes, to some extent.

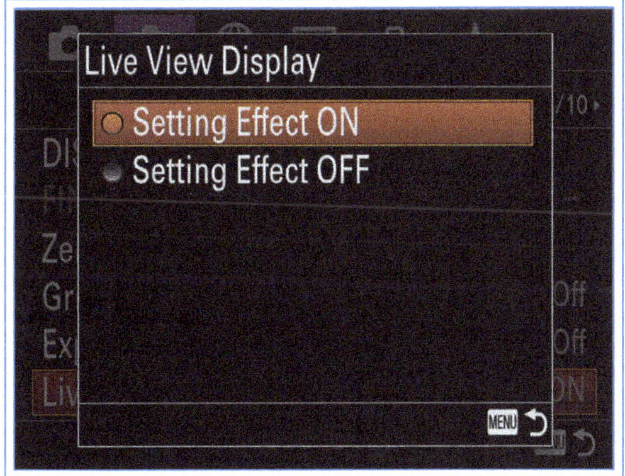

Figure 5-38. Live View Display Options Screen

In some cases, it may be helpful to see what effect a particular setting will have on the final image, and in other cases that feature might be distracting or might even make it difficult to take the shot.

For example, when you are setting white balance, it can be helpful to see how the various options will alter the appearance of your final images. If you have selected Setting Effect On, then, as you scroll through the white balance menu options, you will instantly see the effect of each setting, such as Daylight, Cloudy, Shade, and Incandescent. That change in the display is not distracting; it is actually quite informative.

However, if you are using the Picture Effect option and experimenting with a setting such as Posterization, which drastically alters the appearance of your images, you might find it difficult to compose the image with Setting Effect On selected.

There is one particular use for the Live View Display menu option that I find practically indispensable. On occasion, I use the RX100 VI to trigger external optical slave flash units, with the camera set to Manual exposure mode. For some of these shots, I use settings such as f/9.0, 1/200 second, and ISO 80. This shot will be exposed properly with the flash units I am using, but, with Setting Effect On selected, the camera's screen is completely dark as I compose the shot. That is because the camera's programming does not account for the fact that flash units will be fired.

If I use the Setting Effect Off setting, then the camera displays the scene using the available ambient light, ignoring the settings I have made. In this way, I can see the scene on the camera's display in order to compose the shot properly.

The Setting Effect On option, though, can be useful when using Aperture Priority, Shutter Priority, or Manual exposure mode when you are shooting in unusually dark or bright conditions, because the camera's display screen will change its brightness to alert you that a normal exposure may not be possible with the current settings. (You should see the aperture, shutter speed, M.M., or exposure compensation value flashing to alert you to this situation, also.)

With the Picture Effect setting, some of the options will not change the appearance of the display, even with Setting Effect On activated. Those options are

Soft Focus, HDR Painting, Rich-tone Monochrome, Miniature, Watercolor, and Illustration. You can see the effects of those settings in playback mode, after you have captured an image using one of the settings.

When Setting Effect Off is selected, the camera will display a VIEW icon on the screen, as shown in Figure 5-39, to remind you that the camera's display is not showing the effects of all your settings.

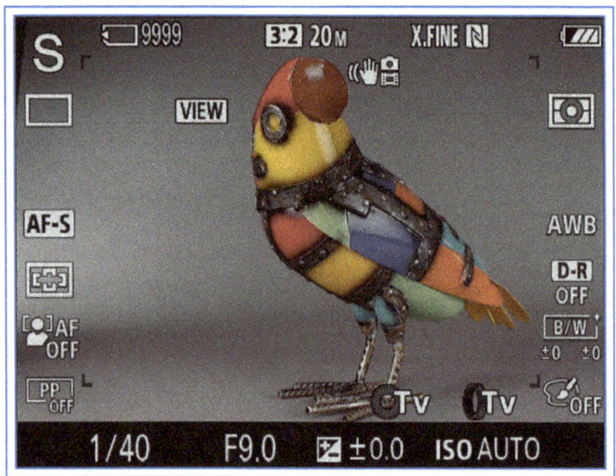

Figure 5-39. VIEW Icon on Shooting Screen for Setting Effect Off

My recommendation is to leave this option at Setting Effect On unless it is difficult to compose a shot, either because the display is too dark or light, or because a setting such as Picture Effect interferes with your ability to view the subject clearly.

In the Intelligent Auto, Scene, Sweep Panorama, HFR, and Movie modes, this option is forced to Setting Effect On and cannot be changed.

The single item on screen 8 of the Camera Settings2 menu is shown in Figure 5-40.

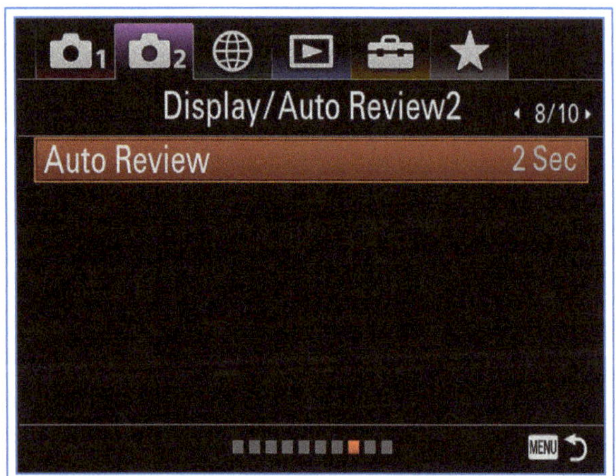

Figure 5-40. Screen 8 of Camera Settings2 Menu

Auto Review

The Auto Review option, shown in Figure 5-41, sets the length of time that an image appears on the display screen immediately after you take a still picture.

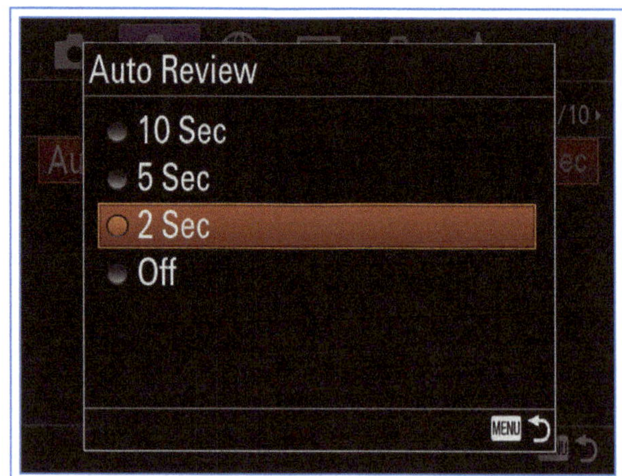

Figure 5-41. Auto Review Options Screen

The default is two seconds, but you can set the time to five or ten seconds, or you can turn the function off. If you turn it off, the camera will return to shooting mode as soon as it has saved a new image to the memory card. When this option is in use, you can always return to the live view by pressing the shutter button halfway. The Auto Review option does not apply to movies; the camera does not display the beginning frame of a movie that was just recorded until you press the Playback button.

While the new image is being displayed, you can use the various functions of playback mode, such as enlarging the image, bringing up index screens, moving to other images, or pressing the Delete button to delete the image. If you start one of these actions before the camera has reverted to shooting mode, the camera will stay in playback mode until you take further action to change out of that mode.

The items on screen 9 of the Camera Settings2 menu are shown in Figure 5-42.

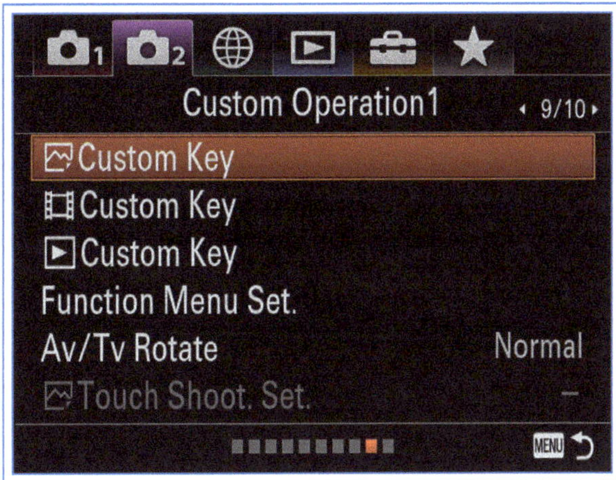

Figure 5-42. Screen 9 of Camera Settings2 Menu

Custom Key (Still Images/Movies/Playback)

As I will discuss in Chapter 6, four of the camera's control buttons and the control ring can have their functions changed through menu options, for when they are activated in shooting mode for still images or movies, and one control (the Function button) can have its function changed for playback mode. The Custom Key (Still Images/Movies/Playback) menu option is the mechanism for changing the functions of physical controls.

These options are provided in three separate menu options on screen 9 of the Camera Settings2 menu: Custom Key (Still Images), Custom Key (Movies), and Custom Key (Playback), as shown in Figure 5-42. I will discuss these three options individually below.

Custom Key (Still Images)

When you select this first Custom Key option, you will see the screen shown in Figure 5-43, which shows the five controls that can be assigned. Move to the line for a control and press the Center Button. You will see a list of all the options that can be assigned to that control. In most cases, these choices are self-explanatory. When you assign a function, such as ISO, to a button, pressing the button calls up the menu screen for the option, which lets you adjust it as if you had selected it from the Shooting menu.

However, there are differences for some assignments, and there are some items that can be assigned through this option that are not available through any menu. I will discuss these details below.

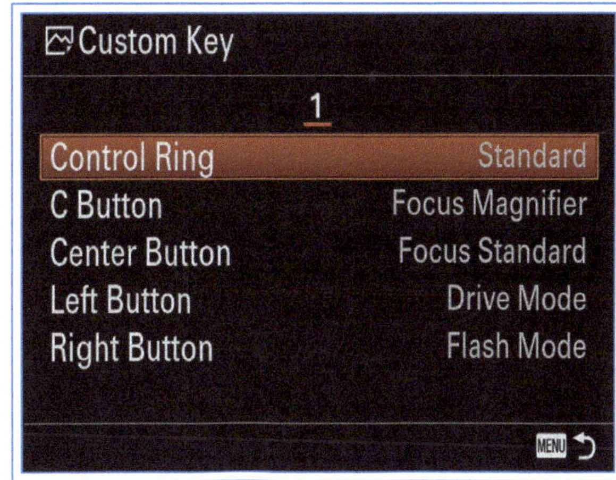

Figure 5-43. Custom Key (Still Images) Options Screen

Control Ring

The first control on the Custom Key (Still Images) menu screen is the control ring. This control is a special case, because, of course, it is not a button but a ring. The options that can be assigned to the ring are Standard, Aperture, Shutter Speed, Exposure Compensation, ISO, white balance, Creative Style, Picture Effect, Zoom, or Not Set, the first five of which are shown in Figure 5-44. You have to scroll from one menu screen to the next using the Right button to see the remaining options, which are on four screens.

The ability to assign a function to the control ring is powerful because, when you assign a setting such as ISO to this ring, you can use the ring to adjust the setting instantly. For example, if you choose ISO, then, when the camera is in shooting mode, all you have to do is turn the control ring and the ISO setting will change. You can then immediately press the shutter button to take a picture with the new setting.

However, you cannot get access to all aspects of these settings by turning the ring. For example, if you assign ISO to the ring, you can select a numerical ISO value or Auto ISO, but you cannot set the minimum and maximum settings for Auto ISO, and you cannot select a value for the Multi Frame Noise Reduction setting.

Similarly, if you assign white balance to the control ring, you can select a preset option, including Custom or Color Temperature, but you cannot set a new custom white balance or choose a new Color Temperature setting, and you cannot fine-tune the white balance using the color axes. For those options, you need to use the White Balance menu option. Likewise, with Creative Style assigned to the ring, you cannot adjust the contrast, sharpness, and saturation parameters of a selected setting, though you can select a custom setting that has been saved with adjustments to those parameters.

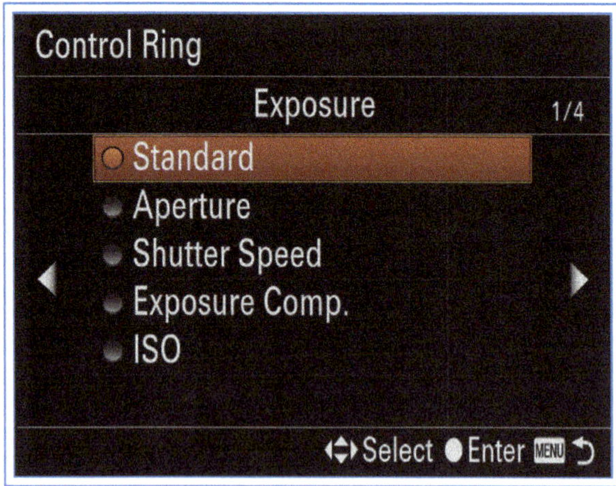

Figure 5-44. First Screen of Options for Control Ring

However, with Picture Effect, you can select any of the settings or sub-settings, because the control ring will cycle through all of the options, including, for example, the sub-settings for Toy Camera, which are Normal, Cool, Warm, Green, and Magenta.

When the control ring has been assigned to a function, the camera puts an icon representing the ring in the bottom right of the screen next to an icon or label indicating the setting currently assigned to the ring. For example, Figure 5-45 shows the screen as it appears when ISO has been assigned to the control ring.

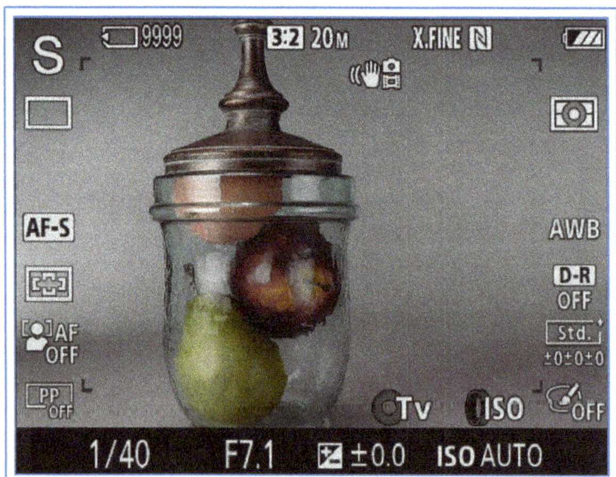

Figure 5-45. Icon Showing Control Ring Controls ISO

By default, the control ring's function is set to Standard. In that case, the ring controls various functions in the various shooting modes, as shown in Table 5-2.

Table 5-2. Control Ring: Standard Setting—Shooting Modes vs. Assigned Functions

Shooting Mode	Assigned Function
Intelligent Auto	Zoom
Superior Auto	Zoom
Program	Program Shift
Aperture Priority	Aperture
Shutter Priority	Shutter Speed
Manual Exposure	Aperture
Scene	Scene Selection
Sweep Panorama	Direction
Movie/HFR	Depends on Movie or HFR exposure mode setting
Memory Recall	Depends on saved setting

Or you can choose the final option, Not Set, in which case the ring will control only manual focus from the shooting screen. (It also will select items with the Function menu and Quick Navi system.) In my opinion, the Standard option is the most useful, but you might prefer to use the control ring for one specific purpose, such as controlling exposure compensation, ISO, or zoom for all shooting modes.

C (Custom) Button

If you select C Button from the Custom Key (Still Images) menu screen, the camera will display a screen like that shown in Figure 5-46, which lists up to six of the many options that can be assigned to the Custom button. The whole list takes up 20 screens; scroll through those screens using the Left and Right buttons.

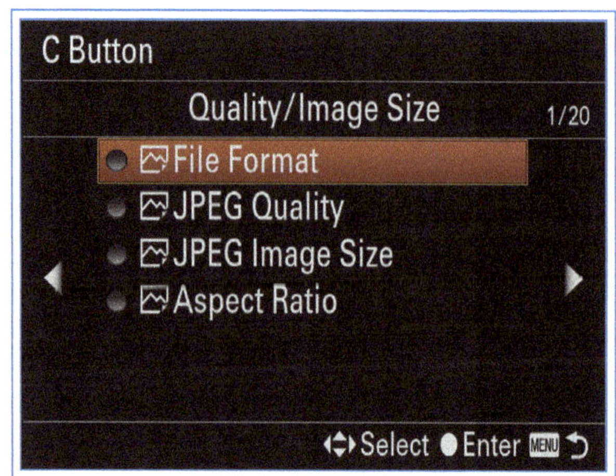

Figure 5-46. One Screen of Options for C Button

The complete list includes the following choices, any one of which can be assigned to this button:

- File Format (Still Images)
- JPEG Quality
- JPEG Image Size
- Aspect Ratio
- Drive Mode
- Self-timer During Bracketing
- Memory
- Focus Mode
- AF/MF Control Hold
- AF/MF Control Toggle
- Focus Standard
- Focus Area
- Registered AF Area Hold
- Registered AF Area Toggle
- Center Lock-on AF
- Face Priority in AF
- Eye AF
- Exposure Compensation
- ISO
- ISO Auto Minimum Shutter Speed
- Metering Mode
- Face Priority in Multi Meter
- AEL Hold
- AEL Toggle
- Spot AEL Hold
- Spot AEL Toggle
- Flash Mode
- Flash Compensation
- White Balance
- Priority Set in Auto White Balance
- DRO/Auto HDR
- Creative Style
- Picture Effect
- Picture Profile
- Soft Skin Effect
- Focus Magnifier
- Peaking Display Select
- Peaking Level
- Peaking Color
- Smile Shutter
- Auto Object Framing
- In-Camera Guide
- MOVIE (start/stop movie recording)
- Frame Rate (HFR)
- Auto Dual Recording
- SteadyShot (Movies)
- Marker Display Select
- Shutter Type
- SteadyShot (Still Images)
- Smart Teleconverter
- Finder/Monitor Select
- Zebra Display Select
- Zebra Level
- Grid Line
- Live View Display Select
- Bright Monitoring
- Audio Signals
- Send to Smartphone

- Playback
- Monitor Brightness
- Gamma Display Assist
- Touch Operation Select
- TC/UB Display Switch
- Not Set

Scroll through the list and press the Center button to make your selection. The dot next to the chosen option will turn orange to mark the choice.

Many of these options are self-explanatory because, when the button has the option assigned, pressing the button will simply call up the menu screen for that option, if the option is available in the current shooting mode. For example, if the Custom button is assigned to drive mode, then, when you press the button, the camera displays the drive mode menu, just as if you had used the Menu button to get access to that option. (In some cases, the screen looks different from the menu screen called up with the Menu button, but the regular menu options are available in every case.) I will not discuss those options here; see Chapter 4 for discussion of the Camera Settings1 menu, Chapter 5 for the Camera Settings2 menu, Chapter 8 for the Setup menu, and Chapter 10 for discussion of the Network menu.

With the following choices, the assigned button switches between menu options without first calling up a menu screen: Peaking Display Select, Marker Display Select, Finder/Monitor Select, Zebra Display Select, Live View Display Select, Touch Operation Select, and TC/UB Display Switch. (TC/UB Display Switch selects counter, time code, or user bit display for movie recording.)

There are several other selections for the Custom button (and the other control buttons) that do not call up a menu screen. Instead, they perform a function that is not available from a menu option. I will discuss those selections below.

AF/MF Control Hold

If you select AF/MF Control Hold for the Custom button's function, pressing the button switches the camera between autofocus and manual focus, but only while you hold down the button. If the camera is set to any autofocus mode, pressing and holding the Custom button will switch the camera into manual focus mode. Releasing it will switch to the autofocus mode that was originally set. If the camera is set to manual focus mode, pressing and holding the button will switch to single-shot AF mode. In this situation, when you press the Custom button, the camera will also evaluate the focus and lock focus, if possible. Releasing the button will switch back to manual focus mode. If the camera is set to DMF mode, pressing the button will toggle between DMF and manual focus.

This function is useful in situations when it is difficult to use autofocus, such as dark areas, extreme closeups, or areas where you have to shoot through obstructions such as glass or wire cages. You can switch quickly into manual focus mode and back again, as conditions warrant.

Also, this capability is helpful if you want to set zone focusing, so you can shoot quickly without having to wait for the autofocus mechanism to operate. For example, if you are doing street photography, you can set the camera to single-shot autofocus mode and focus on a subject at about the distance you expect to be shooting from—say, 25 feet (7.6 meters). Then, once focus is locked on that subject, press and hold the Custom button to switch the camera to manual focus mode, and the focus will be locked at that distance in manual focus mode. You can then take shots of subjects at that distance without having to refocus. If you need to set another focus distance, release the Custom button to go back to autofocus mode and repeat the process.

Finally, it is convenient to quickly get the camera to use autofocus when it is set to manual focus mode. With this function, as noted above, when you press and release the Custom button, the camera will quickly focus using autofocus, and then go back to manual focus mode for any further adjustments you may want to make. This capability is sometimes called "back button focus," meaning you can press a button on the back of the camera to force it to use its autofocus mechanism.

AF/MF Control Toggle

If you select AF/MF Control Toggle for the setting of the Custom button's function, pressing the button switches the camera between autofocus and manual focus. This option works the same as AF/MF Control Hold, except that you do not hold down the button; you just press it and release it. The switched focus mode then stays in effect until you press the button again. However, with this setting, the camera will not use its autofocus to focus on the scene when you press the assigned button. For that "back button focus" operation, you have to use the AF/MF Control Hold option, discussed above.

Focus Standard

I discussed this option in Chapter 4, in connection with the focus area menu option. When the Custom button is assigned to Focus Standard, it has two functions when pressed while the shooting screen is displayed. First, if focus area is set to Zone, Flexible Spot, or Expand Flexible Spot, pressing the Focus Standard button makes the focus zone or frame movable, allowing you to re-position it on the display. Second, if Center Lock-on AF is turned on and focus area is set to Wide or Center, pressing the assigned button initiates tracking of the subject in the center of the display.

Registered AF Area Hold/Registered AF Area Toggle

These two options work in conjunction with the AF Area Registration option on screen 5 of the Camera Settings1 menu, which I discussed in Chapter 4. With that option, you can register a particular point on the camera's display as the point where you want the camera to use its autofocus. Once that area is registered, you can assign the Registered AF Area Hold option to a control button. When you press that button in shooting mode, the camera will place the autofocus frame at the registered area on the display. Then, while you hold down the assigned button, you can cause the camera to focus at that area.

If you assign the button to the Registered AF Area Toggle option, you don't have to hold down the assigned button; just press it and release it, and the autofocus area will be placed at the registered point. You then have to press the assigned button again to remove the autofocus area frame from the display.

It's useful to remember that the registered AF area will be flashing on the screen in shooting mode, to remind you of its location, so you can compose the shot with that frame at the proper position.

This function works only in the Program, Aperture Priority, Shutter Priority, and Manual shooting modes.

Eye AF

If you assign Eye AF to the Custom button, then, if the camera is set to an autofocus mode, when you press this button the camera will look for human eyes and focus on them if possible. If the camera detects an eye, it will display a small green frame to show that it has focused on the eye, as shown in Figure 5-47.

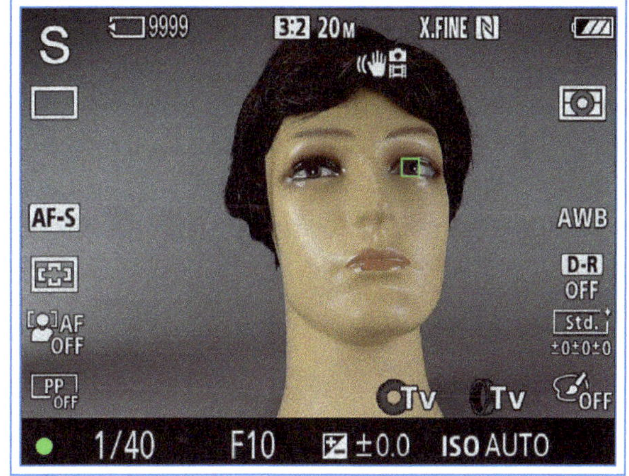

Figure 5-47. Green Frame for Eye AF

Continue to hold down the assigned button to lock focus on the eye while you press the shutter button to take the picture. The camera does not have to have face detection activated for this option to work, and it functions with single AF, automatic AF, continuous AF, and DMF. It does not function when manual focus is in effect.

Eye AF can be especially useful when depth of field is shallow, such as when the lens is zoomed in to a long focal length or you are shooting a closeup, to make sure the focus is sharpest on the subject's eyes rather than on the nose or some other feature. A portrait generally looks best when the eyes are in sharp focus.

This option also is useful to give you an instant way to focus on a face when you were not expecting to take a portrait. You can just press and hold the assigned button to focus on the nearest eye, which should result in a well-focused portrait. Eye AF is not available when recording movies.

AEL Hold

If you set the Custom button to the AEL Hold (Autoexposure Lock Hold) option, then, when the camera is in shooting mode, pressing this button will lock exposure at the current setting as metered by the camera, as long as you hold down the button. You also can lock exposure by pressing the shutter button halfway, if AEL with Shutter is in effect, as discussed earlier in this chapter. If that option is not in effect, you can use AEL Hold instead.

You might want to use AEL Hold to calibrate exposure for an object that is part of a larger scene, such as a dark painting on a light wall. You could lock exposure while holding the camera close to the painting, then move back to take a picture of the wall with the locked exposure ensuring the painting will be properly exposed.

Assuming the camera is in Program mode, hold the camera close to the painting until the metered aperture and shutter speed appear on the screen. Press and hold the Custom button and an asterisk (*) will appear in the lower right corner of the screen, as shown in Figure 5-48, indicating that exposure lock is in effect.

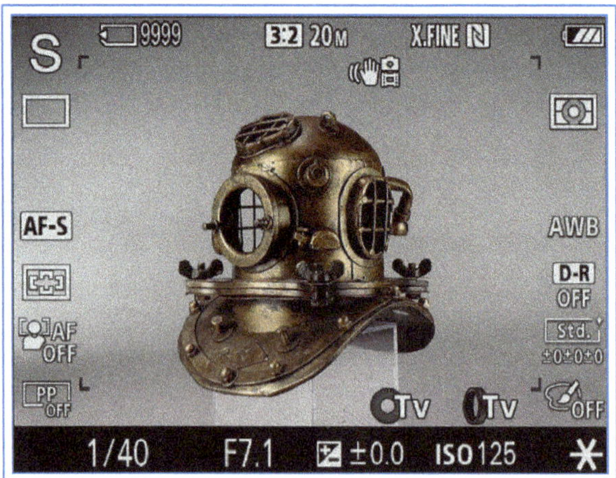

Figure 5-48. Asterisk Indicating AEL Hold in Effect

Now you can move back (or anywhere else) and take the photograph using the exposure setting that you locked in. Once you have finished using the locked exposure setting, release the Custom button to make the asterisk disappear. The camera is now ready to measure a new exposure reading.

If the camera is set to Manual exposure mode, pressing a control button assigned to AEL Hold activates Manual Shift, which I discussed in Chapter 3. While you hold down the button for AEL Hold, if you change the aperture or shutter speed, the camera will select a corresponding shutter speed or aperture to maintain the original exposure. This feature operates whether ISO is set to ISO Auto or to a numerical value.

AEL Toggle

If you set the Custom button to the AEL Toggle option, then, in shooting mode, pressing the button will lock exposure just as with AEL Hold. The difference with this setting is that you just press and release the button; the exposure will remain locked until you press the button again to cancel the exposure lock.

Spot AEL Hold

The next option for the Custom button is AEL Hold with a spot icon before the name. The spot icon means that, with this setting, when you press the button and hold it, the camera will lock exposure as metered by the spot-metering area in the center of the display, no matter what metering method is currently in effect. This option can be useful if you want to switch to spot-metering just for one or two shots. You can hold down the Custom button, make sure the center of the display covers the area you want to use for evaluating exposure, and take the shot with the exposure adjusted for that spot.

Spot AEL Toggle

The Spot AEL Toggle option is similar to the AEL Toggle option, except that the camera meters only in the spot area in the very center of the display, as with the Spot AEL Hold option.

In-Camera Guide

With this option, when the camera is displaying a menu you can press the assigned button to display a brief help screen with guidance or tips about the menu option that is highlighted. The help screen varies depending on the context.

If the camera is displaying the main page of a menu screen with the highlight on a particular feature, pressing the C button will bring up a screen with a brief message explaining the use of that feature. For example, Figure 5-49 shows the message that is shown when the camera is displaying screen 3 of the Camera Settings1 menu, with the drive mode item highlighted.

If you select a sub-option for a menu item and press the C button, the camera will display a message with details about that option. For example, Figure 5-50 shows the help screen that was displayed when I pressed the C button after highlighting the Continuous Shooting option for drive mode, with the Hi option selected for speed of shooting.

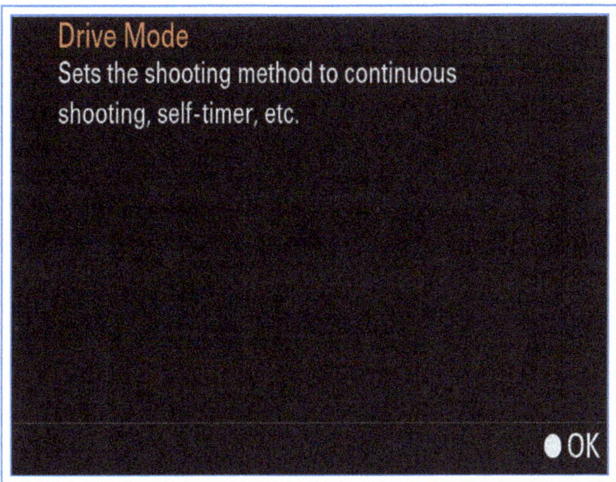

Figure 5-49. Help Screen for Drive Mode Menu Item

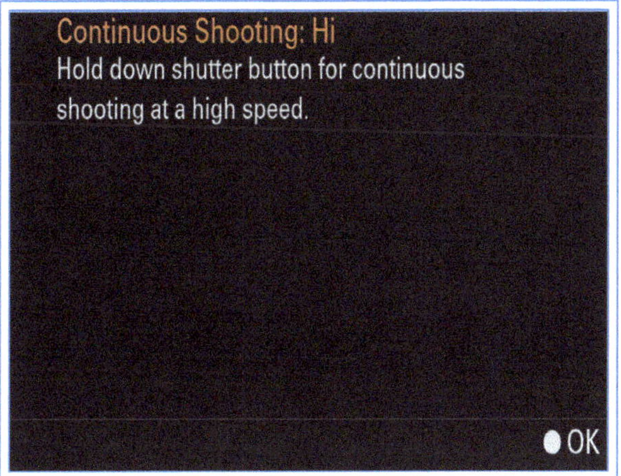

Figure 5-50. Help Screen for High-speed Burst Shooting Item

This help system is quite detailed; for example, it provides guidance even for different ISO settings, such as ISO 100, 320, and 1600, with tips about when to use each setting. The help function operates with all of the RX100 VI menu systems, including Camera Settings1 and 2, Playback, Network, and Setup. It also works with the Function menu and the Quick Navi system to give information about a highlighted option.

Movie

The Movie setting does not call up a menu option. When you assign a button to this setting, the button takes on the same role as the camera's red Movie button. This option gives you another way to start and stop the recording of a video. If you set the Movie Button menu option to Movie Mode Only, this button will start recording a video only if the mode dial is set to Movie mode.

Smart Teleconverter

The next non-menu choice for assignment to a control button is Smart Teleconverter. With this option, when you press the assigned button and release it, the camera enlarges the current image by a factor of 1.4 times and crops the enlarged image to fill the frame. If you press the button again, the magnification increases to 2.0 times. The camera does not do any enhancement of the image; it just crops away some of the pixels in the image, which results in a loss of some resolution.

Some users like this feature because it gives them a quick way to get an enlarged view of the scene—just press a button and you immediately get a 1.4x magnification. Press again for a 2.0x view, and a third time to return to normal size. With the 20-megapixel sensor of the RX100 VI, you can afford to lose some resolution if you capture an image with this feature in use. Some people like to be able to compose a shot while looking at a magnified view, and then go back to the normal view to capture it. They may want to have the camera's metering system evaluate the exposure for the enlarged area before capturing the final image. In any event, if you find this feature useful, it is available here and easy to use. It is not available when File Format (Still Images) is set to Raw. Also note that this feature conflicts with some other features, such as Clear Image Zoom, Digital Zoom and Lock-on AF.

Bright Monitoring

This option is intended for a specific situation: when you are using manual focus in dark conditions that make it difficult to evaluate the focus on the LCD screen or in the viewfinder. In that situation, when you press the button assigned to Bright Monitoring, the camera increases the display's brightness and sets the Live View Display option to Setting Effect Off, if it was not already set that way. With Setting Effect Off, the display does not darken or brighten to show the effects of exposure settings; instead, it maintains a normal brightness if possible.

If you have the focus mode set to any option other than manual focus, this key assignment will have no effect. It works only in the PASM shooting modes, and it does not work if either MF Assist or Focus Magnifier is turned on. When you have finished using this feature, press the assigned button again to turn it off.

This setting is designed for use when you really can't see the LCD screen, such as when you are trying to make a long exposure outdoors at night or you need to take a portrait in very dim light.

Playback

This option causes the assigned button to act just like the Playback button, to place the camera into playback mode so you can review images and videos in the camera.

Not Set

The last option that can be assigned to the Custom button is called Not Set. If you choose this option, then the button will not be assigned any special function. You may want to select this option if you will be using a limited number of settings and don't want to risk activating a different setting by pressing the button accidentally.

Center Button

Next, you can assign the Center button to any of the same options as for the Custom button, except In-Camera Guide.

Left Button

The possible assignments for the Left button are the same as for the Custom button, except that the following seven choices are not available: AF/MF Control Hold, Focus Standard, Registered AF Area Hold, Eye AF, AEL Hold, Spot AEL Hold, and In-Camera Guide. So, if you want to set the Left button to lock exposure or to switch between autofocus and manual focus, the button will act only as a toggle, not as one that you have to hold down. Presumably, Sony made this choice because it would be awkward to hold down the Left button while pressing the shutter button. (Eye AF and Registered AF Area Hold also require that you hold down the control button while pressing the shutter button.)

Right Button

The Right button has the same options available for assignment as the Left button.

Custom Key (Movies)

This menu option lets you assign a function to any of the same five controls as for the Custom Key (Still Images) option, discussed above. The choices are similar to those for that menu option, but there are some differences. First, for each of the controls, the last option in the list of choices for assignment to the control is called Follow Custom (Still Images). If you assign that option to a control, the control will have the same function as was assigned to that control using the Custom Key (Still Images) menu option.

That assignment will be in place even if it cannot take effect. For example, if the Left button is assigned to the JPEG Image Size option with the Custom Key (Still Images) option, and you then choose Follow Custom (Still Images) for the assignment of the Left Button with the Custom Key Movie option, that assignment will be in place, even though the JPEG Image Size option is not compatible with movie recording. If you press the assigned button with the mode dial set to Movie mode, you will see an error message.

The other difference from the Custom Key (Still Images) option is that the lists of possible assignments for the various controls are in most cases shorter for the Custom Key (Movies) option. The lists are as follows:

Control Ring

The control ring can be assigned to any of the same settings as with the Custom Key (Still Images) option.

Custom Button

The list of possible assignments for the Custom button are as follows:

- Memory
- Focus Mode
- AF/MF Control Hold
- AF/MF Control Toggle
- Focus Standard
- Focus Area
- Center Lock-on AF
- Face Priority in AF
- Exposure Compensation
- ISO
- Metering Mode

- Face Priority in Multi Meter
- AEL Hold
- AEL Toggle
- Spot AEL Hold
- Spot AEL Toggle
- White Balance
- Priority Set in Auto White Balance
- DRO/Auto HDR
- Creative Style
- Picture Effect
- Picture Profile
- Focus Magnifier
- Peaking Display Select
- Peaking Level
- Peaking Color
- In-Camera Guide
- MOVIE
- Frame Rate (HFR)
- Auto Dual Recording
- SteadyShot (Movies)
- Marker Display Select
- Finder/Monitor Select
- Zebra Display Select
- Zebra Level
- Grid Line
- Audio Signals
- Send to Smartphone
- Playback
- Monitor Brightness
- Gamma Display Assist
- Touch Operation Select
- TC/UB Display Switch
- Not Set
- Follow Custom (Still Images)

Center Button

The Center button can be assigned any of the same options as the Custom button, except for In-Camera Guide.

Left Button

The Left button can be assigned any of the same options as the Custom button, except for AF/MF Control Hold, Focus Standard, AEL Hold, Spot AEL Hold, and In-Camera Guide.

Right Button

The Right button can be assigned any of the same options as the Left button.

Custom Key (Playback)

This next menu option lets you assign the Function button to handle a single function when the camera is in playback mode. The main screen for this option is shown in Figure 5-51.

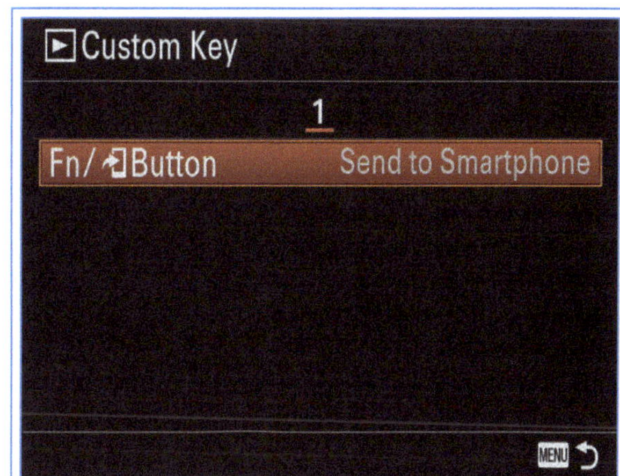

Figure 5-51. Custom Key (Playback) Options Screen

The options that can be assigned to the Function button are the following:

- Finder/Monitor Select
- Send to Smartphone

- Protect
- Rotate
- Delete
- Rating
- Beauty Effect
- Photo Capture
- Enlarge Image
- Image Index
- Touch Operation Select
- TC/UB Display Switch
- Not Set

The list of options for Custom Key (Playback) does not include the Follow Custom (Still Images) option.

Function Menu Settings

As I will discuss in Chapter 6, when you press the Function button in shooting mode, the camera displays up to 12 options in blocks at the bottom of the display.

Move through the options with the direction buttons. Adjust main settings with the control wheel and control ring, and adjust some secondary settings with the control ring. Use the Function Menu Settings menu item to assign options to the 12 blocks of the Function menu. When you select this option, the camera displays the screen shown in Figure 5-52, showing the assignments for the upper six blocks of the Function menu.

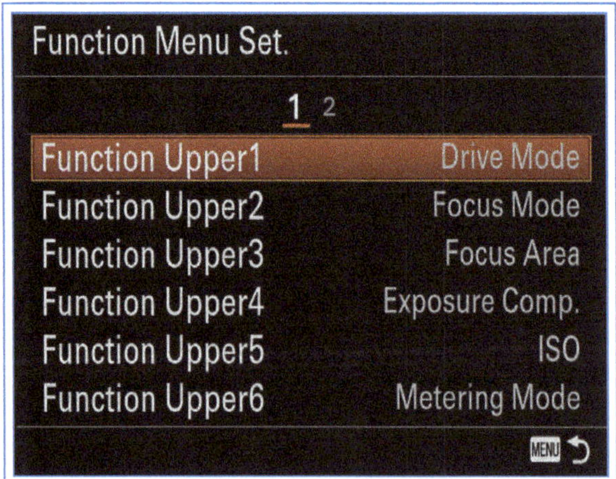

Figure 5-52. Assignments for Upper Function Menu Blocks

When you press the Center button on any one of those lines, you will see a screen like that in Figure 5-53, listing the options that can be assigned to that block.

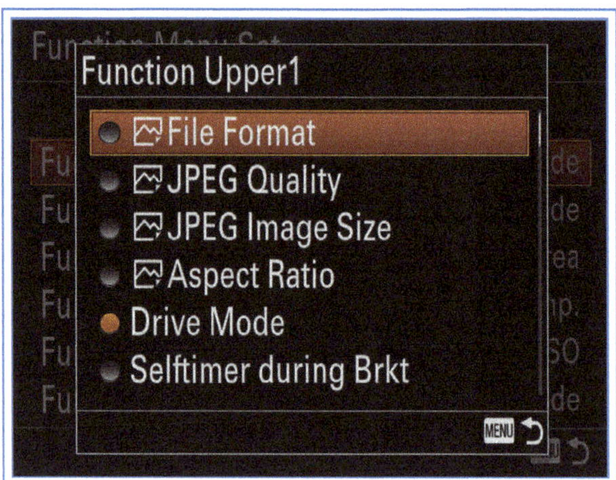

Figure 5-53. List of Assignment Options for Function Menu Block

For each block, the options that can be assigned are:

- File Format (Still Images)
- JPEG Quality
- JPEG Image Size
- Aspect Ratio
- Drive Mode
- Self-timer During Bracketing
- Focus Mode
- Focus Area
- Center Lock-on AF
- Face Priority in AF
- Exposure compensation
- ISO
- ISO Auto Minimum Shutter Speed
- Metering Mode
- Face Priority in Multi Meter
- Flash Mode
- Flash Compensation
- White Balance

- Priority Set in Auto White Balance
- DRO/Auto HDR
- Creative Style
- Picture Effect
- Picture Profile
- Soft Skin Effect
- Peaking Display
- Peaking Level
- Peaking Color
- Smile Shutter
- Auto Object Framing
- Frame Rate (HFR)
- Auto Dual Recording
- SteadyShot (Movies)
- Marker Display
- Shutter Type
- SteadyShot (Still Images)
- Zebra Display
- Zebra Level
- Grid Line
- Live View Display
- Audio Signals
- Gamma Display Assist
- Touch Operation
- Shoot Mode
- Not Set

Press the Center button when the option you want to assign to a given block is displayed, and the camera will place an orange dot on that line to indicate that that feature is assigned to that block.

I recommend you assign a function to each of the 12 blocks and experiment to find the best setup. Remember that you can use the control ring and the Custom, Center, Left, and Right buttons for your most important settings, such as, perhaps, ISO, AEL Toggle, drive mode, white balance, and focus mode, so you can reserve these 12 blocks for other options.

Av/Tv Rotate

This menu item lets you change the direction of rotation when you use the control wheel to adjust aperture or shutter speed in Aperture Priority, Shutter Priority, or Manual exposure mode, or in Movie mode or HFR mode with Exposure Mode set to A, S, or M. The choices are normal or reverse. This is strictly a matter of personal preference, which I have never found a need to use.

Touch Shooting Settings

This menu option has two sub-options, touch shutter and touch focus, discussed below, which control how the camera uses the touch screen for focusing and for capturing still images. For both of these features, Touch Operation must be turned on through screen 3 of the Setup menu and Center Lock-on AF must be turned off.

Touch Shutter

This first sub-option lets you turn on the touch shutter function, which is available for capturing images in still image shooting modes. When touch shutter is turned on, you will see a special icon in the upper right corner of the monitor, as shown in Figure 5-54.

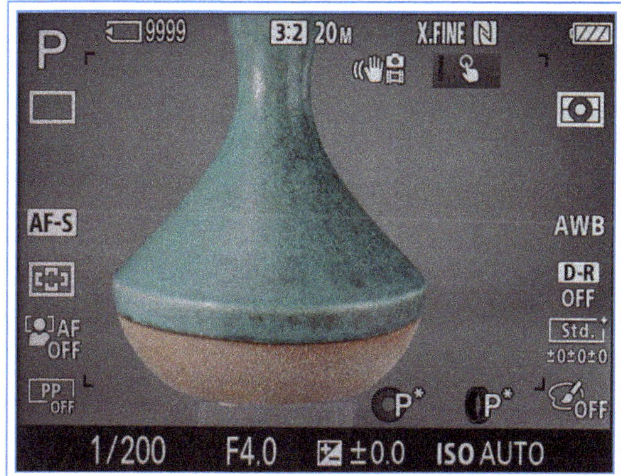

Figure 5-54. Touch Shutter Icon on Shooting Screen

When you touch that icon with your finger, the camera will add an orange bar at the icon's left side, indicating that the touch shutter option is active. Then, the next time you touch the screen, the camera will focus on the spot you touched and take a picture at the same time. To cancel the touch shutter function, touch the touch shutter icon again. If burst shooting or bracketing is turned on, you can press the monitor to activate those operations.

The touch shutter option is not available when using the viewfinder or in the Movie, HFR, or Panorama modes. It also is not available when Smile Shutter is turned on, with manual focus, digital zoom, clear image zoom, or when focus area is set to Flexible Spot or Expand Flexible Spot.

Touch Focus

This option is similar to the previous one, except that it sets the camera only to focus at the spot where you touch the monitor, not to take a picture also. For still images, touch the subject on the monitor where you want the camera to focus. The camera will place a focus frame there. When you press the shutter button halfway down, the camera will focus on the subject within that frame. If you are using the viewfinder, you can move the focus area around by dragging your finger on the monitor.

If you are recording a movie, touch the monitor where you want focus to be directed. The camera will direct its focus to the spot you touched and will activate manual focus temporarily to let you make a further adjustment using the control ring. (Sony calls this function "spot focus.") You can cancel the spot focus operation by pressing the hand icon with an X, or by pressing the Center button.

Touch focus is not available in Sweep Panorama mode or when actually using clear image zoom or digital zoom.

The items on screen 10 of the Camera Settings2 menu are shown in Figure 5-55.

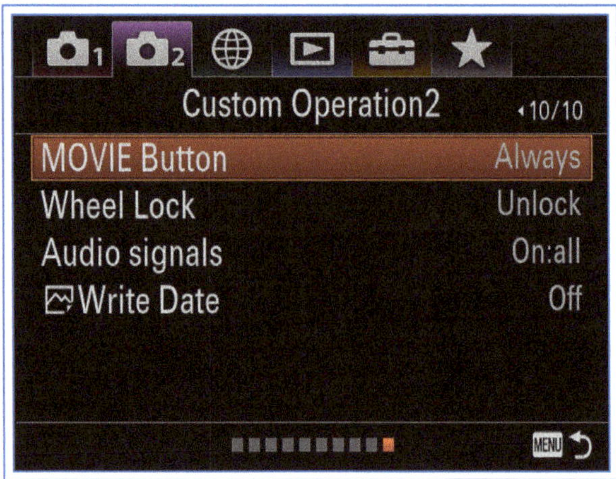

Figure 5-55. Screen 10 of Camera Settings2 Menu

Movie Button

This menu item, whose options are shown in Figure 5-56, lets you lock out the operation of the Movie button to avoid accidentally starting a video recording.

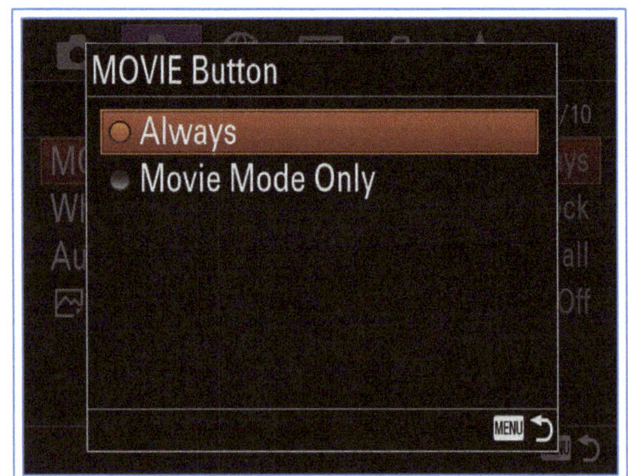

Figure 5-56. Movie Button Options Screen

The two choices are Always and Movie Mode Only. If you want to be able to start recording a video at any time without delay, you should leave the Movie Button option set to Always. With this setting, you can start recording a movie by pressing this button, no matter what shooting mode is set on the mode dial (except HFR, which uses a special procedure and records only high frame rate movies).

This is a convenient setting, because you can start shooting a video at a moment's notice without having to turn the mode dial to the Movie position.

As I will discuss in Chapter 6 in the section on the Movie button, the main reason to choose the Movie

Mode Only option is if you are afraid you may press the Movie button by mistake.

With the models in the RX100 series, I have pressed the Movie button many times by mistake, resulting in unwanted recordings and the need to stop a recording and delete it. So, unless you expect to make movie recordings fairly often in other shooting modes, you should consider setting this option to Movie Mode Only to avoid unwanted uses of the button.

As discussed earlier, if you assign a control button to have the Movie function, which gives that button the same function as the red Movie button, this menu option affects the operation of that button also.

Wheel Lock

This next option on screen 10 of the Camera Settings2 menu has two possible settings, Lock and Unlock, as seen in Figure 5-57.

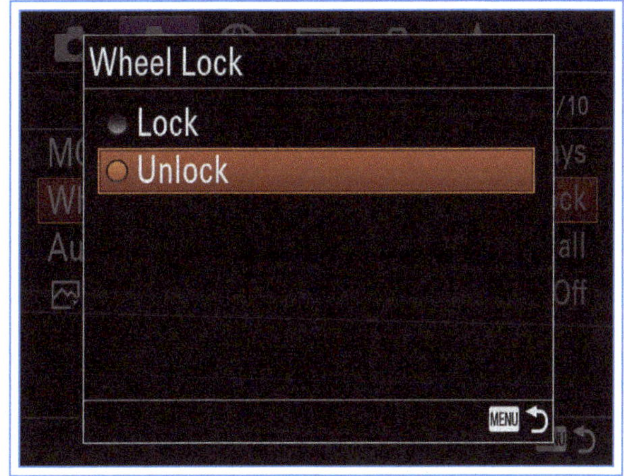

Figure 5-57. Wheel Lock Options Screen

If you select Lock, you can lock the functioning of the control wheel. To engage the actual lock, after this menu item is set to Lock, press and hold the Function button for several seconds when the shooting screen is displayed, until a Locked message appears on the screen.

After that, you will see an icon in the lower right corner of the display indicating that the lock is in effect, as shown in Figure 5-58. Once the lock is in effect, turning the control wheel will not have any effect on the camera's settings.

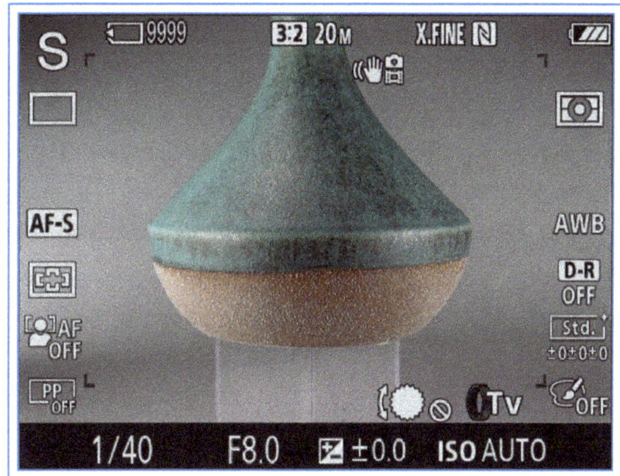

Figure 5-58. Icon Showing Wheel Lock in Effect

For example, the control wheel will not adjust aperture or shutter speed in modes where it can be adjusted. However, the wheel will still carry out its function of navigating through menu screens, even with the lock in effect. The control ring will continue to function to adjust aperture or shutter speed, if it is set to that operation in the current shooting mode.

This option can prevent the wheel from accidentally moving and changing your settings. If you make an important adjustment to your settings, you can lock the wheel so the setting will stay in place. When you are ready to change settings, press and hold the Function button again to remove the lock.

I have not had occasion to use this feature myself, but I can see its value for situations in which you need to keep a setting locked in and want to guard against accidental slipping of the wheel.

Even when the Lock option is turned on, the Function button can be used to call up the Function menu. A quick press of the button will call up that menu, and a longer press-and-hold will lock or unlock the wheel. However, if the AF Area Registration option is turned on through screen 5 of the Camera Settings1 menu, the Wheel Lock option will be unavailable, because the AF Area Registration option requires a long press of the Function button to register an AF area.

Audio Signals

This option lets you choose whether or not to activate the various sounds the RX100 VI makes when some operations take place, such as pressing the shutter button or Movie button, using the self-timer, or confirming focus. By default, the sounds are turned on, but it can be helpful to silence them in a quiet area, during a religious ceremony, or when you are doing street photography and want to avoid alerting your subjects that a camera is being used. There is a separate entry for Shutter, so you can leave the shutter sound turned on while silencing sounds such as self-timer and focus beeps if you want.

Write Date

This final setting on the Camera Settings2 menu can be used to embed the current date in orange type in the lower right corner of your still images as you record them, as shown in Figure 5-59.

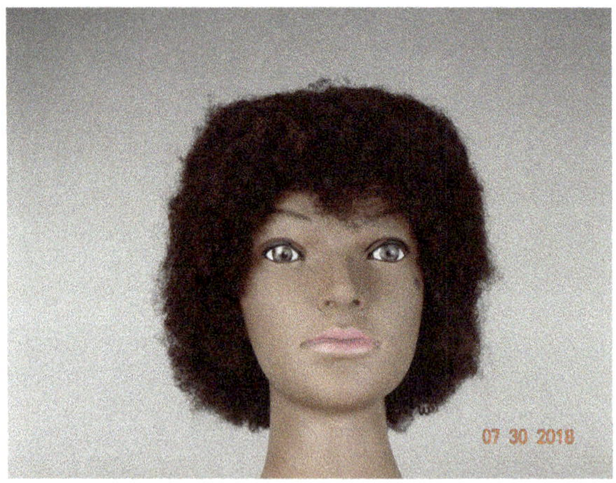

Figure 5-59. Write Date Option in Use on Image

This embedding is permanent, which means the information will appear as part of the image and cannot be deleted, other than through cropping or other editing procedures. You should not use this function unless you are certain you want the date recorded on your images, perhaps for pictures that are part of a scientific research project.

You can always add the date in other ways after the fact in editing software if you want to, because the camera records the date and time internally with each image (if the date and time have been set accurately), so think twice before using this function. This option is not available when File Format (Still Images) is set to Raw or Raw & JPEG, with panoramas, bracketing, continuous shooting, with the continuous self-timer, or in Movie or HFR mode.

Chapter 6: Physical Controls

The Sony RX100 VI, like other compact cameras, does not have very many physical controls. It relies largely on its menus for changing settings. But the RX100 VI is a high-quality compact camera, and one aspect of its quality is that its controls can be configured to adjust many settings. In this chapter, I'll discuss each of the camera's physical controls and how they can be used to best advantage, starting with the controls on top of the camera, shown in Figure 6-1.

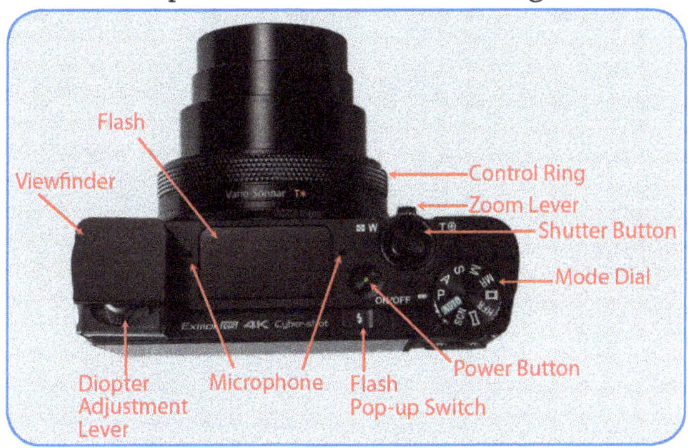

Figure 6-1. Controls on Top of Camera

Mode Dial

The mode dial has just one function—to select a shooting mode. I discussed the shooting modes in Chapter 3. To take a quick still picture, turn this dial to the AUTO position, select either Intelligent Auto or Superior Auto for the shooting mode, and fire away. To record a video sequence, turn the dial to that same position and press the red Movie button, just below the mode dial at the top of the camera's back.

There are two movie-oriented modes on this dial, one marked by a movie-film icon and one marked by HFR for high frame rate, but you do not have to select either of those icons to record movies. You can record a normal-speed movie with the mode dial set to any position except HFR (which is used for high frame rate movies).

Note that screen 10 of the Camera Settings2 menu has an option called Movie Button for locking out the use of the Movie button unless the camera is in Movie mode. If the mode dial is set to any position other than Movie, the Movie button will not start a movie recording if the Movie Button menu option is set to Movie Mode Only. (To record high frame rate movies, a different procedure is used, as discussed in Chapter 9.)

Shutter Release Button

When you press the shutter release button halfway, the camera evaluates and locks focus and exposure if you're using standard settings, including single autofocus. You can change this behavior in various ways. For example, as discussed in Chapter 4, you can use manual focus and adjust the focus yourself, or you can use continuous autofocus, which does not lock focus when you press the shutter button halfway. You also can go to screen 7 of the Camera Settings1 menu and set the AEL w/Shutter option to Off, in which case the camera will never lock exposure when you press the shutter button halfway. I discussed that option in Chapter 4.

In Manual exposure mode, the camera evaluates exposure when you press the shutter button halfway, but it does not change the aperture or shutter speed settings you have made. If Auto ISO is in effect, the camera will adjust the ISO to achieve a normal exposure if possible, and you can lock that exposure by half-pressing the shutter button, assuming AEL w/Shutter is turned on.

Once you are satisfied with the settings, press the button all the way to take the picture. When the camera is set for continuous shooting, you hold this button down to cause the camera to fire repeatedly. You also can press this button halfway to exit to the live view from playback mode, menu screens, and help screens. You can half-press this button to wake the display up after it has blacked out because of the Auto Monitor Off option on screen 2 of the Setup menu.

When the mode dial is set to Movie mode, the behavior of this button depends on the setting of the Movie w/ Shutter option on screen 4 of the Camera Settings2 menu. If that option is turned off, pressing the shutter button in Movie mode has no effect unless a movie is being recorded. Pressing the shutter button during movie recording will capture a still image in most circumstances, in any mode in which movies can be recorded. Details of that function are in Chapter 9.

If the Movie w/Shutter option is turned on, then pressing the shutter button in Movie mode will start or stop the recording of a movie, but in that case you cannot capture still images during movie recording.

When the mode dial is set to the HFR position, pressing the shutter button has no effect in any situation.

Zoom Lever

The zoom lever is a small ring with a short handle surrounding the shutter button. Its primary function is to vary the focal length of the lens between its wide-angle setting of 24mm and its telephoto setting of 200mm. If you have the camera set for Clear Image Zoom or Digital Zoom through the Zoom Setting item on screen 6 of the Camera Settings2 menu, the lever will take the zoom to higher levels, as discussed in Chapter 5.

You can also zoom using the control ring, if you assign the zoom function to the control ring using the Custom Key (Still Images) or Custom Key (Movies) option on screen 9 of the Camera Settings2 menu. And, you can set the control ring to use the Step Zoom function, which causes the lens to zoom in a predefined step each time you turn the ring. (That function is controlled by the Zoom Function on Ring option on screen 6 of the Camera Settings2 menu.) The Step Zoom function does not work with the zoom lever, though. When you use the zoom lever, the lens zooms continuously, even if Step Zoom is turned on for the control ring. You adjust the speed of zooming with the lever using the Zoom Speed item on screen 6 of the Camera Settings2 menu.

In playback mode, moving the zoom lever to the left produces an index screen, and moving the lever to the right enlarges the current image. Those operations are discussed in Chapter 7.

Power Button

This button is used to turn the camera on and off. An orange light in the center of the button glows when the battery is being charged in the camera. A green light in the button glows when the camera is powered on. You also can turn the camera's power on by pressing the Playback button, which places the camera into playback mode, or by popping up the EVF with the Finder switch.

There are two items to discuss on the front of the camera, as seen in Figure 6-2.

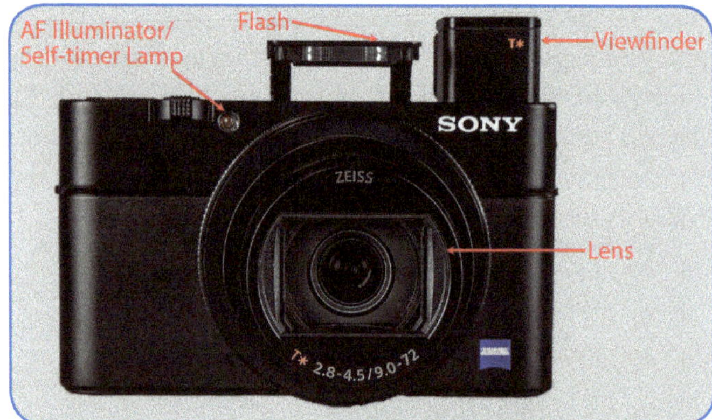

Figure 6-2. Items on Front of Camera

AF Illuminator/Self-Timer Lamp

The reddish light on the front of the camera near the control ring blinks to signal the operation of the self-timer, and it turns on in dark environments to assist with autofocusing. You can control its function for helping with autofocus through the AF Illuminator item on screen 4 of the Camera Settings1 menu, as discussed in Chapter 4. If you set that menu item to Auto, the lamp will light as needed for autofocus; if you set it to Off, the lamp will never light for that purpose, though it will still illuminate for the self-timer.

Control Ring

Whenever the camera is set to manual focus or DMF (direct manual focus) using the focus mode option on screen 4 of the Camera Settings1 menu, the control ring adjusts focus. The ring also has other functions, depending on the settings you make.

To assign functions to the control ring, use the Custom Key (Still Images) or Custom Key (Movies) option on screen 9 of the Camera Settings2 menu. The first sub-option for this menu item is Control Ring, whose first screen of options is shown in Figure 6-3.

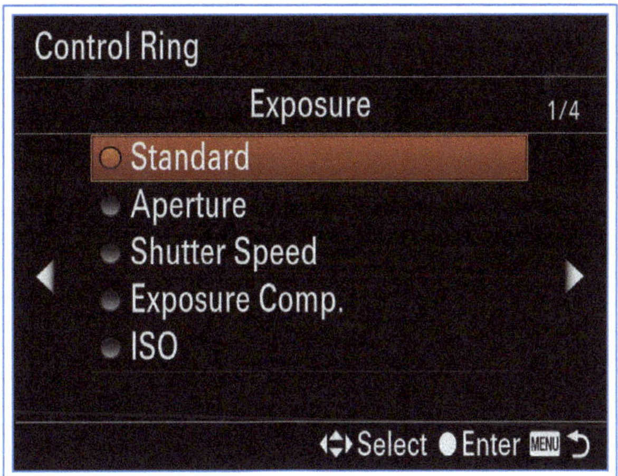

Figure 6-3. First Screen of Options for Control Ring

By default, the Control Ring item is set to Standard. When the Standard setting is in effect, the control ring controls just one function in any given shooting mode; the function it controls depends on which shooting mode the camera is set to. For example, if the camera is set to the Aperture Priority mode, the control ring adjusts aperture; in Shutter Priority mode, the ring adjusts shutter speed. In the Scene shooting mode, the ring controls selection of scene types. I usually leave the Control Ring menu item set to Standard because the functions the ring controls in the various shooting modes in that case are quite useful.

However, if you want to use the ring for one dedicated function no matter what shooting mode is in effect, you can use the Control Ring menu item to choose one of the following items that will stay assigned to the ring until you make another change. Under the Custom Key (Still Images) menu item, the options are: Standard, Aperture, Shutter Speed, Exposure Compensation, ISO, white balance, Creative Style, Picture Effect, or Zoom. You also can choose Not Set, in which case turning the ring will have no effect (unless you activate a function, such as manual focus, that requires use of the ring).

Under the Custom Key (Movies) menu item, the choices are the same as for still images, with the addition of the choice of Follow Custom (Still Images), which assigns the ring to the same function for movies as for still images.

A function assigned to the ring only works if the context permits it. For example, if you assign Aperture to the control ring, the ring will control aperture if the camera is set to Aperture Priority or Manual exposure mode, or the Aperture Priority or Manual Exposure setting for Movie mode or HFR mode. In any other shooting mode, turning the ring will have no effect (except for adjusting manual focus) because aperture cannot be controlled manually in other modes. Table 6-1 lists the functions that are assigned to the control ring with the Standard setting.

Table 6-1. Control Ring: Standard Setting—Shooting Modes vs. Assigned Functions

Shooting Mode	Assigned Function
Intelligent Auto	Zoom
Superior Auto	Zoom
Program	Program Shift
Aperture Priority	Aperture
Shutter Priority	Shutter Speed
Manual Exposure	Aperture
Scene	Scene Selection
Sweep Panorama	Panorama Direction
Memory Recall	Depends on Saved Setting
Movie	Depends on Movie exposure mode setting
HFR	Depends on HFR exposure mode setting

The control ring also is used in a few other situations, regardless of how you have set its assigned function. When you press the Function button (discussed later in this chapter) in shooting mode, the camera activates a menu that shows several options—including items such as white balance, ISO, exposure compensation, etc.—depending on the settings you have chosen for that menu. Once you have pressed the Function button to display that menu, you can turn the control ring (or the control wheel) to select the value for the setting that is highlighted on the menu. The control ring also is used to adjust settings using the Quick Navi system, which is also called up with the Function button.

When the camera is set to manual focus or DMF (direct manual focus), you use the control ring to adjust focus. If the MF Assist option is turned on through screen 11 of the Camera Settings1 menu, the display will be magnified to assist with focusing as soon as you start turning the control ring. (With DMF, you have to half-press the shutter button while turning the control ring to use MF Assist.) When the camera is set to either of those focus modes, you cannot use the control ring for any other function when the shooting screen is displayed. (It will still adjust items on the Function menu and Quick Navi menu.)

The controls on the back of the RX100 VI are seen in Figure 6-4.

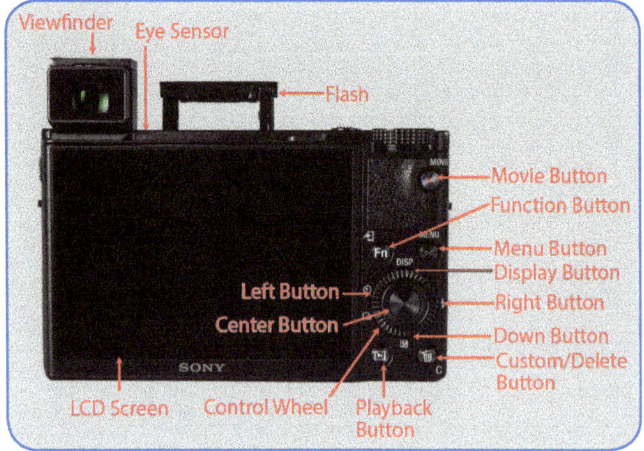

Figure 6-4. Controls on Back of Camera

Electronic Viewfinder

One of the most useful features of the Sony RX100 VI is its retractable electronic viewfinder, or EVF. With this option, the camera can be used in bright conditions even if the LCD display is washed out by sunlight. In addition, you can hold the camera up to your eye and keep it steady against your forehead while viewing a high-resolution image that includes the same information that is available with the LCD display.

To use the EVF, first pop it up by pressing down on the Finder switch on the left side of the camera. If the camera was not already powered on, popping up the viewfinder will turn the camera on. Adjust the EVF for your vision using the diopter adjustment lever on top of the eyepiece, shown in Figure 6-5. How you use the EVF, of course, is a matter of personal preference. You can hold it up to either your left or right eye, depending on which feels more comfortable to you. If you wear glasses, you may find it more comfortable to take them off and use the diopter adjustment lever to compensate.

By default, the camera switches automatically between the EVF and the LCD. That is, when the EVF is popped up and your head is against the EVF, the EVF is active and the LCD is turned off. When you move your head away from the EVF, the LCD screen becomes active and the EVF is turned off. If you want the EVF to be active whenever it is popped up, regardless of the position of your head, use the Finder/Monitor option on screen 7 of the Camera Settings2 menu; set that option to Viewfinder (Manual) to keep the EVF active at all times when it is popped up. (The eye sensor that detects the presence of your head near the screen is shown in Figure 6-4.)

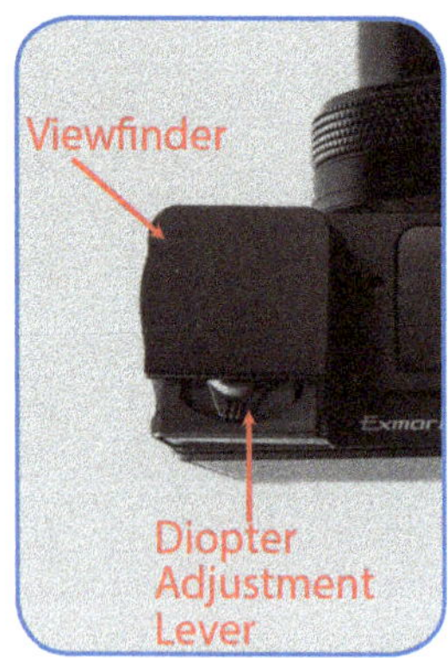

Figure 6-5. Diopter Adjustment Lever

To adjust the EVF's brightness, use the Viewfinder Brightness option on screen 1 of the Setup menu, as discussed in Chapter 8. The information displayed in the EVF is independent of what is displayed on the LCD screen. That is, with two exceptions, you can have the EVF display all of the screens that can be shown on the LCD, but you don't have to do that. The two exceptions are the For Viewfinder display and the blanked-out monitor, which are available only for the LCD. To set the display screens for the LCD and EVF, use the Display Button option on screen 7 of the Camera Settings2 menu. When the shooting screen is displayed, cycle from one display to another by pressing the Display button. I discussed that menu option and the available information displays in Chapter 5.

When you have finished using the EVF, stow it inside the camera by pressing it down gently until it clicks into place. The eyepiece, which extends automatically when the EVF pops up, will automatically be retracted into the EVF when it is pressed down.

When you stow the EVF, the camera will turn off or stay powered on, depending on a menu setting. To determine what happens in that situation, go to the Function for VF Close option, the last item on screen 2 of the Setup menu. The choices are Power Off or Not Power Off. If you choose Power Off, the camera will turn off when you press the EVF down into the camera's body. If you choose Not Power Off, the camera will remain powered on when the EVF is stowed. I prefer to have the camera stay powered on, but it is good to have this choice available.

Built-in Flash and Flash Pop-up Switch

The camera's built-in flash unit is normally retracted and hidden in the center area of the camera's top. If you want the flash to be available for use, you first have to pop it up using the flash pop-up switch, located directly behind the power button, and shown earlier in Figure 6-1.

Once you have popped up the flash unit, if you want it to fire, you need to make an appropriate setting using the flash mode menu on screen 8 of the Camera Settings1 menu. You also can bring up that menu by pressing the Right button on the control wheel, unless that button has been assigned to a different function using the Custom Key (Still Images) option on screen 9 of the Camera Settings2 menu.

Once you have popped up the flash unit and selected a flash mode, the flash may fire when you press the shutter button, depending on the settings that are in effect and the lighting conditions. I discussed the flash mode options in Chapter 4.

To stow the flash away, press it gently back down into the camera until it clicks into place. To use "bounce flash," which causes the flash to be reflected by the ceiling or wall to reduce its intensity, you can pull the flash unit back carefully with your finger and hold the flash so that it is aiming upward while it fires.

As discussed in Appendix A, you can use an optical slave unit to fire a more powerful flash that is triggered by the light from the camera's built-in flash unit.

Playback Button

This button to the lower left of the control wheel, marked with a small triangle, is used to put the camera into playback mode, which allows you to view your images on the LCD screen or in the EVF. It also can be used instead of the power button to turn the camera on, placing the RX100 VI immediately into playback mode with the lens retracted. When the camera is in playback mode, you can press the shutter button halfway or press the Playback button again to switch the camera into shooting mode.

Movie Button

The red button at the upper right of the camera's back has just one function—to start and stop the recording of a movie sequence. As I noted in discussing the mode dial earlier in this chapter, you can control how the Movie button operates. If you want to be able to start recording a movie in any shooting mode (except HFR), go to the Camera Settings2 menu and select the first option on screen 10, called Movie Button. If you set that menu option to Always (the default setting), the Movie button will operate in any shooting mode except HFR. If you set the option to Movie Mode Only, the Movie button will not start recording a movie unless the camera is set to Movie mode using the mode dial. (Movie mode is the mode marked by a movie-film icon.)

This is a fairly important decision to make, and it depends on your preferences and likely uses of the camera. If you want to be able to start recording a video at any time without delay, leave the Movie Button option set to Always. The reason you might not want to do this is that it is easy to press the Movie button by mistake. I have done that often with the small cameras in the RX100 series. When you press the button by mistake, you have to press it again to stop the recording, and wait for the camera to finish processing the movie before you can use any other controls. And, of course, the camera will have an unwanted file cluttering the memory card, until you delete it.

My preference is to limit use of the Movie button to when the camera is in Movie mode, but if I were going on a vacation and wanted to be able to start recording a movie in Auto mode without delay, I would enable the button for use in all modes.

There are differences in how the camera operates for video recording in different shooting modes. I will discuss movie making in detail in Chapter 9.

Menu Button

The Menu button, to the upper right of the control wheel, is straightforward in its basic function. Press it to enter the menu system, and press it once more to return to whatever mode the camera was in previously (shooting mode or playback mode). The button also cancels out of sub-menus, taking you back to the previous menu screen. In playback mode, when an image has been enlarged using the zoom lever, you can press the Menu button (or the Center button) to return it to the normal-sized view.

Function Button

The button marked Fn, for Function, has different functions in shooting mode and playback mode.

Shooting Mode: Function Menu

When the camera is in shooting mode, the Function button gives you options for setting up the RX100 VI according to your own preferences. With the Function Menu Settings option on screen 9 of the Camera Settings2 menu (discussed in Chapter 5), you can assign up to 12 functions to the Function menu from 44 choices, including items such as ISO, drive mode, white balance, metering mode, and Picture Effect. The last option is Not Set, which leaves a slot on the Function menu blank.

Scroll through the lines from Function Upper1 through Function Upper6 on the first sub-screen of this menu option and Function Lower1 through Function Lower6 on the second screen. On each line, press the Center button and then scroll through the 44 options to highlight the one you want, and press the Center button to confirm that selection.

Once you have assigned up to 12 options to this button, it is ready for action. To use an option, press the Function button when the camera is in shooting mode, and a menu will appear at the bottom of the display in two rows with six choices each, as shown in Figure 6-6.

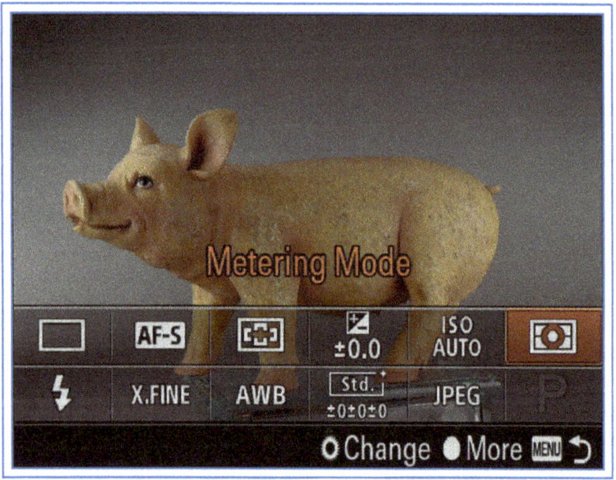

Figure 6-6. Function Menu on Shooting Screen

Use the four direction buttons to move to and highlight an option to adjust. Then turn either the control wheel or the control ring to change the value of that option. For example, if you have moved the orange highlight block to the File Format (Still Images) item, turn the control wheel or the control ring until the setting you want to make appears, as shown in Figure 6-7, where Raw & JPEG is selected.

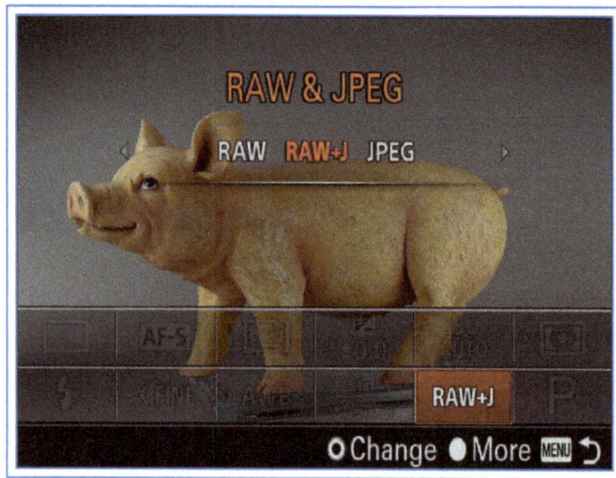

Figure 6-7. Raw & JPEG Selected on Function Menu

Then, press the Function button to confirm the setting and exit from the Function menu screen. Or, if you want to make multiple settings from the Function menu options, after changing one setting you can press the Center button to go back to the Function menu and make more settings before you press the Function button to exit to the shooting screen.

If the setting you are adjusting needs to have a sub-option set, you can press the Center button to go directly to the menu screen for that setting. For example, suppose you want to set a particular color temperature for white balance. First, from the shooting screen press the Function button to bring up the Function menu, and use the four direction buttons to scroll to the white balance block. Then, instead of choosing a value with the control wheel or control ring, press the Center button, and the camera will display the regular white balance menu screen, as shown in Figure 6-8.

From that screen, you can navigate to the Color Temperature/Filter option and select the color temperature you want to set. When you have finished, press the Menu button to return to the Function menu. From there, you can press the Function button to return to the shooting screen.

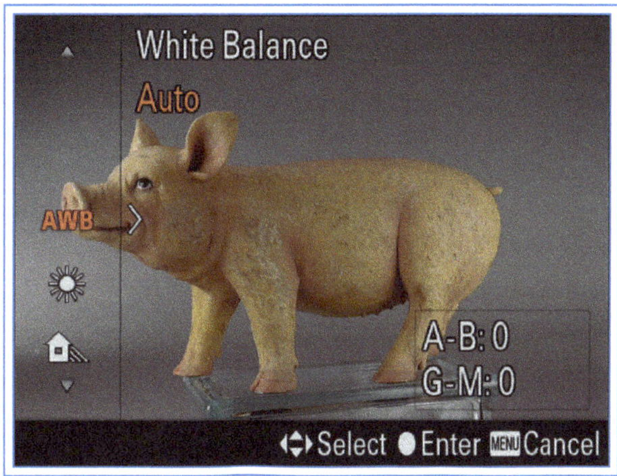

Figure 6-8. White Balance Menu Screen from Function Menu

There may be items on the Function menu whose icons are dimmed because the item is unavailable for selection in the current context. If you move the highlight to one of those items and then try to change the setting, the camera will display an error message.

Also, the selections I discussed above may not be available because they have not been assigned to the Function menu. If that is the case, you can use the Function Menu Settings menu option to assign them if you want to follow the examples.

I strongly recommend that you develop a group of 12 items to assign to the Function menu and make use of this speedy way to change important settings.

Quick Navi System

In shooting mode, the Function button also gives you access to the Quick Navi system for changing settings rapidly. This system has similarities to the Function menu system I just discussed, but there are significant differences.

The Quick Navi system comes into play in only one situation—when you have called up the special display screen shown in Figure 6-9, which Sony calls the "For Viewfinder" display.

This is the only shooting mode display that displays information but does not include the live view. It is called "For viewfinder" because this screen is designed for use when you are using the viewfinder to frame your composition, so you can see the live view through the viewfinder and see the details of your settings on this display, which appears only on the LCD screen.

The For Viewfinder display is summoned by pressing the Display button, but only if you have selected it for inclusion in the cycle of display screens.

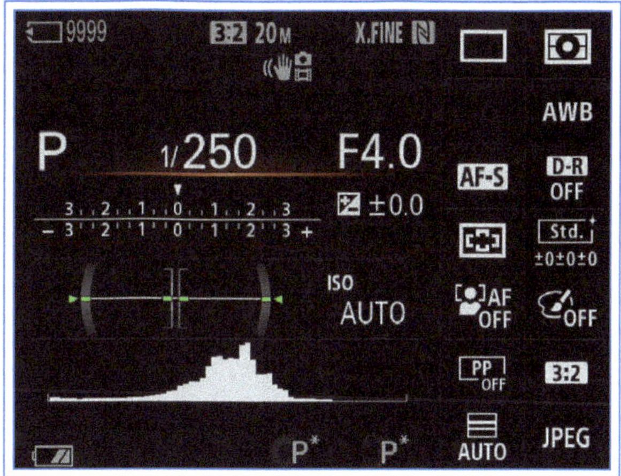

Figure 6-9. For Viewfinder Display Screen

You do that using the Display Button option on screen 7 of the Camera Settings2 menu. From that option, select the sub-option for Monitor, then check the box for the For Viewfinder item on the next screen, as shown in Figure 6-10.

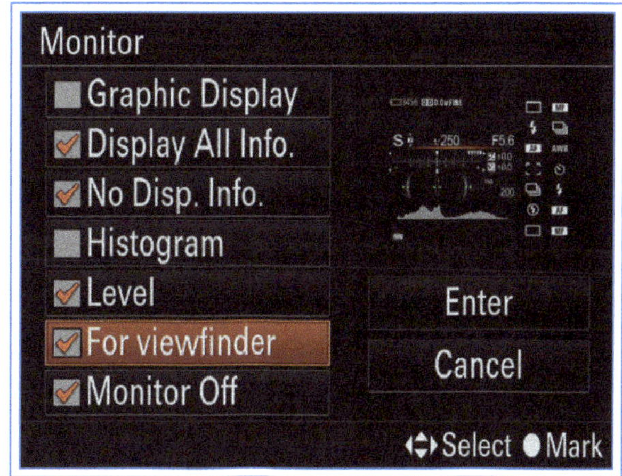

Figure 6-10. For Viewfinder Screen Selected for Monitor

As seen in Figure 6-9, the For Viewfinder screen displays a lot of information at the right, including drive mode, white balance, focus area, DRO, Picture Effect, Picture Profile, Shutter Type, and several others.

Normally, these items are displayed for information; you cannot adjust them on this screen. But, if you press the Function button, an orange highlight appears at the right, as shown in Figure 6-11, indicating that the Quick Navi system is in use.

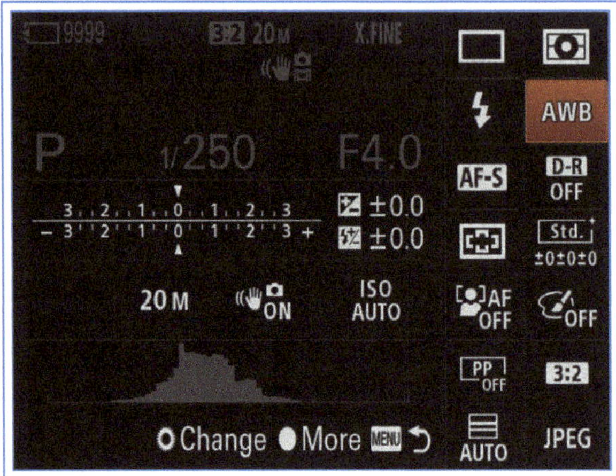

Figure 6-11. Quick Navi System in Use

Use the direction buttons to move through the settings. You can press the Left button to move the orange highlight to the left, to settings such as ISO, SteadyShot, and JPEG Image Size. When you have highlighted a setting to adjust, turn the control wheel or the control ring to scroll through the available values and make the adjustment quickly.

When you use the control wheel or control ring to adjust a setting, such as Aspect Ratio, a secondary window opens in the top part of the display, as shown in Figure 6-12, showing the options available for the setting.

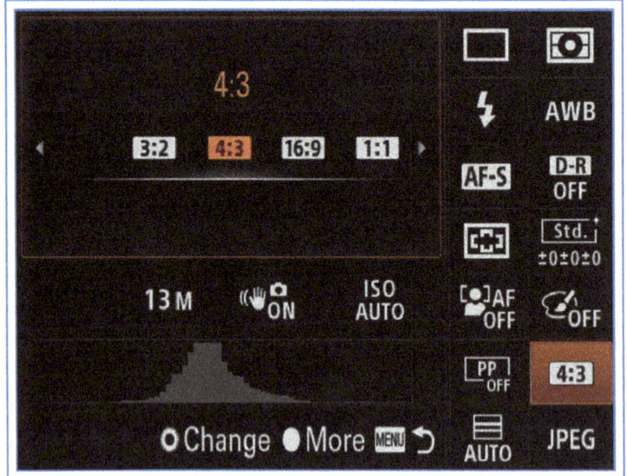

Figure 6-12. Aspect Ratio Setting on Quick Navi Screen

After changing a setting, you can move to other settings using the direction buttons. If a setting is displayed in gray instead of white, it is not currently adjustable. Once you have made all of your changes, press the Function button again to exit to the static For Viewfinder display, which will now show the new settings in place.

If you select an option that requires a sub-setting, the steps are slightly different. For example, suppose you want to turn on HDR using the maximum setting of 6.0EV. From the Quick Navi screen, highlight the DRO option and, instead of turning the control wheel or control ring to change the setting, press the Center button. You will be taken to a special menu screen for the DRO option, as shown in Figure 6-13.

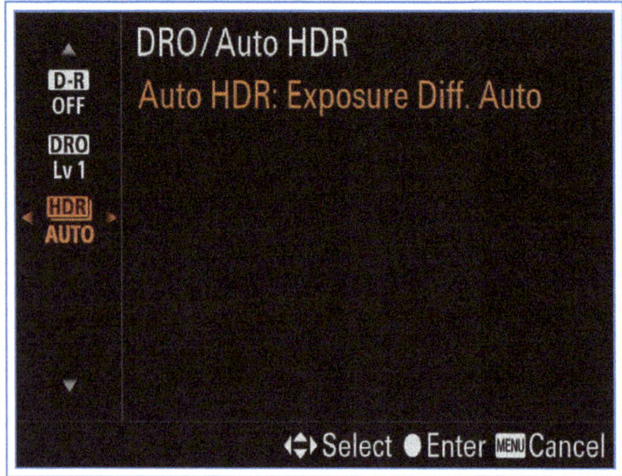

Figure 6-13. DRO Options Screen from Quick Navi System

On that screen, you can select HDR and set it to 6.0EV. Press the Center button to select this setting and exit to the For Viewfinder display.

You also can press the Center button when an option is highlighted, even if a sub-setting is not needed, if you prefer to use a menu screen to make the adjustment. For example, when Aspect Ratio is highlighted on the Quick Navi screen, you can press the Center button to call up a menu, rather than just turning the control wheel or control ring.

The Quick Navi system can streamline your ability to change settings once you get used to it. I recommend you devote some time to practicing with it, if speed is important to you.

Wheel Lock

The Function button also can carry out the Wheel Lock operation in shooting mode, depending on how a Camera Settings2 menu option is set. The second item on screen 10 of that menu is the Wheel Lock option. If that option is set to Lock, then, when you press and hold the Function button for several seconds when the shooting screen is displayed, the shooting-related operations that are adjusted by turning the control wheel are locked. The wheel will still operate to navigate through menu screens and menu settings, but turning it will not set items such as ISO, shutter speed, and scene types. The control ring and the buttons at the edges of the control wheel will still operate normally. I discussed that menu option in Chapter 5.

AF Area Registration

The final function of the Function button in shooting mode is to register the location of an autofocus area, using the AF Area Registration option on screen 5 of the Camera Settings1 menu. As I discussed in Chapters 4 and 5, after you turn on that menu option, you have to press and hold the Function button for several seconds to register the location of the current AF area. You then assign a control button to the Registered AF Area Hold option through the Custom Key (Still Images) option on screen 9 of the Camera Settings2 menu. Then, when you press the assigned button, the camera will place the AF frame at its registered location while you hold down the button.

Playback Mode: Send to Smartphone

When the RX100 VI is in playback mode, the Function button can be assigned one function, which you can choose using the Custom Key (Playback) option on screen 9 of the Camera Settings2 menu. By default, pressing the Function button activates the Send to Smartphone option, just as if you had chosen that menu option from the Wi-Fi menu. So, if you have taken a photo and want to transfer it to your phone for sharing with friends or posting to Facebook, you can press the Function button in playback mode and make the transfer quickly.

However, if you prefer, you can assign any one of 11 other functions to this button for use in playback mode, or you can choose Not Set. I discussed the Custom Key (Playback) menu option in Chapter 5.

Custom/Delete Button

The button marked with a C, to the right of the Playback button, is called the Custom/Delete button. This button can be programmed to perform any one of numerous functions, or it can be designated as Not Set. To make this choice, use the Custom Key (Still Images) or Custom Key (Movies) option on screen 9 of the Camera Settings2 menu, and then select the C Button sub-option. I discussed that menu option in Chapter 5.

When the camera is in playback mode, displaying a recorded image or movie (not a menu screen), this button becomes the Delete button, as indicated by the trash can icon to the lower right of the button. If you press it, the camera displays the message shown in Figure 6-14, prompting you to select Delete or Cancel.

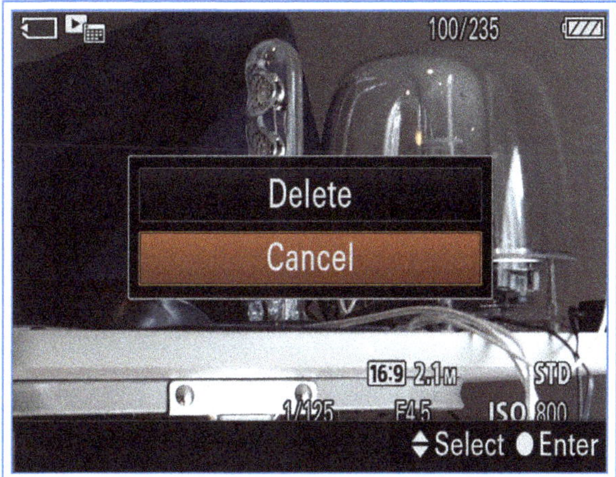

Figure 6-14. Delete Screen from Pressing C Button

If you highlight Delete and press the Center button, the camera will delete the image or video that was displayed. If you choose Cancel, the camera will return to the playback mode screen. This operation also works when an image is being displayed briefly with the Auto Review option, right after the image was captured.

How you program the C button is, of course, a matter of personal preference. The In-Camera Guide option is quite useful, especially when you are first learning the operation of the camera. Once you are more confident with the camera's functions, you might want to use this button for an operation that is not available through the menu system, or not readily available through a menu, such as Eye AF or AF/MF Control Toggle.

Control Wheel and Its Buttons

Several controls are within the perimeter of the control wheel, the ridged wheel with icons around its outer edges. In the middle of the wheel is the Center button, a much-used control. The four edges of the wheel (up, down, left, and right) act as buttons. If you press the wheel's rim at any of those four points, you are, in effect, pressing a button. Each button has at least two functions—as a direction control along with one or more other specific assignments. When they act as direction controls, the buttons are used to navigate through menu options and other choices for controlling the camera's settings. The other main functions of the buttons are indicated by one or more icons at each button's position on the control wheel. I will discuss all of these controls in turn.

Control Wheel

In many cases, to choose a menu item or a setting, you can turn this wheel. In some cases, you have the choice of using the control wheel or pressing the direction buttons. One helpful feature of the RX100 VI is that it places a round icon on the shooting screen representing the control wheel when there is a value that can be adjusted at that point by the wheel. (If you don't see the icon, press the Display button until it appears.)

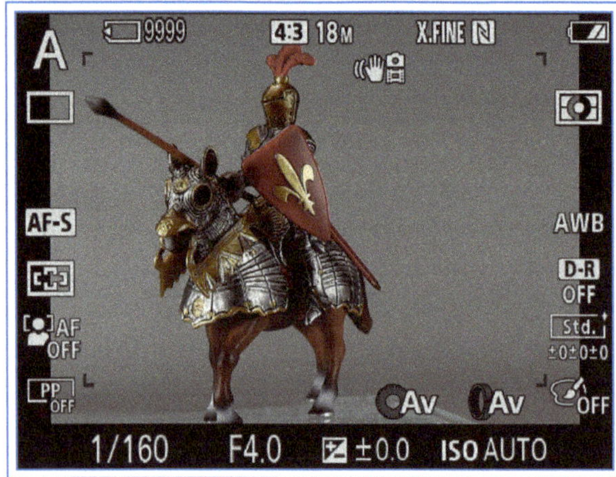

Figure 6-15. Icon Showing Control Wheel Controls Aperture

For example, in Figure 6-15, the icon, which looks like a gray ring lying flat on the screen in the lower right corner, is positioned next to the Av indicator, meaning the control wheel can now control aperture. (The more three-dimensional icon to the right of that one shows that the control ring also can control aperture.)

Figure 6-16 shows the camera in Manual exposure mode, and the icon for the control wheel is next to the Tv indicator, standing for time value or shutter speed, indicating that you can adjust the shutter speed by turning the control wheel. (The icon to the right shows that the control ring now adjusts aperture.)

In Aperture Priority mode, or in Movie mode or HFR mode with the Exposure Mode menu option set to Aperture Priority, the wheel controls aperture, and in Shutter Priority mode and the related Movie and HFR modes, it controls shutter speed. When the camera is in Manual exposure mode or one of the related Movie or HFR modes, the control wheel adjusts shutter speed. However, if you press the Down button, the role of the control wheel changes, and the wheel adjusts aperture.

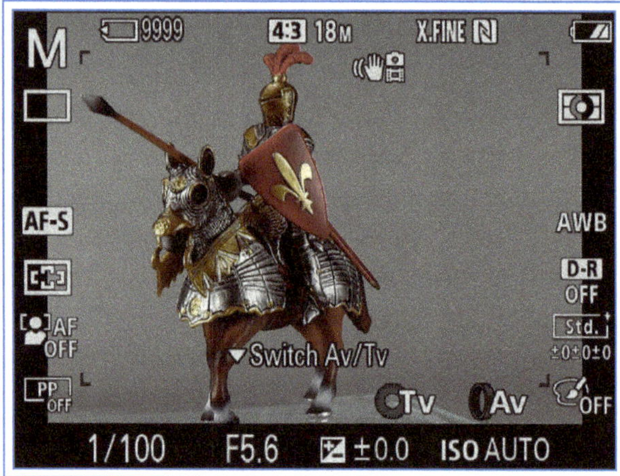

Figure 6-16. Icon Showing Control Wheel Controls Shutter Speed

When the camera is in Scene mode, you can turn the control wheel to change the scene type, such as Portrait, Landscape, and the like. In Sweep Panorama mode, turning the wheel changes the direction of the panorama. In Program mode, it controls Program Shift.

The control wheel has several other functions. When you are viewing a menu screen, you can navigate through the lists of options by turning the wheel. When you are adjusting items using the Function menu or Quick Navi system, you can change the value for the selected setting by turning the control wheel. When you are using manual focus and you have the Focus Magnifier or MF Assist option turned on, you can turn the control wheel to move the area of the scene that is being magnified. With the Flexible Spot setting for the focus area menu option, you can turn the control wheel to adjust the size of the focus frame when the frame is activated for moving around the display.

In playback mode, you can turn the control wheel to navigate through images. Also, when a video is being played in the camera, you can turn the control wheel to fast-forward or rewind, or, when the video is paused, to play it slowly, frame-by-frame, either forward or in reverse. When an image is enlarged, you can turn this wheel to view other images at the same enlargement factor.

Center Button

This button in the center of the control wheel has many uses. On menu screens that have additional options, such as the JPEG Image Size screen, this button takes you to the next screen to view the other options. It also acts as a selection button when you choose certain options. For example, after you select focus mode from screen 4 of the Camera Settings1 menu and navigate to your desired focus option, you can press the Center button to confirm your selection and exit from the menu screen back to the shooting screen.

The Center button also has several other possible uses depending on how it is set up. Screen 9 of the Camera Settings2 menu (discussed in Chapter 5) has an item called Custom Key (Still Images) and a similar item called Custom Key (Movies), each of which has a sub-option for setting the function of the Center button.

One of the many options for assignment to the Center button for still images is Eye AF. If you assign that option to the button, you can press the button to cause the camera to focus on an eye in any human face it detects, as discussed in Chapter 5. That option does not work for movie recording, however.

If you prefer not to use the Eye AF option, you can use the Custom Key menu options to set this button to carry out one of many other functions or to be Not Set.

In playback mode, you press the Center button to start playing a video when its first frame is displayed on the camera's screen. Once the video is playing, press the Center button to pause the playback and then to toggle between play and pause. When a panoramic image is displayed, press the Center button to make it scroll on the screen at a larger size using the full expanse of the display screen. When you have enlarged an image using the zoom lever, you can return it immediately to its normal size by pressing the Center button. When you are selecting images for deletion, protection, or printing using the appropriate Playback menu options, you use the Center button to mark or unmark an image for that purpose.

Direction Buttons

Each of the four edges of the control wheel acts as a button you can press to get access to a setting or operation. This is not immediately obvious, and sometimes it can be tricky to press in exactly the right spot, but these four buttons are important to your control of the camera. You use them to navigate through menus and screens for settings, whether moving left and right or up and down.

You also use these buttons in playback mode to move through your images and, when you have enlarged an image using the zoom lever, to scroll around within the magnified image.

In addition to navigation, the buttons are used for miscellaneous functions in connection with various settings. For example, when the camera is set to Manual exposure mode, you can press the Down button to toggle the action of the control wheel between setting aperture and setting shutter speed. And, as with the Center button, the Right and Left buttons (but not the Up or Down button) can be assigned to carry out other functions through the Custom Key (Still Images) and Custom Key (Movies) options on screen 9 of the Camera Settings2 menu, as discussed in Chapter 5.

Finally, each of the direction buttons has its own separate identity, as indicated by the one or two icons that appear near each of the buttons, as discussed below.

Up Button: Display

The Up button, marked "DISP," switches among display screens on the LCD monitor and in the viewfinder, in both shooting and playback modes. As discussed in Chapter 5, you can change the contents of the shooting mode screens using the Display Button option on screen 7 of the Camera Settings2 menu. The various display screens for playback mode are discussed in Chapter 7.

The Up button cannot be reassigned using the menu system; it is permanently assigned as the Display button.

Right Button: Flash Mode

When the camera is in shooting mode, pressing the Right button brings up a menu on the left of the display showing the options for setting the behavior of the flash unit. The options are Flash Off, Autoflash, Fill-flash, Slow Sync, and Rear Sync, although not all of them are available in any one shooting mode. This menu can also be summoned from screen 8 of the Camera Settings1 menu. I discussed the use of these settings in Chapter 4.

One important point is that you have to use the flash pop-up switch to pop up the flash before it can be used, no matter what option you have selected from the flash mode menu.

You can reassign the function of the Right button using the Custom Key (Still Images) or Custom Key (Movies) option on screen 9 of the Camera Settings2 menu. You can choose any one of numerous options, including flash mode, focus mode, focus area, ISO, white balance, and others; I discussed that menu option in Chapter 5.

Down Button: Exposure Compensation

The Down button is marked with an icon with a plus and minus sign on a black-and-white background. That icon indicates that in the Program, Aperture Priority, Shutter Priority, Movie, HFR, and Sweep Panorama modes, this button controls exposure compensation, discussed below.

In Manual exposure mode, this button toggles the control wheel's function between controlling aperture and controlling shutter speed. In that mode, you can use the Exposure Compensation item on screen 6 of the Camera Settings1 menu to adjust exposure compensation, or you can use the Custom Key (Still Images) or Custom Key (Movies) menu option to assign a control button or the control ring to adjust that setting. (Exposure compensation can be adjusted in Manual exposure mode only if ISO is set to Auto ISO.)

In the Auto and Scene modes, the Down button has no function other than as a direction button. If you press it when the shooting screen is displayed in those shooting modes, you will see an error message.

Exposure compensation can be used to adjust for an unusual, or non-optimal, lighting situation. Figure 6-17 is a photo of a pair of fabric-covered balls in front of a white background, taken in Program mode with metering mode set to Multi.

The camera's metering system measured the light being reflected from the white background along with the light from the dark subject, and because of the bright background, the metering system reduced the exposure setting and underexposed the two balls.

One solution to this problem is to use exposure compensation to increase the overall exposure of the image, so the subject will not be too dark. To accomplish this with the RX100 VI, press the Down button to bring the exposure compensation scale up on the display, as shown in Figure 6-18.

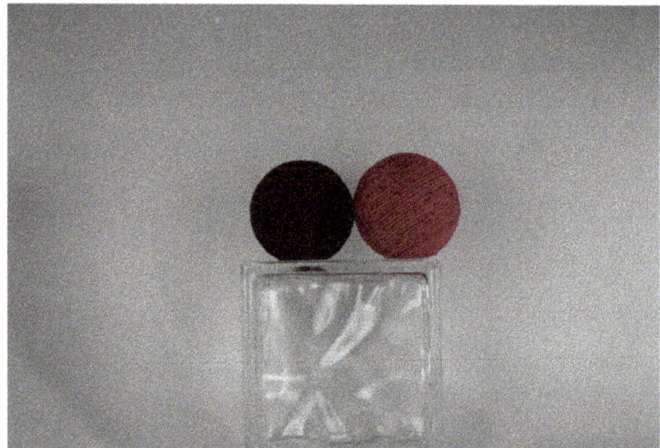

Figure 6-17. Exposure Compensation Example: Before

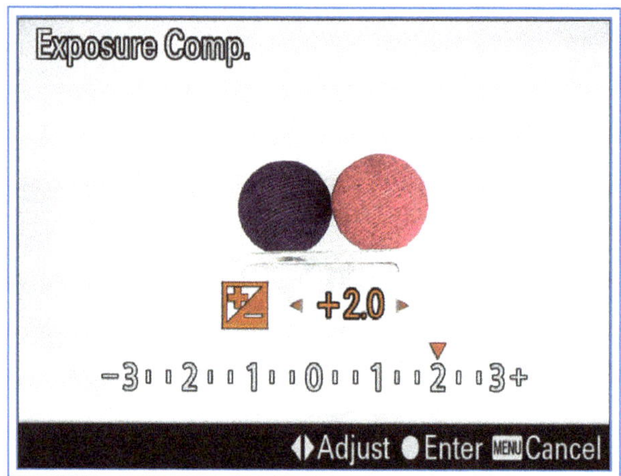

Figure 6-18. Exposure Compensation Scale on Display

Turn the control wheel or press the Left and Right buttons to move the orange triangle above the scale, so it points to a value to the left or right of the zero point.

As you do this, the number above the scale will change. With a negative value, the image will be darker than it otherwise would be; with a positive value, it will be brighter. The camera's display will grow brighter or darker to indicate the effect of the adjustment, if the Live View Display item on screen 7 of the Camera Settings2 menu is set to Setting Effect On.

In this case, with exposure compensation increased by 2.0 EV (exposure value) units, the balls become brighter and are no longer underexposed, as shown in the final image in Figure 6-19.

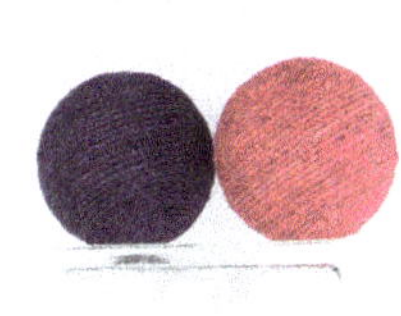

Figure 6-19. Exposure Compensation Example: After

Some photographers follow the practice of generally leaving exposure compensation set at a particular amount, such as negative 0.7 EV. You might do this if you find your images generally are slightly overexposed or if you see that highlights are clipping in many cases. (You can tell if highlights are clipping by checking the histogram, as discussed in Chapter 7. If the histogram is bunched to the right, with no space between the data lines and the right side of the chart, highlights are clipping, or reaching the maximum value.) It is difficult to recover details from images whose highlights have clipped, so it can be a safety measure to underexpose images slightly to avoid that situation.

If you don't plan to leave a permanent exposure compensation setting in place, you should return the setting to the zero point when you are finished with it, so you won't inadvertently change the exposure of later images that don't need the adjustment. (The exposure compensation setting will remain in place even after the camera has been turned off and back on again.) Another way to use an ongoing adjustment to exposure compensation is with the Exposure Standard Adjustment menu option on screen 7 of the Camera Settings1 menu, as discussed in Chapter 4.

If you use exposure compensation often, you can assign it to the control ring using the Custom Key (Still Images) or Custom Key (Movies) menu option. Then you can turn the ring to adjust exposure compensation with a circular scale on the screen, as shown in Figure 6-20.

(The ring will not adjust exposure compensation if the camera is set for manual focus or DMF, because the ring is used to adjust focus with those settings.)

There is one other duty performed by the Down button. In playback mode, when a movie is displayed as ready to play, you can press this button to move to a screen for adjusting the sound level for playback of movies, as shown in Figure 6-21.

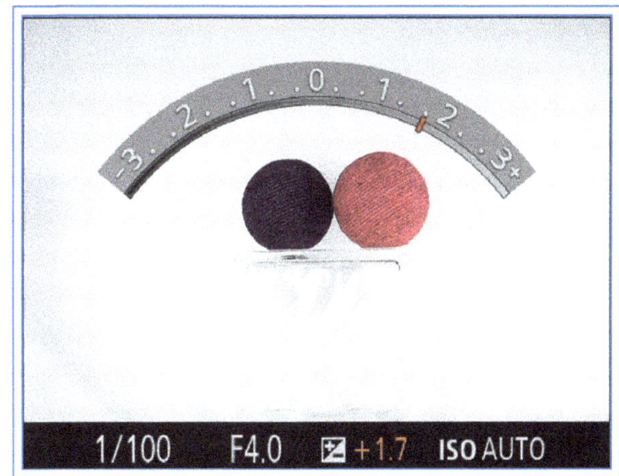

Figure 6-20. Exposure Compensation Adjusted with Control Ring

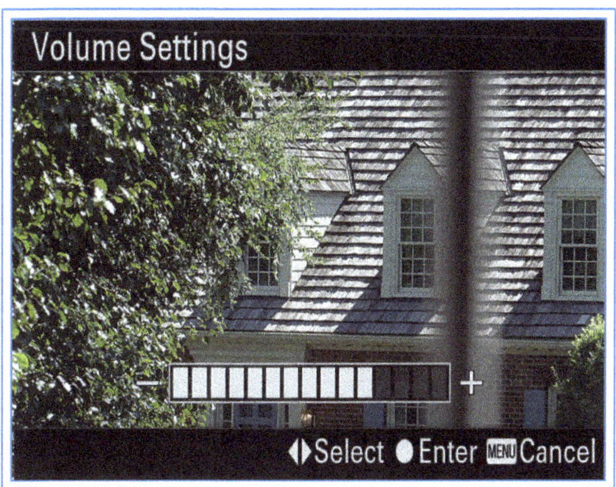

Figure 6-21. Volume Setting Screen from Pressing Down Button

This function also works when a still image is displayed, if the View Mode option on the Playback menu is set to Date View, which includes both still images and movies. When a movie is playing or paused, you can press this button to get access to the full panel of playback controls, as indicated in Figure 6-22 by the down-facing triangle next to the Control Panel label. In some circumstances, as discussed in Chapter 7, you can press this button when a still image or movie is displayed in playback mode to adjust the sound volume for movies.

The Down button is permanently assigned to control exposure compensation when the shooting screen is displayed. This button cannot be reassigned to other operations through the Custom Key menu options.

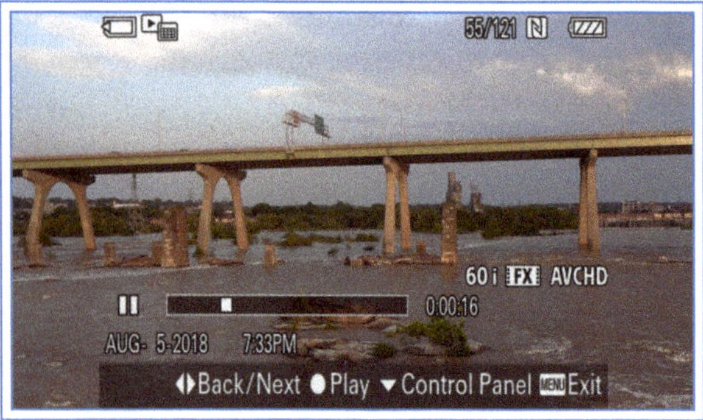

Figure 6-22. Panel of Movie Playback Control Icons

Left Button: Self-Timer/Drive Mode

The Left button is labeled with the timer dial icon for the self-timer and the stack-of-frames icon for continuous shooting. When you press this button, the camera brings up the drive mode menu with its options for self-timer, continuous shooting, and several types of bracketing. I discussed these options in Chapter 4 in connection with the drive mode option on the Camera Settings1 menu.

You can reassign the function of the Left button using the Custom Key options on screen 9 of the Camera Settings1 menu, as discussed in Chapter 5.

LCD Screen: Tilting Features

The next item to be discussed is the tilting ability of the LCD screen. This screen, even without its tilting ability, is a notable feature of the camera. It has a diagonal span of three inches (7.5 cm) and provides a resolution of about 920,000 dots.

The screen can tilt to assist with various types of shots. First, it can tilt downward as much as 90 degrees, as shown in Figure 6-23. You can grab the small tab sticking out at the upper left of the screen to pull it away from the camera.

When the LCD is tilted downward, you can hold the camera above your head and view the scene as if you were an arm's length taller or were standing on a small ladder. If you attach the camera to a monopod or other support and hold it up in the air, you can extend the height even farther and still view the LCD screen quite well. You can activate the self-timer before raising the camera up in the air to take the photo. You also can use a smartphone or tablet connected to the camera by Wi-Fi to trigger the camera by remote control while it is raised overhead, as discussed in Chapter 10, or you can use a wired or wireless remote control device, as discussed in Appendix A.

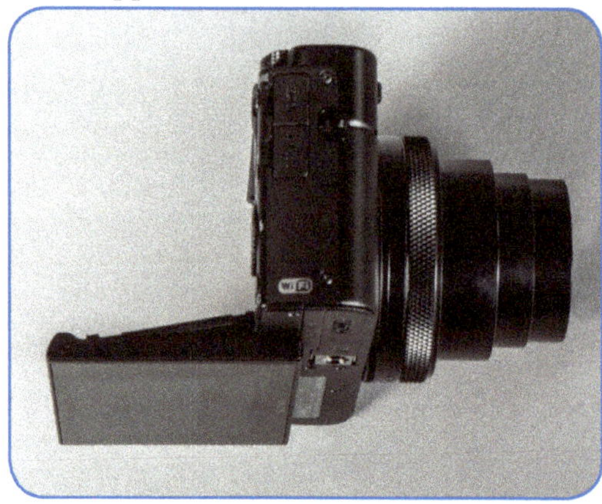

Figure 6-23. LCD Monitor Tilted Downward for Overhead Shots

On the other hand, if you need to take images from a vantage point near ground level, you can rotate the screen so it tilts upward toward your eye, as shown in Figure 6-24, and hold the camera down as far as you need to get a low-angle view of the world.

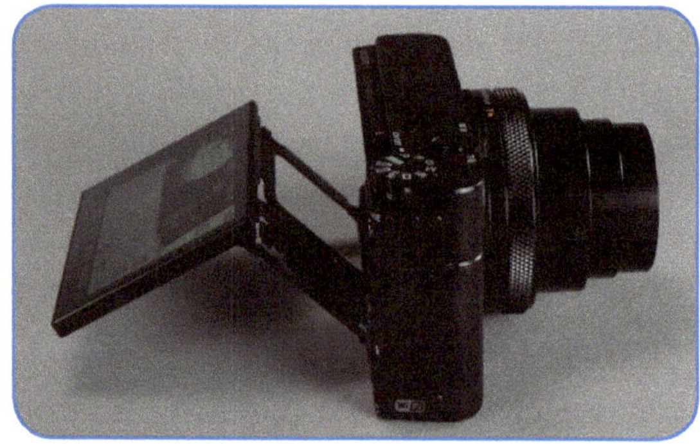

Figure 6-24. LCD Monitor Tilted Upward for Low-angle Shots

It can be helpful to shoot upward like this when your subject is in an area with a busy, distracting background. You can hold the camera down low and shoot with the sky as your background to reduce or eliminate the distractions. (Similarly, you may be able to shoot from a high angle to frame your subject against the ground or floor to have a less-cluttered background.)

The tilting display also is useful for street photography: You can fold the screen upward and look down at the camera while taking photos of people without drawing undue attention to yourself.

Finally, you can rotate the screen 180 degrees so it faces in the same direction as the lens, as seen in Figure 6-25. With this orientation, you can take self-portraits. If you turn on the Self-portrait Timer option on screen 12 of the Camera Settings1 menu, then, when the screen is in this position, the camera will count down from three to one with large numbers on the screen, as shown in Figure 6-26. This orientation also is useful if you need to see yourself as you record a video blog.

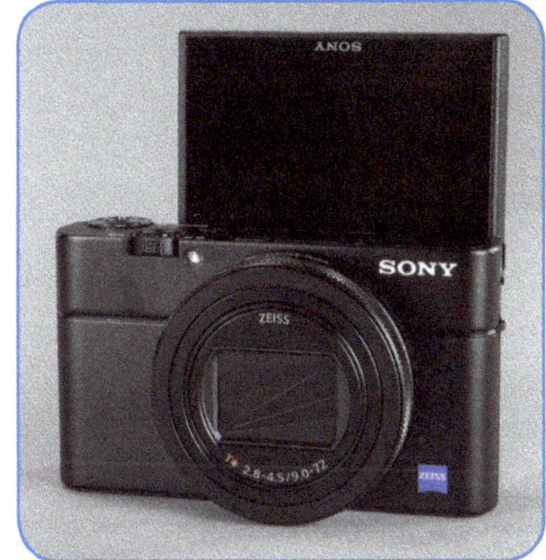

Figure 6-25. LCD Monitor Rotated for Self-portraits

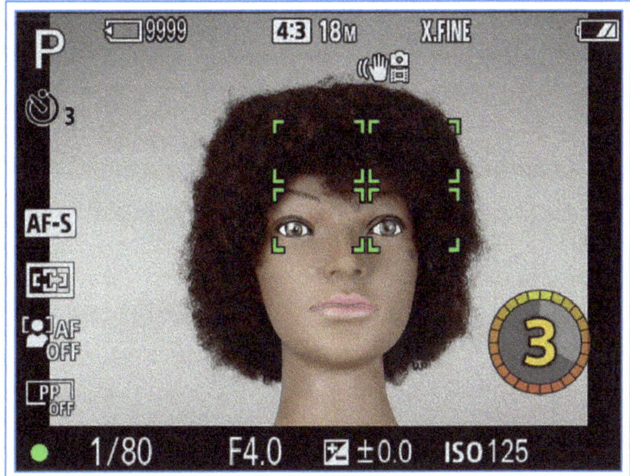

Figure 6-26. Self-portrait Timer on Display

LCD Screen: Touch Screen Features

The second category of special features of the LCD screen is its limited functionality as a touch screen. I have discussed these features to some extent in earlier chapters, and I will provide a summary of these features here.

For touch screen features to work, you first have to make sure the Touch Operation item on screen 3 of the Setup menu is turned on. To have all touch functions working, go to the Touch Panel/Pad item on the same menu screen and choose Touch Panel + Pad for the setting.

Also, on screen 9 of the Camera Settings2 menu, go to the Touch Shooting Settings option and select either Touch Shutter or Touch Focus. (For this discussion, I will assume that Touch Focus is chosen, not Touch Shutter.)

The camera's touch focus capability when shooting still images works in any shooting mode for stills other than Sweep Panorama, and it works with all focus modes except manual focus. The way it works depends on the focus area setting on screen 4 of the Camera Settings1 menu. If that option is set to Wide, Zone, or Center, or to the Wide, Zone, or Center setting for Lock-on AF, you can touch the screen where you want the camera to focus, and it will place a small, black focus frame at that point. (That frame can be hard to see on a dark subject.)

You can then proceed to press the shutter button halfway to focus and all the way down to shoot as you would normally, with the focus point at that location. The camera also places a pointing-finger icon and an X on the screen, as shown in Figure 6-27; you can touch that icon, or press the Center button, to cancel the touch focus operation. At that point, the camera will resume its focusing operations as it would with no touch screen in use, though you can always touch the screen again to set a new focus point. You also can drag the focus frame around the screen with your finger.

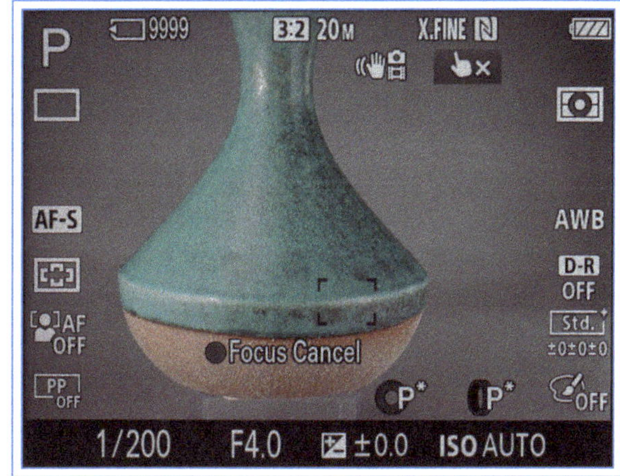

Figure 6-27. Icon to Turn Off Touch Focus

If focus area is set to Flexible Spot or Expand Flexible Spot (or the Flexible Spot or Expand Flexible Spot setting for Lock-on AF), if you touch the screen, you can drag the focus frame to a new location or set a new focus point outside of the existing frame. In this situation, the camera does not place a cancel icon on the screen.

With Lock-on AF in effect, you can touch a point on the screen to lock the tracking frame at that point, or move the existing frame to a new position, depending on which sub-option for Lock-on AF is in effect.

When Center Lock-on AF is in effect, once the tracking frame has been activated, you can touch the screen to set a new location for the frame. After tracking is canceled, you can touch the screen to start it again.

With Face Priority in AF turned on, you can touch the screen to move the focus point to a different face, or to a point that is not on any face. If Touch Shutter is turned on through the Touch Shooting Settings option, you can touch the screen to capture an image.

When the camera is shooting movies, the touch screen operation works somewhat differently than it does with stills. When you touch the screen, the camera uses what Sony calls "spot focus." The camera directs its focus to that point, and it switches the camera into manual focus mode to lock the focus there; you will see the MF icon appear on the screen.

The camera will stay in manual focus mode until you touch the screen again to choose a new focus point, or you touch the finger icon with the X (or press the Center button) to cancel the spot focus feature and let the camera continue with its normal autofocus system. The camera does not display any focus frame at the point where it directs its focus, but you should be able to see that the focus has become sharp at the selected point.

If you want to create a nice "pull focus" effect for a movie, touch one subject to focus on it. Then, when you are ready to switch the focus to the other subject, touch it, and the camera will change its focus point to the new subject. You can control the speed of the pull-focus transition using the AF Drive Speed option on screen 2 of the Camera Settings2 menu. There is a considerable difference in the effects produced by using the Slow, Normal, or Fast setting for that option. If you want a quick, possibly startling focus change, choose Fast; for a leisurely, relaxed transition, choose Slow.

If focus area is set to Flexible Spot or Expand Flexible Spot when recording video, the touch focus operation is somewhat different. In that case, you can still touch a point on the screen to cause the camera to focus at that point, but the camera does not switch into manual focus mode. You can also drag the focus frame to a new position, and the camera will focus at that new location. You can use this dragging action to carry out a "pull focus" effect, as discussed above for the spot focus feature. Note: If you have set focus area to Flexible Spot or Expand Flexible Spot and you find the touch focus does not work as described above for recording movies, check to make sure Auto Dual Recording is turned off on screen 2 of the Camera Settings2 menu. If it is turned on, the camera can only use Wide for Focus area when recording movies.

You also can use the LCD screen as a touch pad to control focus operations when you are viewing the scene through the viewfinder. The touch focus features can work as described above in that case, but you can change their behavior to some extent with a menu option, Touch Pad Settings, on screen 3 of the Setup menu. If you set the Touch Position Mode option of that menu item to Absolute Position, you can touch any point on the operational area of the screen and the focus will be set there. You also can drag the focus frame, depending on the focus area setting. However, if you set Touch Position Mode to Relative Position, you cannot select a new focus point just by touching the screen; you can only drag an existing focus frame to a new point.

Besides focusing, the RX100 VI offers a couple of other touch screen features. First, when the camera is in playback mode, you can tap the screen twice to enlarge an individual still image. You can then scroll the enlarged image around with your finger, and tap twice again to return it to normal size. Sometimes it can be difficult to tap at the right speed to get this function to work, but it does work fairly well.

Also, when the camera is in shooting mode with manual focus in use, you can tap the screen twice to call up the Focus Magnifier feature, which enlarges the screen so you can judge the focus. You can scroll the screen around with a finger, and tap twice again to reduce it to normal size.

Ports and Other Items on Right and Left Sides of Camera

There are two important connection ports on the right side of the camera. Figure 6-28 shows this side of the camera with the protective flaps over those ports opened.

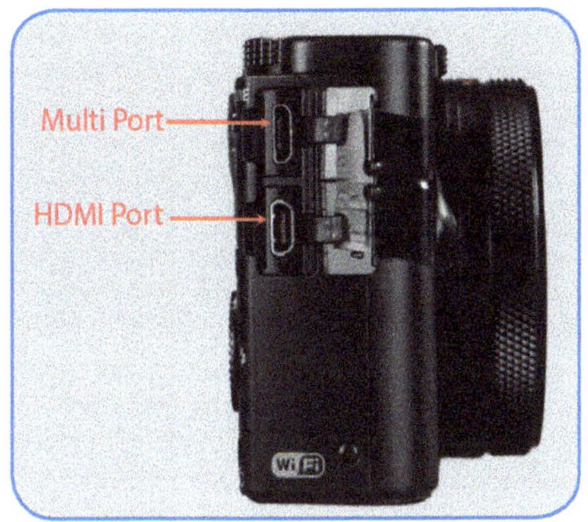

Figure 6-28. Ports on Right Side of Camera

The top port is the Multi port. This is where you plug in the USB cable for charging the battery, powering the camera with an external power source, uploading images and videos to a computer, controlling the camera from a computer using the Remote module of the Imaging Edge software, or connecting the camera directly to a printer to print images. You also can plug in accessories that are compatible with this special terminal, including various models of remote controls, which I discuss in Appendix A.

The lower port is the HDMI port, where you plug in an optional micro HDMI cable to connect the camera to an HDTV for viewing images and videos. You also can view the shooting display from the camera through this connection, so you can connect the camera to an HDTV to act as a monitor for shooting still images or videos. I will discuss that process in Chapter 10. You also can set the camera to output a "clean" HDMI signal, which can be routed through an HDMI cable to an external video recorder. I will discuss that process in Chapter 9.

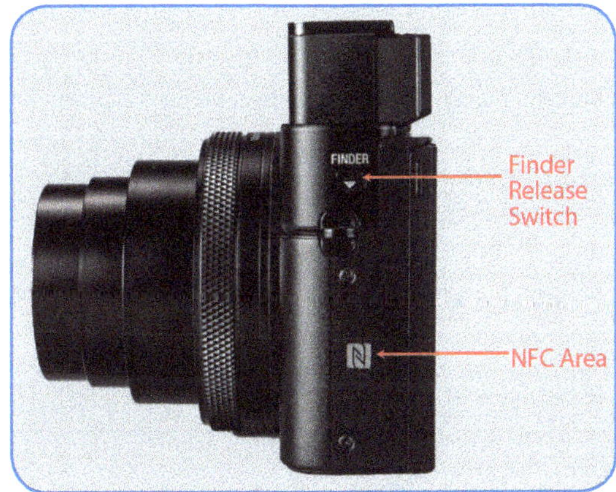

Figure 6-29. Left Side of Camera

The left side of the camera, shown in Figure 6-29, is where the finder release switch is located. Press down on this switch to release the electronic viewfinder so it will pop up. If the camera is turned off, popping up the viewfinder will turn the camera on. Pressing the viewfinder back into the camera's body will power the camera off or leave it powered on, depending on the setting of the Function for VF Close option on screen 2 of the Setup menu.

Below the finder release switch is a decorative letter N, which marks the NFC active area for the RX100 VI. This is where you touch the camera against the similar area on a compatible Android smartphone or tablet that uses the near field communication protocol. As discussed in Chapter 10, when the two devices are touched together at their NFC active areas, they should automatically connect through a Wi-Fi network. Once the connection is established, they can share images, and the phone or tablet can control the camera in some ways.

The bottom of the RX100 VI is shown in Figure 6-30.

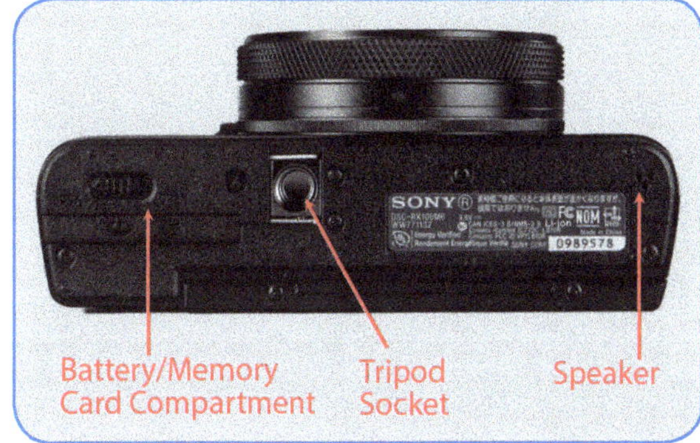

Figure 6-30. Items on Bottom of Camera

The major items here are the tripod socket and the battery/memory card compartment. There is an access lamp inside this compartment, as seen in Figure 6-31.

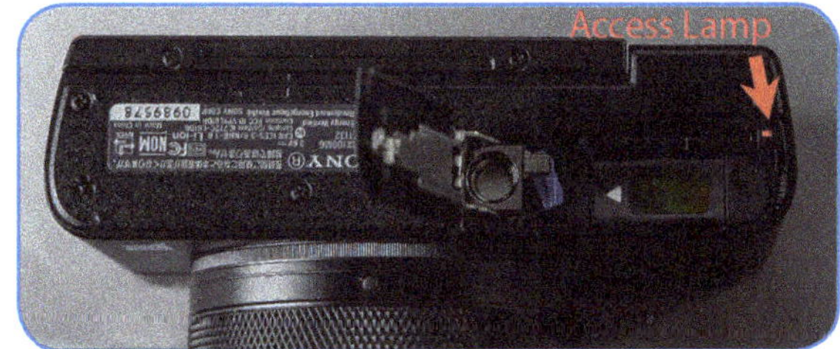

Figure 6-31. Red Access Lamp Inside Battery Compartment

The red access lamp lights when the camera is writing data to the memory card. When the lamp is lit, it's important not to remove the card or the battery from the compartment. Also on the bottom of the camera is the speaker, which emits the sound for movies played in the camera.

Chapter 7: Playback and Printing

You may not spend a lot of time viewing your images and videos in the camera, but even if you don't, it's useful to know how the various in-camera playback functions work. You may need to examine an image closely in the camera to check focus, composition, and other aspects, or you may want to share images with friends and family. So it's worth taking a good look at the playback functions of the Sony RX100 VI. I'll also discuss how to print images directly from the camera.

Normal Playback

First, you should be aware of the Auto Review option on screen 8 of the Camera Settings2 menu. This setting determines whether and for how long the image stays on the screen for review when you take a new picture. If your major interest for viewing images in the camera is to check them right after they are taken, this setting is all you need to be concerned with. As discussed in Chapter 5, you can leave Auto Review turned off or set it to two, five, or ten seconds.

To control how images are viewed later on, you need to work with the options that are available in playback mode. For plain review of images, the process is simple. Once you press the Playback button (marked with a triangle icon), the camera is in playback mode, and you will see an image or video that has been saved to the camera's memory card. (Which item is displayed depends on the setting for View Mode, discussed later, as well as on which one was viewed last.)

To move back through older items, press the Left button or turn the control wheel to the left. To see more recent ones, use the Right button or turn the control wheel to the right. To speed through the images, hold down the Left or Right button.

Index View and Enlarging Images

In normal playback mode, you can press the zoom lever on top of the camera to view an index screen of your images and videos or to enlarge a single image. When you are viewing an individual image, press the zoom lever once to the left, and you will see a screen showing either 9 or 25 images, one of which is outlined by an orange frame, as shown in Figure 7-1.

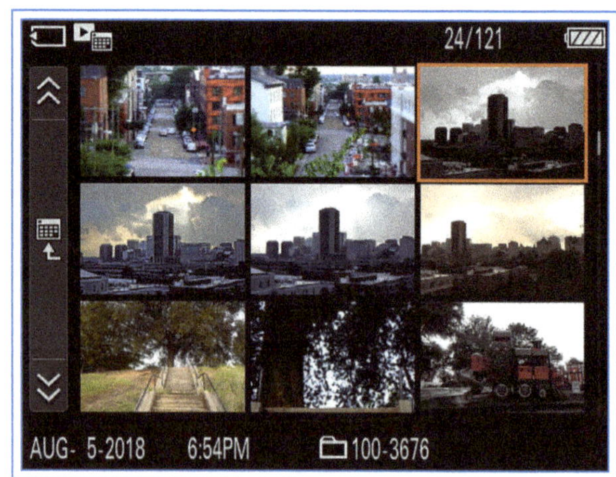

Figure 7-1. Playback Index Screen - 9 Images

(You can choose whether this screen shows 9 or 25 images using the Image Index option on screen 3 of the Playback menu, discussed later in this chapter.)

You can press the Center button to bring up the outlined image on the screen, or you can move through the images on the index screen by pressing the Left and Right buttons or by turning the control wheel. If you move the orange highlight to the far left of the display, as seen in Figure 7-2, you can use the Up and Down buttons to move through the images a screen at a time.

On the 9-image or 25-image index screen, one more press of the zoom lever to the left brings up another screen. For example, if View Mode, discussed later in this chapter, is set to Date View, this next screen will be a calendar display, as shown in Figure 7-3.

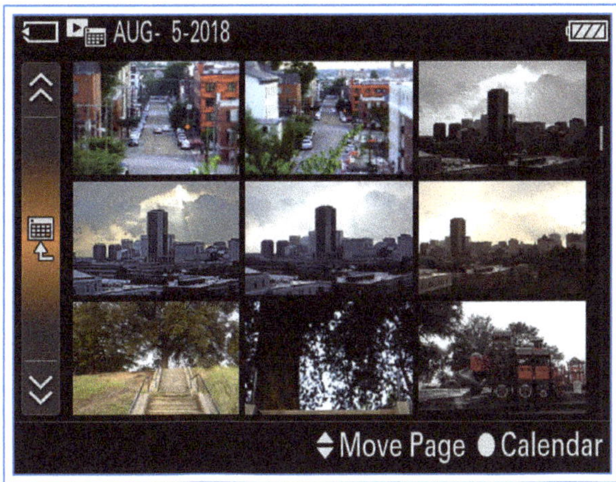

Figure 7-2. Highlight on Screen Navigation Strip

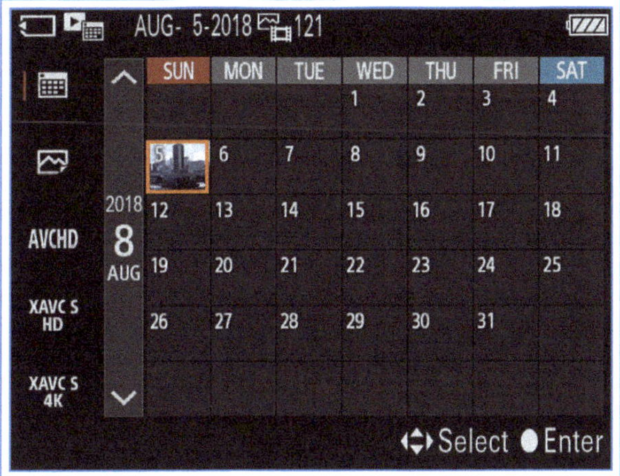

Figure 7-3. Calendar Index Screen

On that screen, you can move the orange frame to any date and press the Center button to bring up a view with images and videos from that date. If you move the orange highlight to the narrow strip to the left of the calendar, as seen in Figure 7-4, you can move through the items by months with the Up and Down buttons.

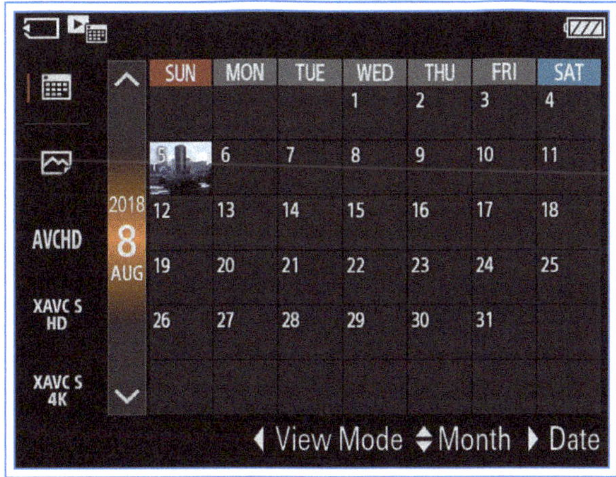

Figure 7-4. Highlight on Month Navigation Strip

If you move the highlight to the far left, as in Figure 7-5, you can use the Up and Down buttons to move through the five icons. You can choose the date view, still-images view, AVCHD videos view, XAVC S HD videos view, or XAVC S 4K videos view. I will discuss those options later in this chapter, in connection with the View Mode item on screen 3 of the Playback menu.

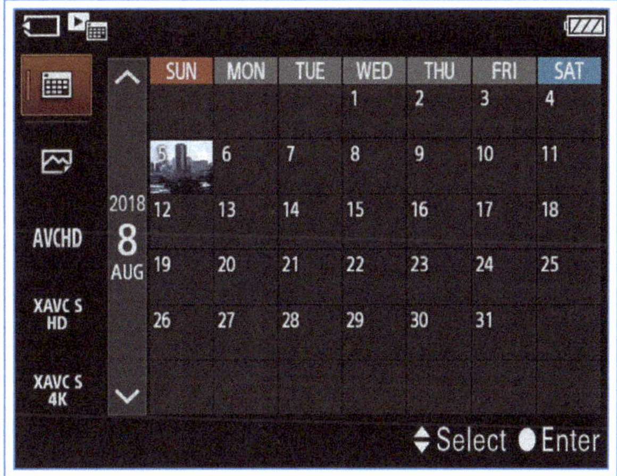

Figure 7-5. Highlight on View Mode Icons Strip

When you are viewing a single still image, a press of the zoom lever to the right enlarges the image, with the enlargement centered on the point where the camera used autofocus, if it did so. If the camera did not use autofocus, the camera will zoom in on the center of the image. (You can change this behavior with the Enlarge Initial Position option on screen 2 of the Playback menu, discussed later in this chapter.) You will see a display in the lower left corner of the image showing a thumbnail with an inset orange frame that represents the portion of the image that is now filling the screen in enlarged view, as shown in Figure 7-6. This feature is useful for quickly checking the focus of the image.

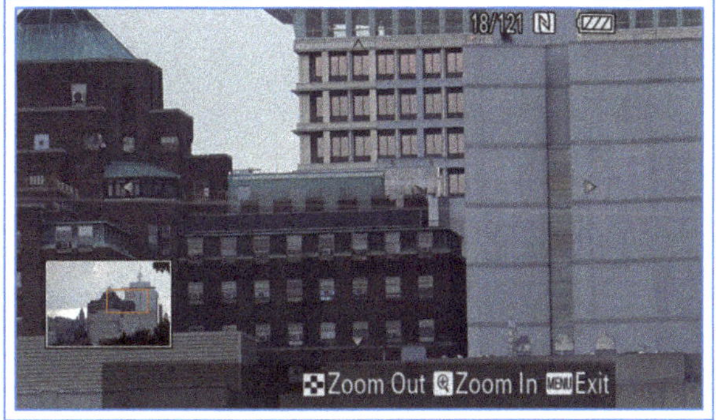

Figure 7-6. Image Enlarged in Playback Mode

If you press the zoom lever to the right repeatedly, the image will be enlarged to increasing levels. While it is magnified, you can scroll in it with the four direction buttons; you will see the orange frame move around within the thumbnail image. To reduce the image size again, press the zoom lever to the left as many times as necessary or press the Center button or Menu button to revert immediately to normal size. You can press the Custom/Delete button to bring up the Delete screen for that image while it is enlarged. To move to other images while the display is magnified, turn the control wheel.

You also can enlarge an image in Playback mode by tapping twice on the LCD screen, if the Touch Operation option on screen 3 of the Setup menu has been set to turn on the touch features of the screen. You can then drag the enlarged image around with a finger, and tap twice again to reduce the image to normal size.

Playback Display Screens

When you are viewing an image in single-image display mode, pressing the Display button (Up button) repeatedly cycles through three playback screens: (1) the full image with no information; (2) the full image with basic information, including date and time it was taken, image number, Aspect Ratio, aperture, shutter speed, ISO, JPEG Image Size, and JPEG Quality, as shown in Figure 7-7; and (3) a reduced-size image with detailed recording information, including aperture, shutter speed, ISO, shooting mode, white balance, focal length, DRO setting, and other data, plus a histogram, as shown in Figure 7-8.

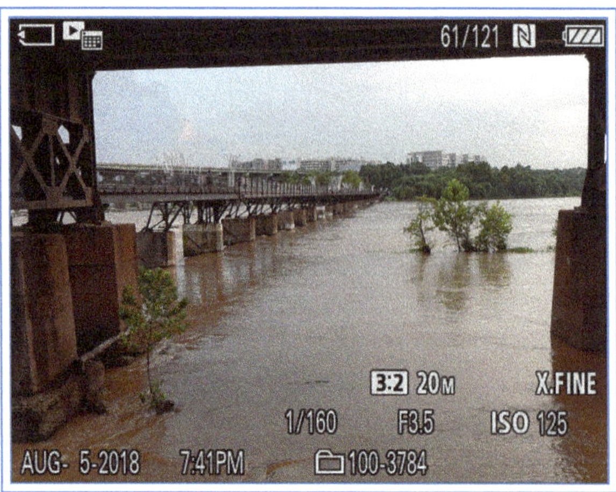

Figure 7-7. Playback Screen with Basic Information

A histogram is a graph showing distribution of dark and bright areas in the image. Dark blacks are represented by peaks on the left and bright whites by peaks on the right, with continuous gradations in between. With the RX100 VI, the graph's top box gives information about the overall brightness of the image. The three lower boxes contain information about the brightness of the basic colors that make up the image: red, green, and blue.

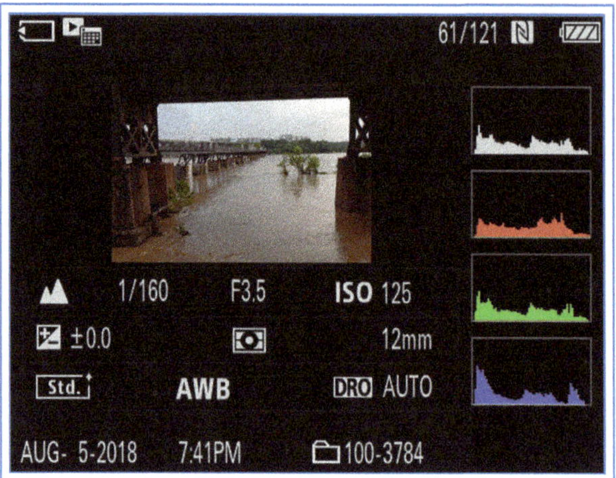

Figure 7-8. Playback Screen with Histogram

If a histogram has brightness values bunched at the left side, there is an excessive amount of black and dark areas (high points on the left side of the histogram) and very few bright and white areas (no high points on the right). If the graph runs into the left side of the chart, it means the shadow areas are "clipped"; that is, the image is so dark that some details have been lost in the dark areas. The histogram in Figure 7-9 illustrates this degree of underexposure.

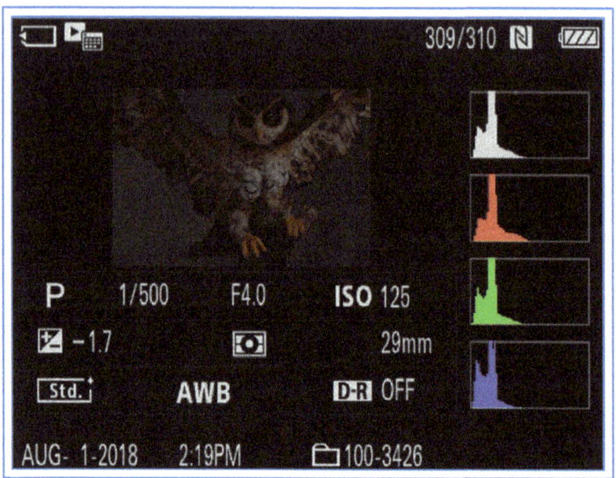

Figure 7-9. Histogram for Underexposed Image

A histogram with its high points bunched on the right means the image is too bright, as shown in Figure 7-10.

If the lines of the graph run into the right side of the chart, that means the highlights are clipped and the image has lost some details in the bright areas.

A histogram for a normally exposed image has high points arranged evenly in the middle. That pattern, illustrated by Figure 7-11, indicates a good balance of light, dark, and medium tones.

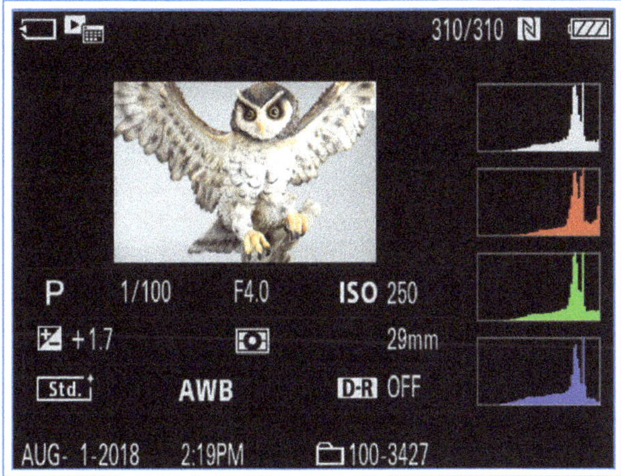

Figure 7-10. Histogram for Overexposed Image

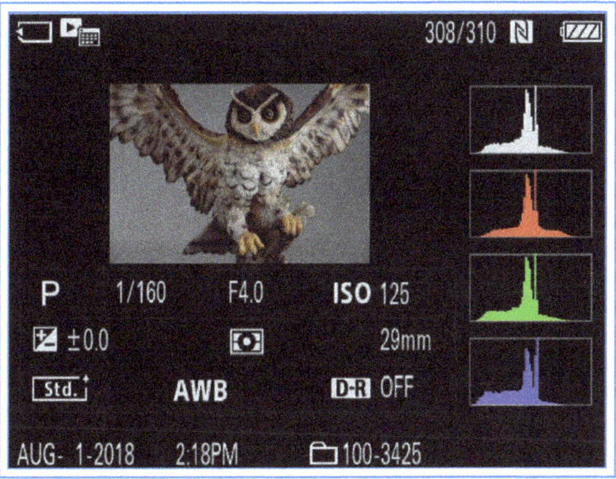

Figure 7-11. Histogram for Normally Exposed Image

When the playback histogram is on the screen, any areas containing highlights that are excessively bright will flash to indicate possible overexposure, alerting you that you might need to take another shot with the exposure adjusted to avoid that situation.

The histogram is an approximation and should not be relied on too heavily. It can give you helpful feedback as to how evenly exposed your image is. There may be times when it is appropriate to have a histogram skewed to the left or right for intentionally "low-key" (dark) or "high-key" (brightly lit) scenes.

If you want to see the histogram when the camera is in shooting mode, you can turn on that option using the Display Button option on screen 7 of the Camera Settings2 menu, as discussed in Chapter 5.

Deleting Images with the Delete Button

As I mentioned in Chapter 6, you can delete individual images by pressing the Delete button, also known as the Custom or C button, at the bottom right of the camera's back. If you press this button when a still image or a video is displayed, whether individually or highlighted on an index screen, the camera will display the Delete/Cancel box shown in Figure 7-12. (You can control how that dialog box is displayed using the Delete Confirmation option on screen 2 of the Setup menu, as discussed in Chapter 8.)

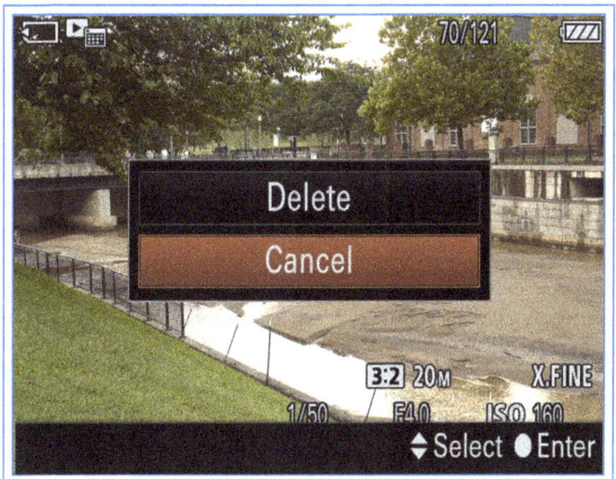

Figure 7-12. Delete Screen from Pressing C Button

Highlight your choice and press the Center button to confirm. You can delete only single images or videos in this way, except for bursts of continuous shots. If you press the C button while a set of continuous shots is displayed as a group, the camera will delete all shots in the group at once, as discussed later in this chapter. If you want to delete multiple items that are not part of the same group, you can use the Delete option on screen 1 of the Playback menu, discussed next in this chapter.

Playback Menu

Other options for controlling playback on the RX100 VI appear as items on the Playback menu, whose first screen is shown in Figure 7-13.

You get access to this menu by pressing the Menu button and navigating to the menu marked by a triangle icon. Following is information about each item on this menu.

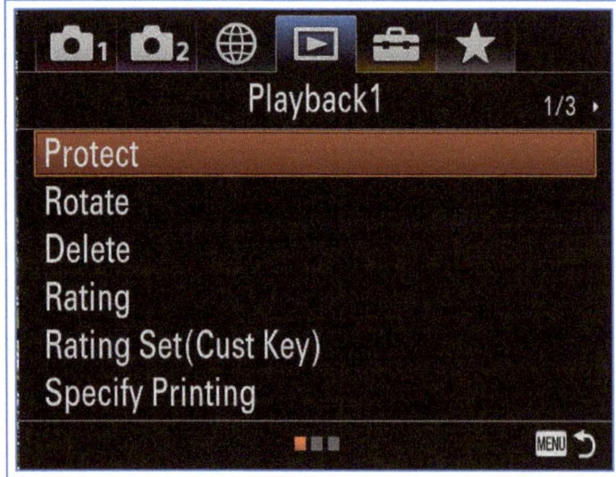

Figure 7-13. Screen 1 of Playback Menu

Protect

With the Protect feature, you can "lock" selected images or videos so they cannot be erased with the normal erase functions, including using the Delete button and using the Delete option on the Playback menu, discussed below. However, if you format a memory card using the Format command on the Setup menu, all data on the card will be erased, including protected images.

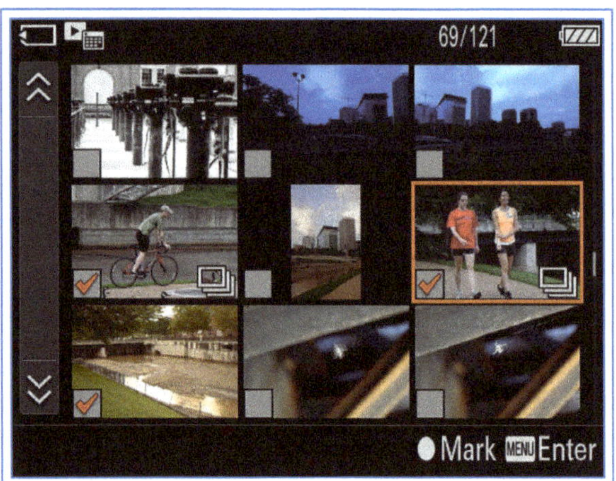

Figure 7-14. Image Selection Screen for Protect Option

When you select this option, the camera will display a screen like that in Figure 7-14, with the choices to select multiple images; all from the same date as the current image or all from the current folder, depending on the current setting for View Mode; or to cancel protection for all images with this date or from this folder.

If you select Multiple Images, the camera will present you with either index screens or individual images. You can scroll through the images and videos and mark any item's check box for protection by pressing the Center button. Press that button again to unmark an image. When you have finished marking them, press the Menu button and the camera will display a confirmation screen. If you select OK to confirm, the marked items will be protected. Any image that is protected will have a key icon at the top center, as shown in Figure 7-15.

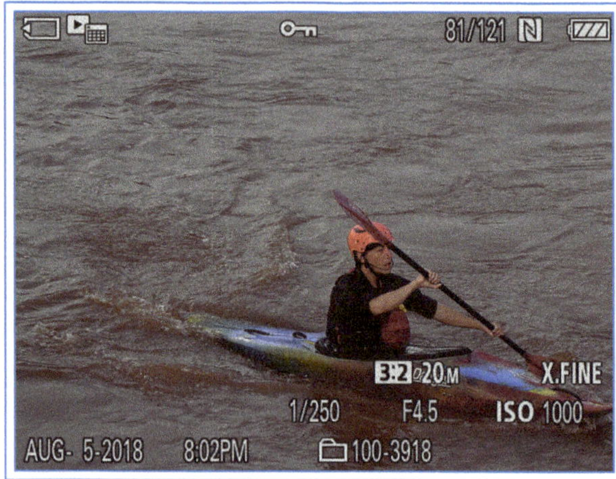

Figure 7-15. Protected Image with Key Icon

To unprotect all images or videos in one operation, select the appropriate Cancel option from the Protect item on the Playback menu. That option will prompt you to Cancel All with this Date or to Cancel All in this Folder, depending on the View Mode setting.

Rotate

The Rotate menu option gives you a way to rotate an image. Select this menu item, and you will see a screen like that in Figure 7-16, prompting you to press the Center button to rotate the image.

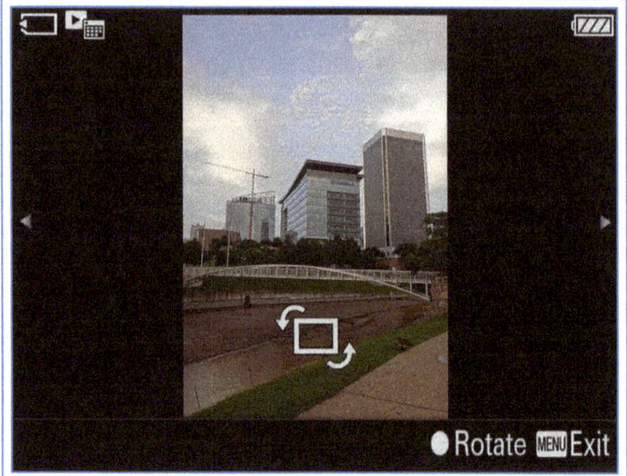

Figure 7-16. Rotate Screen with Arrows

Each time you press the button, the image will rotate 90 degrees counter-clockwise. You can use this option for images taken vertically, when the Display Rotation option on screen 3 of the Playback menu, discussed later in this chapter, is off. This option will be dimmed if View Mode is set to a view for videos only.

Delete

The Delete command lets you erase multiple images and videos from your memory card in one operation. (If you just want to delete one or two items, it's usually easier to display each one on the screen, then press the Delete button and confirm the erasure.) When you select the Delete command, the menu offers you various choices, as shown in Figure 7-17.

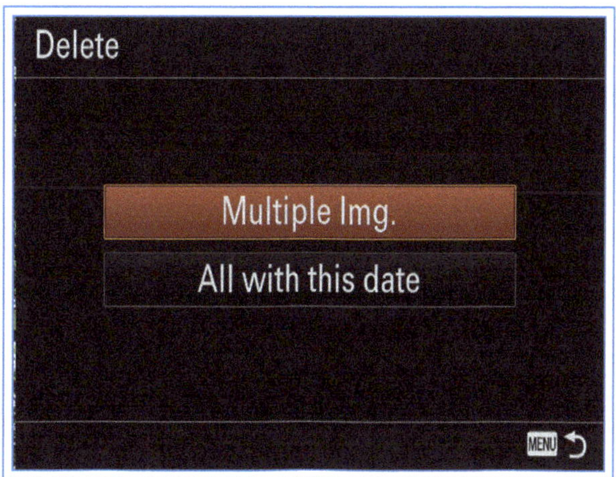

Figure 7-17. Delete Menu Options Screen

These choices may include Multiple Images, All in this Folder, or All with this Date, depending on the current view that has been selected with the View Mode option, discussed later in this chapter.

If you choose Multiple Images, the camera will display the still images or videos with a check box at the left side of each item, as shown in Figure 7-18.

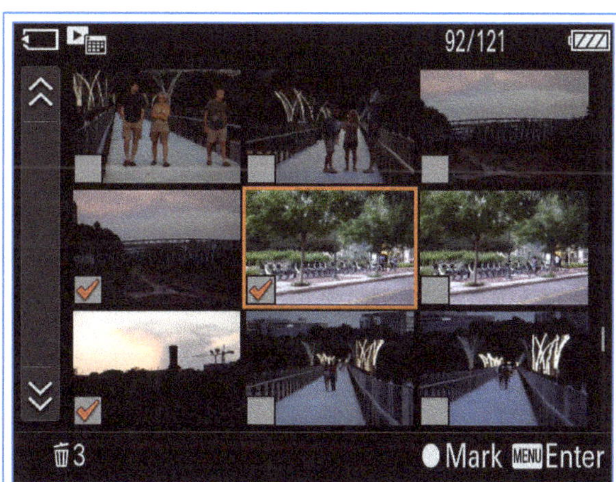

Figure 7-18. Image Selection Screen for Delete Option

The images and videos may be shown individually or on an index screen, depending on whether you started from an individual image or an index screen. You can change between full-screen and index views using the zoom lever, even after choosing the Delete option.

Scroll through the images and videos with the control wheel or the Left and Right buttons. When you reach an item you want to delete, press the Center button to place a check mark in the box for that item. To unmark an image or video, press the Center button again. Continue with this process until you have marked all items you want to delete. Then, press the Menu button to move to the next screen, where the camera will prompt you to highlight OK or Cancel, and press the Center button to confirm. If you select OK, all of the marked items will be deleted. If you want to cancel before you have marked any items, press the Playback button to return to normal playback mode.

If, instead of Multiple Images, you choose All in this Folder or All with this Date, the camera will display a screen asking you to confirm deletion of all of those files.

If any images have a key icon displayed at the top, those images are protected, and they cannot be deleted using this option unless you first unprotect them, as discussed earlier in this chapter.

Rating

This option lets you assign a rating of from one to five stars to any individual still image. (This option does not work for movies or for images displayed as a group, taken in burst mode.) After you select this item, the camera will display a rating selection screen, as shown in Figure 7-19.

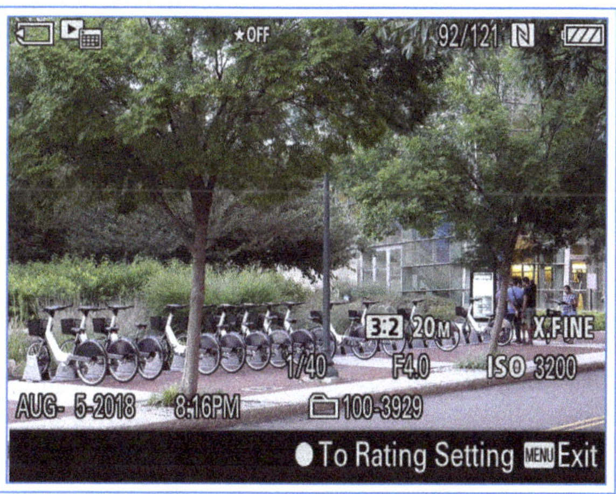

Figure 7-19. Image Selection Screen for Rating Option

Use the Left and Right buttons or turn the control wheel to display an image to be rated. When it is displayed, press the Center button and the camera will display a screen like that in Figure 7-20.

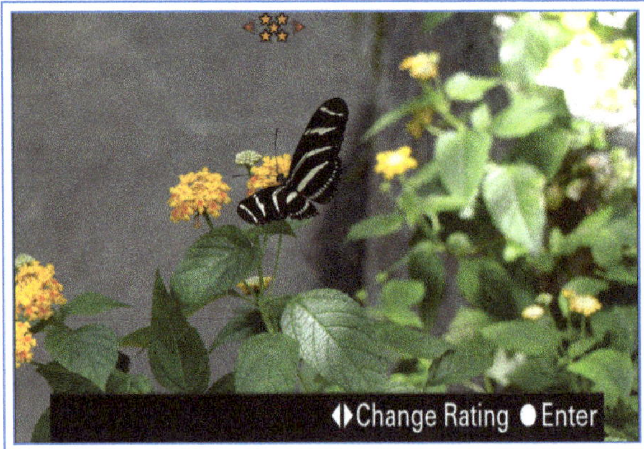

Figure 7-20. Screen to Assign Rating to Image

On that screen, use the Left and Right buttons or the control wheel to select a rating. The camera will change the number of orange stars at the top of the image.

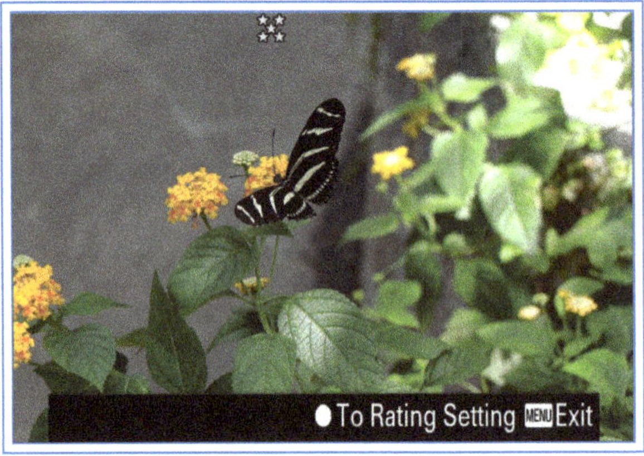

Figure 7-21. Image with Star Rating Assigned

When the star rating is changed as you want, press the Center button to confirm, and the stars at the top of the image will turn white, indicating the final rating, as shown in Figure 7-21. The rating you assigned will show up in software that reads such metadata, such as Adobe Bridge and Sony's Imaging Edge.

Rating Set (Custom Key)

This menu option works in conjunction with the ability to assign a control button to the Rating option using the Custom Key (Playback) option on screen 9 of the Camera Settings2 menu. If you assign a button to the Rating option, you can use the Rating Set (Custom Key) menu option to choose the number of stars to be assigned by that button. So, for example, if you choose three stars, then, in playback mode, if you press the assigned control button when an image is displayed, that image will be assigned a rating of three stars.

Specify Printing

This option lets you use the DPOF (Digital Print Order Format) function, a standard printing protocol that is built into the camera. The DPOF system lets you mark various images on your memory card to be added to a print list, which can then be sent to your own printer. Or, you can take the memory card to a commercial printing company to print out the selected images.

To add images to the DPOF print list, select the Specify Printing option from the Playback menu. On the next screen, shown in Figure 7-22, select Multiple Images.

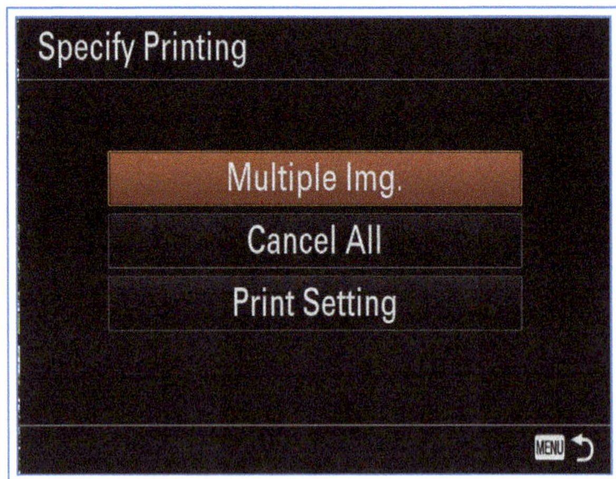

Figure 7-22. Specify Printing Options Screen

The camera will display the first image with a check box at the left, or an index screen with an orange frame around the currently selected image and a check box in the lower-left corner of each image thumbnail, as shown in Figure 7-23.

You can choose to display individual images or index screens using the zoom lever. There will be a small printer icon in the lower left of the display with a zero beside it at first, meaning no copies of any images have been set for printing yet. Use the control wheel or direction buttons to move through the images.

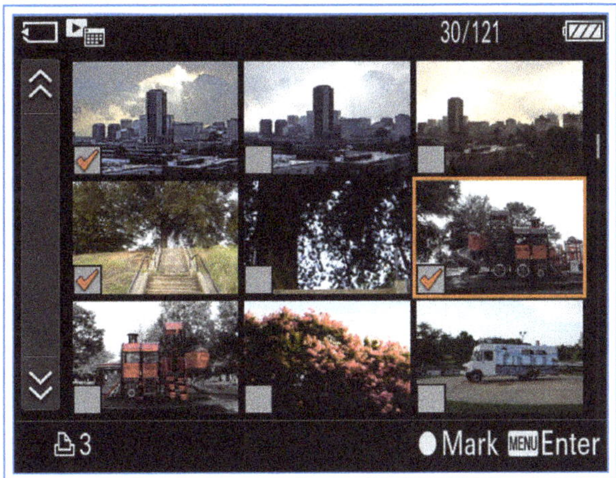

Figure 7-23. Image Selection Screen for Specify Printing Option

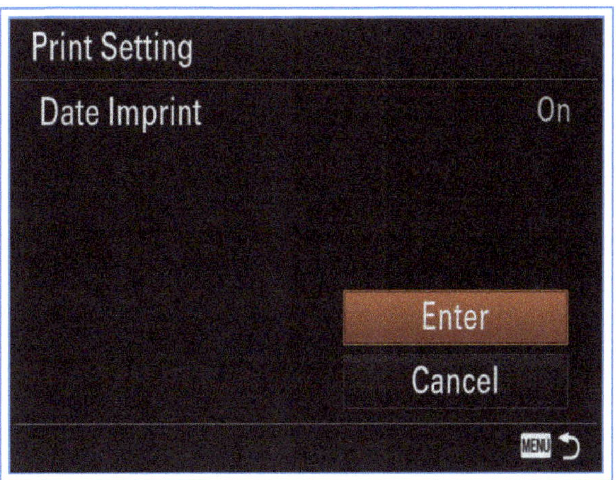

Figure 7-24. Specify Printing Options Screen

When an image you want to have printed is displayed, press the Center button to mark it for printing or to unmark it. If you want to mark all images in a folder or for a date, scroll until you find and highlight with an orange line the box for that folder or date, and press the Center button to mark it. However, if the number of images to be marked exceeds the allowable limit of 100 images, that operation will not succeed.

You can then keep browsing through your images and adding (or subtracting) them from the print list. As you add images to the list, the DPOF counter in the lower left corner of the display will show the total number of images selected for printing. You cannot use this function to print more than one copy of any given image. You cannot specify printing for images in a group of continuous-shooting images while the group is expanded or displayed as a group. If you want to print images from such a group, you have to set the Display Continuous Shooting Group option to Off on screen 3 of the Playback menu, or set View Mode to Folder View (Still).

When you have finished selecting images to be printed, press the Menu button to move to a screen where you can confirm your choices by selecting OK.

You also can turn the Date Imprint option on or off to specify whether or not the pictures will be printed with the dates they were taken. To do this, go to the first screen of the Specify Printing menu option and select Print Setting. On the next screen, shown in Figure 7-24, set Date Imprint to On and then select Enter, to specify that the date should be printed on each image.

You can take the memory card with the DPOF list to a service that prints photos using this system, or you can connect the camera to a PictBridge-compatible printer to print the images. If you want to cancel a DPOF order, select the Specify Printing menu item, and choose the Cancel All option on the next screen.

The items on screen 2 of the Playback menu are shown in Figure 7-25.

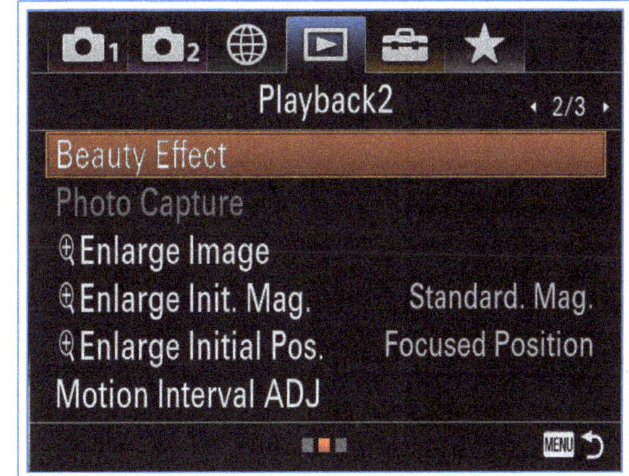

Figure 7-25. Screen 2 of Playback Menu

Beauty Effect

This first option on the second screen of the Playback menu gives you tools for retouching photographs of faces that you have previously taken. To use this feature, navigate to an image of a face in playback mode and select this option from the menu. The camera will display the image with an orange or white frame around any face it detects. If the camera does not detect a face, it will display an error message. If it detects multiple faces, use the Left and Right buttons to select the one to retouch; the selected face will be marked with the orange frame.

After selecting the face, press the Center button to move to the next screen, shown in Figure 7-26.

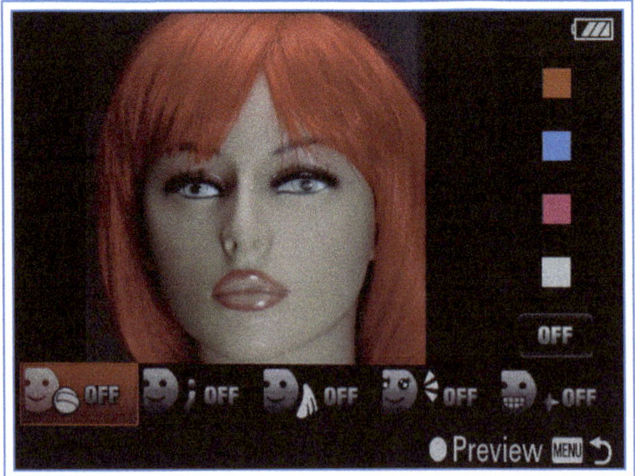

Figure 7-26. Beauty Effect Adjustments Screen

On that screen, the camera displays five controls represented by icons at the bottom of the display, from left to right: Skin Toning, Skin Smoothing, Shine Removal, Eye Widening, and Teeth Whitening. Highlight an adjustment icon using the Left and Right buttons, and adjust each of these settings using the Up and Down buttons or the control wheel.

When they are all adjusted as you want, press the Center button to generate a preview. The camera will display Before and After images on a screen like that shown in Figure 7-27.

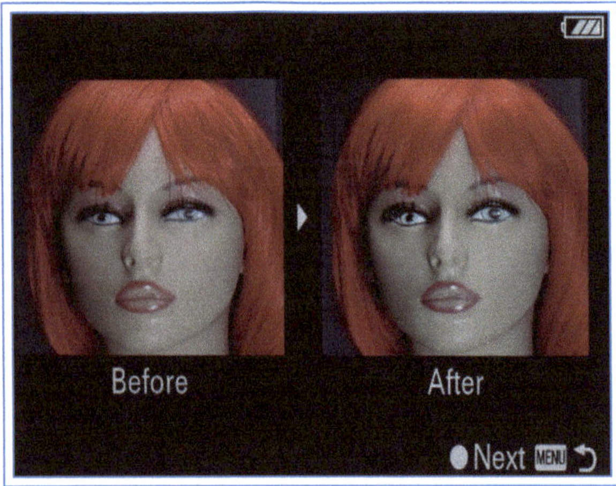

Figure 7-27. Beauty Effect Preview Screen

If you are satisfied, press the Center button, and select OK to confirm on the next screen. The camera will save a new version of the image with the adjustments you selected. If you need to adjust another face in the same image, select that image again and make adjustments for the next face.

Photo Capture

This next option on the Playback menu gives you tools for saving one or more frames from a movie that was recorded with the camera. To use this option, first find the movie that you want to save a still image from. You can use the View Mode option discussed earlier in this chapter to find movies of various formats, to help narrow the search. If View Mode is set to Folder View (Still), this option will not be available for selection.

When you have the chosen movie displayed on the screen in playback mode, select the Photo Capture menu option, and the camera will display the movie again, but this time with a circular area with several icons at the right side of the display that represent the camera's direction buttons and Center button, as shown in Figure 7-28.

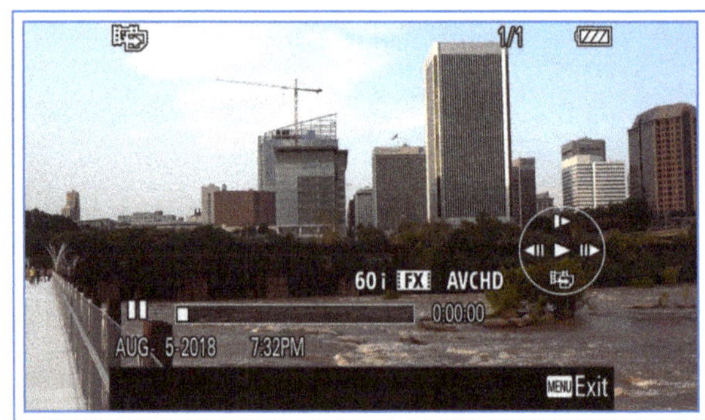

Figure 7-28. Photo Capture Screen with Navigation Controls

The top icon represents slow playback; the right one is for single-frame forward; the left one is for single-frame reverse; the center one is for play or pause; and the bottom one is for photo capture.

Using the four direction buttons and the Center button according to that scheme, play the movie to the exact frame you want to save, then press the Down button to capture the frame as a still image. The camera will display a Processing message briefly, and then will save the image to the memory card. The image will have the same resolution as the movie from which it was saved. For example, if you save a frame from a 4K movie, it will have a resolution of 3840 x 2160 pixels, or about eight megapixels.

If you prefer, you can start the Photo Capture process without using the menu system. To do that, start a movie playing, and press the Center button to pause it. Then press the Down button, and you will see a control panel at the bottom of the screen, as shown in Figure 7-29.

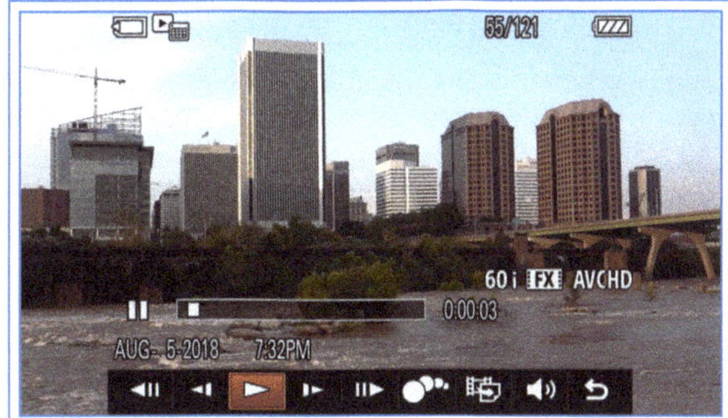

Figure 7-29. Movie Playback Icons with Photo Capture Control

The Photo Capture icon is the third one from the right. Use the direction buttons to navigate to that icon and select it, to start using the Photo Capture feature. Figure 7-30 is a frame that was saved from a 4K video using this feature.

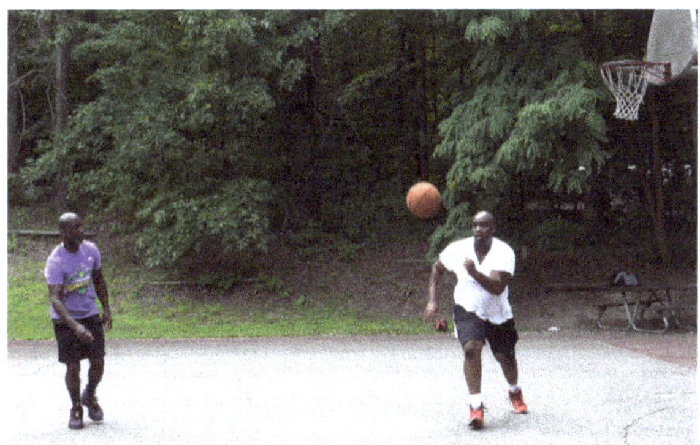

Figure 7-30. Photo Capture Example

Enlarge Image

This option does the same image magnification discussed earlier, which you can also do with the zoom lever, or by tapping on the screen twice, if the touch screen features are enabled. When you select this option, the enlarged image will appear on the screen; you can then use the zoom lever to change the enlargement factor. When the image is enlarged, you can press the Center button or the Menu button, or tap twice on the screen, to return the image to normal size. You can move the enlarged image around the screen with your finger, if the touch screen is turned on, or with the direction buttons. You can turn the control wheel to move to other images at the current magnification level.

Enlarge Initial Magnification

This option lets you choose either Standard Magnification or Previous Magnification, as shown in Figure 7-31. With the Standard Magnification option, when you use the zoom lever to magnify an image, the camera uses the standard magnification factor.

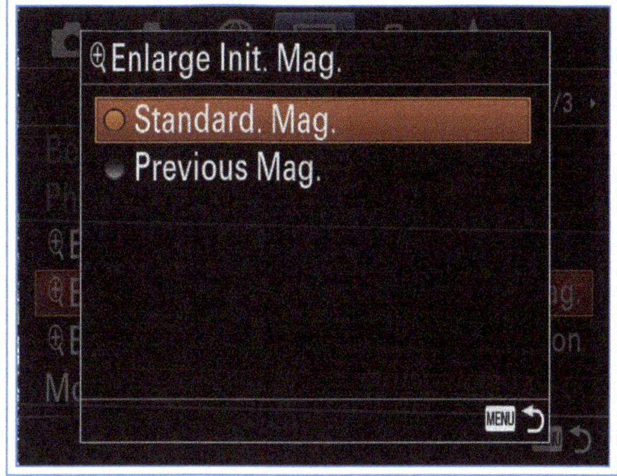

Figure 7-31. Enlarge Initial Magnification Options Screen

If you choose Previous Magnification, the camera will use whatever magnification level was used for the last image that was viewed. So, if you like to zoom your images in with three presses of the zoom lever, you can choose Previous Magnification for this option, and, once you have enlarged one image to that degree, other images will be enlarged to that degree when you first turn the zoom lever to enlarge them.

Enlarge Initial Position

This option lets you choose whether, when an image is enlarged, the camera centers it on the point where focus was achieved (if any), or on the center of the image. The menu options screen is shown in Figure 7-32.

To check focus in playback mode, it can be convenient to have the enlarged image automatically centered on the focus point. For that option, choose Focused Position from this menu screen.

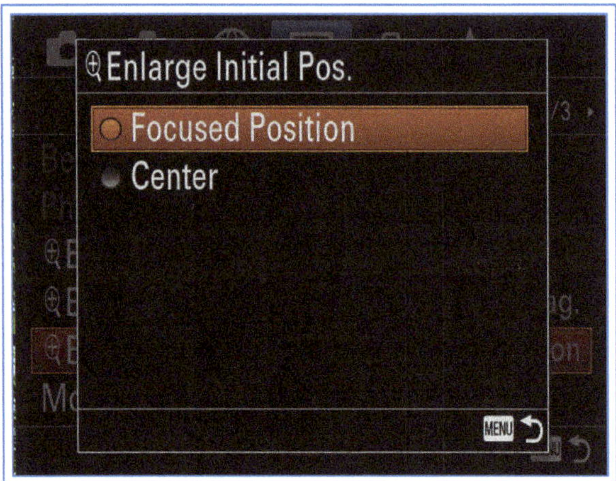

Figure 7-32. Enlarge Initial Position Options Screen

Motion Interval Adjustment

This final option on screen 2 of the Playback menu lets you vary the length of the interval between frames when the camera creates a Motion Shot effect in playing back a movie. The adjustment screen for this option is shown in Figure 7-33.

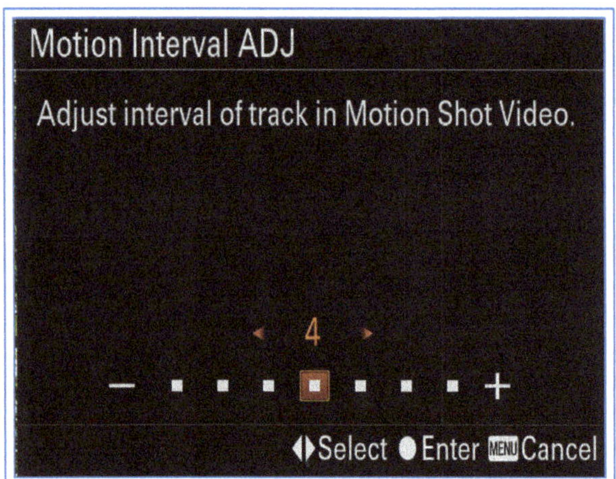

Figure 7-33. Motion Interval Adjustment Screen

The default value is four; you can set the interval to any value from one to seven. The higher the number, the greater the spacing between images in the motion shot. I will discuss this option in Chapter 9, where I discuss movie playback features.

The items on screen 3 of the Playback menu are shown in Figure 7-34.

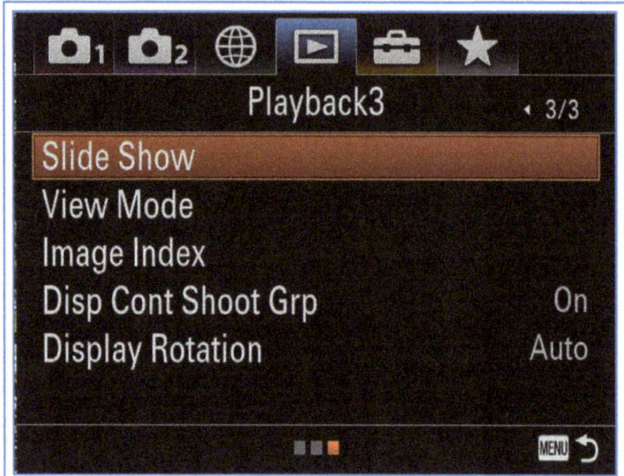

Figure 7-34. Screen 3 of Playback Menu

Slide Show

This feature lets you play your still images and videos in sequence at an interval you specify. This menu option will be dimmed and unavailable if the View Mode option on the Playback menu is set to AVCHD View or either of the two XAVC S View settings. If that is the case, use the View Mode menu option to select either Date View or Folder View (Still). If you select Date View, the Slide Show option will display all of your movies, in all formats, along with your still images. Each movie will play in full before the show advances to the next item, unless you interrupt it with one of the controls. If you select Folder View (Still), the Slide Show option will display only the still images from the folder you selected.

When you select the Slide Show option and press the Center button, the next screen has two options you can set: Repeat and Interval, as seen in Figure 7-35. If Repeat is turned on, the show will keep repeating; otherwise, it will play only once.

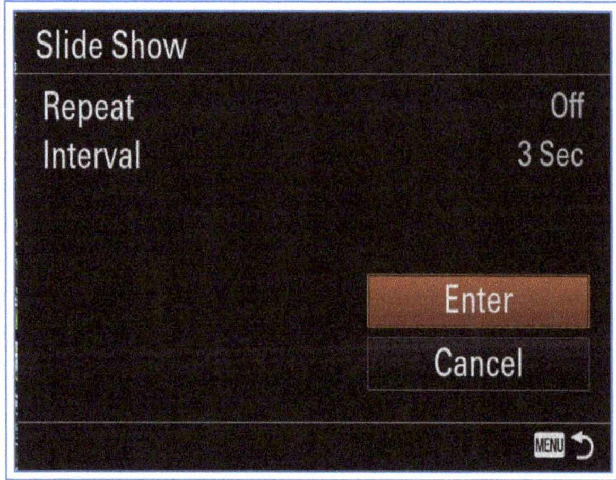

Figure 7-35. Slide Show Options Screen

The camera will not power off automatically in this mode, so be sure to stop the show when you are done with it. The Interval setting, which controls how long each still image stays on the screen, can be set to one, three, five, ten, or 30 seconds. (The Interval setting does not apply to movies, each of which plays to its end.)

With the options set, navigate to the Enter box at the bottom of the screen using the control wheel or the Down button, and press the Center button to start the show. You can move forward or back through the images (and videos, if included) using the Right and Left buttons. Hold the buttons down to move quickly through the images and videos.

You can stop the show by pressing the Menu button or the Playback button. There is no way to pause the show and resume it. When a movie is playing as part of the show, you can control its volume by pressing the Down button and adjusting the sound with the Left and Right buttons or with the control wheel. Each movie plays fully before the next movie or image is displayed, but you can skip to the next movie or image using the Right button.

The Slide Show option does not provide settings such as transitions, effects, or music. You cannot select which images to play; this option just lets you play all of your still images from the selected folder, if you are using Folder View, or all still images and videos starting from the selected date, if you are using Date View.

View Mode

This second option on screen 3 of the Playback menu lets you choose which images or videos are currently viewed in playback mode. The options are Date View, Folder View (Still), AVCHD View, XAVC S HD View, and XAVC S 4K View, as shown in Figure 7-36.

If you select Date View, the camera will display the calendar screen shown earlier in Figure 7-3. You can navigate through the dates for a given month using the control wheel or the direction buttons. Highlight a date and press the Center button; the camera will then display all images and videos from that date. You can move to other months using the navigation bar at the left of the display.

If you select Folder View (Still), the camera will display the screen shown in Figure 7-37, which shows the folders available for selection.

Highlight the folder you want (there may be only one) and press the Center button; the camera will display all still images in that folder. You can navigate through the index screens for those images and select the image or images you want to view.

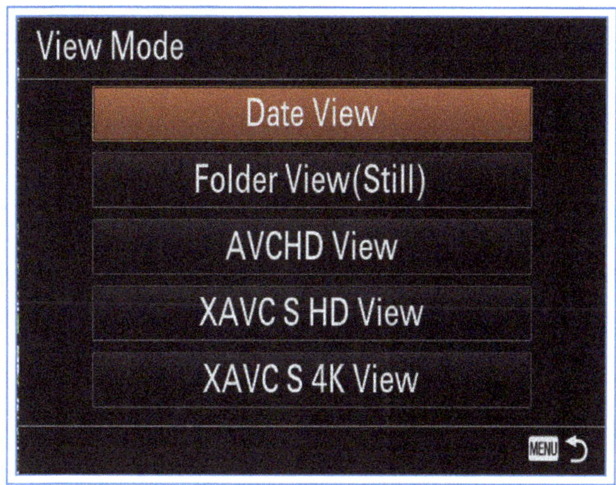

Figure 7-36. View Mode Options Screen

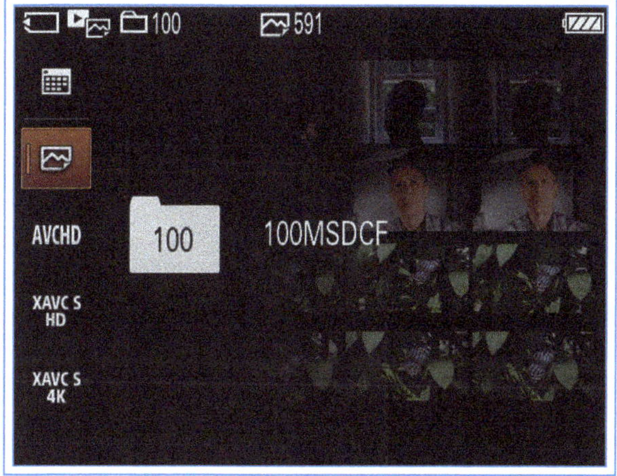

Figure 7-37. Folder View (Still) Selection Screen

If you select AVCHD View, the camera will display a calendar screen with thumbnail images indicating which dates have AVCHD files associated with them. You can highlight any date with a thumbnail image and press the Center button to move to an AVCHD video from that date.

If you select XAVC S HD View or XAVC S 4K View, the camera will display a calendar screen showing the dates on which videos in the selected format were recorded.

My preference is to use the Date View option, because then I can view both images and videos from any date. However, if I want to locate a particular video, it can be quicker to choose one of the video views so I can limit my search to videos only.

You can select a view option from an index screen without using the Playback menu. After moving the zoom lever to the left to call up the calendar display or the folder display, you can move the highlight to the extreme left of the screen to the line of five icons that represent the five view modes, and select one of the modes from that display by highlighting its icon and pressing the Center button.

Image Index

This menu option, shown in Figure 7-38, gives you the choice of having the camera include either 9 images or 25 images when it displays an index screen.

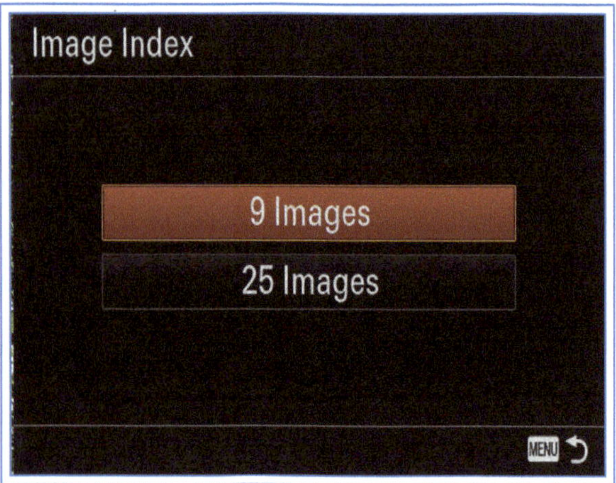

Figure 7-38. Image Index Options Screen

When you make this selection, the camera displays the index screen you chose, and it will display that screen whenever you call up the index screen using the zoom lever, as discussed earlier.

Whether you choose the 9-image screen or the 25-image screen depends on your personal preference as well as some other factors, including how many images you have altogether and how easy it is to distinguish one from another by looking at the small thumbnail images.

The thumbnails on the 9-image screen are considerably larger than those on the 25-image screen, and it may make sense to choose the 9-image screen unless you have so many images that it would be burdensome to scroll through them 9 at a time.

The Image Index menu option will be dimmed and unavailable for selection if there are no items available to view for the currently selected View Mode option. For example, if you have not recorded any 4K videos but View Mode is set to XAVC S 4K View, the Image Index item will not be available for selection.

Display Continuous Shooting Group

This option controls how the camera displays still images that were captured using the Continuous Shooting setting for drive mode. If this option is turned on, those images are displayed as a group that behaves like a single image.

For example, Figure 7-39 shows the playback screen when a group of 99 shots is displayed in the camera. The group is displayed in a stack, as indicated by the edges of the image frames at the right side of the screen. This group of images acts as a single image when scrolling through the images on the memory card. If you press the Custom/Delete button when this group is displayed, the camera displays the message shown in Figure 7-40, announcing that deleting this item will delete all images in the group.

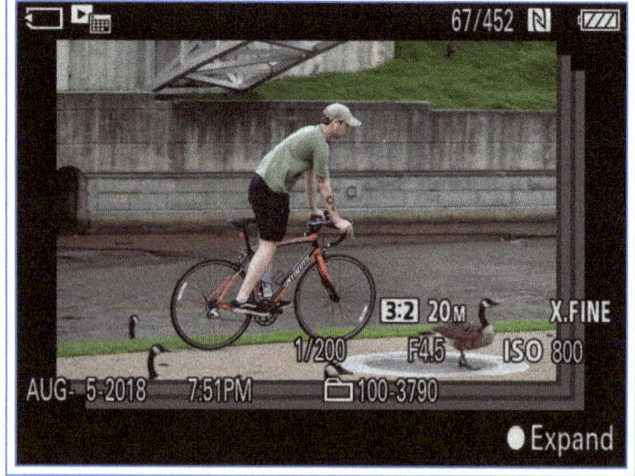

Figure 7-39. Burst of Shots Displayed as Single Group

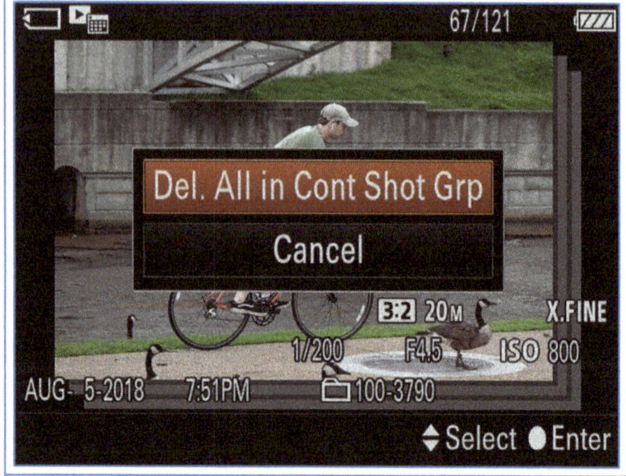

Figure 7-40. Message After Pressing C Button on Group

The message at the lower right of the screen in Figure 7-39 indicates that you can press the Center button to expand the group.

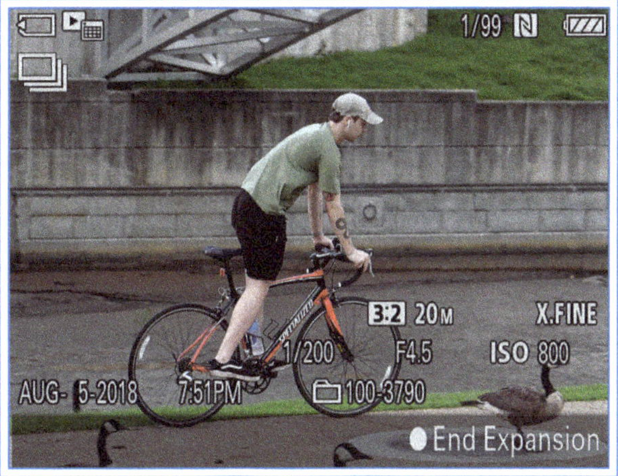

Figure 7-41. Burst of Shots Displayed as Individual Images

If you press that button, the display changes to one like that shown in Figure 7-41, which shows a single image in the group, and indicates by the numbers in the upper right corner that this is the first of 99 images in the group. Now you can scroll through all of those images individually and delete any one of them or otherwise manipulate it as needed. When you are finished viewing the images individually, you can press the Center button again to end the expansion, and view the images as a single group again.

If you turn off the Display Continuous Shooting Group menu option, the images always display individually, rather than as a group. Also, it is important to note that this option works only when View Mode is set to Date View. With any other setting, continuous-shooting images will display individually regardless of the setting for this menu item.

Display Rotation

This final item on the Playback menu controls whether images shot with the camera held vertically appear that way when you play them back on the camera's screen. By default, this option is set to Auto, meaning images taken vertically are automatically rotated so that the vertical shot appears in portrait orientation on the horizontal display, as shown in Figure 7-42.

What is unusual about the Auto setting is that, if you tilt the camera sideways so one side is up, a vertical image will rotate to fill the screen. In this way, you get the best of both worlds: Vertical images display in proper orientation (but smaller than normal) within the horizontal display, and, when you tilt the camera, they display at full size.

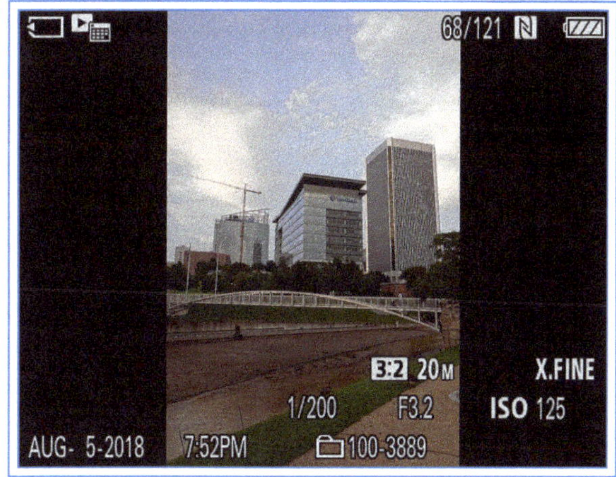

Figure 7-42. Vertical Image Displayed Within Horizontal Screen

If you change the setting to Manual, a vertical image will appear vertically on the horizontal screen, in the same way as shown in Figure 7-42. The difference with this setting from Auto is that, if you tilt the camera, the image will not change its orientation.

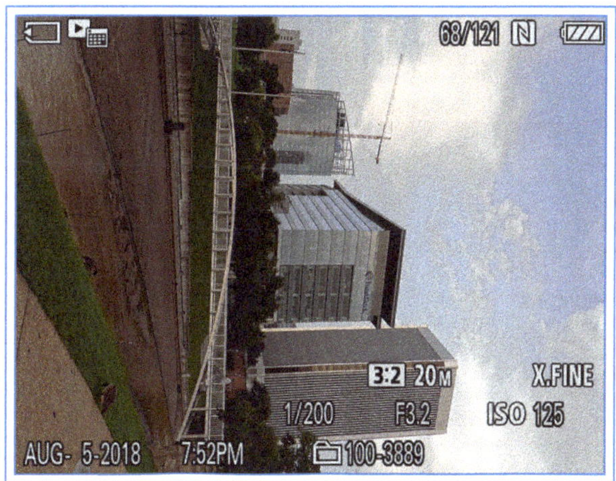

Figure 7-43. Vertical Image Displayed at Full Size

If you set this option to Off, a vertical image will display in landscape orientation on the display, as shown in Figure 7-43, so you would have to tilt the camera to see it in its proper orientation.

With all of these settings, you can use the Rotate option on the Playback menu, discussed later in this chapter, to rotate an image manually to a different orientation.

Chapter 8: The Setup Menu and My Menu

In earlier chapters, I discussed the options available in the Camera Settings1, Camera Settings2, and Playback menu systems. The Sony RX100 VI has one other menu system that helps you set up the camera and customize its operation--the Setup menu. In addition, the camera includes the My Menu feature, which you can use to create your own shortened menu with up to 30 of your most-used options, for quick access. In this chapter, I will discuss the use of the Setup and My Menu options. I'll discuss details of menu options for Movie mode in Chapter 9, and I'll discuss the options on the Network menu in Chapter 10.

Setup Menu

The Setup menu, represented by the toolbox icon, has its tab to the right of the tab for the Playback icon on the list of menu icons. The first screen of the Setup menu is shown in Figure 8-1.

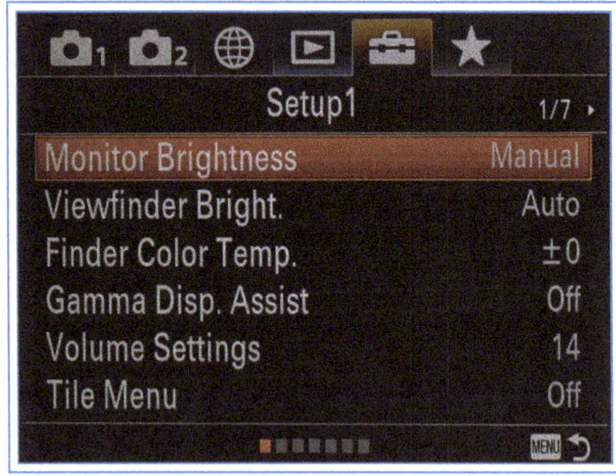

Figure 8-1. Screen 1 of Setup Menu

This seven-screen menu contains options that control technical matters such as computer connections, display brightness, audio volume, file numbering, formatting a memory card, and others. I will discuss each menu item below.

Monitor Brightness

When you highlight and select this menu option, the camera first displays a screen that shows the current setting at the right of the orange highlight block at the top of the screen, as seen in Figure 8-2.

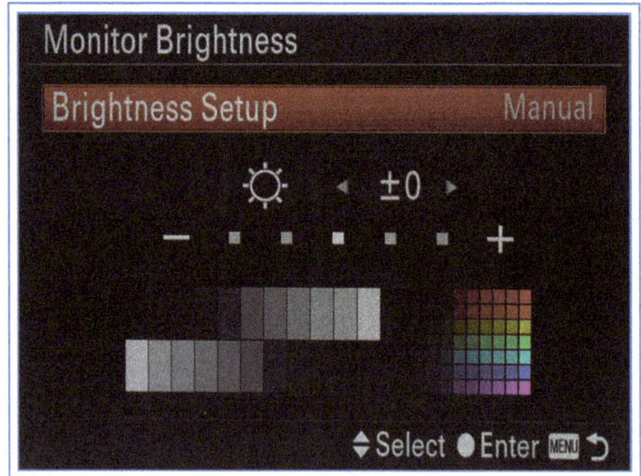

Figure 8-2. Monitor Brightness Main Options Screen

If you press the Center button on that screen, you will see a screen for choosing one of two available settings for controlling the brightness of the LCD display: Manual or Sunny Weather, as shown in Figure 8-3.

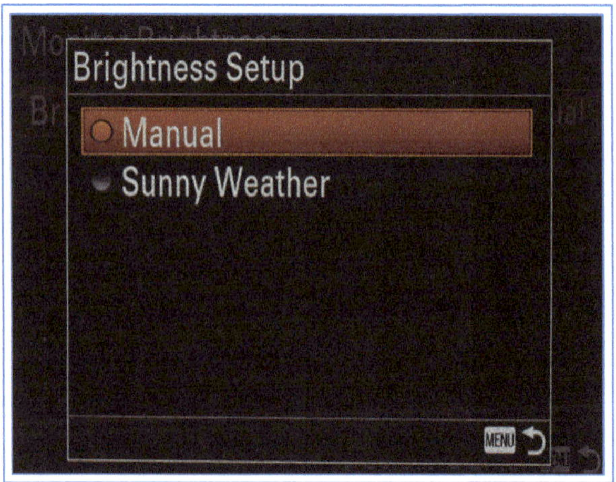

Figure 8-3. Monitor Brightness Screen to Select Setting

If you choose Manual, the camera displays the screen shown earlier in Figure 8-2. Using the controls on that screen, you can adjust brightness to one or two units above or below normal.

When the small orange highlight block is in the brightness scale, press the Left or Right button to make the adjustment.

If your battery is running low and you don't have a spare, you may want to set the monitor to its minimum brightness to conserve power. Conversely, you can increase brightness if you're finding it difficult to compose the image on the screen.

If you are shooting outdoors in bright conditions, you can choose Sunny Weather, which sets the display to a very bright level. Of course, you can switch to using the viewfinder in bright conditions, but there may be times when you want to hold the camera away from your head as you compose the shot, even in bright sunlight. Or, you may want to play back your images for friends while outdoors. The Sunny Weather setting drains the camera's battery fairly rapidly, so you should turn it off when it is no longer needed.

The monitor's brightness will be fixed at the zero level when the camera is recording video with File Format (Movies) set to XAVC S 4K, or to XAVC S HD with Record Setting set to either 120p option (100p for PAL systems); or during high frame rate (HFR) shooting. Brightness is fixed at the -2 level when Wi-Fi operations are active, to conserve battery power.

Viewfinder Brightness

This second option on the Setup menu is similar to the Monitor Brightness selection, discussed above, but it has some differences. With this option, you have to be looking into the viewfinder to make adjustments. There is no Sunny Weather setting, because the viewfinder is shaded from the sun and there is no need for a super-bright setting. You can set the brightness to Auto or Manual. If you select Manual, you can make the same adjustments as with the LCD screen. Again, there is not much need for brightness adjustments because the view is always shielded from outside light.

This option has the same restrictions as the previous one with respect to settings for File Format.

Finder Color Temperature

This option lets you adjust the color temperature of the view through the viewfinder. As with the Viewfinder Brightness setting, you have to look into the viewfinder to make the adjustments. You can use the camera's controls to adjust the color temperature downward by one or two units, which will make the view appear slightly more reddish, or "warmer," or you can adjust upward by one or two units to make it more bluish, or "cooler." I have not found a reason to take advantage of this adjustment, but, if it is helpful to you, it is easy to use.

Gamma Display Assist

This option is a specialized one intended for use only if you are using a Picture Profile setting that includes the S-Log2, S-Log3, HLG, HLG1, HLG2, or HLG3 setting for gamma. As I discussed in Chapter 4, those gamma options are special settings that enable the camera to record video with an extended dynamic range, so it can record scenes clearly even if there is considerable contrast between shadowed areas and bright ones. One characteristic of the S-Log and HLG settings is that the image on the camera's display screen will appear quite dark and low in contrast. In order to take advantage of the high dynamic range available with the S-Log settings, the footage needs to be processed with video software that can deal with the video files properly. For the HLG settings, the footage needs to be viewed on an HDR-compatible monitor to be appreciated fully.

Therefore, Sony has provided the Gamma Display Assist option so you can clearly view a scene being recorded or played back with one of the listed gamma settings in effect. When Gamma Display Assist is activated, the images on the camera's display will be boosted in contrast to a level that makes it appear as if a more standard setting was used—specifically, the ITU709(800%) setting, the HLG(BT.2020) setting, or the HLG(709) setting.

This option has five settings: Off, Auto, S-Log2, S-Log3, HLG 2020, and HLG 709, as shown in Figure 8-4.

If you choose Off, the option is not activated in any situation, and video shot with an S-Log or HLG gamma setting will appear rather dark and low in contrast, as it normally would. If you choose Auto, then the camera will boost the contrast of the display if the Picture

Profile setting in use includes an S-Log or HLG gamma setting. (The PP7 setting for Picture Profile includes the S-Log2 setting by default; the PP8 and PP9 settings include S-Log3; and PP10 includes HLG2. You can change any Picture Profile setting to include any of the S-Log or HLG settings, as discussed in Chapter 4.)

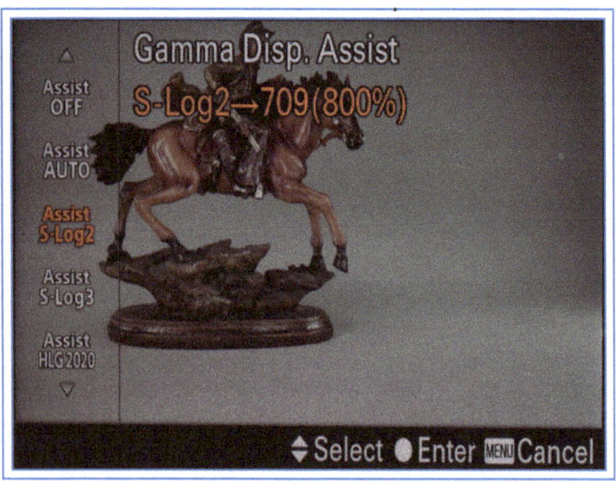

Figure 8-4. Gamma Display Assist Options Screen

If you choose either of the other settings for Gamma Display Assist, labeled as S-Log2, S-Log3, HLG 2020, and HLG 709, the camera always boosts the contrast of the video (or still image) on the display, regardless of the Picture Profile setting.

My preference is to leave this option turned off. I do not have difficulty viewing the display when an S-Log or HLG gamma setting is in use. However, if you are having a problem viewing the scene on the display screen when using one of those settings, this menu option might be useful. It also can be useful to provide a preview of how the footage will look when properly processed or when viewed on the proper type of monitor.

Volume Settings

This option lets you set the volume for video playback at a level anywhere from 0 to 15. You can also set this level when a movie is playing by pressing the Down button to get access to the detailed controls, which include a volume setting option. When a movie is displayed on the screen in playback mode before playback starts, pressing the Down button calls up the volume adjustment screen immediately. Pressing that button when a still image is displayed in playback mode also calls up the volume screen, if View Mode on screen 3 of the Playback menu is set to Date View.

Tile Menu

If you turn this option on, the camera displays a screen with six tiles representing the various menu systems, as shown in Figure 8-5, when you press the Menu button.

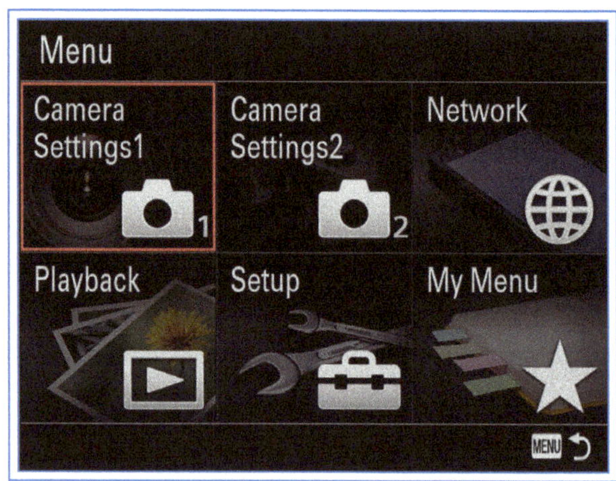

Figure 8-5. Tile Menu Option in Use

This screen is helpful because it gives you a graphic representation of which menu is which, and lets you choose a menu and get quick access to it. You navigate through the six tiles using the direction buttons or the control wheel.

I prefer to leave this option turned off, because, without it, pressing the Menu button takes me right into the last menu option I was using. From there, I can navigate quickly to any other menu system. But for those who are new to this camera or who like having a large display to show the menu choices clearly, the Tile Menu option may be worth using.

Screen 2 of the Setup menu is shown in Figure 8-6.

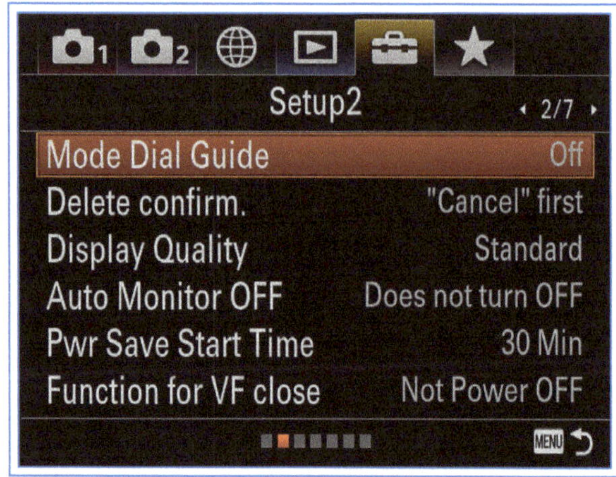

Figure 8-6. Screen 2 of Setup Menu

Mode Dial Guide

This menu item gives you a way to turn on or off the Mode Dial Guide, a graphic display that appears on the camera's screen when you turn the mode dial to select a shooting mode, as shown in Figure 8-7.

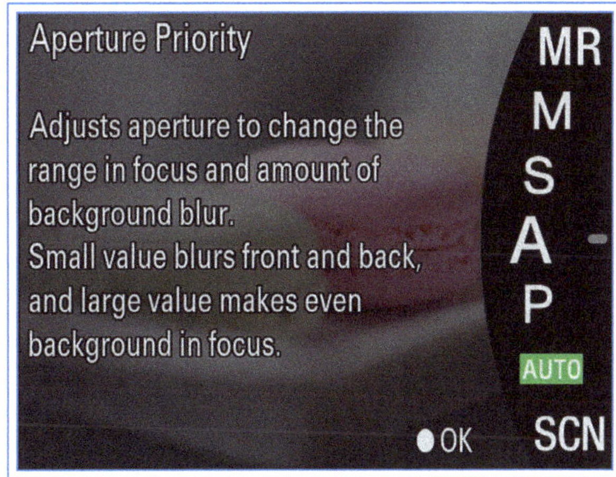

Figure 8-7. Mode Dial Guide in Use

This guide can be helpful when you first get the camera, but it can be annoying if you don't need reminders, and you have to press a button to dismiss the screen. (You can press the Center button or Menu button or press the shutter button halfway; you also can press the Playback button, which puts the camera into playback mode.) I leave this option turned off to speed up my shooting.

Delete Confirmation

This menu item has two options as shown in Figure 8-8: "Delete" First or "Cancel" First.

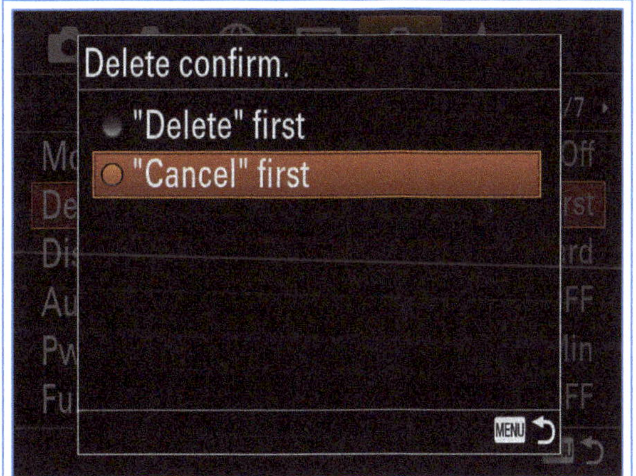

Figure 8-8. Delete Confirmation Options Screen

This option lets you fine-tune the way the menu system operates for deleting images. Whenever you press the Delete button to delete an image or video in playback mode, the camera displays a confirmation screen, as shown in Figure 8-9, with two choices: Delete or Cancel.

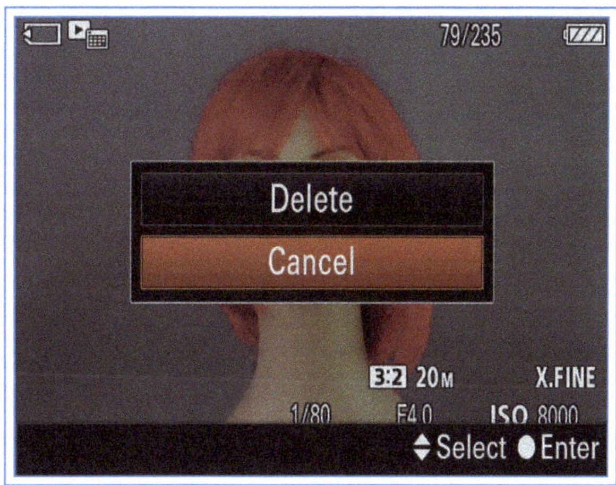

Figure 8-9. Delete Screen from Pressing C Button

One of those choices will be highlighted when the screen appears; you can then just press the Center button to accept that choice and the operation will be done. Of course, you also can use the control wheel or the Up or Down button to highlight the other choice before you press the Center button to carry out your choice.

Which option you choose to be highlighted depends on your habits, and how careful you want to be to guard against the accidental deletion of an item. If you like to move quickly in deleting images and videos, choose "Delete" first. Then, as soon as the confirmation screen appears you can press the Center button to carry out the deletion. If you prefer to have some assurance against an accidental deletion, choose "Cancel" first, so that, if you press the Center button too quickly when the confirmation screen appears, you will only cancel the operation, rather than deleting an image.

Unless you use this process often and need to save time, I recommend you leave this menu item set at the "Cancel" First setting to be safe.

Display Quality

This menu item lets you choose Standard or High for the quality of the display. According to Sony, with the High setting the camera displays the live view on the LCD screen or in the viewfinder at a higher resolution than with the Standard setting, at the expense of additional drain on the battery.

I have tried experiments with these settings, viewing small print from a catalog using both the viewfinder and the LCD display with both Display Quality settings, and I have not found a noticeable difference. There may be situations in which this option has a more obvious impact on the display, but my recommendation is to leave it at Standard to conserve battery life.

Auto Monitor Off

This option lets you choose whether the camera automatically blacks out the LCD monitor in shooting mode after a set period of time to save power. It can be left turned off, or set to two, five or ten seconds. If it is turned on, the monitor goes black after the specified time, if you have not operated any controls during that time. To restore the view on the monitor, press any control button. This function does not operate in playback mode, when a menu is displayed, when the monitor is rotated forward for a self-portrait, when the camera is set to Sweep Panorama mode, or when the Power Save Start Time option is not turned on. (That option is discussed immediately below.)

Power Save Start Time

This menu option lets you set the amount of time before the camera turns off automatically to save power, when no controls have been operated. With this option you can choose one, two, five, or thirty minutes, as shown in Figure 8-10.

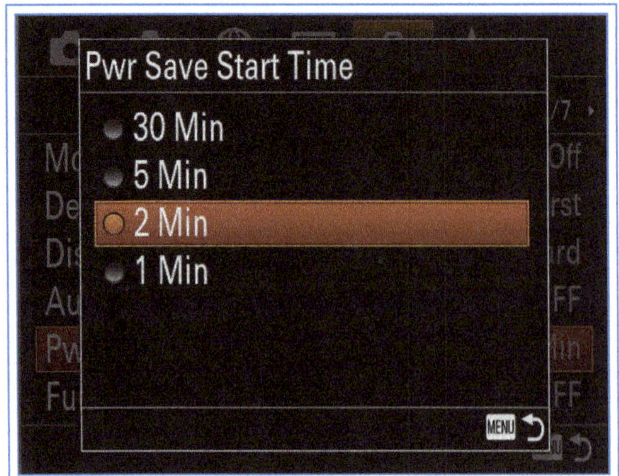

Figure 8-10. Power Save Start Time Options Screen

When the camera goes to sleep with this option, you have to turn the power back on using the power button, the Playback button, or the Finder switch.

You cannot turn the power-saving function off. However, the camera will not power off automatically when you are recording movies, when a slide show is playing, when the camera is connected to a computer, or when it is being powered through the USB port.

The setting you use depends on your habits and needs. In my case, I am usually well aware of the camera's status, and I like to use the maximum thirty-minute period for this option so the camera does not power down just when I am about to use it again. I always have extra batteries available and I'm not too concerned if I have to replace the battery. If you are out in the field and running low on battery power, you might want to choose a shorter time for this option to conserve battery life.

Function for VF Close

This option controls what happens when you push the viewfinder back down into the camera. The choices are Power Off or Not Power Off. If you choose Power Off, the camera will turn off when you stow the viewfinder back in its housing. If you choose Not Power Off, the camera will stay powered on. I prefer the Not Power Off option, so I can keep shooting or using playback functions after the viewfinder has been retracted. But, if you use the viewfinder primarily, you may like the convenience of turning the camera on and off by lifting the viewfinder into place and pushing it back into its slot.

The options on screen 3 of the Setup menu are shown in Figure 8-11.

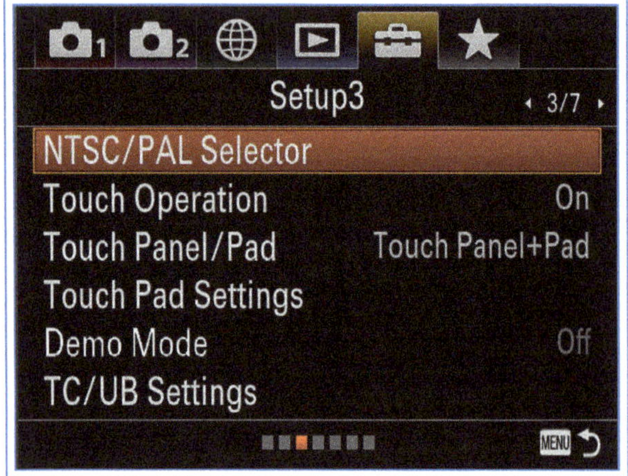

Figure 8-11. Screen 3 of Setup Menu

NTSC/PAL Selector

This menu option controls which television system the camera uses for recording videos—NTSC or PAL. The

NTSC system is used in the United States and other parts of North America, as well as Japan, South Korea, and some other countries. The PAL system is used in many parts of Asia, Africa, and Europe.

For purposes of using the RX100 VI camera, the difference between the two settings is that the NTSC system uses multiples of 30 for video frame rates (such as 30, 60, or 120 frames per second), while the PAL system generally uses multiples of 25, such as 25, 50, or 100 frames per second. You will see these differences in the options for the Record Setting item on screen 1 of the Camera Settings2 menu. If you choose NTSC, the options will be mostly in multiples of 30, although there will be some entries for 24 fps, another NTSC standard. If you choose PAL, the options will be in multiples of 25.

In general, you should use the setting that is standard for the area where you will be using the camera. I live in the United States, so I set the camera to NTSC, where the frame rates are in multiples of 30 (except for the few 24p options).

It is important to choose this setting before you start recording files on your memory card. Once you have started using a card under one of these systems, you cannot change to the other system without re-formatting the card. When you select this menu option, you will see the message shown in Figure 8-12, warning that you will have to re-format the card to continue.

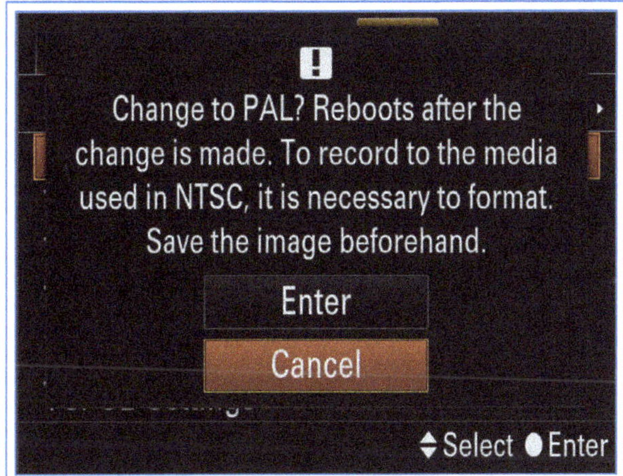

Figure 8-12. Warning Message for Switching from NTSC to PAL

If you then select Enter and press the Center button, the camera will proceed to format the card for the other video system.

Touch Operation

One of the new features added to the RX100 series with the RX100 VI is the ability to control some operations by touching the LCD screen on the back of the camera. As discussed in Chapter 6, with these functions activated, by touching the LCD screen you can select a focus point for a still photo or capture an image, and you can "pull" the focus from one point to another while recording video. In addition, you can use the LCD screen as a touch pad while you are viewing the scene through the camera's viewfinder.

You can enlarge an image in playback mode by tapping twice on the LCD screen and return it to normal size by tapping twice again, and you can enlarge the shooting screen by tapping twice when the camera is using manual focus mode. When the manual focus screen is enlarged, you can drag on the screen to move the area that is magnified. When the Focus Magnifier frame is on the shooting screen, you can drag it around with your finger.

This menu option lets you turn the camera's touch operations on or off. If you find the touch screen options distracting, turn this option off and they will not be active. If you leave this option turned on, though, you can control the use of those operations more specifically using the next menu option, discussed below.

Touch Panel/Pad

This menu option has three choices: Touch Panel + Pad, Touch Panel Only, and Touch Pad Only, as shown in Figure 8-13.

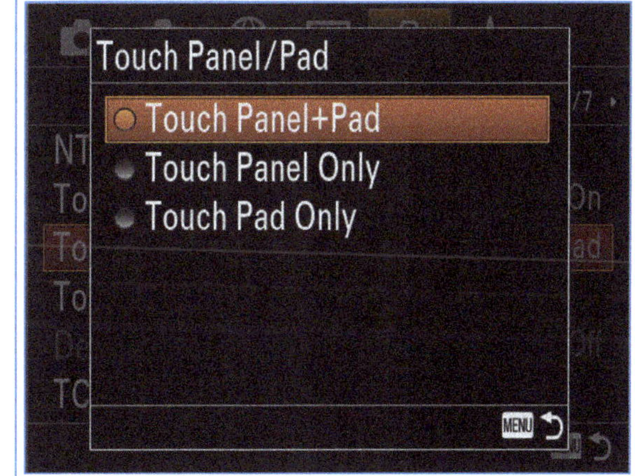

Figure 8-13. Touch Panel/Pad Options Screen

Choose one of these options to determine which of the camera's touch functions will be active when Touch

Operation is turned on with the previous menu option. In order to activate the ability to enlarge the screen by tapping, both in playback mode and in shooting mode, select either Touch Panel + Pad or Touch Panel Only. If you select Touch Pad Only, the enlargement features will not work. You can make similar choices to activate the touch focusing operations using the panel or pad.

Touch Pad Settings

As noted above, using the Touch Operation and Touch Panel/Pad menu options, you can activate the LCD screen on the back of the RX100 VI as a touch pad to select a focus point when you are viewing the scene through the viewfinder. The Touch Pad Settings menu option gives you several ways to control how this capability works in practice. It provides three options: Operation in Vertical Orientation; Touch Position Mode; and Operation Area, as shown in Figure 8-14.

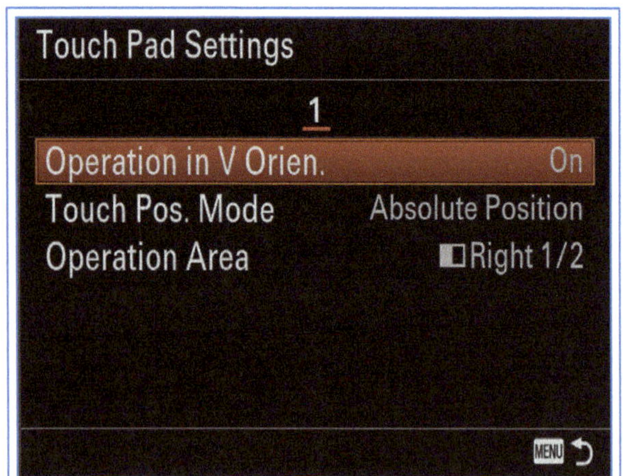

Figure 8-14. Touch Pad Settings Options Screen

The first sub-option, Operation in Vertical Orientation, can be turned either on or off. If it is turned on, the LCD screen can be used as a touch pad even when the camera is rotated to one side to capture vertically oriented images or videos. You may want to disable this option if you feel that your nose may accidentally touch the screen in that orientation, causing an unwanted movement of the focus point.

The second sub-option, Touch Position Mode, can be set to Absolute Position or Relative Position. With Absolute Position, the camera will set the focus point in the viewfinder at the same point you have touched on the LCD screen, and you can also drag a focus frame to a new location. With Relative Position, the camera will move the focus point to a new location based only on the direction and distance of your dragging an existing frame with a finger on the LCD screen, without regard to the actual location that you touch on the screen. If focus area is set to Wide with this setting, the camera will place a focus frame in the center of the screen if you tap; you can then drag that frame to a new location.

The final sub-option, Operation Area, comes into play only if you chose Relative Position for Touch Position Mode. In that case, you can restrict the area of the screen that can be used for re-positioning the focus point, in order to make it easier to move the focus point with a short movement of your finger. When you select this sub-option, the camera displays numerous options, which take more than a full screen to display. The first screen of options is shown in Figure 8-15. The whole list is as follows: Whole Screen; Right Half; Right Quarter; Upper Right; Lower Right; Left Half; Left Quarter; Upper Left; and Lower Left.

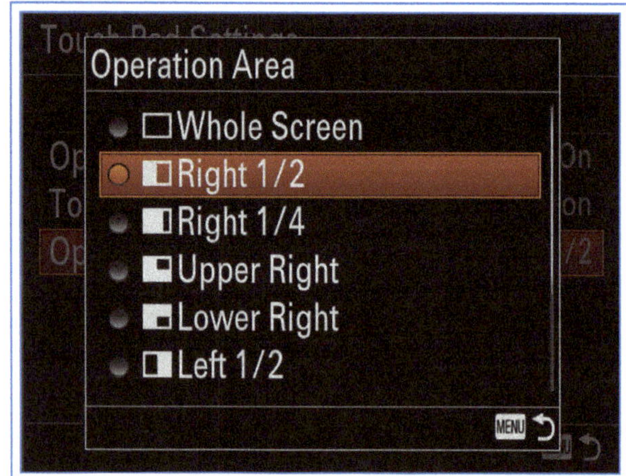

Figure 8-15. Operation Area Options Screen

As you can see in Figure 8-15, each selection has a small diagram next to it to indicate where the operational area on the screen would be. This choice is a matter of personal preference. You may want a small area so you don't have to move your finger very far to carry out a movement, but the choice is yours.

You can make a setting for Operation Area even if Absolute Position is selected for Touch Position Mode, but, in that case, the camera will use the entire area of the screen, regardless of the setting for Operation Area.

Demo Mode

When the Demo Mode menu item is turned on, the camera automatically plays a movie if it has not had any controls operated for about one minute. This feature is designed for use by retail stores, so they can leave the camera turned on with a continuous demonstration on its screen. But you can use it for your own purposes, if you want to create a movie that demonstrates the camera's features for friends, for example, or if you just like the idea of having the camera play a movie when it's not otherwise occupied.

For this feature to be available for selection on the menu screen, as shown in Figure 8-11, the camera has to be plugged into AC power using an AC adapter. Otherwise, this line on the menu will be dimmed.

When Demo Mode is turned on and the camera is in shooting mode, after one minute of inactivity the camera enters Demo Mode. At that point, the camera will automatically play a movie, which you have to provide. It cannot be just any movie. The movie the camera will play in Demo Mode must be recorded in the AVCHD format, it must be protected using the Protect option on the Playback menu, and it must be the oldest AVCHD movie on the memory card. So, if you have a reason to use this option, you may want to use a fresh memory card and record a single AVCHD movie on the card, and then use the Protect function to protect it. When the movie plays, it plays audio as well as video, and it will keep repeating in a loop. To exit from Demo Mode, you can press the Center button or just turn the camera off.

TC/UB (Time Code/User Bit) Settings

This menu item provides several sub-options that are helpful if you use the RX100 VI for advanced video production. For example, because of its ability to shoot 4K video (discussed in Chapter 9), the RX100 VI camera can be used as part of a multi-camera setup for shooting a professional production. In such a setup, it can be useful to control whether and how the camera outputs time code, a type of metadata that is used when editing video sequences. The user bit is another form of metadata that also can be used as an organizing aid.

This option will have all but one of the sub-options dimmed and unavailable for selection unless the mode dial is at the Movie or HFR position. If it is in any other position, you can get access only to the first sub-option, TC/UB Display Setting. For this discussion, I will assume the mode dial is at the Movie position. (Some options work differently when the mode dial is at the HFR position.)

I won't discuss the use of time code in detail in this book, but I will give a brief overview. Time code for video files includes numbers in a format like the following: 02:12:23:19, which stands for hours, minutes, seconds, and frames. In this example, the time code shown would mark the point in the video clip at 2 hours, 12 minutes, 23 seconds, and 19 frames into the next second.

Because video (in the NTSC system) is played back at 30 fps or 24 fps, the number in the final position is based on those values, even if the video is recorded in a format such as XAVC S HD with Record Setting set to 120p 100M. With a Record Setting value of 120p, 60p, 60i, or 30p, the number of frames can be set from 00 to 29. When Record Setting is set to 24p, the number of frames can be set only to 00, 04, 08, 12, 16, or 20. If you are using the PAL video system, the number of frames can go from 00 to 24, because the video is played back at 25 fps.

When you see a time code like the one in the above example, you know what frame of the video is being identified, so you can make an edit at that point or synchronize this video clip with another video clip, as long as both clips are using the same time code format and had the time code recorded in synchronization.

If you are not going to use your camera for that sort of video production, you can largely ignore this menu option, though it is helpful to know what settings you can control. The sub-options are discussed below.

TC/UB Display Setting

This first option controls what figures display in the lower left corner of the camera's screen during video recording. There are three choices—Counter; TC, for time code; or U-Bit, for user bit—as shown in Figure 8-16.

No matter which you choose, the display appears on the screen during recording in all shooting modes and before recording in Movie or HFR mode. The characters are not recorded visibly with the video and will not appear during playback, although they can be used as reference points in appropriate video-editing software.

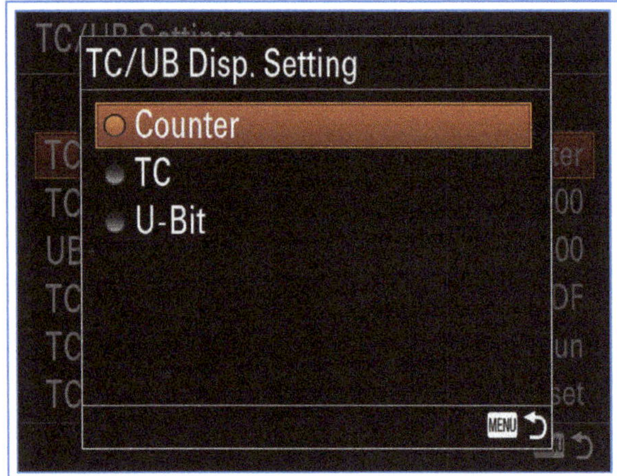

Figure 8-16. TC/UB Display Setting Options

The first choice, Counter, produces a simple display of minutes and seconds of elapsed recording time, as shown in Figure 8-17. This is the default choice, and it is what you probably will want to leave in place for general use. As I noted above, the only reason to use time code (or user bit) is for advanced-level video production.

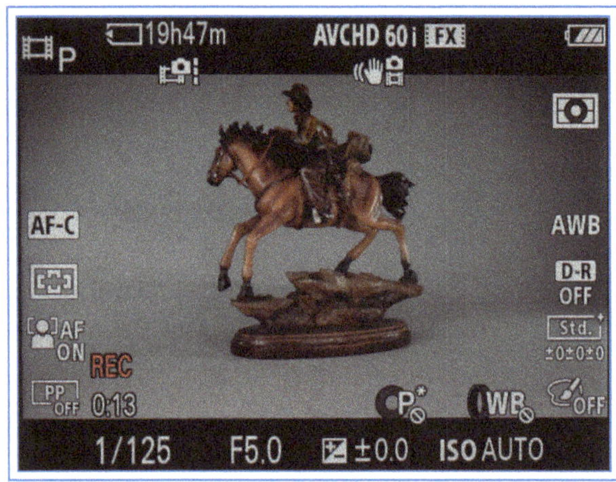

Figure 8-17. Counter in Use on Recording Screen

The second choice places time code on the screen, as shown in Figure 8-18. You may want to use this setting for advanced video production, not just to display on the screen but to output to another device, such as a video recorder, through the camera's HDMI cable, as I will discuss later in this chapter.

The third choice, user bit, lets you set the camera to display a set of four figures in hexadecimal notation, in the format 0B 76 11 F8, as shown in Figure 8-19. This amounts to a string of four numbers, each of which, in hexadecimal notation, can range from 00 (0 in decimal notation) to FF (255 in decimal notation).

In actual practice, I have never used the user bit for video production. Some videographers use this capability to place notes in the video file, using the few available letters (A through F) and the numbers to make notations like C1 for camera 1.

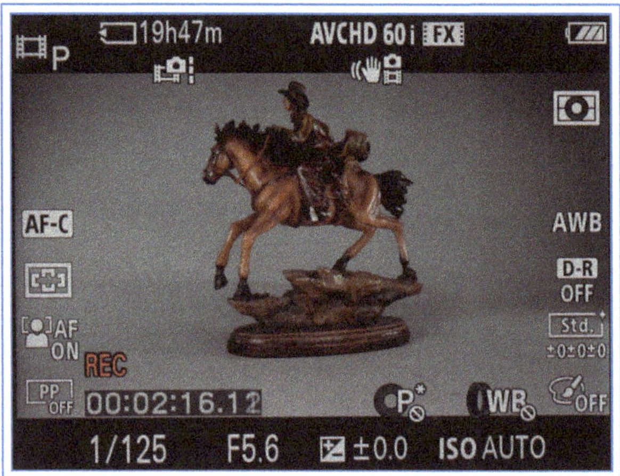

Figure 8-18. Time Code in Use on Recording Screen

If you don't need to include a customized notation using the user bit option, the RX100 VI gives you a way to have the user bit provide a running display of the current time, as shown in Figure 8-19. To do that, go to the last sub-option under TC/UB Settings, UB Time Record, and set it to On. That option sets the user bit to display the current time in the lower left corner of the display. To make that display appear, you also have to set the TC/UB Display Setting option to U-Bit.

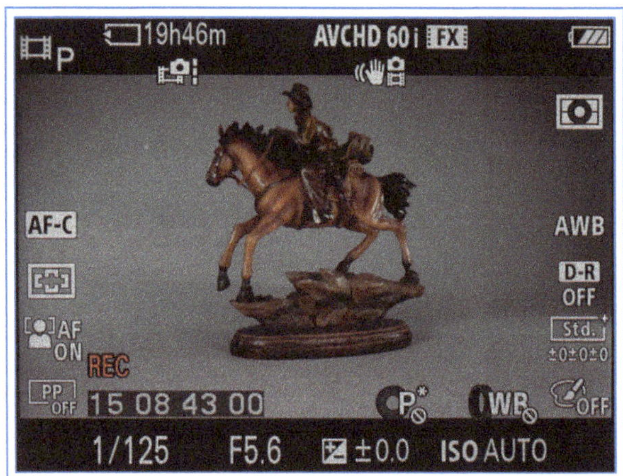

Figure 8-19. User Bit Displaying Current Time

TC Preset

This next option lets you set the initial time code for your video recording. You can set the code anywhere from all zeroes, the default, to 23:59:59:29 for some NTSC formats. As I noted earlier, the final figure can go as high as 29 for most NTSC settings and 20 for the 24p settings. For PAL systems, the highest value for that figure is 24.

You might want to use this option if you need to start with a particular time code for a technical reason, in order to synchronize your footage with existing footage or that from another camera. In addition, in some production environments the practice is to set the hours position to a particular value, such as 01, to designate some item, such as the reel number. Unless you have a need to make a setting of that nature, you can leave these values all at zero.

UB Preset

This option lets you set the user bit, as discussed above. Each of the four positions can be set anywhere from 00 to FF, using the hexadecimal system.

TC Format

This option lets you select either DF (drop-frame) or NDF (non-drop-frame) format for the time code, assuming you are using time code and are using the NTSC video system with a Record Setting option other than 24p. (Drop-frame time code is not used for PAL video.)

This is a technical setting you may need to make in order to be sure the time code you use is compatible with that of other cameras and with your editing facilities. Drop-frame time code is used because the NTSC standard of 30 frames per second does not record exactly 30 frames every second. For technical reasons, the actual rate is 29.97 frames per second. To count the frames accurately, video editors use the drop-frame system, which drops a few frames from the counting process at specified intervals, so the actual number of frames is counted accurately.

You can leave this option set to DF if you are using the NTSC system, unless you know of a specific reason to use NDF.

TC Run

This option lets you choose either Rec Run or Free Run for the time code. With Rec Run, the time code increases only while the camera is actually recording. With Free Run, the time code continues to run all the time. Which system to choose is a matter of preference, depending on how you will use the time code for editing. With Rec Run, there should be no gaps in the time code, which can be an advantage. With Free Run, you can set up the time code to match the time of day, which can be useful if you need to find a clip that corresponds to a particular time during the day's video recording.

Free Run time code continues to run even when the camera is powered off. When you turn the camera on again and set it to Movie mode, the current time should be displaying in the lower left corner of the display, assuming you set the initial value for the time code to the current time.

TC Make

This setting is what you use to set the camera to record the time code option you have selected. The two choices are Preset or Regenerate. If you choose Preset, the camera starts recording time code using the value you entered for TC Preset, discussed earlier. If you choose Regenerate, the camera starts the time code recording based on the last value recorded previously.

UB Time Record

This last option, found on the second screen of the TC/UB Settings menu item, lets you choose whether or not to set the user bit option to display and record the time instead of a user bit formula that you set yourself. If you select On for this option and set the TC/UB Display Setting option to U-Bit, the camera will display the current time in the lower left corner of the screen as the video is recorded, as shown in Figure 8-19. The display shows the hour (in the 24-hour format), minute, and second; the last set of digits is left at zeroes. In this case, the time was 43 seconds after 3:08 p.m.

Screen 4 of the Setup menu is shown in Figure 8-20.

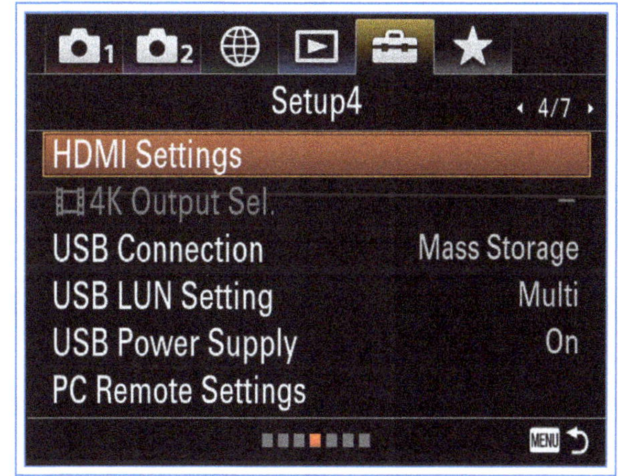

Figure 8-20. Screen 4 of Setup Menu

HDMI Settings

The HDMI Settings menu option has seven sub-options on its two screens.

HDMI Resolution

The HDMI Resolution option can be set to Auto, 2160p/1080p, 1080p, or 1080i. This setting controls how the camera displays images and videos on an HDTV in playback mode. Ordinarily, the Auto setting will work best; the camera will set itself for the optimum display according to the resolution of the HDTV it is connected to. If you experience difficulties with that connection, you may be able to improve the image on the HDTV's screen by trying one of the other settings. The 2160p/1080p setting is designed for connection to 4K-capable TV sets, which often have a resolution of 3840 x 2160 pixels.

24p/60p Output

This menu option is present only on cameras sold in NTSC areas. It is labeled with a movie-film icon, meaning it is for use when the camera is set to Movie mode, and it has a specific, limited use. It is applicable only when you have recorded video with Record Setting set to 24p 50M, using the XAVC S HD File Format setting, or with Record Setting set to 24p 60M or 100M using the XAVC S 4K File Format setting, and you have set the HDMI Resolution item, discussed above, to 1080p or 2160p/1080p.

If all of those conditions are met, that means you have some video footage recorded at 24 frames per second. As I will discuss in Chapter 9, that setting is slower than the standard NTSC setting of 30 frames per second, and produces what some people consider to be a more "cinematic" look for the footage.

When you send your 24p video footage out through an HDMI cable to an HDTV set, you may prefer to send it in a way that looks more like standard TV video, using the 60p setting. That is the function of this menu option. If all of the conditions described above are met, you can select 60p for the 24p/60p Output option, and your 24p footage will be sent out through the HDMI cable to the HDTV in a way that simulates 60p video.

This option also may be of use when you are sending this one variety of 24p video footage out through the HDMI cable to an external video recorder, if 60p footage is a better option for use by the recorder.

HDMI Information Display

This feature also controls the behavior of the camera when you connect it to an HDTV set or other external device using an optional micro HDMI cable. However, unlike the HDMI Resolution option discussed above, which controls what happens when the camera is in playback mode, playing your images and videos on an HDTV set, this menu option controls what happens in shooting mode when the HDMI connection is active.

If this menu option is set to On, which is the default setting, then, when the camera is connected to an HDTV or external recorder in shooting mode, the screen of the external device displays exactly what you would see on the camera's display in that mode if the camera were not connected to the device, including icons and figures showing camera settings.

With the On setting, the HDTV acts as a large, external monitor for the RX100 VI, and the screen of the RX100 VI itself is blank. I use this setting a great deal myself, because this is how I capture screen shots for this book. Once the camera is connected, I can capture all of the information and settings that appear on the shooting screens and menu screens of the camera, with a few exceptions for special settings that are not output through the HDMI port, such as the Zebra stripes.

If this menu option is set to Off, then, when the camera is connected to an HDTV or other external device in shooting mode, the external device's screen displays only the image that is being viewed by the camera, with no shooting information displayed at all. If you press the Display button, nothing will happen on the external screen; the view will not switch to another display with more information on it. However, at the same time, the camera's screen continues to display all of the shooting information it normally would, including the image and whatever information is chosen by presses of the Display button. You can even use the menu system on the camera while the external device is receiving the live image.

You might use the Off setting when you want to display images from the camera's shooting mode on a large HDTV screen, possibly at a wedding or other gathering, and not have the images cluttered or marred by any shooting information at all. For example, a camera may focus on an unsuspecting person in the audience at the event, and that person's image suddenly will appear on the large screen for everyone to see.

Also, this option is useful for video production when you need to output a "clean" video signal that does not include any shooting information from the camera. That signal can be sent through an HDMI cable to a video recorder for recording to another medium, or for display on a large monitor being viewed by the production team. For example, you can record video directly from the camera to a computer by outputting the clean HDMI signal to a device such as the Intensity Pro by Blackmagic Design. There are similar devices available from companies such as Epiphan, AverMedia, Hauppage, and Elgato. You also can send the clean signal to an external 4K video recorder such as the Atomos Shogun, as I will discuss in Chapter 9.

With the On setting, you can press the Display button to show a screen with very minimal shooting information, but that screen still shows the basic information of aperture, shutter speed, exposure compensation, and ISO value at the very bottom of the screen. If you don't want even that minimal level of information to interfere with the video display, choose the Off setting.

This setting does not change the behavior of the camera for playback of images; its only effect is on the display of information in shooting mode through an HDMI connection.

TC Output

This option works together with the TC/UB Settings option discussed earlier. If you have set up the camera to record time code, you can use this option to have the time code output through the HDMI cable to an external recorder, so the time code will be available in the recorded footage for use in editing. The choices are On or Off.

Rec Control

This next sub-option for HDMI Settings is another one that applies only when recording to an external device by sending a clean signal through the HDMI cable. In this case, the option controls whether the camera sends a start-recording or stop-recording signal through the cable. If you turn this option on, you can control the external recorder using the camera's controls, if the external recorder is compatible with this camera.

For example, you can connect an Atomos Shogun 4K recorder with an HDMI cable and control the recorder's starting and stopping using the camera's Movie button, if the Rec Control option is turned on. (You also can use the shutter button to control movie recording, if the Movie w/Shutter option is turned on through screen 4 of the Camera Settings2 menu.) The Rec Control option can be turned on only if the TC Output option, discussed above, also is turned on.

CTRL for HDMI

This next sub-option is of use only when you have connected the camera to an HDTV and you want to control the camera with the TV's remote control, which is possible in some situations. If you want to do that, set this option to On and follow the instructions for the TV and its remote control. This option is intended to be used when you connect the camera to a Sony Bravia model HDTV.

HDMI Audio Output

This final option for HDMI Settings controls whether the RX100 VI sends the audio being recorded for a movie through the HDMI cable, when the camera is connected to an external device through the HDMI port. Turn this option on if you want to send the camera's audio recording signal to an external video recorder, for example. If you are recording the sound through a different system, such as a microphone connected to the external recorder, leave this option turned off.

4K Output Select

This next option on the Setup menu is for use only when the camera is connected to a 4K-capable external video recorder, such as the Atomos Shogun. Unless that connection is active, this option will be dimmed and unavailable for selection. Once the connection to the external recorder is made, the following sub-options are available:

Memory Card + HDMI

With this option, the camera will record video to the memory card in the camera and also output the signal to the external recorder through the HDMI cable. This option gives you an immediate backup copy of your footage.

HDMI Only (30p)

With this option, the camera sends a 4K video signal in 30p format to the external recorder but does not record the video to the camera's memory card. This option lets you record 4K video without having a memory card that meets the specifications for that format, and, in fact, it lets you record with no memory card in the camera at all.

If you choose this option or the next one, for 4K/24p video with no card in the camera, the File Format (Movies) and Record Setting items on the Camera Settings2 menu become unavailable, because the recording format has already been selected by choosing this option or the next one.

I tested this option with the RX100 VI connected by an HDMI cable to an Atomos Shogun external 4K recorder. The camera sent a clean 4K signal through the HDMI cable and the Shogun recorded the video with no problems. If you turn on the Rec Control menu option on the camera, you can control the operation of the Shogun recorder by pressing the Movie button on the camera to start and stop the recording.

HDMI Only (24p)

This option is the same as the previous one, apart from the use of the 24p frame rate instead of 30p.

HDMI Only (25p)

This setting is available only when the NTSC/PAL Selector option is set to PAL.

USB Connection

This option sets the technical standard that the camera uses for connecting to a computer using the USB cable. This menu item has four choices, as shown in Figure 8-21: Auto; Mass Storage; MTP, which stands for Media Transfer Protocol; and PC Remote.

If you choose Auto, the RX100 VI should detect which standard is used by the computer you are connecting the camera to. If the camera does not automatically select a standard and start transferring images, you can try one of the other settings to see if it works better than the Auto setting.

The fourth setting, PC Remote, adds an important function to the camera. If you select this option, you can connect the camera to a computer with the camera's USB cable and control the camera from the computer using Sony's Imaging Edge software. Imaging Edge can be downloaded at no charge from http://support.d-imaging.sony.co.jp/app/imagingedge/en/download/. Imaging Edge comes as part of a software suite that includes image viewing and editing in addition to remote control of the camera.

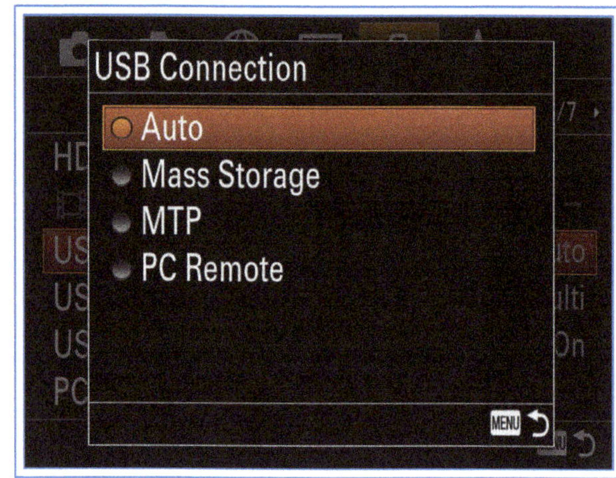

Figure 8-21. USB Connection Options Screen

Once the remote control software is installed on your computer, set this menu option to PC Remote, connect the camera to the computer with the Sony micro USB cable (or, preferably, a longer cable than the one that comes with the camera), and turn the camera on. Then start the software application. You will see on the computer a window like that in Figure 8-22, showing the various items you can control from the computer. The view on the computer will also include a large window at the left with a live view of the subject, but I have cropped that out of Figure 8-22 so I can show the remote control icons at a legible size.

You will have to turn the camera's mode dial to select the shooting mode, but you can control quite a few items from the software, depending on what mode is selected. These include the drive mode settings for continuous shooting, bracketing, and the self-timer; white balance; Picture Effect; DRO/Auto HDR; File Format; JPEG Quality; JPEG Image Size; and Aspect Ratio.

You can set autoexposure lock by clicking on the AEL icon near the top of the window. To control exposure compensation, click on the arrows next to the exposure compensation value, below the EV label. The same technique works for flash exposure compensation to the right of exposure compensation. You also can control ISO by clicking on the arrows next to the ISO reading.

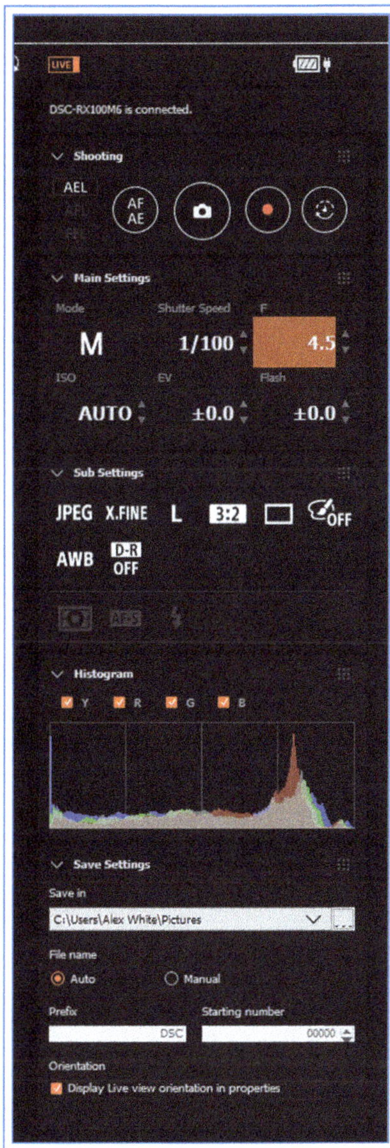

Figure 8-22. PC Remote Window on Computer

When the mode dial is set to Shutter Priority or Manual exposure, you can control the shutter speed by clicking on the arrows next to that setting. When Aperture Priority or Manual exposure mode is selected, you can control the aperture from this software. You can click on the button with the AF/AE label in the upper left of the window to simulate a half-press of the shutter button, locking focus and exposure, if autofocus is in effect.

You can click on the red button at the top of the window to start or stop a video recording. Click on the camera icon to the left of that button to capture a still image. Click and hold down on the camera icon to fire a burst of shots when continuous shooting is selected for drive mode.

If you want to use this tethered-shooting capability to save images to your computer, use the Save In . . . dialog box at the bottom of the remote control window and select a folder; the images captured using this feature will then be stored in that folder. You can set the camera to store images to only the computer, or to both the computer and the camera, using the PC Remote Settings option on screen 4 of the Setup menu. That option also lets you set the storage destinations for files taken with the Raw & JPEG setting for File Format.

If you click on the small button with a timer dial, to the right of the red video recording button, a new window will open up with options for interval shooting. In that window, you can set the interval between shots to a value from ten seconds to 180 minutes and the number of shots from two to 1000, or leave the number of shots unspecified. Using this feature, you can create a time-lapse movie. For example, if you set the camera up on a tripod and aim it at a construction project, taking one picture per minute for 600 minutes, you will end up with 600 images that cover a period of ten hours. If you assemble those images into a movie and play it back at 30 frames per second, the actions for those ten hours will play back in 20 seconds.

If you use this capability for a fairly long sequence, you will probably need to power the camera with the AC adapter or some other external power source, as discussed in Appendix A.

There is a less cumbersome way to carry out interval shooting or time-lapse photography with the RX100 VI. You can do this without connecting the camera to a computer, using a remote control device that includes an intervalometer, such as one of the Vello Shutterboss devices discussed in Appendix A.

USB LUN Setting

This next item on screen 4 of the Setup menu is a technical option that should not often be needed. LUN stands for logical unit number. This item has two possible settings—Multi or Single. Ordinarily, it should be set to Multi, the default. In particular, it should be set to Multi when the RX100 VI is connected to a Windows-based computer and you are using Sony's PlayMemories Home software to manage images. If you have a problem with a USB connection to a computer, you can try the Single setting to see if it solves the problem.

USB Power Supply

The USB Power Supply option, which can be turned either on or off, controls whether or not the camera's battery will be charged or the camera will be powered through the USB cable when the camera is connected by its USB cable to a computer.

If you use the AC adapter provided with the camera or an external USB battery, as discussed in Appendix A, to provide power to the camera, you do not need to have this menu option turned on. When the USB cable is connected to an external power supply, power will be provided to the camera even with this option turned off.

Turning this option on gives you another avenue for keeping the RX100 VI's battery charged. The only problem is that if your computer is running on its battery, that battery will be discharged more rapidly than usual. If you are connecting the camera to a computer that is plugged into a wall power outlet, there should be no problem in using this option.

As I will discuss in Appendix A, it's a good idea to get an external battery charger and at least one extra battery for the RX100 VI. Even though you can charge the battery in the camera using the USB cable, you don't have the ability to insert a fully charged battery into the camera when the first battery is exhausted, unless you have a way to charge a battery outside of the camera.

I recommend leaving this menu option at its default setting of On, unless you will be connecting the camera to a battery-powered computer or other device and you don't want to run down the battery on that device.

PC Remote Settings

This menu option provides a couple of ways to control how the camera saves images when you have it set up for tethered shooting by connecting it to a computer using a USB cable. (Tethered shooting was discussed above in this chapter, under the USB Connection menu option.)

The two sub-options are Still Image Save Destination and Raw+JPEG Save Image. The Still Image Save Destination sub-option has two choices: PC Only or PC + Camera. If you choose PC Only, the images you capture during tethered shooting are saved only to the computer that the camera is connected to. If you choose PC + Camera, the images are saved to both the computer and the memory card in the camera. With this setting, you have to have a suitable memory card in the camera, or else the camera will not release the shutter, even if the Release w/o Card menu option is set to Enable on screen 5 of the Camera Settings2 menu.

The setting you choose for this option depends on your workflow. If you can see the computer's screen while you operate the camera, you may not need to save the images to a card in the camera. However, if that screen is not readily visible, you may want to have the images saved to a card in the camera so you can view them on the camera's LCD screen as they are captured. You also might want to have the second copy as a backup.

The other sub-option for PC Remote Settings, Raw+JPEG Save Image, is available for selection only when the File Format (Still Images) option on screen 1 of the Camera Settings1 menu is set to Raw & JPEG and the Still Image Save Destination option is set to PC + Camera. In that case, you can use this sub-option to decide whether, during tethered shooting, the camera sends both the Raw and JPEG images to the computer, just the Raw image, or just the JPEG image. You might want to limit which versions are transferred in order to speed up the transfer of images to the computer, because they cannot be viewed on the computer's screen until they have been transferred.

Screen 5 of the Setup menu is shown in Figure 8-23.

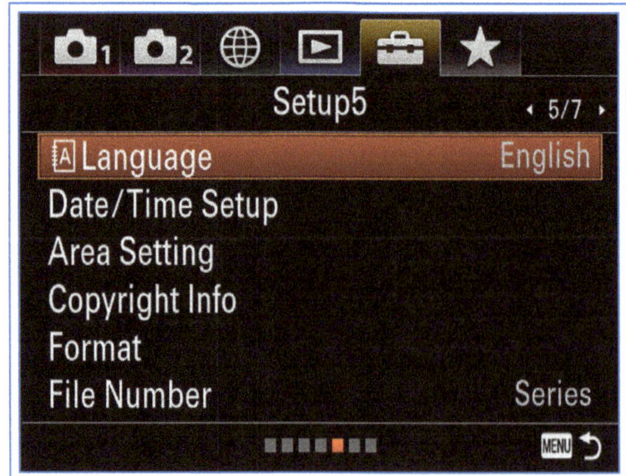

Figure 8-23. Screen 5 of Setup Menu

Language

This option gives you the choice of language for information on the camera's menus and display screens. Once you have selected this menu item, as shown in Figure 8-24, scroll through the language choices using the control wheel or the direction buttons and press the Center button when your chosen language is highlighted.

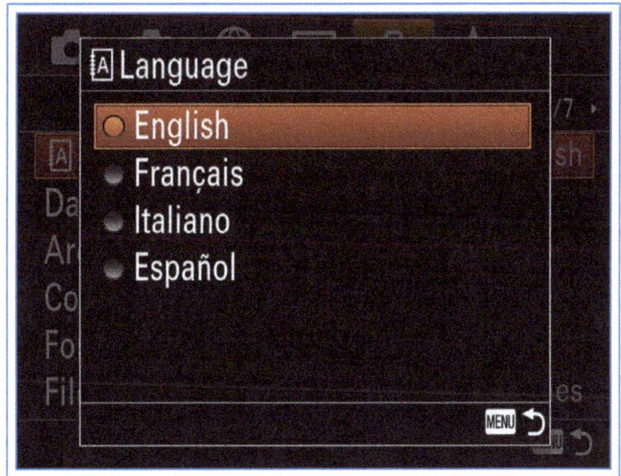

Figure 8-24. Language Selection Screen

Date/Time Setup

I discussed this item in Chapter 1. When the camera is new or has not been used for a long time, it will prompt you to set the date and time and will display this menu option. If you want to call up these settings on your own, you can do so at any time.

When you press the Center button on this menu line, you will see a screen like that in Figure 8-25, which gives you the choice of adjusting Daylight Savings Time (On or Off), Date/Time, or Date Format.

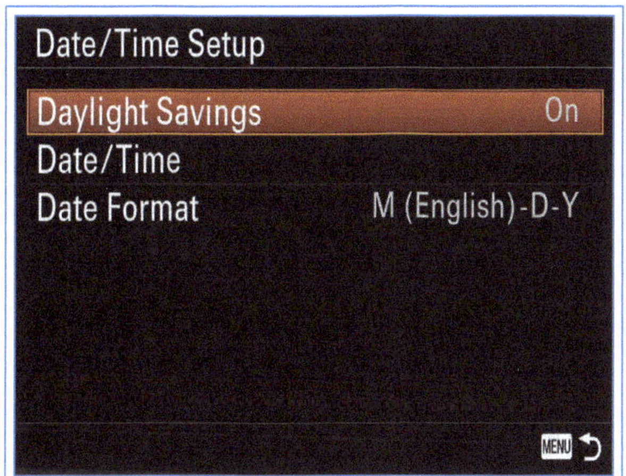

Figure 8-25. Date/Time Setup Options Screen

To adjust Date/Time, select that option and press the Center button. The camera will display a screen like that shown in Figure 8-26.

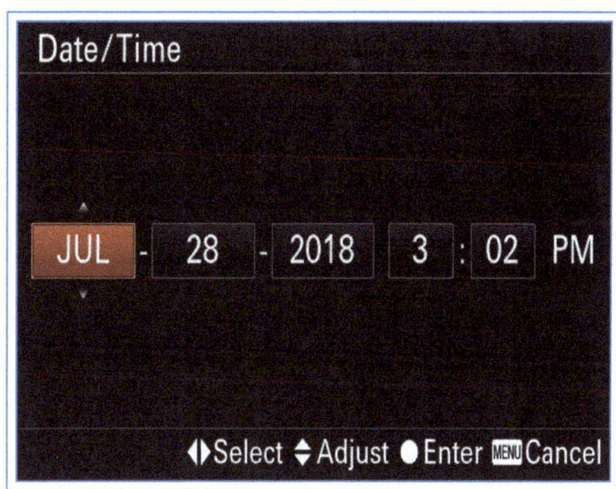

Figure 8-26. Date and Time Settings Screen

Scroll through the options for setting month, day, year, and time by turning the control wheel or pressing the Left and Right buttons. As you reach each item, adjust its value by using the Up and Down buttons. When all of the settings are correct, press the Center button to confirm them and exit from this screen.

You can also go back to the first menu screen and turn Daylight Savings Time on or off depending on the time of year, and you can choose a date format according to your preference.

Area Setting

The Area Setting option lets you select your current location so you can adjust the date and time for a different time zone when you are traveling. When you highlight this item and press the Center button, the camera displays the map shown in Figure 8-27.

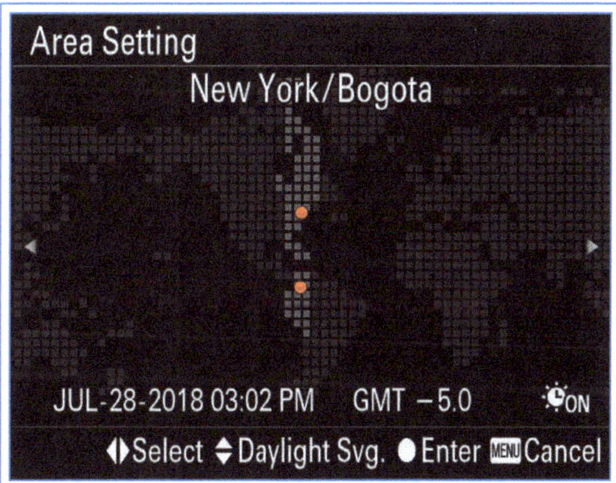

Figure 8-27. Area Setting Map Screen

Turn the control wheel or press the Left and Right buttons to move the light-colored highlight over the map until it covers the area of your current location, then press the Center button. The date and time will be adjusted for that location until you change the location again using this menu item. You also can press the Up or Down button when this screen is displayed to turn the Daylight Savings Time setting on or off.

Copyright Info

This next item on the Setup menu gives you a way to add information about the photographer and copyright holder to the metadata for images taken with the camera.

The first sub-option, Write Copyright Info, determines whether the copyright information entered for this item will be written to still images that you take. If you turn this option on, the copyright information (names of photographer and copyright holder) will be added to the metadata for any still images captured after the option is turned on. The information will not appear on the images themselves, but can be read by any program that reads EXIF data for images, such as Adobe Bridge.

The second option, Set Photographer, lets you enter the name of the photographer using up to 46 characters. When you select this option, you will see a screen with a window for entering the name. Press the Center button when the window is highlighted, and you will see the data-entry screen. Use that screen to enter any name you want. Use the control wheel or the direction buttons to move the orange highlight bar to the first block on the left under the name window. When that block is highlighted, press the Center button to toggle between letters, numbers and symbols. Then move the highlight bar to the block for the letter you want. Move to the up arrow to shift to uppercase letters. Press the Center button repeatedly to choose the character you want from each group of characters.

For example, to type the letter "e," move the highlight bar to the "def" block and press the Center button quickly two times to select e. After a second or two, the blinking white cursor will move to the right, and you can repeat this process. You can move the cursor forward or back using the left and right arrows at the upper right in the blocks of characters.

When you have finished entering the name, highlight OK and press the Center button to accept the name.

The third option, Set Copyright, lets you set the name of the company or person who holds the copyright for the images to be taken with the camera, using up to 46 characters.

Finally, the Display Copyright Info option lets you see what names are currently entered in the camera for these items.

Format

The next option—Format—is an important one. This command is used to prepare a new memory card with the appropriate data structure to store images and videos. The Format command also is useful when you want to wipe all the data off a card that has become full or when you have copied a card's images to your computer or other device. Choose this process only when you want or need to completely wipe all of the data from a memory card.

When you select the Format option, as shown in Figure 8-28, the camera will warn you that all data currently on the card will be deleted if you proceed. If you reply by highlighting Enter and pressing the Center button to confirm, the camera will format the card that is in the camera and the result will be a card that is empty and properly formatted to store new images and videos recorded by the camera.

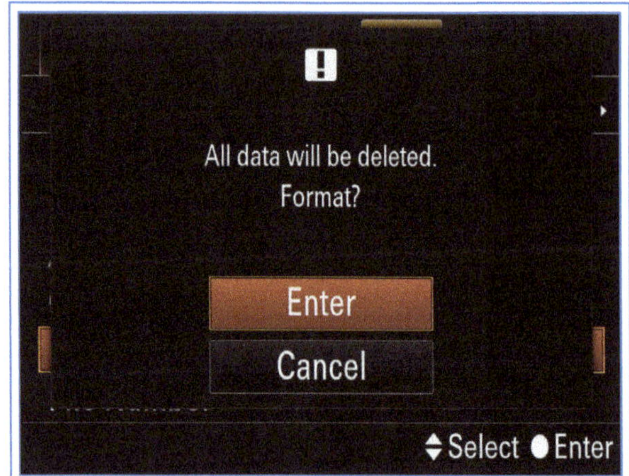

Figure 8-28. Format Confirmation Screen

With this procedure, the camera will erase all images and videos, including those that have been protected from accidental erasure with the Protect function on the Playback menu.

It's a good idea to periodically save your images and videos to your computer or other device and re-format your memory card to keep it properly set up for recording new images and videos. It's also a good idea to use the Format command on any new memory card when you first insert it into the camera. Even though it likely will work without that procedure, it's best to make sure the card is set up with Sony's method of formatting for the RX100 VI.

If the current battery charge is below one per cent, the Format command will not operate.

File Number

This option controls the way the camera assigns numbers to images and videos. There are two choices: Series and Reset, as shown in Figure 8-29.

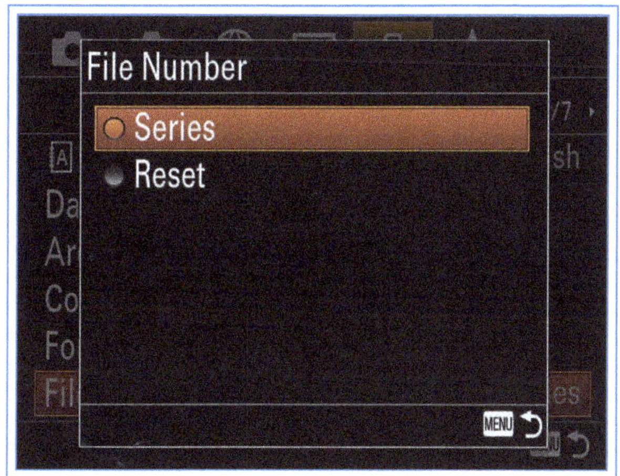

Figure 8-29. File Number Options Screen

With Series, the camera continues numbering where it left off, even if you put a new memory card in the camera. For example, if you have 112 images on your first memory card, the last image likely will be numbered 100-0112: 100 for the folder number and 0112 for the image number.

If you then switch to a new memory card with no images on it, the first image on that card will be numbered 100-0113 because the numbering scheme continues in the same sequence. If you choose Reset instead, the first image on the new card will be numbered 100-0001 because the camera resets the numbering to the first number.

Screen 6 of the Setup menu is shown in Figure 8-30.

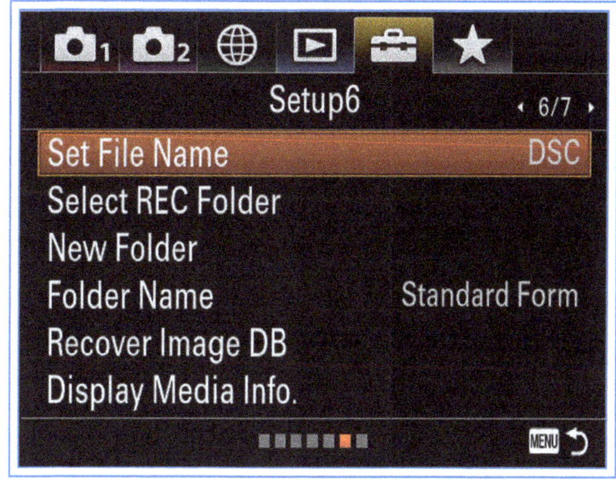

Figure 8-30. Screen 6 of Setup Menu

Set File Name

This menu item lets you specify the first three characters for file names of your images. By default, those characters are DSC, so a typical image might be DSC00150.jpg. You can choose any other characters by using the data-entry screen for this option, shown in Figure 8-31. Those three characters will then appear at the beginning of the file name for any images captured after you change this setting, if the images use the sRGB color space. If the images use the Adobe RGB color space, the camera will add an underscore character before the file name, as shown in Figure 8-31.

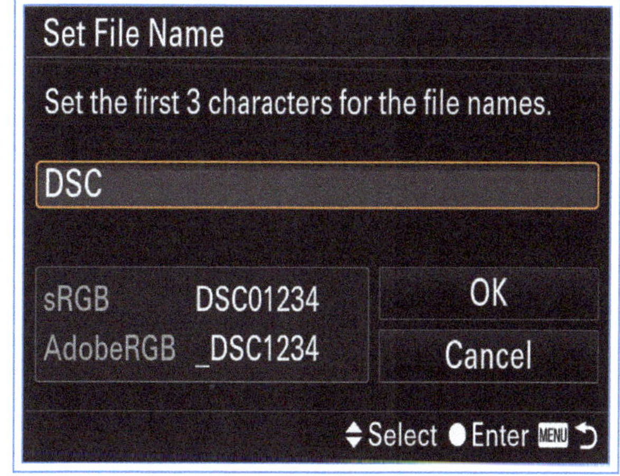

Figure 8-31. Set File Name Options Screen

Select REC Folder

When you select this item, the camera displays an orange bar with the name of the current folder, as shown in Figure 8-32. You can use the Up and Down buttons or turn the control wheel to scroll to the name of another folder if one exists, so you can store future images and videos in that folder. It might be worthwhile to use this function if you are taking photos or movies for different purposes during the same outing.

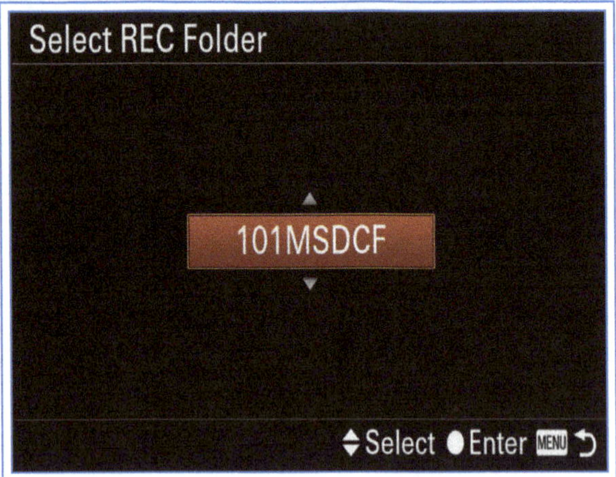

Figure 8-32. Select REC Folder Selection Screen

For example, if you are taking some photos for business and some for pleasure, you can create a new folder for the business-related shots (see the next menu item, below). The camera will then use that folder. Afterward, you can use the Select REC Folder option to select the folder where your personal images are stored and take more personal images that will be stored in that folder.

New Folder

This menu item lets you create a new folder on your memory card for storing images and videos. Highlight this item on the menu screen and press the Center button; you will then see a message announcing that a new folder has been created, as shown in Figure 8-33.

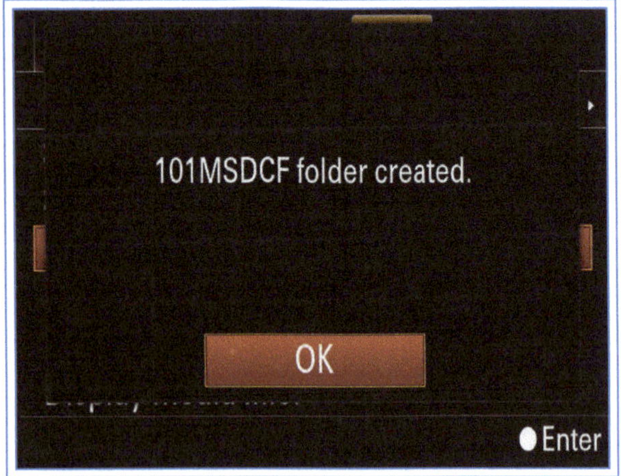

Figure 8-33. Message On Creation of New Folder

Creating a new folder can be a good way to organize images and videos from a particular shooting session. If you are going to view and process the files on your computer, it can be useful to have images from different locations arranged in different folders, for example.

Folder Name

This menu option gives you a choice of two methods for naming the folders used for storing still images on your memory card, as shown in Figure 8-34: Standard Form or Date Form. The Standard Form option uses the folder number, such as 100, 101, or higher, followed by the letters MSDCF. An example is 100MSDCF. If you choose Date Form, folder names will have the same 100 or higher number followed by the date, in a form such as 10080722 for a folder created on July 22, 2018, using only one digit to designate the year.

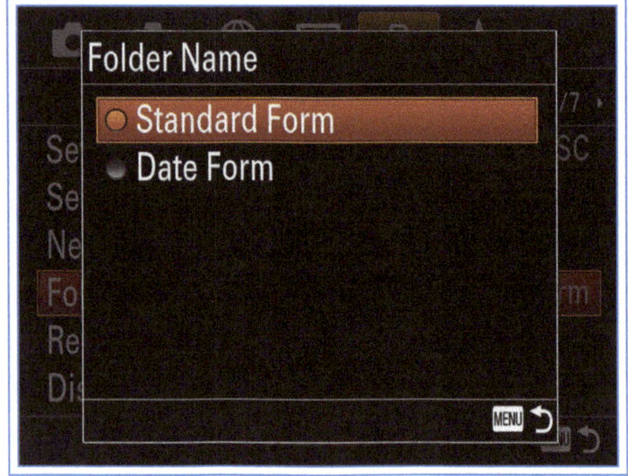

Figure 8-34. Folder Name Options Screen

I find the date format confusing and hard to read, and I am used to the MSDCF format. If you use the date format, you will end up having a folder for every date on which you record still images. You may prefer having your image folders organized in that way so you can quickly locate images from a particular date. I prefer having fewer folders and organizing images on my computer according to my own preferences.

Recover Image Database

This menu item activates the Recover Image Database function. If you select this option and press the Center button to confirm it on the next screen, as shown in Figure 8-35, the camera runs a check to test the integrity of the file system on the memory card. I have never used this menu option, but if the camera is having difficulty reading the images on a card, possibly because the files were altered while the card was in a computer, using this option might recover the data.

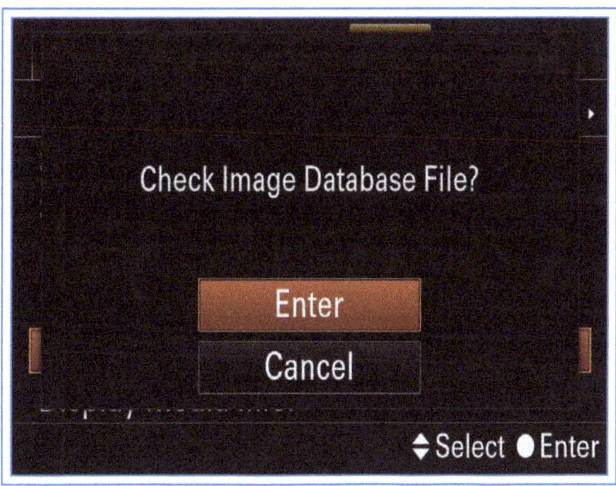

Figure 8-35. Recover Image Database Confirmation Screen

Display Media Info

The last item on screen 6 of the Setup menu screen gives you another way to see how much storage space is remaining on the memory card that is currently in the camera. When you select Display Media Info and press the Center button, the camera displays a screen like that in Figure 8-36, with information about the number of still images and the hours and minutes of video that can be recorded using the current settings for File Format (Still Images), JPEG Image Size, JPEG Quality, File Format (Movies), and Record Setting.

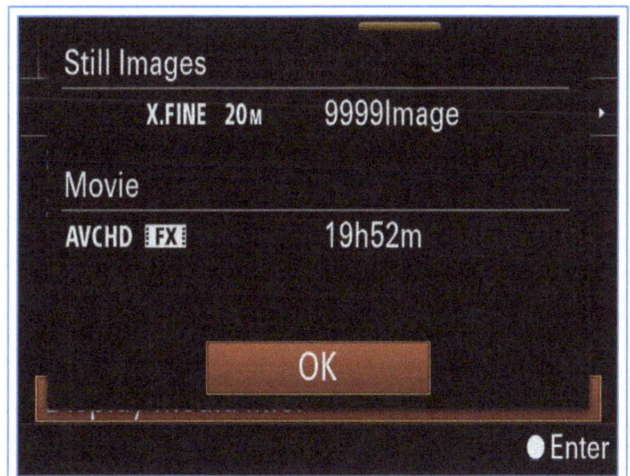

Figure 8-36. Display Media Information Screen

It is nice to have this option available, although the number of images that can be recorded is also displayed on the detailed shooting screen, and the available video recording time appears on the video recording screen once a recording has been started.

Screen 7 of the Setup menu is shown in Figure 8-37.

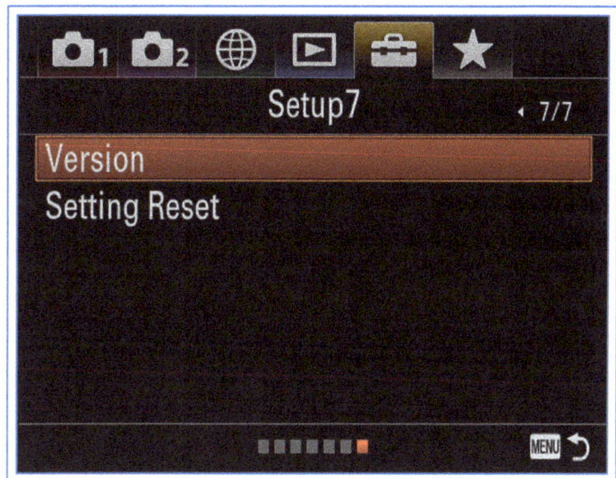

Figure 8-37. Screen 7 of Setup Menu

Version

This first option on the final screen of the Setup menu tells you the current version of the firmware in your camera. The RX100 VI, like other cameras, is programmed at the factory with firmware, which is a set of electronically implanted computer instructions. These instructions control all aspects of the camera's operation, including the menu system, functioning of the controls, and in-camera image processing.

You may want to see what version is installed because the manufacturer may release an updated version of the firmware to fix problems or bugs in the system, provide minor enhancements, or, in some cases, provide major improvements, such as adding new shooting modes or menu options.

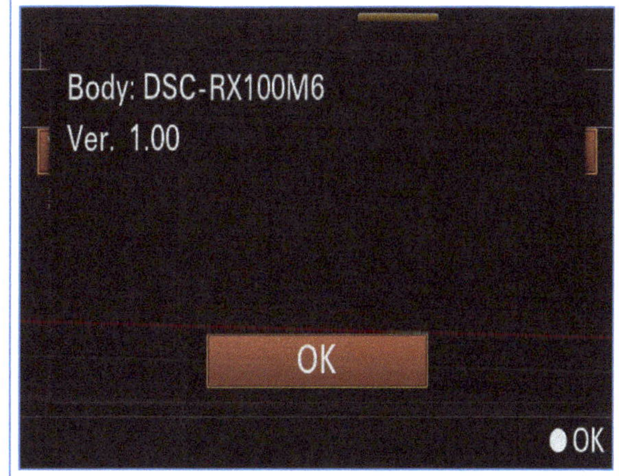

Figure 8-38. Version Screen for RX100 VI Camera

To determine the firmware version installed in your camera, highlight this menu option, then press the Center button, and the camera will display the version number, as shown in Figure 8-38. As you can see, my camera had Version 1.00 installed when this image was captured.

To see if firmware upgrades have been released, I recommend you visit Sony's support website, whose Internet address is http://esupport.sony.com. Find the link for Drivers and Software, then the link for Cyber-shot Cameras, and then a link to any updated version for the DSC-RX100 VI. The site will provide instructions for downloading and installing the new firmware.

Setting Reset

This final option on the Setup menu is useful when you want to reset some or all of the camera's settings to their original (default, or factory) values. This action can be helpful if you have been experimenting with different settings and you find that something is not working as expected.

When you select this item, the camera displays two choices: Camera Settings Reset and Initialize, as shown in Figure 8-39.

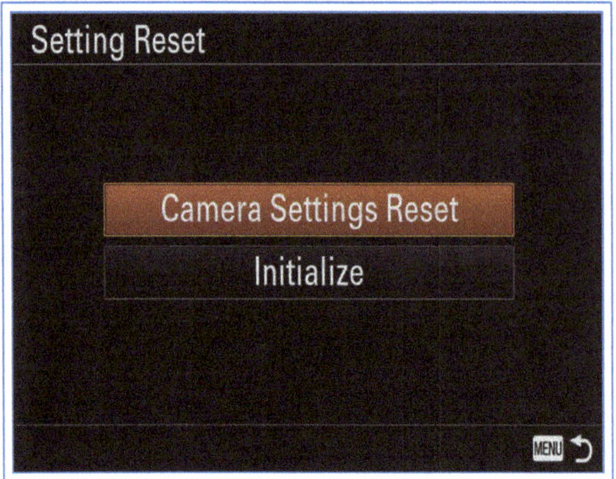

Figure 8-39. Setting Reset Options Screen

With Initialize, the camera resets all major settings to their original values and deletes registered data, such as faces. With Camera Settings Reset, only the values that affect shooting of images and videos are reset. Picture Profile settings will not be reset with either option.

My Menu

The final menu system for the RX100 VI, marked by a star icon at the far right of the main menu screen, is the My Menu system. This menu does not contain any options of its own, other than options for adding and organizing items from other menu systems. My Menu is a blank system that is provided for you to add your most-used options from the main menu systems, for quick access. You can include up to 30 items from any of the menus except the Playback menu. You also cannot add the View on TV item from the Network menu. That leaves a large number of very useful options that can be selected from the Camera Settings1, Camera Settings2, Network, and Setup menus.

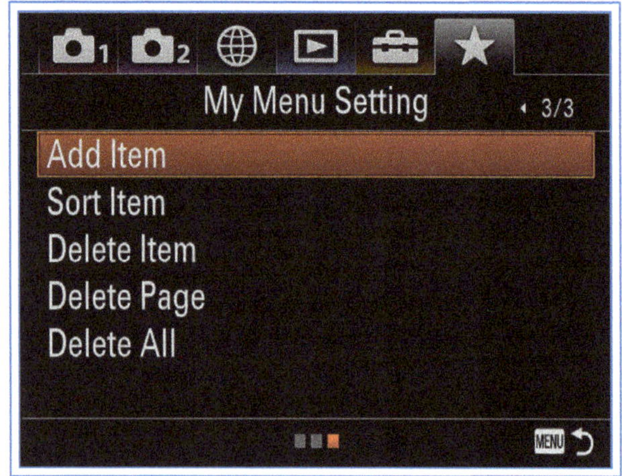

Figure 8-40. My Menu - Screen for Adding Items

To add an item, first, navigate to the screen shown in Figure 8-40, with choices for adding, sorting, and deleting menu items. If no items have been added to My Menu yet, this will be the only screen available. If items have been added, you may have to navigate to a higher-numbered screen. The highest-numbered screen is the one where you can add, sort, and delete items. You will see numbers in the upper right corner, such as 1/3 or 3/3, as shown in Figure 8-40. Those numbers indicate which screen is being displayed.

Once you have reached the screen shown in Figure 8-40, highlight and select Add Item. The camera will display the screen shown in Figure 8-41, which is one of 31 screens of menu options that you can choose from to add to your personalized menus. Scroll through these screens by a full screen at a time using the Left and Right buttons; scroll through the items on a given screen using the Up and Down buttons or the control wheel.

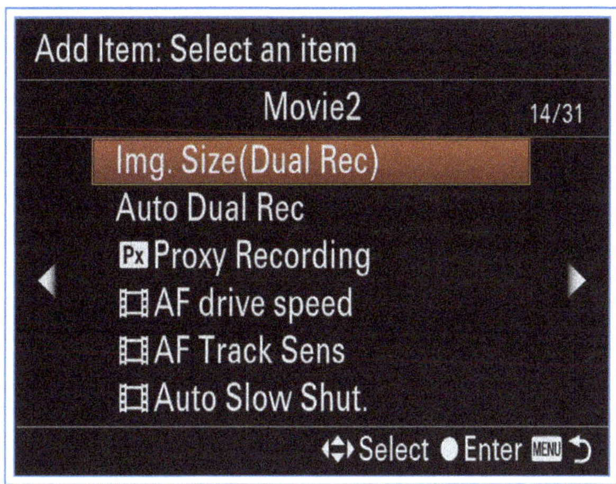

Figure 8-41. One of 31 Screens of Items to Add to My Menu

When you have highlighted a menu item you want to add to My Menu, press the Center button to select it. The camera will then prompt you to select a location for the selected item. For the first item you add, there is only one location possible. For later selections, the camera will place an orange line at the end of the list of the items that are currently included in My Menu, as shown in Figure 8-42.

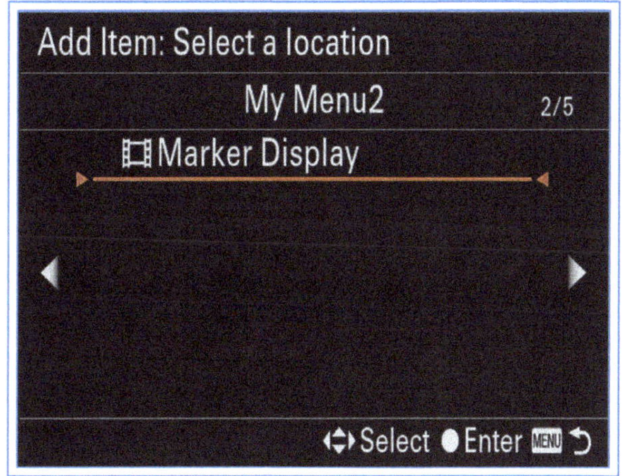

Figure 8-42. Screen to Select Location for Added Item

You can leave the orange line in that location or move it to a different position, and the new item will be added in that location. If you navigate to a screen that is already filled with menu items and highlight an item, the camera will ask if you want to overwrite the item that you have highlighted. If you select OK, the highlighted item will be replaced with the new item you are adding.

When you have finished adding items, press the Menu button to return to the My Menu screen. From there you can navigate to another menu system or press the Menu button again to return to the shooting screen.

After you have added all of the items you have chosen for My Menu, you can later move them around to get the most convenient arrangement. To move an item, while My Menu is displayed, press the Right button enough times to get to the last screen of My Menu, which holds the options for managing the menu. Choose Sort Item from the My Menu screen. Then navigate to the item to move and select it by pressing the Center button. You can then move it to the new location you select. You also can delete an item, a whole page of items, or all items, by using the Delete Item, Delete Page, or Delete All option. Eventually, you will have a system with one or more screens like that in Figure 8-43, with a convenient arrangement of your most-used menu options.

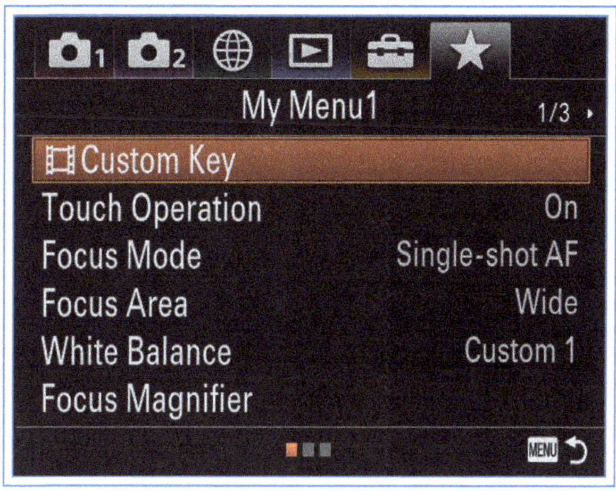

Figure 8-43. My Menu with Some Items Added

Chapter 9: Motion Pictures

The RX100 VI is a stellar performer for capturing still images, and it must be considered primarily a camera for stills. But Sony has added a strong set of movie-recording features to this camera. Although a compact camera like this is not one you might think of for professional-level video shooting, it is equipped with features that would allow you to produce footage for many high-end applications. Before I discuss specific settings you can make for your movies, I'll begin with a brief overview of the process.

Movie-Making Overview

In one sense, the basics of making movies with the RX100 VI can be stated in four words: "Push the red button." (That is, the red Movie button at the top right of the camera's back.) In most situations, you can press and release that button while aiming at your subject and get results that are quite usable. You do not need to worry about special settings, particularly if you set the camera to one of the more automatic modes, such as Auto or Scene. (You can record a normal-speed movie with the mode dial at any position except HFR, as discussed later in this chapter.)

To stop recording, press the red button again. If you prefer not to run the risk of recording unwanted movies by pressing the Movie button accidentally, you can change the button's operation so it activates movie recording only when the camera is in Movie mode, as discussed in Chapter 6.

If you're mainly a still photographer with little interest in movie making, you don't need to read further. Be aware that the red button exists, and if an interesting event starts to happen, you can turn the mode dial to Auto, press the Movie button, and capture footage to post on YouTube or elsewhere with a minimum of effort. But for those RX100 VI users who want to use this camera's strong motion picture capabilities, there is much more information to discuss.

First, there is a requirement that may decide what memory card you get for your camera. To record movies using the high-quality XAVC S 4K or XAVC S HD format, or high frame rate (HFR) movies, you have to use an SDHC or SDXC memory card with a speed of at least Class 10 or UHS Speed Class 1. If you want to record XAVC S 4K or XAVC S HD video using a Record Setting value of 100M, meaning 100 megabits per second, you have to use an SDHC or SDXC card rated in UHS Speed Class 3. These are not just recommendations. If you do not use a card with the listed specifications, the camera will display an error message and will not record video using the format in question. (As I will discuss later in this chapter, 4K is a designation for video files that have higher resolution than high-definition video.)

I have used the SanDisk Extreme 256 GB SDXC card, shown in Figure 9-1, which is rated in UHS Speed Class 3, for recording the highest-level formats with no problems, but there are other choices available, as discussed in Chapter 1.

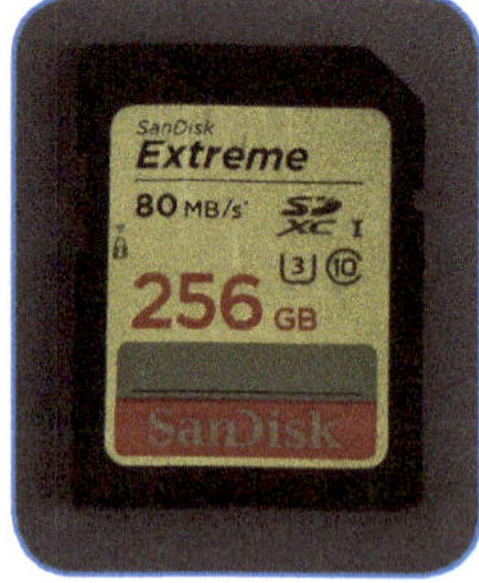

Figure 9-1. SDXC Card Rated in Speed Class UHS-3

Of course, if you are not going to use the highest-level formats, you can use a less-powerful card. And, as I'll discuss later in this chapter, you can actually record 4K video with no card at all, if you connect the RX100 VI to an external video recorder.

Also, the RX100 VI, like most cameras in its class, has built-in limitations that prevent it from recording any sequence longer than about 29 minutes. For 4K video or XAVC S HD video using a Record Setting of 120p (100p for PAL systems), the limit is five minutes, because of overheating issues. You can, of course, record multiple sequences adding up to any length, depending on the amount of storage space available on your memory cards.

If you plan on recording a large amount of HD video, you should get a high-capacity and high-speed card. For example, a 64 GB card can hold about 75 minutes of the highest quality of 4K video, or about 8 hours and 15 minutes of the lowest-quality AVCHD video. (I will discuss these video formats later in this chapter.)

Details of Settings for Shooting Movies

As I noted above, the one necessary step for recording a movie with the RX100 VI is to press the Movie button. However, there are numerous settings that affect the way the camera records a movie when that button is pressed.

I will discuss four categories of settings: (1) the movie-related selections you make on the Camera Settings2 menu; (2) the position of the mode dial on top of the camera; (3) the selections you make on the Camera Settings1 menu and other menus; and (4) the settings you make with the camera's other physical controls.

Movie-Related Menu Options

First, I will discuss the movie-related options on the Camera Settings2 menu, because those options control the format and several other important settings for the movies you record with the RX100 VI. I discussed this menu in Chapter 5, but I did not provide details about all of the movie-oriented options in that chapter.

As noted above, you can press the Movie button to start a normal-speed video recording at any time and in any shooting mode (except for HFR), as long as the Movie Button option on screen 10 of the Camera Settings2 menu is set to Always. Because of this ability to shoot movies in almost any shooting mode, you can always change the settings for movie recording using the Camera Settings2 menu, no matter what shooting mode the camera is set to. I will discuss each item on the Camera Settings2 menu that has an effect on your shooting of videos.

At this point, I will discuss the Camera Settings2 menu options that apply only to movies; later in this chapter, I will discuss the options on other menus that affect movies as well as still images, such as white balance, ISO, Creative Style, Picture Effect, Picture Profile, and others.

Exposure Mode (Movies)

This menu item, the first option on screen 1 of the Camera Settings2 menu, can be selected only when the camera's mode dial is set to Movie mode, as shown in Figure 9-2. In other shooting modes, this menu option is dimmed and unavailable.

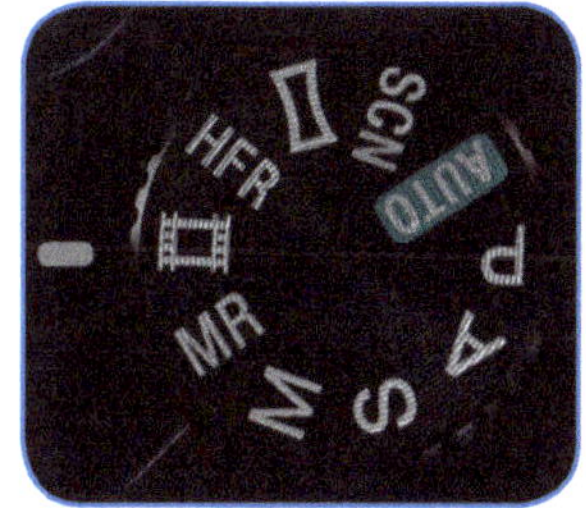

Figure 9-2. Mode Dial at Movie

When the camera is in Movie mode, this option lets you select an exposure mode for shooting movies. If you have the Mode Dial Guide option turned on through screen 2 of the Setup menu, you won't need to use the Exposure Mode option when you first select the Movie mode. When you turn the mode dial to the Movie position and then press the Center button, the screen with choices for the Exposure Mode item will appear automatically. If the Mode Dial Guide option is not active or if the mode dial is already set to Movie mode, you get to this screen by selecting Exposure Mode from the Camera Settings2 menu.

With the mode dial set to Movie mode, highlight and select this menu option and a screen will appear with four options: Program Auto, Aperture Priority, Shutter Priority, and Manual Exposure, as shown in Figure 9-3. Move through these choices by turning the control wheel or by pressing the Up and Down buttons.

You also can call up that screen by assigning Shoot Mode to the Function menu using the Function Menu Settings option on screen 9 of the Camera Settings2 menu. If you do that, then, with the mode dial set to Movie, you can press the Function button to activate the Function menu, scroll to the Shoot Mode item, and select your choice of movie exposure mode. (The Shoot Mode item will be labeled Exposure Mode in the Function menu when the mode dial is at the Movie position.)

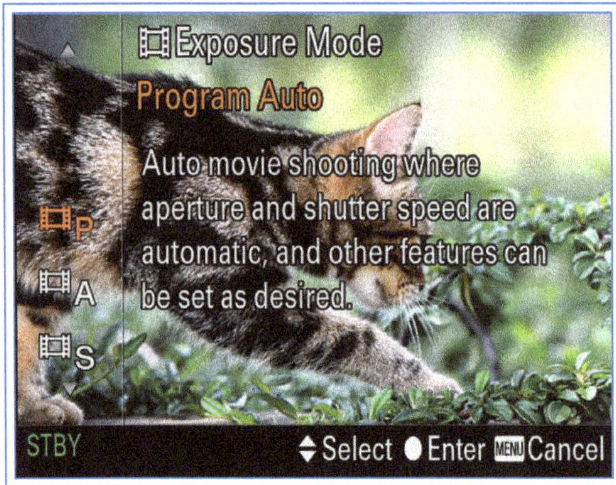

Figure 9-3. Exposure Mode (Movies) Options Screen

Following are details about the behavior of the RX100 VI when shooting movies with each of these settings.

Program Auto

With the Program Auto setting, which is highlighted in Figure 9-3, the RX100 VI sets aperture and shutter speed according to its metering, and it uses settings from the Camera Settings1 menu that carry over to video recording, including ISO, white balance, metering mode, face detection, and DRO.

In this mode, the camera can set the aperture anywhere in its normal range of f/2.8 to f/11.0, and it can use a shutter speed as fast as 1/12800 second. The camera will normally not use a shutter speed slower than 1/25 second, 1/30 second, 1/50 second, 1/60 second, or 1/125 second, depending on the settings for File Format (Movies) and Record Setting. It can use a slightly slower speed if you turn on the Auto Slow Shutter option, discussed later in this chapter.

Aperture Priority

With the Aperture Priority setting, shown in Figure 9-4, you set the aperture, just as in the similar mode for still images, and the camera will set the shutter speed based on its metering. You can set the aperture anywhere in the full aperture range from f/2.8 to f/11.0, though the widest aperture changes to f/4.5 when the lens is zoomed in to its full telephoto setting. As with the Program Auto exposure mode for movies, discussed above, the camera will not use shutter speeds slower than those listed for that mode, unless you turn on the Auto Slow Shutter option.

With this setting, you can adjust the aperture during a video recording. This may not be something you need to do often, but it can be useful in some situations. For example, you may be recording at a garden show, and at some point you may want to open the aperture wide to blur the background as you focus on a small plant. Afterward, you may want to close the aperture down to a narrow value to achieve a broad depth of field to keep a large area in focus.

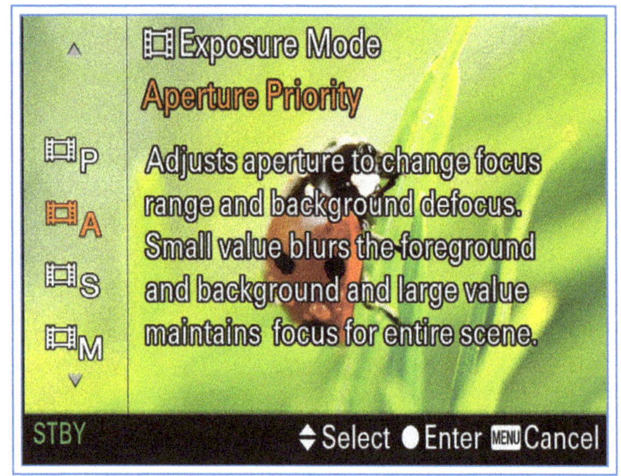

Figure 9-4. Aperture Priority Setting for Exposure Mode

Also, you can use the aperture setting to accomplish an in-camera fadeout. For example, in normal indoor conditions, you may start with the aperture set to f/2.8 and ISO set to 640, with Auto Slow Shutter turned off. Press the Movie button to start recording. When you're ready, turn the control wheel smoothly to the f/11.0 setting. You should get a nice fade to black. In brighter conditions, you may need to reduce ISO to its minimum setting for movies, which is 125.

Shutter Priority

With the Shutter Priority mode for movies, shown in Figure 9-5, you set the shutter speed, and the camera will set the aperture.

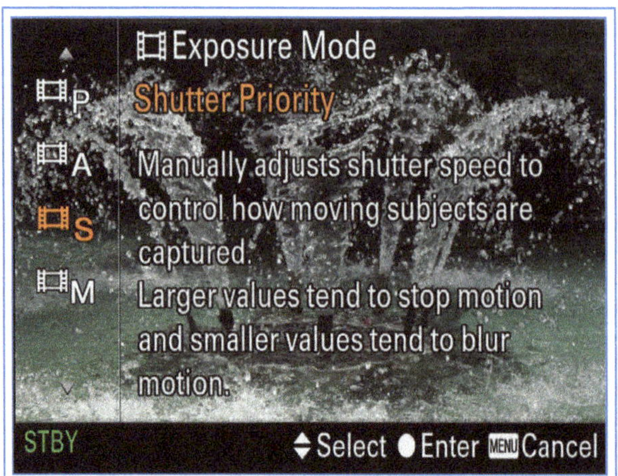

Figure 9-5. Shutter Priority Setting for Exposure Mode

Unlike the situation with the Aperture Priority exposure mode for movies, in which the camera normally will not set the shutter speed slower than 1/25 second (or a higher value for some formats), you are able to set the shutter speed as slow as 1/4 second in this mode in most cases, even if Auto Slow Shutter is turned off. (If Record Setting is set to 120p for XAVC S HD video, the slowest shutter speed available is 1/125 second.) You can select a shutter speed from 1/4 second all the way to the maximum shutter speed for movies, which is 1/12800 second. The camera will use its full range of aperture settings, from f/2.8 to f/11.0.

To expose your video normally at a shutter speed of 1/12800 second or other fast settings, you must have bright lighting, a high ISO setting, or both. Using a fast shutter speed for video can yield a crisper appearance, especially when there is considerable movement, as when shooting sports or other fast-moving events. In addition, having these very fast shutter speeds gives the camera flexibility for achieving a normal exposure when recording video in bright conditions.

With slower shutter speeds, particularly below the normal video speed of 1/30 second (equivalent to 30 fps), footage can become blurry with the appearance of smearing, especially with panning motions. If you are shooting a scene in which you want to have a drifting, dreamy appearance that looks like motion underwater, this option may be appropriate. You will not be able to achieve good lip sync at the slower shutter speeds, so this technique would not work well for realistic recordings of people talking or singing.

One interesting point is that you can preview this effect on the camera's display even before you press the Movie button to start recording. If you have the shutter speed set to 1/4 second in Movie mode, you will see any action on the screen looking blurry and jerky as if it had already been recorded with this slow shutter speed. (The Live View Display option on screen 7 of the Camera Settings2 menu is forced to the Setting Effect On option in Movie mode, and you cannot change it.)

With the Shutter Priority exposure mode for movies, you also can achieve a fadeout effect, as with Aperture Priority mode, discussed above. Just turn the control wheel smoothly to increase the shutter speed to its fastest speed of 1/12800 second, and the scene may go black, depending on the lighting conditions. You may need to use a low ISO setting to achieve full darkness.

Manual Exposure

The last setting for the Exposure Mode item, shown in Figure 9-6, Manual Exposure, gives you more complete control over the exposure of your videos.

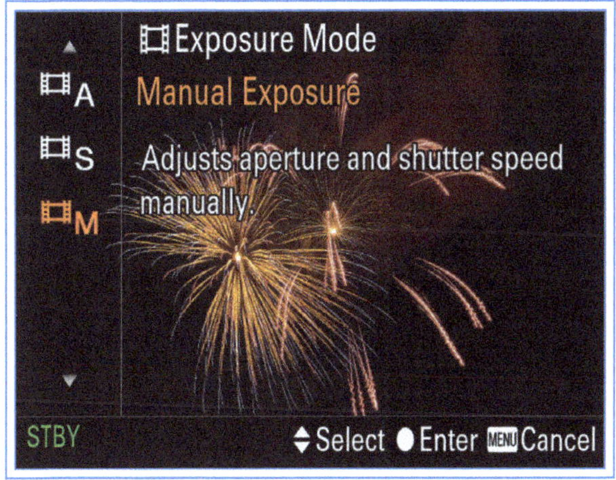

Figure 9-6. Manual Exposure Setting for Exposure Mode

As with Manual exposure mode for stills, with this setting you can adjust both the aperture and the shutter speed to achieve a desired effect. With video shooting, you can adjust the aperture from f/2.8 to f/11.0, and you can adjust the shutter speed from 1/12800 second to 1/4 second. (If Record Setting is set to 120p for XAVC S HD video, the slowest shutter speed available is 1/125 second.) Using these settings, you can create effects such as fades to and from black as well as similar fades to and from white.

For example, if you begin a recording in normal indoor lighting using settings of 1/60 second at f/3.2 with ISO set to 800, you can start recording the scene, and, when you want to fade out, start turning the control wheel slowly to the right, increasing the shutter speed smoothly until it reaches 1/12800 second. Depending on how bright the lighting is, the result may be complete blackness. Of course, you can reverse this process to fade in from black.

If you want to fade to white, here is one possible scenario. Suppose you are recording video with shutter speed set to 1/400 second and aperture set to f/2.8 at ISO 6400. When you want to start a fade to white, turn the control wheel smoothly to the left until the shutter speed decreases all the way to 1/4 second. (You may have to press the Down button to make the control wheel adjust shutter speed.) In fairly normal lighting conditions, such as in my office as I write this, the result will be a fade to a bright white screen.

There are, of course, other uses for Manual Exposure mode when recording videos, such as shooting "day for night" footage, in which you underexpose the scene by using a fast shutter speed, narrow aperture, low ISO, or all three of those settings, to turn day into night for creative purposes. Also, you might want to use Manual Exposure mode when you are recording a scene in which the lighting may change, but you do not want the exposure to change. In other words, you may want some areas to remain dark and some to be unusually bright, rather than have the camera automatically adjust the exposure. In some cases, having a constant exposure setting can be preferable to having the scene's brightness change as the metering system adjusts the exposure.

Note that you can set ISO to Auto ISO with the Manual Exposure setting. With the Auto ISO setting, you can maintain a constant aperture and shutter speed, but the camera will adjust exposure using the ISO setting to the extent that it can. You might want to use that setup if you need to maintain a narrow aperture to have a broad depth of field.

Exposure Mode (HFR)

This second option on screen 1 of the Camera Settings2 menu lets you select an exposure mode when the mode dial is at the HFR position, for recording high frame rate video. I will discuss the process for that mode of recording later in this chapter.

File Format (Movies)

The File Format (Movies) option gives you a choice of the three available movie recording formats on the RX100 VI—XAVC S 4K, XAVC S HD, and AVCHD, as shown in Figure 9-7. This setting determines the format the camera will use to record movies when you press the Movie button. The formats have different characteristics, as discussed below.

XAVC S 4K

The XAVC S format is a consumer version of the XAVC format, developed for use with 4K video recording, sometimes known as Ultra HD. The term "4K" refers to a horizontal resolution of roughly 4,000 pixels, instead of the 1920 pixels in standard HD video (sometimes called "2K" video). On the RX100 VI, video recorded with the 4K format has a pixel count of 3840 x 2160. Because of its high resolution, this option provides excellent quality for your videos.

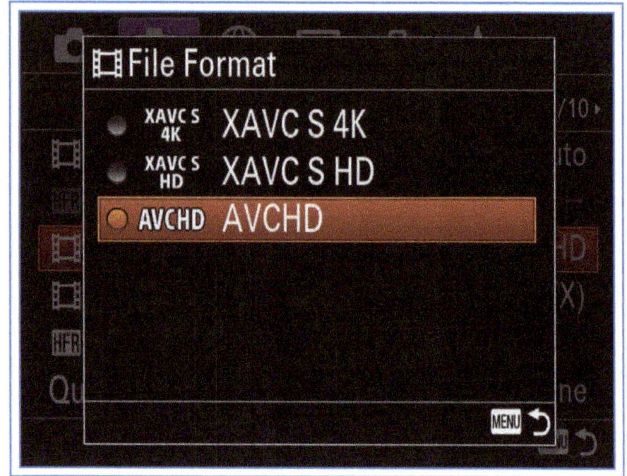

Figure 9-7. File Format (Movies) Options Screen

To enjoy the full benefit of the format, you need to view the videos on a TV set that is equipped for 4K viewing. However, even without that type of TV, you can edit 4K videos with appropriate software, such as Adobe Premiere Pro, Sony Vegas Pro, and others. Sony provides a list of such programs at the following website: http://support.d-imaging.sony.co.jp/www/support/application/nle/en.html. In the editing process, you can downsample the 4K video clips to a standard HD format, such as 1920 x 1080 pixels, and they will have greater quality than videos originally recorded in an HD format.

As noted above, if you use this format, you have to use a memory card rated at least in Speed Class 10 or UHS Speed Class 1. If you use the highest-quality Record Setting options, the card must be rated in UHS Speed Class 3.

However, as I will discuss later in this chapter, you can avoid this restriction if you connect the RX100 VI to an external video recorder, such as the Atomos Shogun, using an HDMI cable, and record to the Shogun recorder without recording to the camera's memory card. I'm not suggesting that that system is simple or inexpensive, but it is available if you need to use the RX100 VI for 4K video recording without having to use a particular type of memory card.

XAVC S HD

This second option for File Format (Movies) uses the high-quality XAVC S format, but records using an HD resolution of 1920 x 1080 pixels rather than the higher 4K resolution. This option will give you excellent quality without requiring the use of a 4K-capable TV set. However, it carries with it the same requirement for a high-speed memory card as the 4K format.

AVCHD

If you don't want to purchase the high-speed memory card required for the XAVC S format, you can choose AVCHD. This format, developed jointly by Sony and Panasonic, has become increasingly common in advanced digital cameras. It provides excellent quality, and movies recorded in this format on the RX100 VI can be used to create Blu-ray discs.

Record Setting

The Record Setting item on screen 1 of the Camera Settings2 menu is another quality-related option for recording video. (The accent is on the second syllable of "Record.") The choices for this item are different depending on whether you choose XAVC S 4K, XAVC S HD, or AVCHD for File Format. I will discuss these options assuming you have your camera set for NTSC, the video standard used in the United States, using the NTSC/PAL Selector option on screen 3 of the Setup menu, as discussed in Chapter 8. If your camera is set for PAL, the choices for Record Setting will include numbers such as 50p and 25p instead of 60p, 30p, and 24p.

XAVC S 4K

If you choose XAVC S 4K for File Format, the four options for Record Setting are 30p 100M, 30p 60M, 24p 100M, and 24p 60M, as shown in Figure 9-8.

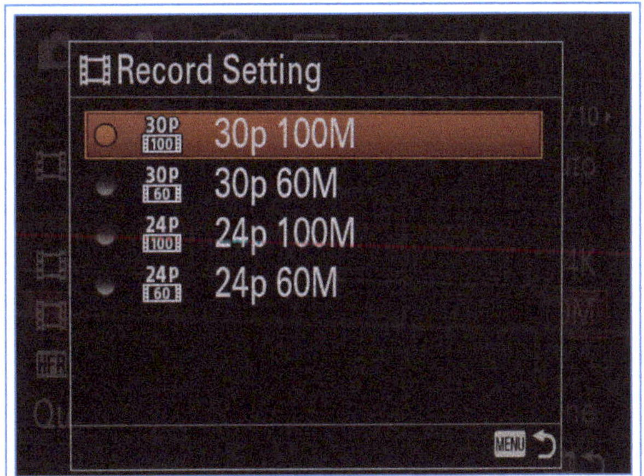

Figure 9-8. Record Setting Options for XAVC S 4K Format

For these choices, the letter "p" stands for progressive, which means the camera records 30 or 24 full video frames per second. (The other option, used with some AVCHD formats, as discussed below, is designated by the letter "i," standing for interlaced. With those options, such as 60i, the camera records 60 fields, or half-frames, per second, which yields lower quality and fewer possibilities for editing.)

The standard speed for recording video in the United States is 30 frames per second, and using either of the 30p settings will yield excellent quality.

If you select 24p 100M or 24p 60M, your video will be recorded and played back at 24 fps. The 24p rate is considered by some people to be more "cinematic" than the 30p format. This may be because 24 fps is a standard speed for movie cameras that shoot with film. My preference is to use the 30p format, but if you find that 24p suits your purposes better, you have that option with the RX100 VI.

The 60M or 100M designation means that these formats record video with a bit rate up to a maximum of 60 or 100 megabits per second, which are high rates that yield excellent quality. As noted earlier, when you record using the 100M setting, you have to use a memory card rated in UHS Speed Class 3.

My recommendation for this setting is to use 30p 60M unless you have a definite need for the super-high quality of the 30p 100M setting.

XAVC S HD

If you choose XAVC S HD for File Format, the seven choices for Record Setting are 60p 50M, 60p 25M, 30p 50M, 30p 16M, 24p 50M, 120p 100M, and 120p 60M, as shown in Figure 9-9.

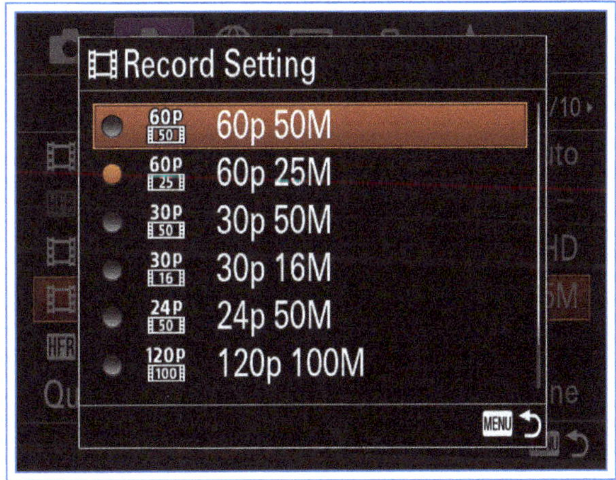

Figure 9-9. Record Setting Options for XAVC S HD Format

(The last of these settings is not visible in this figure; you have to scroll down to see it.) If you use a 60p or 120p option, the camera will record at two or four times the normal speed, and therefore will record two or four times as much video information as with the 30p choice. If you use one of those higher speeds, you will be able to produce a slow-motion version of your footage at very high quality. For example, 60p footage is recorded with twice the number of full frames as 30p footage, so the quality of the video does not suffer if it is played back at one-half speed.

If you think you may want to slow down your footage significantly for playback, you should choose the 60p setting, or, for even slower motion, the 120p setting.

A video recorded with the 60p or 120p setting will play back at normal speed in the camera. To play it back in slow motion, you can use a program such as iMovie, Adobe Premiere Elements, or PlayMemories Home. Just set the playback speed to a factor such as 0.5x or 0.25x to play the footage at the slower speed.

The 24p option is not a substantially slower rate than the 60p format or the 120p format, because the video playback rate in the United States is 30 fps, and the 60p and 120p formats are converted to 30 fps for playback in the camera.

All of these options are recorded in full HD, meaning the pixel count for each video frame is 1920 x 1080. The 120p selections (100p for cameras using the PAL system) are not available with the Auto and Scene shooting modes. With either of the 120p options, the camera cannot use Face Priority in AF, DRO/Auto HDR, Monitor Brightness, Viewfinder Brightness, Center Lock-on AF or Lock-on AF, non-optical zoom, the AF Tracking Sensitivity option, Phase Detection autofocus, the AF Drive Speed option, Auto Dual Recording, Proxy Recording, or Auto Slow Shutter, while recording a video.

Here again, as with the 4K settings, you have to use a memory card rated in UHS Speed Class 3 card if you use the 100M setting, and at least a Speed Class 10 or UHS Speed Class 1 card for the other settings.

AVCHD

If you choose AVCHD for File Format, the two choices for Record Setting are 60i 24M(FX) and 60i 17M(FH), as shown in Figure 9-10. Both of these are recorded with a pixel count of 1920 x 1080, which is full HD. As noted earlier, the letter "i" stands for interlaced. With 60i interlaced video, the camera records 60 fields per second; a field is equal to one-half of a frame, and the two halves are interlaced to form 30 full frames. The video frame rate of 30 frames per second (fps) is the standard video playback rate in the United States.

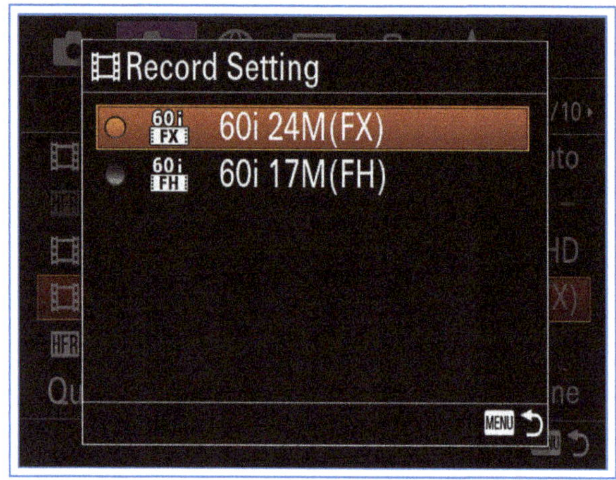

Figure 9-10. Record Setting Options for AVCHD Format

The 24M or 17M figure states the maximum bit rate, or volume, of video information that is recorded—either 24 or 17 megabits per second. The higher rate provides greater quality at the cost of using more storage capacity on the memory card and requiring greater computer resources to edit.

The final designations, FX and FH, are proprietary labels used by Sony for two qualities of video. They have no particular meanings; they are just labels for these levels of video quality.

Choose 60i 24M for excellent quality, or 60i 17M for excellent quality that takes up fewer resources.

HFR Settings

This menu option lets you set up the camera for super-slow-motion video, which you can record when you turn the mode dial to the HFR position, for high frame rate shooting. I will discuss these options later in this chapter, in a section on HFR shooting.

Quality (Dual Recording)

This next option on the Camera Settings2 menu sets the quality of still images that are captured during video recording. When you have started recording a video, with some limitations you can press the shutter button at any time to capture a still image. You also can use the Auto Dual Recording option, discussed below, to set the camera to capture still images automatically during video recording. The options available for this setting are Extra Fine, Fine, and Standard. The Raw setting is not available. I will discuss the process for capturing still images during video recording later in this chapter.

Image Size (Dual Recording)

This first option on screen 2 of the Camera Settings2 menu is related to the previous one. This option sets the size of still images that are captured during video recording. Choices for Image Size are L:17M, M:7.5M, and S:4.2M, for Large, Medium, and Small.

Auto Dual Recording

This menu option lets you set the camera to capture still images automatically during a video recording, when the camera detects what it considers to be "impressive compositions, including people." If this feature is turned on when a video sequence is being recorded, the camera may, from time to time, snap a still image during the recording, if the camera believes a particular scene with human faces is worthy of a still photo.

When you highlight the icon for turning this option on, you can press the Left and Right button to select a shooting frequency of Low, Standard, or High. This setting controls how often the camera is likely to capture a still image. When the camera does take a still photo, the word CAPTURE appears in green letters at the top of the display screen.

The size and quality of the still images captured with this feature are controlled by the Image Size (Dual Rec) and Quality (Dual Rec) items, discussed immediately above. The choices for Image Size are L:17M, M:7.5M, and S:4.2M. The options for Quality are Extra Fine, Fine, and Standard. If you are going to use this feature, I recommend using the L:17M and Extra Fine settings, for the best results. I also recommend using the High setting for frequency, unless you find the camera takes too many still images with that option.

I cannot imagine many situations in which I would want to use this feature, because it provides you with very little control over what the camera does. If you want to capture still images while recording video, you can press the shutter button to do so at any time you choose. However, if you have placed the camera unattended on a tripod to record an event, such as a family gathering or a wedding, it might be interesting to use this feature to set the camera to take some still photos if it detects a good composition with family members or guests.

Proxy Recording

This option is somewhat like a video version of the Raw & JPEG setting for still images. When it is turned on and File Format is set to XAVC S 4K or XAVC S HD, the camera also saves a copy of the video in a smaller file format (XAVC S HD, 1280 x 720 pixels, at 9 Mbps bit rate), giving you a second video file that is easier to share through social media and other means.

Because the copy is equivalent to the original in terms of frame rate and other attributes, it also can be used as a proxy file in video editing software that uses proxy editing. With that system, you can edit the smaller proxy file easily without having to wait for the computer to process effects and handle large files that can strain the memory and processor. Then, at the final editing stage, you can substitute the original, larger file for the final rendering of the video.

Proxy recording is not available when File Format is set to AVCHD, when Record Setting is set to 120p (100p with PAL systems), or when SteadyShot (Movies) is set to Intelligent Active.

I recommend leaving this option turned off unless you have a specific reason to use it.

AF Drive Speed

This option controls the speed at which the camera's autofocus system changes focus when recording video. The choices are Fast, Normal, or Slow. The Fast option is suitable for sports or other activities when the most important goal is to keep the subject in focus, and quick focus shifts are not a problem. The slower options are for use when you are shooting static or slow-moving subjects, and it may be preferable for focus to adjust gradually, to avoid jarring the audience with abrupt focus changes.

This option is particularly useful when you are using the touch screen features of the camera to carry out a "pull focus" action. As discussed in Chapter 6 in connection with the LCD screen, you can touch one spot on the screen, and then another, to shift the focus point, or you can drag the focus frame to a new location, depending on the focus area setting. The choice you make for AF Drive Speed will have a clear impact on the nature of the pull focus effect.

The setting you choose for this menu option depends on your preference and what you are trying to accomplish; you may want to experiment with all three and see which one suits your taste best for a given situation. This option is not available when Record Setting is set to a 120p setting (100p for PAL systems).

AF Tracking Sensitivity

This option, located after AF Drive Speed on the menu, controls how quickly the autofocus system tracks a moving subject when recording video. The choices are Responsive and Standard. With Responsive, the focus will shift quickly, to track a fast-moving subject. With Standard, the focus shifts at a moderate pace.

With the Standard setting, there is less risk that the camera will shift focus when an unwanted subject comes between the camera and the actual subject. For example, if a person walks in front of the camera while you are recording a scene in the distance, with the Standard setting the camera is likely to maintain focus on your actual subject, rather than quickly shifting focus to the person who is temporarily in the way. I recommend using the Standard setting unless you need to track a fast-moving subject, such as a runner in a track meet or a moving vehicle. This option is unavailable with the 120p/100p settings.

Auto Slow Shutter

This last item on screen 2 of the Camera Settings2 menu can be set either on or off. When it is turned on and the RX100 VI is recording a movie with autoexposure, the camera will automatically use a slower shutter speed than normal if the lighting is too dim to achieve proper exposure otherwise. The details of this option depend on the setting for Record Setting on screen 1 of the Camera Settings2 menu. (The File Format setting does not matter; the rules stated here apply for all File Format settings.)

If Record Setting is at a 60p or 60i setting, the camera normally will not use a shutter speed slower than 1/60 second. (In order to record 60 fields or frames per second with good quality, a shutter speed of 1/60 second is needed.) If Auto Slow Shutter is on, the camera can use a shutter speed as slow as 1/30 second.

If Record Setting is at one of the 30p settings, the camera ordinarily will use a shutter speed no slower than 1/30 second, but it will go down to 1/15 second with Auto Slow Shutter turned on.

If Record Setting is at a 24p setting, the camera ordinarily will use a shutter speed no slower than 1/50 second, but it will go down to 1/25 second with Auto Slow Shutter turned on. However, if Record setting is at one of the 120p settings (available only when File Format is set to XAVC S HD), the slowest shutter speed available is 1/125 second, and the Auto Slow Shutter option is not available.

Rather confusingly, the camera will let you turn on Auto Slow Shutter when the mode dial is set to Movie and Exposure Mode (Movies) is set to Shutter Priority or Manual Exposure. However, the setting you make for shutter speed will stay in place and the Auto Slow Shutter option will have no effect, even when the menu item is turned on. The same situation is true when the mode dial is set to the Shutter Priority or Manual exposure mode for stills. You can shoot video in those modes while adjusting the shutter speed and you can turn on Auto Slow Shutter, but that setting will have no effect; the shutter speed you set will take priority.

In addition, for the Auto Slow Shutter option to work, ISO must be set to Auto ISO.

The use of an unusually slow shutter speed can produce a slurred or blurry appearance because the shutter speed may not be fast enough to keep up with the motion in the scene. But, if you are recording in a dark area, this option can help you achieve properly exposed footage, so it is worth considering in that situation.

Audio Recording

Audio Recording, the first item on screen 3 of the Camera Settings2 menu, can be set either on or off. If you are certain you won't need the sound recorded by the camera, you can turn this option off. I never turn it off, because I can always turn down the volume of the recorded sound when playing the video. Or, if I am editing the video on a computer, I can delete the sound and replace it as needed—but there is no way to recapture the original audio after the fact if this option was turned off during the recording.

Micref Level

This option, whose screen is shown in Figure 9-11, can be set to Normal or Low. This setting controls how the camera records audio for movies using its built-in stereo microphone. With Normal, the default setting, the camera uses an automatic gain control to boost the level of quiet sounds to an audible volume. However, it also boosts the level of ambient sounds from sources such as heating or air conditioning equipment. You might want to use this setting if you are recording a speech or a small, relatively quiet event, so the camera will not miss any important sounds.

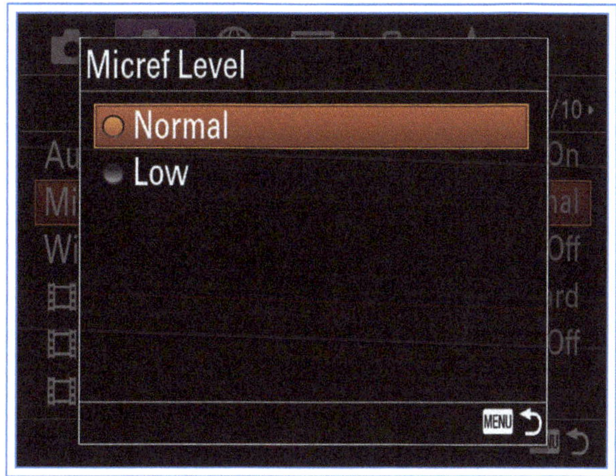

Figure 9-11. Micref Level Options Screen

The Low setting would be more appropriate when you are recording an event such as a concert, and you want to let the sound level vary according to the sound levels of the music without any artificial boosting or limiting.

Wind Noise Reduction

This option, if turned on, activates an electronic filter designed to reduce the volume of sounds in the frequencies of wind noise. I recommend not activating this feature unless the wind is strong, because it limits the sounds that are recorded. With video (or audio) editing software, you can remove sounds in the frequencies that may cause problems for the sound track, but using this built-in wind noise filter may permanently remove or alter some wanted sounds.

SteadyShot (Movies)

This SteadyShot (Movies) item on screen 3 of the Camera Settings2 menu, shown in Figure 9-12, is different from the SteadyShot (Still Images) item on screen 5 of that menu. (The Movies and Still Images designations are indicated by icons on the menu—a movie film icon for Movies and a mountain/landscape icon for Still Images.)

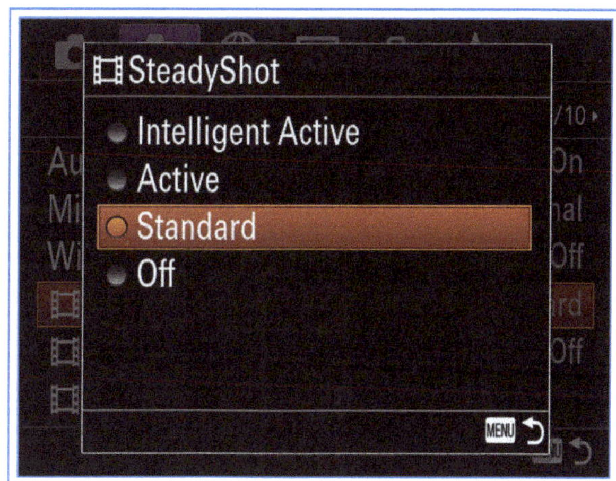

Figure 9-12. SteadyShot (Movies) Options Screen

As shown in Figure 9-12, the SteadyShot (Movies) setting offers four options: Off, Standard, Active, and Intelligent Active, unlike the Still Images version, which is limited to being turned on or off. With the Movies version, if you select Standard, the camera uses the same stabilization system used for shooting stills. If you select Active or Intelligent Active, the camera uses an additional electronic stabilizing system that can compensate for unwanted camera movement to a greater extent.

The Active and Intelligent Active settings are not available when File Format is set to XAVC S 4K or when Record Setting is set to a 120p setting (100p for PAL systems).

With the Active setting, the camera crops out parts of the image at the edges to compensate for the required processing of the image. With Intelligent Active, the camera uses an even stronger stabilizing effect and crops the frame even more heavily.

Figures 9-13 through 9-16 illustrate the cropping that results with the various settings of SteadyShot (Movies), using the same scene in each case. In Figure 9-13, SteadyShot (Movies) was turned off; in Figure 9-14 it was set to Standard; in Figure 9-15 to Active; and in Figure 9-16 to Intelligent Active.

As you can see, the Standard setting does not crop the frame, but the Active setting crops pixels from all four sides of the frame, and Intelligent Active crops even more pixels from all four sides.

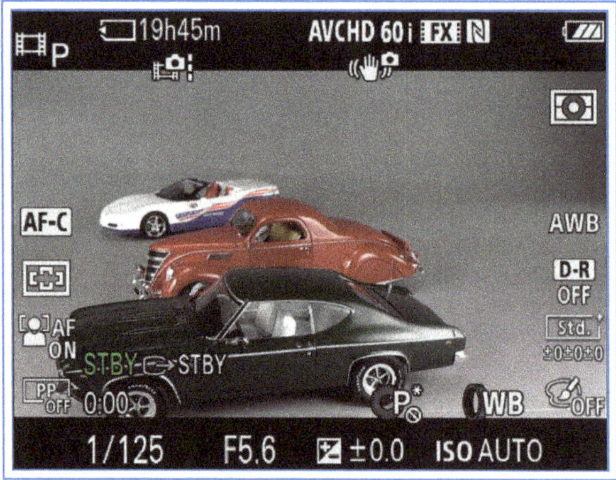

Figure 9-13. SteadyShot (Movies) Off

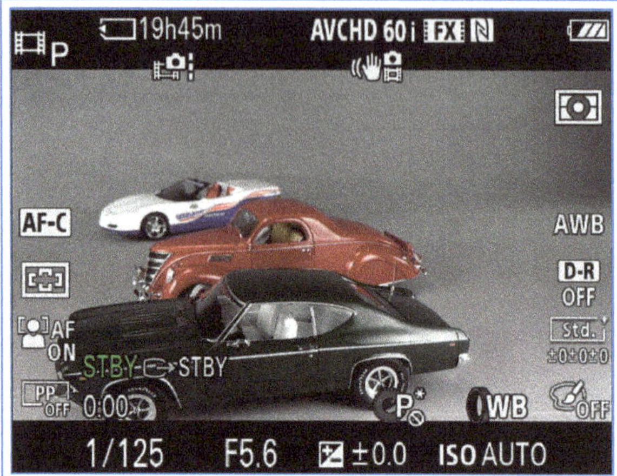

Figure 9-14. SteadyShot (Movies) Standard

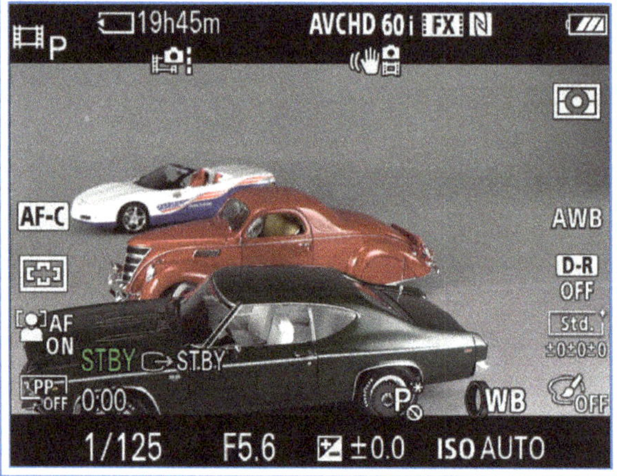

Figure 9-15. SteadyShot (Movies) Active

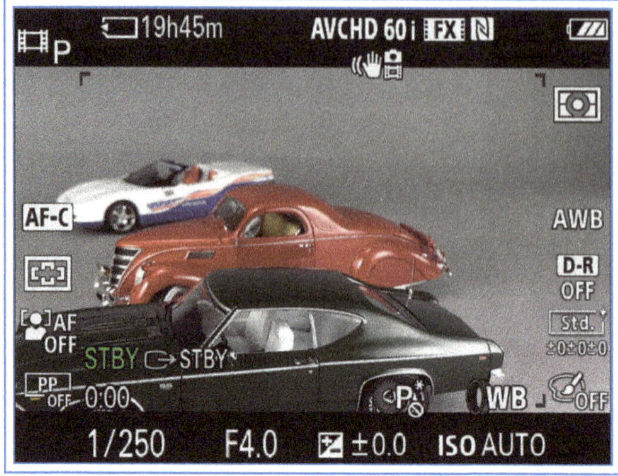

Figure 9-16. SteadyShot (Movies) Intelligent Active

I recommend using Standard in most cases to avoid the cropping that comes from using the Active or Intelligent Active setting. If you need to shoot movies when there is a great likelihood of camera movement, though, those two settings can be useful. They can be especially helpful if you need to hand-hold the camera as you walk. If the camera is on a tripod, you should turn SteadyShot (Movies) completely off.

Marker Display

This option, which can be turned either on or off, determines whether or not various informative guidelines, called "markers," are displayed on the camera's screen for movie recording. There are four special markers available, which outline the aspect ratio and other areas on the screen. Any or all of them can be selected for use with the Marker Settings menu option, directly after this one on this menu screen. If you turn Marker Display on, then any of the four markers that you have selected will be displayed on the shooting screen while a movie is being recorded in any mode. The markers also will be displayed while the mode dial is set to the Movie mode position or the HFR position, even before recording starts.

If this option is turned on, the selected markers will display on the camera's display screen, but they will not be recorded with the movie.

Marker Settings

This menu option works together with the Marker Display option, discussed above. This option lets you activate any or all of the four available markers—Center, Aspect, Safety Zone, and Guideframe.

If you turn on the Center marker, it places a cross in the center of the display, as illustrated in Figure 9-17. If you are shooting video in a busy or hectic environment, this marker may help you keep the main subject centered in the display so you don't cut it off.

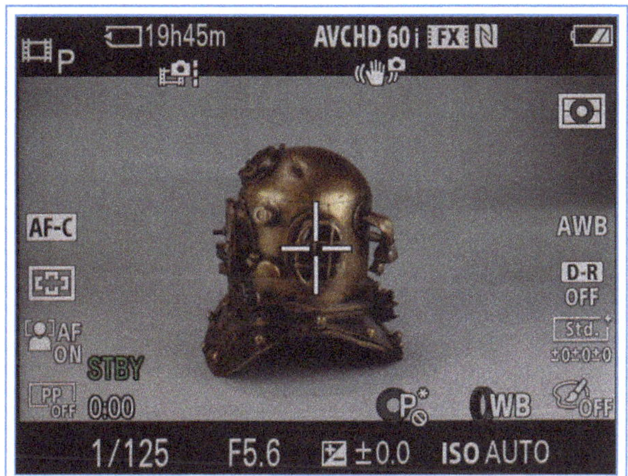

Figure 9-17. Center Marker in Use

The Aspect marker can be off or set to any one of seven settings: 4:3, 13:9, 14:9, 15:9, 1.66:1, 1.85:1, or 2.35:1. Figure 9-18 shows the display with the 2.35:1 setting.

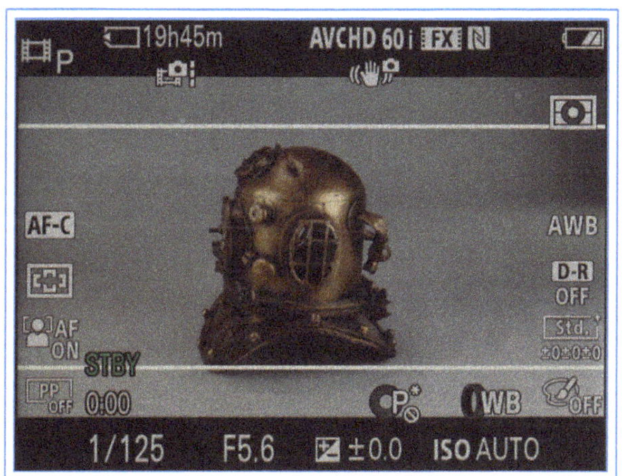

Figure 9-18. Aspect Marker 2.35:1 in Use

This setting places vertical white lines at the sides of the frame or horizontal white lines at the top and bottom of the frame, to outline the shape of the movie frame for the chosen aspect ratio. These lines are useful if you plan to alter the aspect ratio of your footage in post-production, to show what parts of the image will be cut off and help you frame your shots accordingly.

The Safety Zone marker can be off, or set to outline either 80% or 90% of the area of the display. The purpose of this marker's guidelines is to provide a margin for safety, because the average consumer television set may not display the entire video signal provided to it. If you set these lines to mark a safety zone, you can make sure your important subjects are included in the area that definitely will be displayed on most television sets. Figure 9-19 shows the display with the 80% safety zone activated.

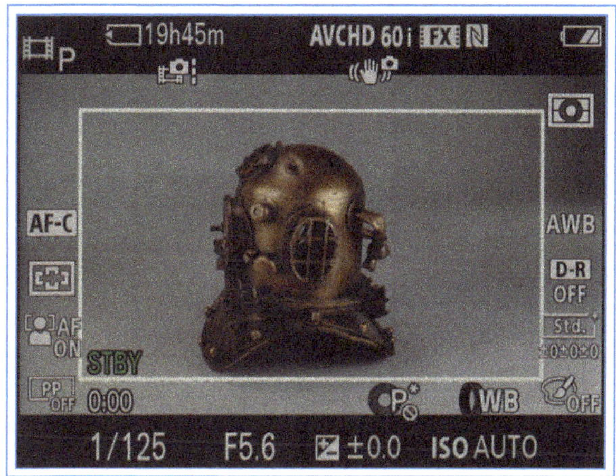

Figure 9-19. 80% Safety Zone in Use

Finally, the Guideframe option, if turned on, displays a grid that is similar to the Rule of Thirds grid available with the Grid Line option, discussed earlier in this chapter. That option uses thin, black lines, which may be hard to see when you are shooting video under difficult conditions. The bold, white lines of the Guideframe setting should be more useful for video shooting. You cannot use both options at the same time; Grid Line is not available when Marker Display is turned on. Figure 9-20 shows the Guideframe option in use.

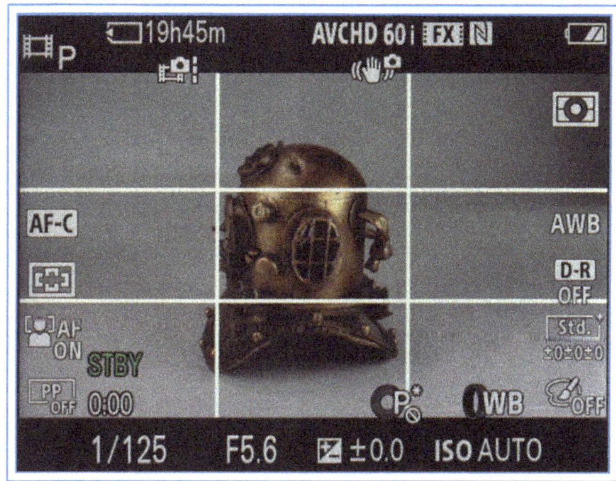

Figure 9-20. Guideframe Option in Use

Movie w/Shutter

This single option on screen 4 of the Camera Settings2 menu can be turned either on or off. If it is turned on, you can start and stop movie recording by pressing the shutter button when the camera is set to Movie mode or HFR mode, for high frame rate. If it is left off, you have to press the red Movie button to start or stop movie recording. Some people find it more natural to use the shutter button to control the recording process, because the button is directly under the right index finger.

Turning this option on does not reduce the functionality of the shutter button for taking still images when the camera is not recording video, because you cannot take still images when the mode dial is at the Movie or HFR position when the camera is not recording video. When the camera is recording video with the mode dial at the Movie position, you normally can take still images, depending on other settings. However, if you turn on the Movie w/Shutter option, pressing the shutter button during video recording with the mode dial at the Movie position will stop the video recording, and will not capture a still image. So, with this setting turned on you give up the ability to capture still images during video recording in Movie mode.

Zoom Setting

This first option on screen 6 of the Camera Settings2 menu lets you choose Clear Image Zoom or Digital Zoom, to expand the zoom range of the lens beyond the normal optical limit of 200mm. It functions for movie recording as it does for capturing still images, as discussed in Chapter 5. However, the settings beyond optical zoom are not available for use when Record Setting is set to 120p (100p for cameras using the PAL system), or when recording high frame rate video with the mode dial at the HFR position. In addition, although this is not a feature of the Zoom Setting menu option, the Smart Zoom function, which increases zoom range when the JPEG Image Size setting is lower than Large, does not work when shooting movies.

Zoom Speed

This second option on screen 6 of the Camera Settings2 menu lets you select Normal or Fast for the speed of zooming the lens using the zoom lever. It works to increase the speed of zooming for movie recording also, though that speed is slower than for still images, with either setting for this menu item. With the Fast setting, there is more risk of recording the sound of the zooming lens.

Zoom Function on Ring

This final option on screen 6 of the Camera Settings2 menu determines how the control ring zooms the lens, when it is set to that function. It works for movies as for still images. However, as with the Zoom Speed option, discussed above, although the Quick setting increases the speed of zooming, that speed still is slower for movies than for still images. In addition, if you choose Step for this option, the step zoom function does not work when recording movies.

Zebra Setting

This third option on screen 7 of the Camera Settings2 menu controls the use of the Zebra stripes to help you gauge exposure. This option is very useful for video recording, and it functions for movie recording in the same way as for still images, as discussed in Chapter 5.

Movie Button

This first item on screen 10 of the Camera Settings2 menu is the final video-related option to be discussed here. As discussed earlier, you can set this option to Always or Movie Mode Only, to control whether the red Movie button (or another button assigned to the same function) can start and stop a movie recording with the mode dial at any position (except HFR), or only when the mode dial is at the Movie position. I generally leave it set to Always.

Effects of Mode Dial Position on Recording Movies

The second category of setting that affects video recording with the RX100 VI is the position of the mode dial. As I discussed above, you can shoot normal-speed movies with the dial in any position except HFR (if the Movie Button menu option is set to Always), and you can get access to many movie-related menu items no matter what position the dial is in. However, as I noted above, the shooting mode does make some difference for your movie options.

First, the position you select on the mode dial determines whether you can adjust the aperture and/or shutter speed for your movies. If the dial is set to the Auto, Scene, Program, or Sweep Panorama mode, the camera will set both aperture and shutter speed automatically. However, if the dial is set to the Aperture Priority, Shutter Priority, or Manual exposure position, you will be able to adjust the aperture, shutter speed, or both aperture and shutter speed, just as you can when shooting still images. The range of available shutter speeds is different for movies than for still images, but you can make those adjustments at any time.

You also can make those adjustments when the mode dial is set to the Movie position and you select one of the more advanced exposure modes using the Exposure Mode (Movies) item on screen 1 of the Camera Settings2 menu. For example, as discussed earlier in this chapter, if you select Manual Exposure for Exposure Mode with the mode dial at the Movie position, you can adjust both aperture and shutter speed for your movies, in the same way as if the mode dial were set to the M position. (If you set the mode dial to the HFR setting, you can shoot high frame rate movies, which will play back as slow-motion movies. I will discuss those options in a separate HFR section later in this chapter.)

Because of the ability to adjust aperture and shutter speed in the advanced still-shooting modes, you might wonder why you would ever use the Movie position on the dial—why not just set the dial to A, S, or M if you want to adjust aperture and/or shutter speed while recording a movie, or to P if you want the camera to set the aperture and shutter speed automatically?

The answer is that several options or settings are available only when the mode dial is at the Movie position. For one thing, you will see how the video recording will be framed before you press the Movie button to start recording. If the mode dial is at one of the still-oriented positions such as Auto, Scene, or one of the PASM modes, the display will show the live view according to the current setting for Aspect Ratio on screen 1 of the Camera Settings1 menu. If that setting is 3:2, 4:3, or 1:1, it will not correspond to the framing of the video, which will be recorded in a widescreen format, until you press the Movie button to start recording. (If Aspect Ratio is set to 16:9, the framing will show approximately how the video framing will look before you press the Movie button.)

With the mode dial at the Movie position, the camera adjusts the view to show how the video will look before you press the Movie button, so you will know before you start recording how to set up the shot to include all of the needed background and foreground elements.

In addition, when the mode dial is at the Movie position, you can take advantage of the Movie Button menu option, on screen 10 of the Camera Settings2 menu, to limit normal-speed video recording to that one shooting mode. In this way, you can make it impossible to start a recording accidentally by pressing the Movie button when the mode dial is set to a still-oriented mode such as Auto, Scene, or one of the PASM modes. If that option is set to Movie Mode Only, you will need to turn the mode dial to the Movie position in order to record a video.

Moreover, several menu options are not available unless the mode dial is at the Movie position. In particular, on screen 4 of the Setup menu, the 4K Output Select option is not available, nor are most of the sub-settings of the TC/UB Settings option on screen 3 of that menu. All of these settings can be useful when recording to an external video recorder. In addition, the Marker Display option on screen 3 of the Camera Settings2 menu can be selected in any shooting mode, but any marker you have selected for display will not appear in still-oriented modes until you actually start recording a video. When the mode dial is at the Movie position (or the HFR position), you will see the marker on the display before the recording starts, so you can set up your composition ahead of time.

Also, the camera's shooting mode has an effect on what options are available on the Camera Settings1 menu and with the control buttons, as discussed in following sections of this chapter. For example, if the mode dial is set to Auto, Sweep Panorama, or Scene, the Camera Settings1 menu options are limited. If the mode dial is set to Program, Aperture Priority, Shutter Priority, or Manual exposure, the options are greater. This point is important for video shooting because, as discussed below, several important Camera Settings1 menu options carry over to movie recording.

If the camera is set to Program mode (P on the mode dial), you can make several settings that will affect the recording of videos while the mode dial is in that position. The camera will set the aperture and shutter speed automatically, as it does with still-image shooting. You can use exposure compensation to vary the exposure, but only within the range of plus or minus 2 EV, instead of the 3-EV positive or negative range for still shooting.

If the camera is set to Aperture Priority mode (A on the mode dial), you will have the same Camera Settings1 menu options as in Program mode, and you can also set the aperture; the camera will set the shutter speed automatically, but the range of available shutter speeds will be somewhat different than for still images. That range is also affected by the Record Setting option selected and the setting of the Auto Slow Shutter menu option, as discussed earlier in this chapter.

If the camera is set to Shutter Priority mode (S on the mode dial), you will have the same Camera Settings1 menu options as in Program mode, and you can also set the shutter speed. You can set it anywhere from 1/4 second (the camera's slowest setting for movies) to 1/12800 second (the camera's fastest setting for movies), regardless of the Record Setting or Auto Slow Shutter settings, with one exception. The one exception is that the slowest setting available is 1/125 second when Record Setting is set to either of the 120p settings (100p for the PAL system), which are available when File Format (Movies) is set to XAVC S HD.

If the camera is set to Manual exposure mode (M on the mode dial), you will have the same Camera Settings1 menu options as before. You can set both shutter speed and aperture, with the same restrictions for shutter speed settings noted above for Shutter Priority mode.

If the camera is set to Sweep Panorama mode, it will act largely as if it were set to Movie mode with the Program Auto exposure mode selected. If it is set to Scene mode, it will shoot movies as if it were set to Intelligent Auto mode, in which limited menu options are available. It will not change its behavior for scene settings such as Portrait, Sports Action, or Sunset. However, according to Sony, it will alter settings for the High Sensitivity setting. (I was not able to verify that point.)

There is a lot of information involved in outlining the differences in the RX100 VI's behavior for video recording in different shooting modes, so I am including here a table that lays out the more important differences, for reference.

Table 9-1. Behavior of RX100 VI for Video Recording in Various Shooting Modes

Shooting Mode:	Auto	Scene	Panorama	HFR	Movie	M	S	A	P
Adjust Aperture During Video Recording	No	No	No	Before recording only; depends on Exposure Mode (HFR) menu option setting	Depends on Exposure Mode (Movies) menu option setting	Yes	No	Yes	No
Adjust Shutter Speed During Video Recording	No	No	No	Before recording only; depends on Exposure Mode (HFR) menu option	Depends on Exposure Mode (Movies) menu option setting	Yes	Yes	No	No
See Video Framing Before Recording Starts	No	No	No	Yes	Yes	No	No	No	No
Use 4K Output Select	No	No	No	No	Yes	No	No	No	No
Use All TC/UB Settings Options	No	No	No	All except TC Run	Yes	No	No	No	No
See Marker Display Items Before Recording Starts	No	No	No	Yes	Yes	No	No	No	No
Use 120p/100p Record Setting Options	No	No	Yes	No	Yes	Yes	Yes	Yes	Yes
Can record video if Movie Button Menu Option is set to Movie Mode Only	No	No	No	HFR video only	Yes	No	No	No	No

Effects of Camera Settings1 Menu Settings on Recording Movies

Although the settings on the Camera Settings1 menu are largely oriented toward still images, several of them affect the recording of movies. I will discuss those options in this section.

One of the main reasons the shooting mode is important for movies is that, just as with still photography, some menu options are not available in some modes. For example, in an advanced still-shooting mode like Aperture Priority or Program, video recording is affected by the settings for focus area, ISO, metering mode, white balance, DRO, Creative

Style, Picture Effect, Picture Profile, Focus Magnifier, Face Priority in AF, and Face Priority in Multi Meter. In some cases, you can adjust these settings while the video is being recorded. You cannot get access to the Camera Settings1 menu by pressing the Menu button; you have to use a control button, the Function menu, or the control ring to call up the item to adjust. Of course, you have to have that setting assigned to the button, menu, or ring ahead of time.

For example, you can adjust ISO while recording a video, but only if you have assigned ISO to the control ring or one of the control buttons using the Custom Key (Movies) option on screen 9 of the Camera Settings2 menu, or to the Function menu.

Another option from the Camera Settings1 menu that is particularly useful for video recording is Picture Profile, found on screen 9 of that menu. Although Picture Profile is applicable for both still images and video recording, it is really oriented for shooting video. I discussed the details of its settings in Chapter 4. If you want to have the greatest amount of dynamic range available in your video sequences and are willing to go through the effort of color grading your clips with post-processing software, you can choose PP7, PP8, PP9, or PP10 for the Picture Profile setting, to take advantage of one of the S-Log or HLG settings for gamma curve. Otherwise, choose one of the lower-numbered profiles, or no profile at all. If you want to get involved with parameters such as gamma, black level, detail, and knee, you can create your own profile with the settings you prefer.

If you want to experiment with different Picture Profile settings, you can assign this menu option to one of the control buttons using the Custom Key (Movies) option on screen 9 of the Camera Settings2 menu or to the Function menu. You can then call up different Picture Profile settings while recording a video, to see how they affect the recording.

If you use a profile that includes an S-Log or HLG gamma setting, you can use the Gamma Display Assist option, discussed in Chapter 8, to increase the apparent contrast of the footage as it is displayed by the camera during recording and playback, so it will be easier to judge matters such as composition, exposure, and focus.

Table 9-2 shows which of these settings can be adjusted while a video recording is in progress, when the camera is set to a shooting mode in which that adjustment is possible.

Table 9-2. Camera Settings1 Menu Items that Affect Movies and Can Be Adjusted Before or During Video Recording

Camera Settings1 Menu Item	Carries Over to Video if Adjusted Before Video Recording	Can Adjust During Video Recording
Focus Mode	Yes	Yes
Focus Area	Yes	Yes
Center Lock-on AF	Yes	Yes
Set Face Priority in AF	Yes	No
Display Contin. AF Area	No	No
Phase Detection Area	No	No
Exposure Compensation	Yes	Yes
ISO	Yes	Yes
Metering Mode	Yes	No
Face Priority in Multi Mtr	Yes	No
Spot Metering Point	Yes	No
White Balance	Yes	No
Priority Set in AWB	Yes	No
DRO	Yes	No
Creative Style	Yes	No
Picture Effect	Yes	No
Picture Profile	Yes	Yes
Focus Magnifier	N/A	Yes
Focus Magnif. Time	Yes	No
Peaking Display	Yes	Yes
Peaking Level	Yes	Yes
Peaking Color	Yes	Yes

There are built-in limitations with some of these settings. Exposure compensation can be adjusted to plus or minus 2.0EV only, rather than the 3.0EV range for still images. The ISO range includes Auto ISO and specific values from 125 to 12800, omitting the two lowest settings. Also, you cannot set ISO to Multi Frame Noise Reduction, which would cause the camera to take multiple shots. With Picture Effect, you can use some of the sub-settings, but not all. The settings that are unavailable for movie recording are Soft Focus, HDR Painting, Rich-tone Monochrome, Miniature, Watercolor, and Illustration. (As noted on the table, you cannot get access to the Picture Effect settings during video recording.)

Also, you can use the focus mode option to change focus modes while recording a movie. However, the only two modes available for video recording are continuous autofocus and manual focus. If you set the mode to the S, A, C, or DMF option, the camera will use continuous autofocus. If you choose MF, the camera will use manual focus.

There are some other options on the Camera Settings1 menu that have no effect for recording movies. Some of these settings are clearly incompatible with shooting movies, such as drive mode, flash mode, and Auto Object Framing. Some are less obvious, such as AF Illuminator.

There are two other points to make about using Camera Settings1 menu settings for movies. First, you have a great deal of flexibility in choosing settings for your movies, even when the camera is not set to the Movie position on the mode dial. You can set up the camera with the ISO, metering mode, white balance, Creative Style, Picture Effect (to some extent), or other settings of your choice, and then press the Movie button to record using those settings. In this way, you could, for example, record a black-and-white movie in a dark environment using a high ISO setting. Or, you could record a movie that is monochrome except for a broad selection of red objects, using the Partial Color-Red effect from the Picture Effect option, with the red color expanded using the color axis adjustments of the white balance setting. (Note that you can't use Creative Style and Picture Effect settings at the same time.)

Second, you have to be careful to check the settings that are in effect for still photos before you press the Movie button. For example, if you have been shooting stills using the Posterization setting from the Picture Effect menu option and then suddenly see an event that you want to record on video, if you press the Movie button, the movie will be recorded using the Posterization effect, making the resulting footage practically impossible to use as a clear record of the events.

Of course, you may notice this problem as you record the video, but it takes time to stop the recording, change the menu setting to turn off the Picture Effect option, and then press the Movie button again, and you may have missed a crucial part of the action by the time you start recording again.

One way to lessen the risk of recording video with unwanted Camera Settings1 menu options is to switch the mode dial to the Auto position before pressing the Movie button. That action will cause the camera to use more automatic settings and will disable the Creative Style and Picture Effect options altogether. (Of course, you have to have the Movie Button item on screen 10 of the Camera Settings2 menu set to Always for this approach to work.)

Effects of Physical Controls When Recording Movies

The next settings that carry over to some extent from still-shooting to video recording are those set by the physical controls. In this case, as with Camera Settings1 menu items, there are differences depending on the position of the mode dial. I will not try to describe every possible combination of shooting mode and physical control, but I will discuss some settings to be aware of.

First, the touch screen operates during video recording, but in a somewhat different way than it does for shooting still images, assuming the touch screen features are turned on through the Touch Operation item on screen 3 of the Setup menu and the touch panel is turned on through the menu option below that one.

If focus area is set to Wide, Zone, or Center and Center Lock-on AF is off, you can touch the screen to select a focus point, and the camera will direct its focus to that point. It will not display a focus frame, but the focus will become sharp at that point. At the same time, the camera will switch the focus mode to manual focus so focus will stay locked at that point. It stays in manual focus mode until you touch the screen at another point, or touch the finger icon with an X that turns off the touch focus feature. You can use this feature, which Sony calls "spot focus," to carry out a "pull-focus" operation by touching one subject and then another. The speed of that operation is governed by the setting for AF Drive Speed on screen 2 of the Camera Settings2 menu.

If focus area is set to Flexible Spot or Expand Flexible Spot, you can drag the focus frame to a new location, and the camera will focus at the new point. You can use this operation for a "pull focus" effect by dragging the focus frame from one subject to another. You also can tap any spot to set a new focus frame, but the camera does not switch to manual focus as it does when focus area is set to Wide or Center, as discussed above.

If manual focus mode is in use, you can tap twice on the screen to enlarge the view.

Second, the Function button operates normally. For example, if the mode dial is set to P for Program mode, then, after you press the Movie button to start recording a movie, you can press the Function button and the Function menu will appear on the screen. This menu will let you control only those items that can be controlled under current conditions.

If you start recording a movie while the mode dial is set to a mode such as Auto in which most options on the Function menu are not available, the RX100 VI will display the menu, but few items will be available for selection.

Third, if you assign the Custom, Center, Left, or Right button or the control ring to carry out an operation using the Custom Key (Movies) option on screen 9 of the Camera Settings2 menu, you can use that button or ring to perform the operation while recording a movie if the action is compatible with movie recording in the current shooting mode.

There are numerous options that can be assigned to a control button or the control ring that will function during video recording, if the current context permits that control. For example, if the Left button is set to control ISO and you are shooting a movie with the mode dial set to P, pressing the Left button will bring up the ISO menu and you can select a value while the movie is recording. If the mode dial is set to Auto, though, pressing the button will have no effect during recording, because ISO cannot be adjusted in that shooting mode.

If the Center button is assigned the Focus Standard setting through the Custom Key (Movies) menu option and Center Lock-on AF is turned on through screen 4 of the Camera Settings1 menu, you can press the Center button during video recording to activate tracking focus. Of course, to use tracking focus, you have to have an autofocus mode selected for the focus mode.

If you set a control button to the AEL Hold or AEL Toggle function, you can press that button while recording a movie to lock the exposure setting. This ability can be useful when recording a movie, when you don't want the exposure to change as you move the camera over different areas of a scene.

Following is a list of functions that can be assigned to one of the control buttons, the control ring, or the Function menu and that can be controlled during video recording by pressing the assigned button, turning the ring, or using that menu. I created this list by checking each item that appears on the menu screens under the Custom Key (Movies) item on screen 9 of the Camera Settings2 menu. Each of these items can be activated during the recording of a video.

- Focus Mode
- AF/MF Control Hold
- AF/MF Control Toggle
- Focus Standard
- Focus Area
- Center Lock-on AF
- Exposure Compensation
- ISO
- AEL Hold
- AEL Toggle
- Spot AEL Hold
- Spot AEL Toggle
- Picture Profile
- Focus Magnifier
- Peaking Display Select (on or off)
- Peaking Level
- Peaking Color
- In-Camera Guide (can be used if Fn menu displayed)
- Movie (button operates to start/stop video recording)
- Frame Rate (HFR)
- Auto Dual Recording
- Marker Display Select
- Finder/Monitor Select (if viewfinder is popped up)

- Zebra Display Select
- Zebra Level
- Grid Line
- Audio Signals
- Gamma Display Assist
- Touch Operation Select (on or off)
- TC/UB Display Switch (switches among counter, time code, and user bit displays)

High Frame Rate Recording

The RX100 VI camera is equipped with an excellent ability to record video at a higher-than-normal frame rate, which results in slow-motion sequences when played back at a normal rate. If you are using the NTSC system, you can record at a rate as high as 960 frames per second (fps); with the PAL system, you can record at up to 1000 fps. With either system, you can create a video sequence to be played back in the camera at up to 40 times slower than normal. Because there are several settings and steps to be taken to use this feature, I will provide a step-by-step guide.

1. Make sure the camera has a memory card inserted that meets the requirements for HFR recording—an SDHC or SDXC card rated in speed class 10, speed class UHS-1, or faster.
2. Set the mode dial to HFR, as shown in Figure 9-21.

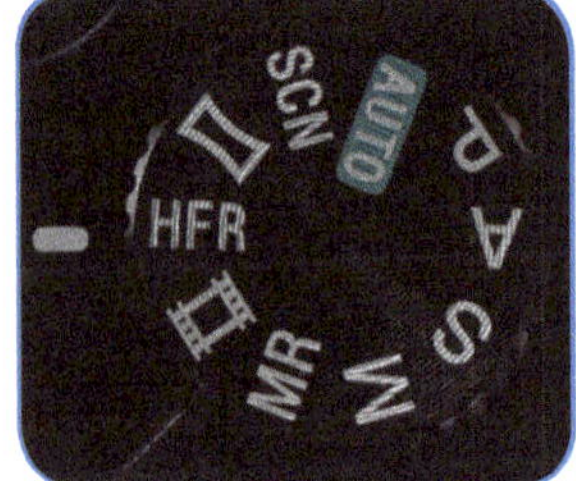

Figure 9-21. Mode Dial at HFR

3. On screen 1 of the Camera Settings2 menu, highlight the second option, Exposure Mode (HFR), and select one of the available exposure modes, as shown in Figure 9-22—Program Auto, Aperture Priority, Shutter Priority, or Manual Exposure.

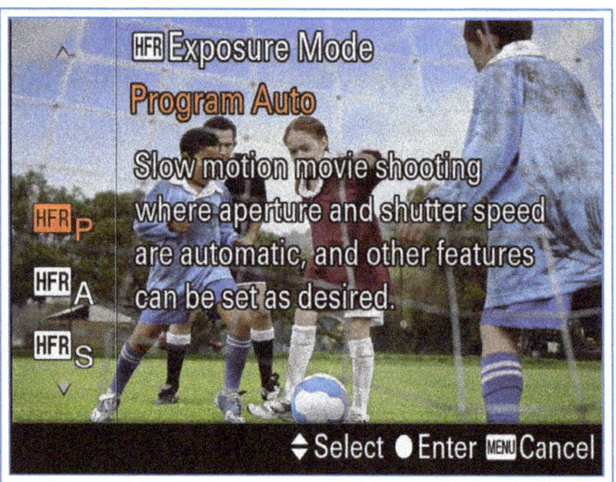

Figure 9-22. Exposure Mode (HFR) Options Screen

4. These modes are similar to those for normal-speed movie shooting, discussed earlier in this chapter. If you choose S or M, the shutter speed that can be set will depend on the Frame Rate setting you make in Step 8. For example, if you select 480 fps for the Frame Rate, the shutter speed will have to be 1/500 second or faster.
5. Make any control or menu adjustments that are needed. For example, if you selected Aperture Priority for the exposure mode, set the aperture. Set ISO, metering mode, white balance, and any other available settings, if needed. Set the focus mode to AF-C or MF, as you wish. Select the zoom amount for the lens and adjust the focus for your subject. None of these items can be adjusted after the screen has been switched to standby mode for HFR shooting.

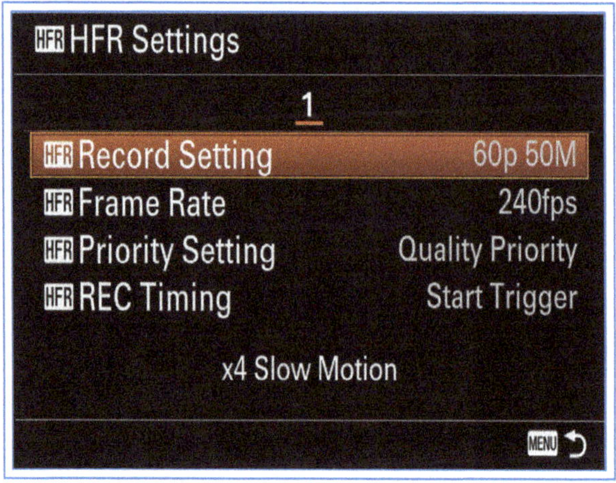

Figure 9-23. HFR Settings Options Screen

6. On screen 1 of the Camera Settings2 menu, highlight HFR Settings and press the Center

button. You will see a screen like that in Figure 9-23.

7. On this screen, set Record Setting as you want it. This setting is not related to the more general Record Setting option on the same menu screen. This setting sets the frame rate for playback of your slow-motion videos. If your camera is set for the NTSC system, the choices for Record Setting are 60p, 30p, or 24p. The bit rate is set at 50M for each of the three settings. The video will be recorded using the XAVC S HD format. For highest quality of the final video, select 60p. For the greatest amount of slowing down of the final video, select 24p.

8. Go back to the menu options and select Frame Rate. The choices are 240 fps, 480 fps, or 960 fps. You can determine how slow the slow-motion footage will be by dividing this number by the Record Setting figure. For example, if Frame Rate is 480 and Record Setting is 30, the final video will be slowed down 16 times when played back in the camera.

9. For Priority Setting, choose Quality Priority or Shoot Time Priority. This setting lets you decide whether it is more important to shoot for a longer time or with higher quality. If you choose Quality Priority, you can record for about three or four seconds; with Shoot Time Priority, you can record for about six or seven seconds but at considerably lower resolution.

10. For Rec Timing, choose Start Trigger, End Trigger, or End Trigger Half. With Start Trigger, the camera will start the brief recording when you press the Movie button, and will record for the next few seconds. With End Trigger, it will end the recording when you press the Movie button, and will capture whatever action it was aimed at for the previous few seconds. With End Trigger Half, it will record only half the time of End Trigger, and the recording process will be finished twice as soon, so you can return to recording a new sequence more quickly. If the action you are trying to record is predictable, you can use the Start Trigger option. If you need to wait and see which few seconds are most worth capturing before you decide, choose End Trigger and push the Movie button quickly after seeing the action you want to record. To avoid having the camera tied up in a long recording process, choose End Trigger Half. Press the Menu button to return to the live view.

11. You will see a screen like that in Figure 9-24, with a message indicating to press the Center button to enter Shooting Standby mode. At this point, you can still press the Menu button to adjust menu options if needed. (If you don't see this screen, press the Display button until it appears.)

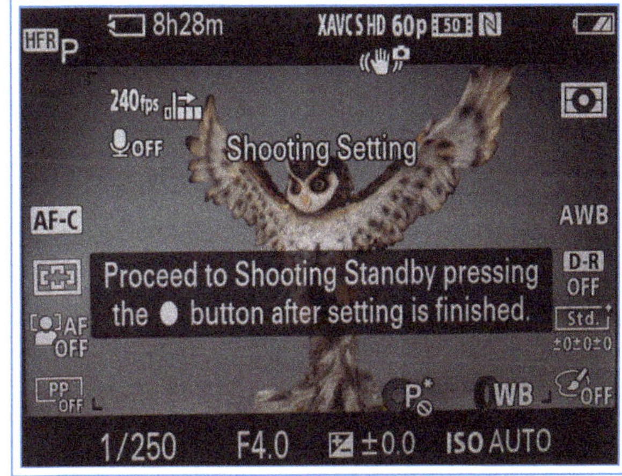

Figure 9-24. Message: Press Center Button for Standby

12. When you are ready to start recording, press the Center button. The camera will briefly display a Preparing . . . message, followed by a message saying Starts Recording with MOVIE Button, and then the screen shown in Figure 9-25, with a green STBY label, for Standby, in the lower left corner.

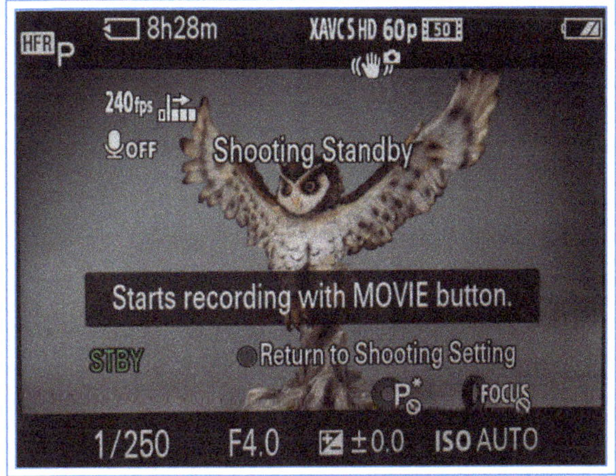

Figure 9-25. HFR Recording Standby Screen

13. The camera is now in standby mode, waiting for you to press the Movie button to mark the start or end of the brief HFR sequence. (To adjust settings at this point, press the Center button to exit standby

mode and make the settings; press the Center button again to return to standby mode.)

14. If you selected Start Trigger for the recording option, wait until you believe the few seconds of action you want to capture is about to start, and press the Movie button just before it starts, if possible. If you selected End Trigger or End Trigger Half, wait until the few seconds of action has just happened, and immediately press the Movie button. In either case, the camera will display a Buffering . . . label, then a red Recording . . . label near the top of the screen and a red REC label in the lower left corner. It will then show a recording screen. This screen may appear for a fairly long time—much longer than the few seconds of action that was captured—depending on the settings used. You can press the Center button to cancel the recording while that screen is displayed.
15. When the Shooting Standby screen returns, you can press the Playback button to view the recording. On the memory card, the video will have a file path such as Untitled:PRIVATE:M4ROOT:CLIP:C0112.mp4.

The HFR feature can produce beautiful videos under the right conditions. Because of the very fast recording rate, it is important to have as much light as possible to achieve excellent quality. I recommend using Quality Priority for the Priority Setting option, unless you have a definite need to record for six or seven seconds instead of three or four seconds. Note that the video quality decreases as the slowdown factor increases, so take that factor into consideration when choosing settings. Finally, note that high frame rate videos are recorded with no sound.

Recording to an External Video Recorder

For recording everyday videos such as clips of vacations or family events, the RX100 VI will serve you well. However, Sony also has equipped this camera with options that make it suitable for some aspects of professional video production. Several of these options are designed for use when the camera sends video to an external video recorder. I will not try to discuss all possible scenarios for using the RX100 VI with a recorder, but I will describe the steps I took to record video with the camera connected to an Atomos Shogun 4K recorder, discussed in Appendix A. I will describe the process I used for doing this, with the caveat that there undoubtedly are many other approaches that will work; this happens to be one that worked for me.

First, make sure the Shogun is powered by a battery or power supply and has a formatted storage disk installed. I used a SanDisk Extreme Pro 480 GB solid state drive (SSD). Connect headphones to monitor sound. On the Input menu, enable HDMI input and HDMI Trigger. I selected Apple ProRes HQ as the recording format.

Connect the HDMI input port of the Shogun to the HDMI output port of the RX100 VI using a micro HDMI cable. Make sure the camera has an SDHC or SDXC memory card with a speed of UHS Speed Class 3. Then turn on both the camera and the recorder and make the settings on the camera shown in Table 9-3.

Table 9-3. **Recommended Settings on RX100 VI Camera for Recording 4K Video to an Atomos Shogun Recorder**

CAMERA SETTINGS1 MENU	
Focus Mode	AF-C
Focus Area	Wide
Switch V/H AF Area	Off
AF Illuminator	Auto
Center Lock-on AF	Off
Set Face Priority in AF	Off
ISO	ISO Auto
Metering Mode	Multi
White Balance	Auto White Balance
Priority Set in AWB	Standard
DRO/Auto HDR	Off
Creative Style	Standard
Picture Effect	Off
Picture Profile	PP1, or other preferred
CAMERA SETTINGS2 MENU	
Exposure Mode (Movies)	Program Auto
File Format	XAVC S 4K
Record Setting	30p 100M
Quality (Dual Recording)	Extra Fine
Image Size (Dual Recording)	L:17M
Auto Dual Recording	Off (Not Available)
Proxy Recording	Off
AF Drive Speed	Normal
AF Tracking Sensitivity	Standard
Auto Slow Shutter	Off
Audio Recording	On

MicRef Level	Normal
Wind Noise Reduction	Off
SteadyShot (Movies)	Standard, or Off if using tripod
Marker Display	On if needed
Marker Settings	As needed
Movie w/Shutter	On if desired
Zoom Setting	Optical Zoom Only
Zoom Speed	Normal
Zoom Function on Ring	Standard
Zebra Setting	Off unless needed
Grid Line	Off
Exposure Settings Guide	Off
Av/Tv Rotate	Normal
SETUP MENU	
Gamma Display Assist	Off unless needed
NTSC/PAL Selector	NTSC (in U.S., etc.)
Touch Operation	On
Touch Panel/Pad	Touch Panel+Pad
TC/UB Settings	
TC/UB Display Setting	TC
TC Preset	00:00:00:00
UB Preset	00 00 00 00
TC Format	DF
TC Run	Rec Run
TC Make	Preset
UB Time Rec	Off
HDMI Settings	
HDMI Resolution	Auto
24p/60p Output	60p
HDMI Info Display	Off (Not Available)
TC Output	On
REC Control	On
HDMI Audio Output	On
4K Output Select	Memory Card + HDMI

Some of the above settings are optional or unnecessary and some, such as white balance and metering mode, can be changed according to your preferences. The important ones are File Format, Record Setting, the TC/UB settings, and the HDMI settings. I have not listed some other settings that are unlikely to be needed, such as Touch Pad Settings, CTRL for HDMI, and several others.

Once the connections and settings are made, press the Movie button on the RX100 VI. The screen on the Shogun recorder should indicate that the recording has begun. Use the controls on the camera to zoom or adjust settings as needed. When you are ready to stop the recording, press the Movie button again, and the recorder should stop.

I tried a modified version of these settings with no SD card in the camera, setting 4K Output Select on the Setup menu to HDMI Only (30p). The Shogun recorded as expected, and I was able to record well beyond the normal five-minute limit for 4K recording because there was no memory card in the camera.

Shooting Still Images During Video Recording

The RX100 VI can shoot still images while recording video, with some limitations. You cannot capture stills when File Format (Movies) on screen 1 of the Camera Settings2 menu is set to the XAVC S 4K format. If File Format is set to XAVC S HD, you have to have Record Setting set to the 60p, 30p, or 24p setting. You can use any Record Setting values for AVCHD videos. The camera can be set to any shooting mode, except HFR.

You cannot capture still images during video recording if Picture Profile is turned on through screen 9 of the Camera Settings1 menu or if Proxy Recording is turned on through screen 2 of the Camera Settings2 menu. If the camera is set to Movie mode, you can capture still images during video recording, but you cannot capture still images when the camera is not recording video. If you press the shutter button when the camera is not recording, you will see an error message (unless you have turned on the Movie w/Shutter option on screen 4 of the Camera Settings2 menu, in which case the camera will start recording a movie).

To control the size and quality of the still images you capture, use the Quality (Dual Recording) and Image Size (Dual Recording) items on screens 1 and 2 of the Camera Settings2 menu. The choices for quality are Extra Fine, Fine, or Standard. The choices for size are L:17M, M:7.5M, or S:4.2M. The images will be captured in the widescreen format of the video (aspect ratio of 16:9). There is no option for capturing Raw images during video shooting.

Assuming you have the mode dial set to a compatible shooting mode and File Format (Movies) and Record Setting set to compatible values, with no conflicting settings in place, once the movie is recording, just press the shutter button at any time to capture a still image. The camera will display a green CAPTURE message at the top of the screen. (If it is not possible to capture a still image with current settings, the camera will display a camera icon with a negative symbol next to it.) There is no limit on the number of still images you can capture in this way, other than the space available on the memory card. You cannot use the camera's built-in flash when shooting still images during video recording.

There is another option to be aware of for shooting still images during video recording—the Auto Dual Recording feature, found on screen 2 of the Camera Settings2 menu. I discussed this option earlier in this chapter. When you turn this setting on, the camera is programmed to automatically capture still images during video recording when it detects what it determines to be an "impressive" composition including people. As I noted earlier, I do not often use this feature, but it might be useful if you were to have a camera set on a tripod, unattended, at a gathering and wanted to have some interesting stills captured while the video was being recorded. This option has the same limitations as shooting stills by pressing the shutter button. You can still press the shutter button to capture images when this option is activated.

Finally, there is one other way to capture still images in connection with video recording—by using the Photo Capture feature, as discussed in Chapter 7. For example, if you record video using the XAVC S 4K format, the video clips will have the relatively high resolution of 4K video, giving you the option to save a still frame that is of high enough quality to stand on its own. If you use an exposure mode that lets you set the shutter speed, you can choose a fast shutter speed to stop action, and use this technique as a type of super burst shooting. Figure 7-30 in Chapter 7 is an example using this approach.

Summary of Options for Recording Movies

As I have discussed, there is some complication in trying to explain all of the relationships among the controls and settings of the RX100 VI for recording movies. To simplify matters, I will provide a summary of options for recording movies with the RX100 VI.

To record a video clip with standard settings, set the mode dial to the Auto or Scene position and press the Movie button. The camera will adjust exposure automatically, and you can use either continuous autofocus (set for video recording using AF-S, AF-A, AF-C, or DMF for focus mode) or manual focus (MF setting). In those shooting modes, you cannot adjust many shooting options, such as ISO, white balance, DRO, Creative Style, or Picture Effect. You can use options such as Center Lock-on AF, face detection, and SteadyShot (Movies). You can choose File Format (Movies) and Record Setting options to control the video quality.

For more control over video shooting, set the mode dial to the P, A, S, or M position. Then you can control several additional Camera Settings1 menu options, including ISO, white balance, metering mode, Creative Style, and Picture Effect, among others. You can choose continuous autofocus or manual focus in the same way as for the more automatic shooting modes. You can adjust aperture, shutter speed, or both, or let the camera set them, depending on which shooting mode you select.

For maximum control over movie recording, set the mode dial to the movie film icon for Movie mode. Then select an option for the Exposure Mode (Movies) item on screen 1 of the Camera Settings2 menu. To control aperture, choose Aperture Priority; to control shutter speed, choose Shutter Priority; to control both aperture and shutter speed, choose Manual Exposure. Other options can be selected from the Camera Settings1 and Camera Settings 2 menus.

Control buttons and dials operate during movie recording if the context permits, as discussed earlier. If you want a set of functions tailored for video recording, use the list in Table 9-4 to start, and adjust it for your own needs:

Table 9-4. **Suggested Control Assignments for Movie Recording**

Control	Function
Control Ring	ISO
Custom Button	AF/MF Control Toggle
Left Button	Picture Profile
Right Button	Focus Magnifier
Center button	Zebra Display

To record good, standard video footage at a moment's notice without having to remember a lot of settings, I recommend that you set up one of the seven registers of the Memory Recall shooting mode with a solid set of movie recording settings. Table 9-5 lists one group of settings to consider. (Settings not listed here can be set however you like.) The Record Setting option and the Picture Profile setting in this table make some other settings unavailable, as noted in the table. If you want to use those settings, turn Picture Profile off and use a different option for Record Setting. I am assuming the mode dial is at the Movie position.

Table 9-5. **Suggested Menu Settings for Recording Movies in Movie Mode**

Camera Settings1 Menu	
Focus Mode	AF-C
Focus Area	Wide
Center Lock-on AF	Off
Face Priority in AF	Off
Face Detection Frame Display	Off
ISO	ISO Auto
Metering Mode	Multi
Face Priority in Multi Meter	Off
White Balance	Auto White Balance
Priority Set in AWB	Standard
DRO/Auto HDR	Off
Creative Style	Standard
Picture Effect	Off
Picture Profile	PP1
Camera Settings2 Menu	
Exposure Mode (Movies)	Program Auto
File Format (Movies)	XAVC S HD
Record Setting	60p 25M
Quality (Dual Recording)	Extra Fine
Image Size (Dual Recording)	L:17M
Auto Dual Recording	Off
Proxy Recording	Off
AF Drive Speed	Normal
AF Tracking Sensitivity	Standard
Auto Slow Shutter	Off
Audio Recording	On
Micref Level	Normal
Wind Noise Reduction	Off unless needed
SteadyShot (Movies)	Standard; Off if using tripod
Marker Display	Off unless needed
Marker Settings	Use as needed
Movie w/Shutter	Off unless needed
Zoom Setting	Optical Zoom Only
Zoom Speed	Normal
Zoom Function on Ring	Standard
Zebra Setting	Use as needed

Other Settings and Controls for Movies

Following are several other points about the effects of the camera's menu options and controls for recording and playing back movies.

The step zoom function is not available for video recording, even if the Zoom Function on Ring option is set to Step on screen 6 of the Camera Settings2 menu. The zoom operates continuously for movies.

The Display button operates normally to change the screens displayed during video recording. Those screens are chosen by the Display Button option on screen 7 of the Camera Settings2 menu. However, the For Viewfinder screen does not appear for video shooting, or when the mode dial is at the Movie position, even if it was selected through that menu option.

In playback mode, the Display button operates normally for movies. The screen with space for a histogram will display, but the spaces for histogram and other information will be blank.

The MF Assist option on screen 11 of the Camera Settings1 menu does not operate for video recording, so the camera will not magnify the display when you turn the control ring to adjust manual focus. However, you can assign the Focus Magnifier function to one of the control buttons and use that capability to enlarge the screen when using manual focus. After you press the assigned control button to put the orange frame on the display, press the Center button to enlarge the area within the frame to 4.0x normal. (This is less than the 5.3x enlargement factor for still shooting.) Then turn the control ring to adjust the focus. Half-press the shutter button to dismiss the Focus Magnifier frame.

The Setting Effect Off choice for the Live View Display option on screen 7 of the Camera Settings2 menu does not function for video recording; the Setting Effect On choice is locked in. So, for example, if you are shooting movies in Movie mode using Manual Exposure for the Exposure Mode setting and you have the aperture and shutter speed set for strong underexposure, you cannot adjust this option to make the display more visible.

Program Shift does not function during video recording. If you turn the control wheel or control ring while the camera is set to Program mode, the exposure settings will not change while the camera is recording a movie. The menu button and Playback button do not operate during video recording.

Finally, when the focus mode is set to MF for manual focus, you can tap the LCD screen twice to magnify the shooting screen during a video recording, just as when shooting still images, as long as the Touch Operation features are turned on through screen 3 of the Setup menu. You can then drag the magnified image around the display, and you can tap twice again to return the screen to its normal viewing size.

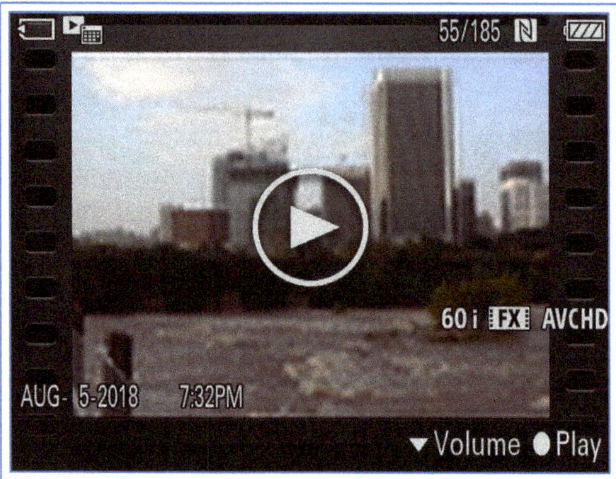

Figure 9-26. Movie Ready to Play in Camera

Movie Playback

As with still images, you can transfer movies to a computer for editing and playback or play them back in the camera, either on the camera's display or on a TV connected to the camera.

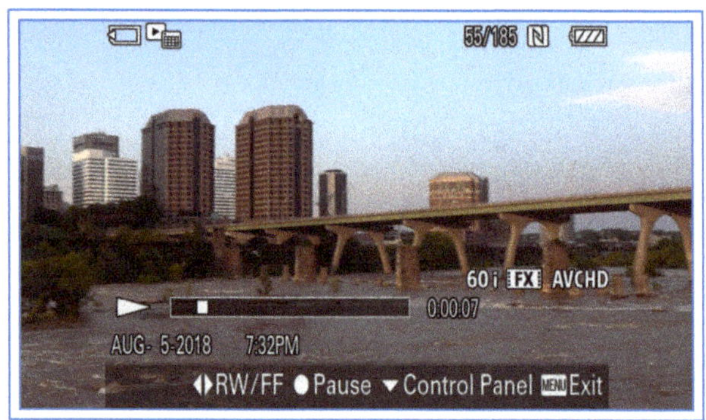

Figure 9-27. Initial Movie Playback Icons

When you play your movies in the camera, there is one aspect of the RX100 VI to be mindful of. As I discussed in Chapter 7, the View Mode option on screen 3 of the Playback menu controls what images or videos you will see in playback mode. If you don't see the video you are looking for, check to make sure this menu option is set to display all files from a certain date (Date View), AVCHD View, XAVC S HD View, or XAVC S 4K View.

Once you have selected a proper mode to view your video, navigate to that file using the direction buttons or the control wheel. When the first frame of the selected video is displayed, you will see a playback triangle inside a circle, as shown in Figure 9-26.

In the lower right corner of the screen will be a Play prompt with a white circle icon indicating that you can press the Center button to play the video. (If you don't see that prompt, press the Display button one or more times until it appears.)

After you press the Center button to start playback, you will see more icons at the bottom of the screen, as shown in Figure 9-27. From the left, these icons indicate: Rewind/Fast Forward; Pause; Open Control Panel; and Exit. From this screen, you can press the Left or Right button repeatedly to play the movie rapidly forward or backward; multiple presses increase the speed up to four times.

One icon indicates you can press the Down button to open the Control Panel. While the video is playing, press the Down button, and you will see a new line of controls at the bottom of the screen, as shown in Figure 9-28.

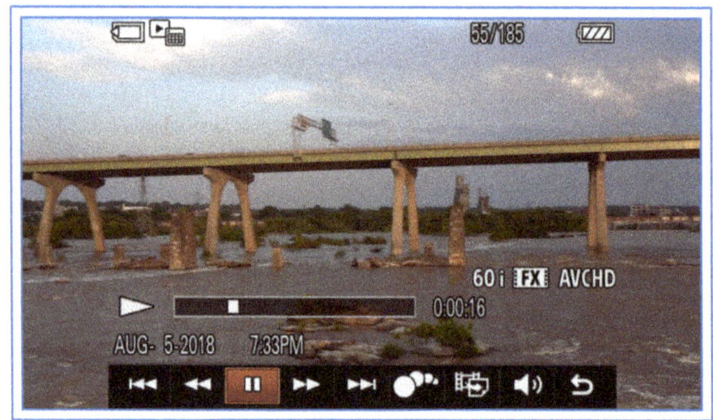

Figure 9-28. Detailed Movie Playback Icons

When the movie is playing, these icons indicate, from left to right: Previous Movie; Fast Reverse; Pause; Fast Forward; Next Movie; Motion Shot; Photo Capture; Volume; and Close Control Panel. When the movie is paused, the icons change, as seen in Figure 9-29. Those icons indicate, from left to right: Previous Frame; Reverse Slow; Normal Playback; Forward Slow; Next

Frame; Motion Shot; Photo Capture; Volume; and Close Control Panel.

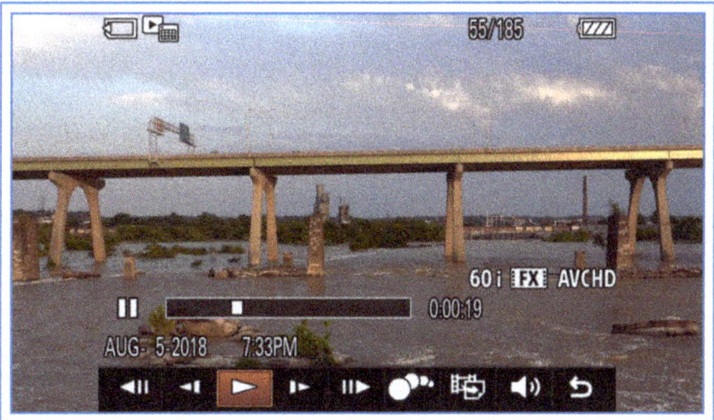

Figure 9-29. Detailed Movie Playback Icons When Paused

In either case, move through the icons with the Left and Right buttons, and press the Center button to select the function for that icon. When a movie is playing, you can fast-forward or fast-reverse through it at increasing speeds by turning the control wheel right or left or by pressing the Right or Left button.

Motion Shot Feature

The icon on the movie playback control panel that is a series of shrinking circles represents the Motion Shot feature. With this option, you can slow down the playback of a movie and display a motion sequence as a series of multiple exposures on the camera's screen, or on a TV screen if you have the camera connected to one.

This feature works only with AVCHD movies, not with movies recorded in either of the two XAVC S formats. To use the feature, let the movie play up to the point where you want to start the effect. For example, suppose you recorded some children playing basketball. You could play the movie up to the point where a child shoots the ball toward the basket. At that point, or just before it, use the Right button to scroll to the Motion Shot icon, highlight it, and press the Center button to select it.

The camera will then play back the video as a series of multiple exposures tracing the path of the object in motion. For example, Figure 9-30 shows how this feature processed a video sequence of a basketball shot. If the images of the moving object overlap too closely on your first attempt, you can make an adjustment using the Motion Interval Adjustment option. On the video control panel, once you have selected the Motion Shot icon, the line of icons will change. The Motion Shot icon will change to an icon for exiting the Motion Shot mode, which looks like a smaller version of the Motion Shot icon.

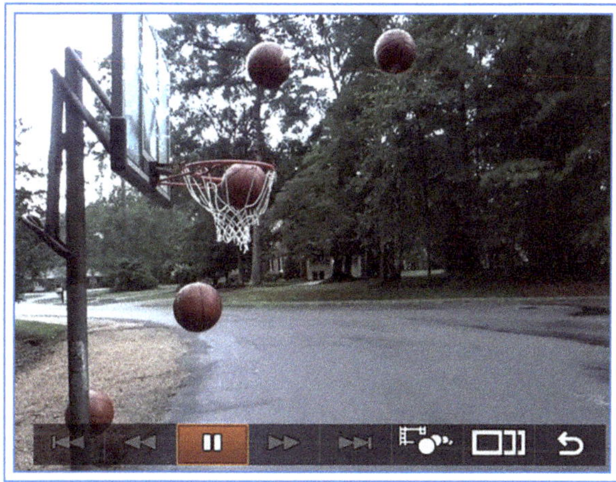

Figure 9-30. Motion Shot Example

The icon to the right of that one, which looks like a set of rectangular frames, lets you adjust the interval between the images. Select that icon and adjust the scale to a lower number to place the images closer together and to a higher number to place them farther apart. You also can adjust the interval using the Motion Interval Adjustment option on screen 2 of the Playback menu.

You cannot save the results of your work with the Motion Shot feature unless you connect the camera to a video capture device using an HDMI cable, as I did for Figure 9-30. I view this feature as an interesting novelty that lets you examine the path of an object in motion in some detail. It might be helpful for checking your golf swing or for adding interest to a video demonstration.

Editing Movies

The RX100 VI cannot edit movies in the camera. If you want to do any editing, you need to use a computer. For Windows, you can use software such as Easy Movie Maker. If you are using a Mac, you can use iMovie or any other movie editing software that can deal with AVCHD files and XAVC S files. I use Adobe Premiere Pro CC on my Mac, and it handles these file types well.

You also can use Sony's PlayMemories Home software. You can download it at https://support.d-imaging.sony.co.jp/app/disoft/en/. This software is revised periodically, so be sure to check the website for updates. You also can refer to the list of programs for editing 4K video provided by Sony at https://support.d-imaging.sony.co.jp/www/support/application/nle/en.html.

Chapter 10: Wi-Fi, Bluetooth, and Other Topics

Wi-Fi Features

The RX100 VI has the ability to connect to computers, smartphones, and tablets using a Wi-Fi network and a Bluetooth connection. Also, with some devices, the RX100 VI can use NFC (near field communication) technology to establish a Wi-Fi connection without going through all the steps that are ordinarily required. Note, though, that the RX100 VI, unlike its predecessor, does not have the ability to download and use camera apps.

In this section, I will describe the Wi-Fi features and give examples of how you can use them.

First, here is one note to remember when using any of the camera's Wi-Fi and Bluetooth features: The Network menu, marked by a globe icon, has an option called Airplane Mode near the bottom of its first screen. If that option is turned on, no wireless features will work. Make sure that menu setting is turned off when using the wireless options.

Sending Images to a Computer

Once you have the RX100 VI camera and a computer set up to communicate over a wireless network, you can use the Send to Computer menu option to transfer images and videos from the camera's memory card over that network. Here are the steps to set up the camera and computer:

1. Install Sony's PlayMemories Home software on the computer. For both Macs and Windows-based computers, the software is available for download at https://support.d-imaging.sony.co.jp/app/disoft/en/.
2. Run the software you downloaded in Step 1. If it does not automatically prompt you to set up your computer for wireless import, do this manually, using the steps below.
3. On the camera, set USB Connection on Screen 4 of the Setup menu to Mass Storage.
4. On a Macintosh, go to the PlayMemories Home menu. Select Preferences, then Wireless Import, and select the option to set this computer as the destination for importing images. When prompted, connect the camera to the computer with the camera's USB cable. Follow further prompts, then disconnect the camera from the computer, using the proper procedure to eject the camera from the computer safely.
5. On a PC using Windows 10, start the PlayMemories Home program, then connect the RX100 VI camera to the computer using the USB cable. When the computer displays a dialog box recognizing the camera, answer Yes when the computer asks if you want to see options for cameras, such as Import Media Files. The computer then will display a screen with several options. Select the option for Wi-Fi Import Settings. Follow the prompts to set up this computer to receive files wirelessly from the RX100 VI. Then disconnect the camera from the computer, using the proper procedure for safe disconnection.
6. Make sure the camera is within range of a wireless access point, also known as a Wi-Fi router. Normally, this will be a private, secured network at your home or office.
7. If the router has a button labeled WPS (Wi-Fi protected setup), you can use the button to connect the camera to the network. Select the Wi-Fi Settings option on screen 1 of the Network menu, then Select the WPS Push sub-option, and the camera will display the screen in Figure 10-1.

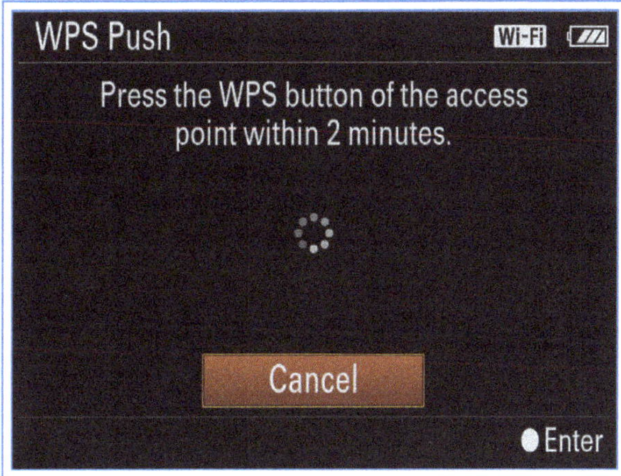

Figure 10-1. WPS Push Screen on Camera

8. Within two minutes, press the WPS button on the router.
9. If the setup is successful, the camera will display a message saying the access point has been registered. Proceed to Step 15.

   –or–

10. If the router does not have a WPS button, or if pushing the button does not work, go to Step 11.
11. Locate the name of the network and its password. (This information may be on a label on the router.)
12. Select the Access Point Settings sub-option under the Wi-Fi Settings option, as shown in Figure 10-2.

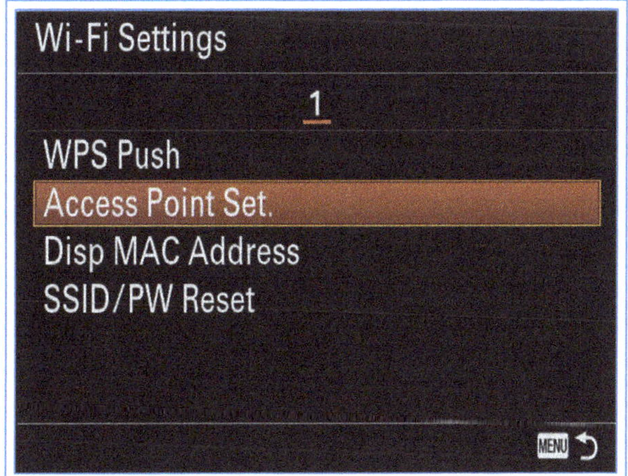

Figure 10-2. Access Point Settings Option Highlighted on Menu

13. If the name of your network appears on the camera's screen, as shown in Figure 10-3, select that network and enter its password, as shown in Figure 10-4. When you press the Center button with the password blank highlighted, the camera will display a virtual keyboard to let you enter the necessary characters.

   –or–

14. If the access point you want to use is not listed on the camera's screen, enter its SSID (network ID), using the Manual Setting option on the menu screen, as shown in Figure 10-5, and then enter the network's password, as shown in Figure 10-4.

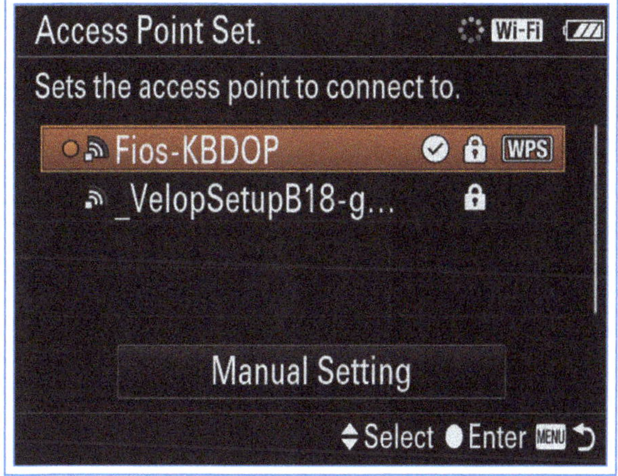

Figure 10-3. List of Available Wi-Fi Networks on Camera's Screen

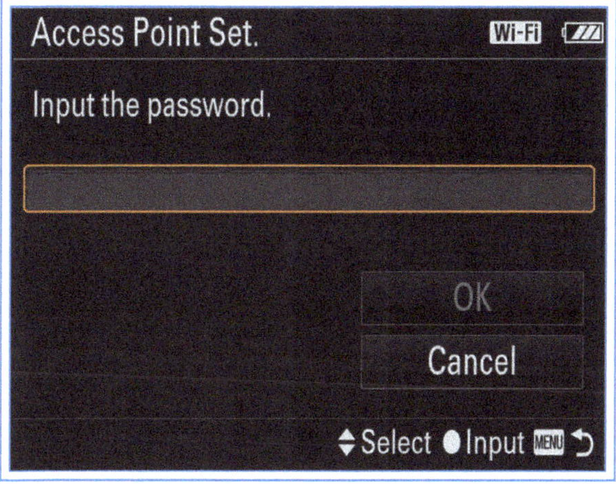

Figure 10-4. Screen to Enter Network Password

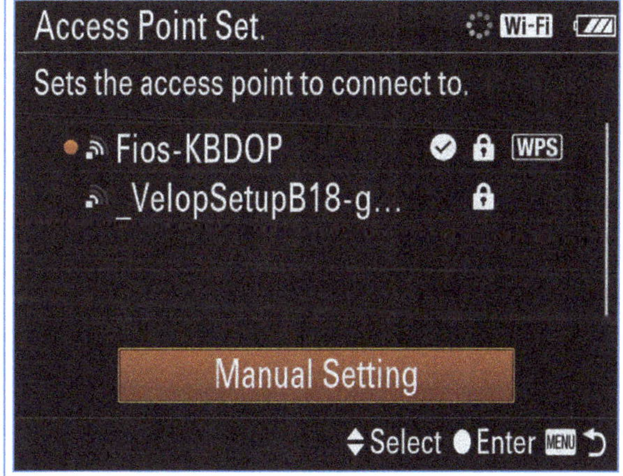

Figure 10-5. Manual Setting Option Highlighted on Menu

15. On the camera's Network menu select Send to Computer, as shown in Figure 10-6.

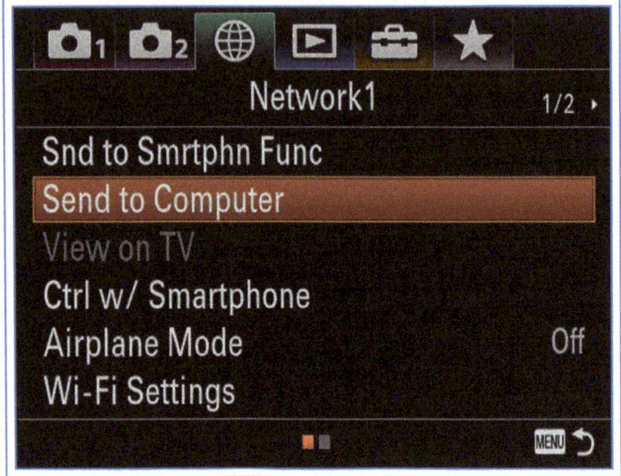

Figure 10-6. Send to Computer Option Highlighted on Menu

16. The camera will display a screen like that in Figure 10-7, reporting the name of the computer it is connecting to.

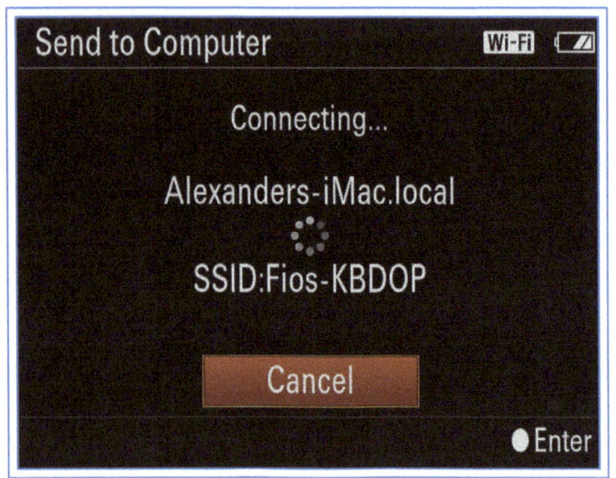

Figure 10-7. Camera's Screen When Connecting to Computer

17. The computer will display a Preparing to Import message, followed by an Importing dialog box showing the names and thumbnails of the images and videos being imported. The images and videos will be uploaded to a folder on your computer. You can designate that folder using the software installed in Step 1. The default folder is the Pictures folder; the computer places the images and videos in a sub-folder bearing the date of the transfer.

The camera will only transfer images and videos that have not previously been transferred wirelessly to the computer, but there is no way to select which items will be transferred. The transfer may take a long time, especially if the transfer includes AVCHD and XAVC S videos. However, I did succeed in sending a 4K video file to a computer using this function.

If you have a fast Wi-Fi network available, this option can be a convenient way to transfer images and videos.

Sending Images to a Smartphone

You may want to transfer images to a smartphone or tablet to share them on social networks, display them on the screen of your tablet, or otherwise enjoy them.

You can transfer images wirelessly from the RX100 VI to a smartphone or tablet that uses the iOS or Android operating system, but you cannot transfer AVCHD videos. For XAVC S 4K videos or XAVC S HD videos recorded with the 120p/100p Record Setting option, you can transfer proxy versions but not the full-sized files. With iOS, you have to use the camera's menu system to connect. With many Android devices, you can use NFC technology, which establishes a Wi-Fi connection automatically when the camera is touched against the smartphone or tablet.

Here are the steps for connecting using the menu system, using an iPhone as an illustration:

1. Install Sony's PlayMemories Mobile app on the phone; it can be downloaded from the App Store for the iPhone or from Google Play for Android devices.
2. Put the camera into playback mode and display an image or video to be transferred to the phone.
3. On the Network menu, select Send to Smartphone Function, then, on the next screen, Send to Smartphone. From that option choose Select on This Device, as shown in Figure 10-8. On the next screen, you can choose to transfer This Image, All with this Date, or Multiple Images.

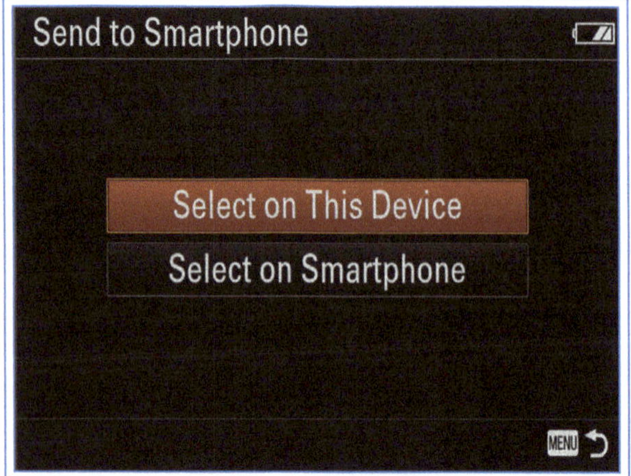

Figure 10-8. Select on This Device Highlighted on Menu

4. On the next screen, as shown in Figure 10-9, the camera will display the SSID (name) of the Wi-Fi network it is generating.

Figure 10-9. Network ID Displayed on Camera's Screen

5. On the phone, go to the Settings app, select Wi-Fi, and select the network displayed on the camera's screen, as shown in Figure 10-10. The first time you connect to that network, you will have to scan the QR code on the camera's screen with the phone, in the PlayMemories Mobile app. Or, if you prefer, you can press the Custom/Delete button to go to a screen that displays the network password, which you can enter in the phone. After that initial connection, you can connect to the camera's network without entering the password.

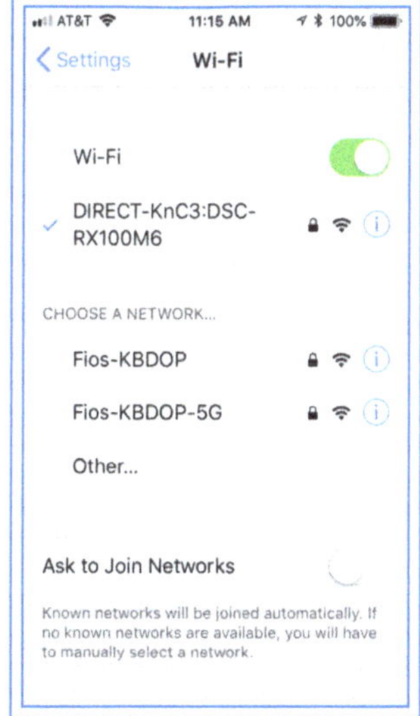

Figure 10-10. Camera's Network ID Displayed on iPhone's Screen

6. The camera will then display a message saying "Connecting." At this point, start the PlayMemories Mobile app, shown by the arrow in Figure 10-11 on the iPhone, unless it was already started so you could scan the QR code from the camera's screen.

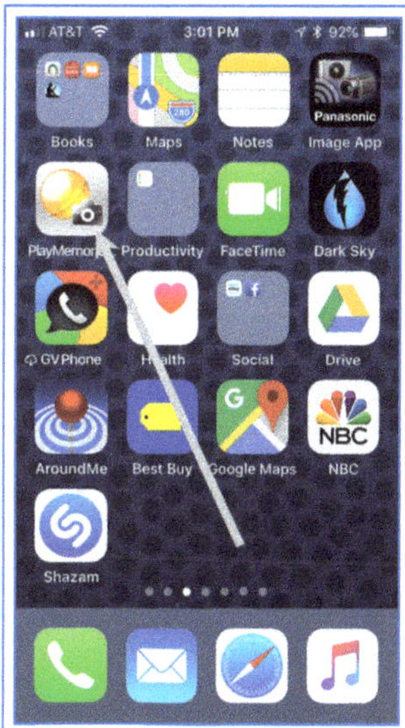

Figure 10-11. Icon for PlayMemories Mobile App on iPhone

7. The phone will display a message saying it is copying items from the camera, and will confirm the copying with a screen like that in Figure 10-12. The images or videos will appear in the Camera Roll area on an iPhone. It can take a long time to transfer a movie.

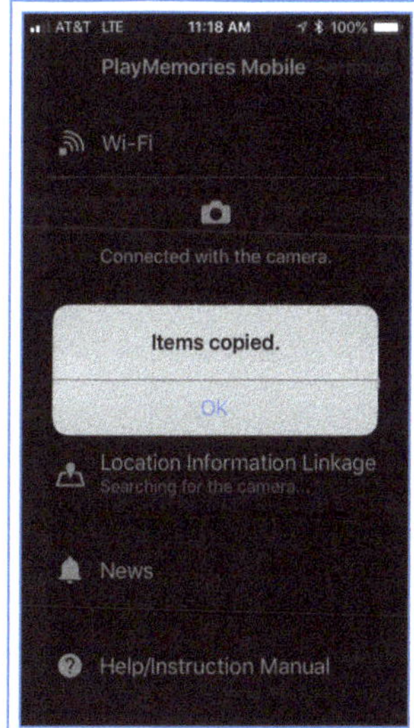

Figure 10-12. Copying Confirmation Message on iPhone

If you prefer, you can initiate the Send to Smartphone process by pressing the Function button when the camera is in playback mode, assuming that button is assigned to that operation. (The Function button is assigned to Send to Smartphone by default, but that operation can be assigned to a different button using the Custom Key (Playback) option on screen 9 of the Camera Settings2 menu.)

Connecting with NFC

If you are using an Android device with NFC, the steps for connecting that device to the RX100 VI are different. I tested the procedure using a Sony Xperia XA2 phone, but the same process should work with many Android devices that have NFC included. Here are the steps:

1. On the Android device, go to the Google Play Store and find and install the PlayMemories Mobile app, as shown in Figure 10-13.

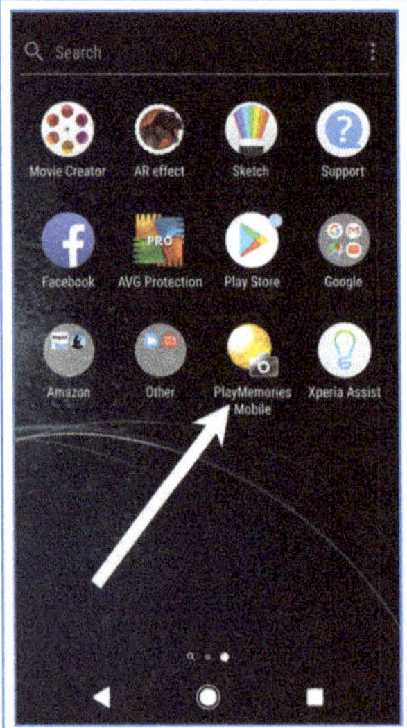

Figure 10-13. Icon for PlayMemories Mobile App on Android Phone

2. On the Android device, go to the Settings app, and choose NFC and Payment. On the next screen, make sure the settings for NFC are turned on, as shown in Figure 10-14.

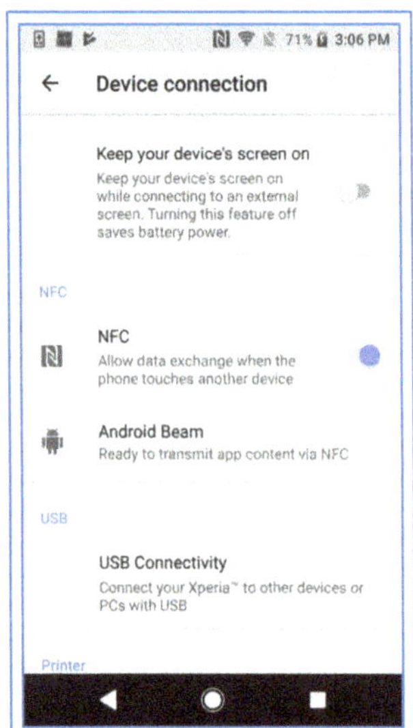

Figure 10-14. NFC Settings Activated on Android Phone

3. Put the RX100 VI into playback mode and display an image you want to send to the Android device.
4. Find the NFC icon on the left side of the camera, which looks like a fancy "N," as shown in Figure 10-15.

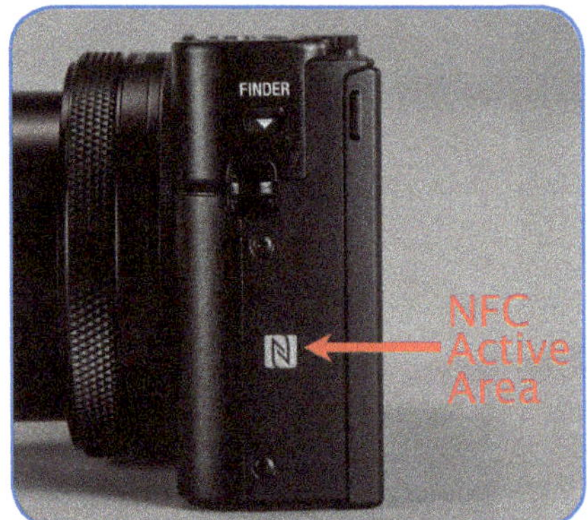

Figure 10-15. NFC Active Area on Camera

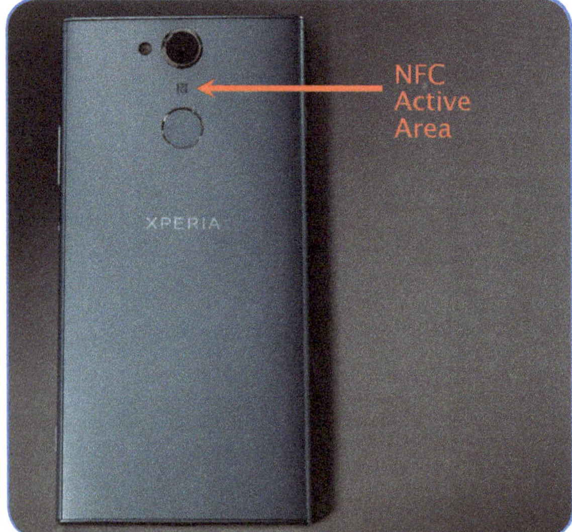

Figure 10-16. NFC Active Area on Sony Xperia XA2 Phone

5. While both devices are active, touch the N on the camera to the NFC area on the Android device. (On the Sony Xperia XA2, this area is on the back below the camera lens, as shown in Figure 10-16.) Be sure the two areas touch; you cannot have the two NFC spots separated by more than about a millimeter, if that.
6. Hold the devices together, and within a few seconds you may hear a sound, depending on settings, and the camera will transfer the image to the Android device; you may see a message on the camera as the connection is established. You may see a message to select an option on the phone such as Connect to Camera to complete the operation. However, if you wait a few seconds, the camera and phone should complete the connection and transfer the image without any further action on your part.

7. The image will appear in the Gallery app on the Android device.
8. If you want to transfer multiple images, select that option from the camera's menu before touching the camera to the Android device to start the transfer.

By default, when you transfer images to a smartphone or tablet, the maximum image size will be 2 MP. If the image originally was larger than that, it will be reduced to that size. You can change this setting to send the images at their original size or at the smaller VGA size. To do that on your device, find the settings for the PlayMemories Mobile app. On an iPhone, go to Settings, then scroll to find PlayMemories Mobile. On an Android device, open PlayMemories Mobile, then tap the Settings icon. If the images were taken with Raw quality, they will be converted to JPEG format before being transferred to the smartphone or tablet, even if the device is set for transfer at the original size.

Using a Smartphone or Tablet as a Remote Control

You can use a smartphone or tablet as a remote control to operate the RX100 VI from a distance of up to about 33 feet (10 meters), as long as the devices are in sight of each other. Here are the steps to do this with an iPhone:

1. On screen 1 of the camera's Network menu, marked by a globe icon, turn on Control with Smartphone, then make a selection for Always Connected, either On or Off. (I recommend Off.) Then highlight the Connection option and press the Center button. The camera will initiate a connection to the phone.
2. The camera will display ID information for its own Wi-Fi network, with a QR code for scanning and a message saying to press the Custom/Delete button to use a password, as shown in Figure 10-17.
3. On the phone, you can open the PlayMemories Mobile app and choose Scan QR Code of the Camera, or you can go to the Wi-Fi tab of the Settings app and select the network ID displayed by the camera, as shown earlier in Figure 10-10. If this is the first time you are making this connection, you will have to press the Custom/Delete button on the camera to display the password, and enter the network password on the phone; you will not have to enter the password for future connections unless the network ID is changed. You may be prompted on the phone to install a profile. If so, follow the prompts.

Figure 10-17. Camera's Display of Network ID for Control with Smartphone Option

4. Set up the camera on a tripod or just place it where you want it, aiming at your intended subject.
5. Open the PlayMemories Mobile app on the iPhone, if it is not already open.
6. The camera will display a screen like that shown in Figure 10-18, with an icon in the upper middle of the display showing that the camera can now be controlled from the phone.

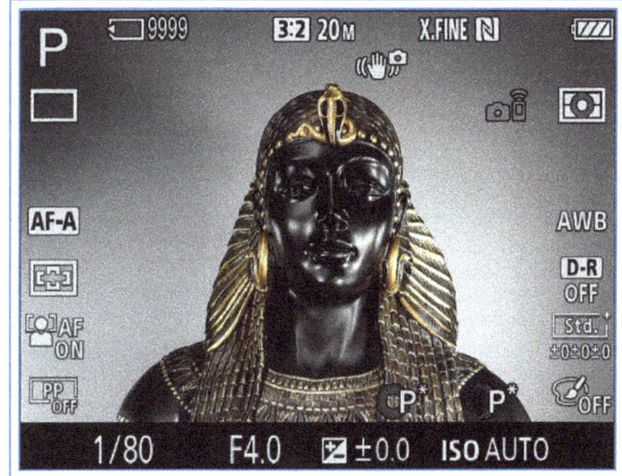

Figure 10-18. Camera's Screen When Controlled by Smartphone

7. The phone will display a screen like that in Figure 10-19, showing the view from the camera's lens and several control icons.
8. Using these controls, you can zoom the lens and control various settings, including exposure compensation, white balance, ISO, aperture, shutter speed, continuous shooting, and self-timer, depending on the shooting mode. You also can adjust several options using the camera's controls.

You can take a still image by tapping the large white circle at the bottom center of the screen.

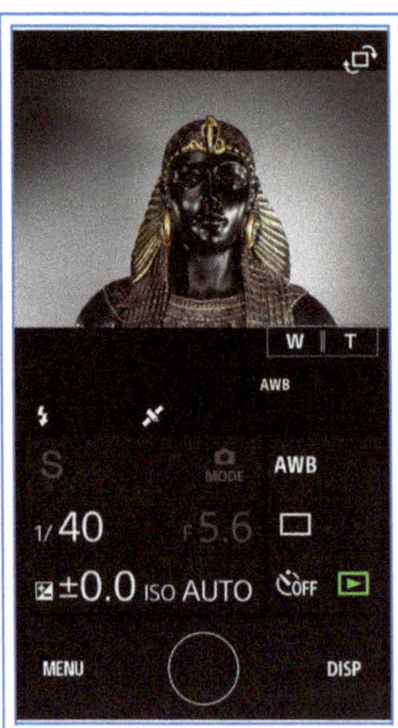

Figure 10-19. iPhone's Screen During Remote Operation

9. You can tap the Menu icon in the lower left corner of the app to get access to a menu that includes options such as flash mode, white balance, self-timer, and others. You can tap the DISP icon in the lower right corner of the app to remove the icons from the screen, leaving only the live view.
10. If you turn the camera's mode dial to the Movie position, the circle at the bottom of the app changes to a red dot, which you can tap to record a movie. You can change the Exposure Mode setting for movies on the camera by tapping the P, A, S, or M icon on the left side of the app. You can change the format for movie recording by tapping the Menu icon, giving access to those settings and others. You can record HFR movies if you turn the mode dial to HFR.
11. When you have set up the shot as you want it, press the camera icon on the iPhone app to take the picture or the red icon to start the video recording.
12. If you are using an Android device with NFC capability, you should be able to connect to the camera by touching the device to the camera, as discussed above in connection with transferring images. First, make sure Control with Smartphone is turned on on screen 1 of the Network menu, and that the camera is in shooting mode with the NFC N logo displayed in the upper right corner of the screen. Then touch the NFC areas of the two devices together.
13. Once the connection has been made, you can separate the devices to the standard remote-control distance of up to about 33 feet (10 meters). If you have difficulty making an NFC connection, start the PlayMemories Mobile App on the Android device before touching the camera to that device. The camera can then be controlled using the PlayMemories Mobile app on the Android device, as noted in the numbered steps above.

You can use the remote-control setup if you want to place your camera on a tripod in an area where birds or other wildlife may appear, so you can control the camera from a distance without disturbing the animals. (The wireless remote will work through glass if you are indoors behind a window.)

Bluetooth Features

As discussed above, the RX100 VI can use a Wi-Fi connection to transfer images to a smartphone, tablet, or computer. In addition, it can use a Bluetooth connection to receive geographical location information from a compatible smartphone or tablet. Bluetooth, like Wi-Fi, is a system for establishing a wireless connection between devices. One advantage of using Bluetooth instead of Wi-Fi is that Bluetooth consumes very little power, so a Bluetooth connection can remain active for a relatively long time without draining the camera's battery excessively.

Adding Location Information to Images

The steps to take for setting up a Bluetooth connection to gather location information with the RX100 VI are set forth below.

1. Install the PlayMemories Mobile app on your smartphone, and use it to transfer at least one image from the camera to the phone, as discussed earlier in this chapter. After that procedure has been done, the Location Information Linkage item will appear on the main page of the app, as shown in Figure 10-20.

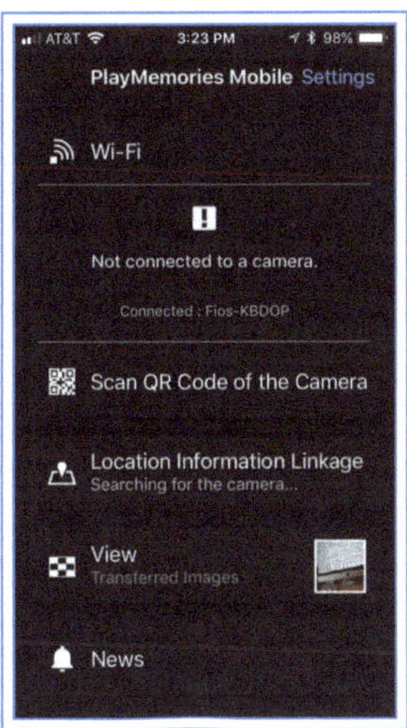

Figure 10-20. Location Information Linkage Item on App Screen

2. Make sure the Bluetooth setting is turned on on the smartphone, but do not initiate a pairing procedure between the phone and the camera yet.

3. On the RX100 VI, go to screen 2 of the Network menu, select Bluetooth Settings, and, on the next screen, set Bluetooth Function to On, as shown in Figure 10-21.

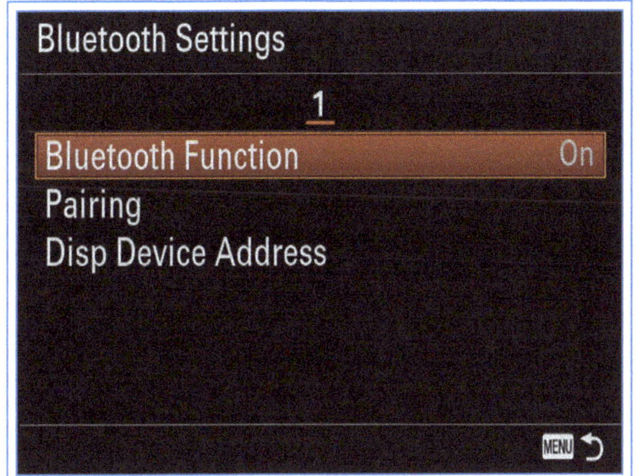

Figure 10-21. Bluetooth Function On Highlighted on Menu

4. On the RX100 VI, on the Bluetooth Settings screen, select Pairing.

5. On the phone, launch the PlayMemories Mobile app and tap Location Information Linkage on the main page. Then turn the button for that setting to the On position, so a green circle appears.

6. On the phone, select the option to Set the Camera, then select the name of the RX100 VI camera from the list on the app's screen.

7. When the camera displays a message prompting you to allow the connection from the RX100 VI, select OK. The app also may ask you to confirm the pairing operation.

8. On the RX100 VI, go to screen 2 of the Network menu, select Location Information Link Setting, and set it to On. The phone and camera will then be paired.

9. As the camera shoots images, it will obtain location information from the smartphone via the Bluetooth connection. As it obtains information, the camera will display the icon seen directly below the X.FINE label in Figure 10-22. It will also display a Bluetooth icon to the right of that icon.

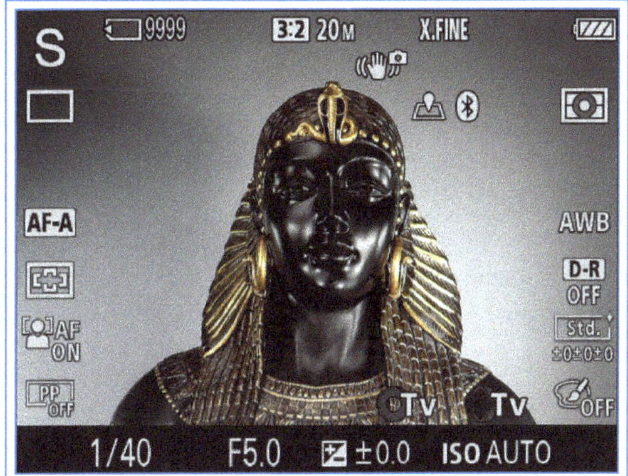

Figure 10-22. Location Information Icon on Camera's Screen

10. You can view the location information using various software programs, such as Adobe Bridge and Sony's Imaging Edge. With PlayMemories Home, each image will have a GPS satellite icon displayed in the upper right corner, and the latitude and longitude can be read using the Properties panel. The location information also will display on the camera's playback screen with detailed information, as seen in Figure 10-23.

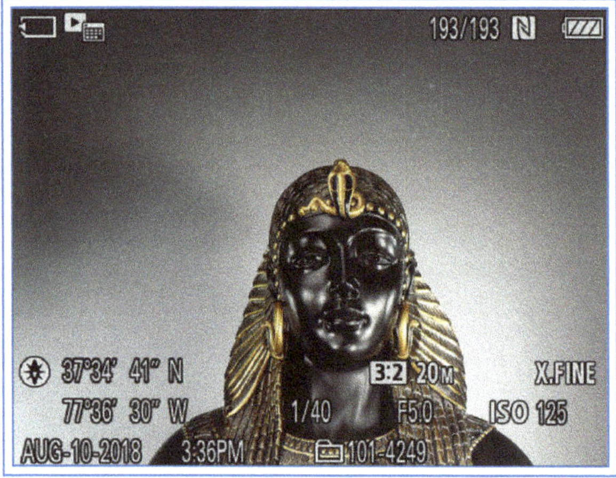

Figure 10-23. Playback Display with Location Information

11. Once the Location Information Link has been established between the smartphone and the camera, you can continue to take pictures and the smartphone will gather location information, as long as the app is running, even in the background. It may take a while for the phone to transmit the GPS data to the camera when the camera is turned on after having been turned off for a while. If you don't need to gather location information for a time, you can save battery power by turning off the Bluetooth settings on the camera.

The Network Menu

I have discussed some of the items on the Network menu, but there are several other options on that menu to discuss. Following is information about each of the items on this menu, whose first screen is shown in Figure 10-24.

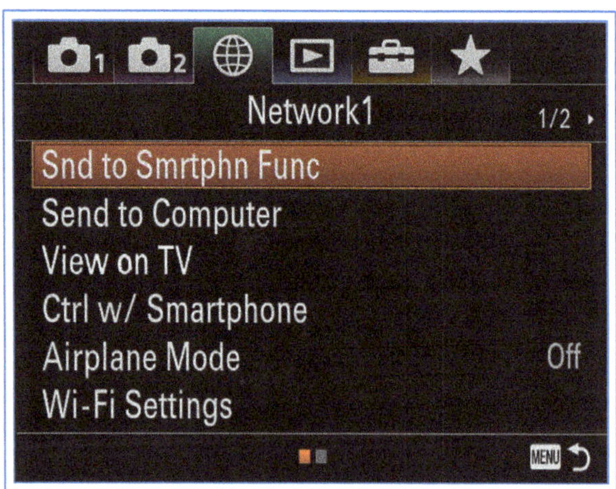

Figure 10-24. Screen 1 of Network Menu

Send to Smartphone Function

This first Network menu option lets you transfer images or videos to a smartphone or tablet. This menu item has two sub-options: Send to Smartphone and Sending Target, as shown in Figure 10-25. I discussed the steps for using the Send to Smartphone option earlier in this chapter. You also can press the Function button (if that button remains assigned to this option) when the camera is in playback mode, to carry out this action.

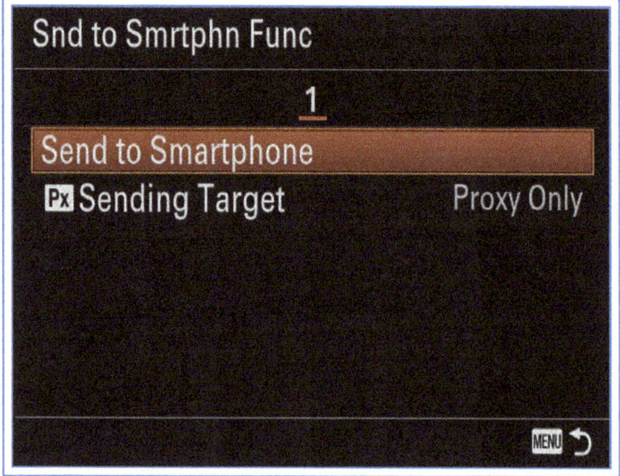

Figure 10-25. Send to Smartphone Function Options Screen

The Sending Target option lets you choose how to transfer movies recorded with the XAVC S HD format—specifically, whether to transfer the original video file, the proxy file, or both. (Proxy recording is turned on with the Proxy Recording item on screen 2 of the Camera Settings2 menu; it creates a smaller version of a video file as the file is recorded.)

You cannot transfer AVCHD movies or XAVC S 4K movies, and you cannot transfer XAVC S HD movies recorded with either of the 120p/100p settings for Record Setting. So, this option controls only the way the camera transfers XAVC S HD movies recorded with a 60p, 30p, or 24p value for Record Setting. The choices for this option are Proxy Only, Original Only, or Proxy & Original.

Make this choice according to your own preference and needs. If you just want to view a particular video on your smartphone, Proxy Only will make the transfer go more rapidly and should be sufficient. Otherwise, select the original, with or without the proxy, but be prepared for it to take a long time to complete the transfer.

Send to Computer

This next option lets you send images and movies directly from the RX100 VI to a computer via a Wi-Fi network. I discussed the steps for this process earlier in this chapter.

View on TV

This option sets up the RX100 VI to transmit still images (not movies) wirelessly to a Wi-Fi–enabled TV, such as a Sony Bravia TV. The procedure will vary with the TV set you are using. Once the connection is established, you can browse through the images using the controls on the camera or the remote control of the TV if the TV is compatible with this setup.

This is a useful option once it is working properly, but I have found it difficult to set up. With this camera, I eventually was able to connect to a device called WD TV Live, by Western Digital. I connected that device to an HDTV using an HDMI cable and connected the WD TV Live device to the same network my RX100 VI was connected to, through the Wi-Fi Settings/Access Point Settings option on the Network menu. Then, with the View on TV option, the camera was able to find and connect to the WD TV Live, as shown in Figure 10-26.

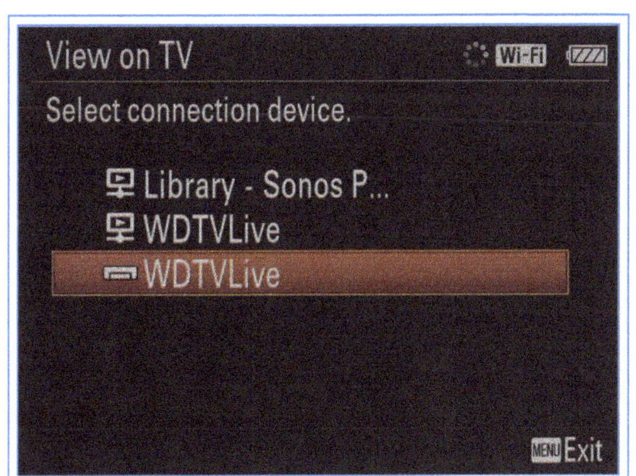

Figure 10-26. Camera's Screen When WD TV Live Found

After the connection was established, the camera sent still images to the TV through the wireless network. The camera showed the screen in Figure 10-27, with a few control icons at the bottom. Once that screen appeared, I pressed the Center button to pause the transmission, and pressed the Down button to display the screen shown in Figure 10-28 with additional options, including 4K display mode, found under the Playback Image Size option.

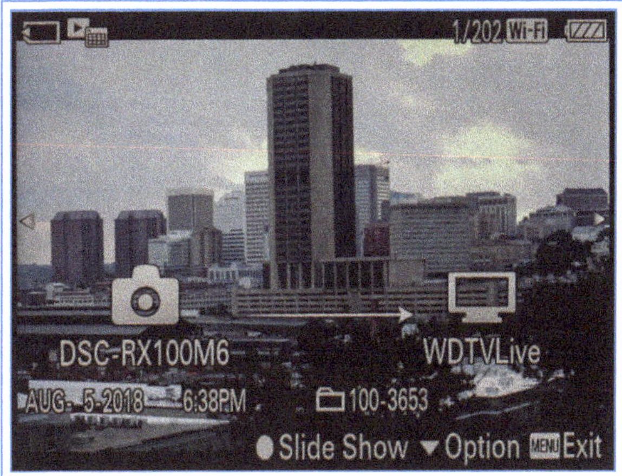

Figure 10-27. Camera's Screen When Sending Images to TV

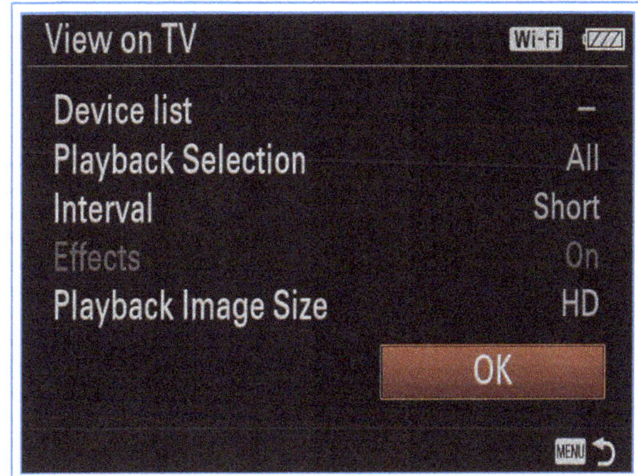

Figure 10-28. Additional Options for View on TV Function

If you have a "smart" TV or are familiar with setting up a media server, this option may be great for you. Otherwise, I recommend that you view your images on a TV using an HDMI cable, a USB flash drive, or some other direct connection.

Control with Smartphone

I discussed this menu option earlier in this chapter, when I discussed the steps for controlling the camera using the PlayMemories Mobile app on a smartphone. The first sub-option, Control with Smartphone, needs to be turned on; you then establish a connection using the Connection sub-option. The third sub-option, Always Connected, can be turned on or off. If it is turned on, the connection between the phone and camera will stay in place and will not need to be re-established. That setting uses up power more rapidly than letting the connection end, so I recommend not enabling the persistent connection unless you have a definite need to do so.

Airplane Mode

This option is a quick way to disable all of the camera's functions related to Wi-Fi, including the camera's own internal Wi-Fi network and its Bluetooth connectivity. As indicated by its name, this option is useful when you are on an airplane and you are required to disable electronic devices. In addition, this setting can save battery power, so it may be worthwhile to activate it when you are on an outing with the camera and you won't need to use any Wi-Fi capabilities for a period of time.

If you try to use any of the camera's Wi-Fi or Bluetooth functions such as Send to Smartphone, Send to Computer, or Bluetooth Function and notice that the menu options are dimmed, it may be because Airplane Mode is turned on. Turn it off and the Wi-Fi options should be available again.

Wi-Fi Settings

This last option on screen 1 of the Network menu has several sub-options, as discussed below.

WPS Push

The WPS Push option gives you an easy way to set up your camera to connect to a computer or other devices over a Wi-Fi network. Ordinarily, to connect to a wireless network, you have to use the Access Point Settings option and then enter the network password into the camera to establish the connection. The WPS Push option gives you a shortcut if the wireless access point or wireless router you are connecting to has a WPS button. That option, if it is present, is likely to be a small button on the back or top of the router, and it is likely to have the WPS label next to it or on it. For example, one router I have used has the button shown in Figure 10-29.

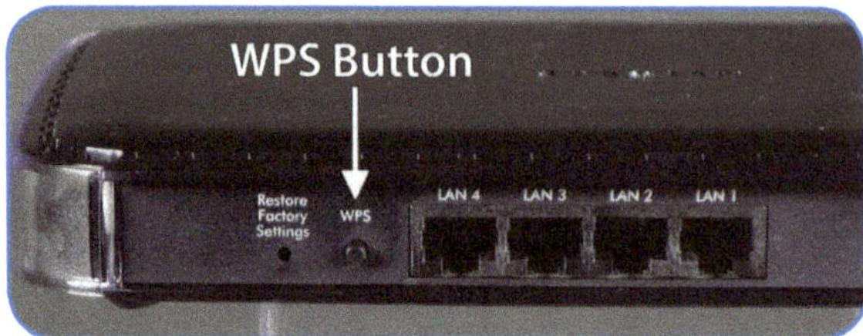

Figure 10-29. WPS Button on Router

If the router has a WPS button, you will not have to make any manual settings or enter a password. All you have to do is select the WPS Push menu option on the RX100 VI, and then within two minutes after that, press the WPS button on the router. If the operation is successful, the camera's display screen will show that the connection has been established, as seen in Figure 10-30.

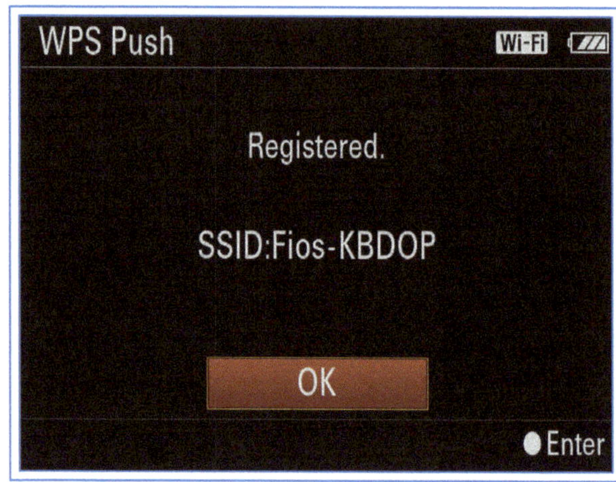

Figure 10-30. Message After Success with WPS Push

Once that connection has been made, you will be able to connect your camera to a computer on that network to transfer images using the Send to Computer option or the View on TV option. If the connection does not succeed using WPS Push, you will need to use the Access Point Settings option, the second sub-option for the Wi-Fi Settings menu item.

Access Point Settings

This option is for connecting the camera to a router if WPS Push, discussed above, is not available or does not work. I discussed the use of this option earlier in this chapter, in connection with sending images and videos to a computer wirelessly.

Display MAC Address

This menu option causes the camera to display a screen like that in Figure 10-31, which shows your camera's MAC address. MAC stands for media access control.

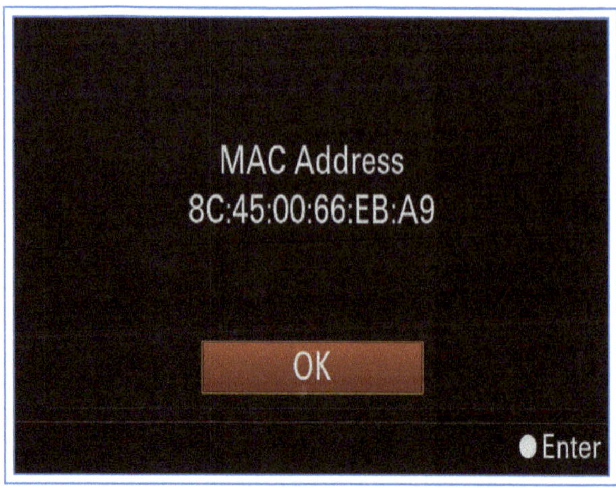

Figure 10-31. Display MAC Address Screen

The MAC address is a string of characters that identifies a device that can connect to a network. In some cases, a router can be configured to reject or accept devices with specified MAC addresses. If you are having difficulty connecting your camera to a Wi-Fi router using the options discussed above, you can try configuring the router to recognize the MAC address of your camera, as reported by this menu item. I have not had to use this option, but it is available in case it is needed.

SSID/PW Reset

When you connect your RX100 VI to a smartphone or tablet, either to transfer images or to control the camera remotely with the other device, the camera generates its own Wi-Fi network internally. With this option, you can force the camera to change the SSID (name) and password of its own wireless network.

You might want to do this if, for example, you have attended a conference where you allowed other people to connect their smartphones to your camera, and now you want to reset the camera's network ID so they will no longer have access to the camera's network.

The second and final screen of the Network menu is shown in Figure 10-32.

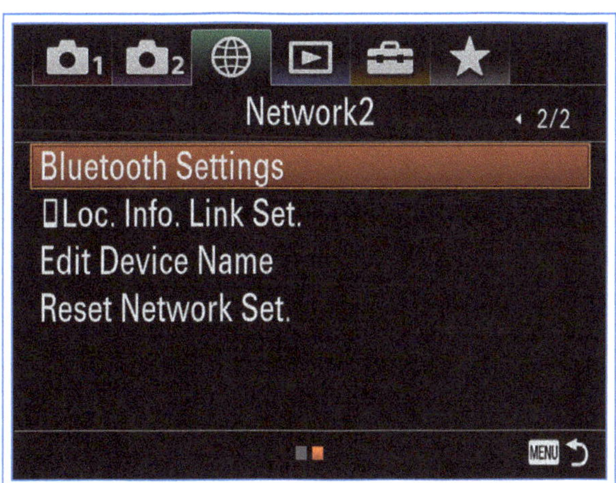

Figure 10-32. Screen 2 of Network Menu

Bluetooth Settings

I discussed this menu option in connection with the procedure for sending GPS location information to the camera from a smartphone. You use this option to turn on or off the camera's Bluetooth functionality and to pair it with a smartphone. You also can use the Display Device Address option to show the BD address, or Bluetooth Device address, of the camera, in case you need that information for troubleshooting or other purposes.

Location Information Link Setting

I discussed this option earlier, in connection with setting up the camera to receive location information. Once you have paired the camera with a smartphone through Bluetooth, you need to turn on the Location Information Link sub-option to cause the phone to send GPS data to the camera. You can also turn on the Auto Time Correction and Auto Area Adjustment options, if you want the camera to obtain updated time and location information from the phone.

Edit Device Name

This next option, shown in Figure 10-33, lets you change the name of your camera as it is displayed on a Wi-Fi network or for a Bluetooth connection. The default name is DSC-RX100M6, and I have found no reason to change it.

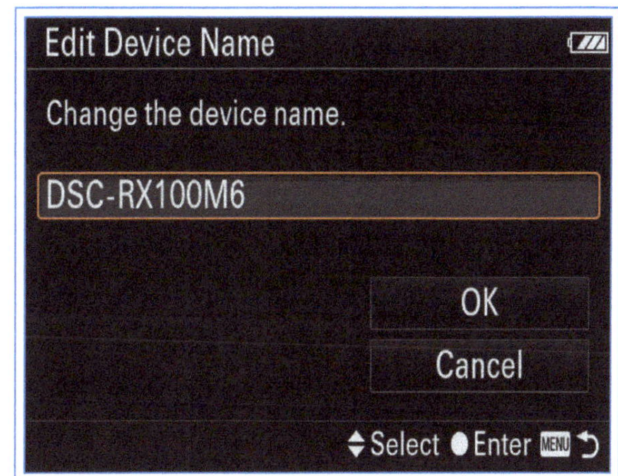

Figure 10-33. Edit Device Name Data Entry Screen

This option could be useful, though, if you are in an environment where other RX100 VI cameras are present and you need to distinguish one camera from another by using different names.

Reset Network Settings

This final option on the Network menu lets you reset all of the camera's network settings, not just the camera's Wi-Fi SSID and password. This option is useful if you are having problems and need to get a fresh start with the wireless functions, if you are switching to a new wireless network where you use the camera, or if you are selling the camera and want to erase these settings.

Other Topics

Astrophotography and Digiscoping

Astrophotography involves photographing sky objects with a camera connected to (or aiming through) a telescope. Digiscoping is the practice of using a digital camera with a spotting scope to get shots of distant objects such as birds and other wildlife.

There are many types of scope and several ways to align a scope with the RX100 VI's lens. I will not describe all of the methods; I will discuss the approach I used and hope it gives you enough guidance to explore the area further.

I used a Meade ETX-90/AT telescope with the RX100 VI connected to its eyepiece. To make that connection, you need a filter adapter, such as one sold by Lensmate or Magfilter, as discussed in Appendix A. You also need adapter rings to connect the filter adapter to the eyepiece. You can get the proper rings for either adapter by purchasing the 52mm Digi-Kit, part number DKSR52T, from telescopeadapters.com. That is the setup shown in Figure 10-34, using the Magfilter adapter.

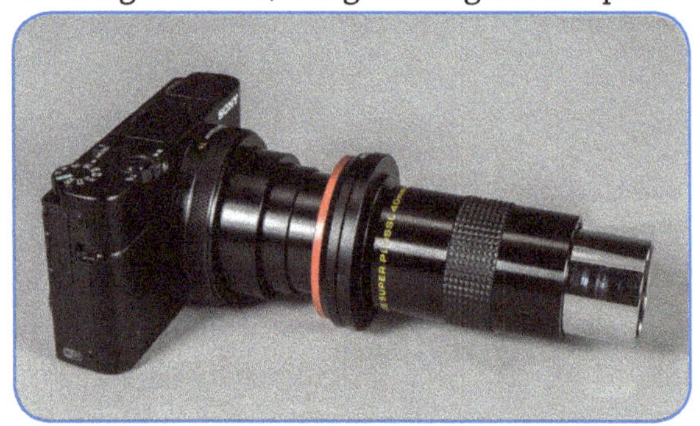

Figure 10-34. Telescope Eyepiece Connected to RX100 VI Camera

I took the image of the moon in Figure 10-35 with the RX100 VI connected to the telescope using the 52mm adapter rings with the Magfilter adapter. I set the camera to Manual exposure mode with settings of 1/200 second, f/4.5, and ISO 1250. I needed a fast shutter speed to avoid motion blur from the unsteadiness of the telescope. I used manual focus, adjusting the telescope's focus control until the image was sharp on the camera's LCD.

At first I used the MF Assist option so I could fine-tune the focus with an enlarged view of the moon's craters. After some experimenting, I found I got better results using the Peaking Level function at High, and Peaking Color set to red. When focus was sharp, I saw a bright, red outline on the outer edge of the moon, which made focusing much easier than relying on the normal manual focus mechanism, even with MF Assist activated.

I set the self-timer to five seconds to minimize camera shake. I set Quality to Raw & JPEG so I would have a Raw image to give extra latitude in case the exposure seemed incorrect. As you can see in Figure 10-35, the RX100 VI did a good job of capturing the crescent moon. Because of the relatively large sensor and high resolution of the RX100 VI, this image can be enlarged to a fair degree without deteriorating.

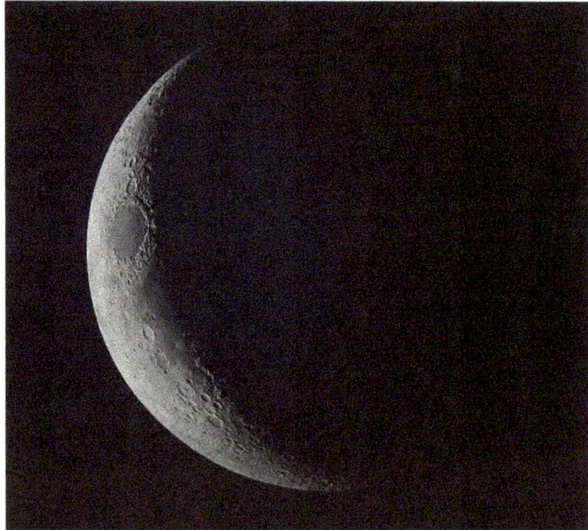

Figure 10-35. Image of Moon Taken with RX100 VI Through Telescope

You can use a similar setup for digiscoping. I attached the RX100 VI to a Celestron Regal 80F-ED spotting scope, using the same eyepiece I used with the telescope.

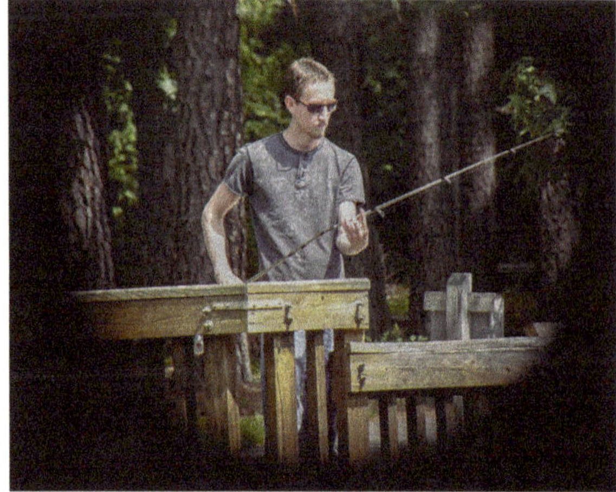

Figure 10-36. Image Taken with RX100 VI Through Spotting Scope

Figure 10-36 is a shot of a man fishing in a park, taken at a considerable distance from the other side of the pond with my RX100 VI through this scope. I turned on burst shooting to catch various views of the man. I used manual focus and also tweaked focus with the controls on the scope. As you can see, there is considerable vignetting, but the overall quality is not bad.

Street Photography

The RX100 VI is well suited for street photography—that is, shooting candid pictures in public settings, often without the subject being aware of your activity. It is small, lightweight, and unobtrusive in appearance, so it can easily be held casually or hidden in the photographer's hands. Its 24mm wide-angle lens takes in a broad field of view, so you can shoot from the hip without framing the image carefully on the screen. You can tilt up the LCD screen and look down at it to frame your shot, which further hides your actions. The f/2.8 lens performs well at high ISO settings, so you can use a fast shutter speed to avoid motion blur. You can silence the camera by turning off its beeps and shutter sounds.

The settings you use depend in part on your style of shooting. One technique that some photographers use is to shoot in Raw, and then use post-processing software such as Photoshop or Lightroom to convert their images to black and white, along with any other effects they are looking for, such as extra grain to achieve a gritty look. (Of course, you don't have to produce your street photography in black and white, but that is a common practice.)

If you decide to shoot using Raw quality, you can't take advantage of the image-altering settings of the Picture Effect menu option. You can, however, use the Creative Style option on the Camera Settings1 menu. (You may have to use Sony's Image Data Converter software for the Creative Style setting to be effective.) You might want to try using the Black and White setting; you can tweak it by increasing contrast and sharpening if you want. Also, try turning on continuous shooting, so you'll get several images to choose from for each shutter press.

You also can experiment with exposure settings. I recommend you shoot in Shutter Priority mode at a fairly fast shutter speed, 1/100 second or faster, to stop action on the street and to avoid blur from camera movement. You can set ISO to Auto, or use a high ISO setting, in the range of 800 or so, if you don't mind some noise.

Or, you can set the image type to JPEG at Large size and Extra Fine quality to take advantage of the camera's image-processing capabilities. To get the gritty "street" look, try using the High Contrast Monochrome setting of the Picture Effect item on the Camera Settings1 menu, with ISO set somewhat high, in the range of 800 or above, to include some grain in the image while boosting sensitivity enough to stop action with a fast shutter speed. You also can use the High Sensitivity setting of Scene mode to convey a gritty feeling.

One interesting approach is to take advantage of the camera's ability to shoot 4K video. You can shoot video in an exposure mode such as Shutter Priority that lets you use a fast shutter speed to avoid motion blur, and record a street scene for several seconds, or even a minute or two. You can then use video-editing software to extract a single frame. You also can use the Photo Capture option on screen 2 of the Playback menu to extract a frame from a movie. Because of the high resolution of 4K video, the quality is likely to be quite acceptable.

For Figure 10-37, I was shooting various scenes with different settings when these two people appeared in front of me. I switched the camera to the Sports Action setting of Scene mode with continuous shooting turned on and grabbed 17 quick shots, of which I chose this one as the best.

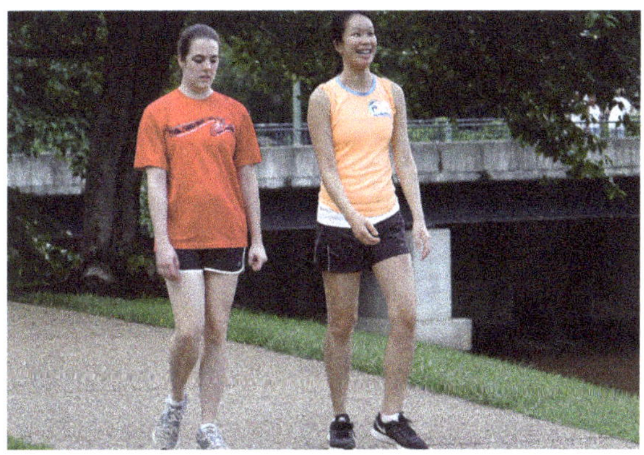

Figure 10-37. Street Photography Example

Connecting to a Television Set

The RX100 VI can play back its still images and videos on an external television set, as long as the TV has an HDMI input jack. The camera does not come with any audio-video cable as standard equipment, so you have to purchase your own cable, with a micro HDMI connector at the camera end and a standard HDMI connector at the TV end. These cables are available through online retailers.

To connect the cable to the camera, you need to open the little flap marked HDMI on the right side of the camera and plug the micro HDMI connector into the port underneath that flap, as shown in Figure 10-38.

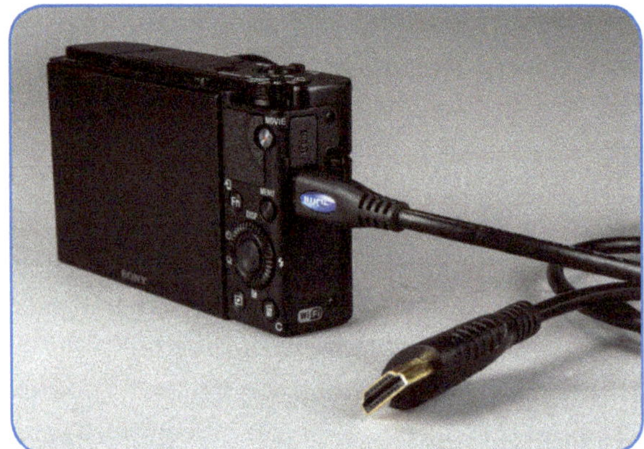

Figure 10-38. HDMI Cable Connected to Camera

Then connect the large connector at the other end of the cable to an HDMI input port on an HDTV set.

Once you have connected the camera to the set, the camera not only can play back images and videos; it also can record. When the RX100 VI is hooked up to a TV while in recording mode, you can see on the TV screen the live image being seen by the camera. In that way, you can use the TV as a large monitor to help you compose your photographs and videos.

You also can use this port and cable to output a "clean" video signal to another device, such as a video recorder. To do that, you have to turn off the HDMI Information Display option under the HDMI Settings item on screen 4 of the Setup menu, as discussed in Chapters 8 and 9.

As noted earlier in this chapter, the RX100 VI also has an option on the Network menu called View on TV, which lets you view your images on a Wi-Fi–enabled TV. As I discussed in that chapter, I have found that option to be difficult to use effectively. Unless you are familiar with using media servers and sharing files over a network, I recommend that you stick to using an HDMI cable for the connection.

Appendix A: Accessories

When people buy a new camera, especially a fairly expensive model like the Sony RX100 VI, they often ask what accessories they should buy to go with it. I will discuss several options, with an emphasis on items I have used personally.

Cases

The RX100 VI is such a small camera that you may find you don't need a case. There is no separate lens cap to deal with, and when the camera turns off and its lens retracts, the RX100 VI is ready to stow easily in your pocket, purse, or other handy location. But I do use a case with my RX100 VI, and I know that other users do also, so I will provide some suggestions.

The Sony case made for the RX100 series of cameras, model number LCJ-RXF, is shown in Figures A-1 and A-2. This case is similar to an earlier version that was made for the original RX100 camera. The older version may not fit the newer camera, so be sure to check the model number of the case. This case is just roomy enough to hold the RX100 VI with its tilting LCD.

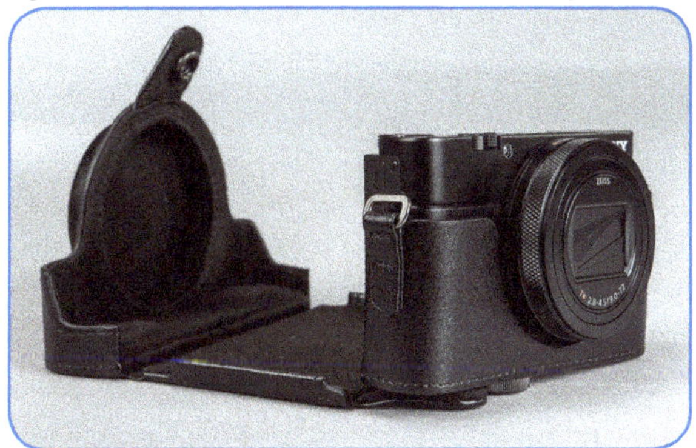

Figure A-1. Sony LCJ-RXF Case Open

This is an attractive case made of synthetic material that looks like leather. It holds the camera securely and comes with a matching shoulder strap. It will hold the camera with a filter adapter attached, but not with an add-on grip installed. It does not have room for holding an extra battery or other items.

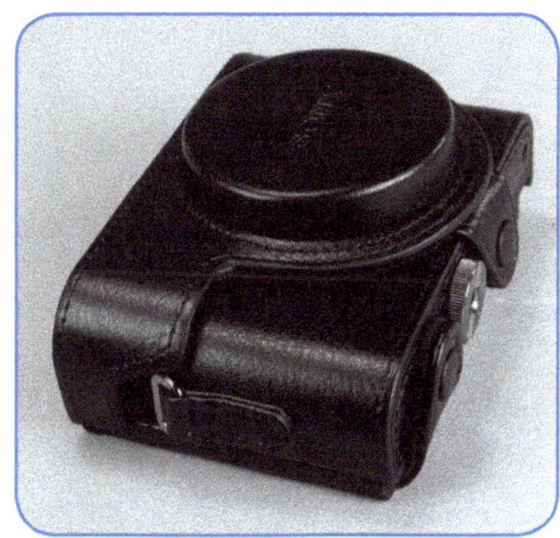

Figure A-2. Sony LCJ-RXF Case Closed

A less expensive option is a generic case like the Camson case shown in Figures A-3 and A-4.

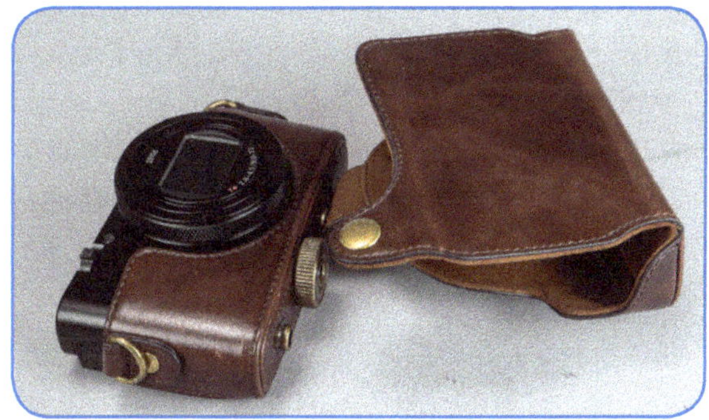

Figure A-3. Camson Case Open

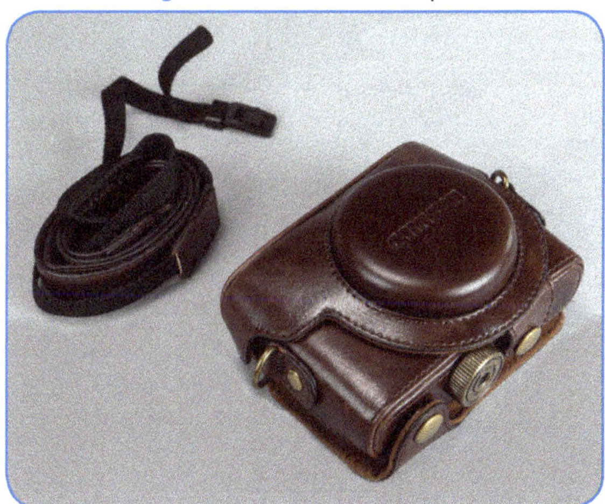

Figure A-4. Camson Case Closed

This brown leather case comes with a matching strap and can hold the camera with filter adapter, but not much else. It has a nice appearance and feel and does not display the Sony label, so it may provide a degree of security because it does not reveal the brand of your camera. I purchased this case from Wall Street Photo in New York.

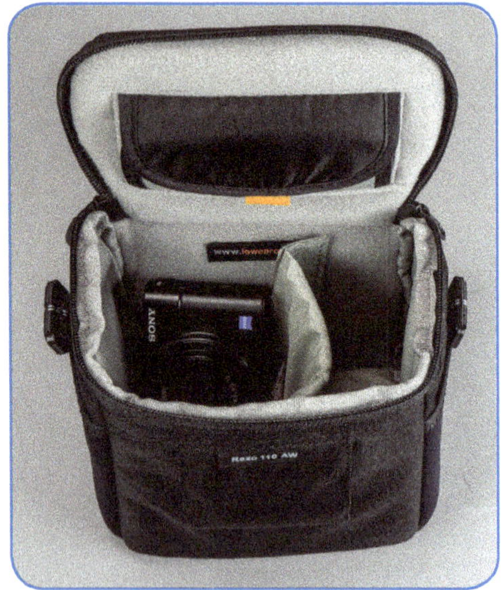

Figure A-5. Lowepro Rezo 110 AW Case

If you want a case with room for other items besides the camera, there are many choices. One I have used successfully is the Lowepro Rezo 110 AW, shown in Figure A-5. This case can hold the camera with grip and filter adapter, and has room for other items such as filters and extra batteries. It has a belt loop, or you can carry it by the padded handle on top. You also could fit a small bottle of water and some snacks for a short trip.

Another good option is a standard waist pack, not designed just for photography, such as the Eagle Creek pack shown in Figure A-6. It can readily accommodate the camera and some small accessories, and it has two mesh pockets for holding small water bottles.

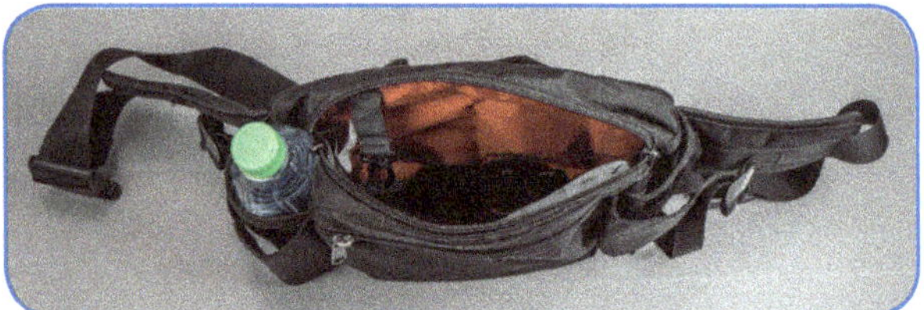

Figure A-6. Eagle Creek Waist Pack

Batteries and Chargers

This is a category of items that I recommend you purchase along with the camera or soon after getting the camera. I use the RX100 VI heavily, and I find it runs through batteries fairly quickly. You can't use disposable batteries, so if you're out taking pictures and the battery dies, you're out of luck unless you have a spare battery (or another power source, as discussed below). The model number of the Sony battery is NP-BX1. You can get a spare Sony battery for about $35 as I write this. It won't do you a great deal of good by itself, though, because the battery is designed to be charged in the camera.

There is an easy solution to this problem. You can find generic replacement batteries, as well as chargers to charge the batteries outside the camera, inexpensively from online sellers. I purchased a package including a generic replacement battery and a charger for about $20 on eBay. You also can get the official Sony external charger, model number BC-TRX. Besides charging a battery externally, the Sony charger can be used with its included USB cable to charge a battery inside the camera. Both the Sony charger and a generic charger are shown in Figure A-7, along with a generic battery and a Sony battery.

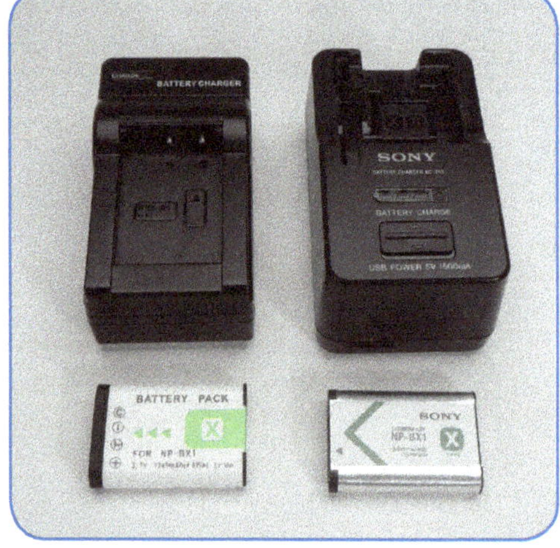

Figure A-7. Battery Chargers and Batteries

Another option for powering the RX100 VI is to use the AC adapter that comes with the camera, which is model number AC-UUD12 in the United States. You can plug the micro USB end of the camera's USB cable into the Multi port on the camera and plug the other end into the AC adapter, and then plug the adapter into an electrical outlet, and it will provide constant power to the camera. If the camera is turned off, the battery inside the camera will be charged. If the camera is turned on, you can operate the camera normally. (The battery will not be charged while the camera is powered externally, though.) There must be a battery installed in the camera for this system to work. If there is no battery installed, the camera will not turn on.

Of course, it is usually not convenient to have the camera plugged into an electrical outlet, unless you are taking shots in a studio or otherwise using the camera indoors. If you want to power the camera from an external source when you are in the field, you can get a good-quality USB power source and connect it to the camera, either for charging the camera's battery or for powering the camera. Figure A-8 shows the Mophie PowerStation XL portable USB battery.

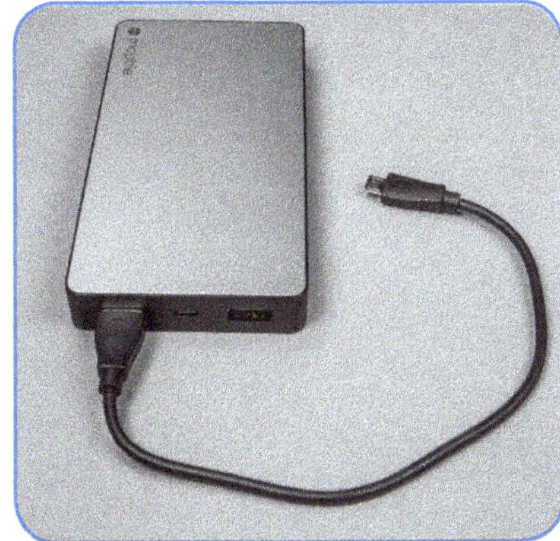

Figure A-8. Mophie PowerStation XL Portable USB Battery

This device has two standard-sized USB ports. You can plug the camera's USB cable into one of those ports and connect the other end to the camera to provide a long-lasting source of power, or to charge the camera's battery. You can charge the power supply through its own micro USB port, using any compatible AC adapter. In fact, you can use the RX100 VI's own AC adapter to recharge the Mophie device. The Mophie device is not very large and weighs about 220 grams (8 ounces).

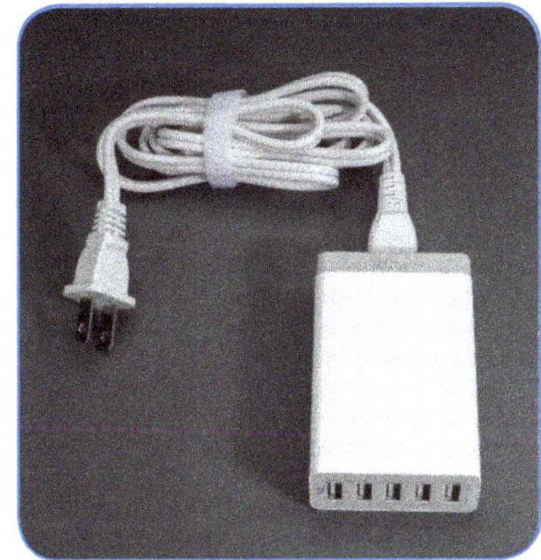

Figure A-9. Anker 40-Watt Desktop USB Charger

Another device I have found useful for providing power for the RX100 VI is the Anker 40-watt desktop USB charger, shown in Figure A-9, which has five slots for charging devices such as phones and tablets. I have used it to charge my iPhone and iPad, and it can charge the Sony battery inside the RX100 VI camera at the same time. You also can use it to charge the Mophie device, discussed above. There undoubtedly are other USB chargers that can handle this process; just make sure the charger meets the necessary specifications. A device rated at 5 volts and 1 amp generally works well.

Add-On Filters and Lenses

There is no way to attach a filter or other item, such as a closeup lens, directly to the RX100 VI's lens, as you can with larger cameras whose lenses are threaded to accept filters and auxiliary lenses. With the RX100 VI, to add such accessory items you need to get an adapter. One such adapter is the Magfilter system, which lets you attach any 52mm-diameter filter to the camera's lens.

The adapter has two parts. The first part, shown already attached to the lens in Figure A-10, is a small metallic ring that you glue onto the front of the lens barrel using an adhesive patch provided by the company.

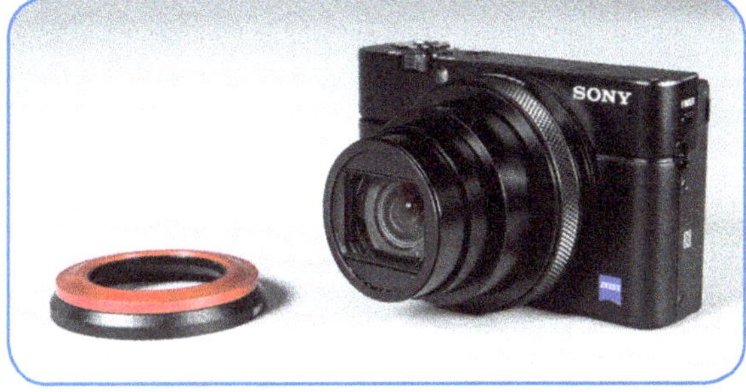

Figure A-10. Filter Adapter Base Ring Attached to Camera

This piece stays in place and does not interfere with the lens or the automatic lens cover. You then attach the actual adapter, the red and black object lying beside the camera in Figure A-10, which attaches by magnetism onto the ring on the lens, as shown in Figure A-11. In this figure, a filter is shown screwed into the adapter.

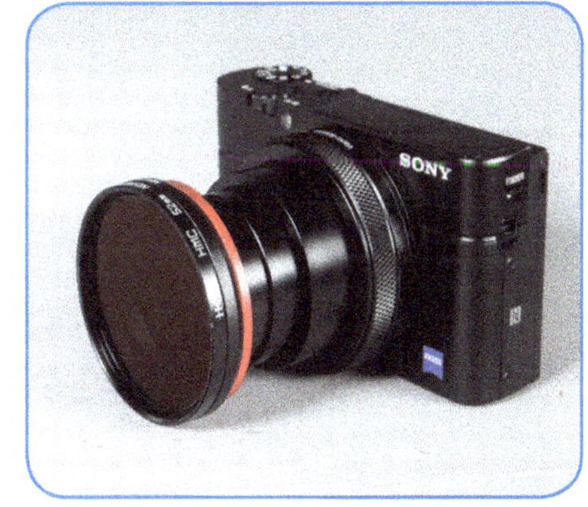

Figure A-11. Filter Adapter Attached to Base Ring

You can screw any 52mm diameter filter or other auxiliary lens into the holder. The base ring is removable if you later want to take it off the lens.

As you might expect, this system is not as sturdy as the natural screw-on capability of other cameras because everything depends on a small ring that is glued in place and the strength of its magnetism. So don't expect to attach large items like teleconverters or anything heavier than a standard 52mm filter. Having the ability to attach filters, however, enhances the usefulness of the camera. You can use neutral density filters, polarizers, or any of a wide assortment of closeup lenses, among others. Also, as discussed in Chapter 10, I used this system to attach the RX100 VI to the eyepiece of a telescope and spotting scope to take pictures through the scopes. You have to be careful not to put too much stress on the adapter in that situation, but the adapter worked well for that purpose.

There is a similar system sold for the RX100 VI by Lensmate, at lensmateonline.com, but that adapter was not available for testing at the time of this writing. I have used past filter adapter models from Lensmate with good success. In fact, I prefer the Lensmate system because it provides a more secure connection between the lens and the filter than the Magfilter system does.

Grips

Some users find it difficult to get a firm grasp of the RX100 VI because it is small and has a smooth front surface with no place to take hold of it. Sony offers a solution to this issue—a custom-made grip, model number AG-R2, shown in Figure A-12. This grip has a somewhat rough texture, making it easy to hold on to the camera. I don't find the grip necessary, but it can provide a degree of security in grasping the camera.

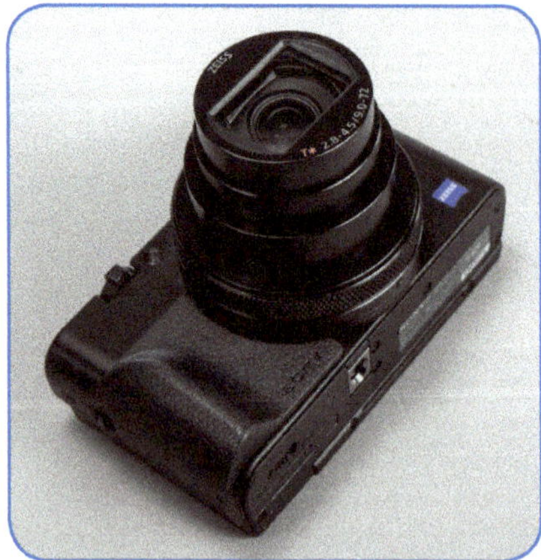

Figure A-12. Sony Grip, Model Number AG-R2, with RX100 VI

Remote Controls

In several situations, it is useful to control a camera remotely. For example, when you are using slow shutter speeds, holding the shutter open with the BULB setting, doing closeup photography, or taking pictures through a telescope, any camera motion during the exposure is likely to blur the image. If you control the camera remotely, you lessen the risk of blurred images from moving the camera as you press the shutter button. Remote control also is helpful when you need to be located away from the camera, as for taking self-portraits or images of wildlife.

As I discussed in Chapter 10, the RX100 VI has a built-in Wi-Fi capability for connecting a computer, smartphone, or tablet to the camera wirelessly. Besides using that feature to transfer images from the camera to the other device, you can use a smartphone or tablet as a wireless remote control. However, it can be tricky to establish and maintain the connection between the camera and the phone or tablet.

Fortunately, Sony offers several remote controls that are compatible with the RX100 VI camera.

Sony's remote control model number RM-VPR1 is shown in Figure A-13.

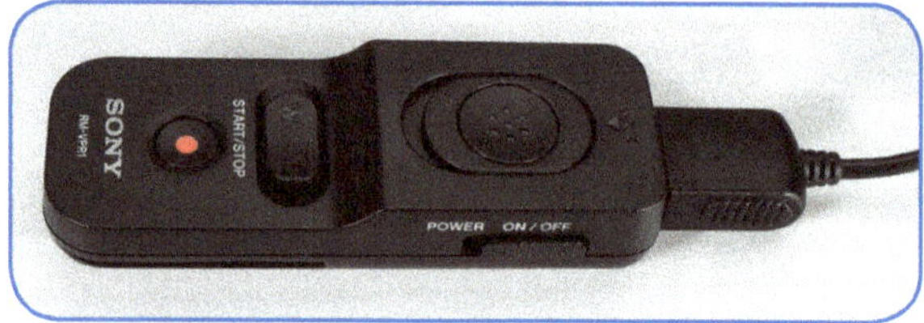

Figure A-13. Sony Remote Control RM-VPR1

You connect this device to the Multi port on the right side of the camera. With this remote, you can turn the camera on and off, use the autofocus system, zoom the lens in and out, take a still image, lock the shutter down for a long exposure, and start and stop video recording.

This remote comes with two cables—one for cameras with a Remote terminal and one for cameras like the RX100 VI, which has the Multi terminal. Take the cable that has identical connectors at each end, and plug the end with the smaller plastic housing into the camera. Plug the other end of the cable, which has a larger housing, into the remote. You also can attach the included clip to the underside of the remote, if you want to clip the remote to a tripod or other support.

You can half-press the shutter button to cause the autofocus system to operate (if the camera is in an autofocus mode), and press the button fully to take a still picture. You can press the shutter button down and then slide it back toward the other controls to lock it in place. This locking is useful when you are taking continuous shots using the drive mode settings, or when you want to hold the shutter open using the BULB setting in Manual exposure mode. Press the shutter button back up in its original direction to release it.

The red button labeled Start/Stop is similar to the Movie button on the RX100 VI camera. Press it once to start recording a movie and press it again to stop the recording.

The power button on the side of the remote control can be used to turn the camera on and off, and to wake it up from power-saving mode. Press the switch back toward yourself as you hold the control to power the camera either on or off.

A more sophisticated remote, Sony model number RMT-VP1K, is shown in Figure A-14.

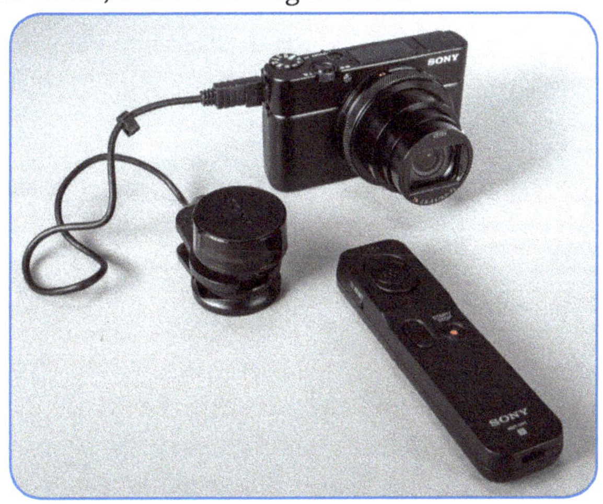

Figure A-14. Sony Remote Control RMT-VP1K

This remote comes with an infrared receiver that plugs into the camera's Multi port. The receiver, a small cylinder, has a foot for attaching to a camera's flash shoe, but, of course, the RX100 VI has no shoe, so you have to let the receiver dangle or attach it somewhere else. The remote kit comes with a clip that you can use to attach the receiver to a tripod leg or other support.

The remote control itself is similar to the wired remote discussed earlier, RM-VPR1, though there are some differences. You can press the shutter button, and you can lock it down for BULB shooting. You can zoom the lens and start and stop a video recording. The remote has a slide switch labeled TC Reset on the left side, which you can operate to reset the camera's time code to zero. With the camera's mode dial at the Movie position, press the TC Reset switch on the remote, and the time code displayed in the lower left corner of the display will be reset to the zero point. The way to accomplish this reset in the camera is to go to the TC Preset option under TC/UB Settings on screen 3 of the Setup menu. With TC Preset highlighted, press the Center button to bring up the screen showing the values of the current time code. While that screen is displayed, press the Custom/Delete button, and the time code will be reset. It is considerably easier to just press the TC Reset button on the remote if you need to reset the time code.

Figure A-15 shows another option, Sony model number RM-SPR1. This device is a very simple wired remote that also connects to the Multi port. It has only one large button, which acts as a remote shutter button.

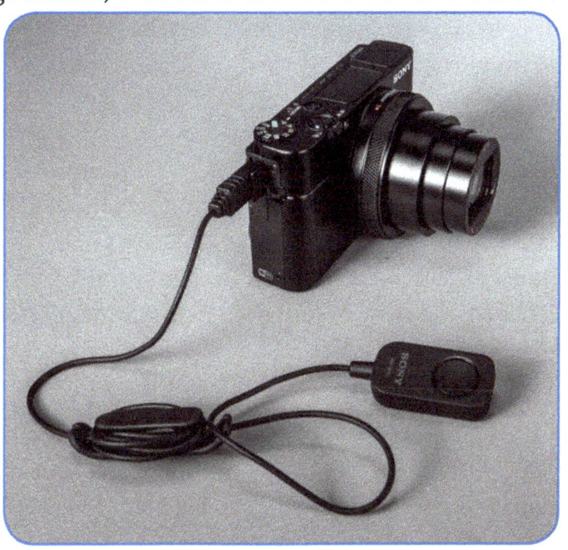

Figure A-15. Sony Remote Control RM-SPR1

You can press it halfway to evaluate focus and exposure, press it all the way to take a still image, or hold it down to fire a burst of shots if drive mode is set for continuous shooting. You cannot use this remote to record a movie or carry out any other functions.

One more device, which has more functionality than an ordinary remote control, is the Vello Wireless ShutterBoss for Sony cameras with the Multi terminal, shown in Figure A-16.

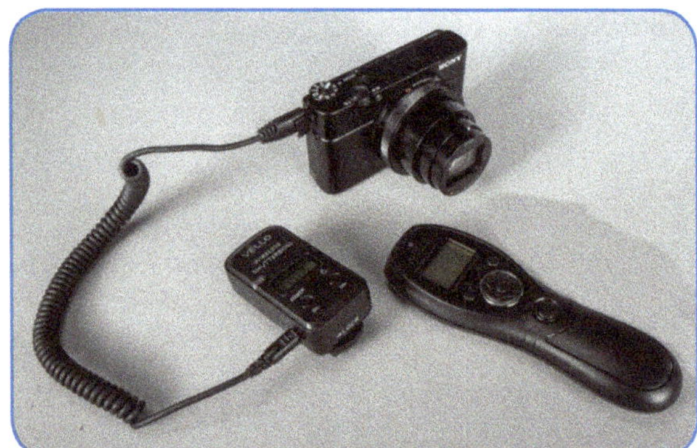

Figure A-16. Vello Wireless Shutterboss

This versatile device, which makes use of a wireless receiver that attaches to the camera's Multi terminal, can act as a remote control, similar to the Sony devices discussed above. In addition, it can serve as a powerful intervalometer, for setting up the camera for a time-lapse sequence. Using the controls and the small LCD screen on the device, you can set up a sequence of up to 399 shots, or an indefinite series, until you command it to stop. You can set the interval between shots to any value from one second up to 99 hours, 59 minutes, and 59 seconds.

Finally, one other remote control to consider is Sony's shooting grip, model number VCT-SGR1. This item, which was announced at the same time as the RX100 VI camera, is a compact handle that screws into the camera's tripod socket, as shown in Figure A-17.

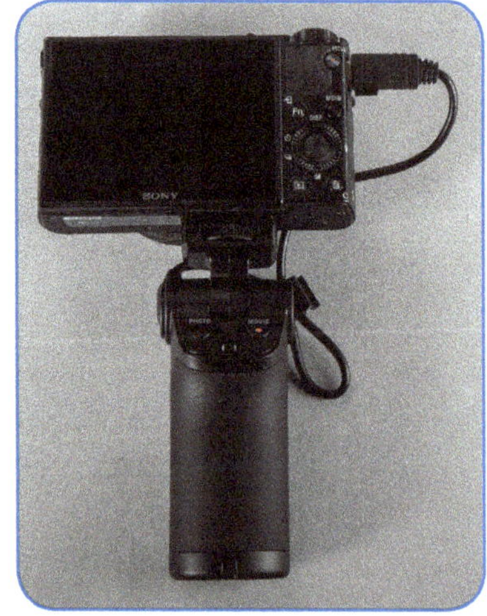

Figure A-17. Sony Shooting Grip, VCT-SGR1

It includes a cable that attaches to the camera's Multi port, so it can serve as a remote control for shooting stills and movies and for zooming the lens. This grip is handy for holding the camera above your head and viewing the tilted LCD screen from below, while operating the camera with the remote control. The grip also folds out into a three-legged tabletop tripod as an added convenience, as shown in Figure A-18.

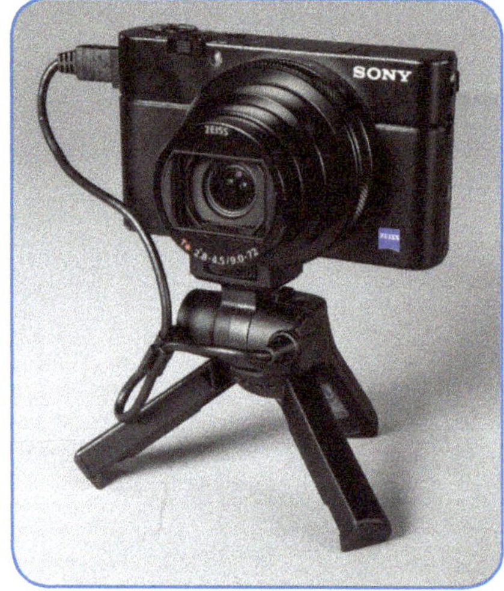

Figure A-18. Sony Shooting Grip, VCT-SGR1, Used as Tripod

External Flash

When Sony designed the RX100 VI, they included the desirable feature of a built-in viewfinder that pops up, but, probably because of that feature, they omitted a hot shoe where you can attach an external flash unit. So, if you want to use an external unit to supplement the light from the camera's small pop-up flash, you have to use an optical slave.

An optical slave is a flash unit that includes a sensor that triggers the flash when it senses the light from the camera's built-in flash. (You also can use a separate optical slave that can be attached to any compatible flash unit.)

One problem with this system is that the RX100 VI fires one or more pre-flashes before it fires the main flash burst to expose the image. The camera uses the pre-flashes to measure the amount of light being reflected from the subject so the image can be exposed properly. If the optical slave is not set to ignore the pre-flashes, it will fire as soon as it "sees" a pre-flash, and the external flash will not be synchronized with the actual exposure.

The solution to this problem is to use an optical slave that can be set to ignore the pre-flashes. One of the best ones I have found for use with the RX100 VI is the LumoPro LP180, shown in Figure A-19. This powerful unit has a head that swivels and rotates, a built-in diffuser, variable power, and settings that allow it to ignore a variable number of pre-flashes. I have had good success using this flash with the RX100 VI by setting the flash to its S2-1 mode.

With this flash, as with any optical slave, you have to use Manual exposure mode on the camera and determine the proper exposure by trial and error or by using a light meter. You can set up the external flash on a light stand or tripod at any location where it can sense the light from the camera's built-in flash.

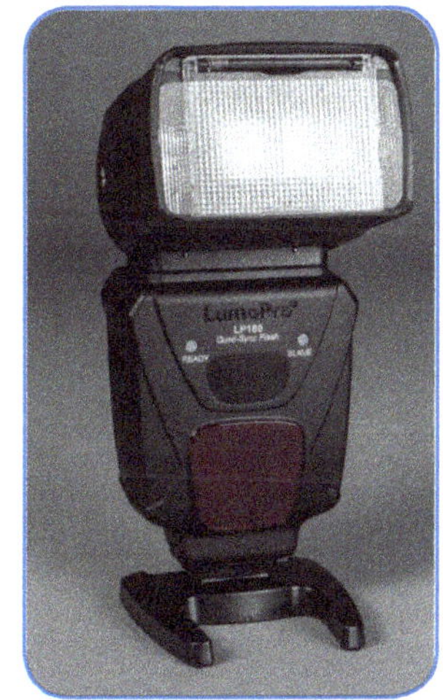

Figure A-19. LumoPro LP180 Flash

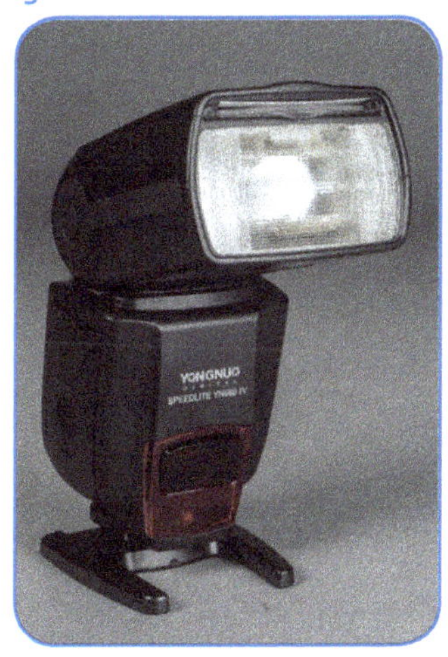

Figure A-20. Yongnuo YN560-IV Flash

Another good unit for use as an optical slave is the Yongnuo YN560-IV, shown in Figure A-20, which also has a built-in optical slave capability.

I had success using this unit with the RX100 VI with the flash set to its S2 optical slave mode. You can attach this, or any, external flash to the RX100 VI using a standard flash bracket with a tripod socket.

When you set the camera to Manual exposure mode, the camera's display screen (or electronic viewfinder display) is likely to be black or very dark because the exposure settings would result in a dark image if you were not using flash, and the camera will not "know" about the effects of the external flash. Therefore, it may be difficult to compose the shot. The solution is to go to screen 7 of the Camera Settings2 menu on the camera, and set the Live View Display option to Setting Effect Off. With that setting, the camera's display will not darken to show the effects of the manual exposure settings, and you will probably be able to view the display clearly enough to compose the image.

External Video Recorder

In Chapter 9, I discussed how to take advantage of the RX100 VI's excellent video features to output its 4K video signal via the HDMI port to an external video recorder. Using this system, you can bypass the five-minute limit on recording 4K video to a memory card, and you can even make a 4K recording with no memory card in the camera at all.

The recorder I used to test this process is the original Atomos Shogun 4K recorder, a very capable device though an expensive one. The original Shogun is no longer available, but the more recent Shogun Inferno and Shogun Flame models are available at this writing for about $1,000 each. As you can see from Figure A-21, the recorder is considerably larger than the camera, and it can be tricky to mount the two devices together. I ended up attaching the camera on top of the recorder using a Pearstone 4.2-inch (10.7 cm) articulating arm, which has tripod screws on two mounting heads, shown here. (With larger cameras, the Shogun often is mounted on top of the camera; the Shogun has standard tripod sockets on its top and bottom edges.)

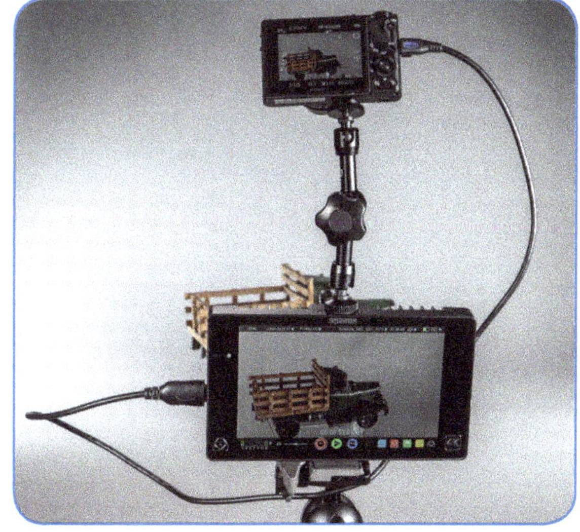

Figure A-21. Atomos Shogun Video Recorder with RX100 VI

Apart from the mounting issues, the combination of RX100 VI and Shogun performed very well in producing 4K video files. The menu system is easy to work with and the recorder produces high-quality files. At the highest quality, the files can be extremely large (more than 190 GB in one case), so be prepared with a strong computer capability for editing. There are other 4K video recorders that might work as well, such as the Odyssey7Q+ recorder from Convergent Design or devices from Blackmagic Design, though I have not tested any of those.

External Audio Recorder

The RX100 VI camera has excellent video features but no provision for connecting an external microphone for high-quality audio. Although the built-in microphone records good-quality audio, you can get better results if you use an external audio recorder and synchronize the audio track from that recorder with the sound recorded by the camera. It is not difficult to sync the audio and video; for one article on the procedure, see https://www.premiumbeat.com/blog/how-to-sync-audio-to-video/.

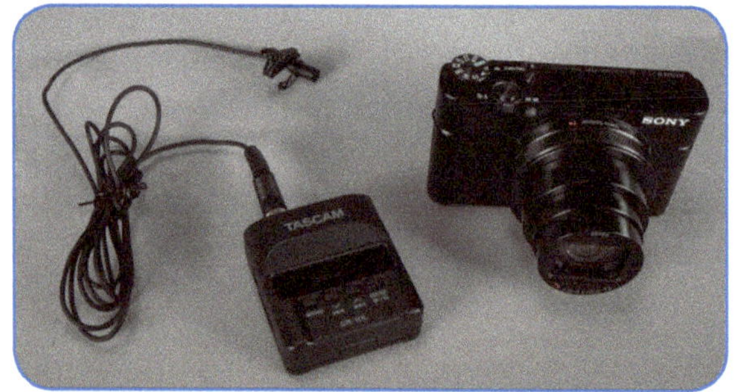

Figure A-22. Tascam DR-10L Audio Recorder with RX100 VI

One excellent piece of equipment for this purpose is the Tascam DR-10L recorder, shown in Figure A-22. This very small device records high-quality audio through its included lavalier microphone, or you can attach another microphone of your choice. There are many other options that will work for this purpose, depending on your budget and needs, including the Shure VP83F, the Tascam DR-40, the Zoom F1, the Zoom H1, and the Zoom H6. Also, if you use the Atomos Shogun video recorder discussed above or a similar model, you can connect high-quality microphones to that device using an audio connection cable from Atomos.

Tripods

I will mention two tripods that I have found to be excellent for traveling with the Sony RX100 VI camera. They are both Manfrotto BeFree tripods, shown in Figures A-23 and A-24.

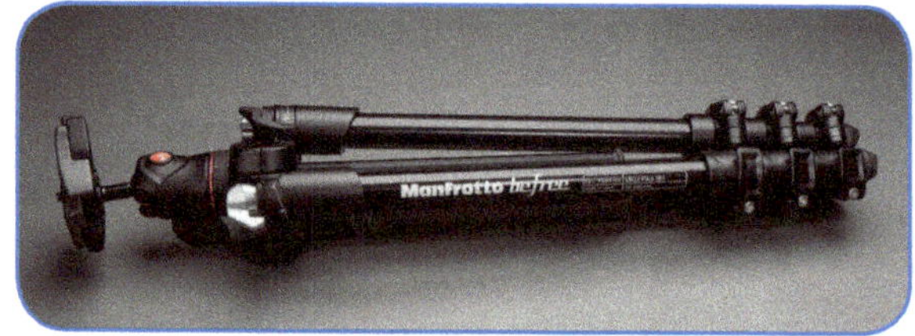

Figure A-23. Manfrotto BeFree Aluminum Tripod

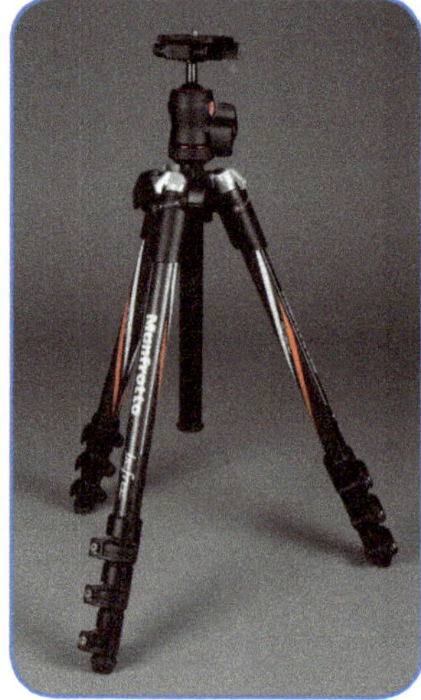

Figure A-24. Manfrotto BeFree Carbon-fiber Tripod

The version in Figure A-23 shows the aluminum version, model no. MKBFRA4-BH. It includes a versatile head, reduces to about 20 inches (50 cm) long just by collapsing the legs, and to about 16 inches (40 cm) if you take the trouble to fold the legs backward. It weighs about three pounds five ounces (1.5 kg). The tripod in Figure A-24 is the carbon-fiber version, model no. MKBFRC4-BH, which is lighter and more expensive than the aluminum one.

External LCD Monitor

There is another accessory to consider for viewing live and recorded images with the RX100 VI. The Sony Clip-On LCD Monitor, model number CLM-FHD5, is an add-on unit with a 5-inch (12-cm) screen. The unit, shown in a closeup view in Figure A-25, includes a short HDMI cable that ends in a micro HDMI plug at the camera end, for connecting to the HDMI port of the camera. It also includes a folding sunshade, which is attached to the screen in this image.

This monitor adds visibility for viewing the shooting screen and for playing back images and videos. The screen can rotate 180 degrees, so you can view the scene from the front of the camera for self-portraits. It also can tilt up or down for viewing from high or low angles. The monitor has numerous controls for settings such as Peaking, brightness, and contrast, and it has a special display mode for boosting the contrast when you are using the S-Log2 gamma curve. This unit costs about $700 at the time of this writing, plus the cost of a battery, but if you need the extra screen size or versatility, it is worth looking into.

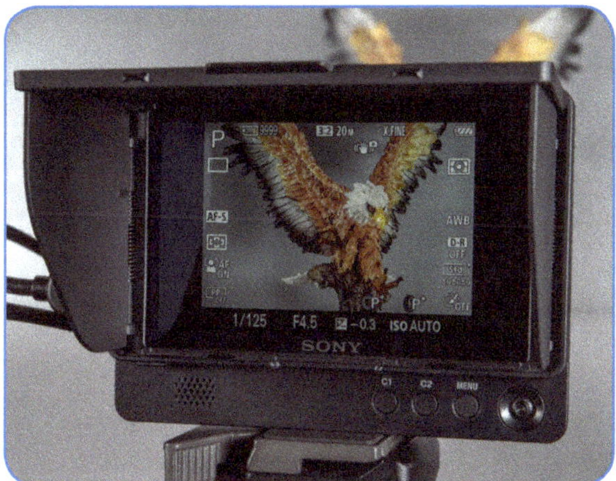

Figure A-25. Sony LCD Monitor CLM-FHD5

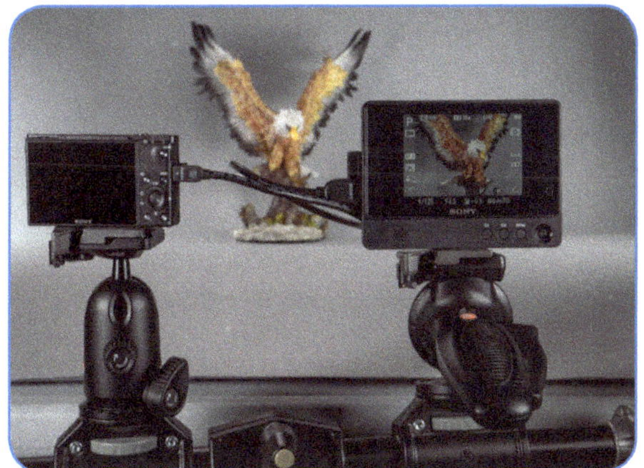

Figure A-26. Sony LCD Monitor and RX100 VI Attached to Same Bar

With a larger camera, the monitor can be attached to an accessory shoe on the camera's top. With the RX100 VI, which has no shoe, you can use a flash bracket or some other accessory to hold the monitor. In Figure A-26, I attached the monitor and the camera to two separate ball heads on a horizontal bar on my tripod, to show how the two devices work together.

Gimbal

Because of the RX100 VI's ability to record 4K video and its other excellent video features, including high speed video, the camera is well suited to cinematography. If you want to maximize its usefulness in this area, you may want to consider a gimbal, like the one shown in Figure A-27.

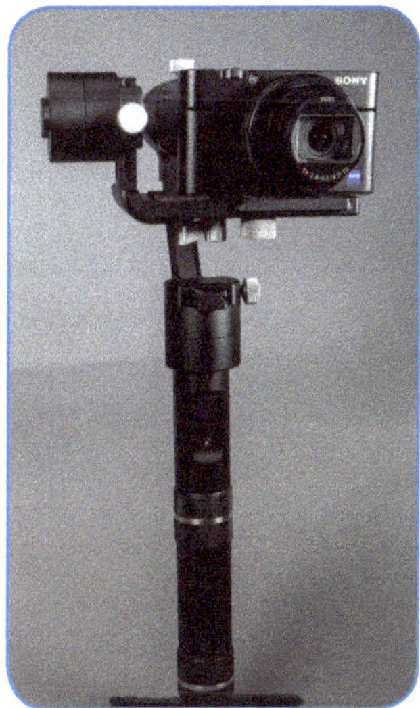

Figure A-27. Zhiyun Crane-M Gimbal with RX100 VI

This device, the Zhiyun Crane-M, is one of many such stabilizing mechanisms now available for video production. The gimbal includes three small motors which constantly level the camera on three axes to counter movements made by the camera, even as you handhold the camera and walk with it. The result is smooth, stabilized video footage. This particular model is well suited for the size and features of the RX100 VI camera.

Appendix B: Quick Tips

In this section, I will list some tips and facts that might be useful as reminders. I have tried to include points that you might not remember from day to day, especially if you don't use the RX100 VI constantly.

Move the focus frame quickly. To adjust the focus frame for use with autofocus, choose Flexible Spot or Expand Flexible Spot for focus area on screen 4 of the Camera Settings1 menu. Then, when the camera is in shooting mode, touch the focus frame to move it around the display. For other options for moving the focus area, see Chapter 4.

Use Auto ISO with Manual exposure mode. With these settings, you can set the shutter speed and aperture and let the camera choose the ISO value to produce a good exposure. This is like having a new shooting mode that lets you stop action and control depth of field at the same time.

Use continuous shooting. Consider turning burst shooting on as a matter of routine, unless you are running out of storage space or battery power, or have a reason not to use it. Even with portraits, you may get the perfect expression on your subject's face with the fourth or fifth shot. Press the Left button (or use the menu system) to call up drive mode, scroll to Continuous Shooting, and turn it on. With the High speed setting, the camera can shoot at up to 24 frames per second while adjusting focus and exposure. Continuous shooting is not available when the camera is set to Sweep Panorama mode or to any Scene mode setting other than Sports Action.

Use 4K video for super continuous shooting. When you use the 4K video format for recording video, you can extract still frames from the video sequence using editing software such as Adobe Premiere Pro or Final Cut Pro, or with the Photo Capture option on screen 2 of the Playback menu. If you shoot with a fast enough shutter speed to stop action, you can use this system to produce still images with good resolution and image quality. In effect, you can do continuous shooting at 30 frames per second for up to five minutes at a time.

Use tethered shooting. With the RX100 VI, you can connect the camera to a Mac or Windows computer and control the camera from the computer using the free Imaging Edge software from Sony. That software can be downloaded from http://www.sony.co.jp/imsoft/Win/ for Windows-based computers and from http://www.sony.co.jp/imsoft/Mac/ for Macintosh computers. Then, on screen 4 of the Setup menu, select PC Remote for USB Connection. Details are in Chapter 8.

Use shortcuts. Speed up access to many settings by placing them on the Function menu for recall with a press of the Function button. In some cases, as with flash mode and drive mode, you can press a button (the Right and Left buttons, respectively) to get access to the features you need. Use the control wheel to move rapidly through the items on a menu screen. Use the Right and Left buttons to move through the menus a screen at a time, and move from one menu system to another by highlighting the icons at the top of the screen and navigating between icons with the Right and Left buttons. Use the Custom Key options on screen 9 of the Camera Settings2 menu to assign functions to control buttons.

Take advantage of the help system. The RX100 VI does a good job of advising you about conflicts between settings. If a menu option is unavailable for selection, you can still highlight it and press the Center button. The camera will display a message telling you what setting is causing the highlighted item to be unavailable. Press the C button when a menu item is highlighted to get information about the item, if In-Camera Guide is assigned to that button through the Custom Key (Still Images) or Custom Key (Movies) menu option.

Use the Memory Recall shooting mode. The MR position on the mode dial lets you save seven favorite groups of settings. You also can use it for more specific purposes.

I like to have one slot set up to remove all "special" settings, such as Creative Style, Picture Effect, and self-timer, so I can quickly set up the camera to take a shot with no surprises. You can use one slot to set the lens at a particular focal length, such as, say, 50mm. To do this, press the zoom lever to move the lens, so you see the desired value below the zoom scale in the upper right corner of the display. When the value is set as you want it, use the Memory menu option to save the settings to one of the MR slots. (You also can use the Step Zoom feature to set a particular zoom amount; to do that, set the Zoom Function on Ring option on screen 6 of the Camera Settings2 menu to Step.)

Use an external power source to power or charge the camera. The RX100 VI can be powered by any compatible USB battery, such as the Mophie unit discussed in Appendix A. A device like that is useful when you need to do extensive photography in the field. It also can recharge the battery inside the camera when the camera is powered off.

Use the extra settings for white balance and Creative Style. When you set white balance, even to Auto White Balance, you can press the Right button and use the amber-blue and green-magenta axes to further adjust the color of your shots. Remember to undo any color shift when you no longer need it. Also, you can press the Right button after selecting a Creative Style option and then adjust the contrast, saturation, and sharpness settings. (Saturation is not adjustable for the Black and White and Sepia settings.)

Play your movies in iTunes, and on iPods, iPhones, and iPads. If you record movies using the MP4 extension (including XAVC S HD and XAVC S 4K movies), you can use iTunes to copy the MP4 files to an iTunes-compatible device, such as an iPad. After transferring the files to your computer, open iTunes on that computer and drag an .mp4 file from the computer's Explorer or Finder window to the Home Videos panel in iTunes. You can then play the movie from iTunes. To play it on an iPod, iPhone, or iPad, select the video in iTunes, and, on the iTunes menu, select File—Convert—Create iPod or iPhone version, or Create iPad or AppleTV version, as appropriate. Then sync iTunes with your device, and the converted movie will play on that device. (If you have trouble locating the .mp4 files on your computer, see the next item in this appendix.)

Find movie files on a memory card. One issue you may encounter when first starting to edit movie files from the RX100 VI is finding the files. When you insert a memory card into a card reader, the still images are easy to find; on my computer, the SD card shows up as No Name or Untitled; then, beneath that level, there is a folder called DCIM; inside it are folders with names such as 100MSDCF, which contain the still images. (If you use the Folder Name option on screen 6 of the Setup menu to select Date Form, the folder names will be based on dates the images were taken; an example is 10080830 for images taken on August 30, 2018.)

The movie files are a bit trickier to find. The XAVC S files that you need to find and import into your software for editing have an .mp4 extension, but they are not the same as the more ordinary .mp4 files. Here is the path to a sample XAVC S file: Untitled\Private\M4ROOT\CLIP\C0007.MP4.

Here is the path to an AVCHD movie file: Untitled\Private\AVCHD\BDMV\Stream\0006.MTS. These files can be difficult to find on a Macintosh, because the Finder may not immediately show the contents of the AVCHD folder. You may have to right-click on the AVCHD item in the Finder and select Show Package Contents in order to view the BDMV folder. You may have to repeat that process to see the contents of the BDMV folder.

Diffuse your flash. If the built-in flash produces light that's too harsh for macro or other shots, try using translucent plastic pieces from milk jugs or broken ping-pong balls as diffusers. Hold the plastic between the flash and the subject. When using Fill-flash out-doors, use the Flash Compensation setting on the Camera Settings1 menu to reduce the intensity of the flash by -2/3 EV. You can bounce the light from the built-in flash off of the ceiling or a wall by holding it back gently with a finger.

Use the self-timer to avoid camera shake. The self-timer is not just for group portraits; you can use the two-second or five-second self-timer whenever you use a slow shutter speed and need to avoid camera shake. It also is useful for macro photography. Don't forget that you can set the self-timer to take multiple shots, which can increase your chances of getting more great images.

Use DMF for focusing. The direct manual focus option combines the camera's autofocus ability with your own manual focus adjustments, to achieve precision for critical focus tasks. You can use the MF Assist option, which enlarges the display when you turn the Control ring to adjust focus, but, with DMF, you have to half-press the shutter button as you turn the control ring for MF Assist to work.

Try time-lapse photography. With time-lapse photography, a camera takes a series of still images at regular intervals, several seconds, minutes, or even hours apart, to record a slow-moving event such as the rising or setting of the moon or sun or the opening of a flower. The images are played back at a much faster rate to show the whole event unfolding quickly. The RX100 VI does not have this feature built in, but you can control interval shooting with Sony's Imaging Edge software when the camera is connected to a computer, or the Vello ShutterBoss II or Wireless Shutterboss intervalometer, as discussed in Appendix A.

Use the self-timer for bracketed exposures. To do this, use the Bracket Settings option on screen 3 of the Camera Settings1 menu and select the first sub-option, Self-timer During Bracket.

Use the camera's automatic HDR option. To do this, go to screen 9 of the Camera Settings1 menu, select DRO/Auto HDR, then HDR. You cannot use certain other settings with HDR, including Raw for Quality, Picture Effect, or Picture Profile.

Use the settings that are available only when assigned to a control button. Use the Custom Key (Still Images) option on screen 9 of the Camera Settings2 menu to assign one of these settings to the Custom, Left, Right, or Center button. These include Eye AF, AF/MF Control Toggle, AEL Toggle, Bright Monitoring, and others, as discussed in Chapter 5. Several options also work during video recording when assigned to control buttons using the Custom Key (Movies) option, including focus mode, focus area, ISO, Focus Magnifier, and Picture Profile, among others, as discussed in Chapter 9.

Use the Playback button to turn on the camera. This is useful if you only need to look at menu items or view your images or videos. The lens will not be activated.

Use the Picture Profile feature to full advantage. If you are really serious about getting the maximum benefit from the Picture Profile feature, including the S-Log2, S-Log3, and HLG options for gamma, you need to use color-grading software. A good software package can take advantage of the profiles and bring out the colors, contrast, and other aspects of your video files in the way you intend. An extremely powerful program is DaVinci Resolve 15, which is available in a free version as well as a professional one. See https://www.blackmagicdesign.com/products/davinciresolve.

Experiment with Picture Profile for still images. Picture Profile is intended primarily for use with video recording, to achieve consistent results among various video cameras and to manage dynamic range efficiently. However, the RX100 VI's Picture Profile menu option includes a wealth of adjustments, some of which might be useful for your still photography. For example, you might take one of the settings, such as PP1, and adjust it for a particular purpose. You could set Color Mode to Black & White, and then adjust the Color Depth options to emphasize the brightness of the various colors (red, green, blue, cyan, magenta, and yellow), in a way similar to the use of glass filters on a camera using black-and-white film.

Avoid the five-minute limit for high-quality video recording. If you record video to an external video recorder, as discussed in Chapter 9, with no memory card in the camera, you can record for longer periods of time, avoiding the five-minute limit for the highest-quality formats.

Appendix C: Resources for Further Information

Websites and Videos

Since websites come and go and change their addresses, it's impossible to compile a list of sites that discuss the RX100 VI that will be accurate far into the future. I will include below a list of some of the sites or links I have found useful, with the caveat that some of them may not be accessible by the time you read this.

Digital Photography Review

Listed below is the current web address for the "Sony Cyber-shot Talk" forum within the dpreview.com site. Dpreview.com is one of the most established and authoritative sites for reviews, discussion forums, technical information, and other resources concerning digital cameras.

http://www.dpreview.com/forums/1009

Reviews and Demonstrations of the RX100 VI

The links below lead to reviews or previews of the RX100 VI by dpreview.com, photographyblog.com, and others.

https://www.dpreview.com/reviews/sony-cyber-shot-dsc-rx100-vi-m6

https://www.cameralabs.com/sony-rx100-vi-review/

https://www.imaging-resource.com/PRODS/sony-rx100-vi/sony-rx100-viA.HTM

https://www.techradar.com/reviews/sony-cyber-shot-rx100-vi

https://www.photographyblog.com/reviews/sony_cybershot_rx100_vi_review

https://www.dpmag.com/cameras/compact/sony-rx100-vi-first-sample-images-and-thoughts/

https://www.pcmag.com/review/361684/sony-cyber-shot-dsc-rx100-vi

https://www.trustedreviews.com/reviews/sony-rx100-vi

White Knight Press

My own site, White Knight Press, provides updates about this book and other books, offers support for download of PDFs and ebooks, and provides a way for readers or potential readers to contact me with questions or comments.

https://www.whiteknightpress.com

The Official Sony Site

The United States arm of Sony provides resources on its website, including the downloadable version of the user's manual for the RX100 VI and other technical information.

http://esupport.sony.com

http://helpguide.sony.net/di/pp/v1/en/index.html

http://helpguide.sony.net/dsc/1750/v1/en/index.html

https://www.sony.com/electronics/cyber-shot-compact-cameras/dsc-rx100m6/specifications

https://esupport.sony.com/US/p/model-home.pl?mdl=DSCRX100M6&LOC=3#/manualsTab

The link below has a list of software that Sony says can be used to edit 4K video files:

http://support.d-imaging.sony.co.jp/www/support/application/nle/en.html

The next link is to a guide for using the Picture Profile feature with the RX100 VI:

http://helpguide.sony.net/di/pp/v1/en/index.html

The next link is a portion of the Picture Profile help guide that discusses the use of HLG and HDR:

http://helpguide.sony.net/di/pp/v1/en/contents/TP0001599018.html

The link below is to the operating instructions for the PlayMemories Mobile app for Android and iOS:

http://support.d-imaging.sony.co.jp/www/disoft/int/playmemories-mobile/en/operation/index.html

The link below leads to a site with information about using the location information linking features of the camera with the PlayMemories Mobile app:

http://support.d-imaging.sony.co.jp/www/disoft/int/playmemories-mobile/en/location/index.html?id=hg_stl

The next link points to a page with information about Sony accessories:

https://www.sony.net/Products/diacc/systemchart/en-gb/index.html#cyber-shot

The link below leads to the site where you can download PlayMemories Home and Imaging Edge software for use with the RX100 VI:

https://support.d-imaging.sony.co.jp/app/disoft/en/

The link below leads to a site where you can find troubleshooting and other information about Sony's Imaging Edge software:

https://support.d-imaging.sony.co.jp/app/imagingedge/en/faqs/

The link below leads to a site where you can download Sony's Catalyst Browse software, which lets you view the metadata of video files more extensively than is possible with other programs:

https://www.sonycreativesoftware.com/download/catalystbrowse

Other Resources

This next link is to a video seminar by video expert Philip Bloom discussing video settings for the Sony a7S camera, much of which is useful for the RX100 VI:

https://youtu.be/zeX-eZXaRtw

The link below is to more information from Philip Bloom, including insights about the video features of Sony cameras:

http://philipbloom.net/blog/rxroadtests/

The next link discusses picture profiles on the Sony FS-700 video camera. Much of the discussion is applicable to the RX100 VI.

http://videogearsandiego.blogspot.com/2013/12/using-picture-profiles-on-sony-fs-700.html

The link below provides a detailed analysis of the differences between S-Log2 and S-Log3:

http://www.xdcam-user.com/2016/12/the-great-s-log2-or-s-log3-debate/

The link below is to an article from dpreview.com on the reasons why you might want to record video using an external video recorder:

https://www.dpreview.com/articles/3388025881/why-would-i-want-an-external-recorder-monitor

This next link has a video with tips on settings for shooting video with the Sony a7S:

http://www.4kshooters.net/2014/10/13/some-useful-sony-a7s-movie-settings-tips-and-tricks/

The link below provides more information about the settings that can be adjusted for Picture Profiles:

http://www.xdcam-user.com/picture-profile-guide/

The link below discusses the HLG setting for video, and how it relates to HDR:

https://www.cinema5d.com/the-link-between-hdr-sdr-and-hlg-explained/

The link below is to a thread at dpreview.com that discusses some issues concerning the use of the HLG settings on the RX100 VI:

https://www.dpreview.com/forums/post/61401784

The link below leads to an article and video tutorial on photographing birds in flight:

https://petapixel.com/2017/11/25/tips-photographing-birds-flight/

Finally, the last link below is to a site that has excellent tutorials on many photographic topics:

http://www.cambridgeincolour.com

Index

Symbols

A

B

D

E

F

G

H

N

O

P

Q

R

T

U

V

W

X

Z

www.ingramcontent.com/pod-product-compliance
Lightning Source LLC
LaVergne TN
LVHW060636110826
845147LV00018B/994

9781937986728